The Wiley Blackwell Handbook of Positive Psychological Interventions

The Wiley Blackwell Handbook of Positive Psychological Interventions

Edited by

Acacia C. Parks
Hiram College

Stephen M. Schueller
Northwestern University

WILEY Blackwell

This edition first published 2014

Registered Office
John Wiley & Sons Ltd, The Atrium, Southern Gate, Chichester, West Sussex, PO19 8SQ, UK

Editorial Offices
350 Main Street, Malden, MA 02148-5020, USA
9600 Garsington Road, Oxford, OX4 2DQ, UK
The Atrium, Southern Gate, Chichester, West Sussex, PO19 8SQ, UK

For details of our global editorial offices, for customer services, and for information about how to apply for permission to reuse the copyright material in this book please see our website at www.wiley.com/wiley-blackwell.

Library of Congress Cataloging-in-Publication Data

The Wiley Blackwell handbook of positive psychological interventions / edited by Acacia C. Parks, Stephen M. Schueller.
pages cm
Includes bibliographical references and index.
ISBN 978-1-119-95056-1 (cloth)
1. Positive psychology–Handbooks, manuals, etc. 2. Psychotherapy–Handbooks, manuals, etc.
I. Parks, Acacia C., editor of compilation. II. Title: Handbook of positive psychological interventions.
BF204.6.W55 2014
150.19′88–dc23

2013050478

A catalogue record for this book is available from the British Library.

Cover image: © Scott Graham
Cover design by Cyan Design

Set in 10.5/13pt Galliard by Aptara Inc., New Delhi, India

1 2014

To CS, for the extraordinary gift of convincing me that there is no such thing as wasted time.

Acacia C. Parks

To my lovely wife, Alyson Zalta, my greatest source of positive emotions.

Stephen M. Schueller

Contents

List of Contributors

Brett Anderson – Northern Illinois University

Thomas C. Ball – University of Kansas, Center for Public Partnerships and Research

Katherine Jacobs Bao – Manhattanville College

Ena Begovic – Eckerd College

Laura E. R. Blackie – Wake Forest University

Linda Bolier – Trimbos Institute – Netherlands Institute of Mental Health and Addiction, Department of Public Mental Health; University of Twente, Department of Psychology, Health and Technology

Giacomo Bono – California State University, Dominguez Hills

Chad R. Breeden – Clemson University

Fred B. Bryant – Loyola University Chicago

Elise M. Clerkin – Miami University

Collie W. Conoley – University of California, Santa Barbara

Jane Close Conoley – University of California, Santa Barbara

Mark H. Davis – Eckerd College

Anne M. Day – Brown University, Center for Alcohol and Addiction Studies

José L. Duarte – Arizona State University

Katherine V. Eichner – Washington State University

Robert A. Emmons – University of California, Davis

Michel Ferrari – University of Toronto, Ontario Institute for Studies in Education

William Fleeson – Wake Forest University

Marie J. C. Forgeard – University of Pennsylvania

Jeffrey J. Froh – Hofstra University

Jane Gillham – University of Pennsylvania

Suzy Green – Coaching Psychology Unit, University of Sydney; The Positivity Institute

Christine E. Guthrie – University of Toronto, Ontario Institute for Studies in Education

Patrick R. Harrison – Loyola University Chicago

William T. Hoyt – University of Wisconsin-Madison

Eranda Jayawickreme – Wake Forest University

Christopher W. Kahler – Brown University School of Public Health, Center for Alcohol and Addiction Studies

Christie L. Kelley – Clemson University

Kasley M. Killam – Queen's University

Young-Hoon Kim – Yonsei University

Amy Kranzler – Rutgers University

Jaime L. Kurtz – James Madison University

Lindsay Liotta – Kean University

Tara Lomas – Hofstra University

Shane J. Lopez – Clifton Strengths Institute, Gallup, and University of Kansas

Michelle C. Louis – Bethel University

Arden Y. Lowndes – Clemson University

Sonja Lyubomirsky – University of California, Riverside

Jeana L. Magyar-Moe – University of Wisconsin-Stevens Point

Katherina Martin Abello – Trimbos Institute – Netherlands Institute of Mental Health and Addiction, Innovation Center of Mental Health & Technology (I.COM)

Paul E. McGhee – President, The Laughter Remedy, Wilmington, DE

Piper S. Meyer – Minnesota Center for Mental Health, University of Minnesota

Anjali Mishra – University of California, Davis

Justin Misurell – Metropolitan Regional Diagnostic and Treatment Center, Newark Beth Israel Medical Center

Hannah J. Murphy – Clemson University

Michelle R. Nario-Redmond – Hiram College

Jennifer Teramoto Pedrotti – California Polytechnic State University, San Luis Obispo

Marla E. Pontrelli – University of California, Santa Barbara

Cynthia L. S. Pury – Clemson University

Ann Marie Roepke – University of Pennsylvania

Willibald Ruch – University of Zurich

Sarah A. Schnitker – Fuller Theological Seminary, School of Psychology

Stephen M. Schueller – Northwestern University

David J. Shernoff – Rutgers University and Northern Illinois University

Joo Yeon Shin – Colorado State University

Jennifer L. Smith – Mather LifeWays

Gordon B. Spence – Australian Institute of Well-Being; Sydney Business School; University of Wollongong

Nichea S. Spillane – Brown University, Center for Alcohol and Addiction Studies

Craig Springer – Metropolitan Regional Diagnostic and Treatment Center, Newark Beth Israel Medical Center

Charles B. Starkey – Clemson University

Michael F. Steger – Colorado State University; North-West University, South Africa

Dianne A. Vella-Brodrick – Centre for Positive Psychology, Melbourne Graduate School of Education, University of Melbourne

Nathaniel G. Wade – Iowa State University

Justin T. Westbrook – Fuller Graduate School of Psychology

Everett L. Worthington Jr. – Virginia Commonwealth University

Preface

When positive psychology was founded in the late 1990s, little work existed on interventions that aimed to increase happiness. Fordyce's (1977, 1983) work was seminal in this domain but only a few studies dotted the literature in the following two decades. At the turn of the twenty-first century, however, prompted by the interest generated by Seligman's American Psychological Association presidential address and spurred on by several initiatives within the field to launch new research, this work began to flourish. Duckworth, Steen, and Seligman (2005) posited that at least 100 positive psychological interventions had been suggested and by the time Sin and Lyubomirsky (2009) conducted a meta-analysis of positive psychological interventions, they were able to identify empirical studies of 51 interventions (with only seven papers published prior to 2000). Despite this growing body of research, no canonical resource for those interested in the current state of affairs of positive psychological interventions existed. In a 2005 update for the field, Seligman, Steen, Park, and Peterson offered a set of interventions (i.e., the Gratitude Visit, Three Good Things, You at Your Best, Using Signature Strengths in a New Way, and Identifying Signature Strengths) that was widely influential, yet was far from a definitive list of interventions and lacked a thorough description of their theoretical rationale.

It was in this nascent period in the development of positive psychological interventions that we received our introduction to and training in positive psychology. A.C.P. started as a graduate student at the University of Pennsylvania working in Martin Seligman's lab, and S.M.S. began working as an undergraduate research assistant with Sonja Lyubomirsky. As students, we saw the utility of edited volumes when we read (and re-read) Snyder and Lopez's *Handbook of positive psychology*, eager to absorb the collected knowledge of the leading experts within the field. That volume served, and has continued to serve, as a collection of chapters that contain positive psychology's conceptual grounding. In the decade since Snyder and Lopez's (2001) initial publication, positive psychology has expanded in its theoretical nature (i.e., learning more about the causes and consequences of happiness, well-being, positive emotions, and various positive characteristics or traits) and has also moved towards applied approaches aimed at developing techniques to increase individuals' happiness. Because of this explosion of applied work, it seemed to us that a parallel volume is now needed: one that focuses on the ways that positive psychology has been and could be used to improve people's lives.

What started as a handful of disparate studies sprinkled throughout the psychological literature has evolved, in the past decade, into a cohesive area of inquiry with many active researchers. Furthermore, a field that once focused exclusively on developing and testing new interventions is now also concerned with other equally important questions: How do these interventions work? How can their efficacy be maximized? For whom are they (and are they not) appropriate? Equally impressive, thousands of therapists, coaches, educators, and executives have put positive psychology-based strategies into practice. Positive psychological interventions are being used for both research and practice, yet no single source has provided a comprehensive guide to this vast and varied work. We felt that the field was ready for such a resource, and we designed *The Wiley Blackwell handbook of positive psychological interventions* to serve the needs of the positive psychology community, both researchers and practitioners, looking to learn more about positive psychological interventions.

We began by creating what seemed to us a comprehensive list of constructs targeted by positive psychological interventions (PPIs). It quickly became clear that some of these were more thoroughly established than others – gratitude (Lomas, Froh, Emmons, Mishra, & Bono, Chapter 1), forgiveness (Worthington, Wade, & Hoyt, Chapter 2), savoring (Smith, Harrison, Kurtz, & Bryant, Chapter 3), strengths (Louis & Lopez, Chapter 4), meaning (Shin & Steger, Chapter 5), and empathy (Davis & Begovic, Chapter 6) all had an extensive empirical basis and numerous interventions that targeted them; on the other hand, creativity (Forgeard & Eichner, Chapter 7), patience (Schnitker & Westbrook, Chapter 8), courage (Pury and colleagues, Chapter 9), humor (Ruch & McGhee, Chapter 10), flow (Shernoff & Anderson, Chapter 11), and wisdom (Ferrari & Guthrie, Chapter 12) had been acknowledged in research as valuable, but were only beginning to be the subject of deliberate intervention. Thus, we created two distinct sections: one for established areas of intervention (Part I) and another for new and emerging areas (Part II).

We realized, too, that we would need contributions showcasing the many contexts in which PPIs have been applied, or have the potential to be applied. Part III contains chapters from researchers and practitioners who have been using PPIs in novel settings: in family therapy (Conoley, Conoley, & Pontrelli, Chapter 13), in individual therapy (Magyar-Moe, Chapter 14), in coaching (Green & Spence, Chapter 15), over the internet (Bolier & Abello, Chapter 16), and with special populations, including children (Kranzler, Liotta, & Gillham, Chapter 17), minorities (Ball & Nario-Redmond, Chapter 18), individuals suffering from schizophrenia (Meyer, Chapter 19), and smokers trying to quit (Day, Clerkin, Spillane, & Kahler, Chapter 20).

Lastly, as people who study PPIs ourselves, we knew there were a number of special considerations that would need to be addressed in order to give the reader a comprehensive understanding of the controversies and "hot topics" in the literature. The last section (Part IV) explores the ways in which the benefits of PPIs can be threatened by hedonic adaptation (Bao & Lyubomirsky, Chapter 21), as well as the roles of person–activity fit (Schueller, Chapter 22) and culture (Pedrotti, Chapter 23), the importance of ethical standards (Vella-Brodrick, Chapter 24), the potential for more diverse means of assessing outcomes in PPI research (Duarte, Chapter 25), the potential dangers of improving self-evaluations too much (Killam & Kim, Chapter 26), and the promise of increasing well-being through altering one's typical behavioral patterns, i.e., personality (Blackie, Roepke, Forgeard, Jayawickreme, & Fleeson, Chapter 27).

We see this volume serving two purposes. First, it offers a description of the current state of the field. Second, and more aspirational, we hope this volume will guide development in the coming decades of work on positive psychological interventions. Although many people use positive psychological principles in practice, the research on the effectiveness of PPI use in applied settings is seriously lacking. Much of the work on PPIs, both applied and experimental, has used comparison conditions that would hardly be considered rigorous by any behavioral researcher (e.g., no-intervention or wait-list control groups, or in some cases, no control group at all). Furthermore, developers of positive psychological interventions could adopt a more principle-focused approach to developing interventions based on theoretical models. The development work, thus far, has been overwhelmingly atheoretical and a tighter linkage between the basic theories resulting from positive psychological research and intervention development could benefit the field. Lastly, we hope to encourage PPI researchers and practitioners to think carefully about the nature of the population they are serving, a question that, until recently, has remained largely unasked; recent research suggests that people interested in PPIs are not a homogeneous group (see Parks, Della Porta, Pierce, Zilca, & Lyubomirsky, 2012), and it may be that what works for one group of happiness seekers would be ineffective or harmful for another group. We need to move beyond the question, "are PPIs effective?" to a more nuanced set of questions: "which PPIs are effective, under what circumstances, and for whom?"

The end result is the volume you are reading, and we are very proud to have been a part of it. Given the overwhelming evidence linking gratitude with a host of benefits (Lomas, Froh, Emmons, Mishra, & Bono, Chapter 1), we would like to bask in those benefits by expressing our gratitude to the various folks who made this volume possible. We are first and foremost grateful to our unbelievable lineup of contributors. We are grateful for the opportunity to collaborate with each of the authors to create what we believe are the most clear, informative, and impactful versions of their chapters possible. The process of reading the works of these pioneers in PPI research was not only interesting and inspiring; it pushed our knowledge and understanding as well, and we are happy to have had that opportunity to grow as a result of our editorial work for this volume.

We are thankful, too, to Wiley, who approached us about doing this book and then gave us considerable autonomy in all aspects of its creation, as well as support in the form of honoraria for contributors, and indexing. Hiram College (A.C.P.'s home institution) generously covered the cost of professional proofreading, and also funded the assistance of a number of students and colleagues at Hiram – Kaytlin Brewster, Susanna Wong, Lisa Shauver, and Kayla Kennedy – in the process of assembling and checking over the manuscript.

Equally important, we wish to acknowledge our intellectual inspirations. Both A.C.P. and S.M.S. have had the good fortune to have Marty Seligman and Sonja Lyubomirsky as mentors and collaborators. A.C.P. also acknowledges the mentorship of her undergraduate advisors, Kathryn Oleson and Keith Herman, as well as her current department chair, Michelle Nario-Redmond. She is grateful for the support of her departmental colleagues, Amber Chenoweth, Ryan Honomichl, and Lisa Shauver, and for the professional cheerleading of Shane Lopez, who has provided life-saving advice on publishing time and time again. S.M.S. would like to acknowledge the mentorship of Ricardo Muñoz and David Mohr and offer the following special words of thanks to those who have been most influential in his thinking on positive psychological interventions. To Sonja for teaching him what it means to be a scientist. To Marty for teaching him to think big and tackle interesting questions. To Ricardo for teaching him to "practice the presence of the good." And lastly, to David for teaching him to understand and maximize the real-world impact of research. S.M.S. would also like to thank a University of California, Los Angeles graduate student, who when he interviewed for graduate school, challenged him by asking what positive psychological interventions he practiced in his own life. This simple question changed the way he thought about research and practice.

Lastly, we want to acknowledge our family, friends, and colleagues for their support as we have put together this book. A.C.P. admits that she often found herself lost in this project, a slave to flow, and she thanks her husband and children for keeping the household running whenever her head was in the clouds. S.M.S. wants to thank his colleagues at the Center for Behavioral Intervention Technologies for creating an intellectually stimulating and fun environment while he completed his work on this volume, and his wife, Alyson Zalta, who filled their household with delicious baked goods to fuel his work.

References

Duckworth, A. L., Steen, T. A., & Seligman, M. E. P. (2005). Positive psychology in clinical practice. *Annual Review of Clinical Psychology*, *1*(1), 629–651.

Fordyce, M. W. (1977). Development of a program to increase personal happiness. *Journal of Counseling Psychology*, *24*, 511–521.

Fordyce, M. W. (1983). A program to increase happiness: Further studies. *Journal of Counseling Psychology*, *30*, 483–498.

Parks, A. C., Della Porta, M. D., Pierce, R. S., Zilca, R., & Lyubomirsky, S. (2012). Pursuing happiness in everyday life: The characteristics and behaviors of online happiness seekers. *Emotion*, *12*, 1222–1234.

Seligman, M. E. P., Steen, T. A., Park, N., & Peterson, C. (2005). Positive psychology progress. *American Psychologist*, *60*, 410–421.

Sin, N. L., & Lyubomirsky, S. (2009). Enhancing well-being and alleviating depressive symptoms with positive psychology interventions: A practice-friendly meta-analysis. *Journal of Clinical Psychology: In Session*, *65*, 467–487.

Snyder, C. R., & Lopez, S. J. (Eds.) (2001), *Handbook of positive psychology*. New York: Oxford University Press.

Part I

Established Areas of Intervention

1

Gratitude Interventions

A Review and Future Agenda

Tara Lomas, Jeffrey J. Froh, Robert A. Emmons, Anjali Mishra, and Giacomo Bono

Gratitude is highly prized. A small sampling of quotes reveals the power and potential of this virtue. "Whatever you are in search of – peace of mind, prosperity, health, love – it is waiting for you if only you are willing to receive it with an open and grateful heart," writes Sarah Breathnach in the *Simple abundance journal of gratitude*. Elsewhere she refers to gratitude as "the most passionate transformative force in the cosmos." Another popular treatment of the topic refers to it as "one of the most empowering, healing, dynamic instruments of consciousness vital to demonstrating the life experiences one desires" (Richelieu, 1996). Lock and key metaphors are especially common; gratitude has been referred to as "the key that opens all doors," that which "unlocks the fullness of life," and the "key to abundance, prosperity, and fulfillment" (Emmons & Hill, 2001; Hay, 1996).

How do these extraordinary claims regarding the power and promise of gratitude fare when scientific lights are shone on them? Can gratitude live up to its billing? In this chapter we review the growing body of work on gratitude and well-being, explore mechanisms by which gratitude interventions elevate well-being, and close by presenting what we consider important issues for the next generation of gratitude intervention studies to address.

What Is Gratitude and How Is It Measured?

Gratitude is a feeling that occurs in exchange-based relationships when one person acknowledges receiving a valuable benefit from another. Much of human life is about giving, receiving, and repayment. In this sense, gratitude, like other social emotions, functions to help regulate relationships, solidifying and strengthening

The Wiley Blackwell Handbook of Positive Psychological Interventions, First Edition.
Edited by Acacia C. Parks and Stephen M. Schueller.

them (Algoe & Stanton, 2011). Feelings of gratitude stem from two stages of information processing: (i) an affirmation of goodness or "good things" in one's life, and (ii) the recognition that the sources of this goodness lie at least partially outside the self. This cognitive process, furthermore, gives rise to behavioral consequences, specifically the "passing on of the gift" through positive action. As such, gratitude serves as a key link in the dynamic between receiving and giving. It is not only a response to kindnesses received, but it is also a motivator of future benevolent actions on the part of the recipient (see Emmons, 2007 for a review).

Since the emergence of gratitude research in the past 20 years, the two main questionnaires that have been widely administered to measure gratitude are the six-item Gratitude Questionnaire (GQ-6; McCullough, Emmons, & Tsang, 2002) and the 44-item Gratitude, Resentment and Appreciation Test or the GRAT (Watkins, Grimm, & Hailu, 1998). Both measures conceptualize gratitude as a trait, or disposition – in other words, a generalized tendency to first recognize and then emotionally respond with thankfulness, after attributing benefits received through benevolence to an external moral agent (Emmons, McCullough, & Tsang, 2003). When measuring dispositional gratitude, researchers examine gratitude as an "affective trait," or an individual's innate tendency toward grateful experience (Watkins, Woodward, Stone, & Kolts, 2003). State gratitude, rather, is experienced after a positive event has occurred and as a result usually promotes further reciprocal, prosocial behavior (Wood, Maltby, Stewart, Linley, & Joseph, 2008). Individuals who reported greater dispositional gratitude also reported experiencing greater state gratitude daily (McCullough, Tsang, & Emmons, 2004); this is largely due to grateful people processing positive events differently than those less grateful. Specifically, people with greater trait gratitude perceived a benefactor's actions toward them more positively (more costly, valuable, and genuine) than their less grateful counterparts, thus demonstrating greater increases in state gratitude (Wood et al., 2008).

The 44-item GRAT includes the three dimensions of trait gratitude: resentment, simple appreciation, and social appreciation (Watkins et al., 1998). Participants complete the GRAT by answering questions such as, "I believe that I am a very fortunate person" and "I'm really thankful for friends and family" using a five-point Likert scale ranging from 1 (strongly disagree) to 5 (strongly agree with the statement) (Watkins et al., 2003). Retrospective self-report is the primary method used when measuring gratitude (Emmons, Froh, & Mishra, in press). Further, the self-report scales noted above such as the GRAT (Watkins et al., 1998) and the GQ-6 (McCullough et al., 2002) are measuring dispositional gratitude. State gratitude on the other hand is measured through gratitude interventions where participants are partaking in positive psychology exercises such as, keeping a gratitude journal, writing a gratitude letter, and then delivering the letter (Emmons et al., in press). The benefits derived from participating in these gratitude-inducing exercises are examined by measuring positive outcome variables such as happiness, life satisfaction, and overall well-being at post-intervention follow-up (Bono, Emmons, & McCullough, 2004; McCullough et al., 2004; Seligman, Steen, Park, & Peterson, 2005). Other means for assessing trait gratitude are through attributional measures and free response. With attributional measures, gratitude is measured indirectly through participants' analysis of helping scenarios and their attribution of the help as being either autonomous or controlled (Emmons et al., in press). For example, grateful individuals are more likely to perceive the help as autonomously motivated versus controlled (Emmons et al., in press). Free response measures ask participants to spontaneously answer questions revolving around the subject of gratitude (Emmons et al., in press). For example, participants may be asked about a time when they felt grateful or about a person for whom they were grateful (Emmons et al., in press).

Findings from the Science of Gratitude

Gratitude is foundational to well-being and mental health throughout the life span. From childhood to old age, accumulating evidence documents the wide array of psychological, physical, and relational benefits associated with gratitude (Emmons & McCullough, 2003; McCullough, Kilpatrick, Emmons, & Larson, 2001). In particular, dispositional gratitude has been shown to uniquely and incrementally contribute to subjective well-being (McCullough et al., 2004; Watkins et al., 2003, Wood, Joseph, & Maltby, 2008), and to result in benefits above and beyond those conferred by general positive affect (Bartlett & DeSteno, 2006; Froh, Yurkewicz, & Kashdan, 2009). For example, dispositional gratitude encourages more positive social interactions, in turn making people better adjusted and accepted by people around them, and finally leading to well-being (McCullough et al., 2001). Dispositional gratitude has also been found to be positively associated with prosocial traits such as empathy, forgiveness, and willingness to help others. People who rate themselves as having a grateful disposition perceive themselves as having more prosocial characteristics, expressed by their empathetic behavior and emotional support for friends within the last month (McCullough et al., 2002). Other benefits have extended to the physical realm including longer sleep and improved sleep quality and more time spent exercising (Emmons & McCullough, 2003).

Interventions to Increase Gratitude in Adults

Numerous research findings, briefly reviewed above, have highlighted gratitude's positive relationship to subjective well-being and psychological functioning. We will now describe and discuss the empirical evidence behind some widely used gratitude interventions for adults.

Counting blessings

In the seminal gratitude interventions study (Emmons & McCullough, 2003), participants were randomly assigned to one of three conditions: counting blessings, listing hassles, or a no-treatment control (Study 1). People who were randomly assigned to keep gratitude journals on a weekly basis exercised more regularly, reported fewer physical symptoms, felt better about their lives as a whole, and were more optimistic about the upcoming week compared to those who recorded hassles or neutral life events (Emmons & McCullough, 2003, Study 1). Study 2 was an extension of the first study in that a fourth condition was added: downward social comparison. Participants completed weekly reports which asked questions pertaining to physical health and psychological well-being, and were also provided instructions for the condition to which they were assigned (counting blessings, listing hassles, downward social comparison). In each condition, participants listed weekly up to five things they were grateful for, listed five hassles they encountered, or made downward social comparisons indicating ways in which they were better off than others. The daily gratitude journal-keeping exercise resulted in higher reported levels of the positive states of alertness, enthusiasm, determination, attentiveness, and energy compared to a focus on hassles or a downward social comparison (Emmons & McCullough, 2003, Study 2). Participants only in the gratitude condition responded to the following instruction, "There are many things in our lives to be grateful about. Think back over the past week and write down on the lines below up to five things in your life that you are grateful or thankful for" (Emmons & McCullough, 2003, p. 379). Results from both Study 1 and Study 2 showed that individuals in the gratitude condition (counting blessings) reported higher instances of prosocial behavior – they were more likely to report having helped someone with a personal problem or having offered emotional support to another, relative to the hassles or social comparison condition. This indicates that, relative to a focus on complaints, an effective strategy for producing reliably higher levels of pleasant affect is to lead people to reflect, on a daily basis, on those aspects of their lives for which they are grateful (Emmons & McCullough, 2003).

In Study 3, participants with neuromuscular disease were assigned to either the gratitude condition (i.e., counting blessings) or a no-treatment control condition. Participants in both conditions completed 21 "daily experience rating forms" that asked questions about their daily affect, subjective well-being, and health behaviors. Results indicated that individuals in the gratitude condition experienced greater positive affect, were more optimistic, and felt more connected to others than those in the control condition. Spouses of individuals in the gratitude condition also confirm the results of this intervention, indicating increases in their partners' positive affect and life satisfaction (Emmons & McCullough, 2003).

Three Good Things

The benefits of gratitude were further confirmed in another study that compared the efficacy of five different interventions that were hypothesized to increase personal happiness and decrease personal depression (Seligman et al., 2005). Participants randomly assigned to the "Three Good Things" intervention were instructed to write down each day three good things that had happened to them over the course of one week and attribute causes to these positive events (Seligman et al., 2005). Although this intervention did not procure immediate benefits, individuals in the Three Good Things condition experienced lasting effects, with an increase in happiness and decrease in depressive symptoms seen three and six months later (Seligman et al., 2005).

Grateful self-reflection

In a cross-cultural intervention study (Chan, 2010) Chinese teachers voluntarily participated in an eight-week-long "self-improvement project" aimed at increasing individual self-awareness through the process of self-reflection. Participants' gratitude, subjective well-being, happiness, meaning derived from life, and teacher burnout were assessed. Participants were asked weekly to record three good things that had occurred, for eight weeks. Teachers then reflected on these positive occurrences using Naikan meditation-inspired questions. The Naikan meditation represents a form of reflection that not only focuses on the self but also on others. Participants were asked to meditate on the following questions: What did I receive? What did I give? What more could I do? These questions appeared to orient the individual not only to think gratefully but also to be more prosocial (e.g., What more could I do?) (Chan, 2010). Teachers who were more grateful (indicated at pre-test) reported more gratitude, less teacher burnout (emotionally drained, depersonalized), and considered meaning in life of greater importance at post-test.

In another cross-cultural study (Boehm, Lyubomirsky, & Sheldon 2011), foreign-born Asian Americans and Anglo Americans participated in an online intervention study to assess cultural differences in reported life satisfaction after a gratitude intervention. A factorial design was utilized where Anglo Americans and Asian Americans were randomly assigned to one of three conditions: practicing optimism, expressing gratitude, and listing the past week's experiences (control). In the optimism condition, participants wrote about "their best possible life in the future," and in the gratitude condition participants wrote letters of appreciation to those for whom they were grateful.

Cultural differences were noted in both the optimism condition and gratitude condition. Overall, Anglo Americans benefited most from the interventions, experiencing the greatest changes in life satisfaction from baseline across all activities (Boehm et al., 2011). Among Asian American participants, the gratitude intervention was most effective, with modest increases in life satisfaction over time; however, Asian Americans in the optimism condition reported very little change in life satisfaction after participating in the intervention (Boehm et al., 2011). This finding suggests that gratitude interventions with a collectivist orientation (i.e., focus on family and others) may be more beneficial in non-American cultures than are activities with an individualistic orientation (i.e., focus on self and personal accomplishments) (Boehm et al., 2011).

The "Gratitude Visit"

Grateful reflection and acknowledgment in the form of gratitude letters helps foster an appreciation of others and encourages a grateful orientation (i.e., appreciating the benefits – big and small – in one's life) (Emmons & McCullough, 2003; Seligman et al., 2005). In a study comparing several positive psychology interventions, individuals were asked to write a letter to someone to whom they were grateful and then to deliver their letter in person. Individuals who completed this activity reported large gains in happiness and reductions in depression up to one month later (Seligman et al., 2005). Although the gains only lasted one month (compared to six months for some of the other interventions), the magnitude of change was the greatest for this gratitude intervention when compared to the other interventions tested. To date, the Gratitude Visit remains *the* most powerful positive psychology intervention in terms of degree of change. It can be speculated that the hyperemotional nature and behavioral follow-through involved in this intervention are two characteristics which foster the powerful effects.

In another study, Lyubomirsky, Dickerhoof, Boehm and Sheldon (2011) assessed the role of self-selection and effort in fostering the positive benefits (positive affect, life satisfaction, happiness) of grateful intervention. Participants unknowingly self-selected the condition they were a part of by choosing to participate in either a "happiness intervention" (high motivation) or a "study involving cognitive exercises" (low motivation) (Lyubomirsky et al., 2011, p. 394). Based on their selection, participants were then randomly assigned to one of three conditions: a gratitude condition, optimism condition, or control group. The variables examined (positive and negative affect, life satisfaction, happiness, and effort) were combined to represent an overall factor: well-being (Lyubomirsky et al., 2011). Within this study, participants in the gratitude condition were asked to write "gratitude letters" but not send them, while participants in the optimism condition envisioned and wrote about their "best possible selves" (Lyubomirsky et al., 2011).

Positive benefits were immediately observed, with "high motivation" participants reporting greater well-being compared to the "low motivation" participants at post-intervention follow-up (Lyubomirsky et al., 2011). Unfortunately, the intervention did not have a lasting effect, even for the "high motivation" group, at the six-month follow-up (Lyubomirsky et al., 2011). These findings suggest that other factors, such as motivation, effort, and willingness, may also contribute to the benefits that derive from gratitude interventions (Lyubomirsky et al., 2011). Further, in this study participants in the "high motivation" gratitude condition who wrote a letter of appreciation but did not send it failed to experience the lasting effects of the intervention at the six-month follow-up compared with the low motivation condition (Lyubomirsky et al., 2011). This suggests that the Gratitude Visit may only have lasting positive effects when both the psychological (writing letter) and social (delivering letter) mechanisms of the intervention are at work.

Summary of gratitude interventions

Gratitude interventions in adults consistently produce positive benefits, many of which appear to endure over reasonably lengthy periods of time. Gratitude interventions lead to greater gratitude, life satisfaction, optimism, prosocial behavior (Emmons & McCullough, 2003), positive affect (PA) (Emmons & McCullough, 2003; Watkins et al., 2003, Study 4), and well-being (Lyubomirsky, Sheldon, & Schkade, 2005; Seligman et al., 2005), as well as decreased negative affect (NA) (Emmons & McCullough, 2003; Seligman et al., 2005; Watkins et al., 2003, Study 3), compared with controls, for up to six months. Similar findings, over shorter follow-up periods, have been documented in youth (Froh, Sefick, & Emmons, 2008). Despite these encouraging results, much remains unknown, including if children and adults can reap similar benefits from gratitude interventions.

Interventions to Increase Gratitude in Children and Adolescents

Given the benefits of the above-described interventions for adults, some researchers have suggested that gratitude interventions should be applied to many settings and populations so as to spread health, functionality, and happiness to more and more people and to society at large (Bono et al., 2004). Although gratitude interventions for youth surfaced only four years ago, initial findings are promising.

Counting blessings

The best evidence that gratitude can improve youths' well-being comes from three gratitude intervention studies. In one study, Froh, Sefick, and Emmons (2008) randomly assigned 11 classrooms of 6th and 7th graders (ages 11–14) to one of three conditions – gratitude, hassles, or a no-treatment control – to partially replicate Emmons and McCullough's (2003) "counting blessings" intervention. Participants completed the intervention activity daily for two weeks and measures of psychological, physical, and social well-being at pre-test, immediate post-test, and a three-week follow-up. Those in the gratitude condition were instructed to count up to five things they were grateful for, and those in the hassles condition were asked to focus on irritants. Gratitude journal entries included benefits such as: "My coach helped me out at baseball practice," "My grandma is in good health, my family is still together, my family still loves each other, my brothers are healthy, and we have fun everyday," and "I am grateful that my mom didn't go crazy when I accidentally broke a patio table."

Counting blessings, compared with hassles, was related to more gratitude, optimism, life satisfaction, and less negative affect. Students who claimed feeling grateful for receiving help from others reported more positive affect. In fact, the relation between feeling grateful for help from others and positive affect became stronger during the two-week intervention and was strongest three weeks after the intervention ended. Gratitude in response to aid also explained *why* students instructed to count blessings reported more general gratitude. Recognizing the gift of aid – yet another blessing to be counted – seemed to engender more gratitude.

Most significantly, students instructed to count blessings, compared with those in the hassles or control conditions, reported more satisfaction with their school experience (i.e., find school interesting, feel good at school, think they are learning a lot, and are eager to go to school; Huebner, Drane, & Valois, 2000) immediately after the two-week intervention and three weeks after completing it. Expressions of school satisfaction included: "I am thankful for school," "I am thankful for my education," and "I am thankful that my school has a track team and that I got accepted into honor society." School satisfaction is positively related to academic and social success (Verkuyten & Thijs, 2002), and many early and late adolescents indicate significant amounts of dissatisfaction with their school experience (Huebner, Valois, Paxton, & Drane, 2005). Therefore, inducing gratitude in students via counting blessings may be a viable intervention for mitigating negative academic appraisals while promoting a positive attitude about school. Holding such a view predisposes students to improving both their academic and social competence and may help motivate them to get the most out of school.

The "Gratitude Visit"

In another intervention study, children and adolescents from a parochial school were randomly assigned to a gratitude intervention or a control condition (Froh, Kashdan, Ozimkowski, & Miller, 2009). This study partially replicated Seligman et al.'s (2005) "Gratitude Visit" study using a youth population. Participants in the gratitude condition were asked to write a letter to a benefactor whom they had never properly thanked, to read the letter to him/her in person, and to then share their experience with others in the same condition. To illustrate, one 17-year-old female wrote and read the following letter to her mother:

> I would like to take this time to thank you for all that you do on a daily basis and have been doing my whole life ... I am so thankful that I get to drive in with you [to school] everyday and ... for all the work you do for our church ... I thank you for being there

> whenever I need you. I thank you that when the world is against me that you stand up for me and you are my voice when I can't speak for myself. I thank you for caring about my life and wanting to be involved … for the words of encouragement and hugs of love that get me through every storm. I thank you for sitting through countless games in the cold and rain and still having the energy to make dinner and all the things you do. I thank you for raising me in a Christian home where I have learned who God was and how to serve him … I am so blessed to have you as my mommy and I have no idea what I would have done without you.

Participants in the control condition were asked to record and think about daily events. Findings indicated that youth low in positive affect in the gratitude condition reported greater gratitude and positive affect at post-treatment and greater positive affect at the two-month follow-up than youth in the control condition. Thus, although 44% of the gratitude studies published to date found support for gratitude interventions compared against conditions inducing negative affect (e.g., recording hassles) (Froh, Kashdan, et al., 2009), this study suggests that there may be specific individuals – namely, those low in positive affect – who may benefit more.

Learning schematic help appraisals

The most promising intervention study, as we hinted earlier, seems to be one conducted by Froh et al. (in press) that increased gratitude by training individuals' benefit appraisals. Using the youngest children targeted by interventions to date, this study employed a novel technique of strengthening children's schematic help appraisals. Classrooms of children (8–11 years) were randomly assigned to a school-based gratitude curriculum or an attention-control curriculum. School psychology interns taught participants in the gratitude condition about the social-cognitive determinants of gratitude via structured lesson plans. Lessons adhered to the following outline: the introduction (session 1), understanding benefactors' intentions when being a beneficiary (session 2), understanding the cost experienced by benefactors when giving a benefit (session 3), understanding the benefits of receiving a gift bestowed by a benefactor (session 4), and the review/summary, which incorporates all components of the previous sessions (session 5). Using the methods of classroom discussions, acting out different role plays, and writing down personal stories in a "gratitude journal," the intern emphasized the connection between positive things happening to them and the actions of a benefactor. Across five sessions the intern explained that whenever others are nice to us, they may be doing so on purpose (illustrating intention), using their resources (illustrating cost), and helping us (illustrating benefit).[1]

Students in the attention-control condition were also provided with structured lesson plans that followed an outline but they focused on neutral topics, such as events of the day. Similar to the gratitude condition, the attention-control condition lessons included classroom discussions, writing assignments, and role-playing activities. Importantly, the general structure of the attention-control sessions closely mirrored that of the gratitude condition lessons in terms of task assignment but not in terms of content.

Across two different studies, the authors found that children can be taught to become more aware of the social-cognitive appraisals involved in circumstances of receiving help from another, and that this schematic change makes children more grateful and benefits their well-being. A weekly intervention obtained such effects in the long term (up to five months later). A daily intervention produced these effects immediately (two days later) and showed further that children behaviorally expressed gratitude more (i.e., wrote 80% more thank you cards to their Parent Teacher Association) and that their teachers even observed them to be happier, compared to those in the control condition. Evidence thus supported the effectiveness of this intervention.

Next Steps for Gratitude Interventions

Use of gratitude in clinical therapy

Many of the gratitude interventions conducted up until now have found gratitude inductions to be effective in improving mental health and well-being in comparison to control groups that induce people to think about hassles or complaints. Many of the studies we have discussed in this chapter examine various outcomes that are clinically relevant. Researchers have also indicated ways to use gratitude interventions in therapeutic contexts and reasons why this would be beneficial (Bono & McCullough, 2006; Duckworth, Steen, & Seligman, 2005; Seligman, Rashid, & Parks, 2006). Further research, however, is needed before this can occur. Wood, Froh, and Geraghty (2010) lay out an agenda for the kinds of gratitude intervention studies that are needed if gratitude interventions are to be used for clinical therapy. First, they argue that more rigorous experimental studies are needed that compare gratitude inductions against true neutral control conditions (using either a no-treatment control or wait-list method) so that we can know the extent to which gratitude inductions actually produce improvements in individuals' health and well-being over doing nothing at all. Wood et al.'s argument for a stronger, more neutral control group is noteworthy as this will allow researchers to more accurately assess and understand the effects of the intervention. However, using an active control group is a wiser alternative to using a no-treatment control group when a fitting, neutral control is unavailable.

Wood et al. (2010) also argue that experiments using clinical samples are needed to examine whether gratitude interventions would be better than other common therapies known to be effective (i.e., "gold standards") for the treatment of mental disorder. Counseling psychologists are increasingly considering the use of gratitude strategies in developing more sustained programs of intervention for a range of client groups, such as those experiencing depression, substance abuse, or bereavement (Nelson, 2009). Two recent studies have directly examined gratitude's potential for treating mental disorder. One study found that over a two-week period daily listing of up to six things for which one was grateful was as effective as daily automatic thought records in helping a community sample of people with severe body image dissatisfaction, compared to a wait-list control (Geraghty, Wood, & Hyland, 2010a); and another made this same finding with a community sample of people with excessive worrying, or generalized anxiety (Geraghty, Wood, & Hyland, 2010b). Notably, in both studies individuals who did the gratitude listing were twice as likely to stay in the treatment, compared to individuals who received the automatic thought record treatment. These studies provide examples of the kind of evidence that is needed for gratitude interventions to be employed for therapeutic purposes.

Other recent research indicates several fruitful avenues for the therapeutic use of gratitude in populations free of mental disorder, but experiencing other distress. For instance, one recent study found that the experience and expression of gratitude may help patients with metastatic breast cancer tap sources of social support and find improved quality of life (Algoe & Stanton, 2011). These findings suggest that gratitude may help people cope with the stress of lifelong or deadly diseases, issues that are becoming more pressing due to the growth of the elderly population in society. Gratitude may also be helpful in counseling married couples toward more fulfilling and satisfied relationships (Gordon, Arnette, & Smith, 2011). This is consistent with Algoe and colleagues' findings that gratitude can help boost sense of connection and satisfaction in romantic relationships (Algoe, Gable, & Maisel, 2010). Therefore, gratitude will likely play a valuable role in bringing comfort to more and more people in our world as such therapeutic applications are developed.

While gratitude is helpful in many populations, recent research has revealed that gratitude interventions can be detrimental to certain personality types. Sergeant and Mongrain (2011) examined the use of gratitude exercises with two vulnerable depressive personality types: self-critical individuals and needy individuals. Participants participated in the intervention for one week and follow-up assessment was conducted one, three, and six months later (Sergeant & Mongrain, 2011). Individuals were randomly assigned to participate in one of three conditions: a gratitude condition (listing daily five things to be grateful for), music condition (listening to uplifting music), or control condition (writing about childhood memories) (Sergeant & Mongrain, 2011). Interestingly, the gratitude exercise and music exercise only procured positive benefits for the self-critical individuals, with reported increases in self-esteem and decreases in physical symptoms. The needy individuals experienced negative effects as a result of participating in the music and gratitude exercises, reporting decreases in happiness and increases in physical symptomology (Sergeant & Mongrain, 2011).

Use of booster sessions to strengthen interventions

Are there ways to strengthen gratitude interventions so that they produce more long-term effects on well-being? Lyubomirsky and her colleagues make the case that gratitude interventions are most effective when they are distributed regularly over time, rather than all in one day, and when individuals intentionally and willfully engage in activities that match their lifestyle and interests (Lyubomirsky et al., 2005). These researchers have found that people are more likely to experience sustained levels of happiness if they endorse and personally commit themselves to positive exercises like optimistic thinking about their future and writing letters of gratitude to others. These findings suggest that including booster sessions would be a powerful method for strengthening gratitude interventions. To extend on Emmons and McCullough's (2003) intervention as an example, participants who previously kept a gratitude journal (see Emmons & McCullough, 2003) might want to do more entries a month or two later to refresh and "boost" the effects of partaking in this gratitude-inducing exercise.

There are at least two good reasons why booster sessions would help. First, they would remind individuals to continue to put gratitude exercises in practice in their daily lives. Second, they would also help refresh individuals' knowledge about how to do this. Because gratitude requires people to focus their attention on experiences of interpersonal benefits and to remember to express thanks, reminders and refreshers would help encourage both the experience and expression of gratitude. As we intimated earlier, combining cognitive and behavioral strategies may be a powerful method for strengthening gratitude interventions. Thus, boosters may encourage individuals to personally apply the intervention exercises to new situations and people in their lives so that the practices are more likely to instill in them an attitude of gratitude and grateful habits. The more gratitude takes root and has time to influence and become a part of people's relationships and life narratives, the more positive an impact it will have on their lives. We could expect more research in the future examining the generative function of gratitude and ways that gratitude interventions could be used to improve the functioning of relationships, groups, organizations, and communities. Undoubtedly, booster sessions will be involved in implementing such interventions so that impacts could permeate and transform such systems.

Consideration of moderators in interventions

There is evidence that gratitude benefits boys more than it does girls (Froh, Kashdan, et al., 2009). So research examining different mechanisms through which gratitude benefits males and females differently will help to produce better interventions. With the use of exercises that are better tailored to the sexes, individuals are more likely to personally "own" and commit to the interventions. The same could be said of other potential moderators, such as positive affect (Froh, Kashdan, et al., 2009), cultural factors, or attitudinal factors. Recent work by

Wood, Brown, and Maltby (2011) suggests that different people will experience different amounts of gratitude for help or gifts they are given, depending on the amount of help or size of gifts they are accustomed to receiving. A better understanding of how gratitude is experienced and expressed in different cultures and in different groups, then, may help improve our ability to use gratitude to promote well-being or peace for instance.

Yet another important moderator variable to consider is personal responsibility. Chow and Lowery (2010) found that in achievement contexts individuals do not experience gratitude without the belief that they are responsible for their success, even when they acknowledge the help they have received. This is a critically overlooked dimension of gratitude, which for the most part has been regarded as a phenomenon that depends on external attributions of responsibility for positive outcomes that one experiences in life. This research suggests that gratitude may serve a social capital function, enabling individuals to better achieve goals when they themselves, and other people, are more invested in the pursuit of those goals. Again, such knowledge can be used to improve upon gratitude interventions, especially those targeting younger populations. As noted above in relation to the Sergeant and Mongrain (2011) study, personality orientation must be considered when treating clinical populations in order to procure efficacious results when using positive psychology exercises for intervention.

Infusing gratitude into existing school curricula

Our intervention research with children aged 8–11 (Froh et al., in press) shows that gratitude could be easily infused into reading and writing programs in schools, something that is in line with the rise of social-emotional learning programs (CASEL, 2003). To positively transform school and community programs for youth, better understanding is needed of how to improve social settings to better promote positive youth development (Shinn & Yoshikawa, 2008). Social-emotional learning programs are one example of such efforts, and there is evidence that they are helping to improve both the academic and social development of students (Jones, Brown, & Aber, 2008). We believe gratitude can enhance literacy programs and complement social-emotional learning programs.

Modern forms of communication and interaction

Last but not least, yet another direction for gratitude interventions in the future will be techniques that use forms of communication that increasingly characterize our interactions in today's world – the use of digital and electronic modes of communication. We live in a wired culture where teenagers and adults are using social networking websites and cell-phones to chat, text, and convey information to each other. Therefore, future research will undoubtedly explore how these modes of communication and interaction can be used to promote the experience and expression of gratitude. There is a book already exploring this very topic, entitled *I am gr8ful for you* (Serafini, 2011).

Conclusion

The research reviewed highlights the success and lasting effects of gratitude interventions on people's physical and psychological well-being. Taken together, these effects indicate improvements in both personal and relational functioning. The evidence, we think, provides implications for the well-being of people, groups, organizations, and society, and personal and global well-being. Specific to the latter, making nations more grateful may be best accomplished by first incorporating gratitude curricula into schools, for children and adolescents. How might the world be if we fostered a grateful generation? In our opinion, we think societies would improve in many ways. Families would enjoy stronger bonds; neighborhoods would become more supportive; schools would better invest in the strengths and possibilities of youth; and quite possibly, societies would become more cohesive, where people will continue to "pass on the gift" of gratitude.

Note

1 The manual is available on the second author's website.

References

Algoe, S. B., Gable, S. L., & Maisel, N. (2010). It's the little things: Everyday gratitude as a booster shot for romantic relationships. *Personal Relationships*, *17*, 217–233.

Algoe, S. B., & Stanton, A. L. (2011). Gratitude when it is needed most: Social functions of gratitude in women with metastatic breast cancer. *Emotion*, *12*, 163–168. doi:10.1037/a0024024

Bartlett, M. Y., & DeSteno, D. (2006). Gratitude and prosocial behavior: Helping when it costs you. *Psychological Science*, *17*, 319–325.

Boehm, J. K., Lyubomirsky, S., & Sheldon, K. M. (2011). A longitudinal experimental study comparing the effectiveness of happiness-enhancing strategies in Anglo Americans and Asian Americans. *Cognition and Emotion*, *25*(7), 1263–1272. doi:10.1080/02699931.2010.541227

Bono, G., Emmons, R. A., & McCullough, M. E. (2004). Gratitude in practice and the practice of gratitude. In P. A. Linley and S. Joseph (Eds.), *Positive psychology in practice* (pp. 464–481). New York: Wiley.

Bono, G., & McCullough, M. E. (2006). Positive responses to benefit and harm: Bringing forgiveness and gratitude into cognitive psychotherapy. *Journal of Cognitive Psychotherapy*, *20*(2), 147–158. doi:10.1891/jcop.20.2.147

CASEL (Collaborative for Academic, Social, and Emotional Learning) (2003). *Safe and sound: An educational leader's guide to evidence-based social and emotional learning (SEL) programs.* Chicago: Author.

Chan, D. W. (2010). Gratitude, gratitude intervention and subjective well-being among Chinese school teachers in Hong Kong. *Educational Psychology, 30*(2), 139–153. doi:10.1080/01443410903493934

Chow, R. M., & Lowery, B. S. (2010). Thanks, but no thanks: The role of personal responsibility in the experience of gratitude. *Journal of Experimental Social Psychology, 46*, 487–493.

Duckworth, A. L., Steen, T. A., & Seligman, M. E. P. (2005). Positive psychology in clinical practice. *Annual Review of Clinical Psychology, 1*(1), 629–651.

Emmons, R. A. (2007). Pay it forward: A symposium on gratitude. *Greater Good, 4*, 12–15.

Emmons, R. A., Froh, J. J., & Mishra, A. (in press). The assessment of gratitude. In S. J. Lopez (Ed.), *Positive psychological assessment* (2nd ed.). Washington, DC: American Psychological Association.

Emmons, R. A. & Hill, J. (2001). *Words of gratitude for mind, body, and soul.* Radnor, PA: Templeton Foundation Press.

Emmons, R. A., & McCullough, M. E. (2003). Counting blessings versus burdens: An experimental investigation of gratitude and subjective well-being in daily life. *Journal of Personality and Social Psychology, 84*(2), 377–389. doi:10.1037/0022- 3514.84.2.377

Emmons, R. A., McCullough, M. E., & Tsang, J. (2003) The assessment of gratitude. In S. J. Lopez & C. R. Snyder (Eds.), *Positive psychological assessment: A handbook of models and measures* (pp. 327–341). Washington, DC: American Psychological Association.

Froh, J. J., Bono, G., Fan, J., Emmons, R. A., Henderson, K., Harris, C. ... & Wood, A. (in press). Nice thinking! An educational intervention that teaches children how to think gratefully. [Special issue: Theoretical Frameworks in School Psychology Intervention Research: Interdisciplinary Perspectives and Future Directions]. *School Psychology Review.*

Froh, J. J., Kashdan, T. B., Ozimkowski, K. M., & Miller, N. (2009). Who benefits the most from a gratitude intervention in children and adolescents? Examining positive affect as a moderator. *Journal of Positive Psychology, 4*, 408–422.

Froh, J. J., Sefick, W. J., & Emmons, R. A. (2008). Counting blessings in early adolescents: An experimental study of gratitude and subjective well-being. *Journal of School Psychology, 46*, 213–233.

Froh, J. J., Yurkewicz, C., & Kashdan, T. B. (2009). Gratitude and subjective well-being in early adolescence: Examining gender differences. *Journal of Adolescence, 32*, 633–650.

Geraghty, A. W. A., Wood, A. M., & Hyland, M. E. (2010a). Attrition from self-directed interventions: Investigating the relationship between psychological predictors, technique and dropout from a body image intervention. *Social Science and Medicine, 71*, 30–37.

Geraghty, A. W. A., Wood, A. M., & Hyland, M. E. (2010b). Dissociating the facets of hope: Agency and pathways predict attrition from unguided self-help therapy in opposite directions. *Journal of Research in Personality, 44*, 155–158.

Gordon, C. L., Arnette, R. M., & Smith, R. E. (2011). Have you thanked your spouse today? Felt and expressed gratitude among married couples. *Personality and Individual Differences, 50*(3), 339–343. doi:10.1016/j.paid.2010.10.012

Hay, L. L. (1996). *Gratitude: A way of life.* Carlsbad, CA: Hay House.

Huebner, E. S., Drane, W., & Valois, R. F. (2000). Levels and demographic correlates of adolescent life satisfaction reports. *School Psychology International, 21*, 281–292.

Huebner, E. S., Valois, R. F., Paxton, R. J., & Drane, J. W. (2005). Middle school students' perceptions of quality of life. *Journal of Happiness Studies, 6*, 15–24.

Jones, S. M., Brown, J. L., & Aber, J. L. (2008). Classroom settings as targets of intervention and research. In M. Shinn & H. Yoshikawa (Eds.), *Toward positive youth development: Transforming schools and community programs* (pp. 58–77). Oxford: Oxford University Press.

Lyubomirsky, S., Dickerhoof, R., Boehm, J. K., & Sheldon, K. M. (2011). Becoming happier takes both a will and a proper way: An experimental longitudinal intervention to boost well-being. *Emotion, 11*(2), 391–402. doi:10.1037/a0022575

Lyubomirsky, S., Sheldon, K. M., & Schkade, D. (2005). Pursuing happiness: The architecture of sustainable change. *Review of General Psychology, 9*, 111–131.

McCullough, M. E., Emmons, R. A., & Tsang, J. (2002). The grateful disposition: A conceptual and empirical topography. *Journal of Personality and Social Psychology, 82*(1), 112–127. doi:10.1037/0022-3514.82.1.112

McCullough, M. E., Kilpatrick, S. D., Emmons, R. A., & Larson, D. B. (2001). Is gratitude a moral affect? *Psychological Bulletin, 127*(2), 249–266. doi:10.1037/0033-2909.127.2.249

McCullough, M. E., Tsang, J., & Emmons, R. A. (2004). Gratitude in intermediate affective terrain: Links of grateful moods to individual differences and daily emotional experience. *Journal of Personality and Social Psychology, 86*(2), 295–309. doi:10.1037/0022-3514.86.2.295

Nelson, M. (2009). Gratitude and the counseling profession. Editorial. *Louisiana Journal of Counseling.*

Richelieu, F. (1996). Gratitude: Its healing properties. In L. L. Hay (Ed.), *Gratitude: A way of life* (pp. 225–232). Carlsbad, CA: Hay House.

Seligman, M. E. P., Rashid, T., & Parks, A. C. (2006). Positive psychotherapy. *American Psychologist, 61*, 774–788.

Seligman, M. P., Steen, T. A., Park, N., & Peterson, C. (2005). Positive psychology progress: Empirical validation of interventions. *American Psychologist, 60*(5), 410–421. doi:10.1037/0003-066X.60.5.410.

Serafini, K. (2011). *I am gr8ful for you.* Eumundi, Qld: Lithos Therapy Pty Ltd.

Sergeant, S., & Mongrain, M. (2011). Are positive psychology exercises helpful for people with depressive personality styles? *Journal of Positive Psychology, 4*, 260–272. doi:10.1080/17439760.2011.577089

Shinn, M., & Yoshikawa, H. (Eds.) (2008). *Toward positive youth development: Transforming schools and community programs.* New York: Oxford University Press.

Verkuyten, M., & Thijs, J. (2002). School satisfaction of elementary school children: The role of performance, peer relations, ethnicity, and gender. *Social Indicators Research, 59*, 203–228.

Watkins, P. C., Grimm, D. L., & Hailu, L. (1998, June). Counting your blessings: Grateful individuals recall more positive memories. Presented at the 11th Annual Convention of the American Psychological Society Convention, Denver, CO.

Watkins, P. C., Woodward, K., Stone, T., & Kolts, R. L. (2003). Gratitude and happiness: Development of a measure of gratitude and relationships with subjective well-being. *Social Behavior and Personality, 31*(5), 431–452. doi:10.2224/sbp.2003.31.5.431

Wood, A. M., Brown, G. D. A., & Maltby, J. (2011). Thanks, but I'm used to better: A relative rank model of gratitude. *Emotion, 11*, 175–180.

Wood, A. M., Froh, J. J., & Geraghty, A. (2010). Gratitude and well-being: A review and theoretical integration [Special issue]. *Clinical Psychology Review, 30*, 890–905.

Wood, A. M., Joseph, S., & Maltby, J. (2008). Gratitude uniquely predicts satisfaction with life: Incremental validity above the domains and facets of the five factor model. *Personality and Individual Differences*, *45*, 49–54.

Wood, A. M., Maltby, J., Stewart, N., Linley, P., & Joseph, S. (2008). A social-cognitive model of trait and state levels of gratitude. *Emotion*, *8*(2), 281–290. doi:10.1037/1528-3542.8.2.281

2

Positive Psychological Interventions for Promoting Forgiveness

History, Present Status, and Future Prospects

Everett L. Worthington Jr., Nathaniel G. Wade, and William T. Hoyt

Introduction

When the positive psychology movement began, Seligman and Csikszentmihalyi (2000) noted that the applied literature on the virtues was underdeveloped, especially in comparison to psychopathology or basic positive psychology. Interventions to promote virtues needed to be designed, broadened, and adapted to a variety of populations, and tested in randomized clinical trials and other program evaluation designs. One virtue, however, with a well-developed empirical foundation was forgiveness, a characteristic with over two decades of amassed research.

Forgiveness studies got a leg up on many of the other virtues of positive psychology through a trade book by Lewis Smedes (1984), *Forgive and forget: Healing the hurts we don't deserve.* Smedes argued that forgiveness should be undertaken because it could be beneficial to oneself. That argument got the attention of both psychotherapists and researchers, who began to write about and advocate forgiveness for its benefits to the forgiver (Fitzgibbons, 1986; Flanigan, 1987; Hope, 1987; Worthington & DiBlasio, 1990). Interventionists reporting clinical studies were not far behind (Al-Mabuk, Enright, & Cardis, 1995; Coyle & Enright, 1997; Freedman & Enright, 1996; Hebl & Enright, 1993; McCullough & Worthington, 1995; McCullough, Worthington, & Rachal, 1997). When, in 1997, the John Templeton Foundation and 14 funding partners under the organization of A Campaign for Forgiveness Research (www.forgiving.org) eventually funded $9.4 million in grant support, numerous research programs that studied forgiveness interventions emerged.

The Wiley Blackwell Handbook of Positive Psychological Interventions, First Edition.
Edited by Acacia C. Parks and Stephen M. Schueller.

Forgiveness interventions are useful for three purposes: promoting healing, preventing problems, and promoting flourishing. Healing includes psychotherapeutic purposes and interventions that could also transform and heal society by fostering reconciliation among conflicting social groups. Forgiveness interventions have also been applied for prevention of individual, couple, family, group, or societal tensions. Forgiveness interventions have also promoted flourishing through enrichment of individuals, couples, families, groups, communities, and societal groups. In enrichment, people broaden their repertoires and build their resources for more fulfilled living. Positive psychology is most concerned with the third use. In the present chapter, therefore, we will examine evidence related to each of these outcomes, but will give the most attention to interventions that help promote flourishing.

Psychotherapeutic interventions to promote forgiveness – in individual, couple, family, or group psychotherapy – can be either focal interventions or interventions in service of other goals. For focal interventions, the client seeks help specifically to forgive some egregious wrong or some troublesome person. Forgiveness therapy is aimed at a goal of increasing forgiveness. Presumably, the client is willing to spend money, time, and effort at complying with the intervention. Such interventions tend to be of long duration because they deal with life-disrupting problems and forgiveness is at the core of healing. For example, Freedman and Enright (1996) treated incest survivors and the mean time of treatment was almost 60 hours. When forgiveness is dealt with in the course of normal psychotherapy, however, clients and psychotherapists are likely to spend less time on it because they want to expend energy on relieving a symptom, such as depression, and forgiveness is merely one of many ways that might be chosen to ameliorate the depression. They do not want a long intervention but an effective and efficient one that accomplishes the maximum amount of forgiveness within a short time. Typically, practitioners are unwilling to spend more than about two hours on forgiveness-specific techniques when forgiveness is not the focus of treatment (DiBlasio & Procter, 1993). This guideline of about two hours of forgiveness-focused intervention in psychotherapy typically produces a $d = 0.20$ (see Wade, Hoyt, & Worthington, 2013 for a meta-analysis) for measures of forgiveness and about $d = 0.15$ for related mental health outcomes such as reductions of depression and anxiety and promotion of hope. Thus, to promote substantial forgiveness and mental health benefits arising from the forgiveness intervention, some adjunctive intervention is needed. Our observations of non-focal psychotherapeutic forgiveness interventions produce two practical lessons. First, clinicians can refer people to (a) adjunctive psychoeducational or process groups, (b) community adjunctive treatments (such as pastoral counseling, church groups, community programs), or (c) resources such as books, DVDs, or web-available material. Second, a future need is to develop a powerful two-hour or less evidence-based treatment that uses the most effective techniques to produce the most change in the shortest time. As we will see in the following review, in forgiveness work a strong dose–response relationship exists. The greater the amount of time spent trying to forgive, the more forgiveness clients experience. Thus, selecting techniques that "beat" the dose-effect regression line might be a challenge.

Evidence-based benefits of forgiving

Forgiveness interventions are made available to people wanting to forgive because forgiveness is presumed to be beneficial. Forgiveness benefits physical health (Worthington, Witvliet, Pietrini, & Miller, 2007), mental health (Toussaint & Webb, 2005), relationships (Fehr, Gelfand, & Nag, 2010), and spirituality (for a meta-analysis, see Davis, Worthington, & Hook, 2013). Societal benefits have also been claimed, but less has been done to establish the empirical basis of such claims (Fincham & Beach, 2001; Worthington & Berry, 2004). To date, the interventions have been designed to promote physical health (Luskin, Ginzberg, & Thoresen, 2005), mental health (Enright & Fitzgibbons, 2000), and relational (Worthington, 2006) and spiritual benefits (Rye et al., 2005). But most have been aimed at mental health benefits.

Other uses of forgiveness interventions

Forgiveness groups have been advocated as being useful as adjunct groups to psychotherapy for people with interpersonal problems, as relationship enhancement and skill building for couples and families, as groups that can promote a religious virtue of forgiving and build religious spirituality, as a way of modifying current responses to an unchangeable past and to open relational possibilities among former conflicting parties in the future (Arendt, 1963; Tutu, 1999), and as part of a societal reparation strategy, called Track III diplomacy (Worthington & Aten, 2010). Montville (2001) suggested two types of peacemaking strategies. Track I diplomacy involves treaties and agreements between conflicting bodies. Track II diplomacy involves bringing leaders of both sides together to hear and empathize with the other side's stories. Presumably the transformed opinion leaders would take their empathic understandings of the former enemies back to their like-minded people. However, how might the transmission of those empathic and forgiving attitudes occur within groups? Worthington and Aten (2010) suggested that an addition was needed, which they called Track III diplomacy. It involves small groups separately within each side aimed at promoting forgiveness and positive attitudes about reconciliation. Thus, overall, forgiveness interventions can benefit individuals, relationships, families, groups, organizations, communities, and societies. Which intervention one elects to use depends on the intended use for the intervention.

For instance, a program in Track III diplomacy has spread throughout South and Latin America. La Fundación para la Reconciliación y Perdón (http://www.fundacionparalareconciliacion.org/) includes Escuelas de Perdón y Reconciliación (ES.PE.RE; schools for forgiveness and reconciliation) which are conducted by lay helpers in over 10 Latin American countries. The schools last about 60 to 80 hours and teach people who are in societies that have been ravaged by war and conflict how to forgive. These programs have included elements of Worthington's (2006) REACH Forgiveness model and of Enright and Fitzgibbons' (2000) process model of forgiveness, the details of which will be discussed later, but the elements of the two programs are but a fraction of the work on reconciliation that is taught. Roman Catholic priest and sociologist Leonel Narváez founded this grassroots movement and disseminates it throughout Mexico, Central America, and South America. In that context, neither REACH Forgiveness nor Enright's process model alone would be adequate. Both are used and combined with many methods appropriate for each locale. This grassroots movement has garnered attention from UNESCO and boasts three completed international conferences. It is a true force for peace in Latin America.

Descriptions of Forgiveness Interventions

In the following sections, we briefly summarize the most used and investigated interventions. Although, the selection of interventions provides a broad overview of available techniques, the scope of this chapter does not allow an exhaustive review. We would direct interested readers to the following sources for more thorough reviews of available interventions: Worthington, 2005; Wade, Hoyt, and Worthington, 2013; Wade, Worthington, and Meyer, 2005. In the following sections, we survey group and couple interventions. However, the strategies within virtually all of the interventions are applied to individuals in psychotherapy as well. We will lead you through the therapeutic protocols for the most investigated group and couple interventions. Before we embark on that journey, though, let us make three orienting remarks.

First, the interventions are presented in a set of steps. These are not stages in a natural forgiveness process, but they are steps in therapeutic protocols that are meant to lead clients through a series of sequenced experiences that might lead to forgiveness. Thus, they are subject to clinical flexibility.

Second, reading the different listings of steps, one might easily get lost in the trees and miss the forest. All of the protocols follow a similar pattern – reviewing hurts, increasing empathy for the offender, and solidifying the gains. Reviewing the hurts helps motivate the person to forgive. Increasing empathy for the offender involves therapeutic maneuvers intended to help the person become ready to forgive. Almost always those maneuvers involve having the victim take the cognitive perspective of the offender and, if possible, experience emotional empathy. Most protocols make some distinctions between making a decision to forgive, experiencing emotional forgiveness, and saying "I forgive you." Most seek to bring people through a decision and emotional experience of forgiving, with the couple therapies much more focused on interpersonal interactions than the group (or individual) applications of forgiveness. At the end of each protocol, there is usually some attempt to make one's successful experience of having forgiven more concrete than a mere internal process, so some kind of symbolic gesture reflecting forgiveness is often employed.

Third, typically forgiveness is the explicit focus of these protocols, but each one might be tailored to emphasize mental health or physical health outcomes, too. The usual focus is also forgiving a particular event rather than forgiving a person who might have perpetrated many harms on the forgiver. If forgiveness of a person is one's target, the therapeutic guidance is usually to forgive the most salient harms first, working one's way to lesser hurts until generalization to forgiving the person can occur. There are more commonalities than differences among the different treatments, with the major differences being in packaging and in which aspects of experience are emphasized – emotion, cognition, or behavior.

Group interventions

Enright's psychotherapeutic and psychoeducational forgiveness interventions Perhaps the most investigated intervention has been based on Enright's process model of forgiveness (Enright & Fitzgibbons, 2000). He and others have applied this model to treat people for whom unforgiveness poses serious physical and mental health problems. It has been used to treat diverse populations including survivors of incest (Freedman & Enright, 1996), men working through a partner's abortion (Coyle & Enright, 1997), and individuals who have experienced emotional abuse. Enright has applied it in dealing with past emotional abuse (Reed & Enright, 2006), individuals with alcoholism (Lin, Mack, Enright, Krahn, & Baskin, 2004), as well as adolescents and children (for a review, see Worthington, Jennings, & DiBlasio, 2010). The evidence supports its efficacy at promoting forgiveness with early, middle, and late adolescents, but not with children.

Enright's intervention is arrayed in 20 steps that are grouped into four phases, which are briefly described below. Units 1–8 represent the Uncovering Phase. Working through these eight units allows the offended or hurt person to experience both the pain and reality of the injury and how it has affected him or her. Feeling pain from the recall of the psychological or physical injury motivates some people to see a need for change and to move toward forgiving. Units 9–11 represent the Decision Phase, which Enright treats as the critical part of the forgiveness process intervention. In the Decision Phase the person thinks about forgiving before committing to forgive. The person might decide to forgive even though the person does not feel like it at the time. The Work Phase of the model (Units 12–15) begins with seeing the offender with new eyes (i.e., reframing; Unit 12), and moves to empathy (Unit 13), compassion (Unit 14), and acceptance (Unit 15). The Deepening Phase represents the last five units in the model – finding meaning in suffering and forgiveness, realizing one has previously needed others' forgiveness, insight that one is not alone, embracing a new purpose in life after forgiving, and awareness of less negative and more positive affect.

Worthington's REACH Forgiveness model for psychoeducational interventions Worthington's (2006) REACH model is based on the assumption that a forgiveness intervention should accomplish three tasks. First, it must motivate people to forgive. Second, it must help people integrate forgiveness into their lives. Third, it should provide a step-by-step guide to forgiveness. All tasks are important. The intervention is based on the idea that forgiving often involves both a decision and an emotional transformation, which may require a protracted struggle. Emotional transformation usually requires sustained and intense effort.

The REACH Forgiveness intervention provides a five-step model to lead people through a decision to forgive and then emotional replacement of unforgiving emotions with more forgiving emotions. Each step coincides with a letter of the REACH acronym. First, participants recall the hurt (R), which includes recalling the transgression while lessening the blame and emphasis on one's victim status. People are invited to make a decision to forgive the hurt, but that offer is repeated later, after they have experienced more emotional forgiveness. Second, participants empathize (E) with the offender to promote empathy and other positive, other-oriented emotions toward the offender, such as sympathy, compassion, or even love. Third, participants give an altruistic (A) gift of forgiveness. That is, an appeal is made to forgive as a way of releasing the offender from the justice that he or she deserves due to offending or hurting the forgiver. To give the altruistic gift of forgiving, the person is engaged in exercises to stimulate (a) empathy, (b) gratitude for having been graciously forgiven oneself in the past by people such as parents, teachers, or friends, and (c) humility. Fourth, participants make a commitment (C) to the emotional forgiveness they have experienced by making their experience more public than a mental decision. For example, they might write a certificate of forgiveness, a letter to the offender, or perform a symbolic act such as writing the offense on a piece of paper and burning it. Finally, the intervention helps participants to hold (H) on to forgiveness in the face of doubts through referring back to commitments and planning strategies for dealing with triggers for unforgiving thoughts, ruminations, emotions, or behaviors. Leader and participant manuals are available without cost at www.people.vcu.edu/~eworth, and can be modified for use. This includes six-hour secular and Christian versions of the intervention and an 18-hour version of psychoeducational group exercises, and instructions for obtaining no-cost DVDs illustrating how to lead the secular and the Christian groups (a small fee is charged for postage and handling).

Rye's forgiveness groups for divorce or relationship termination Rye and colleagues (Rye & Pargament, 2002; Rye et al., 2004) have developed an intervention targeting individuals' experience of anger and bitterness post-divorce that is designed to increase their levels of forgiveness toward their ex-spouse. Loosely based upon Worthington's REACH model, and conducted in a group, this treatment contains five steps: (a) discussion of feelings of betrayal, (b) coping with anger, (c) forgiveness education, obstacles to forgiveness, and strategies for achieving forgiveness, (d) self-care and self-forgiveness, and (e) relapse prevention and closure. Both religious and secular versions have been tested and are available.

Luskin's forgive-for-good model Luskin's (2001) model incorporates cognitive-behavioral therapy methods within his approach to forgiving. He summarizes his forgive-for-good model in nine steps: (a) Survey one's feelings and what does not feel OK about the offense. (b) Commit to oneself to feel better. (c) Do not confuse forgiveness with reconciliation. Learn to take the offenses less personally than before treatment. (d) Recognize that one's primary distress is coming from the hurt feelings, thoughts, and physical upset, not from the hurt. (e) When one feels upset, practice stress management to soothe sympathetic nervous system activation. (f) Stop expecting that others will provide one's needs. Hope for health, love, friendship, and prosperity, and work hard to get them. But do not demand them. (g) Put your energy into looking for another way to get your positive goals met than through the experience that has hurt you. (h) Remember that a life well lived is your best revenge. Do not focus on wounded feelings, and thereby give power to the offender. Instead, learn to look for love, beauty, and kindness. Appreciate what one has, not focus on what one does not have. (i) Remind oneself of one's heroic choice to forgive.

Luskin has done a couple of studies to investigate the efficacy of the program (e.g., Luskin et al., 2005).

Interventions to promote forgiveness in couples

Gordon, Baucom, and Snyder's forgiveness after infidelity Gordon and colleagues' model (Gordon & Baucom, 1998; Gordon, Baucom, & Snyder, 2004) suggests that forgiveness consists of three components: (a) a realistic, non-distorted, balanced view of the relationship; (b) a release from being controlled by negative affect toward the participating partner; and (c) a lessened desire to punish the participating partner. Violated assumptions from traumatic betrayals often can leave the victim feeling out of control and no longer able to predict future behaviors on the part of his or her partner. Therefore, the forgiveness process results from attempts to reconstruct these former cognitions and regain a sense of interpersonal control, predictability, and safety in the relationship. Forgiveness is therefore thought to pass through three major stages: (a) impact, (b) a search for meaning, and (c) recovery, or moving on. In the impact stage, people recollect details related to the betrayal in an attempt to comprehend what has happened. However, because this betrayal often has major implications for the injured person's well-being, this cognitive process is accompanied by an overwhelming array of emotions such as fear, hurt, or anger. These emotions often alternate with a sense of numbness or disbelief. Additionally, people may find themselves acting toward their partners in ways that are punitive, erratic, or unlike their usual selves. In the meaning stage, people seek to discover why the event happened and to give it meaning. In the recovery or moving on stage, the injured person must move beyond the event and stop allowing it to control his or her life. Forgiveness involves moving on by giving up the control that negative affect can have over the injured person's thoughts and behaviors, and by giving up the right to punish the partner.

Worthington's Forgiveness and Reconciliation through Experiencing Empathy (FREE) approach Worthington's REACH Forgiveness model fits within a larger model called Forgiveness and Reconciliation through Experiencing Empathy (FREE), which has been tested in several studies with couples (Burchard et al., 2003; Ripley & Worthington, 2002; Worthington et al., 2003) and parents (Kiefer et al., 2010). The protocol is made up of two halves of Worthington's hope-focused couples approach (Worthington et al., 1997). HOPE (Handling Our Problems Effectively) is a communication-, conflict resolution-, and intimacy-based approach. FREE (Worthington & Drinkard, 2000) involves four planks to cross the "bridge to reconciliation" – (a) a *decision* about whether, how, and when to reconcile; (b) training in *discussion* about transgressions, including making non-blaming reproaches, giving effective accounts, expressing forgiveness, requesting time before granting forgiveness, dealing with failed requests for forgiving, and accepting forgiveness when one does not feel worthy; (c) *detoxification* of the relationship, which includes employing the REACH Forgiveness model and engaging in relational repair strategies; and (d) *devotion* to building a positive couple relationship by communicating to strengthen the emotional bond and value the other person.

Greenberg's emotion-focused therapy – couples (EFT-C) Greenberg, Warwar, and Malcolm (2010) created a specialized EFT-C treatment focused on facilitating the resolution of emotional interpersonal injuries specifically by forgiving. The treatment protocol follows seven steps: (a) Identify the impact of the psychological or physical injury and the painful emotions felt by the injured partner. (b) Identify the negative interactional cycle and each partner's position in the cycle. (c) Promote expression of empathy with the offended partner's pain resulting from the offense. (d) Access unacknowledged vulnerable attachment- and identity-related feelings. (e) Reframe the problem in the relationship in terms of underlying feelings, and attachment and identity needs, and connect this to the injury. (f) Promote expression of sincere remorse, regret, and apology. (g) Promote steps toward rebuilding trust.

They earlier had investigated the efficacy of emotion-focused therapy (EFT) using repeated sessions of the Gestalt empty-chair dialogue (Greenberg, Warwar, & Malcolm, 2008). Clients in EFT using empty-chair dialogue showed more improvement than a psychoeducational treatment on forgiveness, letting go, global symptoms, and target complaints, to which they were compared.

DiBlasio's decision-based forgiveness DiBlasio (2000) has developed a forgiveness intervention for couples who are dealing with some transgression in couples therapy. Although a broad assessment evaluates the appropriateness of the intervention, the assumption is that virtually any couple seeking counseling have transgressed against each other and could benefit from forgiveness. DiBlasio begins targeting forgiveness, or at least the decision to forgive, during a single two- to three-hour session. He suggests that this decision to forgive is a cognitive process that can shift the couple onto more positive ground from the beginning of couples therapy and improve the overall therapeutic outcomes. Although DiBlasio acknowledges that emotional forgiveness does take time, he views decision-based forgiveness as the important aspect of couples treatment.

DiBlasio's decision-based forgiveness for infidelity involves 13 steps (DiBlasio, 1998, 2000). The first three steps define decision-based forgiveness, discuss its benefits, and prepare the couple for the decision. Then each partner is given the opportunity to seek forgiveness for his or her own wrongful actions in order to create an atmosphere of personal accountability. During the first three steps, DiBlasio suggests that therapists must attend to their clients' expectations concerning how their partners should respond, and help each person to avoid coercive attempts to make his or her partner admit behaviors that the individual sees as wrong. The couple then take turns going through steps 4–12. During these steps, the offense is stated, the offender provides an explanation for his or her behavior, and the reasons for this behavior are further explored, as are the offended person's reactions. Offenders are encouraged to be empathic about the effects of their behaviors on their partners and to develop a plan to stop or prevent the behaviors. Then, the offended partners are asked to recognize the offenders' emotions such as guilt, shame, or fear, about the offense or the effects of the offense, which can be facilitated by either tracing patterns back to offenders' childhoods or the offended partners identifying their own failures in their relationships. Steps 4 to 12 end by recognizing the "choice and commitment involved in letting go" (DiBlasio, 2000, p. 155), and a formal ritual of seeking and granting forgiveness between partners. This formal ritual is the thirteenth step, and symbolizes the couple's commitment to forgiveness and decision to let go of the pain of the betrayal.

Hargrave and Sells' contextual model of forgiveness Hargrave (1994) developed a theoretical framework of forgiveness for use in family and couple therapy that has received some empirical support (Hargrave & Sells, 1997). The model suggests that forgiveness involves a response to a violation of an innate sense of justice or a disruption between the implicit balance of give (obligations) and take (entitlements) inherent in healthy family functioning. The betraying member, or the one who disrupts this balance and violates the justice standard, has likely experienced a violation of trust in a prior relationship and consequently might feel justified hurting the partner. As a result, the betrayed partner faces the realization that the betraying family member may not be reliable or trustworthy, which can engender a number of emotional reactions such as rage and shame. If this injustice is not satisfactorily resolved, betrayed individuals are likely to carry the results forward into new relationships and thus play out their own roles of destructive entitlement in their own family relationships. Forgiveness is theorized to be an effective method to end the cycle of intergenerational transmission of discord and betrayal.

Thus, Hargrave (1994) suggests that the work of forgiveness in families is made up of both exonerating and forgiving in an attempt to right injustice and rebalance the ratio of obligations and entitlements in the family system. Exonerating is more cognitive in nature and includes gaining insight into and understanding the motive behind the betrayal. The increased insight gained allows the individual to become aware of how familial patterns are repeated and to understand or "identify with the victimizer's position, limitations, development, efforts, and intent" (Hargrave & Sells, 1997, p. 44). On the other hand, forgiving is more behavioral and involves a direct discussion between the victimizer and victim about developing a new trustworthy relationship. In addition, forgiving might involve giving the offender the opportunity for compensation, such as allowing the victimizer to engage in a series of behaviors designed to show increased signs of trustworthiness. We observe that Hargrave treats forgiveness not as an intrapersonal experience – as do all the other theorists – but as an interpersonal process. Other theorists also acknowledge the interpersonal transactions that contextualize forgiveness, but they treat those as something different from forgiveness. Hargrave emphasizes that these components are not stages that people progress through in succession; instead, he hypothesizes that people vary between these strategies as they forgive.

Do Forgiveness Interventions Work?

In a recent review of intervention studies with adolescents and children, Worthington, Jennings, and DiBlasio (2010) concluded that none were effective at promoting forgiveness with children. Since that review, one study has reported positive effects with children in a school setting (see Enright, Enright, Holter, Baskin, & Knutson, 2010). Generally, children might not yet have developed the cognitive skills to do more than copy apologetic and forgiving behavior. They do not seem to develop cognitively until early adolescence. Worthington et al.'s review included three studies with middle school adolescents and eight with high school adolescents – most of which effectively promoted forgiveness, and when investigated, better mental health.

By 2000, enough efficacy studies had been conducted on psychoeducational interventions to conduct a meta-analysis to examine the dose–response effect of psychoeducational interventions to promote forgiveness. Worthington, Sandage, and Berry (2000) graphed effect sizes for 19 clinical trials and Worthington, Kurusu, et al. (2000) graphed effect sizes for 23 clinical trials. Both dose–effect relationships were characterized by correlations between time and effect size on the order of .75. It seemed to matter less which program was being evaluated than how long the program lasted and whether it sought to promote empathy and emotional forgiveness (which had stronger outcomes) rather than a decision to forgive.

In 2004, Baskin and Enright meta-analyzed nine intervention studies to promote forgiveness. They were selective in the studies that they chose to meta-analyze, given that the two earlier meta-analyses reviewed 19 (Worthington, Sandage, & Berry, 2000) and 23 clinical trials (Worthington, Kurusu, et al., 2000). They classified them as decision- versus process-based with process-based interventions further subdivided into group and individual. In analyzing the nature of the interventions, they described the Enright process model as a conceptual baseline and described the similarity of the McCullough et al. (1997) empathy-based model to the Enright process model. They found that the process-individual treatments (i.e., the Enright process model applied to individual counseling) were substantially more effective than the process-group interventions which in turn were much more effective than the decision-based groups. They did not take into account the duration of the treatments although many of the interventions with the largest effect sizes corresponded to the longest interventions (e.g., the effect size for Freedman and Enright was 2.16 for 60 hours of treatment; in contrast, effect size for Coyle and Enright was 1.21 for 18 hours of treatment; and the effect size for McCullough and colleagues was 0.53 for 8 hours of treatment). In addition, Baskin and Enright (2004) did not account for severity of the transgression. Enright's process model was typically used in psychotherapeutic or group therapeutic treatments with serious offenses. Worthington's treatments were always used in psychoeducational treatments with non-clinically disturbed people aimed at forgiving those whom they had struggled to forgive, but to do so more as producing flourishing than as therapeutic treatment.

In 2005, Wade, Worthington, and Meyer conducted a meta-analysis combining 42 effect sizes of psychoeducational groups. Again, the correlation between duration of the intervention and effect size at producing forgiveness was around .75. Acknowledging that treatments discussed their elements differently, Wade et al. (2005) found that components of forgiveness interventions could be described similar to the general framework of the REACH Forgiveness model. They analyzed treatment manuals to determine the approximate time spent at each component, and they correlated that component's time with the effect size of the study (relative to control condition).

In 2008, Lundahl, Taylor, Stevenson, and Roberts meta-analyzed 16 process-based studies of forgiveness. They concluded that Enright's model was superior to Worthington's REACH Forgiveness model (in which they included a study comparing 10-minute videotaped interventions, a five-hour intervention with couples, and an intervention of one hour aimed at decisional forgiveness). However, they also noted that severity of offense was confounded with treatment program.

Recently, Wade, Hoyt, and Worthington (2013) meta-analyzed 64 interventions. The mean effect size was 0.55 relative to no-treatment controls and 0.39 relative to alternative treatments, indicating that on average, treated participants were more forgiving than 71% of those receiving no intervention, and 65% of those receiving an alternative (non-forgiveness-based) intervention. The effect sizes for mental health outcomes were similar. Wade et al. found that individual, couple, and group treatments all had significant effect sizes against no treatment but only individual and group treatments were more effective than alternatives. When they compared individual treatments against group treatments, individual treatments were more effective than group interventions against no-treatment controls and alternatives. Several important moderators were tested including theoretical model, intervention duration, and severity of problem. Enright's (n = 22), Worthington's (n = 21), and all other treatments (n = 21) were compared against each other. First-order analyses showed that Enright's was the most effective. However, as with all of the previous meta-analyses, the outcomes were confounded with both the severity of the offense experienced and the length of treatment. After intervention duration and severity of problem were considered, the significant differences among types of treatments disappeared.

In sum, these reviews suggest that the type of forgiveness intervention is much less important than the context and duration of treatment. We would have to conclude at this point that for serious offenses the evidence supports Enright's program. For offenses of moderate severity, the typically shorter group psychoeducation program (e.g., Worthington's) is equivalent in efficacy to Enright's and both have an established evidence base. Other specific treatments aimed at particular offenses (e.g., Luskin's, DiBlasio's, Greenberg's, Gordon's, etc.) do not have enough studies investigating their efficacy to merit comparing to Enright's and Worthington's models. A single laboratory has investigated most of these with only one or two studies per intervention. Thus although they appear promising, no firm conclusions can be drawn.

Efficacious Components of Forgiveness Interventions

Wade et al. (2005) analyzed 42 studies of psychoeducational treatments to explore possible mechanisms of action. Wade et al. coded intervention treatment manuals for the duration of time spent on crucial components – irrespective of theoretical orientation. Five of the seven identified components paralleled Worthington's REACH Forgiveness model, with two additional components of time spent on arriving at a consensus definition of forgiveness and supplemental interventions (e.g., relaxation). Wade et al. (2005) correlated the duration spent on each component with the effect size on the principal measure of forgiveness. The highest correlations between effect size and duration spent on components were for empathizing with the offender, r = 0.51, and committing to forgive, r = 0.52. The elements of the interventions might be confounded and related to overall time intervening because the effect size for the forgiveness measure was for the global intervention, not individual components. However, this analysis suggests that empathizing and committing to forgive might be doing much of the work in helping participants to achieve forgiveness.

A few investigations have compared components within a single study. For example, Al-Mabuk et al. (1995) first examined a decision-based component before examining the full treatment. The decision-based component alone was not efficacious. The full treatment, including process components, produced a greater effect. This does not account for dose, but does suggesting that the decision alone is not enough to produce change.

Worthington has frequently examined components within the same study. Worthington, Kurusu, et al. (2000) randomly assigned people to eight brief 10-minute mini-interventions. They found few differences between those brief components. However, as previously discussed, duration of intervention corresponds to amount of forgiveness instigated, and statistically detectable differences are unlikely to emerge in 10-minute interventions. In another attempt to study components, McCullough and Worthington (1995) compared a decisional appeal to a motive of self-enhancement (i.e., forgive for your own benefit) to a motive of altruism (i.e., forgive to benefit the offender). The treatment was only one hour and both were aimed at producing a decision to forgive, not emotional forgiveness. Neither decisional component showed much efficacy (which is not surprising given the brief one-hour treatment), although the appeal to self-enhancement outperformed the appeal to altruism.

In investigating these motivational components in a longer intervention study, McCullough et al. (1997) compared an eight-hour empathy-based precursor (using the altruism motive) to the REACH Forgiveness model against an eight-hour decision-based approach (using the self-enhancement motive). They found huge differences favoring the empathy-based focus on emotional forgiveness (see also Sandage & Worthington, 2010). The decision-based approach produced only about the same amount of change in eight hours as it had in the one-hour intervention McCullough and Worthington (1995) tested.

In a final component analysis, Worthington et al. (2003) examined the FREE model (Forgiveness and Reconciliation through Experiencing Empathy) against a conflict and communication-based approach called HOPE (Handling Our Problems Effectively), a communication-based behavioral treatment, in 150 newly wedded couples. They found that both produced substantial changes on multiple measures (relative to no-treatment controls) 5.3 weeks after post-treatment, but that the couples who received FREE maintained their gains at one year post-treatment whereas the changes for HOPE had eroded to one-half their levels at immediate post-treatment. The outcomes included forgiveness, communication, conflict resolution, intimacy, behavioral ratings of videotaped discussions, and salivary cortisol levels.

Experimental studies of components (for a recent meta-analysis, see Wade, Hoyt, Kidwell, & Worthington, in press) and Wade et al.'s (2005) earlier meta-analysis of components across-studies yield similar conclusions. First, forgiveness programs are effective. Second, when duration and offense severity are controlled, different components are comparably effective. Third, the decision or commitment to forgive is important. Fourth, experiencing positive emotion, such as empathy, sympathy, or compassion, toward the offender is vital.

Unresolved Questions about Forgiveness Interventions

What are the theories of change?

David and Montgomery (2011) suggested analyzing the efficacy of not only the treatment package but also the specific theory of change. In an intriguing claim, they note that for a treatment to be considered efficacious it must properly identify the mechanism of action. Take for example the early treatment for malaria. Initially, bad air was thought to cause malaria. A preventative treatment, that was somewhat effective, was to shut the windows, which presumably stopped the bad air from circulating. Given that malaria was actually caused by a pathogen transmitted by the anopheles mosquito, closing the windows could effectively prevent its spread. However, the scientific theory on which the treatment was based was incorrect. We take this critique seriously. Few treatments have explicitly stated theories of change that undergird the treatment protocol.

Enright and Fitzgibbons (2000) treated forgiveness within an intervention as if it followed the same steps in the naturalistic environment. This is not likely. Interventions work by instigating cooperation of clients or participants with a treatment protocol or sequence that is led by the interventionist. Thus, interventions impose a process on most clients; that process is virtually never the same as people might undergo in non-intervention environments. We might more generally, however, assume that Enright's theory of change derives from forgiveness having affective, behavioral, and cognitive components. Forgiveness occurs as, in response to the recall of the transgression event or transgressor, something (in naturalistic or intervention settings) stimulates the person to feel different emotions, do different things, and think different thoughts than when the person was unforgiving. Thus, Enright's intervention is seen as providing a structure and specific interactional exercises to manipulate people's affect, behavior, and cognition. At that general level, the evidence supporting Enright's theory of change is strong. However, what is needed is a more clearly articulated theory of change with the evidence summarized on its behalf.

Worthington's (2006) theory of change is explicit. For decisional forgiveness, he believes that people can decide to forgive if they experience salient emotion-provoking events that inspire forgiveness, or if cognitive processes are activated to lead the person to value forgiveness and motivate the person to pursue consonance with his or her values. The theory of change for emotional forgiveness is what he terms the emotional replacement hypothesis, in which he posits that emotional forgiveness occurs only when negative, unforgiving emotions are replaced by positive other-oriented emotions (i.e., empathy, sympathy, compassion, and love). Chapter 5 of *Forgiveness and reconciliation: Theory and application* summarizes an array of four lines of evidence in support of this hypothesis (Worthington, 2006).

Proposing a clearly articulated theory of change allows rigorous testing of other approaches to promoting forgiveness. Thus far, evidence for intervention packages is robust, but evidence for theories of change is not as convincing.

Are common factors at play in forgiveness interventions?

Strong evidence suggests that therapeutic factors common to different treatments account for a sizable portion of a treatment's effectiveness. For example, the therapeutic alliance that is built between a client and his/her therapist is estimated to account for 5 to 7% of the variance in outcome as compared to the 1% of variance in outcome accounted for by different treatments (based on analysis of many studies, see Wampold, 2001; cf. Siev & Chambless, 2007). These results are based mostly on individual psychotherapy for mental disorders, primarily depression and anxiety. Do these findings generalize to treatments to promote forgiveness?

Some evidence suggests that common factors are at work in treatments to promote forgiveness. First, the forgiveness interventions are based on sound psychotherapeutic and psychoeducational principles and include common factors. These include therapeutic empathy and understanding, active and attentive listening, development of hope, and therapist belief in and commitment to the treatment. Group-based treatments involve additional therapeutic factors such as cohesion among members, altruism, imitative behavior, and interpersonal learning (Yalom & Leszcz, 2005). Developing effective treatments that do not include these common factors is virtually impossible.

Some indirect evidence suggests that common factors may be responsible for the lion's share of forgiveness intervention efficacy when presented in groups. Wade and his colleagues have conducted two treatment studies that have found no differences between explicit forgiveness treatments and alternative treatments (Wade & Meyer, 2009; Wade, Worthington, & Haake, 2009). Although, they did not directly test the degree of common factors present, the equivalent improvement in forgiveness across treatments suggests that a focus on forgiveness might not be required to promote it. Additionally, studies that have found significant differences in forgiveness between treatments tend to confound therapist allegiance with treatment type (i.e., therapists have more allegiance to the forgiveness treatment; e.g., Freedman & Enright, 1996; Reed & Enright, 2006).

If common factors are at work, which ones might be most active? Certainly, a good candidate is therapeutic alliance. Participants seeking to develop forgiveness for a past hurt might be particularly vulnerable to concerns about shame, humiliation, and judgment. To make effective progress with the hurt, participants need to be able to feel safe with the therapist, to have trust that they will not be mocked, belittled, blamed, or judged for the ways that they have been hurt, and to feel free to decide about forgiveness for themselves without external moral obligation. A caring and trusting therapeutic relationship would best mitigate these concerns. Other common factors that are likely at work include therapist empathy for the clients' concerns/predicaments, catharsis related to the sharing of the hurt, and hope for getting better or believing that forgiveness is possible. If a particular treatment approach is providing these therapeutic experiences to someone attempting to forgive a past hurt, then they are likely to be helpful.

On the other hand, it may be that some interventions designed explicitly to promote forgiveness (e.g., Enright's or Worthington's interventions) are better at activating common factors. For example, an intervention that has a clearly understood theoretical base and therapeutic progression might be effective at promoting hope in the treatment and for the future and at inspiring client compliance and investment than an intervention that is more general and perhaps more confusing for clients.

How does forgiveness relate to other virtues?

Classical Aristotelian virtue theory, ancient Christian theorizing (Thomas Aquinas), contemporary Christian theorizing (Wright, 2009), and some research (Berry, Worthington, Wade, Witvliet, & Kiefer, 2005; Peterson & Seligman, 2004) suggest that virtues are interrelated. Ancient sources argued that virtues are unitary – that it is impossible to have forgiveness (for example) without also having the courage to show it, the self-control (or temperance) to exercise and maintain it when emotions are heightened, and a balance with justice to regulate social and societal interactions. In addition, humility and gratitude are necessary to exercise any virtue. Religious writers have also treated virtue as a unitary characteristic. Paul of Tarsus, in the Christian scriptures, argued for a single fruit of the Holy Spirit. Thomas Aquinas, drawing on Aristotle's arguments, concluded the same. Thus, secular and religious virtues might be related in substantive ways. The degree to which virtues or character strengths are unitary or discrete is an important area of investigation in positive psychology.

In our lab at Virginia Commonwealth University, Lavelock, Worthington, Greer, Lin, and Griffin (2013) have just completed a randomized clinical trial, assigning 192 college students to complete one of four six-hour workbooks to promote different virtues (forgiveness, humility, self-control, and patience), a workbook to promote positivity, or a repeated retest control condition. Forgiveness and humility but not self-control and patience workbooks produced substantial forgiveness and humility. All workbooks resulted in people reporting more positive affect and less negative affect, but the positivity workbook was superior to all others. This leads to some initial evidence for both overlapping as well as distinct benefits from practicing the different virtues. In addition, enhancing virtues seemed to promote more positivity, but less so than an intervention with that as its primary aim.

Do forgiveness interventions do more than promote forgiveness?

It is well established that forgiveness groups can promote forgiveness (e.g., Wade et al., in press). However, it is not clear what else might change when one attends a forgiveness intervention, and what supports these additional benefits. For example, research has shown that forgiveness relates to better physical health (Toussaint, Williams, Musick, & Everson, 2001), mental health (Toussaint &

Webb, 2005), relationships (Rusbult, Hannon, Stocker, & Finkel, 2005), and spirituality (Davis, Hook, & Worthington, 2008). But, do forgiveness interventions promote the same benefits that are associated with a lifestyle characterized by a forgiving tendency? Furthermore, if the virtues are indeed interrelated, will the development of forgiveness produce other virtues in the person's character (e.g., justice, prudence, courage, and self-control; faith, hope, and love; humility)? More work is needed to investigate these questions.

Who responds to forgiveness interventions?

Little has been done to determine which character traits might be associated with people who are most likely to benefit from a forgiveness intervention. Might it be people with the most self-control, courage, prudence, orientation toward justice (or to the contrary, mercy), love, faith, hope, or humility? Other potential moderators corresponding to person–activity fit require investigation (see Chapter 22). These might include religious and spiritual variables, emotional styles, problem-solving styles, stress management styles, and the like.

Are cultural adaptations required?

Some interventions have adapted secular forgiveness interventions to Christian populations (see Lampton, Oliver, Worthington, & Berry, 2005; Rye & Pargament, 2002; Rye et al., 2005; Worthington et al., 2010). Besides adapting to religion, many studies have adapted US-formulated interventions to different countries or ethnicities. These include Canada (Greenberg et al., 2010; Struthers, Dupuis, & Eaton, 2005), Northern Ireland (Enright et al., 2010), Hong Kong (Hui & Chau, 2009; Hui & Ho, 2004), and the Philippines (Worthington et al., 2010). These adaptations, however, provide little explicit description about how the interventions take into account aspects of religion, countries, ethnicities, or self-construal as individualists or collectivists. It is critical to specify adaptations and test these against the original version of the intervention. Only then can we discern which adaptations are really necessary.

Conclusion

Forgiveness falls within the recognized boundaries of positive psychology, and many interventions have investigated its promotion in psychotherapeutic, preventive, and (for the purpose of the present review) enrichment or flourishing interventions. Two of the interventions – Enright's process model and the REACH Forgiveness model – have robust evidence to support their use. For other interventions, more research is needed to establish them as efficacious practices. In addition, more nuanced research studies that address more complex questions than simply "Does it work?" are needed.

In particular, the research presented within this chapter contains a number of intriguing findings. First, the duration of treatment is very important in helping people forgive, with greater forgiveness resulting from longer treatments. Second, time spent in an intervention promoting empathy with the offender and time spent on helping solidify one's commitment to one's forgiveness affect outcomes. Third, although all forgiveness interventions seem to be equally efficacious, they have specific effects that differentiate them from other interventions – such as increased forgiveness, positive mood, and mental and physical health. Fourth, forgiveness is clearly related to some character strengths or virtues. Specifically, it appears to be more related to humility (and, we might speculate, to other emotionally warm virtues like sympathy, compassion, or love) but not as strongly related to character strengths or virtues that are expressions of inhibiting impulses or of conscientiousness, like self-control, patience, justice, and responsibility. The intervention research aimed at promoting forgiveness seems to be of therapeutic and enrichment value, but questions still remain about how to make forgiveness interventions more powerful in their effects at promoting forgiveness and enhancing happiness, physical health, mental health, and overall well-being.

References

Al-Mabuk, R. H., Enright, R. D., & Cardis, P. A. (1995). Forgiving education with parentally love-deprived late adolescents. *Journal of Moral Education*, *24*, 427–444.

Arendt, H. (1963). *Eichmann in Jerusalem: A report on the banality of evil.* New York: Viking Press.

Baskin, T. W., & Enright, R. D. (2004). Intervention studies in forgiveness: A meta-analysis. *Journal of Counseling and Development*, *82*, 79–90.

Berry, J. W., Worthington, E. L., Jr., Wade, N. G., Witvliet, C. v. O., & Kiefer, R. (2005). Forgiveness, moral identity, and perceived justice in crime victims and their supporters. *Humboldt Journal of Social Relations*, *29*, 136–162.

Burchard, G. A., Yarhouse, M. A., Kilian, M. K., Worthington, E. L., Jr., Berry, J. W., & Canter, D. E. (2003). A study of two marital enrichment programs and couples' quality of life. *Journal of Psychology and Theology*, *31*, 240–252.

Coyle, C. T., & Enright, R. D. (1997). Forgiveness intervention with post-abortion men. *Journal of Consulting and Clinical Psychology*, *65*, 1042–1045.

David, D., & Montgomery, G. H. (2011). The scientific status of psychotherapies: A new evaluative framework for evidence-based psychosocial interventions. *Clinical Psychology: Science and Practice*, *18*, 89–104.

Davis, D. E., Hook, J. N., & Worthington, E. L., Jr. (2008). Relational spirituality and forgiveness: The roles of attachment to God, religious coping, and viewing the transgression as a desecration. *Journal of Psychology and Christianity*, *27*, 293–301.

Davis, D. E., Worthington, E. L., Jr., & Hook, J. N. (2013). Research on religion/spirituality and forgiveness: A meta-analytic review. *Psychology of Religion and Spirituality*, *5*(4), 233–241.

DiBlasio, F. A. (1998). The use of a decision-based forgiveness intervention within intergenerational family therapy. *Journal of Family Therapy*, *20*, 77–94.

DiBlasio, F. A. (2000). Decision-based forgiveness treatment in cases of marital infidelity. *Psychotherapy, 37*, 149–158.
DiBlasio, F. A., & Proctor, J. H. (1993). Therapists and the clinical use of forgiveness. *American Journal of Family Therapy, 21*, 175–184.
Enright, R. D., Enright, J., Holter, A., Baskin, T., & Knutson, C. (2010). Waging peace through forgiveness in Belfast, Northern Ireland II: Educational programs for mental health improvement of children. *Journal of Research in Education, Fall*, 63–78.
Enright, R. D., & Fitzgibbons, R. P. (2000). *Helping clients forgive: An empirical guide for resolving anger and restoring hope.* Washington, DC: American Psychological Association.
Fehr, R., Gelfand, M. J., & Nag, M. (2010). The road to forgiveness: A meta-analytic synthesis of its situational and dispositional correlates. *Psychological Bulletin, 136*, 894–914.
Fincham, F. D., & Beach, S. R. H. (2001). Forgiveness: Toward a public health approach to intervention. In J. H. Harvey & A. Wenzel (Eds.), *A clinician's guide to maintaining and enhancing close relationships* (pp. 277–300). Mahwah, NJ: Lawrence Erlbaum Associates.
Fitzgibbons, R. P. (1986). The cognitive and emotive uses of forgiveness in the treatment of anger. *Psychotherapy, 23*, 629–633.
Flanigan, B. J. (1987). Shame and forgiving in alcoholism. *Alcoholism Treatment Quarterly, 4*, 181–195.
Freedman, S. R., & Enright, R. D. (1996). Forgiveness as an intervention with incest survivors. *Journal of Consulting and Clinical Psychology, 64*, 983–992.
Gordon, K. C., & Baucom, D. H. (1998). Understanding betrayals in marriage: A synthesized model of forgiveness. *Family Process, 37*, 425–450.
Gordon, K. C., Baucom, D. H., & Snyder, D. K. (2004). An integrative intervention for promoting recovery from extramarital affairs. *Journal of Marital and Family Therapy, 30*, 213–231.
Greenberg, L. S., Warwar, S., & Malcolm, W. (2008). Differential effects of emotion-focused therapy and psychoeducation in facilitating forgiveness and letting go of emotional injuries. *Journal of Counseling Psychology, 55*, 185–196.
Greenberg, L. S., Warwar, S., & Malcolm, W. (2010). Emotion-focused couples therapy and the facilitation of forgiveness. *Journal of Marital and Family Therapy, 36*, 28–42.
Hargrave, T. D. (1994). *Families and forgiveness: Healing wounds in the intergenerational family.* Philadelphia: Brunner-Mazel.
Hargrave, T. D., & Sells, J. N. (1997). The development of a forgiveness scale. *Journal of Marital and Family Therapy, 23*, 41–62.
Hebl, J., & Enright, R. D. (1993). Forgiveness as a psychotherapeutic goal with elderly females. *Psychotherapy, 30*, 658–667.
Hope, D. (1987). The healing paradox of forgiveness. *Psychotherapy: Theory, Research, Practice, Training, 24*, 240–244.
Hui, E. K. P., & Chau, T. S. (2009). The impact of a forgiveness intervention with Hong Kong Chinese children hurt in interpersonal relationships. *British Journal of Guidance and Counseling, 37*, 141–156.
Hui, E. K. P., & Ho, D. K. Y. (2004). Forgiveness in the context of developmental guidance: Implementation and evaluation. *British Journal of Guidance and Counseling, 32*, 477–492.
Kiefer, R. P., Worthington, E. L., Jr., Myers, B., Kliewer, W. L., Berry, J. W., Davis, D. E., Kilgour, J., Jr., Miller, A. J., Van Tongeren, D. R., & Hunter, J. L. (2010). Training parents in forgiveness and reconciliation. *American Journal of Family Therapy, 38*, 32–49.
Lampton, C., Oliver, G., Worthington, E. L., Jr., & Berry, J. W. (2005). Helping Christian college students become more forgiving: An intervention study to promote forgiveness

as part of a program to shape Christian character. *Journal of Psychology and Theology, 33*, 278–290.

Lavelock, C. R., Worthington, E. L., Jr., Greer, C. L., Lin, Y., & Griffin, B. J. (2013). Four virtues: Interventions for goodness' sake. Unpublished manuscript under editorial review, Virginia Commonwealth University, Richmond.

Lin, W.-F., Mack, D., Enright, R. D., Krahn, D., & Baskin, T. W. (2004). *Journal of Consulting and Clinical Psychology, 72*, 1114–1121.

Lundahl, B. W., Taylor, M. J., Stevenson, R., & Roberts, K. D. (2008). Process-based forgiveness interventions: A meta-analytic review. *Research on Social Work Practice, 18*, 465–478.

Luskin, F. M. (2001). *Forgive for good: A proven prescription for health and happiness.* San Francisco: Harper.

Luskin, F., Ginzberg, K., & Thoresen, C. E. (2005). The efficacy of forgiveness intervention in college age adults: Randomized controlled study. *Humboldt Journal of Social Relations, 29*, 163–184.

McCullough, M. E., & Worthington, E. L., Jr. (1995). Promoting forgiveness: A comparison of two psychoeducational group interventions with a waiting-list control. *Counseling and Values, 40*(1), 55–68.

McCullough, M. E., Worthington, E. L. Jr., & Rachal, K. C. (1997). Interpersonal forgiving in close relationships. *Journal of Personality and Social Psychology, 73*, 321–336.

Montville, J. V. (2001). Religion and peacemaking. In R. G. Helmick, S. J. Peterson, & R. L. Peterson (Eds.), *Forgiveness and reconciliation: Religion, public policy, and conflict transformation* (pp. 97–116). Philadelphia: Templeton Foundation Press.

Peterson, C., & Seligman, M. (2004). *Character strengths and virtues: A handbook and classification.* Washington, DC: American Psychological Association.

Reed, G. L., & Enright, R. D. (2006). The effects of forgiveness therapy on depression, anxiety, and posttraumatic stress for women after spousal emotional abuse. *Journal of Consulting and Clinical Psychology, 74*, 920–929.

Ripley, J. S., & Worthington, E. L., Jr. (2002). Hope-focused and forgiveness-based group interventions to promote marital enrichment. *Journal of Counseling and Development, 80*, 452–472.

Rusbult, C. E., Hannon, P. A., Stocker, S. L., & Finkel, E. J. (2005). Forgiveness and relational repair. In E. L. Worthington, Jr. (Ed.), *Handbook of forgiveness* (pp. 185–206). New York: Brunner-Routledge.

Rye, M. S., & Pargament, K. I. (2002). Forgiveness and romantic relationships in college: Can it heal the wounded heart? *Journal of Clinical Psychology, 58*, 419–441.

Rye, M. S., Pargament, K. I., Pan, W., Yingling, D. W., Shogren, K. A., & Ito, M. (2005). Can group interventions facilitate forgiveness of an ex-spouse? A randomized clinical trial. *Journal of Consulting and Clinical Psychology, 73*, 880–892.

Sandage, S. J., & Worthington, E. L., Jr. (2010). Comparison of two group interventions to promote forgiveness: Empathy as a mediator of change. *Journal of Mental Health Counseling, 32*, 35–57.

Seligman, M. E. P., & Csikszentmihalyi, M. (2000). Positive psychology: An introduction. *American Psychologist, 55*, 5–14.

Siev, J., & Chambless, D. L. (2007). Specificity of treatment effects: Cognitive therapy and relaxation for generalized anxiety and panic disorders. *Journal of Consulting and Clinical Psychology, 75*, 513–522.

Smedes, L. B. (1984). *Forgive and forget: Healing the hurts we don't deserve.* New York: Harper & Row.

Struthers, C., Dupuis, R., & Eaton, J. (2005). Promoting forgiveness among co-workers following a workplace transgression: The effects of social motivation training. *Canadian Journal of Behavioural Science*, *37*, 299–308.

Toussaint, L., & Webb, J. R. (2005). Theoretical and empirical connections between forgiveness, mental health, and well-being. In E. L. Worthington, Jr. (Ed.), *Handbook of forgiveness* (pp. 349–362). New York: Brunner-Routledge.

Toussaint, L. L., Williams, D. R., Musick, M. A., & Everson, S. A. (2001). Forgiveness and health: Age differences in a U.S. probability sample. *Journal of Adult Development*, *8*, 249–257.

Tutu, D. M. (1999). *No future without forgiveness*. New York: Doubleday.

Wade, N. G., Hoyt, W. T., Kidwell, J. E. M., & Worthington, E. L., Jr. (in press). Meta-analysis of psychotherapeutic interventions to promote forgiveness. *Journal of Consulting and Clinical Psychology*.

Wade, N. G., Hoyt, W. T., & Worthington, E. L., Jr. (2013). Forgiveness interventions: A meta-analytic review of effects and moderators. Unpublished manuscript, under editorial review, Iowa State University, Ames, Iowa.

Wade, N. G., & Meyer, J. E. (2009). Comparison of brief group interventions to promote forgiveness: A pilot outcome study. *International Journal of Group Psychotherapy*, *59*, 199–220.

Wade, N. G., Worthington, E. L., Jr., & Haake, S. (2009). Promoting forgiveness: Comparison of explicit forgiveness interventions with an alternative treatment. *Journal of Counseling and Development*, *87*, 143–151.

Wade, N. G., Worthington, E. L., Jr., & Meyer, J. (2005). But do they really work? Meta-analysis of group interventions to promote forgiveness. In E. L. Worthington, Jr. (Ed.), *Handbook of forgiveness* (pp. 423–440). New York: Brunner-Routledge.

Wampold, B. (2001). *The great psychotherapy debate: Models, methods, and findings*. Mahwah, NJ: Lawrence Erlbaum.

Worthington, E. L., Jr. (Ed.) (2005). *Handbook of forgiveness*. New York: Brunner-Routledge.

Worthington, E. L., Jr. (2006). *Forgiveness and reconciliation: Theory and application*. New York: Brunner-Routledge.

Worthington, E. L., Jr., & Aten, J. (2010). Forgiveness and reconciliation. In E. Martz (Ed.), *Post-conflict rehabilitation: Creating a trauma membrane for individuals and communities and restructuring lives after trauma* (pp. 55–72). New York: Springer.

Worthington, E. L., Jr., & Berry, J. W. (2004). Can society afford not to promote forgiveness and reconciliation? In R. L. Hampton and T. P. Gullotta (Eds.), *Promoting racial, ethnic, and religious understanding and reconciliation* (pp. 159–192). Washington, DC: Child Welfare League of America.

Worthington, E. L., Jr., Berry, J. W., Canter, D. E., Sharp, C., Yarhouse, M., & Scherer, M. (2003, October). Forgiveness and communication in marital enrichment with parents. Paper presented at the Conference on Scientific Findings about Forgiveness, Atlanta, GA.

Worthington, E. L., Jr., & DiBlasio, F. A. (1990). Promoting mutual forgiveness within the fractured relationship. *Psychotherapy*, *27*, 219–223.

Worthington, E. L., Jr., & Drinkard, D. T. (2000). Promoting reconciliation through psychoeducational and therapeutic interventions. *Journal of Marital and Family Therapy*, *26*, 93–101.

Worthington, E. L., Jr., Hight, T. L., Ripley, J. S., Perrone, K. M., Kurusu, T. A., & Jones, D. R. (1997). Strategic hope-focused relationship-enrichment counseling with individual couples. *Journal of Counseling Psychology*, *44*, 381–389.

Worthington, E. L., Jr., Hunter, J. L., Sharp, C. B., Hook, J. N., Van Tongeren, D. R., Davis, D. E., Miller, A. J., Gingrich, F. C., Sandage, S. J., Lao, E., Bubod, L., & Monforte-Milton, M. M. (2010). A psychoeducational intervention to promote forgiveness in Christians in the Philippines. *Journal of Mental Health Counseling, 32*, 75–93.

Worthington, E. L., Jr., Jennings, D. J., II, & DiBlasio, F. A. (2010). Interventions to promote forgiveness in couple and family context: Conceptualization, review, and analysis. *Journal of Psychology and Theology, 38*, 231–245.

Worthington, E. L., Jr., Kurusu, T. A., Collins, W., Berry, J. W., Ripley, J. S., & Baier, S. N. (2000). Forgiving usually takes time: A lesson learned by studying interventions to promote forgiveness. *Journal of Psychology and Theology, 28*, 3–20.

Worthington, E. L., Jr., Sandage, S. J., & Berry, J. W. (2000). Group interventions to promote forgiveness: What researchers and clinicians ought to know. In M. E. McCullough, K. I. Pargament, & C. E. Thoresen (Eds.), *Forgiveness: Theory, research and practice* (pp. 228–253). New York: Guilford Press.

Worthington, E. L., Jr., Witvliet, C. V. O., Pietrini, P., & Miller, A. J. (2007). Forgiveness, health, and well-being: A review of evidence for emotional versus decisional forgiveness, dispositional forgivingness, and reduced unforgiveness. *Journal of Behavioral Medicine, 30*, 291–302.

Wright, T. (2009). *Virtue reborn*. London: SPCK.

Yalom, I. D., & Leszcz, M. (2005). *The theory and practice of group psychotherapy* (5th ed.). New York: Basic Books.

3

Nurturing the Capacity to Savor

Interventions to Enhance the Enjoyment of Positive Experiences

Jennifer L. Smith, Patrick R. Harrison, Jaime L. Kurtz, and Fred B. Bryant

Numerous coping-related interventions have been developed and evaluated with respect to their effectiveness in helping people regulate emotional distress in response to a wide variety of negative life events, including bereavement (Sikkema, Hansen, Kochman, Tate, & Difranceisco, 2004), loneliness (Pavri & Monda-Amaya, 2000), natural disasters (Prinstein, La Greca, & Verberg, 1996), physical illness (Ironson et al., 2002), radiation therapy (Johnson, 1996), substance abuse (Conrod, Stewart, Pihl, Côté, Fontaine, & Dongier, 2000), work-related stress (van der Klink, Blonk, Schene, & van Dijk, 2001), childhood psychopathology (Kendall, 1985), homelessness (Kidd, 2003), and disability (Singer & Powers, 1993). Yet, psychologists have only recently begun to develop and investigate strategies aimed at enhancing people's ability to savor positive experiences. Finding the joy in life is not always easy. As the Austrian poet Rainer Maria Rilke (1923/2005) aptly noted, "the most visible joy can only reveal itself to us when we've transformed it, within" (p. 51). But how do people transform positive experiences into joy within themselves? And are there effective techniques that people can use in order to savor their lives more fully?

In this chapter, we explore these critical questions and examine a variety of structured activities that research psychologists have developed to help people boost levels of positive emotions. The central, unifying concept in our chapter is the construct of *savoring*, or the capacity to notice and appreciate positive experience. We begin by briefly reviewing prior theory and research on savoring, to explicate the conceptual and empirical lenses though which we will interpret relevant positive interventions. We then describe a variety of empirically based, savoring-related interventions and the effectiveness of these interventions in promoting positive

The Wiley Blackwell Handbook of Positive Psychological Interventions, First Edition.
Edited by Acacia C. Parks and Stephen M. Schueller.

emotions and life satisfaction. Finally, we propose a set of recommendations for improving the quality of future research on savoring-related interventions.

Conceptual and Empirical Background to Savoring

Conceptual background

What does it mean to "savor" a positive experience? Although this term might seem at first glance to be synonymous with pleasure, to savor an experience is more than simply feeling good. The concept of savoring (Bryant, 1989, 2003; Bryant, Chadwick, & Kluwe, 2011; Bryant, Ericksen, & DeHoek, 2008; Bryant & Veroff, 2007) refers to processes through which people regulate their positive feelings by attending to: (a) memories of *past* positive experiences (through reminiscence); (b) ongoing positive experiences in the *present* (by savoring the moment); or (c) *future* positive experiences (through anticipation). Savoring is distinct from pleasure or enjoyment in the sense that savoring is a mindful process of attending to pleasurable feelings and either amplifying or dampening them, prolonging or curtailing them. Although savoring requires focused attention on or "meta-awareness" of pleasurable feelings, pleasure alone does not necessarily produce savoring (Smith, Harrison, & Bryant, in press).

How have theorists conceptualized savoring? In explicating the concept of savoring, Bryant and Veroff (2007) highlighted four critical conceptual components: savoring experiences, savoring processes, savoring strategies, and savoring beliefs. To begin with, a *savoring experience* consists of "the totality of a person's sensations, perceptions, thoughts, behaviors, and emotions when mindfully attending to and appreciating a positive stimulus, outcome, or event, along with the accompanying environmental or situational features of that encounter" (Bryant & Veroff, 2007, p. 13). Experiences that are conducive to savoring include soaking in a warm bubble bath, reading a spell-binding mystery novel, or spending the day with your best friend.

Somewhat more abstract than the savoring experience is the *savoring process*. A savoring process is "a sequence of mental or physical operations that unfolds over time and transforms a positive stimulus into positive feelings to which a person attends" (Bryant & Veroff, 2007, p. 13). Savoring processes include thanksgiving (regulating gratitude in response to good fortune), marveling (regulating awe in response to perceived grandeur), basking (regulating pride in response to personal accomplishment), and luxuriating (regulating pleasure in response to positive sensations).

A *savoring strategy* or *response* is the operational component of the savoring process – that is, a specific concrete thought or behavior that amplifies or dampens the intensity, or prolongs or shortens the duration, of positive feelings. Examples of savoring responses or strategies include carefully taking a "mental photograph" of a spectacular vista for later recall, mentally congratulating oneself in response to a personal achievement, and closing one's eyes to focus attention while tasting a delicious wine.

And lastly, *savoring beliefs* reflect people's perceived ability to enjoy positive experiences, as distinct from their ability to obtain positive outcomes (Bryant, 2003; Bryant et al., 2008, 2011; Bryant & Veroff, 2007). Savoring beliefs encompass three time frames: the ability to reminisce about past positive experiences, the ability to savor positive experiences in the present, and the ability to anticipate positive experiences that may happen in the future.

Empirical background

A growing body of research has identified key individual and situational differences in savoring, and has linked savoring to important psychosocial outcomes. When asked to rate their savoring capacities, people typically report being most capable of savoring through reminiscence, moderately capable of savoring the moment, and least capable of savoring through anticipation (Bryant, 2003). Females, compared to males, typically perceive themselves as more capable of savoring positive experiences – a sex difference that emerges as early as age 10, persists throughout older adulthood, and exists in the US, Canada, Australia, and Japan (Bryant & Veroff, 2007). People in individualistic Western cultures more often savor in ways that amplify enjoyment, whereas it is more culturally appropriate for people in collectivistic Eastern cultures to regulate their positive emotions by using savoring strategies that dampen enjoyment (e.g., kill-joy thinking; Lindberg, 2004; Miyamota & Ma, 2011). Both amplifying and dampening strategies may thus represent different types of savoring responses that regulate positive emotional experience in normatively appropriate ways in different cultures or contexts (Bryant et al., 2011; Lindberg, 2004). People's personalities also predict their savoring beliefs, as well as their savoring responses to positive events. Higher levels of trait mindfulness (Beaumont, 2011), extraversion, optimism, and affect intensity, and lower levels of neuroticism, guilt, and hopelessness, are associated with a greater perceived capacity to savor the moment (Bryant, 2003).

The tendency to savor has also been linked to higher levels of happiness, life satisfaction, and perceived control in adolescents (Meehan, Durlak, & Bryant, 1993), college students, and older adults (Bryant, 2003). Differences in the specific types of savoring responses that people use have been associated with variations in subjective well-being. In particular, whereas savoring responses that amplify enjoyment predict higher levels of positive affect and life satisfaction, savoring responses that dampen enjoyment predict lower levels of these outcomes (Quoidbach, Berry, Hansenne, & Mikolajczak, 2010). When they experience positive affect, people high in self-esteem are especially likely to amplify that affect, whereas people low in self-esteem are especially likely to dampen it (Wood, Heimpel, & Michela, 2003) – the latter tendency being linked prospectively to depressive symptoms (Raes, Smets, Nelis, & Schoofs, 2012). Longitudinal experience-sampling research also shows that daily positive events predict greater momentary savoring, which in turn predicts greater daily happiness (Jose, Lim, & Bryant, 2012). Moreover, regulatory diversity, or using many savoring strategies rather than a few specific ones, predicts higher levels of happiness (Quoidbach et al., 2010).

Several theorists have expanded upon the notion of savoring and used it as an explanatory mechanism in other conceptual models. For instance, savoring has been proposed as a mechanism through which positive affect broadens awareness, encourages exploration, and expands behavioral skills (e.g., Tugade & Fredrickson, 2007). Because pleasurable experiences are typically reinforced more than neutral ones, savoring may also promote learning (Frijda & Sundararajan, 2007). In addition, savoring may facilitate the formation and strengthening of social interconnections as well as the discovery of meaning in life (Bryant & Veroff, 2007). Ultimately, savoring not only increases the breadth and depth of feelings and strengthens the connection between pleasure and instrumental learning, but also "expands the world of experience, leading from pleasure to meaning, thereby expanding the individual's worldview and their sense of belonging" (Frijda & Sundararajan, 2007, p. 237).

Interventions Intended to Enhance Enjoyment of Positive Experiences

We now consider specific positive interventions that are conceptually grounded in savoring and designed to enhance people's ability to enjoy positive experiences. By *positive intervention*, we mean a structured activity "aimed at cultivating positive feelings, positive behaviors, or positive cognitions" (Sin & Lyubomirsky, 2009, p. 467), in which participants engage for an extended period of time during their everyday lives. We will restrict our focus to studies that have administered savoring-related interventions to participants outside the laboratory for at least two days. Additionally, we have concentrated our review on the outcome measures of happiness, positive affect, and life satisfaction. We have excluded negative outcomes, such as depression and negative affect, from these analyses, because savoring is a process that underlies positive rather than negative experience (Bryant, 1989; Bryant & Veroff, 2007). We have excluded interventions specifically designed to increase gratitude (see the chapter by Lomas et al. in this book), because feeling grateful is different from savoring or enjoying positive experiences.

In reviewing savoring interventions, we distinguish between interventions that consist of one specific type of savoring-enhancing activity versus multi-faceted interventions that combine savoring-enhancing activities with other types of wellness-enhancing activities within the same intervention (e.g., Fordyce, 1977, 1983; Seligman, Rashid, & Parks, 2006). Because multi-faceted interventions make it impossible to determine which specific treatment component(s) caused observed effects, we have restricted our review to single-pronged interventions, so as to maximize the validity of our inferences about the causal constructs that underlie effective interventions (Cook & Campbell, 1979). We have also excluded experimental manipulations that were implemented in the laboratory or field, but that were not formalized into interventions that participants used in their everyday lives for an extended period of time beyond a few minutes (e.g., Mitchell, Thompson, & Peterson, 1997; Wirtz, Kruger, Scollon, & Diener, 2003). We have organized our review in terms of the temporal focus that interventions have adopted in directing participants' attention to the past, present, or future.

Past-Focused Savoring Interventions

When looking back on events from the past, people often remember the good times more than the bad. This sense of "rosy retrospection" (Mitchell et al., 1997) helps individuals savor past positive experiences and thereby feel happy in the present. Past-focused savoring interventions aim to increase people's awareness and enjoyment of earlier positive experiences. We review seven past-focused interventions designed to enhance savoring (see Table 3.1).

Thinking about positive events

One approach to boosting people's capacity to appreciate past positive events is to provide general cognitive strategies they can use to enhance their savoring of these memories. Lyubomirsky, Sousa, and Dickerhoof (2006) provide suggestions for how best to savor positive events from the past. After choosing one experience that they considered most "joyful or happy for them" (p. 699), participants were asked to spend 15 minutes each day for three days (a) writing about that positive experience, (b) talking about that positive experience into a tape recorder, (c) simply thinking about that positive experience by exploring "your deepest thoughts and emotions ..." (p. 696), or (d) not recalling any experience. Results indicated that simply thinking about – or being mindfully aware of – positive experience was the most effective strategy for improving well-being and positive affect four weeks after the intervention began. These findings suggest that the most effective way to facilitate the savoring of past positive events is not to analyze a positive event systematically, but rather simply to become more mindful of its positive attributes.

Positive reminiscence

A similar approach relies not only on thinking about these experiences, but also on conjuring up mental images related to that positive experience. Along these lines, Bryant, Smart, and King (2005) developed a week-long intervention with two 10-minute sessions each day designed to teach participants how to use cognitive imagery and memorabilia (e.g., souvenirs, photographs) to reminisce about past positive events. Participants were randomly assigned to (a) a cognitive-imagery condition where they were asked to think about a positive experience from the

Table 3.1 Summary of past-focused savoring interventions

Nature of the intervention			*Nature of the study*			*Nature of the sample*			*Effect size*			
Name	*Dosage & duration*	*Author*	*Design*	*Control group task*	*Manip check*	*Type of pop.*	*Mean age*	*% Female*	*Outcome measure*	*Time after intervention*	*d*	*r*
Thinking about past positive events	15 min each day for 3 days	Lyubomirsky et al. (2006)	4-group, pretest–posttest	no intervention (untreated)	yes	US college students	19.43 (2.59)	74	Satisfaction with Life Scale (SWLS; 1985)	4 weeks	0.25	.12
									PANAS (1988)	4 weeks	–.21	–.10
Positive reminiscing with imagery	10 min twice a day for 1 week	Bryant et al. (2005)	3-group, pretest–posttest	think about current concerns	no	US college students	19.98 (3.30)	63	Fordyce Happiness Measure (FHM; 1988)	immediate	0.65	.31
Positive reminiscing with memorabilia	10 min twice a day for 1 week	Bryant et al. (2005)	3-group, pretest–posttest	think about current concerns	no	US college students	19.98 (3.30)	63	FHM (1988)	immediate	0.50	.25
	once each day for 1 week	Seligman et al. (2005)	6-group, pretest–multiple posttest	recall early memories	yes	US general pop.	–	58	Steen Happiness Index (SHI; 2005)	6 months	0.39	.19

(continued)

Table 3.1 (*Continued*)

Nature of the intervention			*Nature of the study*			*Nature of the sample*			*Effect size*			
Name	*Dosage & duration*	*Author*	*Design*	*Control group task*	*Manip check*	*Type of pop.*	*Mean age*	*% Female*	*Outcome measure*	*Time after intervention*	*d*	*r*
Recalling three good things	six times over 10 days	Carlton (2009)	3-group, pretest–posttest	description of activities	no	multinational workplace	34 (12.4)	80	Subjective Happiness Scale (1999)	1 month	0.03	.02
	once each day for 1 week	Anselmo (2010)	4-group, pretest–posttest	recall early memories	no	Canada general pop.	33	83	SHI (2005)	6 months	0.16	.08
Basking	10 min each day for 2 days	Keeney (2009)	3-group, post–test only	write about neutral topic	yes	US college students	–	73	PANAS (1988) SWLS (1985)	immediate immediate	0.54 −0.01	.26 .00
Acknowledging others	10 min each day for 2 days	Keeney (2009)	3-group, post-test only	write about neutral topic	yes	US college students	–	73	PANAS (1988) SWLS (1985)	immediate immediate	0.40 0.15	.20 .07
Reflecting on past kindness	once daily for 1 week	Otake et al. (2006)	2-group, pretest–posttest	no intervention (untreated)	no	Japan college students	18.70 (0.77)	100	Japanese Subjective Happiness Scale	4 weeks	.60	.29

past and "allow images relating to the memory to come to mind" (p. 242); (b) a memorabilia condition where they were asked to "think about memories associated with that memento" (p. 242); or (c) a control condition where they were asked to think about any current concerns. After the intervention, participants in the two reminiscing conditions reported significantly greater increases in frequency of happy feelings over the last week compared to the control condition. Furthermore, the cognitive-imagery intervention produced greater increases in happiness than did the memorabilia intervention. These findings suggest that positive reminiscing, especially using cognitive imagery, can increase happiness over the course of a week-long intervention.

Recalling three positive daily events

Savoring can also be facilitated by increasing people's mindfulness of positive events that have just recently happened. In the Three Good Things intervention (Seligman, Steen, Park, & Peterson, 2005), individuals are encouraged to become mindful of the good things that have happened to them that day. Seligman and colleagues (2005) randomly assigned individuals to complete one of six intervention conditions for one week. Participants in the Three Good Things condition were asked to write down three positive events that happened to them each day and explain why those good events occurred. Compared to a control condition (i.e., writing about early memories), writing about three positive events was more effective at improving happiness levels one month, three months, and six months after the intervention. The Three Good Things intervention has been replicated with general adult (Anselmo, 2010), adolescent (McCabe-Fitch, 2009), and workplace (Carlton, 2009) samples. These findings suggest that simply spending a week listing and considering three good things that happen every day increases savoring of these positive events and boosts happiness, both long-term (i.e., six months post-intervention; Anselmo, 2010; Seligman et al., 2005) and short-term (i.e., one month post-intervention; Carlton, 2009).

These findings may initially seem contradictory to those of Lyubormirsky and colleagues (2006) above, in which writing about a past positive event was not as effective as simply thinking about it. One reason for this difference in findings is that writing about a positive experience can encourage the construction of a logical narrative, which sometimes leads one to "explain it away" (Wilson, Centerbar, Kermer, & Gilbert, 2005). When reflecting on the past, then, one should resist focusing on the whys and hows surrounding the experience and simply focus instead on the positive feelings the memory generates.

Basking in achievement/acknowledging the role of others

Another approach to encourage individuals to savor positive events from the past involves increasing inward awareness of a personal achievement attributable to internal, controllable causes. Keeney (2009) developed and tested two savoring interventions designed to help participants savor the success of their recent admission to college. Shortly after receiving an admission letter, participants were asked to spend 10 minutes each day for two days writing about either (a) their personal role in this achievement and "what obstacles were there that [you] overcame" (p. 98) (basking condition); (b) the role of others (e.g., teachers, parents) in this achievement and "things that would not have been possible if it were not for [their] support" (p. 99) (acknowledging the role of others condition); or (c) the room around them (control condition). Results indicated that both savoring interventions significantly increased positive affect, but not life satisfaction, relative to the control task. Furthermore, basking was more effective than acknowledging others, suggesting that focusing on one's own contribution to a success may especially enhance one's ability to savor these positive experiences.

Reflecting on recent personal acts of kindness

Individuals not only savor the good things that have happened to them personally, but also the good things they have done for others. In the "Counting Kindness" intervention, Otake, Shimai, Tanaka-Matsumi, Otsui, and Frederickson (2006) encouraged individuals to keep track of acts of kindness (e.g., holding a door open, comforting a friend) and to compute a daily count of these acts for one week. Compared to a no-treatment control group, individuals who recorded the positive things they had done for others exhibited greater increases in happiness over the course of the week. These findings suggest that savoring the positive effects of our own actions on others may improve happiness.

Present-Focused Savoring Interventions

Everyday concerns and responsibilities may distract people from the positive events in their lives. Present-focused savoring interventions aim to increase people's awareness and enjoyment of positive experiences while these events are unfolding. Sometimes these interventions also provide people with techniques and strategies for enhancing and extending these positive experiences. We review five present-focused interventions designed to enhance savoring (see Table 3.2).

Increasing the use of savoring strategies

One approach to boosting people's capacity to appreciate ongoing positive experience is to give them cognitive and behavioral strategies that can enhance savoring in everyday life. Along these lines, Hurley and Kwon (2012) tested the

Table 3.2 Summary of present-focused savoring interventions

Nature of the intervention			*Nature of the study*			*Nature of the sample*			*Effect size*			
Name	*Dosage & duration*	*Author*	*Design*	*Control group task*	*Manip check*	*Type of pop.*	*Mean age*	*% Female*	*Outcome measure*	*Time after intervention*	*d*	*r*
Savoring the moment	once daily for 2 weeks	Hurley & Kwon (2011)	2-group, pretest–posttest	no intervention (untreated)	no	US college students	19.48 (2.06)	69	PANAS-X (1999)	immediate	.18	.09
Positive-focus walk	20 min once a day for 1 week	Bryant & Veroff (2007)	3-group pretest–posttest	walk with normal focus	no	US college students	18.67	68	FHM (1988)	immediate	.82	.41
Mindful photography	15 minutes twice weekly for 2 weeks	Kurtz (2012)	3-group pretest–posttest	neutral photo	no	US college students	18.97 (1.26)	71.8	SHS (1999) positive mood	immediate immediate	.26 −.07	.13 −.03
Savoring	once daily for 1 week	Schueller (2010)	quasi-experimental, 1-group pretest–posttest	within subject (pre-test)	no	US general pop.	53.5 (11.98)	77.5	Authentic Happiness Inventory (AHI; 2005)	immediate	.16	.08
Active/Constructive Responding	once daily for 1 week	Schueller (2010)	quasi-experimental, 1-group pretest–posttest	within subject (pre-test)	no	US general pop.	53.5 (11.98)	77.5	AHI (2005)	immediate	−.04	−.03

effectiveness of an intervention designed to teach participants ways of savoring in the moment, such as sharing positive experiences with others, building memories by taking mental snapshots, and counting blessings (Bryant & Veroff, 2007). Participants in the intervention condition received training on each of the ways of savoring, which included imagining ways in which they could have savored three recent positive events. Then, participants were instructed to "use any of the savoring-the-moment strategies discussed or their own personalized savoring-the-moment strategies to savor naturally occurring positive events over the next two weeks" (Hurley & Kwon, 2012, p. 5). Participants were given a log to record how often they savored positive events, and they received daily reminders to savor. Controlling for baseline levels of positive affect, however, participants who received the savoring-the-moment intervention did not differ from those in a no-intervention control condition in levels of positive affect (although they showed greater reductions in negative affect).

Adopting a positive focus

Another present-focused positive intervention designed to enhance savoring the moment involves instructing people to adopt a more positive attentional focus by purposefully noticing pleasurable features in their environment (Bryant & Veroff, 2007). Specifically, participants are instructed to take a daily 20-minute walk during which they should "try to notice as many positive things around them as they could (e.g., flowers, sunshine, music), to acknowledge each of these things in their mind when they noticed it, and to identify what it was about each thing that made it pleasurable" (Bryant & Veroff, 2007, pp. 184–185). After one week, participants randomly assigned to adopt a positive focus during daily walks showed greater increases in happiness, compared both to participants assigned to adopt a negative focus during daily walks and to those assigned simply to take daily walks. These results suggest that simply making people more aware of positive stimuli can make them happier.

Taking mindful photographs

People's mindfulness of pleasant aspects of their environment can also be enhanced by having them complete structured photography exercises (Bryant & Veroff, 2007; Kurtz, 2012). In the "mindful photograph" intervention (Kurtz, 2012), participants were instructed to spend at least 15 minutes taking photographs of a specific subject (e.g., campus architecture, their friends) twice a week for two weeks. Participants were told to "try to make your pictures creative, beautiful, and meaningful to you ... Do not rush through this exercise. Instead, try to take everything in and take the best pictures that you can" (Kurtz, 2012, p. 6). Participants who took mindful photographs reported significantly more positive mood, compared to participants who took neutral, factual photographs. Mindful photography may boost short-term mood by making people more aware of positive stimuli in their environment.

Engaging in daily savoring exercises

Another positive intervention is designed to boost present-focused savoring by giving people daily practice at savoring the moment. For example, Schueller (2010) instructed participants to complete a sequence of up to six positive interventions (three of which were designed to boost savoring), each lasting one week. Participants' levels of happiness were measured at the beginning and end of each week. For the daily savoring exercise, participants were instructed to "reflect each day for at least 2–3 minutes on two pleasurable experiences and to make the pleasure last as long as possible" (Schueller, 2010, p. 194). Participants who completed the daily savoring exercise reported a significant, positive change in happiness levels after one week.

Enhancing active-constructive communications

Schueller's (2010) study also assessed the effectiveness of another intervention designed to encourage savoring the moment through active-constructive communication – a response style associated with greater relationship well-being and intimacy (e.g., Gable, Reis, Impett, & Asher, 2004). An active-constructive response to other people's recounting of positive events "includes genuine happiness and displays excitement as well as active questioning about the event [which] ... enhances the event by encouraging, retelling, and re-experiencing" (Schueller, 2010, p. 193). Participants were instructed to respond for one week in an active-constructive manner whenever people shared positive information with them. Contrary to hypotheses, however, participants who completed the week-long active-constructive response intervention showed no significant pretest–posttest changes in levels of happiness.

Future-Focused Savoring Interventions

Much of the value of a desirable experience comes from anticipation – that is, savoring beforehand what that experience might be like. In fact, a sample of vacationers reported that the most pleasant part of their trip happened before they even left home, as they imagined just how enjoyable their vacation would be (Nawijn, Marchand, Veenhoven, & Vingerhoets, 2010). Indeed, across a wide variety of life experiences, anticipating the future is considered to be even more emotionally intense and impactful than retrospection (Van Boven & Ashworth, 2007). Therefore, this mental orientation has potential implications for savoring, whereby the way people think about the future may have a strong, positive impact on their ability to savor the present. We review four future-focused interventions designed to enhance savoring (see Table 3.3).

Table 3.3 Summary of future-focused savoring interventions

Nature of the intervention			*Nature of the study*			*Nature of the sample*			*Effect size*			
Name	*Dosage & duration*	*Author*	*Design*	*Control group task*	*Manip check*	*Type of pop.*	*Mean age*	*% Female*	*Outcome measure*	*Time after intervention*	*d*	*r*
Positive mental time travel	once daily for 15 days	Quoidbach et al. (2009)	4-group pretest–posttest	no projection	no	US college workers	32.54 (12.31)	65.1	SHS (1999)	1 day	.68	.32
	20 minutes once a day for 4 days	King (2001)	4-group pretest–posttest	focus on plans for the day	no	US college students	21.04 (3.15)	85.2	Positive affect (Diener & Emmons, 1984)	immediate	−.08	−.04
									SWLS (Diener, Emmons, Larsen, & Griffin, 1985)	3 weeks	.10	.05
Best Possible Selves	at least twice over 4 weeks	Sheldon & Lyubomirsky (2006)	3-group pretest–posttest	focus on daily details	no	US college students	–	74.6	PANAS – positive affect (Watson, Clark, & Tellegen, 1988)	4 weeks	.53	.25
	15 minutes per week for 8 weeks	Lyubomirsky et al. (2011)	3-group pretest–posttest	list what they did for the last week	yes	US college students	19.66 (2.91)	69.8	Well-being (averaged across affect, SHS, & SWLS)	6 months	.11	.06
Temporal scarcity	10 minutes twice weekly for 2 weeks	Kurtz (2008)	3-group pretest–posttest	write about typical day	no	US college students	–	77.6	SHS (1999)	immediate	.18	.09
									happy mood	immediate	.04	.02
Life Summary exercise	once daily for 1 week	Schueller (2010)	quasi-experimental, 1-group pretest–posttest	within subject (pre-test)	yes	US general pop.	53.5 (11.98)	77.5	AHI (2005)	immediate	.16	.08

The power of positive imagination

Although lowering one's expectations might seem reasonable as a way to prevent disappointment, research demonstrates that expecting positive future outcomes can actually enhance one's enjoyment of the present. In a recent study Quoidbach and colleagues (2009) asked participants to "please try to imagine, in the most precise way, four positive events that could reasonably happen to you tomorrow. You can imagine all kinds of positive events, from simple everyday pleasures to very important positive events" (Quoidbach, Wood, & Hansenne, 2009, p. 351). After engaging in this activity for 15 consecutive days, participants showed greater increases in happiness than those asked to imagine negative or neutral things. This study suggests that imagining positive future outcomes may make one feel better in the present.

The benefits of positive imagination also apply to how people think about their lives in the long term. In the "Best Possible Selves" paradigm, participants are told, "Think about your life in the future. Imagine that everything has gone as well as it possibly could. You have worked hard and succeeded at accomplishing all of your life goals. Think of this as the realization of all of your life dreams. Now, write about what you imagined" (King, 2001, p. 801). Researchers have found that positive mood scores significantly increase after doing this exercise once in the laboratory (King, 2001) and after four weeks (Sheldon & Lyubomirsky, 2006) or six weeks (Boehm, Lyubomirsky, & Sheldon, 2011) of practice on one's own. The "Best Possible Selves" intervention is more effective when participants choose to participate in a "happiness intervention," as opposed to a study whose true purpose is masked (Lyubomirsky, Dickerhoof, Boehm, & Sheldon, 2011). This exercise may be beneficial partly because it encourages people to notice and savor in the present moment the progress they are making toward their future goals.

Similarly, using a future-focused "life summary review," Schueller (2010) instructed each participant to write a "description of how he or she would like to have his or her life relayed to his or her grandchildren" (p. 194), and a few days later the participants were asked to review this life summary and to identify what changes were needed to reach this desired life. After one week, participants reported a marginally significant increase in happiness compared to pre-test scores.

The benefits of scarcity

In many ways, it would seem adaptive to believe that the good things in life should exist in abundance and last indefinitely. Ironically, however, abundant resources may actually detract from savoring, because when a resource is scarce, it is much more likely to be attended to, valued, and savored (Cialdini, 1993). Consider a case in point.

In a recent experiment (O'Brien & Ellsworth, 2012), participants taste-tested several different chocolates. When the fifth chocolate in the series was delivered, participants were told either, "Here is the last chocolate" or "Here is the next chocolate." Those who were told they were receiving their *last* chocolate enjoyed it more, were more likely to report that it was their favorite, and reported greater overall enjoyment of the experiment. Although this experimental manipulation does not fit our definition of an intervention, adding some scarcity into even a simple, everyday activity may help a person see the experience as special and worthy of attention and appreciation.

This sense of temporal scarcity can be harnessed on a larger scale by thinking about the end of particular phases of life. Six weeks before graduation, for example, Kurtz (2008) asked a sample of college seniors to write for 10 minutes about their college experience. One group was told, "As you write, keep in mind that you only have a short amount of time left to spend in college. In fact, you have about 1200 hours before graduation." A second group was told, "As you write, keep in mind that you still have a significant amount of time left to spend in college. In fact, you still have about 1/10th of a year left before graduation" (p. 1239). In other words, one group thought about graduation as being temporally near, and the other thought about it as being temporally distant. After being encouraged for two weeks to adopt this mindset, participants who thought of graduation as near were significantly happier than they were at the start of the study, whereas participants who thought of graduation as far away showed no change in happiness. Counterintuitive as it may seem, this activity promotes savoring by encouraging a now-or-never kind of motivation. As Kurtz (2008) speculated, "being struck with the realization that a meaningful or pleasurable activity is soon ending brings its positive qualities to the forefront of one's attention along with a sense of motivation to make the most of it" (p. 1238).

A Supplementary Meta-Analysis

Having described a variety of savoring-related interventions qualitatively, we conducted a small-scale meta-analysis to assess the overall effectiveness of these savoring interventions quantitatively. In particular, we coded each of the 16 studies described in our narrative review for the following information: (a) sample characteristics (size, population type, mean age, percentage of female participants); (b) study methods (type of design, type of control condition, presence or absence of a check on the manipulation or fidelity of treatment implementation, type of outcome measures); (c) nature of the intervention (temporal focus, type of intervention, dosage and duration of the intervention); and (d) effect sizes (Cohen's *d* and Pearson *r*). For two-group pretest–posttest studies, we computed effect size adjusting for pre-test group differences (Grissom & Kim, 2011; Wortman & Bryant, 1985), to estimate standardized group differences in change over time. For one-group studies, we computed effect size as standardized within-subjects change. For studies that reported multiple follow-up post-tests, we have followed the practices of the authors of these studies and highlighted the particular post-test that showed the strongest effects.

Combined, these 16 studies reported data from a total of 1,702 participants, with sample size ranging from 27 to 329 (M = 106.38, SD = 82.17). Over two-thirds (69%) of the studies used college student samples, and three-quarters (74%) of the participants were female, on average. Mean age of study participants ranged from 18 to 43 years (M = 25.82, SD = 10.65); and 69% of the studies were from published journal articles, whereas around a third (31%) were unpublished manuscripts, master's theses, or dissertations.

Overall, the 16 studies contributed 26 effect sizes for 16 different types of savoring interventions (7 past-focused, 5 present-focused, and 4 future-focused). On average, each treatment "dose" of the intervention lasted 12 minutes (M = 12.50, SD = 4.52), and the treatments were administered roughly once a day (M = 0.84, SD = 0.47) for a total of 13 days (M = 12.63, SD = 13.18). Roughly a third (31%) of the 16 studies included multiple outcome measures for the same intervention, and one-fifth (19%) evaluated multiple independent interventions simultaneously. Happiness, measured using scales such as the Subjective Happiness Scale (SHS; Lyubomirsky & Lepper, 1999) and Steen Happiness Index (SHI; Seligman et al., 2005), was the most common outcome measure (50% of the 26 effect sizes), followed by positive affect (31%) and satisfaction with life (15%).

The individual Cohen's d effect sizes ranged from −.21 to +0.82 (rs ranged from −.10 to +.41). Across all 26 effect sizes, the sample-size weighted overall effect size was d = +0.20, and the 95% confidence interval did not include zero (CI = +0.13 to +0.27). Thus, savoring interventions overall had a "small" but significant positive effect (equivalent to r = +.10; Cohen, 1988) on measured outcomes. Examining only studies that used more rigorous two-group pretest–posttest designs, we found the same pattern of results when analyzing: (a) the eight effect sizes assessing the impact of savoring interventions on positive affect (overall weighted d = +0.26; 95% CI = +0.11 to +0.41); as well as (b) the 10 effect sizes assessing the impact of savoring interventions on happiness (overall weighted d = +0.38; 95% CI = +0.24 to +0.53). Considered together, these findings suggest that effect sizes for savoring interventions are strongest when measuring happiness as the outcome using a two-group pretest–posttest design. Happiness measures may be better suited to capture changes in savoring across time because they reflect a more global, stable construct, whereas positive affect (mood) scores may be more variable and situation-specific. One-group pretest–posttest designs, which lack a control group, may underestimate intervention effects by ignoring temporal decreases in positive emotions that often occur in the absence of treatment.

We conducted follow-up analyses to determine whether effect size was related to characteristics of the intervention or sample. Based on research about "rosy retrospection" and "rosy prospection" (Mitchell et al., 1997), we hypothesized that past- and future-focused interventions would be more effective than present-focused interventions. Contrary to expectations, however, Cohen's *d* did not significantly differ across the past- (M = 0.28, SD = 0.28), present- (M = 0.21, SD = 0.32), and future-focused (M = 0.21, SD = 0.25) savoring interventions, $F(2,23) = 0.17$, $p = .844$, $h^2 = .01$. Neither sample age, $r(24) = -.15$, $p < .47$, nor percentage of female participants, $r(24) = -.27$, $p < .17$, significantly predicted effect size.

We also tested the hypothesis that greater treatment dosages would predict stronger effect size. Confirming expectations, effect size was positively correlated with both (a) total number of treatment doses (i.e., how long the intervention lasted in days × how many times per day the treatment was administered), $r(24) = .43$, $p < .03$, as well as (b) total dosage (i.e., frequency of treatment × how many minutes per day people engaged in the intervention), $r(18) = .48$, $p < .03$. However, effect size was less strongly related to daily dosage (i.e., how many minutes per day × how many times per day), $r(18) = .36$, $p < .12$, and duration of intervention, $r(24) = .01$, $p < .95$.

Recommendations and Future Directions

The studies reviewed in this chapter have made considerable strides toward creating interventions for enhancing people's ability to enjoy their lives. Building on this foundation, we now offer suggestions for developing new past-, present-, and future-focused savoring strategies. We then discuss several methodological recommendations for improving design and implementation in future studies of savoring-related interventions.

Designing new interventions

Researchers should continue to draw on existing theory and research to develop novel past-, present-, and future-focused savoring interventions. Based on successful laboratory experiments and on theory-grounded concepts not yet implemented as naturalistic interventions, we propose some promising possibilities. Potentially effective *past*-focused treatments include encouraging people to imagine ways in which past positive events might never have happened (Koo, Algoe, Wilson, & Gilbert, 2008) and to recall earlier times when they had looked forward to ongoing positive events (i.e., recalled anticipation; Bryant & Veroff, 2007). Potentially effective *present*-focused treatments include increasing the frequency with which people seek out savoring experiences (Harrison, Smith, & Bryant, in press) and enhancing people's awareness of uncertainty which can make them more mindful during positive experiences (Wilson et al., 2005). Potentially effective *future*-focused treatments include increasing awareness of the ending of positive experiences (O'Brien & Ellsworth, 2012) and enhancing attentional focus and memory-building during ongoing positive events by encouraging people to plan to tell stories in the future about these events (i.e., anticipated recall; Bryant & Veroff, 2007).

Researchers should keep the following methodological prescriptions in mind as they design future studies to evaluate the effectiveness of savoring interventions.

Use experimental designs. Random assignment to experimental or control conditions with pretest–posttest measurements remains the gold standard in evaluating the efficacy of interventions (Cook & Campbell, 1979; Wilson, 2011).

Administer independent interventions. To enhance the construct validity of causal inferences, researchers should avoid multi-faceted interventions in favor of single-pronged interventions (Cook & Campbell, 1979). Single-pronged interventions make it easier for researchers to label in theory-relevant terms the causal constructs responsible for observed effects. However, a benefit of multi-pronged interventions is that they may have greater ecological validity than single-pronged interventions. Recent research suggests that people naturally choose to use multiple types of happiness interventions, and greater variety in intervention types is associated with greater increases in mood (Parks, Della Porta, Pierce, Zilca, & Lyubomirsky, 2012). Clearly, combinations of multiple treatments may have different effects than the same treatments implemented on their own.

Include fidelity and manipulation checks. Experiments should include a fidelity check assessing whether participants implemented the savoring intervention as instructed at the intended dosage and for the intended duration. Experiments should also include "manipulation checks" to determine whether interventions actually produced reliable group differences in the level of the intended independent variable. We note that only 20% of the studies we reviewed included a manipulation check, and none assessed the fidelity with which participants actually put the intervention into practice. One simple method of assessing fidelity of implementation is to ask participants to report a subjective self-assessment of how much they adhered to the prescribed dosage of the intervention. Alternatively, Lyubomirsky and colleagues (2011) had naïve coders rate the perceived effort the participants put into completing the intervention (i.e., writing a response to a best possible selves prompt or other topics). Emphasizing the importance of assessing how the intervention is implemented, Lyubomirsky et al. (2011) found that greater perceived effort predicted greater increases in well-being for participants in the intervention condition.

Measure potential mediating mechanisms. Researchers can more effectively advance conceptual understanding of underlying causal processes by measuring and testing potential mediational mechanisms (MacKinnon & Fairchild, 2009). For instance, Kurtz (2008) suggested that the relation between scarcity and savoring may be mediated by increased salience of positive features of the experience or by the motivation to seize the moment and savor the opportunity. Another potential mediator of the scarcity effect is that people may be motivated to avoid future regret for having failed to take full advantage of the experience while they had the chance. Assessing such potential mediators might well improve our ability to design more effective future interventions.

Recruit diverse samples. Roughly 70% (11 of 16) of the studies we reviewed used college students as participants. Wider, more diverse samples are needed to expand the external validity of findings. For instance, interventions aimed at savoring the past, such as life reviewing, may be most effective for older participants, especially if they experience lower satisfaction with their past life (Coleman, 1974). Furthermore, compared to the general population, depressed populations and people living in deprived environments may have lower baselines for savoring due to lower levels of positive affect. These populations may be especially sensitive to interventions designed to boost savoring because they have more room to increase their positive affect. Also, different types of savoring interventions may be more or less effective for different personality types (Bryant & Veroff, 2007). For example, in response to positive events, extroverts typically use amplifying strategies of sharing with others, memory building, and behavioral expression more than introverts; and optimists tend to amplify positive affect by counting their blessings, whereas pessimists tend to dampen positive affect by engaging in kill-joy thinking (Bryant & Veroff, 2007).

Boost statistical power. As a sobering reminder of the need for large samples in evaluating savoring interventions, a prospective power analysis reveals that the total N required to obtain sufficient (i.e., 80%; Cohen, 1988) statistical power to detect the average unweighted within-study effect size when assessing happiness with a two-group pretest–posttest design ($d = +0.43$ or $r = .21$) at two-tailed $p < .05$ is 175 (i.e., 88 participants per group). Retrospectively, we note that the average total sample size in the 10 two-group pretest–posttest happiness studies we reviewed was 79.1, which provides only about a 50–50 (46%) chance of finding statistical significance for the typical savoring-related intervention. Besides using larger samples, researchers can also boost statistical power by enhancing the fidelity of treatment implementation (see Cohen, 1988; Cook & Campbell, 1979).

Unresolved Issues and Concluding Thoughts

Numerous unanswered questions remain concerning the nature of savoring-related interventions and their intended effects. What exactly are the key conceptual ingredients responsible for treatment effectiveness? And from a practical standpoint, what is the optimal level of "dosage" for savoring interventions? Researchers might well increase the strength of savoring interventions by increasing the dosage or duration of experimental conditions. However, no method currently exists for determining *a priori* for how many minutes, how often, and for how long participants should engage in a given intervention activity, so as to maximize its effectiveness. Future researchers might systematically vary the dosage and duration of the intervention, to help pinpoint optimal dose–response effects. For instance, performing five acts of kindness per week led to an increase in well-being for participants who completed all five acts of kindness in one day, but the intervention was not effective for participants who performed the five acts of kindness over the course of a week (see Lyubomirsky, Sheldon, & Schkade, 2005). Also, one should consider the role of person–activity "fit" when considering effective savoring strategies, because some strategies will be better suited to certain types of people but not others (Sheldon & Lyubomirsky, 2006).

Finally, given that people may become habituated to positive experiences over time (Frederick & Loewenstein, 1999), how long do the effects of savoring-related interventions last? Do the benefits of some interventions gradually fade, while others actually take time to accumulate and fully develop (Seligman et al., 2005)? We look forward with great anticipation to the new interventions that future researchers will investigate, as the field of positive psychology continues to explore ways to nurture people's capacity to transform visible joys within, to use Rilke's (1923/2005) poetic phrase, and savor their lives more fully.

Acknowledgment

The authors wish to thank Linda Perloff for her thoughtful feedback on an earlier version of this chapter.

References

*Study included in meta-analysis.

*Anselmo, T. T. (2010). *Positive psychology interventions: Targeting needy and self-critical individuals.* Unpublished master's thesis. York University, Toronto, Canada.

Beaumont, S. L. (2011). Identity styles and wisdom during emerging adulthood: Relationships with mindfulness and savoring. *Identity, 11*, 155–180.

Boehm, J. K., Lyubomirsky, S., & Sheldon, K. M. (2011). A longitudinal experimental study comparing the effectiveness of happiness-enhancing strategies in Anglo Americans and Asian Americans. *Cognition and Emotion, 25*, 1152–1167.

Bryant, F. B. (1989). A four-factor model of perceived control: Avoiding, coping, obtaining, and savoring. *Journal of Personality, 57*, 773–797.

Bryant, F. B. (2003). Savoring Beliefs Inventory (SBI): A scale for measuring beliefs about savouring. *Journal of Mental Health, 12*, 175–196.

Bryant, F. B., Chadwick, E. D., & Kluwe, K. (2011). Understanding the processes that regulate positive emotional experience: Unsolved problems and future directions for theory and research on savoring. *International Journal of Wellbeing, 1*, 107–126. doi:10.5502/ijw.v1i1.5

Bryant, F. B., Ericksen, C. L., & DeHoek, A. H. (2008). Savoring. In S. J. Lopez (Ed.), *Encyclopedia of positive psychology* (Vol. 2, pp. 857–859). New York: Wiley/Blackwell.

*Bryant, F. B., Smart, C. M., & King, S. P. (2005). Using the past to enhance the present: Boosting happiness through positive reminiscence. *Journal of Happiness Studies, 6*, 227–260.

*Bryant, F. B., & Veroff, J. (2007). *Savoring: A new model of positive experience* (pp. 184–185). Mahwah, NJ: Erlbaum Associates.

Carlton, E. L. (2009). *Happiness at work: Using positive psychology interventions to increase worker well-being.* Unpublished master's thesis: St. Mary's University, Halifax, NS.

Cialdini, R. B. (1993). *Influence: Science and practice.* New York: HarperCollins.

Cohen, J. (1988). *Statistical power analysis for the behavioral sciences* (2nd ed.). Hillsdale, NJ: Erlbaum Associates.

Coleman, P. G. (1974). Measuring reminiscence characteristics from conversation as adaptive features of old age. *International Journal of Aging and Human Development, 5*, 281–294.

Conrod, P. J., Stewart, S. H., Pihl, R. O., Côté, S., Fontaine, V., & Dongier, M. (2000). Efficacy of brief coping skills interventions that match different personality profiles of female substance abusers. *Psychology of Addictive Behaviors, 14*, 231–242.

Cook, T. D., & Campbell, D. T. (1979). *Quasi-experimentation: Design and analysis issues for field settings.* Chicago: Rand McNally.

Diener, E., & Emmons, R. A. (1984). The independence of positive and negative affect. *Journal of Personality and Social Psychology, 47*, 1105–1117.

Diener, E., Emmons, R. A., Larsen, R. J., & Griffin, S. (1985). The Satisfaction with Life Scale. *Journal of Personality Assessment, 49*, 71–75. doi:10.1207/s15327752jpa4901_13

Fordyce, M. W. (1977). Development of a program to increase personal happiness. *Journal of Counseling Psychology, 24*, 511–521.

Fordyce, M. W. (1983). A program to increase happiness: Further studies. *Journal of Counseling Psychology, 30*, 483–498.

Frederick, S., & Loewenstein, G. (1999). Hedonic adaptation. In D. Kahneman, E. Diener, & N. Schwarz (Eds.), *Well-being: The foundations of hedonic psychology* (pp. 302–329). New York: Russell Sage Foundation.

Frijda, N. H., & Sundararajan, L. (2007). Emotion refinement: A theory inspired by Chinese poetics. *Perspectives on Psychological Science, 2*, 227–241.

Gable, S. L., Reis, H. T., Impett, E. A., & Asher, E. R. (2004). What do you do when things go right? The intrapersonal and interpersonal benefits of sharing positive events. *Journal of Personality and Social Psychology, 87*, 228–245.

Grissom, R. J., & Kim, J. J. (2011). *Effect sizes for research: Univariate and multivariate applications* (2nd ed.). New York: Taylor & Francis.

Harrison, P. R., Smith, J. L., & Bryant, F. B. (in press). The savoring expedition. In J. J. Froh & A. Parks-Sheiner (Eds.), *Positive psychology in higher education: A practical workbook for the classroom.* Washington, DC: American Psychological Association.

*Hurley, D. B., & Kwon, P. (2012). Results of a study to increase savoring the moment: Differential impact on positive and negative outcomes. *Journal of Happiness Studies, 13*, 579–588.

Ironson, G., Antoni, M. H., Schneiderman, N., Chesney, M. A., O'Cleirigh, C., Balbin, E., Greenwood, D., Lutgendorf, S., LaPerriere, A., Klimas, N., & Fletcher, M. A. (2002). Coping: Interventions for optimal disease management. In M. A. Chesney & M. H. Antoni (Eds.), *Innovative approaches to health psychology: Prevention and treatment lessons from AIDS* (pp. 167–195). Washington, DC: American Psychological Association.

Johnson, J. E., (1996). Coping with radiation therapy: Optimism and the effect of preparatory interventions. *Research in Nursing and Health, 19*, 3–12.

Jose, P. E., Lim, B. T., & Bryant, F. B. (2012). Does savoring increase happiness? A daily diary study. *Journal of Positive Psychology, 7*(3), 176–187.

*Keeney, J. (2009). *Savoring success: Effects of basking and acknowledgment of others in response to achievement.* Unpublished master's thesis. Michigan State University, East Lansing, MI.

Kendall, P. C. (1985). Toward a cognitive-behavioral model of child psychopathology and a critique of related interventions. *Journal of Abnormal Child Psychology, 13*, 357–372.

Kidd, S. A. (2003). Street youth: Coping and interventions. *Child and Adolescent Social Work Journal, 20*, 235–261.

*King, L. A. (2001). The health benefits of writing about life goals. *Personality and Social Psychology Bulletin, 27*, 798–807.

Koo, M., Algoe, S. B., Wilson, T. D., & Gilbert, D. T. (2008). It's a wonderful life: Mentally subtracting positive events improves people's affective states, contrary to their affective forecasts. *Journal of Personality and Social Psychology, 95*, 1217–1224.

*Kurtz, J. L. (2008). Looking to the future to appreciate the present: The benefits of perceived temporal scarcity. *Psychological Science, 19*, 1238–1241.

*Kurtz, J. L. (2012). Seeing through new eyes: An experimental investigation of the benefits of photography. Unpublished manuscript.

Lindberg, T. L. (2004). *Culture and savoring of positive experiences.* Unpublished doctoral dissertation. University of British Columbia, Vancouver, Canada.

*Lyubomirsky, S., Dickerhoof, R., Boehm, J. K., & Sheldon, K. M. (2011). Becoming happier takes both a will and a proper way: An experimental longitudinal intervention to boost well-being. *Emotion, 11*, 391–402.

Lyubomirsky, S., & Lepper, H. S. (1999). A measure of subjective happiness: Preliminary reliability and construct validation. *Social Indicators Research, 46*, 137–155.

Lyubomirsky, S., Sheldon, K. M., & Schkade, D. (2005). Pursuing happiness: The architecture of sustainable change. *Review of General Psychology, 9*, 111–131.

*Lyubomirsky, S., Sousa, L., & Dickerhoof, R. (2006). The costs and benefits of writing, talking, and thinking about triumphs and defeats. *Journal of Personality and Social Psychology, 90*, 692–708.

MacKinnon, D. P., & Fairchild, A. J. (2009). Current directions in mediation analysis. *Current Directions in Psychological Science, 18*, 16–20.

McCabe-Fitch, K. A. (2009). *Examination of the impact of an intervention in positive psychology on the happiness and life satisfaction of children.* Unpublished doctoral dissertation. University of Connecticut, Storrs, CT.

Meehan, M. P., Durlak, J. A., & Bryant, F. B. (1993). The relationship of social support to perceived control and subjective mental health in adolescents. *Journal of Community Psychology, 21*, 49–55.

Mitchell, T. R., Thompson, L., & Peterson, E. (1997). Temporal adjustments in the evaluation of events: The "rosy view." *Journal of Experimental Social Psychology, 33*, 421–448.

Miyamoto, Y., & Ma, X. (2011). Dampening and savoring positive emotions: A dialectical cultural script guides emotion regulation. *Emotion, 11*, 1346–1357.

Nawijn, J., Marchand, M., Veenhoven, R., & Vingerhoets, A. (2010). Vacationers happier, but most not happier after a holiday. *Applied Research in Quality of Life, 5*, 35–47.

O'Brien, E., & Ellsworth, P. C. (2012). Saving the last for best: A positivity bias for end experiences. *Psychological Science, 23*, 163–165.

*Otake, K., Shimai, S., Tanaka-Matsumi, J., Otsui, K., & Frederickson, B. L. (2006). Happy people become happier through kindness: A counting kindness intervention. *Journal of Happiness Studies, 7*, 361–375.

Parks, A. C., Della Porta, M. D., Pierce, R. S., Zilca, R., & Lyubomirsky, S. (2012). Pursuing happiness in everyday life: The characteristics and behaviors of online happiness seekers. *Emotion, 12*(6), 1222–1234.

Pavri, S., & Monda-Amaya, L. (2000). Loneliness and students with learning disabilities in inclusive classrooms: Self-perceptions, coping strategies, and preferred interventions. *Learning Disabilities Research and Practice*, *15*, 22–33.

Prinstein, M. J., La Greca, A. M., & Verberg, E. M. (1996). Children's coping assistance: How parents, teachers, and friends help children cope after a natural disaster. *Journal of Clinical Child Psychology*, *25*, 463–475.

Quoidbach, J., Berry, E. V., Hansenne, M., & Mikolajczak, M. (2010). Positive emotion regulation and well-being: Comparing the impact of eight savoring and dampening strategies. *Personality and Individual Differences*, *49*, 368–373.

*Quoidbach, J., Wood, A., & Hansenne, M. (2009). Back to the future: The effect of daily practice of mental time travel into the future on happiness and anxiety. *Journal of Positive Psychology*, *4*, 349–355

Raes, F., Smets, J., Nelis, S., & Schoofs, H. (2012). Dampening of positive affect prospectively predicts depressive symptoms in non-clinical samples. *Cognition and Emotion*, *26*, 75–82.

Rilke, R. M. (2005). *Duino elegies* (G. Miranda, Trans.). Falls Church, VA: Azul Editions. (Original work published 1923.)

*Schueller, S. M. (2010). Preferences for positive psychology exercises. *Journal of Positive Psychology*, *5*, 192–203.

Seligman, M. E. P., Rashid, T., & Parks, A. C. (2006). Positive psychotherapy. *American Psychologist*, *61*, 774–788.

*Seligman, M. E. P., Steen, T. A., Park, N., & Peterson, C. (2005). Positive psychology progress. *American Psychologist*, *60*, 410–421.

*Sheldon, K, M. & Lyubomirsky, S. (2006). How to increase and sustain positive emotion: The effects of expressing gratitude and visualizing best possible selves. *Journal of Positive Psychology*, *1*, 73–82.

Sikkema, K. J., Hansen, N. B., Kochman, A., Tate, D. C., & Difranceisco, W. (2004). Outcomes from a randomized controlled trial of a group intervention for HIV positive men and women coping with AIDS-related loss and bereavement. *Death Studies*, *28*, 187–209.

Sin, N. L., & Lyubomirsky, S. (2009). Enhancing well-being and alleviating depressive symptoms with positive psychology interventions: A practice-friendly meta-analysis. *Journal of Clinical Psychology: In Session*, *65*, 467–487.

Singer, G. H. S., & Powers, L. E. (Eds.) (1993). *Families, disability, and empowerment: Active coping skills and strategies for family interventions.* Baltimore, MD: Paul H. Brookes Publishing Co.

Smith, J. L., Harrison, P. R., & Bryant, F. B. (in press). Enjoyment. In A. C. Michalos (Ed.), *Encyclopedia of quality of life research.* New York: Springer.

Tugade, M. M., & Fredrickson, B. L. (2007). Regulation of positive emotions: Emotion regulation strategies that promote resilience. *Journal of Happiness Studies*, *8*, 311–333.

Van Boven, L., & Ashworth, L. (2007). Looking forward, looking back: Anticipation is more evocative than retrospection. *Journal of Experimental Psychology: General*, *136*, 289–300.

van der Klink, J. J., Blonk, R. W., Schene, A. H., & van Dijk, F. J. (2001). The benefits of interventions for work-related stress. *American Journal of Public Health*, *91*, 270–276.

Watson, D., Clark, L. A., & Tellegen, A. (1988). Development and validation of brief measures of positive and negative affect: The PANAS scales. *Journal of Personality and Social Psychology*, *54*, 1063–1070.

Wilson, T. D. (2011). *Redirect: The surprising new science of psychological change.* New York: Little, Brown.

Wilson, T. D., Centerbar, D. B., Kermer, D. A., & Gilbert, D. T. (2005). The pleasures of uncertainty: Prolonging positive moods in ways people do not anticipate. *Journal of Personality and Social Psychology*, *88*, 5–21.

Wirtz, D., Kruger, J., Scollon, C. N., & Diener, E. (2003). What to do on spring break? The role of predicted, on-line, and remembered experience in future choice. *Psychological Science*, *14*, 520–524.

Wood, J. V., Heimpel, S. A., & Michela, J. L. (2003). Savoring and dampening: Self-esteem differences in regulating positive affect. *Journal of Personality and Social Psychology*, *85*, 566–580.

Wortman, P. M., & Bryant, F. B. (1985). School desegregation and black achievement: An integrative review. *Sociological Methods and Research*, *13*, 289–324.

4

Strengths Interventions

Current Progress and Future Directions

Michelle C. Louis and Shane J. Lopez

Practitioners in several fields are committed to identifying and developing personal strengths in an attempt to make lives, organizations, and communities better. This chapter presents the foundational tenets of a strengths perspective and highlights the most common approaches to conceptualizing and measuring psychological strengths. It continues with a description of the status of contemporary strengths interventions – that is, what types of interventions currently are being conducted, and the existing evidence for the efficacy of such interventions. The chapter concludes with recommendations for ongoing strengths intervention practice as well as suggestions for future research in the field.

An Overview of the Strengths Perspective

A strengths approach begins with "efforts to label what is right" within people and organizations (Buckingham, 2007, p. 6) and is built upon the assertion that every individual has talents or psychological resources that can be leveraged toward the attainment of desirable outcomes in many areas of life (Anderson, 2005; Saleebey, 2006). This perspective assumes that human strengths are not "secondary, derivative, illusory, epiphenomenal, parasitic upon the negative, or otherwise suspect" (Peterson & Seligman, 2004, p. 4) and affirms the development of strengths as a legitimate avenue for invoking academic and vocational success, well-being, and personal growth.

These assumptions undergird the programs within educational, organizational, coaching, and therapeutic settings that promote the achievement of positive goals and aims (Biswas-Diener, 2010; Frey, Jonas, & Greitemeyer, 2003; Linley & Burns, 2010; Lopez & Louis, 2009; Park & Peterson, 2009). Emerging strengths-based approaches are viewed as a way to challenge some of the professional conventions that accompany a deficit-driven understanding of the human condition

The Wiley Blackwell Handbook of Positive Psychological Interventions, First Edition.
Edited by Acacia C. Parks and Stephen M. Schueller.

(Peterson, 2006), and can be employed as a self-help technique or avenue for personal growth (Seligman, Steen, Park, & Peterson, 2005). Based upon the conviction that people have a greater proclivity for productive change when their strengths and capabilities are highlighted (Clifton & Nelson, 1992; Delgado, 2000), a central charge of a strengths intervention is to "create a language of strength, hope, and movement" (Kaplan & Girard, 1994, p. 53). This model places the person, not the problem, at the center of practice (Kisthardt, 2006). It suggests that strengths-oriented practitioners may aid in the process of uncovering their clients' suppressed areas of potential or resilience (Barnard, 1994; Saleebey, 1997) and help people cultivate the ability to apply personal resources or skills to solve a problem or attain a goal (Aspinwall & Staudinger, 2003).

At the individual level, strengths interventions are designed to help people grow by developing core aspects of themselves. Such interventions seek to identify positive personal and interpersonal traits or talents, integrate them into a participant's view of self, and inform subsequent behavioral changes (Clifton & Harter, 2003). Strengths practitioners explore ways to empower individuals to flourish or thrive and are guided by the belief that capitalizing on one's areas of strength is more likely to yield high levels of success than would be possible by making a comparable investment of effort into overcoming personal weaknesses or deficiencies (Buckingham, 2007; Clifton & Harter, 2003). The strengths approach therefore underscores the importance of intentionally choosing to focus one's attention and energy into cultivating that which will yield the most significant growth, which is accomplished not by ignoring weaknesses, but by instead seeking to understand and manage areas of deficiency while optimizing effort by building on strengths (Clifton & Harter, 2003; Shushok & Hulme, 2006).

A strengths-oriented philosophy also contributes to contemporary scholarship on organizational behavior by directing attention to the positive dynamics and productive practices that exist at the communal or organizational level through approaches such as appreciative inquiry (Cameron, Dutton, & Quinn, 2003; Cooperrider & Whitney, 2000). This arena of study within organizational science focuses on the strengths or qualities present in an organization that catalyze positive feelings, employee engagement, effective teamwork, and other indicators of thriving at the collective level (Cameron & Caza, 2004). It examines topics such as the positive outcomes, processes, and attributes of organizations and their members as well as the environmental conditions or dynamics within organizations that support excellent performance. Based on an examination of research findings in this field, Drucker (as cited in Cooperrider & Whitney, 2005) encourages organizational leaders to identify and capitalize on their strengths, claiming that "the task of organizational leadership is to create an alignment of strengths in ways that make a system's weaknesses irrelevant" (p. 2). Regardless of whether a strengths perspective is used to generate understanding and inform practice at the individual or group level, its central aim is to discover and amplify the promising characteristics of individuals, groups, and communities (Saleebey, 2006).

Various Approaches to Conceptualizing and Assessing Strengths

Strengths interventions have broad cross-disciplinary appeal and applicability, informing practice in organizational leadership (Buckingham & Clifton, 2001; Clifton & Harter, 2003), education (Louis & Schreiner, 2012; Schreiner, Hulme, Hetzel, & Lopez, 2009), ministry (Winseman, Clifton, & Liesveld, 2004), social work (Saleebey, 2006; Staudt, Howard, & Drake, 2001; Weick, Rapp, Sullivan, & Kisthardt, 1989), and psychology (Biswas-Diener, 2010; Seligman, Rashid, & Parks, 2006). Although intervention practices vary between each of these fields, many of the core elements of existing strengths initiatives are derived from one of the two predominant approaches to conceptualization and measurement. One model for understanding strengths frames them as developed *talents* that produce consistently excellent performance in executing specific activities. The other strengths approach views strengths as elements of *character* that can be used to display virtue. Each of these schools of thought has created assessments to measure human strength, and both have advanced scholarly thought and dialogue regarding the application and optimization of positive human characteristics. The following section will highlight the central ideas that constitute each of these strengths models, and it will also describe the strengths assessments associated with each of these paradigms.

Strengths as Developed Talents: The Gallup Model

Based upon a systematic review of the results of a large sample of semi-structured interviews conducted over the course of three decades with high-performing individuals in a variety of fields, analysts at Gallup pinpointed a series of personal characteristics associated with success (Lopez, Hodges, & Harter, 2005). This information provided the initial framework for a talent-based strengths model. According to this framework, strengths are most accurately conceptualized as well-developed talents that produce excellence. *Talents* are defined as "naturally occurring patterns of thought, feeling, or behavior that can be productively applied" (Hodges & Clifton, 2004, p. 257) and include an individual's patterns of interacting with others, processing information, or navigating the environment. As these talents are believed to be naturally occurring, individuals often use them without conscious awareness of their presence (Clifton, Anderson, & Schreiner, 2006; Drucker, 2000). Clusters of similar talents form *talent themes*, which are viewed as proclivities that can be developed through the addition of acquired knowledge and skill to form *strengths*. Within this model, strengths are evidenced in the ability to produce "consistent, near-perfect performance in a given activity" (Clifton & Anderson, 2002, p. 8) and also can be revealed in psychologically energizing or rewarding activities that one performs with excellence (Buckingham, 2007).

Because strengths are specific to a particular activity or context, they are not listed comprehensively within the Gallup strengths model.

Based upon information gleaned throughout the inductive process of analyzing the interview responses of two million highly successful individuals, researchers at Gallup were able to create the initial version of an instrument called the *Strengths-Finder* (Gallup, 1999). This online instrument was the first to provide an omnibus assessment of human talent and was designed for use in personal development, not as a measure of psychological illness or wellness (Lopez et al., 2005). Subsequently renamed the *Clifton StrengthsFinder*, this assessment contains 177 item-pairs designed to measure talent in 34 possible themes (Lopez et al., 2005). The Clifton StrengthsFinder provides information regarding the respondent's five most predominant clusters of talent (called *signature talent themes*), which are conceptualized as qualities that can be transformed into strengths if they are developed through the addition of knowledge and skill (Buckingham & Clifton, 2001). Examples of the talent themes identified by the instrument include *Activator* (the theme used to describe people who have a propensity to quickly initiate action or activity in response to a problem or situation) and *Relator* (the theme used to identify people who enjoy cultivating close relationships with others). Related supporting materials pertinent to a variety of settings are also available, and these resources are designed to offer strategies for developing signature talent themes into strengths within the spheres of business (Buckingham & Clifton, 2001), education (Clifton et al., 2006; Liesveld & Miller, 2005), leadership (Rath & Conchie, 2008), or ministry (Winseman et al., 2004).

Strengths as Elements of Character: The Values in Action Model

The other main strengths classification system, known as the *Values in Action (VIA) Classification of Strengths*, was developed through the efforts of a collaboration of scholars in positive psychology at the Values in Action Institute (Seligman & Peterson, 2003). The character strengths that appear in the VIA model are the result of an extensive deductive process that included collaborative brainstorming among noted scholars and a review of literature addressing character in several disciplinary fields, resulting in items that were subsequently subjected to psychometric examination (Peterson & Seligman, 2004). Similar to the format used in the Linnaean classification of species, these psychologists categorize positive traits according to several conceptual levels of increasing specificity. The broadest category consists of the *virtues*, which are defined as "core characteristics [ubiquitously] valued by moral philosophers and religious thinkers" (Peterson & Seligman, 2004, p. 13); these include wisdom, courage, humanity, justice, temperance, and transcendence. These six virtues are cultivated through the use of 24 *character strengths*, which are positive traits that are relatively stable across situations and are believed to be "the psychological ingredients – processes or mechanisms – that define the virtues" (Peterson & Seligman, 2004, p. 13). For example, the virtue of justice may be revealed through the use of constituent character strengths such as citizenship, fairness, or leadership.

The authors of the VIA classification system believe that it embodies an explicit recognition that strengths and disorders exist in degrees. Peterson (2006) notes that embedded within the VIA system are classifications of health, absence of health, and illness in that the character strengths are manifest in gradations. This continuum ranges from the *opposite* or antithesis of a particular strength at one extreme that progresses to the mere *absence* of the strength, to the *presence* of the strength, and finally to the *exaggeration* of the strength at the other end of the continuum. For example, the character strength of *citizenship* is opposed by *narcissism*; an absence of citizenship manifests in *selfishness*; and citizenship taken to the unhealthy extreme is *chauvinism* (Peterson, 2006).

As an outgrowth of the VIA classification system and as a way to operationalize its constructs, a 240-item strengths assessment known as the *Values in Action Inventory of Strengths* (VIA-IS; Seligman, Park, & Peterson, 2004) was developed. This inventory is currently available in paper and online formats with separate versions for youth and adults (Park & Peterson, 2007). The VIA-IS utilizes a five-point Likert scale to assess the degree to which respondents affirm inventory items that are reflective of the 24 character strengths in the VIA classification. It generates a report that ranks and describes the respondent's five most strongly endorsed strengths (Peterson & Seligman, 2004; Values in Action Institute, 2007).

The Current Nature of Strengths Interventions

Depending on the context and desired outcomes, strengths development may assume a variety of forms and encompass a range of strategies. As a means of offering individualized feedback to participants, practitioners often administer one of the aforementioned instruments – the Values in Action Inventory of Strengths (VIA-IS; Seligman et al., 2004) or the Clifton StrengthsFinder (Rath, 2007). More recently, some practitioners have also begun to use an instrument called the Realise2 (Centre for Applied Positive Psychology, 2010). A recent poll of a sample of strengths practitioners indicates that most do use some sort of formal assessment as a part of their strengths intervention process (Biswas-Diener, Kashdan, & Minhas, 2011).

However, some practitioners indicate that it is also possible to conduct strengths interventions without requiring the formal completion of a specific strengths assessment tool by instead asking participants to self-identify personal strengths (e.g., Seligman et al., 2006). Exclusive of the use of an assessment, Clifton and Nelson (1992) propose that strengths can be identified by becoming attuned to four clues that are indicative of their existence. Specifically, these authors note that individuals are intuitively drawn to activities that will facilitate strengths utilization, and so they advocate for people to cultivate an awareness of these types of "yearnings" (p. 43). A second signal that a strength may be in use is when an individual derives great satisfaction and energy from investment in an activity, experiencing a sense of engagement and timelessness that mirrors Csikszentmihalyi's (1990) description of *flow* (Peterson & Seligman, 2004). Rapid learning is another sign that a strength may be present, and the fourth indicator of a strength in action is that "glimpses of excellence" (Clifton & Anderson, 2002, p. 52) are demonstrated when an individual attempts an activity that requires the use of a particular strength (Buckingham, 2007, Clifton & Anderson, 2002).

Some strengths programs may simply seek to help participants use their strengths more readily and with greater frequency, a strategy that is derived from the notion that strengths are augmented through regular use (Buckingham & Clifton, 2001) and that successful individuals spend most of their time leveraging their areas of strength while managing their weaknesses (Clifton & Harter, 2003). Using strengths practice to encourage the increased use of strengths is beneficial in that greater strengths use has been associated with increased levels of well-being over time (Wood, Linley, Maltby, Kashdan, & Hurling, 2011), as people who "have the opportunity every day to do what they do best – to act on their strengths – are far more likely to flourish" (Fredrickson, 2009, p. 189). The majority of existing strengths practice tends to focus on identifying positive attributes and encouraging participants to use them with greater frequency (see Louis, 2009 for a review), an approach called "talent identification" (Louis, 2008, p. 16) or the "identify and use" approach (Biswas-Diener et al., 2011, p. 108).

More nuanced and contextualized strengths development strategies include a consideration of how to use strengths more effectively as opposed to simply more frequently. Some areas of focus within these strengths development interventions include modifying the use of strengths in accordance with situational demands, and the inclusion of activities explicitly designed to cultivate strengths and expand their potency – a process that may actually involve learning how to reduce their use in some settings or apply them with greater insight (Kaplan & Kaiser, 2010). Strengths development strategies of this type may also require an evaluation of how the presence of various strengths combinations produces certain tendencies, contemplating which activities may be helpful in catalyzing strengths growth (Lopez & Louis, 2009), or considering how strengths can be applied in novel ways (Seligman et al., 2005).

Although many practitioners are highly attentive to the responsibility of designing interventions that are theoretically based and reflective of current research, a problem can arise when the pace of practice-based innovations surpasses that of meaningful research to inform such adjustments. Biswas-Diener and colleagues (2011) note that some strengths practitioners are proceeding on an *ad hoc* basis, creating a "chasm between what is researched, what is marketed, and what is practiced" (p. 107), a state of affairs that is unbecoming of a field that identifies itself as being theoretically grounded and evidence-based. In the final sections of this chapter, we offer some suggestions for ongoing strengths development practices that align with current research in this area.

Scope of This Chapter

As researchers in strengths psychology, we value multiple models for understanding strengths and believe that each offers unique and important contributions to the field. We also find it critical to maintain a focus and scope for this chapter that allows for an in-depth examination of strengths interventions as opposed to offering a more cursory description of a greater range of intervention types. As the Clifton StrengthsFinder is the most widely used strengths assessment tool in the world, we have opted to focus our attention in this chapter on a description of strengths interventions that are based upon Gallup's definition of strengths and the interventions that are built upon this understanding. Data indicate that the Clifton StrengthsFinder has been completed by more than six million people, including more than a million students attending over 600 postsecondary institutions across the globe (M. Pogue, personal communication, August 24, 2011). This level of prevalence demands an examination of the types of interventions that currently are being conducted in association with the use of this instrument and a consideration of how to advance the science and practice in this area.

Readers who are more familiar with other models or strengths assessments are likely to note that many of our recommendations for ongoing research and strengths practice are as readily applicable to other approaches to strengths assessment and intervention as they are to the Gallup model. In addition, although there are numerous published studies on specific psychological strengths such as hope, courage, or resilience, this chapter does not detail the literature on any individual strength but instead describes strengths more generally.

Review of Existing Strengths Intervention Research

In the following section, we review the existing research on strengths interventions that employ the Gallup model within educational and workplace settings. We describe the state of the available evidence regarding the efficacy of such interventions, highlight what remains unknown in the literature, and offer suggestions for ongoing research.

Strengths interventions in educational settings

Research on the impact of strengths interventions within education has emerged in recent years. Many of the existing studies on this topic are doctoral dissertations that utilize a variety of methodologies to assess the impact of strengths interventions on variables associated with student success. In most cases, these interventions have been conducted using the Clifton StrengthsFinder as the foundation for integrating some type of strengths-oriented curriculum or program. The following section describes each of these intervention studies and highlights their key findings. The majority of studies have examined how first-year college student populations respond to strengths interventions, although other groups have been examined as well.

Classroom-based strengths interventions with first-year college students Williamson (2002) selected a convenience sample of 80 students enrolled in first-year English courses at a private, liberal arts college and randomly assigned them to conditions. Participants received the results of their Clifton StrengthsFinder assessments, two one-hour strengths training sessions conducted in large groups, a brief individual strengths consultation, and a small group discussion on this topic facilitated by the researcher. The control group did not receive any strengths-related information. At the end of the semester, Williamson found that students who experienced the strengths intervention had completed a greater mean number of credit hours and also earned significantly higher grade point averages than had the students in the control group. This researcher also assessed students' intent to re-enroll at their current institution and found no significant differences between the two groups, although he noted that the second semester retention rate for the treatment group was 97%, compared to 87% for the control group. A small sample size and a non-equivalent control group in this study limit the reliability of the findings, but this research provides initial evidence to suggest that strengths-based approaches may positively influence academic achievement in first-year students.

A related study compared whether a strengths-oriented approach to teaching an introductory college-level public speaking course would result in students reporting increased academic engagement and demonstrating better proficiency in desired learning outcomes than would a traditional teaching approach (Cantwell, 2005). This researcher used a quasi-experimental, pretest–posttest non-equivalent control group design and designated those students enrolled in one section of a public speaking course as those who were taught from a distinctly strengths perspective, whereas students enrolled in another section of the same course were simply exposed to the curriculum that had been used in the course during previous semesters (the control condition). The strengths intervention consisted of four class sessions that were devoted to exposing students to their Clifton StrengthsFinder results and discussing information found in the *StrengthsQuest* text (Clifton & Anderson, 2002). In addition, the instructor for the intervention group employed a strengths-based approach to offering feedback to student coursework, emphasizing what students were doing well and encouraging them to consider how to capitalize on their strengths in completing the assignments associated with the course. As the researcher taught both sections of the public speaking course participating in this study, she controlled for extraneous variables in the research design by asking a blind independent rater to assess the uniformity of her teaching behaviors. After also controlling for pre-existing levels of academic engagement and public speaking ability, Cantwell found that students who were exposed to the strengths intervention reported significantly higher levels of academic engagement at the end of the semester than did their counterparts in the control condition. In addition, students in the experimental group attained higher levels of proficiency in course-relevant outcomes, as demonstrated by significantly higher scores on objective examinations and evaluations of public speaking skill. The findings of Cantwell's research therefore lend initial support to the notion that the use of classroom-based strengths interventions is associated with subsequently elevated levels of academic engagement and course performance.

Cantwell's (2005) findings dovetail with the work of Estévez (2005), who used a phenomenological approach to explore the impact of a strengths intervention on academic engagement and perceived social capital of 30 underprepared students enrolled in a first-year seminar course. Following the completion of the Clifton StrengthsFinder, students in this course participated in four class sessions related to strengths, and the information presented was supplemented with the StrengthsQuest text (Clifton & Anderson, 2002). Estévez conducted individual interviews with study participants and invited some of these students to participate in a focus group to gain additional information. Estévez noted that "students who engaged courses on the premises of their strengths more readily engaged the academic demands of the course" (p. 72), and these students reported elevated levels of academic motivation after learning about their personal strengths, a better understanding of how to apply their strengths to meet academic challenges, and a positive impact on their ability to form social networks.

To examine the relative impact of two different types of strengths interventions, Louis (2008) used a pretest–posttest waiting-list control group design with random assignment to compare how students enrolled in a first-year seminar course would respond to these interventions. In this study, 388 students were assigned to participate in four class sessions that used either the institution's traditional first-year curriculum (the control condition), an intervention that emphasized the identification of strengths, or one which focused on developing strengths after they were identified.

Louis found that, as predicted by the literature, students in the control group reported significantly declining levels of perceived academic control during the early weeks of college. However, students exposed to strengths interventions were able to maintain stable levels of perceived academic control during this same time period, a finding that is predictive of students' tendencies to work harder on academic tasks, obtain better grades, and remain enrolled in their classes (Perry, Hladkyj, Pekrun, & Pelletier, 2001). After the students in the waiting-list control group engaged in a strengths intervention, their levels of perceived academic control increased significantly. Participants in Louis' study who were exposed to a strengths intervention that focused on merely labeling and understanding their strengths reported a significant shift toward an entity self-theory at the post-test, a trend that was not witnessed in the other groups. As a fixed mindset is associated with underperformance relative to ability over time (Robins & Pals, 2002), this research suggests the importance of including a developmental component in strengths interventions.

Another group of researchers conducted two related studies to examine the impact of strengths-based approaches on students enrolled in a first-year seminar course (Anderson, Schreiner, & Shahbaz, 2003, 2004). The first study used a one-group pretest–posttest design and required the 611 student participants to complete the Clifton StrengthsFinder and attend six one-hour class sessions focused on the topic of strengths. Prior to this intervention and after its completion, students completed the *Self-Reflection Scale* (Clifton, 1997), and the data revealed significant increases in optimism, personal strengths awareness, self-acceptance, goal directedness, self-confidence, awareness of others' strengths, and realistic expectations following the intervention (Anderson et al., 2003). However, this study lacked a control group, so the observed pretest–posttest differences may therefore be attributed to non-intervention factors.

The second study conducted by this team of researchers assigned 849 incoming students enrolled in a required first-year seminar course to either a strengths intervention group or a waiting-list control condition (Anderson et al., 2004). The strengths intervention included completing the Clifton StrengthsFinder and using the *StrengthsQuest curriculum outline and learning activities* (Anderson, 2003) during four one-hour class sessions focused on helping students identify and capitalize on their strengths. Students in the intervention group also attended an unspecified number of small group meetings with a peer leader for strengths-oriented discussions, and received an individual strengths coaching session with a trained faculty or staff member. These researchers again used the *Self-Reflection Scale* (Clifton, 1997) to measure academic self-confidence, strengths awareness, ability to see others according to their strengths, and perception of personal ability to apply strengths to academic tasks and relationships. They found that students in the strengths intervention group scored significantly higher on all of these variables than did students in the control group (Anderson et al., 2004). However, these results should be interpreted with a full consideration of the design of the study, as it is unclear whether students in the control group received the equivalent experience of meeting with a peer leader in a small group or having individual sessions with a faculty or staff member. It is possible that the mere presence of these experiences within the curriculum, and not the strengths intervention specifically, contributed to the observed results.

Finally, Cave (2003) sought to assess whether a strengths intervention embedded into a first-year seminar course for college students would influence their academic motivation. In this study, students in the intervention group completed the Clifton StrengthsFinder and attended three 50-minute large group plenary sessions designed to teach students about their strengths. During these same time periods, students in the control group attended individual first-year seminar classes consisting of 12–15 students, and which utilized the institution's existing curriculum for this course. Cave hypothesized that exposing students to information about their strengths would increase their academic motivation, but found no significant impact of the intervention on her measures of this variable. This researcher noted some instrumentation problems and outlined various methodological concerns that she encountered during the implementation of her study, and so the results of this work should be interpreted cautiously.

Research examining the use of strengths approaches with postsecondary students beyond the first year of college In addition to research on the effects of strengths interventions on first-year college students, there are also studies that have examined how other student populations respond to these interventions. The first is an investigation conducted by Hodges (as cited in Clifton & Harter, 2003). This research involved 150 undergraduate business students at a public university, who participated in one of three strengths intervention conditions to assess the impact of different degrees of exposure to information about personal strengths on their levels of hope. Students in the first group completed the Clifton StrengthsFinder and received written feedback that identified their signature themes of talent. A second group of students was exposed to the same intervention as were those in the first group but these participants were also granted access to an online learning program that helped them learn more about their talents. The third group of students was given all of the previously noted information and also participated in a 30-minute personal telephone consultation with a trained strengths consultant. Following a pre- and post-administration of the *State Hope Scale* (Snyder et al., 1996), the researchers determined that students in the third group reported a significantly greater increase in state hope than did the other groups. The results of this study suggest that certain types of strengths interventions may be associated with an increase in hope, although the study is limited by the lack of a control group.

Another study involving undergraduate business students is Mostek's (2010) research. This author used a case study method to retrospectively examine the impact of exposure to the Clifton StrengthsFinder assessment and associated curriculum during business students' first year of college on their self-knowledge, goals, and priorities while they were in their junior or senior year. Students interviewed for this research indicated that knowing their strengths provided increased self-knowledge and a heightened sense of confidence, and that they also aligned their priorities and decisions with their identified strengths. Although this study suggests some promising outcome possibilities, the very small sample size of five participants limits the scope of these findings.

Strengths interventions in academic advising, leadership, and mentoring programs Outside of a classroom setting, Swanson (2006) sought to understand the effect of a strengths approach to academic advising with first-year students on their subsequent retention. In Swanson's investigation, students were randomly assigned to one of three groups. The control group met with a faculty member to determine a class schedule for the spring semester, as was the traditionally implemented advising method at the institution where the research was conducted. The first intervention simply required students to meet with their faculty advisor for two 30-minute sessions for the purpose of building a relationship and facilitating integration into the campus community. The third group received a strengths intervention, which meant that these students were required to complete the Clifton StrengthsFinder and to attend two 30-minute advising sessions in which the results of the Clifton StrengthsFinder were interpreted and discussed in relation to the student's academic plans. Attrition data were collected, and Swanson (2006) found that students who had been randomly assigned to the condition in which the Clifton StrengthsFinder was utilized in the advising process had significantly higher retention rates than did the other two groups. One possible confound to this study is that the strengths-oriented advising sessions were conducted with student affairs staff, whereas the other types of advising sessions in this study were faculty-led.

Strengths interventions have also been used to encourage college students to become more effective leaders. Lehnert (2009) conducted a study in which participants in the strengths intervention group completed six online strengths development learning modules, whereas students in the control group engaged in standard leadership development learning modules that were not related to strengths. Exemplary leadership practices were measured by the Student Leadership Practice Inventory (SLPI; Kouzes & Posner, 2003), and results indicated that students who engaged in the strengths intervention reported greater gains on measures of effective student leadership practices than did those in the control group.

Pritchard (2009) used a constructivist approach and a grounded theory methodology to explore the personal attitudes of university students in the United Kingdom following a strengths-based intervention for student leaders. Participants in the study completed the Clifton StrengthsFinder, received their results, and then attended educational sessions over the course of two consecutive days designed to help them understand and apply their signature themes of talent. Following the intervention, Pritchard conducted a semi-structured interview with each student, inquiring about students' reactions to their assessment results and the overall impact of the strengths intervention. Students then engaged in online journaling about the experience for four months, a process that concluded with a second interview that inquired about the degree to which the participants were still reflecting upon and implementing the information presented during the strengths intervention. Participants noted that exposure to the strengths intervention produced immediate, short-term positive personal and relational effects including increased confidence and self-understanding as well as heightened appreciation for the strengths of others. These effects were positively mediated by factors such as the participant's degree of resonance with the results of the strengths assessment and the projection of the use of personal strengths in the future. At follow-up, although nearly all students in Pritchard's study reported that the initial impact of the intervention had diminished, this effect was not as pronounced for students who made efforts to develop their strengths and who continued to use strengths-oriented terminology in their regular vocabulary. Factors that were negative mediators of the long-term intervention effect included lack of ongoing curricular follow-up or training beyond the initial intervention and personal factors such as distraction or lack of interest in continued engagement with the strengths assessment results.

Outside of a postsecondary setting, one recent study (Gallup, 2011) evaluated the effectiveness of in-school mentoring with a strengths component. In a waiting-list control study, 249 students from kindergarten through grade 12 attended, on average, 25 weekly mentoring sessions with an adult from the community that emphasized strengths development. Specifically, mentors used a deck of cards prompting interactions focused on strengths and asked students how they might use their strengths to respond to daily problems at school and home. During this same time period, 121 students completed a comparable number of standard mentoring sessions without a strengths component. The study indicated that students receiving strengths-based mentoring were more likely to look forward to their mentoring sessions and had significantly higher school engagement than their control group counterparts.

Strengths interventions in the workplace

Research in workplace settings has revealed that a strengths-based approach to employee development can result in significant growth in individuals and teams (Asplund, Lopez, Hodges, & Harter, 2009). The following section describes archival evidence accumulated across multiple workplace studies conducted in 11 companies with over 90,000 employees. The bulk of these studies focus on engagement (defined in this research as the extent to which an employee is involved in and enthusiastic about work), a factor associated with productivity and retention. As available data allow, we evaluate the degree to which these companies' investment in strengths development yielded significant returns.

Strengths interventions in the workplace typically involve a manager completing a one-hour strengths coaching session (or a series of such sessions) with a highly trained professional strengths consultant. To date, 896 business units have been studied using a waiting-list control design, with managers in the active intervention group receiving some strengths feedback (typically a one-hour conversation focused on understanding one's strengths) and the other managers receiving no strengths feedback until later in the study. The units of the managers undergoing strengths development showed significantly more improvement in employee engagement over time relative to those units where the manager received no strengths feedback (Asplund et al., 2007).

In addition, of the 896 workplaces (i.e., business units) with managers participating in strengths development, 530 provided productivity data (e.g., number of sales made, amount of products manufactured). The workplaces with managers receiving strengths feedback showed 12.5% greater productivity post-intervention relative to those workplaces where managers did not receive strengths feedback. In one company, team sales increased significantly after a manager completed just one strengths coaching session. Profit data were available for 469 business units, ranging from retail stores to large manufacturing facilities. Those units whose managers received strengths feedback showed 8.9% greater profitability post-intervention relative to units where the manager did not receive strengths feedback (Asplund et al., 2007). Productivity data in the form of sales numbers for 1,874 individual employees from the sales industry were also examined for the effects of strengths development. For employees receiving a strengths intervention, productivity improved by 7.8% relative to employees without the intervention (Asplund et al., 2007).

Occasionally, strengths feedback and coaching are provided to all employees on a team. Among those employees receiving strengths feedback (n = 12,157), engagement also improved significantly over time relative to employees without feedback. Among employees receiving some strengths feedback, turnover rates were 14.9% lower than for those employees receiving no feedback, controlling for job type and tenure (Harter, Schmidt, & Hayes, 2002; Harter, Schmidt, Killham, & Asplund, 2006).

Given the data gathered from business units and employees across the world, the strengths-based approach to management and employee development seems to improve employee engagement within an organization and, in turn, increase productivity and retention.

Recommendations for Practice

The studies described in this chapter highlight the benefits that can be derived from attending to strengths, and yet there has been insufficient consideration given to how best to translate research findings into a concrete set of guidelines for strengths practice. It may be the case that forming a strong linkage between research, theory, and practice has been complicated by several factors. Perhaps one reason for the existing disconnect is that there is interest in psychological strengths across multiple fields, including education, organizational development, social work, and psychology (among others), and yet the interdisciplinary dialogue on the topic of strengths is not as robust as it might be. For practitioners, maintaining ongoing familiarity with current strengths research findings and contemporary intervention techniques across several disciplinary bodies of literature may prove to be a daunting endeavor, made increasingly complex by the varied conceptual frameworks and definitions of strengths, the existence of several instruments for assessing psychological strengths, and significant variations in the types of settings in which strengths interventions are conducted. Based upon our own observations regarding the current status of strengths intervention research and trends in the literature on this topic, we offer a series of recommendations for ongoing strengths intervention practice.

Recommendation 1: Conceptualize strengths as dynamic capacities that can be developed, not as fixed entities that are either present or absent

Strengths assessments can be beneficial in that they offer a classification and terminology for positive personal attributes and can stimulate an increase in self-knowledge. However, if these descriptors are presented in a manner that suggests that the assessment results represent immutable traits, then initial interest in and enthusiasm for one's results can be followed by a period of stagnation. Moreover, the literature on implicit self-theories cautions that when interventions consist of little more than providing affirming descriptive labels, they may actually be detrimental. Specifically, this body of research indicates that when people are given information suggesting that their personal qualities are innate and stable entities, they develop a fixed mindset about their abilities and tend to doubt their capacity for meaningful change through effort (Dweck, 1999). This fixed mindset can undermine one's motivation for working hard when confronted with challenging activities because it implies that having to apply prolonged effort reveals a lack of innate ability and is therefore to be avoided (Blackwell, Trzesniewski, & Dweck, 2007; Mueller & Dweck, 1998).

Research indicates that mindset type can be altered even through brief interventions (Aronson, Fried, & Good, 2002; Kamins & Dweck, 1999). In a study comparing the effects of various strengths intervention strategies, Louis (2011) found that when interventionists describe strengths as static traits that one either possesses or lacks, participants are more likely to adopt a fixed mindset than they are when strengths are framed as dynamic capacities. Whether a person approaches activities with a fixed versus a growth mindset is not simply a nominal distinction. Longitudinal research indicates that a fixed mindset is problematic because it is predictive of long-term underperformance relative to ability (Robins & Pals, 2002). In contrast, people with a growth mindset believe that personal attributes are responsive to developmental efforts, and therefore tend to believe that exerting themselves and working toward personal growth is something desirable (Dweck, 1999).

The clear implication is that it is important for practitioners to carefully consider the explicit and implicit messages they communicate about the nature of strengths during an intervention, as these messages have implications for the outcomes that are generated during the intervention and beyond. For example, a strengths intervention that focuses solely on helping participants understand and appreciate their assessment results may imply that descriptive labeling is the essence of the strengths approach. In contrast, a more sophisticated strengths intervention frames assessment results as merely introductory information that provides impetus for ongoing dialogue or activities designed to refine strengths and exercise them with greater insight and skill. It is critical for practitioners to conceptualize strengths as malleable qualities that can be honed through deliberate effort, and to bring an emphatically development-oriented approach to the intervention process. As Buckingham (2007) notes, strengths interventions are more effective when participants "learn how to go beyond the affirming power of a label, and … figure out how to use [their] strengths to make a tangible contribution" (p. 7).

A complicating factor in this discussion is that practitioners may believe that they are engaging in strengths development although the reality is that their interventions would be more accurately described as involving only exercises designed to help participants understand the labels or strengths terminology generated by their assessment results. An examination of several initiatives referred to as "strengths development programs" reveals that many of these programs actually do very little to help participants learn to develop their strengths, as they focus almost exclusively on identifying strengths and talents (see Louis, 2009 for a review). In such programs, participants may even be verbally encouraged to develop their strengths but are provided with little tangible instruction as to how to do so. Some practitioners note that implementing interventions that merely offer descriptive strengths is not typically a conscious choice, but instead reflects factors such as limitations on time for implementing a strengths program or uncertainty regarding how best to engage in developing clients' strengths.

A developmental approach to strengths interventions might adopt several forms. It could require a consideration of how strengths can be applied to new situations or emerging challenges, how various strengths work together within an individual to produce desired outcomes, a discussion of "strength–environment fit," and whether particular strengths have the potential for associated liabilities if misused (Louis, 2011). Strengths development may also include encouragement to understand and appreciate the diverse strengths of others, as well as an analysis of how to modulate the use of a particular strength in accordance with situational demands by using it more or less frequently (Kaplan & Kaiser, 2010), with greater insight, or in accordance with personal values. Biswas-Diener and colleagues (2011) suggest that strengths development requires a consideration of contextual factors and consists of at least three components, including *proficiency* (using a strength to optimize performance), *frequency* (using a strength with greater regularity), and *regulation* (discerning when and to what degree a strength should be used). These authors emphasize that environmental or situational factors interact with an individual's strengths to influence how they are expressed, and therefore advocate that practitioners cultivate a more holistic approach to strengths development that considers the role of these contributions.

Recommendation 2: Remember that strengths are manifested in relationship with each other rather than in isolation, and that they exist in degrees rather than as qualities that an individual either possesses or lacks

To provide a manageable starting point for engaging in thought and dialogue regarding one's strengths, the authors of the most commonly used strengths assessments encourage a focus on the top five most prominent results provided by their respective inventory, whether these include five "signature strengths" (VIA-IS) or five "signature themes" (Clifton StrengthsFinder). As previously described, these signature profiles represent an individual's most strongly endorsed subset of strengths or talent themes, and are believed to indicate the respondent's most dominant personal tendencies. Although this narrowed scope may help to bring depth and focus to thinking about strengths, the unfortunate result of this approach is that it may unintentionally convey the erroneous idea that people can be reduced to their "top five" strengths or that their signature themes provide a complete description of their positive qualities and capabilities. An exploration of an individual's five most prevalent themes is a somewhat arbitrary distinction that obscures the possibility that an individual possesses many unidentified strengths that are present in lesser degrees, that are not elicited by the demands of their current environment, or which are simply underdeveloped. In many cases, instead of viewing strengths dichotomously as qualities that are either present or absent, it may be helpful to adopt a more holistic view of strengths that recognizes that they exist in varying degrees.

In addition, it may be most helpful to consider strengths pairings or groupings as opposed to viewing them as discrete entities. There is an interplay that exists between strengths as they are expressed because the relative dominance of several strengths within an individual may influence the way that other strengths manifest. Examining strengths in relationship or in combination may lead to more nuanced understandings of how strengths produce desired outcomes. In addition, instead of conceptualizing strengths as independent or solitary entities that are consistent across individuals and situations, considering strengths in context – alongside relevant values, interests, and situational factors – can provide a more comprehensive understanding of their appropriate use for a particular individual.

Recommendation 3: Design strengths interventions by first delineating the desired outcomes and then integrating empirically supported strategies for their attainment into the intervention plan

At the planning or design phase of a strengths intervention, it is critical to begin with a consideration of its intended goals or outcomes. These preferred results then serve as guides for shaping the nature and content of the intervention and also provide tangible outcomes by which to subsequently gauge the intervention's effectiveness. As mentioned in the research review, strengths interventions have been used to heighten engagement, promote hope, facilitate more effective learning, promote personal growth, help students maintain feelings of control over their academic outcomes, and increase leadership effectiveness – among many additional possibilities. Once practitioners have clearly articulated *why* they are using a strengths intervention, these objectives then become the central focus in determining *how* the intervention will be designed to achieve these outcomes. Although strengths interventions may share some philosophical commonalities, they will likely be diverse in their implementation when they are individualized to the specific goals of the setting into which they are integrated.

Once the outcomes are determined, practitioners would ideally seek to use intervention strategies that epitomize a strengths perspective and that also address the target variables or outcomes in ways that the literature reports have been effective in previous studies. As an example, a strengths interventionist seeking to increase participants' hope would benefit from an understanding of literature which suggests that hope consists not only of positive beliefs about personal motivation to attain goals, but also entails specific strategies for doing so (Snyder, Rand, & Sigmon, 2002). In essence, one contemporary understanding of hope is that it consists of *agency*, which is "the motivational component to propel people along their imagined routes to goals" (Snyder, 2000, p. 10), and *pathways*, which are "workable routes to goals" (Snyder et al., 2002, p. 258). Therefore, a strengths intervention designed to impact hope must attend to factors such as goals, motivation, and planning specific strategies for attaining goals and circumventing obstacles – addressing these issues within a strengths-oriented framework. In the design of the intervention, research on successful hope interventions may be instructional in the types of components to include in the process (Lopez et al., 2004; Marques, Ribeiro, & Lopez, 2011).

Recommendation 4: Create a strengths intervention plan that contains elements that are designed to reinforce learning over a long time horizon

Although the literature reviewed in this chapter describes some studies in which brief, stand-alone strengths interventions have produced positive effects, many researchers also highlight the importance of seeking to extend the impact of an intervention over a longer time span to reinforce and solidify these gains. As such, strengths interventions should be considered to be less like a brief or singular event and more like an ongoing developmental process. This suggestion is compatible with our earlier recommendation to conceptualize strengths as dynamic qualities that can be developed. It is also an assertion that is founded in the literature. Specifically, Pritchard's (2009) emerging theory of factors that mediate the impact of a strengths intervention includes the assertion that ongoing efforts to develop one's strengths lengthen the duration of the intervention effect whereas lack of continued follow-up on the initial strengths assessment and on strengths-related learnings are negative mediators of a long-term intervention effect. Another researcher notes that one of the defining qualities present in situations in which people are best able to capitalize on personal strengths is that they receive regular reinforcement of the benefits of their strengths (Janowski, 2006), an idea which suggests that strengths interventions may be most effective if the core learnings can be reinforced over a span of time.

Suggestions for Future Research

A fundamental issue that has implications for the ongoing development of strengths interventions is related to one's understanding of the nature and significance of human strengths. Specifically, some might argue that strengths are valuable in their own right and that the aim of strengths-focused interventions therefore ought to be helping people to identify and understand their strengths and live in ways that are an authentic reflection of these qualities. Others might suggest that strengths are primarily important because mobilizing them is associated with other positive outcomes such as engagement, performance, or well-being. Whether strengths are viewed as an inherently valued end or as a gateway to other desired outcomes may have implications for the kind of intervention strategies that are deemed most appropriate and the metrics by which their effectiveness is measured.

In addition, existing research has tended to focus on the overall impact of strengths interventions, but the field could also benefit from a more nuanced understanding of which components of these approaches are most potent and the mechanisms by which they exert their effect. Investigations of that nature could offer insight to individuals seeking to determine the optimal content, structure, and timing of strengths interventions.

It is also important to gain a better understanding of the role that formal strengths assessments play within intervention efforts. Specifically, researchers might seek to differentiate the impact of exposure to the results of strengths assessments such as the Clifton StrengthsFinder or the VIA-IS from the influence that strengths-oriented programs or curricula themselves exert on participants. *Treating* these two components of a strengths intervention as distinct and separable parts could help researchers discover the relative contribution of each of these elements in catalyzing desired outcomes.

Little is known about whether strengths interventions have enduring psychological or behavioral effects, as researchers have primarily focused on measuring immediate or short-term outcomes. From a theoretical perspective, it is plausible that when strengths interventions generate positive emotions among participants, they have the potential for durability. Specifically, the broaden-and-build theory of positive emotions (Cohn & Fredrickson, 2009; Fredrickson, 1998, 2001) notes that positive emotions are associated with a temporary broadening of awareness, cognition, and behavioral repertoires, and when experienced repeatedly, these broadened states can help people develop meaningful and lasting personal resources. Future strengths intervention research could examine the long-term effectiveness of strengths interventions and the role of positive emotions in predicting durability. In a broad sense, the question of how to increase the longevity of impact of strengths interventions remains, as there is little known about how best to facilitate the process of helping intervention participants maintain conscious awareness of their strengths, lengthen the duration of positive emotional response, or maintain behaviors that are indicative of a commitment to strengths development.

Our hope is that as strengths interventions progress, they will mature from a one-size-fits-all approach into offering a broader repertoire of intervention techniques that are reflective of individual differences and preferences – a strategy that is resonant with the strengths philosophy. This type of progress requires that researchers devote heightened attention to routinely examining the conditional effects in addition to the general effects of strengths interventions, as it is possible that the same intervention may differ in the magnitude or direction of its impact when experienced by individuals with different background characteristics, values, or preferences, or by those in different contexts. Implicit in this recommendation is the charge to involve more diverse samples in future research, and to examine the utility of strengths intervention strategies within a variety of settings based on the possibility that individual, cultural, or other contextual factors may influence the appropriateness and effectiveness of a specific intervention strategy.

References

Anderson, E. C. (2003). *StrengthsQuest: Curriculum outline and learning activities.* Princeton, NJ: Gallup.

Anderson, E. C. (2005). Strengths-based educating: A concrete way to bring out the best in students – and yourself. *Educational Horizons, 83*(3), 180–189.

Anderson, E. C., Schreiner, L. A., & Shahbaz, P. (2003). Research and evaluation of strengths counselors in a New Beginnings course. Unpublished raw data, Azusa Pacific University, Azusa, CA.

Anderson, E. C., Schreiner, L. A., & Shahbaz, P. (2004). Research and evaluation of strengths counselors in a New Beginnings course. Unpublished raw data, Azusa Pacific University, Azusa, CA.

Aronson, J., Fried, C., & Good, C. (2002). Reducing the effects of stereotype threat on African American college students by shaping theories of intelligence. *Journal of Experimental Social Psychology, 38,* 113–125.

Aspinwall, L. G., & Staudinger, U. M. (2003). A psychology of human strengths: Some central issues of an emerging field. In L. G. Aspinwall & U. M. Staudinger (Eds.), *A psychology of human strengths: Fundamental questions and future directions for a positive psychology* (pp. 9–22). Washington, DC: American Psychological Association.

Asplund, J., Lopez, S. J., Hodges, T., & Harter, J. (2009). *The Clifton StrengthsFinder 2.0 technical report: Development and validation.* Princeton, NJ: Gallup.

Barnard, C. (1994). Resiliency: A shift in our perception? *American Journal of Family Therapy, 22*(2), 135–144.

Biswas-Diener, R. (2010). A positive way of addressing negatives: Using strengths-based interventions in coaching and therapy. In G. W. Burns (Ed.), *Happiness, healing, and enhancement: Your casebook collection for applying positive psychology in therapy* (pp. 291–302). Hoboken, NJ: John Wiley and Sons.

Biswas-Diener, R., Kashdan, T. B., & Minhas, G. (2011). A dynamic approach to psychological strength development and intervention. *Journal of Positive Psychology, 6*(2), 106–118.

Blackwell, L. S., Trzesniewski, K. H., & Dweck, C. S. (2007). Implicit theories of intelligence predict achievement across an adolescent transition: A longitudinal study and an intervention. *Child Development, 78*(1), 246–263.

Buckingham, M. (2007). *Go put your strengths to work.* New York: The Free Press.

Buckingham, M., & Clifton, D. O. (2001). *Now, discover your strengths.* New York: The Free Press.

Cameron, C. S., & Caza, A. (2004). Contributions to the discipline of positive organizational scholarship. *American Behavioral Scientist, 47,* 731–739.

Cameron, K. S., Dutton, J. E., & Quinn, R. E. (Eds.) (2003). *Positive organizational scholarship: Foundations of a new discipline.* San Francisco, CA: Berrett-Koehler.

Cantwell, L. (2005). A comparative analysis of strengths-based versus traditional teaching methods in a freshman public speaking course: Impacts on student learning and engagement. *Dissertation Abstracts International, 67*(02A), 478–700. (UMI No. AAT3207574)

Cave, S. L. R. (2003). The effects of strengths education on the academic motivation of first-year college students. *Dissertation Abstracts International, 64*(02A), 417–570. (UMI No. AAT3082036)

Centre for Applied Positive Psychology (CAPP) (2010). *Realise2.* Accessed online at http://www.cappeu.com/realise2.htm

Clifton, D. O. (1997). *The Self-Reflection Scale.* Princeton, NJ: The Gallup Organization.

Clifton, D. O., & Anderson, C. E. (2002). *StrengthsQuest: Discover and develop your strengths in academics, career, and beyond.* Washington, DC: The Gallup Organization.

Clifton, D. O., Anderson, C. E., & Schreiner, L. A. (2006). *StrengthsQuest: Discover and develop your strengths in academics, career, and beyond* (2nd ed.). New York: Gallup Press.

Clifton, D. O., & Harter, J. K. (2003). Investing in strengths. In K. S. Cameron, J. E. Dutton, & R. E. Quinn (Eds.), *Positive organizational scholarship* (pp. 111–121). San Francisco, CA: Berrett-Koehler.

Clifton, D. O., & Nelson, P. (1992). *Soar with your strengths.* New York: Dell.

Cohn, M. A., & Fredrickson, B. L. (2009). Positive emotions. In C. R. Snyder & S. J. Lopez (Eds.), *Handbook of positive psychology* (2nd ed., pp. 13–24). New York: Oxford University Press.

Cooperrider, D. L., & Whitney, D. (2000). A positive revolution in change: Appreciative inquiry. In D. L. Cooperrider, P. F. Sorensen, Jr., D. Whitney, & T. F. Yaeger (Eds.), *Appreciative inquiry: Rethinking human organization toward a positive theory of change* (pp. 3–27). Champaign, IL: Stipes Publishing.

Cooperrider, D. L., & Whitney, D. (2005). *Appreciative inquiry: A positive revolution in change.* San Francisco, CA: Berrett-Koehler.

Csikszentmihalyi, M. (1990). *Flow: The psychology of optimal experience.* New York: HarperCollins.

Delgado, M. (2000). *Community social work practice in an urban context: The potential of a capacity-enhancement perspective.* New York: Oxford University Press.

Drucker, P. (2000). Managing knowledge means managing oneself. *Leader to Leader, 16,* 8–10.

Dweck, C. S. (1999). *Self-theories: Their role in motivation, personality, and development.* Philadelphia, PA: Psychology Press.

Estévez, E. F. (2005). The role of strengths-based case management strategies in the promotion of social capital and academic success of underprepared students. *Dissertation Abstracts International, 66*(08A), 2852–2975. (UMI No. AAT3185052)

Fredrickson, B. L. (1998). What good are positive emotions? *Review of General Psychology, 2,* 300–319.

Fredrickson, B. L. (2001). The role of positive emotions in positive psychology: The broaden-and-build theory of positive emotions. *American Psychologist, 56,* 218–226.

Fredrickson, B. L. (2009). *Positivity.* New York: Crown Publishers.

Frey, D., Jonas, E., & Greitemeyer, T. (2003). Intervention as a major tool of a psychology of human strengths: Examples from organizational change and innovation. In L. G. Aspinwall & U. M. Staudinger (Eds.), *A psychology of human strengths: Fundamental questions and future directions for a positive psychology* (pp. 149–164). Washington, DC: American Psychological Association.

Gallup (1999). *Clifton StrengthsFinder.* Washington, DC: Author.

Gallup (2011). *Measuring the impact of strengths-based mentoring on student hope, engagement, and well-being: Findings for the Teammates Mentoring Program.* Omaha, NE: Author.

Harter, J. K., Schmidt, F. L., & Hayes, T. L. (2002). Business-unit-level relationship between employee satisfaction, employee engagement, and business outcomes: A meta-analysis. *Journal of Applied Psychology, 87,* 268–279.

Harter, J. K., Schmidt, F. L., Killham, E. A., & Asplund, J. W. (2006). *Q12 Meta-analysis.* Omaha, NE: Gallup.

Hodges, T. D., & Clifton, D. O. (2004). Strengths-based development in practice. In P. A. Linley & S. Joseph (Eds.), *International handbook of positive psychology in practice: From research to application* (pp. 256–268). New York: Wiley.

Janowski, K. M. (2006). A theory of capitalizing on personal strengths. *Dissertation Abstracts International, 67*(04A). (UMI No. AAT3215161)

Kamins, M., & Dweck, C. S. (1999). Person versus process praise and criticism: Implications for contingent self-worth and coping. *Developmental Psychology, 35,* 835–847.

Kaplan, L., & Girard, J. (1994). *Strengthening high-risk families.* New York: Lexington.

Kaplan, R. E., & Kaiser, R. B. (2010). Toward a positive psychology for leaders. In P. A. Linley, S. Harrington, & N. Garcea (Eds.), *Oxford handbook of positive psychology and work* (pp. 107–117). New York: Oxford University Press.

Kisthardt, W. E. (2006). The opportunities and challenges of strengths-based, person-centered practice. In D. Saleebey (Ed.), *The strengths perspective in social work practice* (4th ed., pp. 171–196). Boston, MA: Pearson.

Kouzes, J. M., & Posner, B. Z. (2003). *The Leadership Practices Inventory* (2nd ed.) San Francisco, CA: John Wiley and Sons.

Lehnert, A. B. (2009). The influence of strengths-based development on leadership practices among undergraduate college students. *Dissertation Abstracts International.* (UMI No. 3377758)

Liesveld, R., & Miller, J. A. (2005). *Teach with your strengths: How great teachers inspire their students.* New York: Gallup Press.

Linley, P. A., & Burns, G. W. (2010). Strengthspotting. In G. W. Burns (Ed.), *Happiness, healing, and enhancement: Your casebook collection for applying positive psychology in therapy* (pp. 3–14). Hoboken, NJ: John Wiley and Sons.

Lopez, S. J., Hodges, T., & Harter, J. (2005). *The Clifton StrengthsFinder technical report: Development and validation.* Princeton, NJ: Gallup.

Lopez, S. J., & Louis, M. C. (2009). The principles of strengths-based education. *Journal of College and Character, 10*(4), 1–8.

Lopez, S. J., Snyder, C. R., Magyar-Moe, J., Edwards, L. M., Pedrotti, J. T., Janowski, K., Turner, J. L., & Pressgrove, C. (2004). Strategies for accentuating hope. In P. A. Linley & S. Joseph (Eds.), *Positive psychology in practice* (pp. 388–404). Hoboken, NJ: John Wiley & Sons.

Louis, M. C. (2008). A comparative analysis of the effectiveness of strengths-based curricula in promoting first-year college student success. *Dissertation Abstracts International, 69*(06A). (UMI No. AAT 3321378)

Louis, M. C. (2009). *A summary and critique of existing strengths-based educational research utilizing the Clifton StrengthsFinder.* Omaha, NE: Gallup.

Louis, M. C. (2011). Strengths interventions in higher education: The effect of identification versus development approaches on implicit self-theory. *Journal of Positive Psychology, 6*(3), 204–215.

Louis, M. C., & Schreiner, L. A. (2012). Helping students thrive: A strengths development model. In L. A. Schreiner, M. C. Louis, & D. Nelson (Eds.), *Thriving in transitions: A research-based approach to college student success* (pp. 19–40). National Resource Center for the First-Year Experience and Students in Transition. Columbia, SC: University of South Carolina Press.

Marques, S. C., Ribeiro, J. P., & Lopez, S. J. (2011). Building hope for the future: A program to foster strengths in middle school students. *Journal of Happiness Studies, 12*, 139–152.

Mostek, J. A. (2010). *Understanding the influence of strengths on the college experience: A qualitative case study of undergraduate business students.* Master's thesis, University of Nebraska at Lincoln. Accessed online at http://digitalcommons.unl.edu/cehsedaddiss/24

Mueller, C. M., & Dweck, C. S. (1998). Intelligence praise can undermine motivation and performance. *Journal of Personality and Social Psychology, 75*, 33–52.

Park, N., & Peterson, C. (2007). Methodological issues in positive psychology and the assessment of character strengths. In A. D. Ong & M. H. M. van Dulmen (Eds.), *Oxford handbook of methods in positive psychology* (pp. 292–305). New York: Oxford University Press.

Park, N., & Peterson, C. (2009). Character strengths: Research and practice. *Journal of College and Character, 10*(4), 1–10.

Perry, R. P., Hladkyj, S., Pekrun, R., & Pelletier, S. (2001). Academic control and action control in the achievement of college students: A longitudinal field study. *Journal of Educational Psychology, 93*, 776–789.

Peterson, C. (2006). The Values in Action (VIA) classification of strengths: The un-DSM and the real DSM. In M. Csikszentmihalyi & I. Csikszentmihalyi (Eds.), *A life worth living: Contributions to positive psychology* (pp. 29–48). New York: Oxford University Press.

Peterson, C., & Seligman, M. E. P. (2004). *Character strengths and virtues: A handbook and classification.* New York: Oxford University Press; Washington, DC: American Psychological Association.

Pritchard, G. M. (2009). A grounded theory of the factors that mediate the effect of a strengths-based educational intervention over a four-month period. *Dissertation Abstracts International.* (UMI No. 3376400)

Rath, T. (2007). *StrengthsFinder 2.0.* New York: Gallup Press.

Rath, T., & Conchie, B. (2008). *Strengths-based leadership.* New York: Gallup Press.

Robins, R. W., & Pals, J. L. (2002). Implicit self-theories in the academic domain: Implications for goal orientation, attributions, affect, and self-esteem change. *Self and Identity, 1*, 313–336.

Saleebey, D. (1997). The strengths approach to practice. In D. Saleebey (Ed.), *The strengths perspective in social work practice* (2nd ed., pp. 49–57). New York: Longman.

Saleebey, D. (2006). *The strengths perspective in social work practice* (4th ed.). Boston, MA: Pearson.

Schreiner, L., Hulme, E., Hetzel, R., & Lopez, S. (2009). Positive psychology on campus. In S. J. Lopez and C. R. Snyder (Eds.), *Oxford handbook of positive psychology* (2nd ed., pp. 569–578). New York: Oxford University Press.

Seligman, M. E. P., Park, N., & Peterson, C. (2004). The Values in Action (VIA) classification of character strengths. *Ricerche di Psicologia, 27*(1), 63–78.

Seligman, M. E. P., & Peterson, C. (2003). Positive clinical psychology. In L. G. Aspinwall & U. M. Staudinger (Eds.), *A psychology of human strengths: Fundamental questions and future directions for a positive psychology* (pp. 305–317). Washington, DC: American Psychological Association.

Seligman, M. E. P., Rashid, T., & Parks, A. C. (2006). Positive psychotherapy. *American Psychologist, 61*(8), 774–788.

Seligman, M. E. P., Steen, T. A., Park, N., & Peterson, C. (2005). Positive psychology progress: Empirical validation of interventions. *American Psychologist, 60*(5), 410–421.

Shushok, F., & Hulme, E. (2006). What's right with you: Helping students find and use their personal strengths. *About Campus, 11*(4), 2–8.

Snyder, C. R. (2000). Hypothesis: There is hope. In C. R. Snyder (Ed.), *Handbook of hope: Theory, measures, and applications* (pp. 3–18). San Diego, CA: Academic Press.

Snyder, C. R., Rand, K. L., & Sigmon, D. R. (2002). Hope theory: A member of the positive psychology family. In C. R. Snyder & S. J. Lopez (Eds.), *Handbook of positive psychology* (pp. 257–276). New York: Oxford University Press.

Snyder, C. R., Sympson, S. C., Ybasco, F. C., Borders, T. F., Babyak, M. A., & Higgins, R. L. (1996). Development and validation of the state Hope Scale. *Journal of Personality and Social Psychology, 70*, 321–335.

Staudt, M., Howard, M. O., & Drake, B. (2001). The operationalization, implementation, and effectiveness of the strengths perspective: A review of empirical studies. *Journal of Social Service Research, 27*(3), 1–21.

Swanson, J. E. (2006). Success in the first year: Impact of alternative advising on students at a liberal arts college. *Dissertation Abstracts International.* (UMI No. AAT 3246327)

Values in Action Institute (2007). *VIA strengths measurement instruments.* Retrieved from http://www.viastrengths.org/index.aspx?ContentID=34

Weick, A., Rapp, C., Sullivan, W. P., & Kisthardt, W. (1989). A strengths perspective for social work practice. *Social Work, 34*, 350–354.

Williamson, J. S. (2002). *Assessing student strengths: Academic performance and persistence of first-time college students at a private church-affiliated college.* Unpublished doctoral dissertation, University of Sarasota, New York.

Winseman, A. L., Clifton, D. O., & Liesveld, C. (2004). *Living your strengths: Discover your God-given talents and inspire your community* (2nd ed.). New York: Gallup Press.

Wood, A. M., Linley, P. A., Maltby, J., Kashdan, T. B., & Hurling, R. (2011). Using personal and psychological strengths leads to increases in well-being over time: A longitudinal study and the development of the Strengths Use Questionnaire. *Personality and Individual Differences, 50*, 15–19.

5

Promoting Meaning and Purpose in Life

Joo Yeon Shin and Michael F. Steger

Do you feel that your life is meaningful? What purpose guides your life? Why do you do what you do and where are you heading? These can be challenging – and yet fundamental – questions. People throughout history have asked and tried to answer questions about meaning and purpose in life, particularly within the contexts of philosophy, art, and religion. Since Frankl (1963) claimed that human beings have an innate drive to find meaning and significance that enables people to endure life's hardships, questions of meaning have been part of psychological inquiry. The scientific study of meaning and purpose has been further prompted by the "positive psychology" movement that aimed to further understand positive traits and psychological strengths (Ryan & Deci, 2001; Seligman & Csikszentmihalyi, 2000). This confluence of inquiry has led to substantial growth in empirical research on meaning in life.

Meaning in life has been defined in various ways by many researchers, including a sense of coherence and order to one's life (e.g., Antonovsky, 1987; Reker & Wong, 1988), an understanding of relationships among things and people (e.g., Baumeister, 1991; Baumeister & Vohs, 2002), the pursuit of worthwhile goals and life purposes (e.g., Battista & Almond, 1973; Damon, Menon, & Bronk, 2003; Frankl, 1963; Reker, 2000; Ryff, 1989), and a general sense that one's life is significant (e.g., Crumbaugh & Maholick, 1964; Yalom, 1980). Efforts to generate its operational definition have advanced the measurement of meaning and purpose (e.g., Battista & Almond, 1973; Crumbaugh & Maholick, 1964; Reker & Wong, 1988; Ryff & Singer, 1998; Steger, Frazier, Oishi, & Kaler, 2006), which, in turn, has led to fruitful findings on the potential benefits of having meaning and purpose in life. Although definitions of meaning and purpose in life vary, accumulated empirical findings have consistently indicated that meaning in life is an indicator of psychological and spiritual well-being, psychological strengths, and positive development (e.g., Ryff, 1989), a facilitator of adaptive coping and adjustment (Park & Folkman, 1997; Thompson, Coker, Krause, & Henry, 2003),

The Wiley Blackwell Handbook of Positive Psychological Interventions, First Edition.
Edited by Acacia C. Parks and Stephen M. Schueller.

a marker of therapeutic growth (Crumbaugh & Maholick, 1964), a significant predictor of desirable outcomes such as academic achievement (DeWitz, Woolsey, & Walsh, 2009), occupational adjustment (Steger & Dik, 2009; Steger, Pickering, Shin, & Dik, 2010), happiness (e.g., Ryff & Keyes, 1995; Steger, Oishi, & Kashdan, 2009), and life satisfaction (Steger et al., 2006; Steger & Kashdan, 2006; Steger, Kashdan, Sullivan, & Lorentz, 2008), a protective factor for psychological and physical health as indicated by health risk behavior (Brassai, Piko, & Steger, 2011; Steger, Mann, Michels, & Cooper, 2009), and cognitive decline in later life and longevity (Boyle, Barnes, Buchman, & Bennett, 2009; Boyle, Buchman, Barnes, & Bennett, 2010; Krause, 2009).

Given the growing appreciation of the benefits of meaning and purpose, the question of how to develop and cultivate a sense of meaning and purpose naturally holds significance. Yet, upon entering the second decade of positive psychology, we must admit that knowledge remains limited in terms of how to promote meaning and purpose. In this chapter, we try to fill this void. First, we briefly review existing meaning-oriented interventions. Despite their important contributions, we note that these existing intervention efforts tend to (i) focus on overall happiness or well-being instead of addressing the construct of meaning itself, (ii) limit the scope of meaning to its restorative or defensive functions within particular life contexts rather than taking a broader normative developmental perspective, or (iii) draw upon conceptual frameworks that are insufficiently systematic to counter the lack of data about interventions. Therefore, we next provide several intervention strategies based on Steger's (2009) conceptual framework of meaning. Finally, we suggest directions for future research on meaning-enhancing interventions.

Meaning-Oriented Interventions

The literature on palliative/end-of-life/terminal illness care has provided several meaning-oriented intervention approaches. These interventions commonly encourage patients to explore existential themes and find meaning and purpose in life as important resources for coping with emotional and existential suffering as one confronts hardships or crises. For example, Meaning-Centered Group Psychotherapy (MCGP) is one type of short-term existential group therapy for cancer patients. Its goal is to help them find a sense of meaning and to increase spiritual well-being while struggling with cancer illness and treatment (Breitbart, Gibson, Poppito, & Berg, 2004; Greenstein & Breitbart, 2000). MCGP utilizes didactics, structured group discussion, and experiential exercises that focus on exploring the concepts and sources of meaning and understanding the relationship and impact of cancer on one's sense of meaning and identity. For example, group members are asked to describe one or two meaningful events in their lives, considering Frankl's suggestion about three basic sources of finding meaning: (i) creative/significant work such as achievements and good deeds, (ii) valued experiences of art, beauty, and relationships, and (iii) the attitude one takes toward unavoidable suffering or an unchangeable situation. Members also reflect on negative and positive changes in self due to cancer and discuss topics such as what they would consider a good or meaningful death and how they would be remembered by their loved ones (Breitbart et al., 2010; Greenstein & Breitbart, 2000).

Another example is a one-week two-session short-term life review interview (Ando, Morita, Okamoto, & Ninosaka, 2008). In the first session, patients review their lives by answering several questions (e.g., What is the most important thing in your life and why? What are the most impressive memories in your life? In your life, what was the event that or the person who affected you the most?). The patients' narratives are recorded and then transcribed verbatim. The therapist makes an album: both good and bad things are included and feelings or re-framed thoughts in the patients' answers are written in the album. Key words and phrases are selected and written in the album as often as possible. Photos or drawings related to the patients' words or phrases are selected from various books or magazines and pasted into the album to make it more beautiful and more memory-provoking. In the second session, the patient and therapist view the album, and confirm the contents with appreciation. The authors suggest that this interview may help patients confirm their roles in life and modify their original purpose or goal.

The Meaning-Making intervention (MMi; Henry et al., 2010; Lee, 2004; Lee, Cohen, Edgar, Laizner, & Gagnon, 2006) is a brief, individualized, manualized, and therapist-led existential therapeutic approach designed to facilitate the search for meaning following a cancer diagnosis. It consists of one to four intervention sessions of 30–90 minutes each with a therapist who promotes self-exploration that focuses on three main tasks: (i) review the impact and meaning of the cancer diagnosis; (ii) explore past significant life events and successful ways of coping, as related to the present cancer experience; and (iii) discuss life priority and goal changes that give meaning to one's life, while considering cancer-related limitations (Lee, 2004; the MMi manual can be obtained by contacting Dr Virginia Lee: virginia.lee@muhc.mcgill.ca).

Wong (2010) introduces Meaning-Centered Counseling and Therapy (MCCT) which is primarily based on Frankl's classic logotherapy but also assimilates constructs and skills from cognitive-behavioral therapies. Frankl's logotherapy is a therapeutic approach that focuses on the central role of meaning in human adaptation and survival, based on the philosophical insights of existential psychology. Logotherapy has a well-established theoretical foundation and potential efficacy and applicability across a broad range of physical and emotional difficulties (Schulenberg, Hutzell, Nassif, & Rogina, 2008). Logotherapy also employs several therapeutic strategies such as paradoxical intention, de-reflection, and Socratic dialogue (Schulenberg et al., 2008). However, it lacks a clear conceptual analysis and a wide range of therapeutic skills and tools (Wong, 2010, 2012). MCCT adopts the basic tenets of logotherapy but extends it by translating its philosophical insights into cognitive/behavioral processes and operationalizing its key concepts (Wong, 2010).

MCCT suggests two major intervention strategies: the PURE intervention and the ABCDE intervention. The PURE intervention posits that meaning is comprised of four main components: Purpose, Understanding, Responsible action, and Evaluation. MCCT emphasizes the importance of managing and regulating our personal meanings. Meaning helps people predict and control their environment and perform purposeful behaviors through understanding the significance of events happening to them. Drawing on this conceptual basis, clients are encouraged to work on the four main components of meaning by (i) reviewing their personal goals and directions (Purpose), (ii) making sense of their situation and self (Understanding), (iii) taking appropriate/value-congruent actions (Responsible action), and (iv) assessing their satisfaction or dissatisfaction with the situation or life as a whole (Evaluation). The ABCDE strategy is suggested as the main tool in dealing with negative life experiences, where clients are encouraged to (A) Accept and confront the reality, (B) Believe that life is worth living, (C) Commit to goals and actions, (D) Discover the meaning and significance, and (E) Evaluate the processes above.

Thus, several meaning-oriented interventions have been developed and tested to address patients' existential plight (see LeMay & Wilson, 2008 for details). However, these interventions have several limitations. First very little experimental research has been conducted to test whether these interventions work as designed (see Ando et al., 2008; Breitbart et al., 2010; Henry et al., 2010, for exceptions). Reports about these interventions tend to be descriptive rather than evaluative, so it is not necessarily clear that they are effective. Second, when tested, researchers often evaluate whether these interventions improve well-being or quality of life. This is similar to positive psychology interventions in general that use positive mood, cognition, and spirituality as main outcome measures. With few exceptions (e.g., Henry et al., 2010), meaning and purpose are not directly measured, thus providing limited information on whether these meaning-oriented interventions actually impact meaning. Third, many of these interventions were developed originally to help people, mostly adults, under adverse life conditions, traumatic life events, or terminal/chronic illness. Therefore, they focus on meaning-making as a form of coping with specific stressors. Although finding meaning in adverse events is a kind of meaning and plays a crucial role in restoring well-being, it is not the same thing as meaning and purpose in life under normative life conditions. Lastly, most of these intervention efforts were based – loosely in some cases – on the theory of Frankl's logotherapy, which was not designed to develop specific therapeutic tools and techniques. Given that few data are available to evaluate the effectiveness of these approaches, the theoretical foundation on which they are built should have clear, testable, and specific implications for how to work with important change mechanisms of meaning and purpose in life. At the same time, logotherapy's perspective is highly compatible with positive psychology and can be applied in numerous settings (Wong, 2010). Thus, a new theoretical framework is needed to supplement logotherapy-derived approaches. This would enable the development of theory-driven interventions that are rooted less in a particular perspective, no matter how wise, and more in a distillation of relevant empirical and theoretical work.

Toward New Approaches

A theoretical model of meaning in life

Many of the definitions of meaning comprise two commonly used referents for understanding meaning in life (e.g., King, Hicks, Krull, & Del Gaiso, 2006): (i) forming a coherent understanding of life (Battista & Almond, 1973; Reker & Wong, 1988) that accompanies people's understanding of who they are, what the world is like, and how they fit into it (Heine, Proulx, & Vohs, 2006); and (ii) investing in important lifelong aspirations, which has been referred to as goal-directedness or purposefulness in the literature (e.g., Klinger, 1977; Ryff & Singer, 1998). Drawing upon this perspective, Steger (2009, 2012) has provided a conceptual model of meaning in life that integrates both cognitive and motivational dimensions, referred to in this model as comprehension (i.e., an individual's understandings of who they are, what the world is like, and how they fit in and interact with the world around them) and purpose (i.e., an individual's long-term and overarching goal or mission to which they are highly committed and actively engaged).

Comprehension helps people establish a continuous narrative, organize fragmented daily experiences, forge links between familiar experiences and new ones, integrate new experiences into their lives, bring unity to their phenomenological lives, and anticipate and regulate their behaviors in adaptive ways. People achieve these understandings as they become able to find patterns, consistency, and significance in the many events and experiences in their lives. A sense of purpose is developed when an individual discerns, commits to, and engages in their personally meaningful goals. Purpose provides significant and renewable sources of engagement and meaning because it offers direction that helps an individual organize and stimulate goals, manage behaviors, and make daily decisions through the use of finite personal resources (McKnight & Kashdan, 2009).

Steger (2009) has argued that there is a feedback loop between purpose-directed effort and people's comprehension of their lives such that when people are functioning well, they are pursuing purposes that are self-concordant, autonomously chosen, and positively reinforcing. Steger (2009) also argued that the very broad time frame and hierarchically integrative level of meaning, and the reciprocal interaction between comprehension and purpose, distinguishes meaning from other psychological constructs, which is facilitated by goal-directed activities.

A new approach to promoting meaning

In this section, we suggest several intervention approaches to promoting meaning development based on Steger's empirically based conceptualization of meaning.

According to this model (see above), people are likely to experience a greater sense of meaning in life when (i) they have a well-established comprehension of self and the world, which leads to the development of meaningful and beneficial goals, (ii) they engage in purposeful activities and continuously monitor and revise their own personally meaningful goals using the results of goal pursuit, and (iii) they weave those life goals and purposes into their comprehension as a central and predominant theme (McKnight & Kashdan, 2009).

In the following section, we suggest intervention strategies to promote comprehension and purpose focusing on concepts that have been regarded as central mechanisms of developing comprehension and purpose in the existing literature. Promoting comprehension mostly relates to cognitive aspects of intervention efforts, and in particular, to composing integrative narratives. Promoting purpose, in contrast, mostly relates to motivational-behavioral aspects of intervention, including goal-pursuit activities. We incorporate a social-cognitive perspective, emphasizing modeling and social-cognitive variables such as self-efficacy belief, outcome expectation, and goal-relevant environmental supports and resources (Bandura, 1997, 2001; Cantor & Sanderson, 1999; Lent, 2004; Locke & Latham, 2002).

Promoting comprehension

Individuals obtain comprehension of their lives by understanding who they are (e.g., one's distinct self-attributes such as abilities, characters and personality, preferences, weaknesses and strengths), the nature of the world around them (e.g., worldview, beliefs, external resources), and their unique niche within the world (e.g., one's roles, one's opportunities and limitations). Given this framework, how do people build this comprehensive understanding and knowledge? Literature suggests that identity formation (Erikson, 1968) and life-narrative construction (McAdams, 1993) help people to unify the various aspects of their self-knowledge and provide a sense of personal meaning and direction.

Helping identity formation Identity exploration typically has been considered as a cognitive process involving rational thought, problem-solving, and decision-making to determine what is meaningful in one's life. More recently, however, the idea of identity exploration as an emotional process has emerged, wherein individuals use affective states arising from the attainment of flow, personal expressiveness, and self-actualization to decide what is meaningful (Schwartz, 2002; Waterman, 1992). The state of flow is experienced when the challenges posed by an activity or goal are balanced with the skills that one brings to it. This generates an unconstrained sense of time and intense engagement in the activity or pursuit of the goal (Csikszentmihalyi, 1990; Waterman et al., 2003). Personal expressiveness refers to the deep satisfaction from engagement in activities or goals that capitalize on one's unique or innate potentials (Waterman, 1990). Self-actualization refers to fulfilling one's potentials and living up to one's ideals on a consistent basis (Maslow, 1968). People may become more aware of the situations in which they feel that they are "authentic," or being their "true self," as they examine these affective processes and attempt to achieve them (Waterman, 1992, 2004). Meaning in life has been closely linked to these concepts in eudaimonic well-being theory (Ryff, 1989; Steger et al., 2008) and research findings show that a greater sense of meaning is related to "true self-concept" accessibility (Schlegel, Hicks, Arndt, & King, 2009), a sense of contact with the self (Debats, Drost, & Hansen, 1995), and people's beliefs that their behavior is authentic (Kernis & Goldman, 2006).

While the emotional process of identity formation focuses on discovering an intuitive fit between identity alternatives and one's true self, the cognitive process of identity formation relates to constructing a sense of self through rational problem-solving and decision-making (Schwartz, 2002). In this approach, effective exploration involves developing problem-solving competence, with which people can generate and evaluate potential identity alternatives and select one that most fits themselves. Developing an information-oriented identity-processing style is also emphasized, which refers to one of the individual's typical approaches toward exploration characterized by a willingness to identify and sort through prospective alternatives by evaluating relevant information (Berzonsky, 1990).

Because cognitive and affective processes of identity exploration are distinct and impact different outcomes, individuals may benefit from both; indeed, one study reported that cognitively focused intervention strategies were most efficacious in fostering information-oriented identity style and critical problem-solving, while emotionally focused intervention strategies were most efficacious in increasing personal expressiveness, flow, and self-actualization (Schwartz, Kurtines, & Montgomery, 2005). Intervention strategies that target both processes may help individuals approach identity development from a broader perspective, which may also help them consolidate the foundation of meaning.

Example: Participants would be asked to (i) identify one or two important life choices or dilemmas, (ii) engage in structured exploration about the self and the world (e.g., values, abilities, worldviews, roles, environmental resources and barriers, etc.), (iii) generate potential solutions to their life issues, and (iv) critically evaluate each of the solutions to make the most favorable life choices. Then, they would (i) participate in goal-directed activities, and (ii) explore their emotional reactions to those experiences by associating each activity with descriptions of feelings (e.g., feelings of special fit or meshing, feelings of intensely being alive, feelings of completeness or fulfillment, a feeling that this is what one was meant to do) (adapted from Schwartz et al., 2005).

Cultivating life narratives A substantial body of literature suggests that cultivating life narratives is central to people's formation of meaning (e.g., Butler, 1974; McAdams, 1995). Narratives help an individual to re-evaluate and integrate prior experiences into their current and future life context. In doing so, they develop a sense of identity (Erikson, 1968), as well as coherent autobiographical themes, self-continuity, and individuality (Singer, 2004). "Self-authorship," which refers to one's internal capacities to define one's beliefs and values, identity, and relations with others through "reflective judgments," also relates to one's meaning-making (Magolda, 1992, 2008). Based on this understanding of life narratives, we propose several considerations for intervention efforts to facilitate narrative meaning-making.

(1) Growth-oriented narrative. A growth narrative refers to interpreting people's lives as involving progressive and prosocial development in both the past (autobiographical memories) and the future (personal goals) (Bauer, McAdams, & Pals, 2008). In contrast, a security narrative emphasizes security, maintenance, protection of the self, and the acquisition of pleasure. Although engaging in a security narrative may be necessary to preserve a sense of safety and regulate affect, it does not encourage personal meaning-making or achieving progress or improvement in a cognitive and experiential understanding of one's life. Research suggests that life stories with themes of growth facilitate the formation of a growth-oriented identity, which tends to precede increases in meaning-making and adaptation (e.g., Bauer & McAdams, 2010; King & Smith, 2004; Pals, 2006). Therefore, helping people to create growth-oriented narratives may promote meaning development.

Example: An intervention would ask participants to reflect on their past life episodes and identify two areas in which growth has occurred (e.g., where they gained a newer, more adaptive and mature self-awareness, insight, or positive self-transformation). Then, they would be asked to anchor them with specific life examples and propose a vignette exemplifying future growth.

(2) Cultivating meaning from earlier ages. Meaning in life has been studied in elderly people and college students, but relatively less attention has been devoted to meaning development in children and adolescents, or to how to promote their sense of meaning (Steger, Bundick, & Yeager, 2012). However, efforts to promote meaning in life can begin at early stages of life (e.g., early adolescence, if not earlier) because cognitive capacities to narrate and comprehend one's life actively develop in this period (Steger et al., 2012). The ability to narrate both fictitious stories and personal experiences has developed by age 5 or 6 years and improves through the end of grade school (Peterson & McCabe, 1983). Adolescence is regarded as a critical period for acquiring and developing the cognitive capacities that allow for the integration of life experiences into a coherent framework for the construction of life stories (Habermas, Ehlert-Lerche, & de Silveira, 2009). For example, the capacity of autobiographical reasoning, which links events with each other as an individual develops, gradually leads to the construction of a skeletal cognitive "life story schema"; such a schema helps people make sense of how various life events have influenced who they are (i.e., the self) and their life trajectories (Habermas & Bluck, 2000; McAdams, 1993; Steger et al., 2012). Given that adolescents seem to have the necessary capabilities required to construct a meaningful life, they would likely benefit from interventions aimed at promoting meaning.

Example: Participants would be asked to write about two meaningful childhood experiences, with a particular focus on (i) whether (and what) lessons were carried from that time to the present, and (ii) how those lessons have influenced their understandings of the self and the world around them.

(3) Social-cognitive approach for promoting meaning. Researchers have suggested that the construction of life narratives involves social-cognitive processes. Social-interactive and collective aspects of human cognition and behavior have long been acknowledged (e.g., Baltes & Staudinger, 1996; Bandura, 2001). Staudinger and Baltes (1996) found that wisdom-related knowledge and judgment were facilitated in a setting in which individuals were engaged in interactive discussion with another person along with the opportunity for individual appraisal. Staudinger (2001) argues that reflecting upon one's life with other people, such as mentors, families, and peers, may facilitate this process because striving for new insights about oneself and one's life is challenging. Shared family narratives, defined as stories that have been repeatedly told to the child, influence children's life narratives and self-understanding (Bohanek, Marin, Fivush, & Duke, 2006; Habermas et al., 2009; Hayden, Singer, & Chrisler, 2006), suggesting the role of significant others in children's meaning-making. Steger and colleagues (2012) have also emphasized the role of social learning and modeling in the development of adolescents' judgments regarding the meaningfulness of their lives, arguing that people around adolescents (e.g., parents, teachers, and peers) and even the media offer ways of finding and defining meaning. Thus, intervention efforts for promoting meaning need to consider the social aspects of meaning development. For example, supporting and encouraging adolescents in their search for meaning may help them actively engage in self-exploration and potentially meaningful activities, while also reducing the likelihood that their natural and healthy search for meaning could transmute into distressing existential rumination (Steger et al., 2012).

Example: An intervention would ask participants to reflect on their ideas and attitudes towards pursuing meaning in their life (e.g., how they define a meaningful life, how they feel about searching for meaning). Then, they would identify important figures who have influenced their conceptions of a meaningful life by answering questions such as who gave them those (either positive or negative) messages, who in their life exemplifies those messages, and who supports or discourages their pursuit of meaning.

(4) Focusing on specific themes. Theories and research suggest that life stories tend to be centered on certain themes, needs, and values, from which people tend to derive a sense of meaning in their lives. Specifically, people use four themes to make sense of their lives (see Baumeister, 1991, for details): purpose (i.e., people wish to interpret events as being purposive/desirable ends and outcomes), efficacy (i.e., people want to make a difference in external events, autonomy, and control), value and justification (i.e., people want to have reliable criteria of right and wrong that can be used to make moral choices and to define one's own actions as good), and self-worth (i.e., positive affirmation of the self). Self-transcendence is also considered to be one of the universally significant themes of meaning; transcending one's own immediate interests (e.g., serving the greater good) has been linked to a more mature form and greater experiences of meaning in life (Reker

& Wong, 1988), and has been referred to as a defining feature of calling (Dik & Duffy, 2009), and meaningful work (Steger & Dik, 2010).

Example: Participants would be asked to review the suggested four basic needs for meaning (i.e., purpose, efficacy, value and justification, and self-transcendence), and learn that they are more likely to have a meaningful life when each of the four needs is satisfied. Then, they would reflect on whether each of the four needs is met in their lives, and identify specific needs with which they feel frustrated or seek more satisfaction. They would be encouraged to generate a list of activities and involvements that would satisfy the particular needs they have identified.

(5) Focusing on particular life domains. Rather than considering meaning a broad concept, it may be productive to promote meaning in specific areas of life. For example, practitioners could try to encourage individuals to recognize and practice their character strengths and positive attributes because meaning comes from the dedication of one's signature talents (see Chapter 4) to some entity beyond one's self (Seligman, 2002). The Values in Action Inventory of Strengths (VIA-IS; Peterson & Seligman, 2004) is a face-valid self-report questionnaire that provides a list of respondents' values and strengths in order. This would be easily incorporated as part of the intervention because the inventory is available online and open to the public. This instrument has been used in a positive psychological intervention context and it was reported that people's use of signature strengths daily in connection with their goal pursuit was associated with being happier and less depressed (Seligman, Steen, Park, & Peterson, 2005).

Career exploration incorporating the constructs of meaning and purpose would also be useful to help people cultivate potential ways of making their lives meaningful. An individual's work and career life may be one of the most important domains where individuals experience and expand the sense of meaning in their lives (e.g., Dik & Duffy, 2009; Steger & Dik, 2010); a person's work life is closely related to their short- and long-term goals, as well as their lifelong purpose(s), and gives them concrete ideas of their roles and unique fit in the world. Prosocial career aspiration (i.e., the intention to contribute to the common good through their future occupation) seems to provide one important avenue for youth, where mattering might be fulfilled (Steger et al., 2012), helping them feel their current school work as well as their present lives are meaningful (Yeager & Bundick, 2009). Questions such as (i) In what way is your schoolwork/work meaningful to you? (ii) What would make your job more meaningful? (iii) In what way would your job be helpful to society or the common good? (Dik, Duffy, & Eldridge, 2009), (iv) What types of work do people do and why do they do it? and (v) What are your unique skills, interests, and values and how can you use them to do something that is personally meaningful? (see Dik, Steger, Gibson, & Peisner, 2011 for intervention activities) could prompt thoughts on their work in the context of meaning and purpose. Recent research on calling and meaningful work also supports incorporating meaning and purpose into career counseling and career development (e.g., Dik & Steger, 2008; Dik et al., 2009; Kosine, Steger, & Duncan, 2008).

Example: College students trying to decide on a major might use the results of their strengths inventory to decide what course of study they might derive the most meaning from. They might be asked to write a brief paragraph about how their personality, interests, skills, and identified strengths could inform their major and career choices.

(6) Helping people understand what is meaningful to them. Along with seemingly universal sources of meaning, helping people identify and express their own sources of meaning will facilitate the integrative comprehension of their lives. Individuals' sources of meaning incorporate modes of conduct, goals, and themes in life (Reker, 2000) that crystallize people's perception of who they are and how they see themselves in their social life (Bar-Tur, Savaya, & Prager, 2001). We are currently evaluating an intervention that uses the auto-photography method (Noland, 2006), in which people are asked to take photographs of the things that make their lives feel meaningful, rate them in terms of importance, and provide brief descriptions of the photographs. This appears to be a useful way to encourage the process of identifying and expressing sources of meaning.

Questions, protocols, and programs have been designed to help guide people to effectively think through their lives. For example, the Purpose-Interview Protocol consists of a series of questions asking about the most important things in the young person's life and the associated explanation for them (e.g., their short- and long-term life goals, their hopes and dreams, their values, their occupational aspirations; Andrews et al., 2006; Yeager & Bundick, 2009). Another example is McAdams' (1985) interviewing technique which was developed to facilitate people's life review process. This interview program asks participants to consider their lives as if they were in a book and to describe specific scenes, including a high point, a low point, a turning point, and an earliest memory, as well as important characters in the story, future chapters, and life-story motifs and messages. Individuals may also benefit from engaging in brief writing projects because the process of telling or writing about life events facilitates the integration of events into a larger meaning system (see King & Pennebaker, 1996), the reconstruction of the life story (Habermas et al., 2009; McLean, Pasupathi, & Pals, 2007; Thorne, 2000), and the creation of coherent narrative sources of meaning (Pennebaker & Seagal, 1999).

Example: Participants would be asked to (i) take 10 photographs of those things that make their lives feel meaningful, (ii) print out the photographs, (iii) reflect on each photograph in terms of importance to how they live their lives, and (iv) describe each photograph briefly.

Summary of comprehension-based approaches In sum, comprehension, a cognitive building block of meaning in life, may be effectively established in a more concrete, comprehensive, and coherently integrated and organized form through engaging in both affective and cognitive identity formation processes and creating growth-oriented narratives with a particular focus on certain life themes, as discussed above. Also, it would be beneficial to begin early in one's youth in socially supportive environments, using specific questions, protocols, inventories, and activities that facilitate self-exploration. Next, let us turn to the motivational components of meaning in life.

Promoting purpose

Purpose comprises the motivational component of meaning and refers to an individual's long-term and overarching goal or mission to which they are highly committed and actively engaged (McKnight & Kashdan, 2009; Steger, 2009). The model of purpose specifies that people may cultivate and elaborate upon their sense of purpose by discerning, committing themselves to, and engaging themselves in personally meaningful goals. Research has suggested that commitment to personal goals lends a sense of agency, life structure, and personal meaning to people's lives (Cantor & Sanderson, 1999; McGregor & Little, 1998) and serves as an important vehicle for self-discovery and psychological need satisfaction (Sheldon & Elliot, 1999; Sheldon & Kasser, 1998). This highlights the essential role of goal pursuit in achieving a sense of meaning in life.

Goal pursuit and purpose are tightly associated, as the model posits. However, there are two things to be considered in promoting meaning in life. First, despite their similarity, purpose and goals are differentiated in that purpose provides a broader motivational component that stimulates goals and influences behavior, whereas goals are more precise in their influence on proximal behaviors (McKnight & Kashdan, 2009). Further, goals are focused on terminal outcomes, while purpose is focused on an ideal future state that may not be attainable in a concrete sense (Wilson & Murrell, 2004). Second, not all goal pursuit is thought to be derived from purpose; only self-concordant goals contribute to a sense of purpose. Self-concordance of an individual's goal-systems (Sheldon & Elliot, 1999) refers to the degree to which one's stated goals are well-integrated with the self, expressing one's own enduring interests and values. The Self-Concordance model (Sheldon & Elliot, 1999) emphasizes that a person's goals should represent that person's authentic self in a deeper sense, including central interests and values. For example, studying hard for a good grade is a self-concordant goal if the person chooses to do that because he or she finds it personally significant and enjoyable. On the other hand, the same goal is a non-self-concordant goal if the person pursues that goal in order to avoid negative emotions (e.g., anxiety or guilt), gain external rewards such as status or money, or satisfy someone else's wishes (e.g., parental expectation), not because of deep personal conviction and/or a strong self-interest.

A variety of programs for improving individuals' goal-directedness are available, and practitioners may combine and tailor those programs. What we propose here is one example of a possible intervention that could be designed to increase individuals' self-concordant goal progress. The following intervention consists of five steps based on the contents of the goal-training program (Sheldon, Kasser, Smith, & Share, 2002) and the goal-setting intervention (Peterson & Mar, 2004).

Step 1: *Brainstorm 12 goals.* Participants would be asked to list the things that they typically and characteristically would be trying to do in daily life at least during the next six weeks (Emmons, 1986). A brief free-writing activity can facilitate this initial "fantasy" step by giving people the chance to consider a number of possible futures and to identify the ones that were most desirable (e.g., their ideal future, qualities they admired in others, things they could do better, their school and career futures).

Step 2: *Learn about self-concordant goals.* Participants would be given information about the four motivational reasons thought to drive goals (i.e., external, introjected, identified, and intrinsic; Sheldon & Elliot, 1998) and the benefits of selecting self-concordant goals, in a format of brief presentation with several examples.

Step 3: *Evaluate your goals.* Using brief scales, participants would evaluate each of the goals generated through their brainstorming according to several criteria. These criteria are drawn from research on optimizing goal progress (i.e., whether the goals are intrinsically valued and autonomously chosen, approached at a feasible level, and facilitated in their daily life context; Cantor & Sanderson, 1999; Ryan & Connell, 1989; Sheldon & Kasser, 1998).

Step 4: *Finalize six goals.* Using their evaluation of each goal, participants would be asked to finalize six goals that they want to keep for a certain time period (e.g., three months, one semester) and to provide a clear and specific description of each goal. They would also be provided with a definition of purpose, and asked to identify the two goals that are considered most closely linked to their purpose in life.

Step 5: *Make progress (enact, monitor, revise, and integrate).* Participants would be asked to make specific implementation plans for goal pursuit. They would set several subgoals that would provide clear benchmarks of progress (e.g., Gollwitzer, 1999; Locke & Latham, 2006) and identify goal-relevant supports, resources, and skills, as well as external and internal barriers such as low self-efficacy (Bandura, 1997, 2001; Cantor & Sanderson, 1999; Locke & Latham, 2002). They would repeat the goal-evaluation process by rating their effort and progress on each goal (Sheldon & Elliot, 1999) and continue to revise their goals and goal-pursuit strategies. Finally, they would be encouraged to integrate their goal pursuit into their meaning system by briefly describing in what way their goal pursuit is meaningful to their life, using narrative approaches focused on comprehension of self, world, and interaction.

Future Directions for Meaning-Enhancing Interventions

In closing, we would like to suggest several considerations for future efforts to advance an understanding of meaning-enhancing interventions. First, testing potential mediators is of importance because it may reveal the change mechanisms that are the building blocks of meaning and purpose in life. Empirical studies on the efficacy of meaning interventions outside of the context of illness or palliative care are still scarce. Although several theoretical suggestions regarding cultivating a sense of meaning have been made (e.g., Wong, 2010; this chapter), it is not known yet whether those suggested interventions generate changes in meaning and, if so, what elements are responsible for those changes. It has been reported that happiness levels could be increased by "shotgun" interventions involving multiple exercises (Parks, Della Porta, Pierce, Zilca, & Lyubomirsky, 2012; Seligman, Rashid, & Parks, 2006), and that may be true regarding increasing meaning and purpose. Until specific components and activities that contribute to the effects are identified, we would have to guess what really generates the effects in multiple exercises packages. Understanding change mechanisms will also improve effective grouping of exercises by informing crucial issues such as optimal combinations and sequencing of intervention activities (Duckworth, Steen, & Seligman, 2005). For example, among the exercises suggested in this chapter, which activities should be selected and in what order should they be presented in order to maximize intervention effects? Based on Steger's model, which emphasizes interactions between cognitive (i.e., self-knowledge) and motivational (e.g., self-concordant goal progress) components, we speculate that an optimal meaning-enhancing intervention would include some combination of exercises targeting both components. Identifying specific combinations and sequencing of activities also needs to be a crucial focus of future research.

Second, future research should try to document various moderators that impact intervention effects. As discussed above, in grouping exercises for meaning-enhancing interventions, it is important to consider change mechanisms. However, intervention effects may also vary according to individual differences such as individual preference of certain activities. For example, previous studies found that individuals engaged in a positive psychology exercise of their own preference tended to show increased adherence for the exercise (Schueller, 2010). Further, participants who received a positive psychology exercise that was selected based on individual preference showed increased preference and efficacy compared to participants who received one selected randomly (Schueller, 2011). These findings speak to the importance of developing individualized packages based on moderators influencing intervention effects.

Another important question in relation to individual differences will be whether meaning-enhancing interventions work equally well with clinical and non-clinical populations. Sin and Lyubomirsky (2009) reported that positive psychological interventions worked better for mildly depressed participants, indicating that depressive states might play a role in generating the intervention effects. Yet, it would also be possible that clinically depressed participants would struggle in achieving adaptive/positive comprehension of themselves and the world due to their tendency to ruminate or the influence of negative cognitive schemata. For clinical populations, successful goal-pursuit would be more challenging because of deficits in motivation and self-efficacy, engagement in activities, and/or other resources such as social support. Thus, more studies are warranted to inform how these populations may respond to these intervention methods.

Third, future research needs to consider cultural contexts of meaning in life and meaning-enhancing interventions. Steger and colleagues (2006) note that people differ not only in how much they experience the sense of meaning (i.e., the presence of meaning), but also in how much they search for meaning (i.e., the search for meaning). Previous studies (e.g., Steger, Kawabata, Shimai, & Otake, 2008) indicated that the relationship between searching for meaning and experiencing meaning in life varies across cultures; the two variables appear negatively correlated in Western cultures, and positively correlated in (some) East Asian cultures. Meaning interventions may be particularly important in Western cultures because the search for meaning is typically negatively related to the presence of meaning, implying some degree of frustration or interference with searching. Still, intervention may have an additive effect on enhancing meaning in life in East Asian culture. Also, whereas interventions might be targeted at meaning-searching to enhance meaning in life among Eastern cultures, such interventions might be directed at buffering the potential negative effects of meaning-searching among Western cultures, perhaps by boosting students' confidence and comfort with uncertainty.

The shift from a pathology-oriented paradigm to a health-oriented one in the field of psychology has advanced the understanding of how to achieve well-being and how to develop human strengths and nurture growth. A large body of empirical research on meaning and purpose has demonstrated a robust relationship between having a higher sense of meaning and purpose and a psychologically, physically, and spiritually healthy life. We believe that the next step is to inform people how to build a sense of meaning and purpose through developing and empirically testing various feasible intervention strategies (Cowen & Kilmer, 2002). We have provided theoretically derived strategies, as well as a review of current interventions, in the hope of making a meaningful and purposeful life accessible for everyone. We hope that future research will continue to accumulate knowledge about promoting meaning and purpose, and guide efforts to help people benefit from cultivating a sense of meaning and purpose.

References

Ando, M., Morita, T., Okamoto, T., & Ninosaka, Y. (2008). One-week Short-Term Life Review interview can improve spiritual well-being of terminally ill cancer patients. *Psycho-Oncology, 17*, 885–890.

Andrews, M. C., Bundick, M. J., Jones, A., Bronk, K. C., Mariano, J. M., & Damon, W. (2006). Youth Purpose Interview Version 2006. Unpublished instrument, Stanford Center on Adolescence, Stanford, CA.

Antonovsky, A. (1987). *Unraveling the mystery of health: How people manage stress and stay well.* San Francisco: Jossey-Bass.

Baltes, P. B., & Staudinger, U. M. (Eds.) (1996). *Interactive minds: Life-span perspectives on the social foundation of cognition.* New York: Cambridge University Press.

Bandura, A. (1997). *Self-efficacy: The exercise of control.* New York: Freeman & Co.

Bandura, A. (2001). Social cognitive theory: An agentic perspective. *Annual Review of Psychology, 52*, 1–26.

Bar-Tur, L., Savaya, R., & Prager, E. (2001). Sources of meaning in life for young and old Israeli Jews and Arabs. *Journal of Aging Studies, 15*, 253–269.

Battista, J., & Almond, R. (1973). The development of meaning in life. *Psychiatry, 36*, 409–427.

Bauer, J. J., & McAdams, D. P. (2010). Eudaimonic growth: Narrative growth goals predict increases in ego development and subjective well-being 3 years later. *Developmental Psychology, 46*, 761–772.

Bauer, J. J., McAdams, D. P., & Pals, J. L. (2008). Narrative identity and eudaimonic well-being. *Journal of Happiness Studies, 9*, 81–104.

Baumeister, R. F. (1991). *Meanings of life*. New York: Guilford Press.

Baumeister, R. F., & Vohs, K. D. (2002). The pursuit of meaningfulness in life. In C. R. Snyder & S. J. Lopez (Eds.), *Handbook of positive psychology* (pp. 608–618). New York: Oxford University Press.

Berzonsky, M. D. (1990). Self-construction over the life-span: A process perspective on identity formation. In G. J. Neimeyer & R. A. Neimeyer (Eds.), *Advances in personal construct psychology* (Vol. 1, pp. 155–186). Greenwich, CT: JAI.

Bohanek, J. G., Marin, K. A., Fivush, R., & Duke, M. P. (2006). Family narrative interaction and children's sense of self. *Family Process, 45*, 39–54.

Boyle, P. A., Barnes, L. L., Buchman, A. S., & Bennett, D. A. (2009). Purpose in life is associated with mortality among community-dwelling older persons. *Psychosomatic Medicine, 71*, 574–579.

Boyle, P. A., Buchman, A. S., Barnes, L. L., & Bennett, D. A. (2010). Effect of a purpose in life on risk of incident Alzheimer disease and mild cognitive impairment in community-dwelling older persons. *Archives of General Psychiatry, 67*, 304–310.

Brassai, L., Piko, B. F., & Steger, M. F. (2011). Meaning in life: Is it a protective factor for adolescents' psychological health? *International Journal of Behavioral Medicine, 18*, 44–51.

Breitbart, W., Gibson, C., Poppito, S., & Berg, A. (2004). Psychotherapeutic interventions at the end of life: A focus on meaning and spirituality. *Canadian Journal of Psychiatry, 49*, 366–372.

Breitbart, W., Rosenfeld, B., Gibson, C., Pessin, H., Poppito, S., Nelson, C., et al. (2010). Meaning-centered group psychotherapy for patients with advanced cancer: A pilot randomized controlled trial. *Psycho-Oncology, 19*, 21–28.

Butler, R. N. (1974). Successful aging and the role of the life review. *Journal of the American Geriatrics Society, 22*, 529–535.

Cantor, N., & Sanderson, C. A. (1999). Life task participation and well-being: The importance of taking part in daily life. In D. Kahneman, E. Diener, & N. Schwarz (Eds.), *Well-being: The foundations of hedonic psychology* (pp. 230–243). New York: Russell Sage Foundation.

Cowen, E. L., & Kilmer, R. P. (2002). "Positive psychology": Some plusses and some open issues. *Journal of Community Psychology, 30*, 449–460.

Crumbaugh, J. C., & Maholick, L. T. (1964). An experimental study in existentialism: The psychometric approach to Frankl's concept of noogenic neurosis. *Journal of Clinical Psychology, 20*, 200–207.

Csikszentmihalyi, M. (1990). *Flow: The psychology of optimal experience*. New York: Harper & Row.

Damon, W., Menon, J., & Bronk, K. C. (2003). The development of purpose during adolescence. *Applied Developmental Science, 7*, 119–128.

Debats, D. L., Drost, J., & Hansen, P. (1995). Experiences of meaning in life: A combined qualitative and quantitative approach. *British Journal of Psychology, 86*, 359–375.

DeWitz, S. J., Woolsey, M. L., & Walsh, W. B. (2009). College students retention: An exploration of the relationship between self-efficacy beliefs and purpose in life among college students. *Journal of College Student Development, 50*, 19–34.

Dik, B. J., & Duffy, R. D. (2009). Calling and vocation at work: Definitions and prospects for research and practice. *The Counseling Psychologist, 37*, 424–450.

Dik, B. J., Duffy, R. D., & Eldridge, B. (2009). Calling and vocation in career counseling: Recommendations for promoting meaningful work. *Professional Psychology: Research and Practice, 40*, 625–632.

Dik, B. J., & Steger, M. F. (2008). Randomized trial of a calling-infused career workshop incorporating counselor self-disclosure. *Journal of Vocational Behavior, 35*, 226–233.

Dik, B. J., Steger, M. F., Gibson, A., & Peisner, W. (2011). Make your work matter: Development and pilot evaluation of a purpose-centered career education intervention. *New Directions for Youth Development, 132*, 59–74.

Duckworth, A., Steen, T. A., & Seligman, M. P. (2005). Positive psychology in clinical practice. *Annual Review of Clinical Psychology, 1*, 629–651.

Emmons, R. A. (1986). Personal strivings: An approach to personality and subjective wellbeing. *Journal of Personality and Social Psychology, 51*, 1058–1068.

Erikson, E. H. (1968). *Identity: Youth and crisis.* New York: W. W. Norton.

Frankl, V. E. (1963). *Man's search for meaning: An introduction to logotherapy.* New York: Washington Square Press.

Gollwitzer, P. M. (1999). Implementation intentions: Strong effects of simple plans. *American Psychologist, 54*, 493–503.

Greenstein, M., & Breitbart, W. (2000). Cancer and the experience of meaning: A group psychotherapy for people with cancer. *American Journal of Psychotherapy, 54*, 486–500.

Habermas, T., & Bluck, S. (2000). Getting a life: The emergence of the life story in adolescence. *Psychological Bulletin, 126*, 248–269.

Habermas, T., Ehlert-Lerche, S., & de Silveira, C. (2009). The development of the temporal macrostructure of life narratives across adolescence: Beginnings, linear narrative form, and endings. *Journal of Personality, 77*, 527–560.

Hayden, J. M., Singer, J. A., & Chrisler, J. C. (2006). The transmission of birth stories from mother to daughter: Self-esteem and mother-daughter attachment. *Sex Roles, 55*, 373–383.

Heine, S. J., Proulx, T., & Vohs, K. D. (2006). The meaning maintenance model: On the coherence of social motivations. *Personality and Social Psychology Review, 10*, 88–110.

Henry, M., Cohen, S., Lee, V., Sauthier, P., Provencher, D., Drouin, P., & … Mayo, N. (2010). The Meaning-Making intervention (MMi) appears to increase meaning in life in advanced ovarian cancer: A randomized controlled pilot study. *Psycho-Oncology, 19*, 1340–1347.

Kernis, M. H., & Goldman, B. M. (2006). A multi-component conceptualization of authenticity: Theory and research. In M. P. Zanna (Ed.), *Advances in experimental social psychology* (pp. 283–357). New York: Academic Press.

King, L. A., Hicks, J. A., Krull, J. L., & Del Gaiso, A. K. (2006). Positive affect and the experience of meaning in life. *Journal of Personality and Social Psychology, 90*, 179–196.

King, L. A., & Pennebaker, J. W. (1996). Thinking about goals, glue, and the meaning of life. In R. S. Wyer, Jr. (Ed.), *Ruminative thoughts: Advances in social cognition, IX.* Hillsdale, NJ: Lawrence Erlbaum.

King, L. A., & Smith, N. G. (2004). Gay and straight possible selves: Goals, identity, subjective well-being, and personality development. *Journal of Personality, 72*, 967–994.

Klinger, E. (1977). *Meaning and void.* Minneapolis: University of Minnesota Press.

Kosine, N., Steger, M., & Duncan, S. (2008). Purpose-centered career development: A strengths-based approach to finding meaning and purpose in careers. *Professional School Counseling, 12*, 133–136.

Krause, N. (2009). Meaning in life and mortality. *Journal of Gerontology: Social Sciences, 64B*(4), 517–527.

Lee, V. (2004). A meaning-making intervention for cancer patients – procedure manual. Unpublished manuscript. McGill University, Montreal, Canada.

Lee, V., Cohen, S. R., Edgar, L., Laizner, A. M., & Gagnon, A. (2006). Meaning-making and psychological adjustment to cancer: Development of an intervention and pilot results. *Oncology Nursing Forum, 33*, 291–302.

LeMay, K., & Wilson, K. G. (2008) Treatment of existential distress in life threatening illness: A review of manualized interventions. *Clinical Psychology Review, 28*, 472–493.

Lent, R. (2004). Toward a unifying theoretical and practical perspective on well-being and psychosocial adjustment. *Journal of Counseling Psychology, 51*, 482–509.

Locke, E. A., & Latham, G. P. (2002). Building a practically useful theory of goal setting and task motivation: A 35-year odyssey. *American Psychologist, 57*, 705–717.

Locke, E. A., & Latham, G. P. (2006). New directions in goal-setting theory. *Current Directions in Psychological Science, 15*, 265–268.

Magolda, M. (1992). *Knowing and reasoning in college: Gender-related patterns in students' intellectual development.* San Francisco: Jossey-Bass.

Magolda, M. (2008). Three elements of self-authorship. *Journal of College Student Development, 49*, 269–284.

Maslow, A. H. (1968). *Toward a psychology of being* (2nd ed.). Princeton, NJ: Van Nostrand.

McAdams, D. P. (1985). *Power, intimacy, and the life story: Personological inquiries into identity.* New York: Guilford Press.

McAdams, D. P. (1993). *The stories we live by: Personal myths and the making of the self.* New York: William Morrow & Co.

McAdams, D. P. (1995). What do we know when we know a person? *Journal of Personality, 63*, 365–396.

McGregor, I., & Little, B. R. (1998). Personal projects, happiness, and meaning: On doing well and being yourself. *Journal of Personality and Social Psychology, 74*, 494–512.

McKnight, P. E., & Kashdan, T. B. (2009). Purpose in life as a system that creates and sustains health and well-being: An integrative, testable theory. *Review of General Psychology, 13*, 242–251.

McLean, K. C., Pasupathi, M., & Pals, J. L. (2007). Selves creating stories creating selves: A process model of self-development. *Personality and Social Psychology Review, 11*, 262–278.

Noland, C. M. (2006). Auto-photography as research practice: Identity and self-esteem research. *Journal of Research Practice, 2*(1). Retrieved May 3, 2010 from http://jrp.icaap.org/index.php/jrp/article/view/19/65

Pals, J. L. (2006). Narrative identity processing of difficult life experiences: Pathways of personality development and positive self-transformation in adulthood. *Journal of Personality, 74*, 1079–1109.

Park, C. L., & Folkman, S. (1997). Meaning in the context of stress and coping. *Review of General Psychology, 1*, 115–144.

Parks, A. C., Della Porta, M. D., Pierce, R. S., Zilca, R., & Lyubomirsky, S. (2012). Pursuing happiness in everyday life: The characteristics and behaviors of online happiness seekers. *Emotion*, *12*, 1222–1234.

Pennebaker, J. W., & Seagal, J. (1999). Forming a story: The health benefits of narrative. *Journal of Clinical Psychology*, *55*, 1243–1254.

Peterson, C., & McCabe, A. (1983). *Developmental psycholinguistics: Three ways of looking at a child's narratives*. New York: Plenum Press.

Peterson, C., & Seligman, M. (2004). *Character strengths and virtues: A handbook and classification*. Washington, DC: American Psychological Association.

Peterson, J. B., & Mar, R. A. (2004). Self-authoring program: The ideal future. Unpublished manuscript, University of Toronto, Ontario, Canada. Retrieved from www.selfauthoring.com

Reker, G. T. (2000). Theoretical perspective, dimensions, and measurement of existential meaning. In G. T. Reker & K. Chamberlain (Eds.), *Exploring existential meaning: Optimizing human development across the life span* (pp. 39–55). Thousand Oaks, CA: Sage.

Reker, G. T., & Wong, P. T. P. (1988). Aging as an individual process: Toward a theory of personal meaning. In J. E. Birren & V. L. Bengston (Eds.), *Emergent theories of aging* (pp. 214–246). New York: Springer.

Ryan, R. M., & Connell, J. P. (1989). Perceived locus of causality and internalization: Examining reasons for acting in two domains. *Journal of Personality and Social Psychology*, *57*, 749–761.

Ryan, R. M., & Deci, E. L. (2001). On happiness and human potentials: A review of research on hedonic and eudaimonic well-being. *Annual Review of Psychology*, *52*, 141–166.

Ryff, C. D. (1989). Happiness is everything, or is it? Explorations of the meaning of psychological well-being. *Journal of Personality and Social Psychology*, *57*, 1069–1081.

Ryff, C. D., & Keyes, C. L. M. (1995). The structure of well-being revisited. *Journal of Personality and Social Psychology*, *69*, 719–727.

Ryff, C. D., & Singer, B. (1998). The contours of positive human health. *Psychological Inquiry*, *9*, 1–28.

Schlegel, R. J., Hicks, J. A., Arndt, J., & King, L. A. (2009). Thine own self: True self-concept accessibility and meaning in life. *Journal of Personality and Social Psychology*, *96*, 473–490.

Schueller, S. M. (2010). Preferences for positive psychology exercises. *Journal of Positive Psychology*, *5*, 192–203.

Schueller, S. M. (2011). To each his own well-being boosting intervention: Using preference to guide selection. *Journal of Positive Psychology*, *6*, 300–313.

Schulenberg, S. E., Hutzell, R. R., Nassif, C., & Rogina, J. M. (2008). Logotherapy for clinical practice. *Psychotherapy: Theory, Research, Practice, Training*, *45*, 447–463.

Schwartz, S. J. (2002). An examination of change processes in identity: Integrating the constructivist and discovery perspectives on identity. *Identity*, *2*, 317–339.

Schwartz, S. J., Kurtines, W. M., & Montgomery, M. J. (2005). A comparison of two approaches for facilitating identity exploration processes in emerging adults: An exploratory study. *Journal of Adolescent Research*, *20*, 309–345.

Seligman, M. E. P. (2002). *Authentic happiness*. New York: Free Press.

Seligman, M. E. P., & Csikszentmihalyi, M. (2000). Positive psychology: An introduction. *American Psychologist*, *55*, 5–14.

Seligman, M. E. P., Rashid, T., & Parks, A. C. (2006). Positive psychotherapy. *American Psychologist*, *8*, 772–788.

Seligman, M. E. P., Steen, T. A., Park, N., & Peterson, C. (2005). Positive psychology progress: Empirical validation of interventions. *American Psychologist*, *60*, 410–421.

Sheldon, K. M., & Elliot, A. J. (1998). Not all personal goals are "personal": Comparing autonomous and controlling goals on effort and attainment. *Personality and Social Psychology Bulletin*, *24*, 546–557.

Sheldon, K. M., & Elliot, A. J. (1999). Goal striving, need satisfaction, and longitudinal well-being: The self-concordance model. *Journal of Personality and Social Psychology*, *76*, 546–557.

Sheldon, K. M., & Kasser, T. (1998). Pursuing personal goals: Skills enable progress but not all progress is beneficial. *Personality and Social Psychology Bulletin*, *24*, 1319–1331.

Sheldon, K. M., Kasser, T., Smith, K., & Share, T. (2002). Personal goals and psychological growth: Testing an intervention to enhance goal-attainment and personality integration. *Journal of Personality*, *70*, 5–31.

Sin, N. L., & Lyubomirsky, S. (2009). Enhancing well-being and alleviating depressive symptoms with positive psychology interventions: A practice-friendly meta-analysis. *Journal of Clinical Psychology*, *65*, 467–487.

Singer, J. A. (2004). Narrative identity and meaning-making across the adult lifespan: An introduction. *Journal of Personality*, *72*, 437–460.

Staudinger, U. M. (2001). Life reflection: A social-cognitive analysis of life review. *Review of General Psychology*, *5*, 148–160.

Staudinger, U. M., & Baltes, P. B. (1996). Interactive minds: A facilitative setting for wisdom-related performance? *Journal of Personality and Social Psychology*, *71*, 746–762.

Steger, M. F. (2009). Meaning in life. In S. J. Lopez (Ed.), *Oxford handbook of positive psychology* (2nd ed.) (pp. 679–687). Oxford: Oxford University Press.

Steger, M. F. (2012). Experiencing meaning in life: Optimal functioning at the nexus of spirituality, psychopathology, and well-being. In P. T. P. Wong (Eds.), *The human quest for meaning* (2nd ed., pp. 165–184). New York: Routledge.

Steger, M. F., Bundick, M., & Yeager, D. (2012). Understanding and promoting meaning in life during adolescence. In R. J. R. Levesque (Ed.), *Encyclopedia of adolescence* (pp. 1666–1677). New York: Springer.

Steger, M. F., & Dik, B. J. (2009). If one is searching for meaning in life, does meaning in work help? *Applied Psychology: Health and Well-Being*, *1*, 303–320.

Steger, M. F., & Dik, B. J. (2010). Work as meaning: Individual and organizational benefits of engaging in meaningful work. In P. Linley, S. Harrington, & N. Garcea (Eds.), *Oxford handbook of positive psychology and work* (pp. 131–142). New York: Oxford University Press.

Steger, M. F., Frazier, P., Oishi, S., & Kaler, M. (2006). The meaning in life questionnaire: Assessing the presence of and search for meaning in life. *Journal of Counseling Psychology*, *53*, 80–93.

Steger, M. F., & Kashdan, T. B. (2006). Stability and specificity of meaning in life and life satisfaction over one year: Implications for outcome assessment. *Journal of Happiness Studies*, *8*, 161–179.

Steger, M. F., Kashdan, T. B., Sullivan, B. A., & Lorentz, D. (2008). Understanding the search for meaning in life: Personality, cognitive style, and the dynamic between seeking and experiencing meaning. *Journal of Personality*, *76*, 199–228.

Steger, M. F., Kawabata, Y., Shimai, S., & Otake, K. (2008). The meaningful life in Japan and the United States: Levels and correlates of meaning in life. *Journal of Research in Personality*, *42*, 660–678.

Steger, M. F., Mann, J., Michels, P., & Cooper, T. (2009). Meaning in life, anxiety, depression, and general health among smoking cessation patients. *Journal of Psychosomatic Research*, *67*, 353–358.

Steger, M. F., Oishi, S., & Kashdan, T. B. (2009). Meaning in life across the life span: Levels and correlates of meaning in life from emerging adulthood to older adulthood. *Journal of Positive Psychology*, *4*, 43–52.

Steger, M. F., Pickering, N. K., Shin, J. Y., & Dik, B. J. (2010). Calling in work: Secular or sacred? *Journal of Career Assessment*, *18*, 82–96.

Thompson, N. J., Coker, J., Krause, J. S., & Henry, E. (2003). Purpose in life as a mediator of adjustment after spinal cord injury. *Rehabilitative Psychology*, *48*, 100–108.

Thorne, A. (2000). Personal memory telling and personality development. *Personality and Social Psychology Review*, *4*, 45–56.

Waterman, A. S. (1990). Personal expressiveness: Philosophical and psychological foundations. *Journal of Mind and Behavior*, *11*, 47–74.

Waterman, A. S. (1992). Identity as an aspect of optimal psychological functioning. In G. R. Adams, T. Gullotta, & R. Montemayor (Eds.), *Advances in Adolescent Development. Vol. 4 Identity Formation during Adolescence* (pp. 50–72). Newbury Park, CA: Sage.

Waterman, A. S. (2004). Finding someone to be: Studies on the role of intrinsic motivation in identity formation. *Identity: An International Journal of Theory and Research*, *4*, 209–228.

Waterman, A. S., Schwartz, S. J., Goldbacher, E., Green, H., Miller, C., & Philip, S. (2003). Predicting the subjective experience of intrinsic motivation: The roles of self-determination, the balance of challenges and skills, and self-realization values. *Personality and Social Psychology Bulletin*, *29*, 1447–1458.

Wilson, K., & Murrell, A. (2004). Mindfulness and acceptance: Expanding the cognitive-behavioral tradition. In S. C. Hayes, V. M. Follette, & M. Linehan (Eds.), *Values work in acceptance and commitment therapy: Setting a course for behavioral treatment* (pp. 120–151). New York: Guilford Press.

Wong, P. P. (2010). Meaning therapy: An integrative and positive existential psychotherapy. *Journal of Contemporary Psychotherapy*, *40*, 85–93.

Wong, P. (2012). From logotherapy to meaning-centered counseling and therapy. In P. P. Wong (Ed.), *The human quest for meaning: Theories, research, and applications* (2nd ed., pp. 619–647). New York: Routledge/Taylor & Francis.

Yalom, I. D. (1980). *Existential psychotherapy*. New York: Basic Books.

Yeager, D., & Bundick, M. (2009). The role of purposeful work goals in promoting meaning in life and in schoolwork during adolescence. *Journal of Adolescent Research*, *24*, 423–452.

6

Empathy-Related Interventions

Mark H. Davis and Ena Begovic

People can be annoyingly selfish. This is to some degree inevitable, of course, because an organism that does not strive to gain advantage within its environment faces long odds against survival. However, far beyond the level of self-interest necessary to survive, humans routinely think and act in ways that reveal a robust egocentrism (Chambers & Windschitl, 2004; Krueger & Clement, 1994). Moreover, such privileging of the self is also extended to the groups to which we belong. It is absurdly easy to think of things that separate "our" groups from others. Ethnicity, nationality, religion, party affiliation, social class, and a host of other factors create the many in-groups and out-groups that make up the geography of our social worlds – and we find it easy to act in ways that benefit those who are closer to us, and disadvantage those who are not. A quick glance at the morning paper will reveal a depressing number of instances of individuals and groups acting in ways that increase their own welfare at the expense of others. This sad reality is echoed, moreover, in more formal investigations of human nature. As readers of this volume already know, psychology's view of humanity has long included a strong emphasis on hedonism and self-interest (e.g., Cialdini, Darby, & Vincent, 1973; Dollard & Miller, 1950; Spencer, 1870). In short, the tendency for humans to see their interests as separate from others', and to act so as to maximize these interests at the expense of others, is widespread and robust.

However, the gap between self and other is not unbridgeable. People do not *always* act in ways that maximize their own self-interest. Our more admirable behavior can spring from many sources, but the psychological process frequently invoked to explain phenomena such as these is empathy (e.g., Batson, 1991; Davis, 1994; Eisenberg & Fabes, 1990; Hoffman, 1982). Definitions of empathy have been nearly as numerous as those interested in defining it, but virtually all such efforts have agreed on at least one core feature: that empathy in some way involves the transformation of the observed experiences of another person into a response within the self. Empathy is therefore the psychological process that at least temporarily *unites* the separate social entities of self and other, and as such can be considered among the most positive of psychological phenomena.

The Wiley Blackwell Handbook of Positive Psychological Interventions, First Edition.
Edited by Acacia C. Parks and Stephen M. Schueller.

As befits such a construct, there have been numerous attempts to develop interventions to make empathic responding stronger or more likely. These attempts have taken many forms. Some have focused on increasing empathy within very specific contexts, while others have been part of larger and more comprehensive efforts to enhance social and emotional competencies in general. Intervention efforts have also varied widely in the techniques they have employed, from brief one-time procedures to long and sustained programs. In addition, these interventions have varied with regard to their definition of empathy. To aid in our understanding of what is to follow, then, it is necessary to briefly consider the nature of empathy.

What Is Empathy?

Attempts to define empathy have a long and convoluted history. Over the years it has been conceived of as a cognitive *process* (e.g., Wispé, 1986), as an accurate *understanding* of another (e.g., Dymond, 1950), as a *sharing* of emotional states with a target (e.g., Hoffman, 1984), and as the specific emotional response of *sympathy* (e.g., Batson, 1991). Previously, Davis (1994) offered a model designed to organize all of these approaches into a comprehensive treatment of the empathy process; Figure 6.1 contains a somewhat revised and updated version of this model. The spirit of this model is deliberately inclusive, designed to emphasize the connections between these constructs. Thus, empathy is broadly defined here as a set of constructs having to do with the responses of one individual to the experiences of another. These constructs specifically include both the *processes* taking place within the observer and the affective and non-affective *outcomes* that result from those processes. This distinction is necessary because while a process can potentially lead to many outcomes, it is also separate from them. For example, the model distinguishes between the *process* of perspective taking, in which

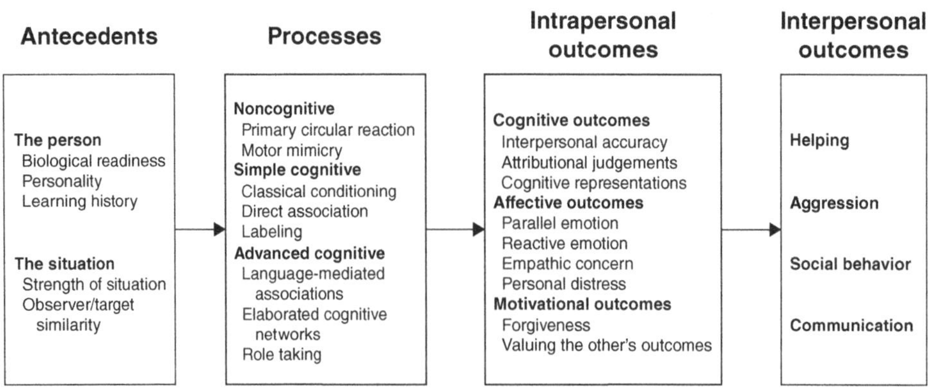

Figure 6.1 A model organizing a variety of empathy-related phenomena (adapted from Davis, 1994)

the observer tries to imagine the target's internal states, and the *outcomes* of perspective taking such as feelings of sympathy for the target (affective) or a more accurate understanding of the target (non-affective). Based on this definition, the model conceives of the typical empathy "episode" as consisting of an observer being exposed in some fashion to a target, after which some response on the part of the observer – cognitive, affective, motivational, and/or behavioral – occurs. Four related constructs can be identified within this prototypical episode, each of which will be elaborated upon below: *antecedents*, which refer to characteristics of the observer, target, or situation; *processes*, which refer to the particular mechanisms by which empathic outcomes are produced; *intrapersonal outcomes*, which refer to cognitive, affective, and motivational responses produced in the observer that are not necessarily manifested in overt behavior; and *interpersonal outcomes*, which refer to behavioral responses directed toward the target.

Antecedents

There are two broad categories of antecedents: those having to do with the *observer* and those having to do with the *situation*. The most important observer factor for the purposes of this chapter is *individual differences* in personality. A variety of measures have been developed over the years for the purpose of assessing the dispositional tendency to engage in empathy-related processes such as perspective taking (e.g., Davis, 1980; Hogan, 1969) or to experience empathy-related affective responses (e.g., Davis, 1980; Mehrabian & Epstein, 1972). Of special note here are two individual differences: the tendency to *take the perspective* of other people and the tendency to experience feelings of *sympathy* for a person in distress. These constructs are frequently assessed by subscales of the Interpersonal Reactivity Index (IRI; Davis, 1980). The IRI is a 28-item instrument that inquires about the respondent's tendency to engage in perspective taking (e.g., "I sometimes try to understand my friends better by imagining how things look from their perspective"), to experience empathic concern (e.g., "I often have tender, concerned feelings for people less fortunate than me"), and to experience personal distress (e.g., "Being in a tense emotional situation scares me"). A fourth dimension of the IRI is less relevant for the purposes of this chapter; it assesses the tendency to imaginatively enter into films, books, plays, etc.

The most relevant situational factor is probably *strength of the situation*, defined as its power to evoke an emotional response from observers. For example, being face-to-face with someone in real distress, especially if that person is weak, helpless, and blameless, can be characterized as a strong situation. It is strong because it is likely to evoke very similar (and substantial) emotional responses in most people. In contrast, weak situations do not produce such uniform responses. Being indirectly exposed to a mildly distressed target who is *not* helpless or blameless may evoke a wider variety of emotions (or no emotion at all), and thus would be characterized as relatively weak. As we will see, interventions vary widely in terms of how intense and sustained an experience they provide to participants.

Processes

The model's second major construct consists of the specific processes that generate empathic outcomes in the observer. Based on the work of Hoffman (1984) and Eisenberg (Eisenberg, Shea, Carlo, & Knight, 1991), the model identifies three broad classes of empathy-related processes, chiefly distinguished from one another by the degree of cognitive effort and sophistication required for their operation. *Noncognitive processes* are those that require very little cognitive activity, or that are unconscious altogether (e.g., motor mimicry). In contrast, *simple cognitive processes* require at least a rudimentary cognitive ability on the part of the observer. Classical conditioning is an example. Imagine an observer and target who simultaneously taste the same unpleasant dish (haggis comes to mind), and react with facial displays of disgust. In the future, when the observer sees that same facial expression, it may well invoke in her the same emotional response because seeing that expression has been paired with experiencing that emotion.

Finally, *advanced cognitive processes* require more sophisticated cognitive activity. The most advanced of these, and the one that has received by far the most empirical attention, is *perspective taking*: the attempts by one individual to understand another by imagining the other's perspective. It is typically conceived of as an effortful process, involving both the suppression of one's own egocentric perspective on events and the active entertaining of someone else's. For example, a woman who tries to understand how her friends view her boyfriend must ignore information that *she* possesses but they do not – such as his occasional hurtful actions that she has never shared with them.

In laboratory investigations the most common method of inducing perspective taking is through instructional sets. In one such instruction (Imagine Target), participants are asked to imagine what the target is currently thinking and feeling. Another form (Imagine Self) asks participants to imagine how they *themselves* would feel if they were in the target's place. Although the two instructional sets are quite similar, and have some of the same effects (e.g., Davis, Conklin, Smith, & Luce, 1996), the Imagine Target instructions are more likely in general to produce feelings of sympathy, while the Imagine Self instructions are more likely to produce personal distress (Batson, 2009). Instructional sets are by far the most common technique for inducing perspective taking, but other methods – for example, asking observers to imagine and write about a day in the life of some target – have also been employed. Promoting perspective taking is a frequent goal of empathy interventions.

Intrapersonal outcomes

The model's third major construct consists of *intrapersonal outcomes* – the cognitive, affective, and motivational responses of the observer that result from exposure to the target. Enhancing one or more of these outcomes is another common goal of intervention efforts. For example, one important cognitive outcome is *interpersonal accuracy*, the successful estimation of other people's thoughts, feelings, and characteristics (e.g., Ickes, 1997). Having an accurate understanding of others' feelings has long been recognized as critical for smooth social interaction (e.g., Mead, 1934). For example, an inability to distinguish between a friend's expressions of fear, sadness, or anger can lead to disastrously awkward and inappropriate responses.

A variety of important affective outcomes are also possible during an empathy episode. One such outcome is to experience *parallel emotions* – that is, to feel the same emotion as the target. Another important affective response is the feeling of compassion for others. This response has been given many names – including sympathy (Wispé, 1986), empathy (Batson, 1991), and *empathic concern* (Davis, 1980). Finally, empathic processes sometimes produce motivational outcomes such as *forgiveness*, which is often conceptualized as a transformation of motivation toward a transgressing partner in which desires for revenge are reduced and desires for reconciliation are increased (McCullough, Worthington, & Rachal, 1997; see Chapter 2).

Interpersonal outcomes

The final construct in the model consists of *interpersonal outcomes*, defined as behaviors directed toward a target that result from prior exposure to that target. The outcome that has attracted the most attention from empathy theorists and researchers is *prosocial behavior*; both cognitive and affective facets of empathy have long been thought to contribute to the likelihood of observers offering help to needy targets. *Aggressive behavior* has also been linked theoretically to empathy-related processes and dispositions, with the expectation that empathy will be negatively associated with aggressive actions. Another interpersonal outcome is the set of behaviors that occur within *social relationships*, such as providing effective and timely social support to friends and family. Finally, an interpersonal outcome that has often been relatively ignored by social psychologists is the *communication* of empathy. That is, independent of any intrapersonal changes in affect, or accuracy, or motivation, how much of this is actually conveyed to the target? As it turns out, improving such empathic communication is the goal of many interventions.

Summary

This overview of empathy-related constructs has at least two broad implications for our consideration of intervention efforts. First, empathy interventions are likely to have a variety of aims. Some will attempt to change a temporary emotional state such as empathic concern; some will try to create a more accurate understanding of the target's circumstances; others will attempt to increase levels of dispositional empathy; still others will seek to improve empathic communication. Thus, intervention efforts will differ considerably with regard to what they are specifically trying to accomplish. Second, while many methods and techniques will be used in these interventions, a significant number of them are likely to be based on the key process of perspective taking. In one form or another – both explicitly and implicitly – intervention efforts by their nature will often encourage observers to understand what another person is thinking or feeling.

Empathy Interventions

The wide variety of empathy interventions makes it somewhat difficult to categorize these efforts. However, it seems reasonable for the purpose of this chapter to organize them according to the particular technique that is employed to enhance empathy. Of course, placement in any given category will be imprecise, especially because many interventions employ more than one technique. Thus, the remainder of this chapter will consist of four sections addressing different kinds of empathy interventions, and a final section discussing some implications of this review. The four intervention techniques are: (i) perspective taking; (ii) instructional approaches; (iii) the use of audio/visual media; and (iv) skills training. In each section details of several studies are provided to illustrate the technique. A full listing of all the studies identified while writing this chapter, and the technique(s) they employ, appears in Table 6.1.

Perspective taking

Many interventions rely on participants (observers) in some way adopting the perspective of the target or target population. The assumption underlying this approach is that when observers "inhabit" the target's world in some fashion, they will come to understand and appreciate the target's point of view, which will ultimately produce desirable outcomes. As noted earlier, considerable laboratory evidence suggests that perspective taking contributes to a number of outcomes, including feelings of sympathy, increased helping behavior, and a greater willingness to forgive. When used in a formal intervention, perspective taking is generally created in one of two ways: either by having participants directly experience the target's situation through some form of active role-playing, or by having participants indirectly experience the target's situation through imagination.

Direct perspective taking The first approach is based upon the idea that engaging in active role-playing will lead the participant to in some way *experience* life in the same way as the target, and that doing so will increase empathy for the target or the target's social group. Such active role-playing can take many forms. For example, some interventions expose participants to the actual sensory experience of the target population, a technique that has been used when attempting to enhance medical students' empathy for their patients. In one study (Pacala, Boult, Bland, & O'Brien, 1995), medical students role-played the experience of

Table 6.1 Intervention techniques used in 44 empathy intervention studies.

	Perspective taking		*Instructional*				
	Direct	*Indirect*	*Didactic instruction*	*Discussion groups*	*Activity-based learning*	*Audio/visual media*	*Skills training*
Armour et al. (2008)			✓	✓	✓	✓	
Bar-On & Kassem (2004)			✓	✓	✓		
Batson et al. (2002)		✓				✓	
Batson et al. (1997)		✓				✓	
Berg et al. (1999)		✓		✓		✓	
Bodenhorn & Starkey (2005)	✓			✓	✓		✓
Bratton & Landreth (1995)	✓		✓	✓	✓		✓
Bunn & Terpstra (2009)	✓						
Chalmers & Townsend (1990)	✓	✓	✓	✓	✓		✓
Chau & Landreth (1997)	✓		✓	✓	✓		✓
Costas & Landreth (1999)	✓		✓	✓	✓		✓
Dow et al. (2007)	✓		✓				✓
Epstein & Jackson (1978)	✓		✓	✓			✓
Foubert & Newberry (2006)		✓	✓	✓		✓	
Garaigordobil (2004)	✓			✓	✓		✓

(*continued*)

Table 6.1 (*Continued*)

	Perspective taking		*Instructional*				
	Direct	*Indirect*	*Didactic instruction*	*Discussion groups*	*Activity-based learning*	*Audio/visual media*	*Skills training*
Glover & Landreth (2000)	✓		✓	✓	✓		✓
Harris & Landreth (1997)	✓		✓	✓	✓		✓
Hatcher et al. (1994)	✓		✓				✓
Herbek & Yammarino (1990)	✓		✓	✓	✓		✓
Hodson et al. (2009)		✓		✓	✓		
Jagers et al. (2007)	✓		✓	✓	✓	✓	
Kimber et al. (2008)	✓		✓	✓	✓		✓
Lane-Garon (1998)	✓		✓	✓	✓		✓
Lee (1987)		✓	✓	✓			
Lee & Landreth (2003)	✓		✓	✓	✓		✓
Long et al. (1999)	✓		✓	✓	✓		✓
Malhotra & Liyanage (2005)	✓		✓	✓	✓	✓	
Newton et al. (2007)					✓		✓
Pacala et al. (1995)	✓						
Paluck (2009)						✓	
Pinezone-Glover et al. (1998)		✓	✓	✓			
Rau et al. (2010)			✓	✓		✓	
Reilly et al. (2012)		✓		✓	✓		✓

Table 6.1 (*Continued*)

	Perspective taking		*Instructional*				
	Direct	*Indirect*	*Didactic instruction*	*Discussion groups*	*Activity-based learning*	*Audio/visual media*	*Skills training*
Roter et al. (1995)	✓		✓	✓	✓		✓
Sanson-Fisher & Poole (1978)			✓				✓
Schewe & O'Donohue (1993)		✓				✓	
Schewe & O'Donohue (1996)		✓	✓		✓	✓	
Shechtman & Tanus (2006)	✓			✓	✓	✓	
Soble et al. (2011)						✓	
Staub et al. (2005)			✓	✓	✓		✓
Uhlemann, Lea, & Stone (1976)			✓				✓
Wilkes et al. (2002)	✓						
Wilson et al. (1999)	✓	✓	✓	✓	✓	✓	
Wilt, Evans, Muenchen, & Guegold (1995)	✓	✓		✓		✓	

elderly people. As part of the experience they wore earplugs in order to simulate a loss of hearing and donned heavy socks to mimic pedal edema (swelling of the feet). They also had popcorn kernels placed in their shoes to simulate the pain of arthritis. Another investigation (Bunn & Terpstra, 2009) had medical students who were beginning their psychiatry rotation go through a role-play designed to approximate the experience of an auditory hallucination. The students listened to a 40-minute recording on individual headphones of a simulated hallucination in which (among other things) voices criticized the participant. While they listened, the students had to carry out a variety of tasks: following written instructions to construct geometric designs out of toothpicks, taking a series of memory and concentration tests, and interacting with peers. Thus, the students experienced (at least slightly) what everyday life can be like for schizophrenic patients. To give medical students a more global sense of what it is like to be a patient, a program at the UCLA Medical Center had students admitted to the Center under assumed names and feigning an illness (Wilkes, Milgrom, & Hoffman, 2002). During their overnight stay, the students were exposed to a wide range of typical patient experiences, including blood draws, IV drips, and repeated examinations. Beyond the medical experiences, they also had to endure the presence of roommates, lack of privacy, and the confusing paperwork associated with a hospital stay.

Outside of the medical context, role-playing interventions typically take a different form, often designed to make participants experience the *emotional* states of the target population. This approach is sometimes used in interventions designed to enhance empathy for a target group toward whom long-standing negative feelings exist. For example, Shechtman and Tanus (2006) carried out an intervention intended to increase Arab students' empathy for Israelis. As part of the multifaceted 10-session intervention, the students were read a letter written by a Jewish mother whose child had been killed in a terrorist attack. The students then had to respond by writing a personal letter to the mother, with the goal of inducing in them some of the grief and sorrow felt by the mother.

Finally, role-playing is often used as a way to practice skills that the intervention is trying to foster in the participants. For example, in an intervention designed to teach perspective taking to peer mediators (Lane-Garon, 1998), trainers had the participants role-play interpersonal disputes in order to practice inferring the thoughts and feelings of the disputants. Landreth's (1991) filial play intervention (described more fully in the section on skills training) employs role-playing as a means of teaching parents how to engage in empathic play with their children. After viewing a videotape of a therapist conducting a play session with a child, pairs of parents then role-play a session themselves, alternating between the roles of parent and child. The goal is to develop and refine their ability to engage in empathic play – in which the parent allows the child to take the lead, and does not initiate or direct the activity. Similar use of role-playing as a form of practice is employed in many skill-training interventions.

Indirect perspective taking The other major approach in this category is to induce perspective taking not through active role-playing but by instructing (or in some way encouraging) the participant to *imagine* the thoughts, feelings, or situation of the target. This approach has frequently been used in laboratory interventions. Often in such settings, the target is another student, and thus broadly similar to the observer. However, this is not always the case. For example, in a series of three experiments Batson et al. (1997) used an instructional set that asked participants to imagine the thoughts and feelings of a target belonging to a stigmatized group

(AIDS patients; the homeless; murderers). Specifically, they were asked to "imagine how the woman (man) who is interviewed feels about what has happened and how it has affected her (his) life. Try to feel the full impact of what this woman (man) has been through and how she (he) feels as a result." Batson, Chang, Orr, and Rowland (2002) used similar instructions and asked participants to take the perspective of a jailed drug addict.

Perspective-taking instructions have also been used outside of the laboratory, often in conjunction with other techniques. For example, several sexual assault prevention interventions (Lee, 1987; Pinzone-Glover, Gidycz, & Jacobs, 1998; Schewe & O'Donohue, 1993, 1996) have tried to induce empathy among participants (typically male college students) by using a combination of methods that included instructing participants to take the perspective of a sexually abused individual, or to imagine how they would feel if they were sexually victimized. A typical approach is that taken by Lee (1987); the male participants were asked to identify with the male presenter, who then read a detailed account of being raped. Participants then discussed their emotional responses to hearing the account.

Instructional approaches

Another widely used intervention technique is essentially instructional in nature and consists of conveying information to the participants, with the nature of the information and the means by which it is conveyed taking a variety of forms. This approach is based on the assumption that a key factor preventing participants from experiencing empathy for a given target is insufficient or inaccurate information. Thus, providing that information should have the desired effect of enhancing empathy for, and positive actions toward, the target population. As one might imagine, such instruction can take many forms. Although it is not an exhaustive list, some of the major instructional methods are: (i) didactic instruction (typically within an educational setting); (ii) discussion groups; and (iii) activity-based learning. However, it must be noted that educational programs frequently employ multiple techniques; thus, some educational interventions use all three of these forms in combination. In addition, the dividing line between these methods – especially between discussion groups and activity-based learning – can be fuzzy, and these techniques often merge.

Didactic instruction Straightforward classroom lectures are a component of many interventions, although almost always in conjunction with other, more interactive techniques. For example, an acquaintance-rape prevention program carried out with college students (Pinzone-Glover et al., 1998) consisted of a single 60-minute session delivered to mixed-gender groups of 15–20 participants. The session had several components. The students were given basic factual information about the prevalence of sexual assault on college campuses, and the legal definition of rape was explained. Students completed a Rape Myths and Facts Worksheet, and then discussed it. The students were also told about typical characteristics and attitudes of offenders (e.g., ignoring the woman's attempts to resist), and several case studies were presented and discussed. Techniques to improve personal safety were also presented.

Lecture presentations have also been part of interventions designed to enhance empathy for members of out-groups (e.g., Malhotra & Liyanage, 2005; Staub, Pearlman, Gubin, & Hagengimana, 2005). For example, an ambitious intervention designed to foster reconciliation in Rwanda between the Hutu and Tutsi ethnic groups was based to a considerable degree on the belief that a greater understanding of certain key concepts would increase the degree of empathy for the other ethnic group. In particular, it was predicted that greater understanding of the causes of genocide, the effects of trauma and victimization, and the nature of certain basic psychological needs would enhance empathy, healing, and reconciliation. Thus, one component of the nine-day intervention was a series of 45–75-minute lectures on these topics. The lectures were subsequently supplemented with more interactive activities (Staub et al., 2005).

Discussion groups Discussion groups are also widely used in educational interventions. A good example of this technique can be found in an elaborate school-based program carried out with Spanish adolescents (Garaigordobil, 2004). The program was designed to broadly enhance socio-emotional skills in adolescents, with empathy enhancement one of these skills. The program consisted of weekly two-hour sessions conducted throughout the entire school year. In a typical session, the topic for the day (e.g., encouraging cooperative behavior) would be introduced by the teacher, and the class would then be divided into groups of five or six students. These groups would discuss the topic, often using one or more specific discussion methods. Thus, sometimes groups would engage in brainstorming, and attempt to generate a wide range of solutions to the day's issue; afterwards the group would discuss the solutions and identify the best ones. Another technique was to present the group with a case study consisting of a real-life example; the group would freely discuss the case and offer their own opinions. Regardless of the particular group activity employed in a given session, the small groups would then re-convene and each group would report their conclusions to the full class, providing an opportunity for a broader discussion under the leadership of the teacher.

This general approach has also been incorporated into interventions carried out in a wide variety of contexts. For example, in the extensive program designed to enhance reconciliation between Hutu and Tutsi in Rwanda, participants not only received some educational content through lectures, they also engaged in small group work designed to enhance empathic listening. Pairs of participants practiced empathic listening, and then reflected on their experiences with the larger group.

Activity-based learning Activity-based learning goes beyond didactic instruction and group discussion by having participants engage in some activity that will help foster a change in their beliefs, attitudes, or values. In part, the logic of this approach is that learning may occur via multiple avenues, and that traditional lecture and discussion only makes use of some of them. By having participants *do* things instead of simply talking, additional learning may be possible. Further, experiential learning may also bypass some of the resistance that can accompany more traditional approaches.

A typical example of activity-based learning comes from the intervention with Spanish adolescents described earlier (Garaigordobil, 2004). In this activity, groups of four students are given 28 geometrical plastic pieces, with each student receiving some of the pieces. The group's goal is to construct a figure (or figures) out of the pieces with no pieces left over at the end. The students must make the decision as to which figure(s) – and how many – to create, and these decisions have to be made by general consent of the group. The groups then spend 30–40 minutes collaboratively constructing the figures. The groups then come together to see what each has created, and to discuss the process by which they did so.

Another interesting use of this approach was developed by Bar-On and Kassem (2004) in an intervention designed to foster greater empathy and understanding between Israelis and Palestinians. Jewish and Palestinian students at Ben Gurion University enrolled in a class on "Jewish-Arab encounters based on storytelling." The key component of the class was that each student had to interview members of their parents' and grandparents' generations; the interviews were designed to elicit the interviewees' life stories. In class, the students would then present the stories to the full group for analysis and discussion. The goal of the exercise was to improve students' ability to listen to the experiences of the "other side," and to develop a more complex and sympathetic image of the other group.

Finally, one especially imaginative example of this approach was that taken by Hodson, Choma, and Costello (2009), who had heterosexual college students participate in small group discussions in which they imagined crash-landing on an alien planet where circumstances paralleled those facing homosexuals in our culture. Specifically, the students were asked to imagine that on this planet all reproduction took place via artificial insemination, and that all sexual activity and displays of affection were strictly forbidden. Thus, in this hypothetical world the students would be forced to constantly hide their romantic feelings and behavior to avoid punishment; they were asked to identify all the ways that they would respond to such a situation. The parallel to homosexuality was never overtly mentioned by the experimenters prior to the group discussion, and the groups did not typically notice it until facilitators eventually pointed it out and had them consider it.

Audio/visual media

A third intervention technique is to use audio/visual media to enhance empathy for targets. The underlying assumption of this approach is that information presented to observers will be more engaging when it has a narrative-like quality, and this greater engagement will allow the viewer to better connect to the target on an emotional and cognitive level. Thus, the most important feature of this technique is not so much the specific content provided but the dramatic form in which it is presented. Importantly, a dramatic narrative quality can be used not only with fictional content, but also when real individuals and/or real stories are presented.

The media used in empathy interventions can take a variety of forms. Some interventions have employed videos or audiotapes of crime victims describing their horrific experiences and the negative consequences they subsequently faced. For example, in one study designed to enhance empathy for rape victims (Berg, Lonsway, & Fitzgerald, 1999), some participants listened to an audiotape of a young woman describing her experience of being raped. On the tape she recounts the circumstances of the assault – that she was acquainted with the man who raped her, and that drinking was involved on the night of her attack. She describes her feelings of powerlessness during the assault, and then goes on to describe her post-rape experience, including feelings of shame and fear and her decision not to report the attack to the police. Similarly, an intervention designed to foster character growth among prisoners included a number of videotapes of crime victims recounting their stories in order to sensitize offenders to the harm caused by their actions and enhance empathy for their victims (Armour, Windsor, Aguilar, & Taub, 2008).

Typically the victims provide a firsthand account of their experiences; however, some interventions have told a victim's story through a third person. For instance, in another rape prevention intervention (Foubert & Newberry, 2006), fraternity men were shown a video in which a police officer, Sergeant Ramon, recounts a story of a fellow male police officer who was raped by two men on the job. Ramon graphically describes the details of the rape and the officer's experience of having a rape examination performed. The officer was further traumatized when his colleagues did not believe that he was a powerless victim of rape; instead they believed he was a participant in a consensual sexual encounter.

Some interventions have used material from professionally produced television programs. For example, to enhance empathy for Blacks, White undergraduates watched a 20-minute clip of an episode from the television series *Primetime Live* in which a Black man and a White man engaged in different activities like shopping in a store and trying to rent an apartment. Hidden cameras revealed how the two men were treated differently, with the Black man clearly receiving more negative treatment (Soble, Spanierman, & Liao, 2011).

In another study (Wilson et al., 1999) middle school students watched a video created by Court TV as part of a school-based program. The video featured three real cases involving teenaged perpetrators and victims. In each case, the teenagers were engaging in typical adolescent behavior that got out of hand; thus, it should be easy for the participants to identify with the teenagers in the videos. For example, in the "Daring Your Friends" case, several teenagers gathered one night to engage in typical teenage activities, such as socializing, drinking, and drug use. As the group wandered through a park, one boy pushed another boy into a river as part of a bet; the boy subsequently drowned. The boy responsible for the actual pushing was arrested, as were the four other individuals who bet him to do it. The video included facts of each case, actual footage of the trials, and interviews with the individuals involved in the cases and their families.

Entertainment movies have long been identified by educators, researchers, and laypeople as a powerful vehicle for captivating audiences and eliciting strong emotions. As such, movies have sometimes been used in empathy interventions. In a study by Shechtman and Tanus (2006), for example, non-Jewish Arab adolescents watched the movie *Life is Beautiful.* This emotional movie tells the story of a Jewish father and son who are sent to a Nazi concentration camp. In order to shelter his son from the horrors of the camp, the father pretends that they are players in a game. He tells his son that the object of the game is to earn 1,000 points, and the first person to do so wins a tank. He goes on to tell his son that performing certain behaviors, such as staying quiet and hiding from the guards, will earn him points; other behaviors, such as crying or complaining about being hungry, will cost him points. The movie was used in an effort to enhance the students' empathy towards the "Jewish narrative."

Finally, in one particularly creative intervention, Paluck (2009) used an "education entertainment radio soap opera" to reduce prejudice and conflict between Hutus and Tutsis. The soap opera (*Musekewaya*) depicts two fictional Rwandan communities facing societal problems mirroring Rwanda's real problems, including violence, casualties, and traumatization. In addition to typical soap opera themes, the program includes educational messages designed to influence listeners' beliefs about prejudice, violence, trauma, and healing and provides a model for peace and cooperation. The 30 characters featured in the program are depicted in a relatable and realistic manner, and serve to convey the education messages to other characters. For example, some characters debunk the idea that traumatized individuals are mentally ill; they teach others that symptoms of trauma can be understood and healing can begin by openly expressing emotions and talking about the past.

Skills training

The final intervention technique used is rather different from the other three. The "skills training" approach seeks to teach the participants behavioral responses that will successfully convey empathy to the target. Thus, this approach is less about enhancing the level of empathy *experienced* by the observer, and is more concerned with increasing the degree of empathy *communicated* by the observer to the target. Theoretically, then, in this approach the observer may not need to experience empathy at all; he or she only needs to be able to convey it. However, it seems reasonable to expect that these two phenomena will typically co-occur.

The skills training approach often focuses on three interrelated skill sets: observation, listening, and responding. The first skill set, *observation*, entails attuning to the target and attempting to interpret: (i) facial expressions, gestures, and other non-verbal behaviors; and (ii) the meaning behind the target's words. *Listening* includes behaviors such as: (i) listening to a target without interrupting or judging; and (ii) showing interest through verbal behaviors (e.g., "please, go on"; "mm-hmm") and non-verbal behaviors (e.g., nodding, maintaining eye contact, slightly leaning forward). The *responding* skill set includes behaviors such as: (i) repeating or paraphrasing statements as a way of verifying understanding (e.g., "I'm hearing you say that …"; "Let me see if I got this right …"; "So you think/feel that …"); and (ii) validating the target's statements (e.g., "You have every right to be angry").

Specific interventions have emphasized each of these general skills to varying degrees, depending upon their particular purpose. For example, some interventions focus primarily on the responding skill. Roter et al. (1995) provided physicians with eight hours of training in communication skills, with an emphasis on minimizing patient distress. During the training, these physicians repeatedly practiced asking patients about their fears and offering reassurance. Similarly, Epstein and Jackson (1978) employed an intervention in which married couples participated in five 90-minute sessions over a three-week period to improve communication with the partner. Using discussion and small group work, the intervention emphasized making assertive requests, clear statement of opinions, and honest statements of emotions.

An intervention aimed at improving the parent–child relationship using play therapy (Guerney, 1976; Landreth, 1991) is a good example of more comprehensive skills training; all three skill sets are included in this "filial play" intervention. The observation and listening skills are addressed by activities designed to teach the parents to detach themselves from their own expectations, and instead stay in the moment while playing with the child; that is, parents are taught to observe, listen, and stay emotionally active. While parents do not have to actually play alongside the child, they are urged to pay attention, show interest, and always be "present." It is especially important for parents to be attuned to their child's needs and to his or her inner, subjective world.

This intervention addresses the responding skill in several ways. For example, parents are taught how to provide *validation* of the child's experience. If a child is sad over losing a crayon, parents are taught to provide a validating response (e.g., "It sure is sad to lose a crayon, isn't it?"), instead of rejecting the experience (e.g., "Don't be sad") or offering false reassurance. Another way in which responding is addressed is by teaching the parents to allow the child self-direction – by *refraining* from telling the child (either verbally or non-verbally) how to act or think. For instance, parents are taught to allow their child to independently choose which toys to play with and how to color a drawing. If a child insists on asking the parent for direction on a task, the parent is taught to reply with a statement that emphasizes the child's freedom (e.g., "You can choose to play with any toy you want").

Another intervention addressing all three components was used by Long, Angera, Carter, Nakamoto, and Kalso (1999), and focuses on improving perspective taking within romantic couples. In one component of this program, participants are shown a silent video of a couple interacting and are instructed to interpret the non-verbal messages the couple were sending each other. The participants then share their thoughts about the couple's relationship based on the nature of their non-verbal communication. In another skills training exercise, the participants first learned about the empathic communication component of responding. Afterwards, couples took turns speaking and responding. The speaker would briefly talk, and then the responder would paraphrase the message. The listener pointed to a particular spot on a target to indicate how accurately the responder understood the message; the bull's-eye represented complete accuracy. If the responder wasn't initially accurate, the couple would repeat the process until a bull's-eye was achieved.

In recent years the use of theater has been a popular approach to teaching empathic communication skills. Dow, Leong, Anderson, and Wenzel (2007) had theater professors deliver training sessions to a group of medical residents. The sessions emphasized expressiveness, body language, and vocal presence. Some specific empathy-conveying skills that were taught included: speaking in the appropriate tone of voice, maintaining congruency between one's voice and body to avoid sending mixed messages, and sitting next to and facing a target. In another intervention (Reilly, Trial, Piver, & Schaff, 2012), medical students and faculty participated in a theater games workshop. In one game participants were asked to choose an emotion and pose in a manner to reflect that emotion. The other participants then tried to interpret the pose. In another game, student pairs were instructed to face each other and closely observe their partner for a few minutes. Next, the partners had to turn around and alter their appearances in three ways. Once finished, the partners faced each other once again and tried to detect the changes.

Empathy Interventions: What Works?

In this final section, we will offer some thoughts regarding the features that characterize the most and least effective types of interventions. Unfortunately, it is quite difficult to provide firm conclusions regarding the relative efficacy of the four intervention techniques discussed thus far. There is evidence – sometimes very strong evidence – that each of the four techniques can be effective. However, comparing the techniques is problematic because so many interventions have employed multiple techniques; the net result is that it is nearly impossible to tell which one (or ones) are the most effective. Nevertheless, some limited conclusions may be drawn, and there are at least three factors to consider when evaluating the question of efficacy: (i) intervention context (e.g., health professions, couples, students), (ii) intervention methodology (e.g., instructional, skills training), and (iii) the intervention's assessment of empathy (e.g., cognitive, affective).

The evidence suggests that efforts to enhance empathy may have the greatest success when the *target of the empathy is someone psychologically close to the participant.* For example, empathy interventions specifically targeted to one's children (filial therapy) and romantic partners (perspective-taking training) are reliably effective. In addition, forgiveness interventions (see Chapter 2) have also proven quite effective in producing empathy for transgressors, and these transgressors are almost always spouses/romantic partners, family members, or close friends. Importantly, all of these approaches also involve fairly intense interventions. The forgiveness and perspective-taking interventions typically consist of multiple sessions in which participants engage in a variety of activities and exercises. In filial therapy participants similarly engage in an intense 10-week program. Finally, it is impressive that these interventions were successful despite employing a wide variety of empathy assessments. The forgiveness interventions typically define empathy in terms of self-reported sympathy and concern for the transgressor; the perspective-taking intervention defines and measures empathy in terms of cognitive empathy (willingness to take the partner's perspective); the filial therapy intervention assesses empathy in terms of actual parental behavior coded from videotaped play sessions.

Evidence also suggests an especially high level of success for interventions that focus on *enhancing the communication of empathy.* For example, the programs designed to teach medical students how to better convey empathy for patients were largely successful (e.g., Roter et al., 1995; Dow et al., 2007). Similarly, the Epstein and Jackson (1978) intervention designed to enhance empathic communication among couples led to greater perceptions of empathy in one's partner – that is, the partners receiving this intervention more successfully conveyed understanding and acceptance. The filial play intervention is another example of a skills-based program with strong evidence of efficacy. As with the forgiveness and perspective-taking approaches, the communication-focused programs typically involved intense multi-session interventions.

At the other end of the efficacy spectrum are the interventions designed to enhance empathy toward victims of sexual assault. Although some of these interventions have increased empathy, a meta-analysis by Anderson and Whiston (2005) found no reliable effect for such programs. Why might this be? One possibility is the relative brevity of the interventions. Compared to the multi-session approach used in the interventions already mentioned, programs designed to enhance empathy for victims of sexual assault are often one-time affairs (e.g., Pinzone-Glover et al., 1998; Schewe & O'Donohue, 1993). A second factor concerns the motivation of the participants. Unlike many of the interventions described in this chapter, participants in sexual assault workshops are often required to attend rather than freely choosing to take part – which seems likely to reduce the effectiveness of the intervention.

Between these two extremes, educational programs designed to enhance empathy among youth have had mixed success. For example, Garaigordobil (2004) and Newton et al. (2007) reported an increase in trait empathy as a result of such programs, but Kimber, Sandell, and Bremberg (2008) found no increase in self-reported empathic behavior. Hatcher et al. (1994) found an increase in trait empathy among college students receiving "peer facilitation" training, but not high school students; Lane-Garon (1998) found no significant increase in trait empathy following peer mediation training. Jagers et al. (2007) reported an increase in trait empathy following an anti-violence program; Wilson et al. found an increase in affective sharing but not in empathic accuracy. One factor contributing to this inconsistent pattern is probably the context – large-scale interventions primarily delivered via the classroom to students who vary widely in their interest and attentiveness. Moreover, in such programs empathy enhancement is only one of many curricular goals, and thus may not receive sustained attention. However, the inconsistent pattern may also result to some degree from the fact that these interventions frequently use measures of trait empathy rather than changes in current emotional states or in overt behavior. Given that personality traits are relatively (although not perfectly) stable, it may be difficult to significantly alter them within the time frame of the intervention.

Finally, and on a more positive note, it appears that intervention efforts carried out in intergroup settings, while not always effective, nevertheless may have a reasonable expectation of success. Even when the groups involved have a long and contentious history, and even when horrific violence has occurred, empathy interventions have had some success. Effective interventions have been reported in Rwanda, Sri Lanka, and with Palestinian/Israeli relations, all of which would certainly qualify as "difficult cases." Importantly, as with the other successful interventions described above, these efforts typically involved multi-session programs. To be sure, there are significant challenges in such interventions, and there is no mistaking the difficulty of the task. However, the fact that increased empathy is achievable even in such seemingly intractable contexts reinforces the promise that empathy interventions can offer.

Conclusion

So what may we conclude from this review? First, and most optimistically, it seems clear that efforts to enhance empathy are frequently successful. This is true for virtually every form of empathy – cognitive, affective, and behavioral. It is also true for almost all of the subject populations with which interventions have been attempted, including ethnic groups with a long history of animosity. To be sure, there are some caveats. Almost all of the evidence for the efficacy of empathy interventions is based on measurement of empathy in the immediate aftermath of the intervention; very little is known about the longevity of these effects. Moreover, there are particular practices, and combinations of practices, that seem to be especially effective. For example, longer-term interventions are more effective than short ones, especially one-shot efforts. Similarly, programs designed to enhance specific skills such as empathic communication seem more reliably effective than more general efforts to improve trait empathy. Nonetheless, it seems broadly true that attempts to enhance empathy are often successful (at least in the short term), and this is very good news indeed.

Second, and less optimistically, it is not at all clear at present exactly which intervention techniques are the most effective – or if in fact such techniques *do* vary in their efficacy. There are two primary reasons for this. One reason is that it is fairly uncommon for an intervention to employ only a single technique. For example, only 5 of the 44 investigations listed in Table 6.1 employed a single intervention methodology. The others all employed multiple techniques, and sometimes dizzying numbers of them. As a result, it is often impossible to determine which of the multiple techniques is the "active ingredient" in the intervention. The other reason why we do not know which empathy intervention techniques are most effective is more fundamental – we have not tried to find out! Virtually none of the investigations in Table 6.1 made an explicit effort to determine the relative efficacy of intervention techniques; instead, the focus was simply on demonstrating the overall effectiveness of some particular intervention program. This focus on demonstrating program effectiveness is completely understandable. However, it does not move us very far toward a deeper understanding of how empathy might most effectively and efficiently be enhanced. Thus, it seems to us that the single biggest shortcoming in the literature on empathy enhancement is the lack of explicit attempts to identify the most effective methods for accomplishing this goal. Until such efforts are made, our understanding of this important issue will be imperfect at best, and woefully inadequate at worst.

References

Anderson, L. A., & Whiston, S. C. (2005). Sexual assault education programs: A meta-analytic examination of their effectiveness. *Psychology of Women Quarterly*, *29*, 374–388.

Armour, M. P., Windsor, L. C., Aguilar, J., & Taub, C. (2008). A pilot study of a faith-based restorative justice intervention for Christian and non-Christian offenders. *Journal of Psychology and Christianity*, *27*, 159–167.

Bar-On, D., & Kassem, F. (2004). Storytelling as a way to work through intractable conflicts: The German-Jewish experience and its relevance to the Palestinian-Israeli context. *Journal of Social Issues*, *60*, 289–306.

Batson, C. D. (1991). *The altruism question: Toward a social-psychological answer*. Hillsdale, NJ: Lawrence Erlbaum Associates.

Batson, C. D. (2009). Two forms of perspective taking: Imagining how another feels and imagining how you would feel. In K. D. Markman, W. M. P. Klein, & J. A. Suhr (Eds.), *Handbook of imagination and mental simulation* (pp. 267–279). New York: Psychology Press.

Batson, C. D., Chang, J., Orr, R., & Rowland, J. (2002). Empathy, attitudes, and action: Can feeling for a member of a stigmatized group motivate one to help the group? *Personality and Social Psychology Bulletin*, *28*, 1656–1666.

Batson, C. D., Polycarpou, M. P., Harmon-Jones, E., Imhoff, H. J., Mitchener, E. C., Bednar, L. L., ... Highberger, L. (1997). Empathy and attitudes: Can feeling for a member of a stigmatized group improve feelings toward the group? *Journal of Personality and Social Psychology*, *72*, 105–118.

Berg, D. R., Lonsway, K. A., & Fitzgerald, L. F. (1999). Rape prevention education for men: The effectiveness of empathy-induction techniques. *Journal of College Student Development*, *40*, 219–234.

Bodenhorn, N., & Starkey, D. (2005). Beyond role-playing: Increasing counselor empathy through theater exercises. *Journal of Creativity in Mental Health*, *1*, 17–27.

Bratton, S., & Landreth, G. (1995). Filial therapy with single parents: Effects on parental acceptance, empathy, and stress. *International Journal of Play Therapy*, *4*, 61–80.

Bunn, W., & Terpstra, J. (2009). Cultivating empathy for the mentally ill using simulated auditory hallucinations. *Academic Psychiatry*, *33*, 457–460.

Chalmers, J. B., & Townsend, M. A. R. (1990). The effects of training in social perspective taking on socially maladjusted girls. *Child Development*, *61*, 178–190.

Chambers, J. R., & Windschitl, P. D. (2004). Biases in social comparative judgments: The role of nonmotivated factors in above-average and comparative-optimism effects. *Psychological Bulletin*, *130*, 813–838.

Chau, I. Y., & Landreth, G. L. (1997). Filial therapy with Chinese parents: Effects on parental empathic interactions, parental acceptance of child and parental stress. *International Journal of Play Therapy*, *6*, 75–92.

Cialdini, R. B., Darby, B. L., & Vincent, J. E. (1973). Transgression and altruism: A case for hedonism. *Journal of Experimental Social Psychology*, *9*, 502–516.

Costas, M., & Landreth, G. (1999). Filial therapy with nonoffending parents of children who have been sexually abused. *International Journal of Play Therapy*, *8*, 43–66.

Davis, M. H. (1980). A multidimensional approach to individual differences in empathy. *JSAS Catalog of Selected Documents in Psychology*, *10*, 85.

Davis, M. H. (1994). *Empathy: A social psychological approach*. Boulder, CO: Westview Press.

Davis, M. H., Conklin, L., Smith, A., & Luce, C. (1996). Effect of perspective taking on the cognitive representation of persons: A merging of self and other. *Journal of Personality and Social Psychology*, *70*, 713–726.

Dollard, J., & Miller, N. (1950). *Personality and psychotherapy: An analysis in terms of learning, thinking and culture*. New York: McGraw-Hill.

Dow, A. W., Leong, D., Anderson, A., & Wenzel, R. P. (2007). Using theater to teach clinical empathy: A pilot study. *Journal of General Internal Medicine*, *22*, 1114–1118.

Dymond, R. F. (1950). Personality and empathy. *Journal of Consulting Psychology*, *14*, 343–350.

Eisenberg, N., & Fabes, R. A. (1990). Empathy: Conceptualization, measurement, and relation to prosocial behavior. *Motivation and Emotion*, *14*, 131–149.

Eisenberg, N., Shea, C. L., Carlo, G., & Knight, G. P. (1991). Empathy-related responding and cognition: A "chicken and the egg" dilemma. In W. Kurtines & J. Gewirtz (Eds.), *Handbook of moral behavior and development* (Vol. *2*) *Research* (pp. 63–88). Hillsdale, NJ: Lawrence Erlbaum Associates.

Epstein, N., & Jackson, E. (1978). An outcome study of short-term communication training with married couples. *Journal of Consulting and Clinical Psychology*, *46*, 207–212.

Foubert, J. D., & Newberry, J. T. (2006). Effects of two versions of an empathy-based rape prevention program on fraternity men's survivor empathy, attitudes, and behavioral intent to commit rape or sexual assault. *Journal of College Student Development*, *47*, 133–148.

Garaigordobil, M. (2004). Effects of a psychological intervention on factors of emotional development during adolescence. *European Journal of Psychological Assessment*, *20*, 66–80.

Glover, G. J., & Landreth, G. L. (2000). Filial therapy with Native Americans on the Flathead Reservation. *International Journal of Play Therapy*, *9*, 57–80.

Guerney, L. F. (1976). Filial therapy program. In D. H. Olson (Ed.), *Treating relationships* (pp. 67–91). Lake Mills, IA: Graphic Publishing.

Harris, Z. L., & Landreth, G. L. (1997). Filial therapy with incarcerated mothers: A five week model. *International Journal of Play Therapy*, *6*, 53–73.

Hatcher, S. L., Nadeau, M. S., Walsh, L. K., Reynolds, M., Galea, J., & Marz, K. (1994). The teaching of empathy for high school and college students: Testing Rogerian methods with the Interpersonal Reactivity Index. *Adolescence*, *29*, 961–974.

Herbek, T. A., & Yammarino, F. J. (1990). Empathy training for hospital staff nurses. *Group and Organization Studies*, *15*, 279–295.

Hodson, G., Choma, B. L., & Costello, K. (2009). Experiencing alien-nation: Effects of a simulation intervention on attitudes towards homosexuals. *Journal of Experimental Social Psychology*, *45*, 974–978.

Hoffman, M. L. (1982). Development of prosocial motivation: Empathy and guilt. In N. Eisenberg (Ed.), *The development of prosocial behavior* (pp. 281–313). New York: Academic Press.

Hoffman, M. L. (1984). Interaction of affect and cognition in empathy. In C. E. Izard, J. Kagan, & R. B. Zajonc (Eds.), *Emotions, cognition, and behavior* (pp. 103–131). Cambridge: Cambridge University Press.

Hogan, R. (1969). Development of an empathy scale. *Journal of Consulting and Clinical Psychology*, *33*, 307–316.

Ickes, W. (Ed.) (1997). *Empathic accuracy*. New York: Guilford Press.

Jagers, R. J., Morgan-Lopez, A. A., Howard, T., Browne, D. C., Flay, B. R., & Aban Aya Coinvestigators (2007). Mediators of the development and prevention of violent behavior. *Prevention Science*, *8*, 171–179.

Kimber, B., Sandell, R., & Bremberg, S. (2008). Social and emotional training in Swedish classrooms for the promotion of mental health: Results from an effectiveness study in Sweden. *Health Promotion International*, *23*, 134–143.

Krueger, J., & Clement, R. W. (1994). The truly false consensus effect: An ineradicable and egocentric bias in social perception. *Journal of Personality and Social Psychology*, *67*, 596–610.

Landreth, G. L. (1991). *Play therapy: The art of the relationship*. Muncie, IN: Accelerated Development.

Lane-Garon, P. S. (1998). Developmental considerations: Encouraging perspective taking in student mediators. *Mediation Quarterly*, *16*, 201–217.

Lee, L. A. (1987). Rape prevention: Experiential training for men. *Journal of Counseling and Development*, *66*, 100–101.

Lee, M., & Landreth, G. L. (2003). Filial therapy with immigrant Korean parents in the United States. *International Journal of Play Therapy*, *12*, 67–85.

Long, E. C. J., Angera, J. J., Carter, S. J., Nakamoto, M., & Kalso, M. (1999). Understanding the one you love: A longitudinal assessment of an empathy training program for couples in romantic relationships. *Family Relations*, *48*, 235–242.

Malhotra, D., & Liyanage, S. (2005). Long-term effects of peace workshops in protracted conflicts. *Journal of Conflict Resolution*, *49*, 908–924.

McCullough, M. E., Worthington, E. L., & Rachal, K. C. (1997). Interpersonal forgiving in close relationships. *Journal of Personality and Social Psychology, 73*, 321–336.

Mead, G. H. (1934). *Mind, self, and society: From the standpoint of a social behaviorist* (C. W. Morris, Ed.). Chicago, IL: University of Chicago Press.

Mehrabian, A., & Epstein, N. (1972). A measure of emotional empathy. *Journal of Personality, 40*, 525–543.

Newton, M., Watson, D. L., Gano-Overway, L., Fry, M., Kim, M., & Magyar, M. (2007). The role of a caring-based intervention in a physical activity setting. *The Urban Review, 39*, 281–299.

Pacala, J. T., Boult, C., Bland, C., & O'Brien, J. (1995). Aging game improves medical students caring for elderly. *Gerontology and Geriatrics Education, 15*, 45–57.

Paluck, E. L. (2009). Reducing intergroup prejudice and conflict using the media: A field experiment in Rwanda. *Journal of Personality and Social Psychology, 96*, 574–587.

Pinzone-Glover, H. A., Gidycz, C. A., & Jacobs, C. D. (1998). An acquaintance rape prevention program: Effects on attitudes toward women, rape-related attitudes, and perceptions of rape scenarios. *Psychology of Women Quarterly, 22*, 605–621.

Rau, T. J., Merrill, L. L., McWhorter, S. K., Stander, V. A., Thomsen, C. J., Dyslin, C. W., … Milner, J. S. (2010). Evaluation of a sexual assault education/prevention program for male U.S. Navy personnel. *Military Medicine, 175*, 429–434.

Reilly, J. M., Trial, J., Piver, D. E., & Schaff, P. B. (2012). Using theater to increase empathy training in medical students. *Journal for Learning through the Arts, 8*.

Roter, D. L., Hall, J. A., Kern, D. E., Barker, L. R., Cole, K. A., & Roca, R. P. (1995). Improving physicians' interviewing skills and reduction in patients' emotional distress: A randomized clinical trial. *Archives of Internal Medicine, 155*, 1877–1884.

Sanson-Fisher, R. W., & Poole, A. D. (1978). Training medical students to empathize: An experimental study. *Medical Journal of Australia, 1*, 473–476.

Schewe, P. A., & O'Donohue, W. (1993). Sexual abuse prevention with high-risk males: The roles of victim empathy and rape myths. *Violence and Victims, 8*, 339–351.

Schewe, P. A., & O'Donohue, W. (1996). Rape prevention with high-risk males: Short-term outcome of two interventions. *Archives of Sexual Behavior, 25*, 455–471.

Shechtman, Z., & Tanus, H. (2006). Counseling groups for Arab adolescents in an intergroup conflict in Israel: Report of an outcome study. *Peace and Conflict: Journal of Peace Psychology, 12*, 119–137.

Soble, J. R., Spanierman, L. B., & Liao, H. (2011). Effects of a brief video intervention on white university students' racial attitudes. *Journal of Counseling Psychology, 58*, 151–157.

Spencer, H. (1870). *The principles of psychology*. London: Williams and Norgate.

Staub, E., Pearlman, L. A., Gubin, A., & Hagengimana, A. (2005). Healing, reconciliation, forgiving and the prevention of violence after genocide or mass killing: An intervention and its experimental evaluation in Rwanda. *Journal of Social and Clinical Psychology, 24*, 297–334.

Uhlemann, M. R., Lea, G. W., & Stone, G. L. (1976). Effect of instructions and modeling on trainees low in interpersonal-communication skills. *Journal of Counseling Psychology, 23*, 509–513.

Wilkes, M., Milgrom, E., & Hoffman, J. R. (2002). Toward more empathic medical students: A medical student hospitalization experience. *Medical Education, 36*, 528–533.

Wilson, B. J., Linz, D., Federman, J., Smith, S., Paul, B., Nathanson, A., … Lingsweiler, R. (1999). *The Choices and Consequences evaluation: A study of Court TV's anti-violence curriculum*. Santa Barbara, CA: Center for Communication and Social Policy, University of California.

Wilt, D. L., Evans, G. W., Muenchen, R., & Guegold, G. (1995). Teaching with entertainment films: An empathetic focus. *Journal of Psychosocial Nursing and Mental Health Services*, *33*, 5–14.

Wispé, L. (1986). The distinction between sympathy and empathy: To call forth a concept, a word is needed. *Journal of Personality and Social Psychology*, *50*, 314–321.

Part II

New and Emerging Areas of Intervention

7

Creativity as a Target and Tool for Positive Interventions

Marie J. C. Forgeard and Katherine V. Eichner

One of the most striking differences between humans and other species is the extent to which they deliberately come up with new ideas, behaviors, or things – in other words, their creativity. Accordingly, creativity is generally viewed as one of the main forces driving the advancement of human culture (Gabora, 1997; Mithen, 1998). Creativity is generally defined as the production of novel and useful ideas or products (Sternberg & Lubart, 1999), and "manifest[s] itself in new types of behavior, going beyond mere re-applications of established scripts or action-patterns" (Carruthers, 2002, p. 226). Creativity therefore contributes to an optimally functioning society by, for example, inspiring great works of art, as well as by driving technological and political progress. In addition to its positive societal and historical impact at the macro level, creativity also benefits individuals at the micro level (Simonton, 2002). Creativity is an important asset for professional success (Florida, 2002) and may foster individual traits that are related to well-being such as flexibility, openness, autonomy, and playfulness (Cropley, 1990, 1997).

The phenomenon of creativity can be conceived of as a quality of a process that individuals engage in (Cropley, 1969), or as a character strength – a somewhat stable positive trait manifested to different degrees and at different frequencies by different individuals (Cropley, 1997; Nicholls, 1972). Accordingly, creativity has become a topic of interest for the field of positive psychology, which is concerned with the study of human flourishing and attempts to delineate what individual, situational, and institutional factors allow individuals to thrive (Seligman & Csikszentmihalyi, 2000). Moving beyond the descriptive level, positive psychologists also attempt to harness such factors by building interventions that can effectively enhance people's flourishing. Broadly speaking, positive interventions are "treatment methods or intentional activities that aim to cultivate positive feelings, behaviors, or cognitions" (Sin & Lyubomirsky, 2009, p. 468). Positive interventions therefore aim to build character strengths and promote well-being, as opposed to simply fixing what is deficient or maladaptive. Such

The Wiley Blackwell Handbook of Positive Psychological Interventions, First Edition.
Edited by Acacia C. Parks and Stephen M. Schueller.

interventions foster positive outcomes by cultivating one or more facets of well-being, including positive emotion/pleasure, engagement, relationships/support, meaning/purpose, and accomplishment/competence (Duckworth, Steen, & Seligman, 2005; Forgeard, Jayawickreme, Kern, & Seligman, 2011; Jayawickreme, Forgeard, & Seligman, 2012; Seligman, 2011).

Where does creativity fit in as a target or tool for positive interventions? Creativity is an important psychological strength found in Peterson and Seligman's (2004) classification of character strengths and virtues. Since Guilford's (1950) presidential address to the American Psychological Association, the study of creativity has attracted increasing attention from researchers (Beghetto, Plucker, & MaKinster, 2001). Beyond merely trying to understand the influence of personal, social, or environmental factors, psychologists have proposed ways to enhance creative thinking. As noted by Simonton (2002, p. 197), "practical new methods are needed for enhancing both personal and societal creativity," an intrinsically valuable goal. Beyond increasing creativity for the sake of creativity, researchers have been interested in using it as a tool to enhance other aspects of psychological well-being. The discipline of art therapy, for example, utilizes creative activities to enhance psychological functioning and health, and is generally less concerned with the quality of the creative output than with the creative process itself and the benefits it confers on the well-being of individuals.

The main goal of this chapter is to provide a concise but comprehensive review of the ways in which creativity interventions have been used to promote human flourishing, and the level of empirical support these interventions have garnered. As explained above, two types of creativity-based interventions will be described: interventions in which creativity is the main target (and is seen as an end in itself), and interventions in which creativity is used as a tool to increase other aspects of psychological well-being.[1] In addition, the present chapter will mainly focus on the enhancement of "little-c" creativity (the everyday creativity of ordinary individuals) and "pro-c" creativity (the creativity of professionals), as much of the research on creativity interventions has occurred in these areas. Less research has looked directly at explicitly enhancing "Big-C" creativity (the extraordinary creativity displayed by eminent individuals) (Kaufman & Beghetto, 2009). We however agree with Simonton (2002, p. 197) that "to become full participants in the positive psychology movement, researchers ultimately must produce real improvements in both everyday and genius-grade manifestations of creativity." This chapter concludes by making suggestions and highlighting directions for future research on creativity-based positive interventions.

Creativity as a Target for Positive Interventions

The intrinsic value of creativity

Many researchers are interested in enhancing creativity for its own sake, not just as a means to another positive outcome. As with other character strengths, creativity is a personal asset that has been intrinsically valued across time and across cultures (Peterson & Seligman, 2004). Creativity, then, "contributes to various fulfillments that constitute the good life, for oneself and for others" (p. 17) and "is morally valued in its own right, even in the absence of obvious beneficial outcomes" (p. 19). In other words, people may want to be creative for the sole purpose of being creative. "Wealth and acclaim may follow in the wake of certain creative acts, but these consequences are probably not why people pursue them in the first place" (p. 96). Indeed, a large body of literature attests to the importance of intrinsic motivation for creativity (Amabile, 1996; Hill & Amabile, 1993). The writer Joyce Carol Oates once described her primary reason for writing in a way that elegantly conveys the intrinsic appeal of engaging in creative behavior: "I write to discover what it is I will have written" (1982, as cited by Amabile, 1996, p. 8).

Approaches to the Enhancement of Creativity

Interventions that aim to increase creativity for its own sake are typically referred to as "creativity-training programs" in the research literature. To date, creativity-training programs have been developed in a wide array of domains and have often (but not always) been the focus of empirical validation efforts. While an exhaustive review of these interventions is beyond the scope of this chapter, it should be highlighted that they present considerable heterogeneity in their content (the techniques learned), their domain-specificity (how generalizable the skills learned become), their length, and their effectiveness (Scott, Leritz, & Mumford, 2004a). Nevertheless, a recent meta-analysis of 70 creativity-training studies found that these programs tend to be effective overall, and that the most effective programs tend to focus on the acquisition of cognitive skills (as opposed to other approaches such as the ones described below) (Scott et al., 2004a; see also Scott, Leritz, & Mumford, 2004b). Creativity was operationalized in these studies using measures of divergent-thinking (the generation of novel ideas), problem-solving, performance, and attitudes/behaviors. Examples of specific methods are provided below in order to illustrate various approaches that may be used to enhance creativity (see also Bull, Montgomery, & Baloche, 1995).

Cognitive/ideational approaches

Cognitive/ideational approaches focus on teaching participants specific thinking techniques in order to help them generate novel ideas. A short intervention developed by Clapham (1997; see also Clapham & Schuster, 1992) helps illustrate what a typical intervention focusing on ideational skills might look like. In Clapham's intervention, participants begin by completing a divergent-thinking task: they are given two minutes to list on a piece of paper as many ideas as they can think of to improve a bathtub. Participants then tally the number of original answers they have come up with. Next, the training phase begins by a group discussion of a proposed definition of creativity as the "recombination of elements which already exist for a useful purpose" (Clapham, 1997, p. 37) (i.e., the notion that creative thinking may occur through associating previously unconnected ideas or things). Finally, participants are introduced to more specific ideational techniques to help them generate additional ideas for the divergent-thinking exercise they completed at the beginning of the session. These techniques include: brainstorming (generating ideas without evaluation), forced relation (integrating something in one's direct environment – for example, while sitting on a chair, thinking of adding a seat to a bathtub), magnification/minimization/rearrangement (changing basic size and organizational features), or cataloging (literally looking through a source of varied information such as a shopping catalog in order to develop ideas one might not otherwise have thought of by staying entirely focused on the task) (for other possible techniques and their empirical support, see Scott et al., 2004a).

Social/motivational approaches

Social/motivational approaches to the enhancement of creativity broadly focus on teaching participants to focus on the right reasons for engaging in creative behavior, and removing social obstacles to creativity. Indeed, social factors such as the provision of rewards or evaluation have been shown to decrease creativity insofar as they decrease intrinsic motivation (for a review, see Amabile, 1996).[2] As a result, Hennessey, Amabile, and colleagues have developed training programs for schoolchildren aimed at preventing the negative effect of potential harmful extrinsic motivators that can rarely be avoided in real-life settings (e.g., business or educational settings). These "immunization programs" (Hennessey, Amabile, & Martinage, 1989; Hennessey & Zbikowski, 1993) teach children how to remain focused on their intrinsic interest for the task at hand, and to cognitively distance themselves from harmful extrinsic motivators. In order to do this, children in the program complete two 20-minute training periods in small groups (3–5 children). During these periods, children begin by watching videotaped segments featuring child actors modeling the importance of intrinsic motivation (for example, in one segment of the training video, the children remark that it is important not to focus too much on grades at school, but instead do their work because it is fun and interesting). Following the videos, children discuss the ideas expressed by the children and talk about their own reasons for doing work (for a description of the procedure, see Hennessey et al., 1989).

Personality approaches

Personality approaches to the enhancement of creativity have been discussed in the literature (Bull et al., 1995) but have not been adequately investigated using empirical tools at this point, perhaps as a result of the notion that personality might be more difficult to change than other determinants of creativity. We include them in this chapter because we believe that they constitute a promising approach to the enhancement of creativity, and will hopefully form the basis for future interventions. Indeed, the personality trait of openness to experience is one of the most reliable and robust predictors of creativity (Feist, 1998; King, McKee, & Broyles, 1996; McCrae, 1987); enhancing this trait would therefore constitute an interesting new approach to enhancing creative thinking. Openness to experience can be defined as one's willingness to engage in novel experiences for their own sake (including aesthetic, emotional, intellectual, and action-oriented experiences, among others) (Costa & McCrae, 1992).

Yet, two recent lines of research suggest that personality may be more amenable to change than previously thought. In a study inspired by Fleeson's Density Distribution approach (Fleeson, 2001, 2012), which proposes that personality traits consist of a person's distribution of trait-relevant behaviors, Fleeson, Malanos, and Achille (2002) found that a short intervention in which participants were asked to act more "bold, talkative, energetic, active, assertive, and adventurous" (p. 1416) succeeded in making them at least temporarily more extraverted. These intriguing findings suggest that it might also be possible to increase individuals' levels of openness to experience by asking them to behave in specific open ways (see Chapter 27). Second, another study found that a training program aimed at enhancing the cognitive abilities of older adults (using training in logical reasoning accompanied by crosswords and Sudoku puzzle practice) was effective at increasing openness to experience (Jackson, Hill, Payne, Roberts, & Stine-Morrow, 2012). These two lines of research suggest that the personality trait of openness to experience may be fostered by the use of simple behavioral and cognitive exercises, which may in turn result in benefits for creativity. As previously mentioned, such an approach to the enhancement of creativity has yet to be tested but represents a promising lead.

Two applied examples in business and education

As most of the research has been conducted in the fields of business and education, we briefly comment on the evidence base supporting creativity-training programs in both fields and provide examples of two popular applied programs utilized in order to enhance creativity (for comprehensive reviews, see Clapham, 2003; Parnes, 1999; Plucker & Runco, 1999).

The importance of creativity in business and education Creative thinking has become an important asset that both employers and teachers wish to cultivate. In the field of business, it is widely agreed that creativity is an essential asset, particularly in the current rapidly changing market (Clapham, 2003; Florida, 2004; Janszen, 2000; Placek, 1988). Creativity forms the basis for innovation: any new invention or advance begins with a creative idea (Puccio & Cabra, 2009). A survey-based study found that 25% of companies with more than 100 employees offered some kind of creativity training for their employees (Solomon, 1990, as cited by Scott et al., 2004a), and many books have been written to help develop creativity for business applications (e.g., de Bono, 1985, 1993, 2008; Henry, 2011; Linkner, 2011). Similarly, creativity is viewed as an important resource to be developed in educational settings. Creativity in the classroom is valued both because it prepares students to have the kinds of innovative problem-solving skills valued in the business world, and also because it develops the capacity to effectively deal with challenges in their daily lives (Hunsaker, 2005).

The evidence base Reviewing the empirical support garnered by creativity-training programs in the fields of business and education is a challenging task given the number and heterogeneity of existing programs. Researchers who have tackled the task of reviewing and integrating results from these literatures have revealed a somewhat imbalanced picture – while education researchers have adequately studied their interventions using empirical tools, little research has been conducted on the effectiveness of creativity-training programs for business settings (Clapham, 2003), in spite of the fact that numerous books and interventions have been developed for practitioners in this field (such as the ones cited above). This has led researchers to question the validity and usefulness of these methods (Sternberg & Lubart, 1999), and given the public the highly problematic impression that "to be a creativity expert, one merely has to profess oneself as such" (Puccio, Firestien, Coyle, & Masucci, 2006, p. 30). In contrast, reviews summarizing the results of empirical tests have concluded that creativity-training programs conducted in schools are generally effective and increase students' scores on outcomes such as divergent-thinking and problem-solving tasks (Meador, Fishkin, & Hoover, 1999; Pyryt, 1999). Next, we provide examples of two programs that have been studied empirically and appear to constitute promising approaches. Since both programs are based on the same theoretical framework, the Creative Problem Solving approach, we begin by reviewing this framework.

The Creative Problem Solving approach The Osborn–Parnes Creative Problem Solving (CPS) approach was developed in the 1950s based on the work of Osborn (an advertising executive who popularized the use of brainstorming) and Parnes (who began investigating this framework using empirical tools) (Parnes, 1999). The CPS model represents one example of a cognitive approach (as defined above) that explicitly delineates basic steps in the creative process. These steps differ slightly according to the particular CPS-based programs that have been developed over the years, but overall include the following three phases: (i) exploring the challenge at hand (by identifying goals, gathering facts and data, and defining a specific problem to be solved); (ii) generating ideas (by finding novel ideas to solve the problem at hand); and (iii) preparing for action (by implementing the solution and putting it into action) (e.g., Basadur, 1994; Miller, Vehar, & Firestien, 2004; Puccio, Murdock, & Mance, 2007; Treffinger, Isaksen, & Dorval, 2000). One of the unique features of the CPS approach is that, at each step of the process, individuals are encouraged to use *both* divergent and convergent thinking strategies – in other words, to generate novel ideas, but also to evaluate and select them carefully (e.g., Puccio & Cabra, 2009; Treffinger et al., 2000).

A review of the literature on the effectiveness of CPS training conducted by Puccio et al. (2006) found 17 studies on the topic, and concluded that CPS-based interventions appear to be effective techniques. Next, we review two interventions based on the CPS model.[3]

Basadur's Simplex program Basadur and colleagues have developed and refined their own version of the Creative Problem Solving approach over the past few decades (Basadur, Graen, & Green, 1982; Runco & Basadur, 1993). The latest iteration of Basadur's intervention is the Simplex program (Basadur, 1994), which addresses three key components of creative thinking. First, clients discuss the *Skills* needed for creative thinking, including imaginative and analytical thinking skills (which can be broadly thought of as divergent- and convergent-thinking skills). Second, clients learn about the *Process* of creative thinking, in the form of a three-phase sequence similar to the one described above. Third, clients are introduced to the notion of a creative *Profile*, which helps them recognize what their specific strengths are. Four strengths or profiles are discussed: (i) *Generators* are adept at recognizing opportunities and coming up with original ideas and solutions to problems; (ii) *Conceptualizers* are good at defining problems and deepening their understanding of challenges at hand; (iii) *Optimizers* think about how to put ideas into practice and get them to work in real-life settings; finally, (iv) *Implementers* put ideas into action and ensure that solutions are accepted by others. In the Simplex framework, all four profiles or strengths are present to varying degrees within all individuals, but one of the interesting aspects of this program is its capacity to recognize and take advantage of individual differences in abilities

Destination ImagiNation Destination ImagiNation (DI) is a competitive educational program aimed at enhancing the creative thinking skills of children, teenagers, and young adults (Destination ImagiNation, 2012). In this program, teams of students solve open-ended challenges and present solutions at yearly tournaments. DI involves approximately 125,000 participants every year. Teams solve two types of challenges: Central and Instant Challenges. Central Challenges are season-long projects. Each team picks one of the challenges proposed in one of the following areas: Community Service, Technical/Mechanical Design, Scientific Exploration, Theater/Literature/Arts, Improvisation, or Structural/Architectural Design. In contrast, Instant Challenges are 5–7-minute challenges in which participants are asked to think on their feet and produce a solution to a previously unknown problem.

In the DI program, participants first form teams of up to seven members (sometimes around previously organized groups such as girl/boy scouts), and then pick a Team Manager (usually a parent or teacher) in charge of facilitating the process. Next, teams participate in icebreaking and team-building activities to learn about each other and increase team cohesiveness. Third, teams select the Central Challenge they wish to work on for the length of the season and learn CPS skills (such as the steps detailed above, using training materials provided by the DI program) and apply them to the challenge at hand. Participants also use CPS skills to practice solving Instant Challenges. Finally, participants present their solutions to Central Challenges and solve Instant Challenges on the spot in front of live audiences and evaluators (in charge of judging solutions) at local tournaments. Teams with the best projects advance to state, country, and global finals. Initial evaluations of the DI program have shown that participants are satisfied with the programs, and outperform control groups (comparable students not participating in the DI program) on multiple creative thinking tasks (Callahan, Hertberg-Davis, & Missett, 2011; Treffinger, Selby, & Schoonover, 2004). Additional research is needed, ideally using longitudinal designs and random assignment, in order to provide further support for the DI program.

Conclusions The past decades of research on creativity training have evidenced promising approaches and programs to enhance the creativity of individuals. More research is, however, needed to provide further support for existing programs, to investigate the generality of the benefits of such programs, and to better understand the mechanisms through which they work. In parallel to these creativity-training programs that specifically target creativity as an end in itself, other interventions have focused on creativity, but this time as a tool for another end – psychological well-being.

Creativity as a Tool for Increasing Well-Being

Researchers have highlighted the numerous potential benefits that creative activities have for well-being, beyond their intrinsic value (Cropley, 1990, 1997; Richards, 2010). Csikszentmihalyi commented that although

> personal creativity may not lead to fame and fortune, it can do something that from the individual's point of view is even more important: make day-to-day experiences more vivid, more enjoyable, and more rewarding. When we live creatively, boredom is banished and every moment holds the possibility of a fresh discovery. (1996, p. 344)

Given their reported benefits, creative activities have been used to increase well-being. The main intervention technique promoting this approach has been art therapy (Malchiodi, 2003). The American Art Therapy Association (AATA) defines art therapy as

> [the use of] the creative process of art making to improve and enhance the physical, mental and emotional well-being of individuals of all ages. It is based on the belief that the creative process involved in artistic self-expression helps people to resolve conflicts and problems, develop interpersonal skills, manage behavior, reduce stress, increase self-esteem and self-awareness, and achieve insight. (American Art Therapy Association, 2011, para. 7)[4]

As a result of growing interest in the discipline, research supporting the benefits of art therapy has started to accumulate. Although art therapy researchers have traditionally preferred qualitative methods (McNiff, 1998), results of quantitative studies including randomized controlled trials (RCTs) are now available, and many call for the development of both kinds of evidence to support the efficacy and effectiveness of art therapy (Kaplan, 2000). Recent reviews have found a total of 17 quantitative studies (including 5 RCTs) published before 1999 (Reynolds, Nabors, & Quinlan, 2000) and 28 studies (including 11 RCTs) published between 1999 and 2007 (Slayton, D'Archer, & Kaplan, 2010). Results were encouraging, as most of the studies reviewed showed some positive effect of art therapy on well-being outcomes.

In a typical art therapy session, an art therapist works collaboratively with a client on a work of art designed to directly or indirectly address issues and themes of concern. Art-making is used both as a tool to explore and understand the issues at hand, as well as to heal. The specific medium used may depend on the art therapist's experience and background, as well as the preferences of the client. In addition, the nature of interactions between therapist and client vary according to the therapist's orientation and practice. Different schools of art therapy have different theories with regard to how art therapy works, and these theories influence how the process unfolds. One school of thought for example proposes that art therapy works by acting as "an adjunct to psychotherapy, facilitating the process through both image making and verbal exchange with the therapist" (Case & Dalley, 1992, p. 2). Art, in this view, is another way for the therapist to understand the patient and for the patient to communicate with the therapist; it is the creative product (the artwork), and not the process, that allows the therapist to facilitate psychological healing. Alternatively, another group of practitioners believe that art therapy is valuable because of "the healing power of the creative process" and often refer to art therapy as "art as therapy" rather than as "art psychotherapy" (Rubin, 2009, p. 25). The majority of art therapists today seem to accept both positions and utilize both art and therapy in their work (St John, 2006; Ulman, 2001).

Some studies have tested mechanisms for the effect of art therapy on well-being. For example, it has been suggested that creating art might reduce the stress response and pain (Anand & Anand, 1997; DeLue, 1999; Gabriels, 1999; Hiltebrand, 1999; Lusebrink, 1990), allow children to repair deficits in attachment with their parents (Riley, 2001), and allow individuals to make meaning of past adverse experiences (Pennebaker, 1997; Zausner, 2007). In addition to these mechanisms, a few laboratory-based empirical studies have tested how creative art-making may affect mood, an important component of psychological well-being. In an experimental study in which adult participants were asked to either view or create art, Bell and Robbins (2007) found that generating a work of art led to significantly larger reductions in both negative mood and anxiety compared with viewing art. In addition, in an experimental study conducted by Petrillo and Winner (2005) in which participants were exposed to tragic images (which provoked negative mood), participants who were subsequently asked to draw a picture based on how they were feeling saw their mood improve significantly more than participants who were simply asked to copy shapes. Thus, the creative act of inventing a picture (using one's feelings as inspiration) appeared to have mood-enhancing properties superior to the simple visual-motor act of tracing lines on paper. In a subsequent study, Petrillo and Winner asked participants to complete word puzzles in order to compare this condition to the creative drawing condition. Results showed that word puzzles also did not enhance mood as much as drawing creatively. A simple distraction therefore did not improve mood as much as a creative activity that allowed participants to express feelings and construct meaning, suggesting that this function may constitute one of the active therapeutic ingredients of creative art-making. Other studies refined these results. Dalebroux, Goldstein, and Winner (2008) for example found that, subsequent to a negative mood induction, expressing positive emotion through drawing improved mood significantly more than expressing negative emotion through drawing (venting). Drake, Coleman, and Winner (2011) found similar results by asking a group of participants to complete either a drawing or a writing task (both creative activities) after a negative mood induction. Results showed that drawing was more effective at improving mood than writing. In addition, participants who reported using the creative activity to distract themselves saw their mood improve more than participants who reported using the creative activity to vent their feelings (at least in the short term).

Taken together, these findings suggest that engaging in creative activities has the potential to improve mood. An important limitation to this conclusion is that the current body of research is limited to artistic creative activities, and it remains unclear whether other kinds of creative involvement (e.g., creative problem-solving) would also have this effect. In addition, the research reviewed examined the short-term mood-enhancing properties of art-making after negative mood inductions. Whether creative activities can also bring people from a neutral to a positive state (rather than from a negative to a neutral state) is a question that has therefore not yet been empirically addressed. More research is called for in order to determine whether creative activities can increase a neutral or even already positive mood, and whether these effects might be sustained over a long period. In addition, more research is needed to continue to examine which creative strategies work best (e.g., venting, meaning-making, distraction, etc.), for whom, and under which circumstances. Also, most of the research so far has focused on exploring the positive affect and sense of meaning resulting from creative activities. Additional empirical work could investigate whether and how creative activities affect other components of well-being such as a sense of engagement, competence, agency, and accomplishment.

Although art therapy has provided convincing evidence that engaging in creative activities improves well-being, it does not quite fit the definition of a positive intervention, insofar as its main focus has been to heal pathology. More work is needed to evaluate the effect of art therapy on positive outcomes.

Nevertheless, the philosophy underlying art therapy is that of a positive intervention, as art therapists seek to both heal pathology and increase well-being by using the creative strength of individuals. Indeed, "the arts therapies [...] build on the positive attributes of patients, assuming that all can be creative at some level" (Waller, 2002, p. 2). One promising area of art therapy research is geriatric art therapy, as it already "tend[s] to focus on quality of life improvement rather than on therapeutic change" (Ravid-Horesh, 2004). Making art may allow older adults to feel a sense of achievement and an increase in self-esteem (Hubalek, 1997), encourage socialization and connection (Harlan, 1991; Rusted, Sheppard, & Waller, 2006; Wald, 2003), and help elderly people acquire adaptability skills (Wadeson, 2000). In a qualitative study, older adults participating in an arts exhibition reported that creative activities allowed them to age successfully by fostering a sense of purpose, competence, and growth (Fisher & Specht, 1999).

Current interventions using creative activities as a tool to improve psychological well-being have provided an important empirical base and laid the groundwork for the invention of additional creativity-based positive interventions. What then, aside from art therapy, could be done to harness the potential of creative activities in order to enhance the well-being of individuals?

Building Creativity-Based Positive Interventions

In addition to future directions for research on creativity training and art therapy discussed above, new positive interventions can be developed to use creative activities as a tool for enhancing well-being. These new interventions can draw on the work of other researchers who have built short, empirically validated interventions to cultivate character strengths other than creativity (e.g., gratitude, mindfulness, kindness, etc.) (Seligman, Steen, Park, & Peterson, 2005; for a review see Sin & Lyubomirsky, 2009). These interventions typically ask participants to engage in a brief, simple activity (or exercise) over the length of a week, and participants are often asked to report back on the benefits they have perceived. One interesting approach might be to inject a creative component into already existing interventions, to see if their effect can be amplified or supplemented (for example, a creativity component may add a sense of competence to an activity that previously mainly acted on positive emotion). For example, the Gratitude Visit exercise (as described in Seligman, 2002; Seligman et al., 2005) asks participants to write and deliver a letter expressing their gratitude for a person they had never properly thanked. This already powerful activity could perhaps become meaningful in new ways if participants were invited to write and deliver their message in another creative form (e.g., a poem, a painting, etc.). Aside from adding a creative component to validated positive interventions, new exercises can be invented on the model of existing short-term positive interventions, and an example in this area is outlined next.

An example of a positive intervention – exploring your creative potential

In a pilot investigation, the first author (Forgeard, 2012) asked a group of 96 undergraduate students to complete a creativity exercise as part of a positive psychology course. Students were asked to take a creative photograph (a medium available to most students, and that did not require extensive training). Students were also asked to write a one-page paper describing what their creative process was like, what their own personal definition of creativity was, and what it felt like for them to be creative. Students then attended a one-hour small group discussion of this assignment. Discussion groups were also assigned to one of two experimental conditions: in half of the groups, students displayed their creative photographs for others; in the other groups, photographs were not shown. Essays written by students provided clues regarding the ways in which a creative activity may affect well-being. One of the students described the emotions he felt after taking his creative photograph as follows:

> Even though it kind of just happened, I could tell that I felt a great sense of joy when I was first inspired to take the picture. It was one of those "eureka!" moments when someone is suddenly hit with a great idea or an elusive solution to a problem.

Essays written by students also suggested that their enjoyment of the activity (and, conversely, their anxiety about the activity) may have been linked to whether they perceived themselves as creative in the first place. This observation highlighted the need for interventions specifically aimed at developing one's perceived creative potential (small group discussions appeared to be helpful in this regard). In addition, results showed that students who displayed their photographs for their peers took more creative photographs (as rated by a panel of judges) and experienced larger increases in positive affect during the small group discussions than students who did not display their creative photographs. This suggests that sharing one's creative output with a supportive audience may constitute one way to amplify the positive consequences of participating in a creative activity. This class assignment therefore illustrated how a short-term creative activity may be used to foster well-being. More research is needed to refine instructions, explore different creative media, and examine the effectiveness of such creativity exercises.

Conclusion

This chapter has reviewed the existing literature on the use of interventions that aim to increase creativity, or that use creativity in order to increase well-being. It has highlighted the existence of at least three bodies of research. First, empirical work on creativity-training programs in business and educational settings has evidenced that creativity, seen as a valuable end in itself, can be enhanced. Second, scholarship on art therapy suggests that creative activities can be used to heal psychopathology and enhance well-being. More research is needed to continue building the evidence base supporting the effectiveness of creativity-training programs and creative art therapies, and investigate which kinds of interventions work best, and for whom. Third, research on short-term positive interventions suggests that the time is ripe for the creation and validation of interventions that use targeted creative exercises to enhance various facets of well-being such as positive emotion and a personal sense of competence (among others). Indeed, it is the creativity of researchers that is now needed to develop, test, validate, and disseminate such exercises. The potential of interventions using creativity as a tool to enhance well-being is evidenced by the following comment written by a student who participated in the photography exercise described above:

> It is such a joy to see something that is yours and yours alone develop from mind to fruition. The joy I feel comes from the satisfaction that I made this how I wanted it to be and it is just as I have imagined it.

Acknowledgments

This publication was made possible through the support of a grant from the John Templeton Foundation. The opinions expressed in this publication are those of the authors and do not necessarily reflect the views of the John Templeton Foundation. Additional funding for this project was generously provided by Eva Kedar, PhD.

We would also like to thank Eranda Jayawickreme for providing comments on an earlier version of this chapter, as well as Stephen Schueller and Eli Tsukayama for advice on ideas discussed in this chapter.

Notes

1 Only creativity interventions that actively ask participants to create something novel and useful will be reviewed here; interventions that make use of outside creative works in order to increase well-being (but do not ask that participants be actively involved in creating) are not included (e.g., exposing people to great symphonies or works of art) (e.g., Ulman, 2001).

2 It should be noted that extrinsic motivators that do not decrease intrinsic motivation do not harm creativity; in addition, certain extrinsic motivators that boost intrinsic motivation (e.g., support from mentors) can increase creative thinking (Amabile, 1996).

3 While we decided to review these two interventions in this chapter, no value judgment is made regarding their effectiveness in comparison to other interventions not reviewed here, which produce comparable reliable increases in creative thinking in participants.

4 As an exhaustive review of the field of creative arts therapies is beyond the scope of this chapter, we focus on visual art therapy rather than other approaches (e.g. music therapy, drama therapy, or dance therapy), as visual art therapy has received the most research attention to date.

References

Amabile, T. M. (1996). *Creativity in context.* Boulder, CO: Westview Press.

American Art Therapy Association. (2011). *History and background.* Retrieved from http://www.arttherapy.org/aata-history-background.html

Anand, S. A., & Anand, V. K. (1997). Art therapy with laryngectomy patients. *Art Therapy: Journal of the American Art Therapy Association, 14,* 109–117.

Basadur, M. (1994). *Simplex: A flight to creativity.* Buffalo, NY: Creative Education Foundation.

Basadur, M., Graen, G. B., & Green, S. G. (1982). Training in creative problem-solving: Effects on ideation and problem finding and solving in an industrial research organization. *Organizational Behavior and Human Performance, 30,* 41–70.

Beghetto, R. A., Plucker, J. A., & MaKinster, J. G. (2001). Who studies creativity and how do we know? *Creativity Research Journal, 13,* 351–357.

Bell, C. E., & Robbins, S. J. (2007). Effect of art production on negative mood: A randomized, controlled trial. *Art Therapy, 24,* 71–75.

Bull, K. S., Montgomery, D., & Baloche, L. (1995). Teaching creativity at the college level: A synthesis of curricular components perceived as important by instructors. *Creativity Research Journal, 8,* 83–89.

Callahan, C. M., Hertberg-Davis, H., & Missett, T. C. (2011). *Destination ImagiNation program evaluation report.* Charlottesville, VA: University of Virginia Curry School of Education.

Carruthers, P. (2002). Human creativity: Its cognitive basis, its evolution, and its connections with childhood pretence. *British Journal for the Philosophy of Science, 53,* 225–249.

Case, C., & Dalley, T. (1992). *The handbook of art therapy.* New York: Tavistock/Routledge.

Clapham, M. (1997). Ideational skills training: A key element in creativity training programs. *Creativity Research Journal, 10,* 33–44.

Clapham, M. M. (2003). The development of innovative ideas through creativity training. In L. V. Shavininia (Ed.), *International handbook on innovation* (pp. 366–376). Oxford: Elsevier Science.

Clapham, M. M., & Schuster, D. H. (1992). Can engineering students be trained to think more creatively? *Journal of Creative Behavior, 26,* 156–162.

Costa, P. T., & McCrae, R. R. (1992). *Revised NEO Personality Inventory and NEO Five Factor Inventory, professional manual.* Odessa, FL: Psychological Assessment Resources.

Cropley, A. J. (1969). Creativity, intelligence, and intellectual style. *Australian Journal of Education, 13,* 3–7.

Cropley, A. J. (1990). Creativity and mental health. *Creativity Research Journal, 3,* 167–178.

Cropley, A. J. (1997) Creativity and mental health in everyday life. In M. A. Runco & R. Richards (Eds.), *Eminent creativity, everyday creativity, and health.* Greenwich, CT: Ablex Publishing Corporation.

Csikszentmihalyi, M. (1996). *Creativity: Flow and the psychology of discovery and invention.* New York: HarperCollins.

Dalebroux, A., Goldstein, T. R., & Winner, E. (2008). Short-term mood repair through art-making: Positive emotion is more effective than venting. *Motivation and Emotion, 32,* 288–295.

de Bono, E. (1985). *Six thinking hats.* Boston, MA: Little, Brown, & Company.

de Bono, E. (1993). *Serious creativity: Using the power of lateral thinking to create new ideas.* New York: HarperCollins.

de Bono, E. (2008). *Creativity workout: 62 exercises to unlock your most creative ideas.* Berkeley, CA: Ulysses Press.

DeLue, C. H. (1999). Physiological effects of creating mandalas. In C. A. Malchiodi (Ed.), *Medical art therapy with children* (pp. 33–50). London: Jessica Kingsley Publishers.

Destination ImagiNation (2012). *Destination ImagiNation – A closer look.* Retrieved from http://www.idodi.org/index.php/a-closer-look

Drake, J. E., Coleman, K., & Winner, E. (2011). Short-term mood repair through art: Effects of medium and strategy. *Art Therapy: Journal of the American Art Therapy Association, 28*, 26–30.

Duckworth, A., Steen, T. A., & Seligman, M. E. P. (2005). Positive psychology in clinical practice. *Annual Review of Clinical Psychology, 1*, 629–651.

Feist, G. J. (1998). A meta-analysis of personality in scientific and artistic creativity. *Personality and Social Psychology Review, 2*, 290–309.

Fisher, B. J., & Specht, D. K. (1999). Successful aging and creativity in later life. *Journal of Aging Studies, 13*, 457–472.

Fleeson, W. (2001). Towards a structure- and process-integrated view of personality: Traits as density distributions of states. *Journal of Personality and Social Psychology, 80*, 1011–1027.

Fleeson, W. (2012). Perspectives on the person: Rapid growth and opportunities for integration. In K. Deaux and M. Snyder (Eds.), *The Oxford handbook of personality and social psychology* (pp. 33–63). New York: Oxford University Press.

Fleeson, W., Malanos, A., & Achille, N. (2002). An intra-individual, process approach to the relationship between extraversion and positive affect: Is acting extraverted as "good" as being extraverted? *Journal of Personality and Social Psychology, 83*, 1409–1422.

Florida, R. (2002, May). The rise of the creative class. *Washington Monthly.* Retrieved from http://www.washingtonmonthly.com

Florida, R. (2004). America's looming creativity crisis. *Harvard Business Review, 82*, 122–136.

Forgeard, M. J. C. (2012). The role of positive emotion in the social facilitation of creative behavior. Manuscript in preparation.

Forgeard, M. J. C., Jayawickreme, E., Kern, M. L., & Seligman, M. E. P. (2011). Doing the right thing: Measuring well-being for public policy. *International Journal of Wellbeing, 1*, 79–106.

Gabora, L. (1997). The origin and evolution of culture and creativity. *Journal of Memetics, Evolutionary Models of Information Transmission, 1.* Retrieved from http://cogprints.org/794/1/oecc.html

Gabriels, R. L. (1999). Treating children who have asthma: A creative approach. In C. A. Malchiodi (Ed.), *Medical art therapy with children* (pp. 95–112), London: Jessica Kingsley Publishers.

Guilford, J. P. (1950). Creativity. *American Psychologist, 5*, 444–454.

Harlan, J. E. (1991). The use of art therapy for older adults with developmental disabilities. In M. J. Keller (Ed.), *Activities with developmentally disabled elderly and older adults* (pp. 67–79). New York: Haworth Press.

Hennessey, B. A., Amabile, T. M., & Martinage, M. (1989). Immunizing children against the negative effects of reward. *Contemporary Educational Psychology, 14*, 212–227.

Hennessey, B. A., & Zbikowski, S. M. (1993). Immunizing children against the negative effects of reward: A further examination of intrinsic motivation training techniques. *Creativity Research Journal, 6*, 297–307.

Henry, T. (2011). *The accidental creative: How to be brilliant at a moment's notice.* New York: Portfolio Penguin.

Hill, K. G., & Amabile, T. M. (1993). A social psychological perspective on creativity: Intrinsic motivation and creativity in the classroom and workplace. In S. G. Isaksen, M. C. Murdock, R. L. Firestien, & D. J. Treffinger (Eds.), *Understanding and recognizing creativity: The emergence of a discipline*. Westport, CT: Ablex Publishing.

Hiltebrand, E. (1999). Coping with cancer through image manipulation: A creative approach. In C. A. Malchiodi (Ed.), *Medical art therapy with children* (pp. 113–135), London: Jessica Kingsley Publishers.

Hubalek, S. K. (1997). *I can't draw a straight line: Bringing art into the lives of older adults*. Baltimore, MD: Health Professions Press.

Hunsaker, S. L. (2005). Outcomes of creativity training programs. *Gifted Child Quarterly*, *49*, 292–299.

Jackson, J. J., Hill, P. L., Payne, B. R., Roberts, B. W., & Stine-Morrow, E. A. L. (2012). Can an old dog learn (and want to experience) new tricks? Cognitive training increases openness to experience in older adults. *Psychology and Aging*, *27*, 286–292.

Janszen, F. (2000). *The age of innovation: Making business creativity a competence, not a coincidence*. London: Pearson Education.

Jayawickreme, E., Forgeard, M. J. C., & Seligman, M. E. P. (2012). The engine of well-being. *Review of General Psychology*, *16*(4), 327–342.

Kaplan, F. (2000). *Art, science and art therapy: Repainting the picture*. London: Jessica Kingsley Publishers.

Kaufman, J. C., & Beghetto, R. A. (2009). Beyond big and little: The four c model of creativity. *Review of General Psychology*, *13*, 1–12.

King, L. A., McKee, L. W., & Broyles, S. J. (1996). Creativity and the five-factor model. *Journal of Research in Personality*, *30*, 189–203.

Linkner, J. (2011). *Disciplined dreaming: A proven system to drive breakthrough creativity*. San Francisco, CA: Jossey-Bass.

Lusebrink, V. B. (1990). *Imagery and visual expression in therapy*. New York: Plenum Press.

Malchiodi, C. A. (Ed.) (2003). *Handbook of art therapy*. New York: Guilford Press.

McCrae, R. R. (1987). Creativity, divergent thinking, and openness to experience. *Journal of Personality and Social Psychology*, *52*, 1258–1265.

McNiff, S. (1998). *Art-based research*. London: Jessica Kingsley Publishers.

Meador, K. S., Fishkin, A. S., & Hoover, M. (1999). Research-based strategies and programs to facilitate creativity. In A. S. Fishkin, B. Crammond, & P. Olszewski-Kubilius (Eds.), *Investigating creativity in youth: Research and methods* (pp. 389–415). Cresskill, NJ: Hampton Press.

Miller, B. J., Vehar, J. R., & Firestien, R. F. (2004). *Creativity unbound: An introduction to the creative process* (4th ed.). Evanston, IL: THinc Communications.

Mithen, S. (1998). *Creativity in human evolution and history*. London: Routledge.

Nicholls, J. G. (1972). Creativity in the person who will never produce anything original and useful: The concept of creativity as a normally distributed trait. *American Psychologist*, *27*, 717–727.

Oates, J. C. (1982, July 11). Stories that define me. *New York Times Book Review*.

Parnes, S. J. (1999). Programs and courses in creativity. In S. R. Pritzker (Ed.), *Encyclopedia of creativity* (Vol. 2, pp. 465–478). San Diego, CA: Academic Press.

Pennebaker, J. W. (1997). Writing about emotional experiences as a therapeutic process. *Psychological Science*, *8*, 162–166.

Peterson, C., & Seligman, M. E. P. (2004). *Character strengths and virtues: A handbook and classification*. Washington, DC: American Psychological Association.

Petrillo, L., & Winner, E. (2005). Does art improve mood? A test of a key assumption underlying art therapy. *Art Therapy*, *22*, 205–212.

Placek, D. (1988, January 18). Common sense, experience, are not enough; It's time to get creative. *Marketing News*, *22*, 7.

Plucker, J. A., & Runco, M. A. (1999). Enhancement of creativity. In S. R. Pritzker (Ed.), *Encyclopedia of creativity* (Vol. 1, pp. 669–675). San Diego, CA: Academic Press.

Puccio, G., & Cabra, J. (2009). Creative problem solving: Past, present and future. In T. Rickards, M. A. Runco, & S. Moger (Eds.), *The Routledge companion to creativity* (pp. 327–337). New York: Routledge.

Puccio, G., Firestien, R. L., Coyle, C., & Masucci, C. (2006). A review of the effectiveness of CPS training: A focus on workplace issues. *Creativity and Innovation Management*, *15*, 19–33.

Puccio, G. J., Murdock, M. C., & Mance, M. (2007). *Creative leadership: Skills that drive change*. Thousand Oaks, CA: Sage.

Pyryt, M. C. (1999). Effectiveness of training children's divergent thinking: A meta-analytic review. In S. Fishkin, B. Cramond, & P. Olszewski-Kubilius (Eds.), *Investigating creativity in youth: Research and methods* (pp. 351–365). Cresskill, NJ: Hampton Press.

Ravid-Horesh, R. H. (2004). A temporary guest: The use of art therapy in life review with an elderly woman. *The Arts in Psychotherapy*, *31*, 303–319.

Reynolds, M. W., Nabors, L., & Quinlan, A. (2000). The effectiveness of art therapy: Does it work? *Art Therapy: Journal of the American Art Therapy Association*, *17*, 207–213.

Richards, R. (2010). Everyday creativity: Process and way of life – Four key issues. In J. C. Kaufman & R. J. Sternberg (Eds.), *The Cambridge handbook of creativity* (pp. 180–215). New York: Cambridge University Press.

Riley, S. (2001). *Group process made visible: Group art therapy*. Philadelphia, PA: Brunner-Routledge.

Rubin, J. A. (2009). *Introduction to art therapy: Sources and resources*. New York: Brunner-Routledge.

Runco, M. A., & Basadur, M. (1993). Assessing ideational and evaluative skills and creative styles and attitudes. *Creativity and Innovation Management*, *2*, 166–173.

Rusted, J., Sheppard, L., & Waller, D. (2006). A multi-centre randomized control group trial on the use of art therapy for older people with dementia. *Group Analysis*, *39*, 517–536.

Scott, G., Leritz, L. E., & Mumford, M. D. (2004a). The effectiveness of creativity training: A quantitative review. *Creativity Research Journal*, *16*, 361–388.

Scott, G., Leritz, L. E., & Mumford, M. D. (2004b). Types of creativity training: Approaches and their effectiveness. *Journal of Creative Behavior*, *38*, 149–179.

Seligman, M. E. P. (2002). *Authentic happiness: Using the new positive psychology to realize your potential for lasting fulfillment*. New York: Free Press.

Seligman, M. E. P. (2011). *Flourish: A visionary new understanding of happiness and well-being*. New York: Free Press.

Seligman, M. E. P., & Csikszentmihalyi, M. (2000). Positive psychology: An introduction. *American Psychologist*, *55*, 5–14.

Seligman, M. E. P., Steen, T. A., Park, N., & Peterson, C. (2005). Positive psychology progress: Empirical validation of interventions. *American Psychologist*, *60*, 410–421.

Simonton, D. K. (2002). Creativity. In C. R. Snyder & S. J. Lopez (Eds.), *Handbook of positive psychology* (pp. 189–201). New York: Oxford University Press.

Sin, N. L., & Lyubomirsky, S. (2009). Enhancing well-being and alleviating depressive symptoms with positive psychology interventions: A practice-friendly meta-analysis. *Journal of Clinical Psychology: In Session*, *65*, 467–487.

Slayton, S., D'Archer, J., & Kaplan, F. (2010). Outcome studies on the efficacy of art therapy: A review of findings. *Art Therapy: Journal of the American Art Therapy Association*, *27*, 108–118.

Solomon, C. M. (1990). Creativity training. *Personnel Journal*, *69*, 64–71.

Sternberg, R. J., & Lubart, T. I. (1999). The concept of creativity: Prospects and paradigms. In R. J. Sternberg (Ed.), *Handbook of creativity* (pp. 3–15). Cambridge: Cambridge University Press.

St John, P. (2006). A short history of art therapy practice in the United States. In S. Brooke (Ed.), *Creative arts therapies manual* (pp. 3–20). Springfield, IL: Charles C. Thomas.

Treffinger, D. J., Isaksen, S. G., & Dorval, K. B. (2000). *Creative problem solving: An introduction* (3rd ed.). Waco, TX: Prufrock Press.

Treffinger, D. J., Selby, E. C., & Schoonover, P. F. (2004). *Destination ImagiNation program evaluation – Phase I report*. Sarasota, FL: Center for Creative Learning.

Ulman, E. (2001). Variations on a Freudian theme. In J. A. Rubin (Ed.), *Approaches to art therapy: Theory and technique* (2nd ed., pp. 289–305). Philadelphia, PA: Brunner-Routledge.

Wadeson, H. (2000). *Art therapy practice: Innovative approaches with diverse populations*. New York: John Wiley & Sons.

Wald, J. (2003). Clinical art therapy with older adults. In C. A. Malchiodi (Ed.), *Handbook of art therapy* (pp. 294–308). New York: Guilford Press.

Waller, D. (2002). *Arts therapies and progressive illness: Nameless dread*. New York: Brunner-Routledge.

Zausner, T. (2007). *When walls become doorways: Creativity and the transforming illness*. New York: Harmony Books.

8

Do Good Things Come to Those Who Wait?

Patience Interventions to Improve Well-Being

Sarah A. Schnitker and Justin T. Westbrook

Patience, defined as the propensity to wait calmly in the face of frustration, adversity, or suffering, is a character strength just beginning to receive substantial psychological inquiry. Initial evidence supports that interventions intending to increase patience also lead to increases in well-being, pointing to favorable prospects of adding patience to the repertoire of positive psychological interventions. Historical perspectives on patience, definition and discrimination of the virtue, and a review of empirically tested patience interventions will be discussed. In addition, future directions in patience interventions research and possible applications of interventions will be proposed.

Historical Perspectives on the Virtue of Patience

Patience has long been considered a crucial component of the virtuous life. Moral philosophers and religious scholars across time and cultures have discussed the ways in which patience promotes attainment of the "good life" and eudaimonia. Religious writings extolling the importance of patience can be found in the sacred texts of Judaism (e.g., Proverbs 14:29), Christianity (e.g., Galatians 5:22), Islam (e.g., Qur'an 11:115), Buddhism (Gyatso, 1991, p. 101)), and Hinduism (e.g., Code of Manu 4:246). Ancient philosophers and writers, from both the East and West, support the importance of patience. Taoist philosopher Lao-tzu stated, "I have just three things to teach: simplicity, patience, and compassion. These three are your greatest treasures" (Lao-tzu, *Tao Te Ching*), and Horace penned, "Patience makes lighter/What sorrow may not heal" (Horace, *Carmina* 1.24).

Harned (1997), however, notes that Western moral philosophy and theology have lost their emphasis on patience since the industrial revolution. In many ways,

The Wiley Blackwell Handbook of Positive Psychological Interventions, First Edition.
Edited by Acacia C. Parks and Stephen M. Schueller.

patience has come to be viewed in Western culture as a concession to society's failures to control the environment through technology, or "an unimaginative failure of nerve" (p. 3), rather than a highly desirable trait. Is it any surprise, then, that Western psychology has taken so long to begin studying patience? In the twentieth century, only Mehrabian (1999) empirically studied patience from a psychological perspective and created a short measure of it. This lack of interest in patience on the part of both theorists and empiricists is disheartening, particularly in light of the potential personal and societal benefits of patience.

Character ethicist Stanley Hauerwas defines patience as "facing life's limits in an optimistic culture that tells us we can overcome all limits" (Stassen & Gushee, 2003, p. 53). Though technological advances have vastly increased modern humans' control over their environment, technology has its limitations and creates its own frustrations (e.g., traffic congestion). Patience becomes an even more important trait in modern times as people's exceedingly high expectations for convenience are continually violated. Harned (1997) pushes this argument a step further and says waiting is not accidental to human lives; if humans are to interact in reciprocal relationships, then waiting is inherent to lived social experience. Constant, active agency is not equivalent to humanness. There is more to being human than constant doing. Perhaps, then, more emphasis should be placed upon patience in positive psychological investigation of virtue.

Defining and Discriminating Patience

The first task in the programmatic study of patience is to define this virtue, yet even the uniqueness of patience in relation to other virtues has been debated. In their classification of virtues and character strengths, Peterson and Seligman (2004) claim that patience is not a separate character strength. Instead, they maintain it is a combination of persistence, open-mindedness, and self-regulation (three strengths from their 24-strength classification). Therefore, they view patience as redundant with other strengths.

Schnitker and Emmons (2007) disagreed and demonstrated patience's distinction (i.e., discriminant validity) from the three proposed constituent strengths, as well as from the entire virtue classification (i.e., the three strengths explain only 4% of the variance in scores on their patience scale, and the whole VIA explains only 26% of the variance in patience scores). This is not to say, however, that patience is completely orthogonal to other virtues. Participants' evaluations of their own patience are positively correlated with Peterson and Seligman's (2004) virtues of temperance (e.g., forgiveness) and justice (e.g., loyalty), and participants' beliefs about the importance of patience positively correlate with the virtues of justice (e.g., fairness) and transcendence (e.g., hope). Schnitker and Emmons (2007) provided evidence that patience adequately meets Peterson and Seligman's virtue criteria. They also demonstrated that patience is not reducible to basic personality, as the Big Five account for only 25% of the variance of the Patience Scale-10

(PS-10; Schnitker & Emmons, 2007) and only 38% of the total patience score on the 3-Factor Patience Scale (3-FPS; Schnitker & Emmons, 2011).

Having established the status of patience as a unique character strength worthy of investigation, how do we understand possible nuances of the virtue? Both moral philosophers and psychologists have suggested that it is a multi-faceted construct. Harned (1997) recognized four interrelated forms of patience, including endurance/suffering, forbearance/tolerance, willingness to wait/expectancy, and perseverance. However, in their initial study of patience, Schnitker and Emmons (2007) created the PS-10 and found that items measuring patience were reducible to two factors: self-evaluation of patience and importance of patience. This seems to fit St Augustine's view that true patience is known only by its cause or internal motivation, revealing outer and inner dimensions of patience (Harned, 1997). Though people tend to think about the outward manifestations of patience (calm and tolerant behavior), it also has an inward, emotional aspect (serene inner states). In fact, this inner component may be the defining feature of the virtue. Gregory the Great wrote that external patient behaviors mean nothing if the person is not also patient internally (Harned, 1997).

Schnitker and Emmons (2011) also maintained that patience has behavioral (external) and emotional (internal) components, but they proposed that the internal state of the individual is the key determinant for marking the presence of patience. Thus, it is the individual person who is best equipped to judge his or her own patience. They found that informants' mean ratings of participants' patience were higher than the participants' mean ratings of their own patience. The authors suggested that the informants could base their assessments solely on the external behaviors of patience, whereas the participants had access to their internal, emotional state to consider in making judgments about their patience. Lacking this internal insight, the informants overestimated the patience of the participants.[1]

In subsequent studies, other distinctions in understanding the virtue of patience have emerged. Schnitker (2010) developed a 3-Factor Patience Scale (3-FPS) comprising the factors of interpersonal, long-term, and short-term patience. The first two factors are more goal-directed in their nature, whereas the third factor represents a more reactive form of patience. Interpersonal patience is distinguished from long-term patience in its focus on patience in relationships with other people, while long-term patience is focused on accomplishing long-term goals or suffering long-term personal hardships. The distinction between interpersonal and long-term patience aligns with Thomas à Kempis' suggestion that patience can be used with others (i.e., interpersonal patience) and with oneself (i.e., intrapersonal patience). The three factors of the 3-FPS are correlated, which fits with Harned's (1997) view that patience is made up of multiple, non-orthogonal facets.

What patience is not

Another essential part of defining patience is defining what it is not. Schnitker and Emmons (2007) argue that patience is not merely self-regulation, in part because patience has an inner, emotional aspect. Therefore, they suggest examining emotion regulation, rather than self-regulation, to better understand patience. Furthermore, patience has moderate correlations with the emotion regulatory strategy of reappraisal (r = .41; Schnitker, 2010) and with Tangney, Baumeister, and Boone's (2004) measure of self-control (r = .38; Schnitker & Emmons, 2007). These correlations indicate that patience is similar to, yet distinct from, self-control and emotion regulation.

Patience is not equivalent to delay of gratification, because delay of gratification involves the choice of whether or not to wait for rewards (Curry, Price, & Price, 2008). In contrast, patience does not always involve a choice of whether or not to wait – the only choice a person may make is deciding how to wait (Schnitker & Emmons, 2007). Moreover, patience is ultimately defined by a person's internal state, whereas delay of gratification is defined by the external behavior of the person.

Philosophers have also argued that patience is not the opposite of impatience. Aristotle claimed that virtues (e.g., patience) are the virtuous mean between the two poles of excess (e.g., recklessness/impatience) and deficiency (e.g., sloth; Rorty, 1980). Perhaps unsurprisingly given psychology's historical emphasis on disorder and dysfunction, psychologists have studied problems of impatience more than the character strength of patience. Though insights may be gleaned from research on impatience (e.g., Type A personality research on impatience-irritability and time urgency; Landy, Rastegary, Thayer, & Colvin, 1991; Spence, Helmreich, & Pred, 1987), patience needs to be considered as a positive construct in contrast to both poles of excess and deficiency.

Patience and Well-Being

The connection between the virtue of patience and well-being has been empirically verified. Patience exerts positive effects on people's lives. Schnitker and Emmons (2007, 2011) found that patience protects against negative affect and increases positive affect in some samples. Patience, as measured by the 3-FPS, is positively correlated with life satisfaction, hope, and self-esteem, and it is negatively correlated with depression and loneliness (Schnitker & Emmons, 2011). Patience is also negatively correlated with depression and health issue occurrences, such as headaches (Schnitker & Emmons, 2007).

Patience has been shown to increase hedonic and eudaimonic well-being by aiding the achievement of goals and affecting the content of goals, respectively. In fact, goal satisfaction completely mediated the effect of patience on well-being (Schnitker & Emmons, 2011). People high in trait patience worked harder on goals in general, and in a longitudinal study, effort exerted on a goal predicted increased patience on that goal over time. This suggests that people use patience as a strategy for successful goal pursuit.

Finally, patience should not be defined as having a dark side, nor should having "too much" patience be construed as a weakness. Patience should not be mistaken for passive resignation, but instead it should be thought of as the demonstration of ego-strength by choosing to actively wait in the face of difficult circumstances. This distinction is supported by the positive correlation between patience and goal effort.

Similarly, patience does not make people doormats that others can walk all over. Instead, Schnitker & Emmons (2011) found that assertiveness had zero correlation with patience, such that having high or low patience was unrelated to assertive behaviors. Moreover, patience moderated the relation between assertiveness and well-being, such that participants high in both patience and assertiveness had the best outcomes, and participants low in assertiveness were buffered from the negative effects of low assertiveness if they were also high in patience.

It may be helpful to conceptualize patience as a character strength akin to Rothbaum, Weisz, and Snyder's (1982) idea of secondary control, where, instead of seeking to change the situation, people exert control by changing themselves to fit the situation. Thus, patient people are not being passive, but are actively adapting to face their circumstances. This may be especially important when people are faced with circumstances that they cannot change, no matter how hard they try. For example, patience may be particularly important in coping with a long-term disability.

Empirically Tested Patience Interventions

To date, only one intervention designed to increase patience and well-being has been developed and empirically tested (Schnitker & Emmons, 2011). In theory, character strengths are malleable and capable of changing (Peterson & Seligman, 2004), and the classification of patience-increasing activities as a positive psychological intervention requires that changes in the character strength also produce changes in well-being.

Schnitker and Emmons (2011) created a patience intervention involving group discussions, individual activities, and guided meditation that they presented to participants as a stress reduction and personality study. Seventy-one participants (61 females) were drawn from a psychology department undergraduate subject pool and ranged in age from 18 to 27 years of age ($M = 20.6$ years, $SD = 1.8$). Participants were primarily Caucasian (40%) and Asian American (34%), though other ethnic minorities were represented (Hispanic 11%, Middle Eastern 7%, African American 3%, other ethnic minority 4%). The intervention began with a 45-minute introduction, which included completion of various measures (e.g., patience, other virtues, personality, and well-being; Time 1). The participants were also randomly placed into the experimental and control groups. The experimental group participated in four sessions (described below) over two weeks, after which they completed all of the measures again via the internet (Time 2). The control group did nothing with the researchers during these two weeks, after which they also completed all of the measures again via the internet (Time 2). One month later, everyone in both the experimental and control groups was sent a link to complete the measures a third time (Time 3).

The experimental intervention was administered to groups of 3–6 participants over four 30-minute sessions. Schnitker and Emmons (2011) developed these sessions by adopting methods and interventions used by other researchers in the meditation, character strengths, Type A personality, cognitive-behavioral therapy, and self-control literatures. The first session consisted of teaching the participants to become aware of both their positive and negative emotions and to recognize what caused and triggered them. The second session consisted of training in emotion regulation, including both preventive and reactionary techniques. The third and fourth sessions consisted of training participants how to cope with stress in interpersonal situations and helping them to have more empathy and compassion for others by reflecting on and reframing (through guiding questions) past experiences. Also, participants were given scenarios and asked to write their usual negative reactions to such situations, followed by writing a positive reframe. For example, participants were given the following scenario –

> You are catching a new release at the movies. The person behind you keeps kicking your chair and chewing her popcorn really loudly. As the movie progresses, she proceeds to answer her phone twice

– and were asked to describe their typical negative response (e.g., "People are so annoying! Can't they understand that I'm trying to watch a movie?"), as well as a reframe of the situation (e.g., "I've probably accidentally kicked the chair in front of me before, so maybe it was an accident").

During all four sessions, 10–15 minutes were used for guided meditation, including breathing and posture techniques. The first two sessions utilized meditation based on replacing negative emotions with positive emotions. The final two sessions utilized loving-kindness meditation (Carson et al., 2005; Fredrickson, Cohn, Coffey, Pek, & Finkel, 2008; Kristeller & Johnson, 2005), which begins with directing positive emotion toward oneself and gradually extending these positive emotions outward to various others. The authors used loving-kindness meditation because of the interpersonal nature of patience.

After the intervention was finished and all of the follow-up measures were completed, Schnitker and Emmons (2011) found significant changes on Time 2 variables as a result of the patience intervention. First, trait interpersonal patience was increased by the patience intervention, controlling for the participants' patience at Time 1. Participation in the intervention also predicted decreased depression and increased positive affect. However, the patience training had no effect on negative affect, life satisfaction, happiness, gratitude, or mindfulness. Though there were no significant effects of the intervention on the emotion regulation strategies of reappraisal and suppression, the effect did approach significance for the reappraisal subscale.

Looking at the results at Time 3, Schnitker and Emmons (2011) did not find statistically significant effects of the intervention. However, this appeared to be a power issue rather than the absence of an effect (the number of participants who completed the Time 3 measures was only N = 42). In fact, many of the non-significant Time 3 effect sizes were similar in magnitude to the effect sizes that were statistically significant at Time 2. For instance, though the effect of the experimental intervention on increased interpersonal patience at Time 3 was not significant, the non-significant beta at Time 3 was actually larger than the significant beta at Time 2. Even more interesting, long-term patience was not significantly changed at Time 2, but it approached significance at Time 3, and the beta was much bigger at Time 3 than it was at Time 2. The authors suggested that this fit their *a priori* hypothesis that the participants would need time to use and notice their newly improved long-term patience before reporting it on the measures.

Thus, Schnitker and Emmons (2011) provided initial evidence that patience can be intentionally increased with an experimental intervention. Moreover, these improvements in patience coincided with improvements in well-being. Though not statistically significant, their results suggest that increases in patience and well-being may be sustainable over time. However, this study should be viewed as the first step toward developing interventions to improve patience. As this was an initial study to test the viability of patience interventions, the authors utilized many different components in their experimental intervention. What is not known is which pieces or combination of pieces (e.g., meditation, cognitive reappraisal training, etc.) have the greatest effect on increasing patience. Moreover, it remains unclear whether the increase in well-being was actually mediated by the increase in patience; though a significant mediating indirect effect for patience was found, other coefficients required to support mediation were not significant. The intervention did not lead to changes in mindfulness or gratitude, which suggests that the intervention was specific to patience, rather than these other character strengths, and that patience was the active mediator for the well-being increase.

Future Directions for Patience Interventions Research

Given the newness of psychological research on the virtue of patience and its well-being correlates, there are countless research questions regarding patience interventions. We outline four areas of inquiry that will best establish rigorous patience interventions based on sound psychological research.

Isolating patience-increasing activities

First, future research studies need to isolate the specific activities that increase patience by separating hypothesized activities into different experimental conditions. Activities from Schnitker and Emmons' (2011) study are prime candidates for these experimental conditions (i.e., loving-kindness meditation, relaxation meditation, positive reframing/reappraisal scenarios, emotion causes and triggers recognition, and teaching emotion regulation techniques could be compared to each other in their ability to increase patience), but other exercises should also be developed and included. For example, participants could be asked to practice patience in a specific life domain, such as driving or parenting, for the duration of the study. Instructions could include specific trigger–action response repertoires that the participant should follow, akin to Gollwitzer's (1999) implementation intentions (e.g., when you get stuck in traffic, practice breathing exercises).

Correspondingly, researchers need to determine which activities particularly increase patience rather than increase character strengths more broadly. For instance, does completing positive reframing scenarios also increase character strengths such as kindness, citizenship, fairness, or self-control? Does loving-kindness meditation increase character strengths such as love, kindness, and forgiveness in addition to patience? If so, mediation analyses or additional control conditions will be needed to isolate the effects of increased patience on well-being.

Improved control conditions for social desirability

Research on patience interventions thus far has relied upon non-treatment control groups. Future studies should utilize more meaningful control conditions to rule out social desirability effects. The evidence thus far does not point to strong social desirability effects or demand characteristics for patience interventions. First, patience is one of the few virtues that it is acceptable to lack in our culture; few people will say, "I am not a loving (or grateful or honest) person" with the same levity that they will say, "I am not a patient person." Second, if demand characteristics were driving the effects of patience interventions, we would expect to observe increased scores on all well-being outcomes equally. Instead, Schnitker and Emmons (2011) found that depression, which is least susceptible to demand characteristics (with non-intuitive items such as "I did not feel like eating; my appetite was poor" and "My sleep was restless"), was alleviated by a patience intervention, whereas life satisfaction and happiness, which are more susceptible to demand characteristics (with transparent items such as "I am satisfied with my life" and "I consider myself a happy person"), did not change as a result of the intervention.

However, it is still possible that demand characteristics could be driving results. Participants may have inferred that the patience training should help lessen their negative emotionality and reflected this in their responses. The inclusion of additional control conditions, such as teaching organization skills or simply tracking daily moods, will further rule out social desirability effects.

Is patience a buffer against negative emotions or a producer of positive emotions?

Patience is dependably related to well-being across studies, but its relation with positive and negative affect is less consistent. Sometimes patience predicts decreased negative emotions (Schnitker & Emmons, 2007), sometimes it predicts increased positive emotions (Study 3: Intervention Study in Schnitker & Emmons, 2011), and sometimes it predicts both increased positive and decreased negative emotions (Studies 1 and 2 in Schnitker & Emmons, 2011). Thus, this presents multiple hypotheses regarding patience in relation to affect.

First, patience can be conceptualized as a buffer against negative emotionality. People high in the virtue of patience may experience fewer negative emotions because their patient disposition prevents the activation of these emotions in frustrating situations and circumstances. Second, patience may be construed as a producer of positive emotionality. Patience may allow people to feel more positive emotions or may directly lead to the activation of certain positive emotions.

It is important to distinguish between low-arousal positive affect (e.g., serene, peaceful, calm) and high-arousal positive affect (e.g., excited, enthusiastic, inspired), as previous research has shown separable effects for the two (e.g., Kessler & Staudinger, 2009). However, low-arousal positive affect has received considerably less attention than high-arousal positive affect in the psychological literature, as evidenced by the dearth of low-arousal positive affect terms in the most widely used measure of affect (Positive and Negative Affect Schedule; Watson, Clark, & Tellegen, 1988). This bias most likely reflects the Western emphasis on high-arousal positivity as the "ideal affect," whereas people from Eastern cultures tend to describe their "ideal affect" as low-arousal positivity (Tsai, Knutson, & Fung, 2006). Care should be taken to avoid this Western bias in the consideration of patience, as the virtue may well be most related to low-arousal positive affect.

Researchers have found that the discrepancy between ideal and actual affect is associated with depression, such that a larger gap between the two predicts increased depression (Tsai et al., 2006). This points to another possible mechanism by which patience interventions may decrease depression: by changing participants' ideal affect. Thus, future research on patience interventions should (a) test if patience buffers against negative emotions, (b) clarify the role of patience in promoting both low- and high-arousal positive emotions, and (c) look for shifts in participants' "ideal affect" resulting from the intervention.

Moving beyond individual well-being: interpersonal outcomes

In addition to accruing benefits for the individual person, patience is hypothesized to improve the relationships and social systems in which a patient person is embedded. Kunz (2002), from the perspective of Levinas' ethics, defines patience as "the uncomplaining endurance of distress," and as "the disposition to suffer as responsible sacrifice ... patience is self-sacrifice inspired in me by others to suffer for their sake" (p. 121). If patient people were willing to suffer for the sake of the other and for the sake of the relationship, we would predict that patience could transform those relationships. We hypothesize that people high in interpersonal patience are able to remain calm and positively (or at least neutrally) engaged with people who are potentially frustrating. This calm demeanor could promote interpersonal interactions such that the relationship itself improves – not just the patient person's sense of individual well-being.

For instance, a wife may notice that her husband has failed to take out the trash (yet again) and decide to confront him about the issue. If she is patient, she will be able to gently remind him he forgot to take out the trash and ask him to remember next time, without getting highly frustrated or angry. Her husband will feel less defensive and will be more likely to comply with her wishes. If she does not enact patience toward her husband, she will become very frustrated or angry, and she will most likely communicate her reminder to take out the trash in a vitriolic and abrasive manner. This will probably initiate a defensive and escalated response from her husband, which promotes a deteriorating cycle of interaction leading to marital dissatisfaction (Gottman, Coan, Carrere, & Swanson, 1998). Over time, the wife's patience, or lack thereof, can change the dynamics of the relationship. Studies could test if a patience intervention could not only increase the wife's well-being and marital satisfaction, but also the marital satisfaction of her spouse. Moreover, if the husband also participated in the intervention, he could learn to react in a non-defensive manner to his wife's complaints. With both parties learning to enact patience in their relationship, the cycle of negativity in conflict could be curtailed.

As another example, consider a teacher who is working with slow-learning students in a classroom. If he is patient, he will be able to explain the lessons clearly and portray the expectation that the students are able to master the material. If he is impatient, his frustration will impair his ability to teach the students. He will either give up trying to explain things to the students, or he will display his frustration to them, conveying an efficacy-reducing message.

Possible Applications of Patience Interventions

Though scientific study pertaining to the virtue of patience and its intervention possibilities is only just beginning, a variety of therapeutic and non-therapeutic applications can be readily envisaged.

One possible application for patience intervention is to use it as an add-on to traditional therapy. Change and personal growth take time, often longer than clients expect. Many times clients withdraw early or fail to complete therapy because their expectations for how long treatment should take do not match the realities of therapeutic interventions (Barrett, Chua, Crits-Christoph, Gibbons, & Thompson, 2008; Beck et al., 1987; Sledge, Moras, Hartley, & Levine, 1991). Current research suggests that a minimum of 11–13 sessions of evidence-based psychotherapy are needed for 50–60% of clients to be considered recovered (Hansen, Lambert, & Forman, 2002; Lambert, 2007), but more than 65% of clients terminate therapy before the tenth session of therapy (Garfield, 1994), with many terminating in 6–8 sessions (Phillips, 1985). It is highly feasible that many clients become frustrated with the slow rate of progress in therapy. By utilizing a brief patience intervention in the therapeutic context, clients may be equipped with a character strength that allows them to become less distressed and frustrated by slow progress, which could enable them to continue the therapeutic process toward full recovery. It is imperative that such an adjunct patience intervention be pithy and powerful. Therapists have many tasks to accomplish early in the therapeutic process, so the intervention must not detract from these essential objectives of treatment.

Patience interventions could also be administered as add-ons to marital or family therapy (administered to one or all individuals involved). Not only could increasing a client's patience improve his or her individual well-being, but it could also increase the functioning of the marriage dyad/family system, improving relationship satisfaction and perhaps decreasing symptomatology. Moreover, the inclusion of a strength-based component to a therapeutic modality that has historically low satisfaction ratings (Seligman, 1995) may activate approach-oriented goals as clients work to build strengths rather than exclusively aim to fix their problems. The activation of approach-oriented goals may increase motivation to engage in the therapeutic process given their excitatory and stimulating nature (Elliott & Dweck, 1988).

A plethora of creative applications of the hypothesized interpersonal benefits of patience interventions can be imagined. Parental enrichment programs could incorporate patience training to improve quality of parenting and parent–child relationships. Schools could offer patience interventions to teachers to improve relational functioning with students, thus improving student performance. Students themselves could also benefit from such training, especially during transitions to high school, college, or graduate school when academic pressures increase and the learning process takes longer than students were accustomed to in their previous schools. Businesses and organizations primarily engaged in customer service could include patience interventions in employee training to facilitate employee well-being and improve service for customers, and patience interventions could facilitate team-building within many businesses. Myriad possibilities abound, so researchers are encouraged to engage in the robust data collection and analysis needed to build a strong empirical and theoretical basis for such potential applications.

Note

1 The authors recognize other possibilities for higher informant scores, such as informants (particularly parents) trying to save face or vicariously improve self-esteem through the participants' possession of this virtue. In addition, the assumption is made that the individual had a more accurate view of his or her own patience, rather than an observer, based on their access to more data. Other measurement modalities (e.g., physiological measurement, emotion expression coding, behavioral measures) are necessary to confirm this increased accuracy.

References

Barrett, M. S., Chua, W. J., Crits-Christoph, P., Gibbons, M. B., & Thompson, D. (2008). Early withdrawal from mental health treatment: Implications for psychotherapy practice. *Psychotherapy: Theory/Research/Practice/Training, 45*, 247–267.

Beck, N. C., Lamberti, J., Gamache, M., Lake, E. A., Fraps, C. L., McReynold, W. T., ... Dunn, J. (1987). Situational factors and behavioral self-prediction in the identification of clients at high risk to drop out of psychotherapy. *Journal of Clinical Psychology, 43*, 511–520.

Carson, J. W., Keefe, F. J., Lynch, T. R., Carson, K. M., Goli, V., Fras, A. M., & Thorp, S. R. (2005). Loving-kindness meditation for chronic low back pain: Results from a pilot trial. *Journal of Holistic Nursing, 23*, 287–304.

Curry, O. S., Price, M. E., & Price, J. G. (2008). Patience is a virtue: Cooperative people have lower discount rates. *Personality and Individual Differences, 44*, 780–785.

Elliott, E. S., & Dweck, C. S. (1988). Goals: An approach to motivation and achievement. *Journal of Personality and Social Psychology, 54*, 5–12.

Fredrickson, B. L., Cohn, M. A., Coffey, K. A., Pek, J., & Finkel, S. M. (2008). Open hearts build lives: Positive emotions, induced through loving-kindness meditation, build consequential personal resources. *Journal of Personality and Social Psychology, 95*, 1045–1062.

Garfield, S. L. (1994). Research on client variables in psychotherapy. In A. E. Bergin & S. L. Garfield (Eds.), *Handbook of psychotherapy and behavior change* (pp. 190–228). New York: Wiley.

Gollwitzer, P. M. (1999). Implementation intentions: Strong effects of simple plans. *American Psychologist, 54*, 493–503.

Gottman, J. M., Coan, J., Carrere, S., & Swanson, C. (1998). Predicting marital happiness and stability from newlywed interactions. *Journal of Marriage and the Family, 60*, 5–22.

Gyatso, T. (1991). *Path to bliss: A practical guide to stages of meditation* (T. Jinpa & G. T. Huboam, Trans., C. Cox, Ed.). Ithaca, NY: Snow Lion Publishers.

Hansen, N. B., Lambert, M. J., & Forman, E. M. (2002). The psychotherapy dose-response effect and its implications for treatment delivery services. *Clinical Psychology: Science and Practice, 9*, 329–343.

Harned, D. B. (1997). *Patience: How we wait upon the world*. Boston, MA: Cowley.

Horace, *Carmina* I, 24, 19.

Kessler, E. V., & Staudinger, U. M. (2009). Affective experience in adulthood and old age: The role of affective arousal and perceived affect regulation. *Psychology and Aging, 24*, 349–362.

Kristeller, J. L., & Johnson, T. (2005). Cultivating loving kindness: A two-stage model of the effects of meditation on empathy, compassion and altruism. *Zygon, 40*, 391–407.

Kunz, G. (2002). Simplicity, humility, patience. In E. E. Gantt & R. N. Williams (Eds.), *Psychology for the other: Levinas, ethics and the practice of psychology* (pp. 118–142). Pittsburgh, PA: Duquesne University Press.

Lambert, M. J. (2007). Presidential address: What we have learned from a decade of research aimed at improving psychotherapy outcome in routine care. *Psychotherapy Research, 17*, 1–14.

Landy, F. J., Rastegary, H., Thayer, J., & Colvin, C. (1991). Time urgency: The construct and its measurement. *Journal of Applied Psychology, 76*, 644–657.

Mehrabian, A. (1999). *Manual for the Revised Achieving Tendency (MACH) and Disciplined Goal Orientation (DGO) scales.* (Available from Albert Mehrabian, 1130 Alta Mesa Road, Monterey, CA 93940.)

Peterson, C., & Seligman, M. E. P. (2004). *Character strengths and virtues: A handbook and classification*. Washington, DC: American Psychological Association.

Phillips, E. L. (1985). *Psychotherapy revised: New frontiers in research and practice*. Hillsdale, NJ: Erlbaum.

Rorty, A. (1980). *Essays on Aristotle's ethics*. Berkeley, CA: University of California Press.

Rothbaum, F., Weisz, J. R., & Snyder, S. S. (1982). Changing the world and changing the self: A two-process model of perceived control. *Journal of Personality and Social Psychology*, *42*, 5–37.

Schnitker, S. A. (2010). *An examination of patience and well-being*. Unpublished doctoral dissertation. University of California, Davis, CA.

Schnitker, S. A., & Emmons, R. A. (2007). Patience as a virtue: Religious and psychological perspectives. *Research in the Social Scientific Study of Religion*, *18*, 177–207.

Schnitker, S. A., & Emmons, R. A. (2011). An examination of patience and well-being. Manuscript submitted for publication.

Seligman, M. E. P. (1995). The effectiveness of psychotherapy: The Consumer Reports study. *American Psychologist*, *50*, 965–974.

Sledge, W. H., Moras, K., Hartley, D., & Levine, M. (1991). Effect of time-limited psychotherapy on patient dropout rates. *American Journal of Psychiatry*, *147*, 1341–1347.

Spence, J. T., Helmreich, R. L., & Pred, R. S. (1987). Impatience versus achievement strivings in the Type A pattern: Differential effects on students' health and academic achievement. *Journal of Applied Psychology*, *72*, 522–528.

Stassen, G. H., & Gushee, D. P. (2003). *Kingdom ethics: Following Jesus in contemporary context*. Downers Grove, IL: InterVarsity Press.

Tangney, J. P., Baumeister, R. F., & Boone, A. L. (2004). High self-control predicts good adjustment, less pathology, better grades, and interpersonal success. *Journal of Personality*, *72*, 271–322.

Tsai, J. L., Knutson, B., & Fung, H. H. (2006). Cultural variation in affect valuation. *Journal of Personality and Social Psychology*, *90*, 288–307.

Watson, D., Clark, L. A., & Tellegen, A. (1988). Development and validation of brief measures of positive and negative affect: The PANAS scales. *Journal of Personality and Social Psychology*, *54*, 1063–1070.

9

Courage Interventions

Future Directions and Cautions

Cynthia L. S. Pury, Charles B. Starkey, Chad R. Breeden, Christie L. Kelley, Hannah J. Murphy, and Arden Y. Lowndes

Although courage has been praised for centuries, like many of the virtues studied by positive psychologists it has received limited empirical attention. Perhaps because courage involves both moral judgment as well as risk to the actor, little to none of the research to date has focused on interventions. In this chapter, we recount what is known about the phenomenon of courage, propose possible targets for intervention based on this limited knowledge, and raise cautions that researchers and clinicians alike should consider when encouraging courage.

Definition

Courage is everywhere; however, we rarely stop to consider what it actually means. Rate and colleagues formulated an empirically derived definition of courage as "(a) a willful, intentional act, (b) executed after mindful deliberation, (c) involving objective substantial risk to the actor, (d) primarily motivated to bring about a noble good or worthy end, (e) despite, perhaps, the presence of the emotion of fear" (Rate, Clarke, Lindsay, & Sternberg, 2007, p. 95).

In contrast with this somewhat universal definition of courage, other researchers have concentrated on explicating the many different types of courage (Lopez et al., 2010; Pury, Kowalski, & Spearman, 2007) or its related construct, heroism (Franco, Blau, & Zimbardo, 2011). When asked to imagine courage, noble actions taken despite intense physical danger are common prototypes, but there is more to the nature of courage than braving the sea, fires, and the battlefield. New research suggests that courage extends to actions that also risk our social and emotional lives (Pury & Starkey, 2010; Putman, 2004, 2010). Of course, this

The Wiley Blackwell Handbook of Positive Psychological Interventions, First Edition.
Edited by Acacia C. Parks and Stephen M. Schueller.

should not diminish those types of acts, but rather point to a distinction between the different types of courage, reviewed below.

Types of Courage

First, those cases which put the actor at risk of bodily injury, physical pain, or death are known as physical courage or valor (Lopez et al., 2010). This type of courage has been acknowledged for a long time, emerging in literature as early as Aristotle in the fourth century BCE (Aristotle, 1999). Courage was one of his proposed virtues, and he considered it a necessity to protect one's self and one's family from harm, emphasizing making a difference through physical action (Putman, 2010). Physical courage has always been celebrated; the ability to act in spite of fear, with confidence on the battlefield or in service of others, is still encouraged today (Walton, 1986).

However, physical courage is not the only way one can be brave. Moral courage is defined as standing up for what is right despite possible social condemnation (Lopez, O'Byrne, & Petersen, 2003), expressing truthfulness in the face of opposition (Larsen & Giles, 1976), or socially beneficial behavior which has no specific reward for the actor but carries a high social cost (Osswald, Greitemeyer, Fischer, & Frey, 2010). These conceptions can bring images to mind as varied as standing up for friends in schoolyard squabbles, whistle-blowing, and acts of civil disobedience. Although there might be physical risk involved – for example, the civil rights protester who risks substantial violent acts against him – there is definitely social risk. Moreover, as implied by its name, moral courage is also defined as much by the moral goodness of its goal as by the type of risk incurred.

Other types of courage have also been described in research, most notably psychological or vital courage, and the more recent workplace courage. Putman (1997) initially proposed psychological courage as the strength to confront destructive habits, irrational anxiety, and controlling relationships. It has since been expanded to describe acts that require facing inner fears, including the idea that we might have a particular problem or that we may become unhappy (Putman, 2004). Those displaying psychological courage stand up to neither physical nor social harm, but rather to their own inner challenges. This type of courage is actually quite common, as we all struggle from time to time with psychological challenges such as stress and sadness. However, this type of courage is not solely limited to mental health issues. Moving away from familiar people and places, ending dysfunctional relationships, and instances of stepping outside one's comfort zone are also relevant to the discussion of psychological courage (Pury et al., 2007). A related construct, vital courage, describes "pushing beyond" the struggle to cope with illness or adversity (Finfgeld, 1995, 1999). Finally, workplace courage is defined by actions which occur in the workplace that require employees risking social ostracism to report counterproductive behaviors, the supervisor risking social and emotional comfort by providing a negative performance review, and even the employee risking a loss of self-esteem to accept criticism (Kelley & Pury, 2011).

Another distinction that can be made is between courage as an accolade and courage as a process (Pury & Starkey, 2010). Accolade courage refers to actions as seen by an observer: does this action appear to be taken for a worthy cause despite risk? Actions extremely high in accolade courage are, by definition, those actions that appear so noble and risky that they merit comment or even awards. Research studies on accolade courage typically examine the extent to which observers rate an action as courageous. Process courage, on the other hand, refers to the process an individual experiences when taking on what personally seems to be a worthy cause despite perceived apparent risks. Research studies on process courage typically involve the extent to which participants engage in a particular action, or first-person accounts of the experience of taking courageous action.

Possible Models Leading to Interventions

At the level of the individual, Hannah, Sweeney, and Lester (2010) propose that courage is facilitated by a courageous mindset, an example of Mischel and Shoda's (2000) Cognitive Affective Processing System (CAPS). In the CAPS model, personality consists of multiple situation-specific self-aspects or social roles, each with its own encoding categories, expectancies, values, affects, goals, and self-regulatory strategies. Applying this to courage, Hannah et al. (2010) propose a courageous mindset occurs when external situations trigger a CAPS module that (i) reduces the fear experienced as the result of a risk and/or (ii) increases the likelihood of action despite fear. Thus, one might engage in a courageous mindset by reminding oneself of a relevant role.

Preliminary research by Osswald and colleagues (2010) found that, compared to a neutral condition, activating a sense of one's self as a just person made it more likely that participants would be willing to discuss their beliefs with a potentially hostile audience. By priming participants to think of themselves as just, the CAPS model would suggest, the participants activated a social role that in turn activated the moral courage needed to agree to the discussion.

At the level of individual actions, Pury, Starkey, Breeden, Murphy, and Kelley (2011) suggest that courage can be understood according to Kruglanski's Goal Systems Theory (GST) model (Kruglanski et al., 2002). Applying this model to process courage, the means to attain the (noble) goal also serves as the means to an undesired (anti-)goal that the actor would rather avoid: in other words, a risk. GST provides the mechanism to explain the common observation of modest heroism, self-regulatory strategies to increase courage (Pury, 2008), and increased appraised courage for successful actions (Pury & Hensel, 2010).

Kruglanski et al. (2002) describe two types of goals: prevention goals, something the actor wants to prevent from happening, and promotion goals, what the actor wants to happen. We propose that the different forms of courage may differ in whether they prime a prevention goal or a promotion goal. Acts of physical and moral courage are commonly undertaken for prevention goals, such as saving someone from a burning building or ending an injustice. Psychological courage, on the other hand, is more likely to occur in the service of a promotion goal, such as attaining a career goal or personal improvement.

The GST model helps organize the cognitive processes that occur when a person considers taking courageous action. We suggest that the network can help better predict the likelihood of courageous action based on the size (or importance) of each node. When the risk, or anti-goal, is smaller than the noble goal, it is expected that the actor will be more likely to pursue the courageous act. Thus, enhancing the nobility of the goal, increasing the efficacy of reaching the goal or avoiding the risk, and/or reducing felt risk may be the most appropriate targets for intervention.

The GST model is compatible with Hannah and colleagues' CAPS model (Hannah et al., 2010). For example, a soldier who needs to overcome stigma to get needed mental health treatment might say to himself, "I am a leader and a soldier. People are counting on me to be able to do my job – I have to do this." The soldier is drawing on a courageous mindset as a soldier and leader. This mindset enhances the value of the goal (getting better will help me do my job better), while drawing on a competent, brave sense of self.

While promising, both of these models of the mechanics of process courage remain in the speculative phase. However, both rely on the idea of the known features of courageous action: a noble goal, personal risk which may lead to fear, and voluntary action. These serve as the most promising targets for intervention, as outlined below.

Encouragement from others

Encouragement is the act of instilling courage, or motivating someone toward a goal (Shelp, 1984). It is a particular form of social support that can incite someone to act courageously. Encouragement can come from close friends or even strangers. It can give a person reason to exercise psychological, physical, or moral courage. Encouragement may also involve a different type of social support than one provided by a network of relationships. For instance, one may subscribe to a certain religion or set of values and be indirectly encouraged to act in the name of one's beliefs. An example of this is an act of terrorism. While terrorists most likely have key people encouraging them to act, they may also be encouraged by their religious doctrine and values.

Encouragement has a long recorded history. The 3,000-year-old *Epic of Gilgamesh*, for example, features numerous exchanges between King Gilgamesh and his friend Enkidu in which one friend loses heart and the other encourages him. In some of these exchanges, the speaker offers direct emotional support intended to reduce fear: "Where you've set your mind begin the journey, let your heart have no fear, keep your eyes on me!" (Anonymous, 1999, p. 114). In others, he tries to help his friend overcome the fear caused by the risk from a formidable foe: "Huwawa ... is not the mountain, he is different altogether ... Come, cast aside your fear" (Anonymous, 1999, p. 135). Other encouragement implores a direct rejection of fearful physiology combined with a focus on their goal: "Let your shout resound like a kettle drum, let the stiffness leave your arms, the tremors [your knees]. Take my hand friend, and we shall go [on] together, [let] your thoughts dwell on combat! Forget death and [seek] life!" (Anonymous, 1999, p. 38). Finally, in other exchanges, the speaker reminds his friend of his own efficacy by employing a reference to the listener's self-aspect: "You were born and grew up in the wild, a lion attacked you, you experienced it all" (Anonymous, 1999, p. 111).

Modern examples of encouragement abound. Have you told someone "You can do it!" or cheered "Go!" or "Looking strong!" at a children's sporting event? Have you pointed out ways that someone has overcome adversity or triumphed in the past? Have you responded to a friend's social media posting with "It's going to be OK" or "Hang in there"? Have you given someone a non-verbal cue that they can accomplish something, like a thumbs-up sign or an encouraging nod? These types of informal encouragement are a part of our everyday life.

More elaborate, formalized encouragement abounds as well: most wedding ceremonies have elements of encouragement in them, both from the new spouses to each other and from the assembled friends and family for the couple. Greeting cards for difficult occasions – get well cards, thinking of you cards, and sympathy cards – frequently offer words of encouragement. More recently, websites, such as CaringBridge.org, provide a more organized way for family and friends to send encouraging words to someone facing an illness or surgery.

Psychotherapists, coaches, teachers, and other experts use encouragement too, of course. As well as the same type of informal encouragement we all engage in, these experts have additional knowledge to share with their clients, and thus may be ideal encouragers. They know, for example, how far a student has progressed. They know how close a medical procedure is to being complete. They know what the criteria are for a successful performance. This broader picture, then, makes them a particularly credible source of encouragement, provided they are giving the person an accurate (even if an optimistically accurate) picture.

Self-encouragement

Within the ongoing argument attempting to distinguish courage as an accolade or a process, one comes across the question of whether an actor has the ability to increase his or her own courage before committing to action. If courage is a personality trait, as opposed to a process that any person has the ability to perform, then logically, people identified as more courageous should predictably participate in courageous actions more often than those acknowledged to be less courageous (Pury & Starkey, 2010). To date, multiple scales for assessing courage as a trait-like entity are undergoing validation tests, including the Woodard–Pury Courage

Scale-23 (WPCS-23; Woodard & Pury, 2007), the Courage Measure (CM; Norton & Weiss, 2009), and the Munich Civil Courage Instrument (MuZI; Kastenmüller, Greitemeyer, Fischer, & Frey, 2007). Despite the implications of the value of the goals and the risks inherent in courageous action, these measures fail to assess the principal question of courage-as-process: how does one decide to execute the task at hand?

During a 2011 pilot study conducted by the first author and undergraduate research assistants, we investigated this self-encouragement process through a series of self-report questionnaires and focus groups assessing different strategies employed before a courageous action. Of the 29 young adolescent female respondents, nearly all reported using some type of personal encouragement prior to their self-reported courageous action. The three conditions investigated for use before initiating, or during commission of, the action were as follows: focusing on the task, which may improve efficacy; focusing on the desired nature of the goal; and avoiding negative thoughts, which may reduce fear.

In the condition regarding a focus on the task, we asked participants if they had specifically attempted to plan out their behavior, or otherwise focused on things learned from previous experiences, as part of their process of personal encouragement. Twenty out of 29 respondents reported utilizing this strategy, implying that while possibly not employed by a large majority, thinking about plans certainly helped many to go forward with their courageous action. A slightly greater number of participants (21 out of 29) stated an emphasis on potential desired outcomes resulting from the choice to act or refrain. Lastly, a large majority of respondents (24 out of 29) elicited the avoidance of negative thoughts and attempting to calm oneself prior to or during the action. Representative personal narratives of how the participants specifically bolstered their own courageousness through this method included thoughts of, "I can do this," "I [told] myself I needed to do it," and "I thought about other brave people overcoming [their] problems."

Assessing the data from the pilot study, it seems probable that people in fact do prepare themselves for a courageous action. None of the conditions from the study were exclusive; 22 out of 27 participants using one type of self-encouragement reported using at least two different methods. Therefore, it may be a particular use, or some type of combination, of these tactics that allows potential courageous actors to follow through with the planned course of action. However, courage is not simply a situation wherein a person properly prepares, initiates, and completes an action others might not; prior to the decision to act, the actor must also assess the goals and risks.

Caution: low or negative value goals

One implication of considering courage as a process (rather than an accolade) is that it becomes possible to think of "bad courage," a term dedicated for when the process of courage is used to pursue a goal that is either harmful to the actor or to society (Pury & Starkey, 2010). For example, suicidal actions and eating-disordered behavior might involve intentionally overcoming a sense of fear or risk to pursue a goal the actor favors at the time, but which is objectively bad for him or her. Likewise, former terrorists describe their actions as noble deeds done despite great risk and fear (Silke, 2004). Even the valued but feared battle Gilgamesh and Enkidu undertake is considered an example of Gilgamesh's immaturity and foolishness by some scholars (George, 1999).

For the clinician seeking to develop a courage intervention, one implication of "bad courage" is that in some cases it may be appropriate to help clients critically assess their goals rather than just encouraging them to focus on the goals to improve their ability to meet those goals in the face of fear-eliciting risks. Consider two examples: a client who wants the resolve to join their friends in a thrill activity of riding on the roof of a car at high speeds, and a client who wants the resolve to orchestrate a risky smear campaign against a co-worker who is a competitor for a promotion. Rather than helping the clients devise ways to meet their goals, one might encourage the clients to call into question how worthwhile or noble the goals are. Note that the recommendation here is to initiate a process on the part of the client of questioning the value of the goal, rather than direct criticism of the goal on the part of the clinician. We believe that the clinician should guide the client and let them determine the merits of their goals, rather than tell the client what to think. But at the same time, the clinician is often ideally situated to provide clients with tools for examining the merit of goals.

These tools take the form of principles that articulate common ethical values. One is the principle of utility (Mill, 2004): the idea that something is good to the extent that it maximizes the overall good of the affected population. A feature that makes a goal worthwhile is the overall good it produces. Another consideration is the principle of autonomy (Dworkin, 1988), or the idea that choice for rational beings is a paramount good. A goal may be more or less worthwhile because of its effect on one's autonomy, defined as the choices that the goal will enable one to make now and in the future. Indeed, it is largely respect for autonomy that drives both the ethics and goals of therapy. The individual has the right to make free choices about their own life. A problem with the goal of those who have Body Integrity Identity Disorder (Stirn, Thiel, & Oddo, 2009), and thus wish to have a limb amputated, is that removing the limb may sharply and permanently reduce the future choices available to the client, and activities that they may capably engage in. A less dramatic example is that of choices that might limit a client's financial future, like making a risky business decision that could dramatically reduce their income. A third principle is that of respect for persons (Kant, 2009). According to this principle, persons, as persons, are inherently entitled to a baseline level of respect, including fair treatment. A goal may be less worthy because it does not adequately respect other people. A goal that involves deception violates this principle of respect, because such deception manipulates people. Lies generally try to manipulate people's behavior in order that a person may choose an option they normally may not if given adequate information. A fourth principle involves a person's general aspirations (see Hinman, 2007). What kind of person are they making themselves in striving toward or achieving that goal? Is that the kind of person they want to be?

As with acceptance and commitment therapy (Hayes, Strosahl, & Wilson, 1999), this approach encourages the client to address their root concerns (i.e. their goals and the values that underlie them). These four principles provide the client with tools to examine the value of their goals. Although the principles can offer different recommendations about the same goal, such as when a goal will probably increase the overall good, but consequently may not treat people with adequate respect, we note that they are more likely to be complementary and thus provide independent but corroborating reasons to judge the goal to be worthy or unworthy. Significantly, since most people are likely to value the ideas behind these principles, the client's assessment of their goals will be by reference to values that they themselves accept. This method thus avoids paternalistic intervention by the clinician.

Caution: genuine risk

A proper assessment of courage includes risks associated with the courageous act. Most conceptions of courage suggest that the action must involve "substantial risk." Risks of action take on a different form in each "brand" of courage. Physical courage involves the risk of bodily harm or even death. An example of a physical risk would be the risk of being burned while trying to save someone from a fire. Moral courage may involve the risk of social disapproval, such as being ostracized after sticking up for an unpopular cause, or in many cases financial and occupational risk such as being fired for speaking out at work. The risk involved with vital courage is a little bit ambiguous. This risk may just be acting courageously despite an uncertain or unsuccessful outcome.

Anyone designing or implementing a courage intervention should be comfortable with techniques to help clients assess the actual, rather than the perceived, risks of a situation. Techniques from cognitive-behavioral approaches to anxiety disorders (e.g., Clark & Beck, 2010) may be useful for clients who have excessive fear in response to the level of actual risk in the situation. For those with a more realistic or even underestimation of the risks involved, we propose that approaches be grounded in the judgment and decision-making literature (e.g., Hardman, 2009; Jacobs & Klaczynski, 2005; Koehler & Harvey, 2004). We envision these approaches giving clients tools to more accurately assess the risks of any given situation, in addition to any particular issue they are dealing with at the time of treatment.

Caution: research outcome concerns

As with any scientific study, there are ethical concerns which must be acknowledged before proceeding with research. With courage, there are some obvious limitations on what researchers can include or present in studies, and in the treatment itself. Placing subjects into an obviously physically dangerous situation to invoke courageous reaction (or lack thereof) is unacceptable, and would never pass ethical review. Similarly, it would be difficult to place individuals in socially or psychologically damaging scenarios solely for the means of assessing courage. As such, many studies of courage are derived from professions which require it (for example, explosive ordinance disposal – see Rachman, 1990), or they are studies that ask people to describe a past action (Pury & Kowalski, 2007; Pury et al., 2007), that mirror a courageous act but are not inherently dangerous (Norton & Weiss, 2009; Osswald et al., 2010), or that simply use survey and scenario methods to garner a response (Rate et al., 2007). Because courage cannot often be manipulated without the presence of these ethical concerns, it requires creative and lateral thinking for assessment and measurement of outcomes.

Conclusion

Courage, a virtue that has been praised for centuries, can enable people to do great things. Unfortunately, it can also be misapplied to allow people to make terrible mistakes. The basic science behind the process of courage is still developing: once it does develop, these findings must be applied in combination with techniques to enable clients to avoid bad courage and unnecessary risks.

References

Anonymous (1999). *The epic of Gilgamesh* (A. George, Trans.). London: Penguin Books.

Aristotle (1999). *Nicomachean ethics* (M. Ostwald, Trans.). Upper Saddle River, NJ: Prentice Hall.

Clark, D. A., & Beck, A. T. (2010). *Cognitive therapy of anxiety disorders: Science and practice.* New York: Guilford Press.

Dworkin, G. (1988). *The theory and practice of autonomy.* Cambridge: Cambridge University Press.

Finfgeld, D. L. (1995). Becoming and being courageous in the chronically ill elderly. *Issues in Mental Health Nursing, 16*(1), 1–11. doi:10.3109/01612849509042959

Finfgeld, D. L. (1999). Courage as a process of pushing beyond the struggle. *Qualitative Health Research, 9*(6), 803–814. doi:10.1177/104973299129122298

Franco, Z. E., Blau, K., & Zimbardo, P. G. (2011). Heroism: A conceptual analysis and differentiation between heroic action and altruism. *Review of General Psychology, 15*, 99–113. doi:10.1037/a0022672

George, A. (1999). Introduction. *The epic of Gilgamesh* (pp. xiii–lii). London: Penguin Books.

Hannah, S. T., Sweeney, P. J., & Lester, P. B. (2010). The courageous mind-set: A dynamic personality system approach to courage. In C. L. S. Pury & S. J. Lopez (Eds.), *The psychology of courage: Modern research on an ancient virtue* (pp. 125–148). Washington, DC: American Psychological Association.

Hardman, D. (2009). *Judgment and decision making: Psychological perspectives.* Malden, MA: Wiley-Blackwell.

Hayes, S. C., Strosahl, K. D., & Wilson, K. G. (1999). *Acceptance and commitment therapy: An experiential approach to behavior change.* New York: Guilford Press.

Hinman, L. M. (2007). *Ethics: A pluralistic approach to moral theory.* Florence, KY: Wadsworth.

Jacobs, J. E., & Klaczynski, P. A. (2005). *The development of judgment and decision making in children and adolescents.* Mahwah, NJ: Lawrence Erlbaum Associates.

Kant, I. (2009). *Groundwork of the metaphysics of morals* (H. J. Paton, Trans.). New York: Harper.

Kastenmüller, A., Greitemeyer, T., Fischer, P., & Frey, D. (2007). Das Münchner Zivilcourage-Instrument (MüZI): Entwicklung und Validierung. *Diagnostica, 53*(4), 205–217. doi:10.1026/0012-1924.53.4.205

Kelley, C., & Pury, C. (2011). Development and validation of a workplace courage scale. Paper presented at the Work, Stress, and Health Conference 2011: Work and Well-Being in an Economic Context, Orlando, FL.

Koehler, D. J., & Harvey, N. (2004). *Blackwell handbook of judgment and decision making.* Malden, MA: Blackwell Publishing.

Kruglanski, A. W., Shah, J. Y., Fishbach, A., Friedman, R., Chun, W. Y., & Sleeth-Keppler, D. (2002). A theory of goal systems. In M. P. Zanna (Ed.), *Advances in experimental social psychology* (Vol. 34, pp. 331–378). San Diego, CA: Academic Press.

Larsen, K. S., & Giles, H. (1976). Survival or courage as human motivation: Development of an attitude scale. *Psychological Reports, 39*(1), 299–302.

Lopez, S. J., O'Byrne, K. K., & Petersen, S. (2003). Profiling courage. In S. J. Lopez & C. R. Snyder (Eds.), *Positive psychological assessment: A handbook of models and measures* (pp. 185–197). Washington, DC: American Psychological Association.

Lopez, S. J., Rasmussen, H. N., Skorupski, W. P., Koetting, K., Petersen, S. E., & Yang, Y.-T. (2010). Folk conceptualizations of courage. In C. L. S. Pury & S. J. Lopez (Eds.), *The psychology of courage: Modern research on an ancient virtue* (pp. 23–45). Washington, DC: American Psychological Association.

Mill, J. S. (2004). *Utilitarianism.* Retrieved from http://www.gutenberg.org/files/11224/11224-h/11224-h.htm

Mischel, W., & Shoda, Y. (2000). A cognitive-affective system theory of personality: Reconceptualizing situations, dispositions, dynamics, and invariance in personality structure. In E. T. Higgins & A. W. Kruglanski (Eds.), *Motivational science: Social and personality perspectives* (pp. 150–176). New York: Psychology Press.

Norton, P. J., & Weiss, B. J. (2009). The role of courage on behavioral approach in a fear-eliciting situation: A proof-of-concept pilot study. *Journal of Anxiety Disorders, 23*(2), 212–217. doi:10.1016/j.janxdis.2008.07.002

Osswald, S., Greitemeyer, T., Fischer, P., & Frey, D. (2010). Moral prototypes and moral behavior: Specific effects on emotional precursors of moral behavior and on moral behavior by the activation of moral prototypes. *European Journal of Social Psychology, 40*(6), 1078–1094. doi:10.1002/ejsp.728

Pury, C. L. S. (2008). Can courage be learned? In S. J. Lopez (Ed.), *Positive psychology: Exploring the best in people* (Vol. 1) *Discovering human strengths* (pp. 109–130). Westport, CT: Praeger Publishers/Greenwood Publishing Group.

Pury, C. L. S., & Hensel, A. D. (2010). Are courageous actions successful actions? *Journal of Positive Psychology, 5*(1), 62–72. doi:10.1080/17439760903435224

Pury, C. L. S., & Kowalski, R. M. (2007). Human strengths, courageous actions, and general and personal courage. *Journal of Positive Psychology*, *2*(2), 120–128. doi:10.1080/17439760701228813

Pury, C. L. S., Kowalski, R. M., & Spearman, J. (2007). Distinctions between general and personal courage. *Journal of Positive Psychology*, *2*(2), 99–114. doi:10.1080/17439760701237962

Pury, C. L. S., & Starkey, C. B. (2010). Is courage an accolade or a process? A fundamental question for courage research. In C. L. S. Pury & S. J. Lopez (Eds.), *The psychology of courage: Modern research on an ancient virtue* (pp. 67–87). Washington, DC: American Psychological Association.

Pury, C. L. S., Starkey, C. B., Breeden, C., Murphy, H., & Kelley, C. (2011). A goal systems theory explanation of courage. Paper presented at the International Positive Psychology World Congress, Philadelphia, PA.

Putman, D. (1997). Psychological courage. *Philosophy, Psychiatry, and Psychology*, *4*(1), 1–11. doi:10.1353/ppp.1997.0008

Putman, D. (2004). *Psychological courage*. Dallas, TX: University Press of America.

Putman, D. (2010). Philosophical roots of the concept of courage. In C. L. S. Pury & S. J. Lopez (Eds.), *The psychology of courage: Modern research on an ancient virtue* (pp. 9–22). Washington, DC: American Psychological Association.

Rachman, S. J. (1990). *Fear and courage* (2nd ed.). New York: W. H. Freeman/Times Books/Henry Holt & Co.

Rate, C. R., Clarke, J. A., Lindsay, D. R., & Sternberg, R. J. (2007). Implicit theories of courage. *Journal of Positive Psychology*, *2*(2), 80–98. doi:10.1080/17439760701228755

Shelp, E. E. (1984). Courage: A neglected virtue in the patient–physician relationship. *Social Science and Medicine*, *18*(4), 351–360. doi:10.1016/0277-9536(84)90125-4

Silke, A. (2004). Courage in dark places: Reflections on terrorist psychology. *Social Research*, *71*, 177–198.

Stirn, A., Thiel, A., & Oddo, S. (2009). *Body Integrity Identity Disorder: Psychological, neurobiological, ethical and legal aspects*. Lengerich, Germany: Pabst Science Publishers.

Walton, D. N. (1986). *Courage: A philosophical investigation*. Berkeley, CA: University of California Press.

Woodard, C. R., & Pury, C. L. S. (2007). The construct of courage: Categorization and measurement. *Consulting Psychology Journal: Practice and Research*, *59*(2), 135–147. doi:10.1037/1065-9293.59.2.135

10

Humor Intervention Programs

Willibald Ruch and Paul E. McGhee

Much of the first decade of positive psychology was devoted to obtaining a better understanding of the virtues and character strengths (Peterson & Seligman, 2004; Chapter 4) and their contribution to happiness and subjective well-being (SWB). A natural next step is using this understanding to develop intervention programs that nurture these character strengths (Sin & Lyubomirsky, 2009). Given the goal of promoting SWB, a logical starting point is to focus on character strengths known to be associated with happiness and well-being.

Humor assumes an important role in contributing to well-being. We offer a brief summary of this research as it is discussed in detail elsewhere (e.g., McGhee, 2010b). Higher levels of humor correspond to greater well-being (Park, Peterson, & Seligman, 2004; Proyer, Gander, Wyss, & Ruch, 2011; Ruch, Proyer, et al., 2010; Ruch, Proyer, & Weber, 2010b), and lower levels of depression (Deaner & McConatha, 1993; Nezu, Nezu, & Blissett, 1988), anxiety (Lefcourt & Martin, 1986; Yovetich, Dale, & Hudak, 1990), and negative emotion (Kuiper & Martin, 1998; Moran & Massam, 1999). Indeed, it typically rates about seventh highest, among the VIA character strengths, in terms of its correlation with life satisfaction (Ruch, Proyer, & Weber, 2010a, 2010b). Peterson, Park, and Seligman (2006) found that recovery from a psychological disorder or serious illness was associated with elevated humor and this increase predicted life satisfaction.

Related to Peterson et al.'s (2006) findings, the use of humor for interventions is often focused on its use as a coping mechanism. Simply watching a comedy video has been shown to both boost positive affect and reduce anxiety (Abel & Maxwell, 2002). Being asked to actively produce humor in the midst of experimentally induced stress reduced the level of negative emotion experienced, in comparison with individuals not asked to actively engage their sense of humor (Martin & Lefcourt, 1983). Those who score higher on measures of sense of humor also show less negative emotion in real-life stressful situations (Martin & Lefcourt, 1983). Interestingly, laughter propensity and negative life events have an interactive effect on positive affect: as the number of negative events one experiences increases, individuals who find more things to laugh at experience more positive affect than

The Wiley Blackwell Handbook of Positive Psychological Interventions, First Edition.
Edited by Acacia C. Parks and Stephen M. Schueller.

those who do not laugh often (Kuiper & Martin, 1998; Kuiper, Martin, & Dance, 1992). Humor, then, does not only reduce negative emotions; it can transform negative emotions into positive emotions.

Given the evidence for humor's contribution to psychological well-being and its effectiveness as a coping mechanism, it seems worthwhile to study how this character strength may be increased. Below, we review existing research attempting to do just that.

What Is Humor?

Poets, philosophers, psychologists, clinicians, and linguists have all addressed humor. Accordingly, humor has been conceptualized as a temperament, coping strategy, ability, attitude, worldview, aesthetic judgment, character strength, and virtue. Labels of instruments include "sense of humor," "styles of humor/comic styles," "humor appreciation," and "humor creation/wit," but more specific terms are also used such as, "irony," "playfulness," or "nonsense." In psychological research, however, the term "humor" is not limited to these domains. Experimental studies of humor use jokes and cartoons and studies of personality examine the liking (appreciation) and creation (production, reproduction) of humorous stimuli (i.e., films, jokes, cartoons). Furthermore, in some assessments, the propensity to laugh is subsumed under humor. Critical forms, such as sarcasm, cynicism, or irony, are also studied, although kept separate. To date no shared conceptualization of a sense of humor exists in the research community.

Measurement Issues

Assessment is essential to the evaluation of humor training. Due to the multifaceted nature of humor, no comprehensive instrument exists. Thus, studies should at least assess the components of humor targeted by the intervention, although it is also instructive to determine if other facets change due to the intervention. We discuss measures that either stem from positive psychology or have been used in prior intervention studies. For those interested, a more thorough review of measures can be found elsewhere (Ruch, 2007, 2008).

The humor scale of the *Values in Action Inventory of Strengths* (VIA-IS; Peterson & Seligman, 2004) consists of 10 items in a 5-point Likert-style format (from 1 = "very much like me" to 5 = "very much unlike me") measuring humor as a stable, dispositional trait. A high scorer is someone "who is skilled at laughing and teasing, at bringing smiles to the faces of others, at seeing the light side, and at making (not necessarily telling) jokes" (Peterson & Seligman, 2004, p. 530). A sample item is "Whenever my friends are in a gloomy mood I try to tease them out of it."

The *Sense of Humor Scale* (SHS; McGhee, 1996) was designed as a means of determining one's progress following completion of humor training. It consists of 40 items in a 7-point Likert-style format (1 = "strongly disagree" to 7 = "strongly agree"), with 8 items each measuring "playful/serious attitude" and "positive/negative mood" and 24 items measuring *sense of humor* (i.e., enjoyment of humor, laughter, verbal humor, finding humor in everyday life, laughing at yourself, and humor under stress). Similar to the VIA-IS humor scale, it is unipolar and unidimensional, and the two are highly correlated (e.g., $r = .63$; Müller & Ruch, 2011).

Several measures tap multidimensional conceptualizations of humor but two specifically assess styles of humor. The *Humorous Behavior Q-Sort-Deck* (HBQD; Craik, Lampert, & Nelson, 1996) consists of 100 statements describing everyday humor behaviors in a 9-point Likert-style format (1 = "very uncharacteristic" to 9 = "very characteristic"). The statements relate to 10 styles (five bipolar factors) of humorous conduct, namely *socially warm vs. cold*, *reflective vs. boorish*, *competent vs. inept*, *earthy vs. repressed*, and *benign vs. mean-spirited humorous style*. The *Humor Styles Questionnaire* (HSQ; Martin, Puhlik-Doris, Larsen, Gray, and Weir, 2003) is designed to distinguish between adaptive (i.e., affiliative, self-enhancing) and maladaptive (aggressive, self-defeating) styles of humor. The HSQ is a self-report questionnaire composed of 32 items in a 7-point Likert-style format (1 = "totally disagree" to 7 = "totally agree") measuring those four dimensions.

The *State-Trait-Cheerfulness-Inventory* (STCI; Ruch, 1997) assesses the temperamental basis for humor: *cheerfulness*, *seriousness*, and *bad mood*. The temperamental foundations of humor are assumed to be universal, even if the expression of humor varies across culture and time. Respondents answer questions in a 4-point Likert-style format (1 = "strongly disagree" to 4 = "strongly agree"). The STCI has both trait (60-item) and state (30-item) versions. The state form is suited to evaluating the effects of humor training both before and after a single session or a longer intervention period.

Finally, assessments might assess the ability to be witty or create humor. In one example, punch-lines written for an ambiguous stimulus (e.g., a captionless cartoon) are rated for quality by a panel of judges. Humor appreciation is typically measured by rating funniness (and aversiveness) of jokes and cartoons (Ruch, 2008). Such tests can provide behavioral measures for whether the humor training enhanced wittiness and enjoyment of humor.

Early Humor Intervention Studies

Some of the earliest studies of humor interventions produced inconsistent results, raising the question of whether boosting humor skills/competence was possible. For example, an early attempt to improve the sense of humor of high school teachers produced no changes on a humor production test, although peer ratings (i.e., fellow participants') of both one's appreciation of humor and ability to produce humor during the meetings increased significantly (Nevo, Aharonson, & Klingman, 1998). This training consisted of seven weekly sessions of about three hours each. Each meeting focused on content ranging from an initial discussion of the nature of humor (and a sense of humor), to emotional barriers to enjoying and producing humor, the role of humor in social life, the benefits of humor, distinctions between positive and negative humor, and possible uses of humor in one's work setting. Little time was spent focusing specifically on building humor skills and habits. Participants noted, "they did not think the program greatly improved their sense of humor but they enjoyed it." Thus, such an intervention may be fun but not effective.

Other early humor intervention studies (e.g., Ruch, 2008; Ruch, Rodden, & Proyer, 2011) yielded increases in trait cheerfulness or coping humor; however, they lacked a manualized intervention or a comparison control group. Thus, more structured interventions and research were needed to determine if humor interventions could work.

The 7 Humor Habits Program

McGhee (1996, 2010a) developed a structured humor intervention program that emphasized strengthening key humor habits and skills. Dubbed the 7 Humor Habits Program (7HHP), it consists of seven core habits listed in Table 10.1 below. The key goals of the program are to: (i) demonstrate that humor can be trained/strengthened, (ii) boost humor, (iii) increase frequency of positive emotions, (iv) decrease frequency of negative emotions, (v) increase emotional resilience and the ability to cope with stress. The program aims to first build or strengthen these core habits and skills on the days when one is in a good mood and then gradually apply the same habits in the midst of stress (when angry, anxious, depressed, etc.). Because sense of humor is often lost in the midst of stress, a minimum of one week of repetition of the habits on "good days" is considered crucial to the ability to later sustain the habits on bad (stressful) days.

Table 10.1 Core habits from the 7 Humor Habits Program

1	Surround yourself with humor (and think about the nature of your sense of humor).
2	Cultivate a playful attitude.
3	Laugh more often and more heartily.
4	Create your own verbal humor.
5	Look for humor in everyday life.
6	Take yourself lightly: laugh at yourself.
7	Find humor in the midst of stress.

Home play and humor log exercises

The 7HHP uses two approaches to strengthen humor habits: "home play" assignments and "humor log" exercises. A "home play" assignment is a list of specific activities to engage in during the week (generally 10–12 per habit). Participants do not need to complete every activity but are asked to choose something from the list to practice every day. This maximizes the chances of finding at least one activity per habit that might benefit them in the long term. Table 10.2 contains examples of "home play" for each humor habit.

"Humor log" exercises get participants to actively think about issues related to each humor habit and their sense of humor, but with no active practice of the habits. Thus, the humor log is a cognitive/reflective exercise, whereas home play represents a behavioral component. Participants also keep a daily humor diary in which they record observations and efforts related to the humor habit being worked on.

Review of research testing the impact of the 7HHP

Several studies have evaluated the 7HHP. Although the exact procedures used in these studies vary somewhat (number of trainers, setting in which the training took place, contents of the meeting), no systematic comparisons of the important factors influencing the outcomes have been conducted. Thus, we first discuss several intervention studies and then organize the section below according to the outcome measures used to evaluate the program.

Discussion of studies The program has been evaluated for adults recruited from a rehabilitation clinic using four comparison groups (Sassenrath, 2001). One group completed the training program as intended, with weekly meetings and completion of home play assignments. A second group received the theoretical discussion during weekly meetings, but did not practice the humor habits. A third discussed socially relevant topics at the meetings (but not humor). The fourth completed only the outcome measures in a group.

Another evaluation of the 7HHP recruited adults of different professions into one of four groups (Rusch & Stolz, 2009). Three experimental groups met every two weeks for two-hour sessions. The fourth, a control group, only met to complete outcome measures. Of the experimental groups, one completed home play activities and exercises, a second completed the same discussions within sessions, but did not receive home play activities, and a third received passive exposure to humor during the sessions, but received no humor-specific training.

Crawford and Caltabiano (2011) tested the 7HHP with adults. The experimental group received eight weekly one-hour training sessions (incorporating home play for each habit), while a "social group" met weekly for tea and "humorous banter," but received no humor training of any kind. A control group only completed the outcome measures.

Table 10.2 The seven humor habits

Step 1	**Surround yourself with humor (and think about the nature of your sense of humor).** Rationale: Many individuals simply do not have humor "on their radar" in everyday life. They rarely seek out humor and fail to find humor in situations considered by others to be funny. Increasing the amount of time and focus people spend actively thinking about humor contributes to the gains made. Home play: Provides specific guidelines for (i) immersing oneself in humor and (ii) thinking about both the strengths and weaknesses of one's current sense of humor and influences on its development. Home play example: Watch several sitcoms and decide which programs you like the best. Use these as a basis for thinking about your sense of humor.
Step 2	**Cultivate a playful attitude.** Rationale: An essential component of humor is the joy and fun that come from play. Humor can be thought of as a form of mental play, playing with ideas. A playful attitude refers to a prevailing frame of mind characterized by a general receptiveness to any form of play or fun. Home play: Participants collect things they have fun doing and then do as many of these as possible every day for two weeks. For most people, physical forms of play are very effective in "jump-starting" mental play and the mental/emotional frame of mind where humor thrives. Home play example: Make a list of things you have fun doing, and do two each day. Keep a prop (silly nose, toy, etc.) handy that puts you in a playful mood.
Step 3	**Laugh more often and more heartily.** Rationale: Although, laughter *per se* is not a humor skill, it is included because the physical act of laughter might explain some of the benefits to physical health, happiness, and resilience resulting from humor. Home play: Participants are instructed to spend more time in situations in which social laughter commonly occurs (e.g., comedy clubs, funny movies, parties, etc.), watch more television sitcoms or funny DVDs, and so on. They are asked to laugh at times and in ways different than one's inclination – for example, to laugh louder and longer than you normally would. Home play example: At some point, try forcing yourself to laugh when you are angry, anxious, or depressed. Notice the effect this has on your emotional state.
Step 4	**Create your own verbal humor.** Rationale: This is the first genuine humor skill – playing with language. Verbal humor is one of the most common forms of humor across cultures, and good verbal humor skills/habits are considered to play an important role in using humor to support a positive daily mood and life satisfaction. Home play: Verbal humor-building exercises begin with simple forms of word play. Many exercises center on the appreciation or generation of puns. Participants actively seek out puns and other forms of verbal humor in newspaper headlines, public signs, everyday conversations. Home play example: Look for ambiguous words or phrases in conversations and in newspaper headlines and on signs. Write them down to build the habit of noticing them.

Table 10.2 (*Continued*)

Step 5	**Look for humor in everyday life.** Rationale: Finding a funny side of one's own daily life is considered to be crucial to the ultimate goal of using humor to cope with stress. McGhee has heard many people in his own humor workshops say, "If I had your life, I'd be laughing too. Nothing funny ever happens in my life!" The goal here is to demonstrate that many opportunities for humor in daily life simply go unnoticed and to show participants how to start noticing them. Home play: Focuses on actively looking for humor at home, at work, on the way to work, while waiting for a bus, and so on. Visual props and other reminders are placed in key areas at home, at work, and in the car as reminders to look for a funny side of things at that moment. Specific requests are made to write funny observations down and share them with others (this is assumed to speed up the development of this habit). Home play example: When watching television sitcoms, relate funny situations that arise in the show to incidents in your own life.
Step 6	**Take yourself lightly: laugh at yourself.** Rationale: Being able to laugh at oneself – at one's own mistakes, weaknesses, perceived flaws, and so on – promotes the use of humor to cope with stress. This is usually the most difficult skill to develop, because awkward or embarrassing incidents or being the butt of a joke (or otherwise being laughed at) typically elicit negative emotions that interfere with the ability to create and enjoy humor. Home play: Individuals make a list of their sensitive zones; that is, areas of their life about which it is very difficult to "lighten up." Items on the list are arranged from smaller or minor ones to major ones. Initial attention is given to minor items because they have less "emotional baggage." Also, prior to joking about their sensitive zones, individuals are first asked to simply verbalize them to others. This is assumed to speed up progress in laughing at them. Home play example: Learn a few self-disparaging jokes. Some of these jokes should have nothing to do with your sensitive zones. Others should relate directly to your sensitivities. Practice telling them to others.
Step 7	**Find humor in the midst of stress.** Rationale: The key challenge here is to extend already-developed humor habits to stressful situations. This is an emotional skill, as much as an intellectual one, because most people find that their sense of humor abandons them in the midst of stress. Negative emotions (e.g., tension, anger, or depression) interfere with accessing the playful mood and mindset required for humor. A central tenet of the 7HHP is that strengthening every humor habit on good-mood days is essential to making the habit accessible in the midst of stress. Home play: Individuals are asked to simply keep doing the kinds of things they have been doing, but focus special attention on doing them in stressful situations – initially focusing on regularly occurring (predictable) and mildly stressful situations and then moving on to more stressful ones.

(*continued*)

Table 10.2 (*Continued*)

	Home play example: Make a list of commonly occurring hassles and problems. Be determined to find a way to maintain a lighter attitude when these come up.
Step 8	**Integrate the habits into everyday life.**
	Rationale: During the week devoted to each humor habit, participants are asked to focus attention only on that specific habit. Once work on the seventh habit is completed, they spend a week working on all seven habits simultaneously. This is done in a final effort to further strengthen the habits and make each readily accessible at any given time.

Measures of humor/sense of humor The 7HHP increases sense of humor using various measures. These include the SHS (Andress, Hoshino, & Rorke, 2010; Rusch & Stolz, 2009; Sassenrath, 2001; also Crawford, 2009, however, only subscales were reported and not total SHS) and Coping Humor Scale (Sassenrath, 2001). These increases were maintained over time at one-month (Sassenrath, 2001), two-month (Rusch & Stolz, 2009), and three-month follow-ups (Crawford & Caltabiano, 2011).

Interestingly, passive humor groups also appear to improve on measures of sense of humor (Rusch & Stolz, 2009; Sassenrath, 2001). Thus even participants who are not specifically trained in building humor skills may experience an improved sense of humor, although perhaps to a lesser extent than groups with skills training (Sassenrath, 2001). However, other work suggests that the improvement experienced by a passive humor group may be comparable to that of an active training group (Rusch & Stolz, 2009); though in this study, the researchers discovered that the group had gotten together on their own several times between sessions to discuss humor. Thus the passive humor groups may help stimulate interest in taking a more active effort to improve one's sense of humor.

Affect, happiness, and life satisfaction Consistent findings suggest that the 7HHP intervention boosts positive emotions and subjective well-being using a broad range of measures. This includes: playfulness or playful attitude (Andress et al., 2010; Crawford, 2009; Sassenrath, 2001), positive mood or positive affect (Andress et al., 2010; Crawford, 2009; Sassenrath, 2001), trait cheerfulness (Rusch & Stolz, 2009), life satisfaction (Rusch & Stolz, 2009), optimism (Andress et al., 2010 – $p < .056$; Crawford & Caltabiano, 2011), perceived sense of self-efficacy, and sense of control over one's internal states (Crawford & Caltabiano, 2011). 7HHP intervention studies have also yielded significant decreases in seriousness (Sassenrath, 2001), negative mood (Sassenrath, 2001), depression (Beh-Pajooh, Jahangiri, & Zahrakar, 2010; Crawford & Caltabiano, 2011), anxiety (Crawford & Caltabiano, 2011), and perceived stress (Crawford & Caltabiano,

2011). Several studies with follow-up assessments show sustained benefits including boosts in trait cheerfulness at two months (Rusch & Stolz, 2009), and sustained changes in positive affect, optimism, self-efficacy, perceived control over internal states, perceived stress, and depression at three months (Crawford & Caltabiano, 2011).

Coping with stress To our knowledge, only two studies have directly examined the impact of 7HHP training on coping with stress. In the first, Gunderson (1998) provided an eight-week version to senior citizens living in a retirement community. One group received the program as described in the manual. Another group spent the meeting time watching comedy videos selected by the participants, playing games, and engaging in friendly banter (passive exposure to humor). While the two groups showed similar scores on measures of coping at the beginning of the study, the active humor-training group scored significantly higher than the passive humor group on the "humor under stress" SHS subscale (the other SHS subscales were not administered because the focus of the study was coping) and two additional measures of coping with stress in general (without consideration of humor). Crawford and Caltabiano (2011) found similar results; their 7HHP intervention reduced scores on two different measures of stress.

Use of the 7 Humor Habits Program in clinical practice

Given that the 7HHP improves sense of humor, positive emotions, and life satisfaction, and decreases negative emotion, stress, and depression in non-clinical samples, it is worth considering whether these same benefits can be demonstrated among clinical samples. Individuals with depression show an inability to experience pleasure and a negative, pessimistic view of their future. Humor has been shown to stimulate pleasure centers in the brain (see McGhee, 2010b for a detailed discussion of this research), and simultaneously boost positive emotion while reducing negative emotion; thus it may well support the ability to pull oneself out of depression. So training effective humor habits and skills in depressed individuals should be an effective means of helping them learn to manage depression on their own.

Three studies of the 7HHP have documented a reduction in clinical depression. In Crawford and Caltabiano (2011), 38% of the participants in the experimental group had clinically elevated levels of stress and depression (using the Depression, Anxiety and Stress Scale; Lovibond & Lovibond, 1995) at the time of the pre-test, and 24% had clinically elevated levels of clinical anxiety. By the post-test, this percentage had dropped to 9.5% for stress and depression and 0% for anxiety. This suggests that the 7HHP is worthy of further investigation specifically targeting its usefulness as a clinical tool.

One study specifically addressed whether the 7HHP could boost the effectiveness of a standard program for the treatment of depression. Patients with depression (n = 11) received an abbreviated (four-week) version of the 7HHP, during the course of standard treatment (consultation and anti-depressant medication; Wilbers, 2009). The abbreviated program included two meetings per week, with each meeting devoted to one of the humor habits. The program significantly boosted the patients' appreciation/enjoyment of cartoon humor, but it did not increase the effectiveness of the regular treatment program. Nor did it significantly increase sense of humor as measured by the SHS. It could be that the 7HHP is not effective for individuals with depression or that four weeks is simply not enough time for the program to have a meaningful impact on sense of humor.

Finally, in a pilot study, the 7HHP was administered to six patients with major depression to see if it could help elevate their mood and enable them to use humor to cope (Falkenberg, Buchkremer, Bartels, & Wild, 2011). Completion of the eight-week program significantly improved mood within most of the weekly sessions, along with significantly increased cheerfulness and decreased seriousness at the end of the program. As a pilot study, the researchers also used an exploratory measure of humor that increased significantly. Depression levels, however, among the patients were not reduced. These patients, though, were very positive about the 7HHP and were "willing to pursue the training until the end." Thus the program may have value in engaging patients. This study, combined with the clinical impressions of the researchers in using the 7HHP with patients with psychological disorders led to the development of a manual for the use of the 7HHP in therapy sessions (Falkenberg, McGhee, & Wild, 2012).

Considerations for Future Humor Intervention Research

Does pre-intervention sense of humor impact the effectiveness of the 7HHP?

While most studies of the 7HHP obtain pre-training assessments of humor, no effort has been made to determine whether individuals scoring low, in the middle, or high on these measures make the strongest (or weakest) gains in humor on various well-being assessments as a result of the training.

Can brief humor interventions be effective?

Research systematically exploring the length and intensity of humor interventions is warranted. Brief interventions may be effective. Gander, Proyer, Ruch, and Wyss (2013), for example, simply had participants "write down the three funniest things they experienced or did, and an explanation of why those things happened to them, on every day for a week." These participants reported reduced self-reported depressive symptoms at the end of the seven days, as well as at a one- and three-month follow-up (but not at a six-month follow-up). Self-reported happiness scores did not increase (relative to pre-test scores) at day 7, but did increase at the one- and three-month follow-up (but not at the six-month follow-up).

Proyer, Ruch, and Buschor (2012) included a brief adaptation of one part of the 7HHP in a brief (one-evening) intervention along with the strengths of curiosity, gratitude, hope, and zest. While this combined-strengths intervention did boost life satisfaction scores of participants, it is impossible to determine if it was due to humor versus the other strengths.

It is possible that not all habits in the 7HHP are necessary, as the Gander et al. (2013) data suggest. Dismantling studies of the 7HHP would help researchers assess which habits are necessary to strengthen humor or improve SWB.

How much engagement in training activities is needed?

So far no systematic appraisals address the amount of effort participants invest in humor-training programs. Motivation and engagement have emerged as important factors contributing to the efficacy of other positive psychological interventions (Lyubomirsky & Layous, 2013), and should be addressed for humor. The 7HHP was designed to be flexible in terms of the specific activities practiced to build a given humor habit. Different individuals, however, may enjoy different strength-building activities and exercises. Thus, although offering a range of choices may help sustain a high degree of engagement, systematically varying the range of choices may produce an optimal dosage of these activities (see Schueller & Parks, 2012, for an investigation of this in other areas of positive psychological interventions).

Likewise, participants vary in their participation in skill-building exercises. Measuring engagement among participants in future studies would help determine just how much practice is required to generate significant improvement in sense of humor, positive and negative emotion, and so on. Likewise such variation might be introduced experimentally. The results would address whether the gain from the 7HHP intervention is a direct function of level of engagement in the habit-building activities provided.

Can morally good forms of humor be promoted?

As mentioned previously, humor contains many critical forms that may be more related to vice than virtue. A training module could be created that helps participants identify virtues (and vices) in humor and then shows how to generate humor that is in the service of these virtues; that is, expressing humanity or justice. Refraining from earthy and mean-spirited humor in favor of more socially acceptable forms of humor might be particularly important. Indeed, indulging in negative forms of humor correlated inversely with both meaningfulness of life and satisfaction with life (Ruch, 2012). The 7HHP already covers the distinction between socially acceptable and less acceptable forms of humor. However, it might be worth adding the notion of virtue and how different humor techniques can support each virtue.

From boosting resilience to well-being and flourishing?

One important remaining question refers to the issue of what to expect from a humor intervention. McGhee's (2010a) original goal in developing the 7HHP was to strengthen one's sense of humor such that it could be actively used in real-life stressful situations to boost resilience and cope more effectively. He assumed this to be an essential prerequisite to the achievement of a high level of happiness and life satisfaction. In this respect, future 7HHP training studies should specifically examine the program's impact on coping with real-life stressors. A study by Beh-Pajooh, Jahangiri, and Zahrakar (2010) showing a significant decrease in depression in patients coping with spinal cord injuries is a good example of this kind of research. A life well-lived, however, goes beyond happiness, depression, and life satisfaction. Humor might also enhance positive relationships or build meaning (while negative humor, such as cynicism, might be deleterious to meaning). Measures addressing these aspects should be included in future evaluations of humor programs.

Conclusion

Research supports that humor is trainable and that training humor in turn leads to other desirable outcomes (i.e., increased positive emotions, decreased negative emotions, increased coping with life stressors). This can be interpreted as justification to list humor among the important character strengths, as the first criterion for a strength is that it should lead to fulfillment in life. Training-induced changes prevail at least for a few months, and if they do enrich people's lives, one can hope that people will continue to practice and refine the use of humor. This hope needs to be verified, however, as the follow-ups of the existing research are too short to make such assertions.

In addition to improving both humor and well-being, humor training might lead to increases in other life variables that are associated with the use of humor (e.g., interactions with others, longer lasting mood, popularity as a friend or company). These variables have yet to be examined in humor interventions and thus this remains an open question. Further research on humor interventions should also begin to test the boundaries of these interventions in terms of the people and contexts for which they might be the most useful, as well as ways to broaden the intervention programs for novel populations and contexts. Then we will know whether humor trainings are useful for everyone, independent of the level of strengths to start with, or whether special modules will have to be developed for use with humor starters, advanced humor users, or groups with special characteristics.

It is also too early to say what aspects of humor can be trained and which ones not. The results of such studies and further refinement of interventions can provide additional support and increase the value of humor training within the arsenal of positive psychological interventions. Its value as an intervention technique corresponds to its practicality, the amount of training needed, the amount of change obtained reliably, and the breadth of the impact of this change in people's daily lives and the sustainability thereof. The results so far provide ample evidence that humor is useful, but further evaluation studies are needed.

Acknowledgment

The preparation of this chapter was facilitated by a grant from the Swiss National Science Foundation (Positive Interventions: Empirical studies on enhancing satisfaction with life (SNF: 100014_132512/1)).

References

Abel, M. H., & Maxwell, D. (2002). Humor and affective consequences of a stressful task. *Journal of Social and Clinical Psychology, 21*, 165–190.

Andress, W. C., Hoshino, M., & Rorke, S. C. (2010, July). Empirical evidence for therapeutic laughter courses on a university campus. Paper presented at the 35th Annual National Wellness Conference, Stevens Point, WI.

Beh-Pajooh, A., Jahangiri, M., & Zahrakar, K. (2010). Humor skills training and reducing depression in patients with spinal cord injury. *Journal of Iranian Psychologists, 6*, 227–236.

Craik, K. H., Lampert, M. D., & Nelson, A. J. (1996). Sense of humor and styles of everyday humorous conduct. *Humor: International Journal of Humor Research, 9*, 273–302.

Crawford, S. (2009). *Humor skills enhancement: A positive approach to emotional well-being.* Unpublished doctoral dissertation, James Cook University, North Queensland, Australia.

Crawford, S. A., & Caltabiano, N. J. (2011). Promoting emotional well-being through the use of humour. *Journal of Positive Psychology, 6*, 237–252.

Deaner, S. L., & McConatha, J. T. (1993). The relation of humor to depression and personality. *Psychological Reports, 72*, 755–763.

Falkenberg, I., Buchkremer, G., Bartels, M., & Wild, B. (2011). Implementation of a manual-based training of humor abilities in patients with depression: A pilot study. *Psychiatry Research, 186*, 454–457.

Falkenberg, I., McGhee, P. E., & Wild, B. (2012). *Humorfähigkeiten trainieren: Ein Manual für die psychiatrisch-psychotherapeutische Praxis* [Humor skills training: A manual for psychiatric and psychotherapeutic practice]. Stuttgart: Schattauer.

Gander, F., Proyer, R. T., Ruch, W., & Wyss, T. (2013). Strength-based positive interventions: Further evidence on their potential for enhancing well-being and alleviating depression. *Journal of Happiness Studies, 14*, 1241–1259. Online first publication.

Gunderson, A. L. (1998). *A comparison of the effect of two humor programs on self-reported coping capabilities and pain among the elderly.* Unpublished master's thesis, Montclair State University, Montclair, NJ.

Kuiper, N. A., & Martin, R. A. (1998). Laughter and stress in daily life: relation to positive and negative affect. *Motivation and Emotion*, *22*, 133–153.

Kuiper, N. A., Martin, R. A., & Dance, K. A. (1992). Sense of humor and enhanced quality of life. *Personality and Individual Differences*, *13*, 1273–1283.

Lefcourt, H. M., & Martin, R. A. (1986). *Humor and life stress: Antidote to adversity.* New York: Springer-Verlag.

Lovibond, S. H., & Lovibond, P. F. (1995). *Manual for the depression anxiety stress scales* (2nd ed.). Sydney: Psychology Foundation.

Lyubomirsky, S., & Layous, K. (2013). How do simple positive activities increase well-being? *Current Directions in Psychological Science*, *22*, 57–62.

Martin, R. A., & Lefcourt, H. M. (1983). Sense of humor as a moderator of the relation between stressors and moods. *Journal of Personality and Social Psychology*, *45*, 1313–1324.

Martin, R. A., Puhlik-Doris, P., Larsen, G., Gray, J., & Weir, K. (2003). Individual differences in uses of humor and their relationship to psychological well-being: Development of the humor styles questionnaire. *Journal of Research in Personality*, *37*, 48–75.

McGhee, P. E. (1996). *Health, healing and the amuse system: Humor as survival training.* Dubuque, IA: Kendall/Hunt.

McGhee, P. E. (2010a). *Humor as survival training for a stressed-out world: The 7 humor habits program.* Bloomington, IN: Author House.

McGhee, P. E. (2010b). *Humor: The lighter path to resilience and health.* Bloomington, IN: Author House.

Moran, C. C., & Massam, M. M. (1999). Differential influences of coping humor and humor bias on mood. *Behavioral Medicine*, *25*, 36–42.

Müller, L., & Ruch, W. (2011). Humor and strengths of character. *Journal of Positive Psychology*, *6*, 368–376.

Nevo, O., Aharonson, H., & Klingman, A. (1998). The development and evaluation of a systematic program for improving sense of humor. In W. Ruch (Ed.), *The sense of humor: Explorations of a personality characteristic* (pp. 385–404). New York: Mouton de Gruyter.

Nezu, A. M., Nezu, C. M., & Blissett, S. E. (1988). Sense of humor as a moderator of the relation between stressful events and psychological distress: A prospective analysis. *Journal of Personality and Social Psychology*, *54*, 520–525.

Park, N., Peterson, C., & Seligman, M. E. P. (2004). Strengths of character and well-being. *Journal of Social and Clinical Psychology*, *23*, 603–619.

Peterson, C., Park, N., & Seligman, M. E. P. (2006). Greater strengths of character and recovery from illness. *Journal of Positive Psychology*, *1*, 7–26.

Peterson, C., & Seligman, M. E. P. (2004). *Character strengths and virtues: A handbook and classification.* Washington, DC: American Psychological Association.

Proyer, R. T., Gander, W., Wyss, T., & Ruch, W. (2011). The relation of character strengths to past, present and future life satisfaction among German-speaking women. *Applied Psychology: Health and Well-Being*, *3*, 370–384.

Proyer, R. T., Ruch, W., & Buschor, C. (2012). Testing strengths-based interventions: A preliminary study on the effectiveness of a program targeting curiosity, gratitude, hope, humor, and zest for enhancing life satisfaction. *Journal of Happiness Studies*, *14*, 275–292.

Ruch, W. (1997). State and trait cheerfulness and the induction of exhilaration: A FACS study. *European Psychologist*, *2*, 328–341.

Ruch, W. (Ed.) (2007). *Sense of humor: Explorations of humor as a personality characteristic.* Berlin: Mouton de Gruyter.

Ruch, W. (2008). The psychology of humor. In V. Raskin (Ed.), *A primer of humor* (pp. 17–100). Berlin: Mouton de Gruyter.

Ruch, W. (2012, April). Humor and positive psychology: A matching couple? Paper session presented at the 25th annual conference of the Association for Applied and Therapeutic Humor, Chicago.

Ruch, W., Proyer, R. T., Harzer, C., Park, N., Peterson, C., & Seligman, M. E. P. (2010). Adaptation and validation of the German version of the Values in Action Inventory of Strengths (VIA-IS) and the development of a peer-rating form. *Journal of Individual Differences, 31*, 138–149.

Ruch, W., Proyer, R. T., & Weber, M. (2010a). Humor as a character strength among the elderly: Theoretical considerations. *Zeitschrift für Gerontologie und Geriatrie, 43*, 8–12.

Ruch, W., Proyer, R. T., & Weber, M. (2010b). Humor as a character strength among the elderly: Empirical findings on age-related changes and its contribution to satisfaction with life. *Zeitschrift für Gerontologie und Geriatrie, 43*, 13–18.

Ruch, W., Rodden, F. A., & Proyer, R. T. (2011). Humor and other positive interventions in medical and therapeutic settings. In B. Kirkcaldy (Ed.), *The art and science of health care: Psychology and human factors for practitioners* (pp. 277–294). Göttingen: Hogrefe Publishers.

Rusch, S., & Stolz, H. (2009). *Ist Sinn für Humor lernbar? Eine Anwendung und Evaluation des 8 Stufen Programs (McGhee, 1999)* [Can a sense of humor be learned? An application and evaluation of the 8-Step Program (McGhee, 1999)]. Unpublished master's thesis, University of Zurich, Switzerland.

Sassenrath, S. (2001). *Humor und Lachen als Stressbewältigungsstrategie* [Humor and laughter as coping mechanism]. Unpublished master's thesis, University of Vienna, Austria.

Schueller, S. M., & Parks, A. C. (2012). Disseminating self-help: Positive psychology exercises in an online trial. *Journal of Medical Internet Research, 14*, e63.

Sin, N. L. & Lyubomirsky, S. (2009). Enhancing well-being and alleviating depressive symptoms with positive psychology interventions: A practice-friendly meta-analysis. *Journal of Clinical Psychology, 65*, 467–487.

Wilbers, J. (2009). *Humour appreciation and emotion regulation: Training humour abilities in depressive patients.* Unpublished master's thesis, Maastricht University, The Netherlands.

Yovetich, N. A., Dale, J. A. & Hudak, M. A. (1990). Benefits of humor in reduction of threat-induced anxiety. *Psychological Reports, 66*, 51–58.

11

Enacting Flow and Student Engagement in the College Classroom

David J. Shernoff and Brett Anderson

Flow is a peak mental state of full immersion in an activity, characterized by a feeling of energized focus, full involvement, and enjoyment in the process (Csikszentmihalyi, 1990, 1997). In flow, one has the feeling of doing the activity well or being successful at it. Emotions are positive and energized, as with joy, rapture, or intense enjoyment, even though happiness or fulfillment is frequently reported only in retrospect since individuals in flow are usually too focused to form larger meanings of the experience at the time. Flow is a central construct in positive psychology, and is considered one of the main paths to happiness (Seligman, Steen, Park, & Peterson, 2005). There has been a fair amount of research on flow, its various applications, and its associations with a variety of psychological benefits (see Csikszentmihalyi, Abuuhamdeh, & Nakamura, 2005; Strati, Shernoff, & Kackar, 2012). Despite the recognized value of flow for one's quality of life, there have been very few interventions attempting to facilitate it as there have been for many other positive psychological constructs such as optimism, gratitude, and hope. In this chapter, we will briefly review research on flow in education – one of the few settings in which flow has been deliberately induced – including those studies that attempt to facilitate flow in domain-specific instruction. We then present an original study in which we attempted to teach, enact, and stimulate flow in undergraduate classrooms, interpret the results, and identify implications for fostering flow.

Flow Theory and Student Engagement

While flow is typically described holistically as a singular experience with certain psychological characteristics (Csikszentmihalyi, 1990), we find it conceptually useful to distinguish between the experience of and the conditions for flow.

The Wiley Blackwell Handbook of Positive Psychological Interventions, First Edition.
Edited by Acacia C. Parks and Stephen M. Schueller.

As described above, the *experience* of flow is characterized by deep immersion and positive emotions, but it also includes a perception of being in control, loss of self-consciousness, and a distorted perception of time (usually time seems to fly) (Csikszentmihalyi et al., 2005; Strati et al., 2012). However, certain *conditions* make flow experiences more likely. Perhaps the most central criterion for flow to occur is an activity that presents a significant challenge paired with a high degree of skill that can be used to meet the challenge. In addition, flow is more typical when the activity is autotelic, or pursued as a goal in and of itself, and when the emphasis is more on the process than the product. Lastly, flow occurs most often in situations when the individual has clear goals, receives immediate feedback on their progress towards those goals, and feels both autonomous and in control.

Flow is inherently related to learning, because in the process of developing one's talents and gaining skills, one needs to continually increase the level of challenge to hold one's interest; further skills are then needed to meet increasingly higher levels of challenge. In this iterative process, both skills and challenges will repeatedly be maximized, and individuals are most likely to enter flow when this occurs. In addition, while facts and rudimentary knowledge may be learned through language and memorization, the learning of most domain-based skills and talents is episodic, characterized by engagement in activities involving motion, rhythm, action, and use of material objects (Shernoff, 2013). We have therefore conceptualized and measured engagement in learning as rooted in the experience of flow, measuring it as the simultaneous occurrence of high concentration, enjoyment, and interest – all experiential components research has shown to be related to learning (Shernoff & Csikszentmihalyi, 2009).

Research on Flow in Educational Settings

Much of the research on flow in educational settings has used the Experience Sampling Method (ESM) in which moment-by-moment snapshots of subjective experience are obtained when participants respond to random signaling prompting them to complete a brief self-report form (Hektner, Schmidt, & Csikszentmihalyi, 2007). In addition to the participants' experience, the survey also solicits information about the environment such as activities and social partners. A repeated finding of ESM research in educational settings is that flow and engagement in learning vary by activity type. For example, studies have found that students reported higher levels of flow and were more engaged in cooperative group work and individual work compared to whole class or large group instruction in both secondary and higher education (Peterson & Miller, 2004; Shernoff, Csikszentmihalyi, Schneider, & Shernoff, 2003).

Recent studies of optimal learning environments have examined the environmental features of classrooms and other educational contexts empirically shown to produce high levels of engagement and/or flow (Shernoff, 2012; Shernoff, Tonks, Anderson, & Dortch, 2011). While most of these studies are correlational, the logical implication is that features of the learning environment give rise to heightened engagement or flow rather than vice versa. The most distinctive characteristic of optimal learning environments is ***environmental complexity***, which combines environmental challenge and environmental support. Features of environmental challenge include challenging tasks, clear goals, perceived relevance, and high expectations, use of domain-specific tools to solve problems or fashion products, and accountability/assessments. Another distinctive characteristic of optimal learning environments is ***environmental support***. Environmental support includes motivational/autonomy support, supportive relations, interactivity, performance feedback, and activity level. While some of these studies were based in traditional classrooms, models of optimal learning environments were found mainly in private or alternative public schools (Shernoff, 2013). For example, Rathunde and Csikszentmihalyi (2005a, 2005b) found that students (n = 290) attending Montessori high schools, which integrate freedom of activity choice (environmental supports) with high developmental demands, reported more positive perceptions and emotions while at school compared to students in traditional public high schools. Similarly, students (n = 80) attending the alternative and democratically governed Nova High School in Seattle, Washington, which promotes egalitarian relationships and creates a community climate of mutual respect, involvement, and fairness, were found to be more engaged than those attending a traditional public school (Johnson, 2008).

ESM research has generally found that adolescent-aged students are more engaged during extra-curriculum activities than they are when doing school work (Csikszentmihalyi & Larson, 1984), and when in non-academic classes compared to their academic classes (Shernoff et al., 2003). Adolescents report especially high levels of engagement in structured after-school programs (Vandell et al., 2005). When in such programs, students reported more positively valenced affective states during structured learning activities such as academic and arts enrichment compared to during academic homework (Shernoff & Vandell, 2007). It appeared that students became highly engaged in learning during activities in which they played an authentic role in activities that had meaning or value in real life, and were not perceived as merely academic exercises. Therefore, in our study to facilitate flow in higher education presented in this chapter, we tested the hypothesis that engagement in learning may be maximized in activities that are project-based, set in the real life of the community, and relevant to the lives of youth.

Toward Interventions to Facilitate Flow and Engagement in Learning

Only a small handful of studies of educational contexts attempt to implement a program, curriculum, or intervention specifically designed to elevate flow. However, several recent studies have attempted to implement domain-specific curricular innovations in an effort to stimulate flow and engagement in learning in high school classrooms. We here review one in the context of science instruction and one in English instruction.

As modeled by Larson (2011), an engaging approach to high school science is a curriculum and instruction that is "backward designed" (Wiggins & McTighe, 2005) to develop interest in working towards a real-world learning goal and to sustain engagement as scientific language and vocabulary improve. Backward design is designing instruction with the educational "ends" in mind, as when identifying the educational goals and specific understandings desired before selecting the instructional method and mode of assessment. In this case, the educational ends were to facilitate and sustain engagement, as well as to build science literacy in biology.

Larson (2011) designed a mixed-methods, quasi-experimental study comparing student engagement and conceptual science understanding among students receiving her backward-designed science curriculum intervention to a control group receiving traditional instruction. The curricular intervention emphasized academic literacy instruction. Academic literacy is fluency with modes of inquiry, expression, and discourse in common across core subjects, such as making a hypothesis or supporting an argument with evidence. The intervention utilized four steps or cumulative stages of engaging instruction including (a) situating scientific inquiry to make it relevant to the lives of students (e.g., beginning a unit on germs and disease by dispensing Glo Germ into students' hands and observing the germs after rounds of hand washing); (b) sustaining interest and engagement for the continued construction of scientific knowledge (e.g., activities to simulate a pandemic); (c) supporting autonomy to synthesize knowledge (e.g., making available a wide variety of related reading materials to be explored voluntarily); and (d) student demonstration of scientific knowledge and literacy (e.g., writing an essay contextualized in real-life products such as an article for the school newspaper, serving as a primary assessment of conceptual knowledge and vocabulary). To assess engagement and learning, Larson used the ESM and authentic learning measures such as science essays in response to a writing prompt, scored with the Illinois state ISAT Writing Rubric aligned with the Illinois Learning Standards. Results indicated that students were significantly more engaged, and obtained significantly higher scientific literacy, reasoned thought, and conceptual understanding compared to a control group using traditional instruction, with high effect sizes (Larson, 2011).

Curricular innovations in English to facilitate a deeper absorption and interaction with literature have been modeled by Wilhelm (2008), by using a methodology similar to the ESM, allowing Wilhelm to obtain repeated snapshots of students' experiences while reading literature. Wilhelm found that proficient readers experientially enter a story, form powerful mental images, and deeply relate to the characters when reading literature; such readers usually proceed to develop higher-level interpretive and reflective skills. Other readers, however, are resistant to high-level engagement while reading, and have difficulty visualizing or participating in the story world (Wilhelm, 2008). Particularly to help this latter group, Wilhelm developed several innovative and engaging approaches to English and literacy instruction based in drama and the arts. Activities to help students experientially enter the story world and progress to more advanced skills included revolving role dramas (taking turns acting out particular scenes paralleling the text), dramatic play (improvisational acting to fill out expected action following a prompt from the story), and guided imagery (writing about or drawing scenes, often guided by visual descriptions or musical accompaniments). Like many effective instructors, Wilhelm considered his students' deep engagement with content materials to be his primary marker of success. As students participated in these activities, reluctant readers began to make the same moves as the engaged readers in terms of entering story worlds, becoming connected to the characters and authors, and reflecting on their meanings contained in the text.

There has been even less research reported on flow or engagement in higher education than there has been in the secondary and elementary levels. One exception was a unique curricular intervention in which an educational video game was designed to teach an undergraduate course in mechanical engineering (Coller, Shernoff, & Strati, 2011). Coller designed a new way to teach the challenging mechanical engineering course, Dynamic Systems and Control. Instead of using the traditional approach based on problem sets from a textbook, Coller centered the course on an educational video game in which students raced a virtual car around a track for all of their lab exercises and homework. Specifically designed to plunge students into deep flow with the virtual world of racing, the program demanded that students employ relevant principles of mechanical engineering in order to race the car well. Coller and colleagues performed a quasi-experimental ESM study comparing student engagement and performance of a cohort of students receiving this experimental intervention to that of a control cohort taking the course as it had traditionally been taught. Results revealed that students in the experimental cohort reported significantly greater flow-like engagement, intrinsic motivation, positive affect, and creativity than the students who completed their coursework in the traditional way.

The Study

The present study sought to isolate and measure various flow conditions as well as the effects of specific activity types during multiple class meetings of two consecutive semesters of an undergraduate educational psychology course (Adolescent Development). The first was a unit on flow and student engagement in order to test whether students could experience flow firsthand while learning about it conceptually. The rationale was that when teaching some educational concepts such as flow, it may be extremely important for instruction to "walk the talk," or enact rather than merely teach the concept. In the subsequent semester, data were gathered in a service-learning class project centered on learning about and creating a community service student organization on campus. This part of the study was to test if students experience flow and student engagement more readily in project-based instruction that focuses on real-life events with real consequences outside of the classroom.

The following research questions were examined:

Research Question 1. Would students' engagement and other experiential variables vary as they moved from one activity to another during a unit on flow in which undergraduate students participated in the ESM? In particular, would students perceive conditions for flow such as challenge and skill, as well as student engagement, to be higher in activities designed to create flow conditions and stimulate engagement?

Research Question 2. Would instructional activities during a service-learning class project in the subsequent semester produce an increase in engagement and other experiential measures compared to the previous semester due to basing activities on issues, events, and outcomes in the "real world?" Which activities produced the highest and lowest engagement across both semesters? Would participants find a project oriented towards community service and social change meaningful?

Method

Participants Participants (n = 54) were undergraduate students enrolled in two consecutive semesters of an undergraduate educational psychology course at a Midwestern university located in a rural, middle-class community. Half of the students (n = 27) were enrolled in the fall 2010 semester, and half (n = 27) were enrolled in the same course in the spring 2011 semester. The gender and ethnic breakdown was similar in both classes: 89% of the sample (n = 24 in the fall and n = 24 in the spring) were female; 68% (n = 17 in the fall and n = 20 in the spring) were Caucasian; 26% (n = 8 in the fall and n = 6 in the spring) were African American; and 6% (n = 2 in the fall and n = 1 in the spring) were Latino. Teacher participants included a Caucasian, male instructor (first author), and three teacher's assistants (TAs): a Caucasian, male graduate student (second author) in the fall semester, and two female undergraduate students in the spring semester, one Caucasian and one Latino.

Procedures

Instrumentation To introduce students to the principal research method for studying flow, and in the process facilitate an awareness of their own emotional fluctuations, students participated in the Experience Sampling Method (or ESM; see Hektner et al., 2007). Students were signaled at one random time point during each of a variety of instructional activities during a designated unit in each semester, described in more detail below. When signaled, students completed an Experience Sampling Form (ESF) on which they rated their perception of the activity and subjective experiences on seven 5-point Likert-type scales ranging from "Not at all" to "Very much." The seven items were: (a) "How important was this activity to you and your future goals?" (b) "Was it interesting?" (c) "Was it challenging?" (d) "Did you enjoy what you were doing?" (e) "How hard were you concentrating?" (f) "Were you using a high level of skill?" and (g) "How much were you learning?" Repeated responses to these items were then utilized as the primary dependent measures of student engagement, flow conditions, and perceived learning. Student engagement was a composite of the items measuring concentration, interest, and enjoyment used in previous research (see Shernoff & Csikszentmihalyi, 2009) reaching an acceptable level of reliability ($\alpha = .77$). Items measuring challenge and skills were the primary conditions for flow measured. The measure of perceived learning was item (g).

Units and activities Units in both semesters included a variety of activity types, which unfolded over the course of multiple class meetings. See Table 11.1 for a description of each activity. To provide a more in-depth example, a detailed description of the flow application intervention tested in the fall semester is provided below.

Activity 9 (fall, class meeting 2) – flow application intervention. The overarching objective of the flow application intervention was for students in small groups to design an activity to foster flow in a given context with a specific population. This was designed as an opportunity not only for students to apply the concept of flow to a real-world context, but also to practice designing and creating the conditions that allow youth to experience flow as future educators. The activity took approximately 35–45 minutes.

First, the classroom was divided into five groups of five or six students. Each group received a packet of materials. Students followed along as instructions were provided orally. For each small group, the Instruction Sheet specified a different, unique population and context for which the group was to design a flow-inducing activity. Example populations included high school students, middle school students, middle school girls, and late adolescents (e.g., ages 17–22); examples of contexts included an after-school club, an art class, a mentoring program to promote resiliency and leadership, a civic action program to promote citizenship and awareness of societal issues, and a computer science class.

The rest of the Instruction Sheet, which was the same for all groups, further directed each small group to identify and describe (a) an activity, (b) defining rules of the activity, (c) instructions for the population, (d) the goals of the activity, and (e) how the group will know if the activity indeed facilitated flow (i.e., method of evaluation). Each student in a group was responsible for describing one of these components on an Activity Structure Worksheet by the end of the activity. In addition, each student was assigned a Specialist Role to be responsible for assuring one of the flow conditions was present in the design of the activity, and described how this responsibility was met in writing.

Table 11.1 Description of activities during the fall and spring semester

Fall semester, class meeting 1	
Activity 1	**Final paper instructions** Instructions for the final paper in the course were distributed and explained orally by the instructor. Students could ask questions.
Activity 2	**Cognitive constructivism video** Students watched a video demonstrating principles of Piaget's cognitive constructivism via a double-digit subtraction task.
Activity 3	**Structured cognitive constructivism video** The video was paused to provide students with instructions and a structured note recording sheet to identify principles of cognitive constructivism depicted in the video.
Activity 4	**Flow presentation and small group discussion** Following a 12-minute PowerPoint presentation describing the experience of flow, students broke into small groups or pairs to share times that they felt like they were in flow.
Activity 5	**Large group discussion on flow** Large group activity to share experiences discussed in Activity 4.
Activity 6	**Flow states presentation** Continuation of PowerPoint presentation focusing on conditions for flow states. Students were given a handout with a 2 × 2 chart of high/low challenge and skill conditions, and were asked to complete the psychological state predicted by flow theory (Csikszentmihalyi, 1997) for each combination, providing an example.
Fall semester, class meeting 2	
Activity 7	**Class discussion on reading** Class discussion about a reading assignment on "Flow in Schools" (Shernoff & Csikszentmihalyi, 2009), in which the instructor and TA facilitated with guiding questions.
Activity 8	**Written reflection** Written reflections about the flow unit and students' experience participating in the ESM. Students wrote answers to the following three questions: (a) "What did you learn about flow, or flow in the life of adolescents, that was most valuable?" (b) "Do you think that the ESM (i.e., beeper) method accurately captured your level of flow and engagement over the course of the unit? Why or why not?" and (c) "Would there be a better way? If so, what?" High-challenge task, requiring reflection, independent thinking, and written expression skills.
Activity 9	**Flow application intervention** Students in small groups design an activity to foster flow in a given context with a specific population.
Activity 10	**Presentation of data** Presentation of research findings on adolescents' quality of experience as measured by the ESM (e.g., high flow activities and low flow activities) from the previous studies, Being adolescent (Csikszentmihalyi & Larson, 1984) and Becoming adult (Csikszentmihalyi & Schneider, 2000).

(*continued*)

Table 11.1 (*Continued*)

Spring semester, class meeting 1	
Activity 11	**Icebreaker** The first three activities in the first class of the group project were ice-breaking activities from PeaceJam's service-learning curriculum. In the first activity, students were to stand up if read-aloud statements applied to them ("Please stand if …"). Example statements were, "You have felt it is not always safe in the neighborhood around your schools," "Someone has threatened you personally in the last three years," "Someone you know personally has been in a situation where a knife was used in a threatening way," and, "… where a gun was used in a threatening way." Follow-up discussion questions included, "What did you notice from our pattern of standing up?" "What does this tell you about our own lives?" and, "How do you think teenagers in other parts of the country or world would respond to these categories?"
Activity 12	**Role-playing** Role-played issues of social inclusion and exclusion. Eight volunteers were taken, with one volunteer asked to leave the room. The remaining volunteers were told that they formed a group of friends, and should stand in a circle with their arms around each other's shoulders, much like a sports huddle. After returning to the room, the solitary volunteer played the role of an "outsider," and was told to try to enter the group using any verbal means possible in three consecutive role-plays: Role-play 1 – the group of "friends" were asked to be exclusive, keeping their backs to the outsider and keeping the outsider on the outside. Role-play 2 – the group of friends were asked to let the outsider inside physically, and put their arms around his shoulders too, but to ignore him and change the topic whenever he tried to speak. Role-play 3 – the group of friends were asked to include the outsider in the group, and to make him feel welcomed. Discussion questions were asked after each role-play, such as "Why do people discriminate against other people?"
Activity 13	**Reflection** This activity was intended to help students reflect on behavioral choices we and others make. Students were broken into groups of six or seven students. They were then provided with descriptions of five basic human needs according to psychiatrist, Dr William Glasser: survival, love and belonging, power, freedom, and fun. They were then asked to explore two scenarios, one in which a young person steals a car, and another in which a young person joins a gang. After each scenario, students were asked how the action might have been done to satisfy each of the needs (e.g., "How could the car theft have helped to meet the need for survival?"). Following consideration of the two scenarios, students proceeded to engage in small group discussions with discussion questions such as, "Does this tell us anything about the possible roots of violence? What?"

Table 11.1 (*Continued*)

Spring semester, class meeting 2	
Activity 14	**Viewing testimonials** Students were introduced to the PeaceJam organization, including its history and mission, how it operates, and its impact on the development of participants. In this activity, students watched a video of testimonials from PeaceJam participants about how participation impacted them personally and their development as an individual.
Activity 15	**Book reading and presentation** Following an assignment in which each student read a chapter from a book on PeaceJam's 10 "Global Calls to Action" about a youth who interacted with a Nobel Peace Laureate in service of that call, all students made a class presentation of what they had learned from the chapter they had read.
Activity 16	**Service phase of project** Following the first phase of the project in which students were educated about PeaceJam, its potential impact on adolescents, and social issues it is intended to address, the service phase of the project began in which the class was intended to "spring into action." The instructor presented plans for forming a PeaceJam Scholars student organization and the class began to discuss strategies for outreach and recruitment.
Activity 17	**Class brainstorm** This was a whole class brainstorming activity on strategies for the PeaceJam club recruitment and outreach, and possibilities for division of labor.
Spring semester, class meeting 3	
Activity 18	**Small group applications** Students worked in small groups to complete a part of the student organization's application to the university's Student Association. This included the writing of a mission statement, a constitution with bylaws according to a template, and election procedures.
Spring semester, class meeting 4	
Activity 19	**Small group discussion** This was a small group activity to discuss outreach activities and division of labor. At the time of the signal, students were reading instructions at the beginning of the activity.
Activities 20 and 21	**Small group discussion 2** Following the reading of instructions, students worked in small groups to discuss strategies for communicating with other classes and organizations; media strategies including print media (e.g., campus newspapers and internet articles), radio, college publicists, and social networking outlets; and strategies for making and distributing materials such as flyers and signs.
Spring semester, class meeting 5	
Activities 22 and 23	**Small group promotional activity** Students worked in small groups to make promotional materials using computer design programs. They were given significant latitude to create promotional materials of interest.

(*continued*)

Table 11.1 (*Continued*)

Spring semester, class meeting 6	
Activities 24 and 25	**Small group promotional activity 2** Students continued work on promotional materials and all students were to complete at least one flyer either independently or as part of a team. Instructions indicated that the best or most creative flyers according to a panel of the PeaceJam Scholars officers (who had now been elected) would be recognized and announced.

Qualitative measures of experience (spring) During the spring semester, students had several opportunities to reflect in writing on the importance of community service to adolescent development and their personal experience with the group project. At the end of the class project, students completed several follow-up measures of experience, including a survey adapted from Jones, Bench, and Warnaar (2010) in which students rated the extent to which their encounter with the class project was meaningful and purposeful on a five-point scale from "agree" to "disagree" (sample items: "Working for social change is personally meaningful"; and "Participating in the class project has motivated me to work for social change"). In addition, a focus group of five students participated in a recorded interview soliciting their reflections on the class project. These follow-up measures will be discussed as a complement to the ESM analysis of data presented below.

Results

Statistical analyses There were 46 student participants who provided at least one of the ESFs ($N_{ESF} = 441$) collected. To answer Research Question 1, we employed One-Way ANOVA comparing mean differences in engagement and other experiential variables, and Duncan's Multiple Range post-hoc tests for significance testing mean differences between activities during the unit on flow. To answer Research Question 2, we conducted a factor and correlational analysis of the experiential items, and examined histograms of experiential items by activity. We also conducted an Independent-Samples t-test comparing the mean difference in engagement and other experiential variables between the fall and spring semester at both the activity and person level, and examined a histogram of engagement combining activities from both semesters.

Findings

Preliminary analyses A factor analysis was conducted to determine what set of experiential variables, if any, were highly intercorrelated with perceived learning and concentration as subjective proxies for learning. Two factors emerged with Eigenvalues greater than 1. Variables loading highly on the first, which accounted for 55% of the variance, included interest (.94), enjoyment (.85), importance

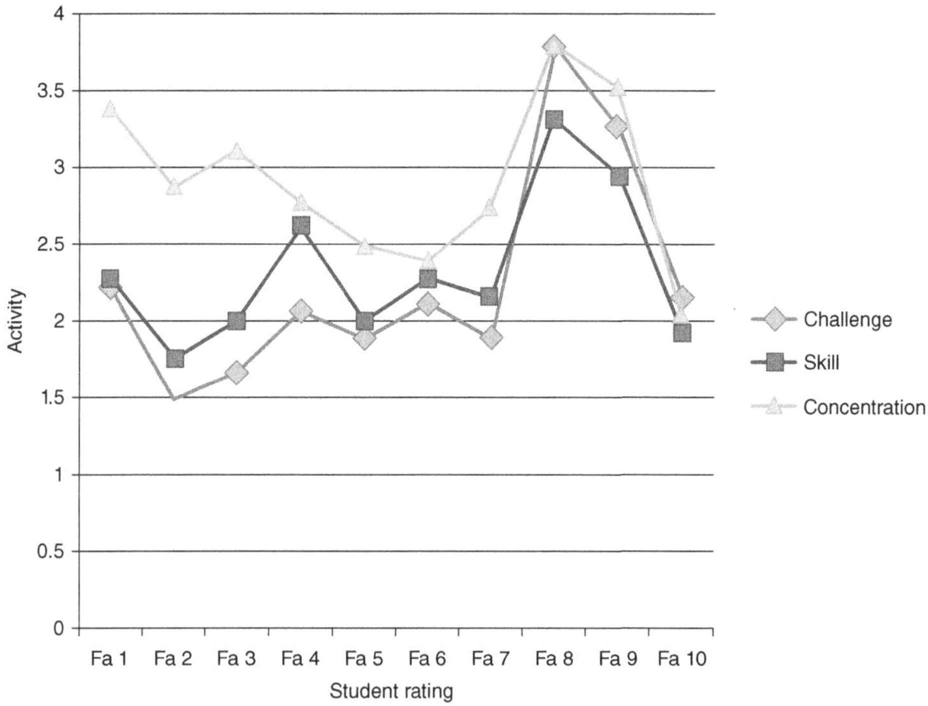

Figure 11.1 Challenge, skill, and concentration by activity during the flow unit

(.75), and perceived learning (.74). This factor appeared to represent intrinsic motivation and relevance as highly related to perceived learning in the college classroom. Variables loading highly onto the second factor, accounting for 16% of the variance, were challenge (.98), skills (.85), and concentration (.52). This factor appeared to represent the flow conditions and its theorized relation to concentration. Figure 11.1 illustrates how challenge, skills, and concentration tended to vary together by activity during the unit on flow, with all three heightened during the flow intervention application and the reflective writing activity. The correlation between engagement and perceived learning at the activity level confirmed a moderately high relationship ($r = .71$, $p < .01$), which was significant despite an N of only 25 activities. Similarly supportive of the factor analysis, challenge, skill, and concentration had a high intercorrelation at the activity level ($\alpha = .84$).

Research Question 1 The overall F-test of the hypothesis of mean differences in engagement among activities during the unit on flow in the fall semester was not significant, $F(9, 174) = 1.47$, ns. Duncan's post-hoc tests revealed one exception, however: the reflective writing activity (Activity 8) was reported as significantly more engaging than Activities 6 and 10, both of which were direct instruction (PowerPoint presentation on flow conditions, and presentation of findings about flow in the life of adolescents). Also, the F-tests for mean differences in the flow conditions of challenge and skill were statistically significant, F (9, 174) = 9.90, p < .001; and F (9, 173) = 3.81, p <.001). Post-hoc comparisons revealed challenge was significantly higher in the reflective writing activity and the flow application intervention than in all of the other activities, and skill level was also higher in these activities than in the five activities in the bottom of the skill level distribution. The lowest skill use was reported in Activity 2 (unstructured viewing of the Piaget video), which was significantly lower than not only the writing activity and flow intervention, but also Activity 4 (sharing flow experiences in small groups). The only other experiential item for which the F-test was significant was concentration, F (9, 174) = 5.50, p <.001, with the highest level of concentration also reported in the reflective writing activity and flow application intervention.

Research Question 2 Results of Independent-Samples t-tests at the activity level (e.g., mean engagement in Activities 1–10 vs. Activities 11–25) reveal that engagement and importance were reported to be significantly higher in the fall semester, t (24) = 2.31, p < .05; and t (24) = 2.12, p < .05, respectively. This indicates that average engagement was actually lower in the service-learning class project activities in the spring than in the flow unit activities in the fall. Figure 11.2 illustrates mean engagement in all 25 activities from lowest to highest. Here we see engagement was reported to be lower in nearly all of the activities in the spring semester

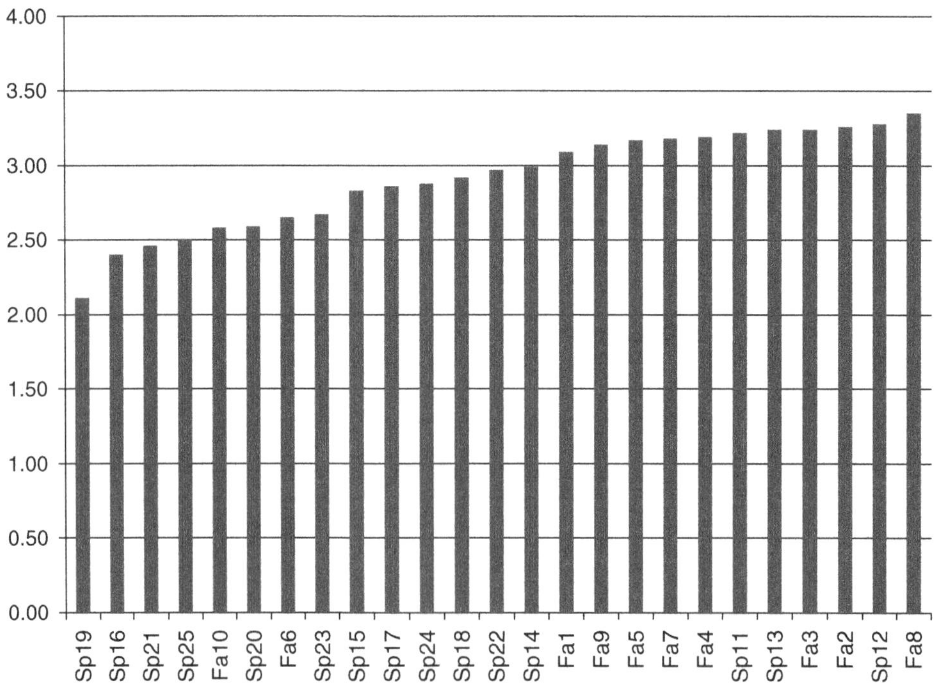

Figure 11.2 Engagement in 25 sampled activities in two semesters, from lowest to highest
Note: Labels indicate fall or spring semester (Fa or Sp) followed by the activity number.

compared to the fall semester with the notable exception of the icebreaker activities to promote awareness and connections around issues of violence and social exclusion (spring activities 11, 12, and 13). Results of t-tests at the student level (e.g., mean engagement of students in the fall vs. students in the spring) yielded higher means among students in the fall (flow unit) for all experiential variables, but none of the differences were statistically significant.

Qualitative findings Qualitative data in the form of open-ended reflections, as well as a survey and focus group interview conducted at the end of the semester, were analyzed to assess if students would experience a project oriented towards community service and social change as meaningful. In their reflections, assignments, and interviews most students consistently demonstrated a sound understanding of how community service was of value to adolescent development. Furthermore, survey results indicated that on average students felt that working for social change was important, personally meaningful, and made them feel good about themselves. Of the 21 items in the survey, on average they more strongly agreed than disagreed with the vast majority of positive statements about the meaningfulness of the project. Strongest agreement was expressed with the statements: "I felt like I could give my opinion, or have a voice, in the class project activities"; "It is important for individuals to work for social change"; "Working on social action projects makes me feel competent or successful"; "Working for social change is personally meaningful"; and "Participating in the class project has made me more tolerant of people's differences." There were only three of the 21 statements with which students disagreed more than agreed, which were: "Participating in the class project is consistent with my spirituality or religious views"; "Participating in the class project has made me think about my place in the world"; and "I felt connected to my class project groups."

Perhaps the strongest theme emerging from student reflections and interviews was a high personal regard and appreciation for community service and service learning in general. Many students claimed that this disposition would inspire action on their part to be more involved with community service initiatives now or in the future. The vast majority of the students were open and honest that they lacked the time to be highly involved in the PeaceJam initiative on campus at this juncture in their undergraduate education, but nevertheless saw enough value in it that they hoped the organization would be successful and maintain a presence within the university. Most students also shared their appreciation for a range of values engendered by the class project, including making a difference in the world, helping others, human diversity, empathy and compassion, teamwork to improve one's community, service-oriented identity development, and making a contribution. They also valued the sense of self-esteem and accomplishment adolescents can gain from making a positive change in one's life and contributing to "something larger" in the outside world. Several students indicated that the values embodied by the class project influenced their educational and career goals.

Discussion

In this chapter, we presented a study comparing a range of college classroom activities both within and between two consecutive semesters of a college educational psychology course in terms of their association with flow and student engagement. With respect to the within-semester comparison of activities during a unit on flow, highest engagement was reported in a reflective writing activity (Activity 8), and secondarily in a flow application intervention (Activity 9), specifically designed to increase flow and engagement. In these activities, it is likely that conditions for flow were operative. For example, both Activity 8 and Activity 9 were high challenge activities, and students confirmed that this was met with a comparably high level of skill use. Moreover, the flow application intervention was specifically designed to (a) provide a sense of control for students by allowing them to design an original flow activity, (b) provide a clear goal for each student (i.e., through the specification of individual roles and responsibilities), (c) provide a challenge demanding the use of skills, requiring focused concentration, (d) provide feedback to each individual from the supervising instructor as well as student collaborators, (e) solicit a variety of skills (e.g., social, verbal, written) and interests, and (f) foster interactivity. With these most fundamental conditions for flow satisfied, according to the theory, the expectation for students to concentrate the hardest in these activities was also fulfilled. On the other hand, the lowest levels of engagement were reported during unstructured video viewing and teacher presentation on flow and related research findings, among the only activities in which the students were strictly consumers of information transmitted to the whole class and were required to surrender their control almost entirely.

Overall, we found that student engagement and sense of importance were higher in the fall semester than in the spring semester. In fact, lower engagement was reported in nearly every individual classroom activity in the spring with the exception of only the initial icebreaker activities designed to introduce issues of violence and social exclusion. These findings indicate that student engagement was actually lower during the service-learning project than during the unit on flow in the fall.

There may be a number of possible reasons why this was the case. First, it should not escape notice that the units were very different in nature. The explicit goal of the unit in the fall was the teaching and enacting of flow, but the class project in the spring seemingly had nothing to do with flow in terms of content (rather, the focus of the service-learning class project in the spring was on the role of community service in supporting adolescent development). It was of interest to test students' experience of flow given this difference because it may be argued that overtly attempting to teach and create flow can have the effect of ironically interfering with the experience of flow, which usually entails unselfconsciousness. However, results suggested that being conscious about the concept of flow did not detract from the experience of engagement in learning about it; on the contrary, student reflections indicated that they found the topic of flow to be a very novel, interesting, and engaging one.

Although one should not underestimate the potentially confounding influence of cohort effects when comparing results between only two classes, results suggest that the overarching dimension of embedding instruction in a real-life project is not a panacea or "mega-factor" for stimulating engagement, the hypothesis tested in the spring semester. On the contrary, results suggest that the more proximal conditions and intentional designing of these activities may take precedence in terms of potential to engage students. Not only was this illustrated in the case of the very methodically designed flow application intervention, but also in the case of the icebreaker activities in the spring, as these activities were also very thoughtfully designed and structured group activities from PeaceJam's official service-learning curriculum. Both activities were designed to foster connectedness and relationship building.

Findings also invite educators to consider the meaning of "instructional relevance," especially in the college classroom. The two-factor structure appearing to represent intrinsic motivation (i.e., interest, enjoyment, positive affect) on the one hand, and flow on the other (i.e., challenge, skills, concentration), is not at all atypical in ESM research on academic engagement at the secondary and university level (e.g., Coller et al., 2011; Shernoff et al., 2003). In high school classrooms, the perception of importance or instructional relevance in classrooms typically loads more highly onto the flow factor; however, in this sample of college students, it loaded more highly onto the intrinsic motivation factor, along with perceived learning. Because college students typically adopt a more consumer-oriented approach to course taking, they may enter courses with firm expectations about the relevance for their interests and career goals. Therefore, relevance may be more individualized and topic-based in college than at the secondary or prior levels of education, and may indeed be a strong catalyst for interest and perceived learning. In elementary and secondary instruction, engagement including importance may be more dependent on pedagogy and activity type.

Given the limitations of time (typically limited to course meeting times within a single semester) and space (typically on the college campus) when designing a course for the college classroom, embedding instruction in community projects may be vulnerable to backfiring by virtue of "trying too hard," ironically becoming perceived as more contrived than more traditional, less "ambitious" instruction. It is possible that service-learning projects may need to be student-selected and embedded in students' interests and career goals in order to generate greater engagement. This may prove challenging in mixed-majors undergraduate classrooms, but may stand a better chance of success at the graduate level where interests among students may be more homogeneous.

Despite relatively lower engagement during the service-learning class project in the spring, qualitative data demonstrate that most students found it to be a personally meaningful experience that enhanced their lives or futures. These somewhat discrepant findings may be indicative of the distinctiveness of two dimensions of engaged living suggested by Froh et al. (2010): absorption (e.g., the experience of flow in the moment), and social integration (e.g., the quality of one's relationships to society and the community). It may be that pursuing socially important, real-life causes in the college classroom has greater effects on global meaning-making and sense of personal meaningfulness than on one's momentary experiences of flow and engagement.

Facilitating Flow in Educational Contexts

Overall, the study supports the proposition that optimal learning environments are created by environmental complexity (i.e., a combination of environmental challenge and support), including a variety of environmental conditions that stimulate flow and engagement in learning. These conditions included optimal challenge, a complex task often involving the use of materials, clear and important student goals for the activity, interactivity, and teacher monitoring and feedback, and good rapport between teacher and students (Shernoff, 2012; Shernoff et al., 2011). When many of these features are present, students are frequently problem-solving, experimenting, or learning by discovery. To a certain extent, some schools with alternative approaches, such as Montessori schools (Rathunde & Csikszentmihalyi, 2005a, 2005b) and the Nova High School in Seattle (Johnson, 2008), suggest that a large factor in creating optimal learning environments is providing the right kind of environment: one in which the classroom is rich with objects of exploration, time and space for autonomous exploration is provided, and a culture of respectful relationships, belongingness, and participation is sustained. Subject-specific research that has successfully stimulated flow within curricular interventions (e.g., Larson, 2011; Wilhelm, 2008) suggests that optimal learning environments are also created by intentionally or "backward" designing a high level of involvement, interaction, and application of domain-specific language and tools into the instructional activity. The present study corroborates these findings, further suggesting that curricular interventions can stimulate flow and engagement in learning when primary conditions for flow are created, including a clear goal and role for each student and performance feedback on reaching that goal.

Overall, this study illustrated that students could simultaneously (a) learn about the concept of flow, its relation to learning, and how to apply it to create optimal learning environments; (b) gain an understanding of a leading methodology used to study flow and student engagement; and (c) experience heightened engagement during activities in which conditions for flow were present. In addition, the conditions most important for creating flow may be identified and discussed as a class, furthering students' understanding. In this manner, students not only learn, but also practice positive psychology.

References

Coller, B. D., Shernoff, D. J., & Strati, A. D. (2011). Measuring engagement as students learn dynamic systems and control with a video game. *Advances in Engineering Education, 2*, 1–32.

Csikszentmihalyi, M. (1990). *Flow: The psychology of optimal experience.* New York: Harper Perennial.

Csikszentmihalyi, M. (1997). *Finding flow: The psychology of engagement with everyday life.* New York: Basic Books.

Csikszentmihalyi, M., Abuuhamdeh, S., & Nakamura, J. (2005). Flow. In A. J. Elliot & C. S. Dweck (Eds.), *Handbook of competence and motivation* (pp. 598–608). New York: Guilford Press.

Csikszentmihalyi, M., & Larson, R. (1984). *Being adolescent: Conflict and growth in the teenage years.* New York: Basic Books.

Froh, J., Kashdan, T., Yurkewicz, C., Fan, J., Allen, J., & Glowacki, J. (2010). The benefits of passion and absorption in activities: Engaged living in adolescents and its role in psychological well-being. *Journal of Positive Psychology, 5*, 311–332. doi:10.1080/17439760.2010.498624

Hektner, J. M., Schmidt, J. A., & Csikszentmihalyi, M. (2007). *Experience sampling method: Measuring the quality of everyday life.* Thousand Oaks, CA: Sage.

Johnson, L. S. (2008). Relationship of instructional methods to student engagement in two public school settings. *American Secondary Education, 36*, 69–87.

Jones, J. N., Bench, J. H., & Warnaar, B. L. (2010, April). The development of youth purpose through social action. Poster presentation at the Annual American Education Research Association Conference, Denver, CO.

Larson, S. C. (2011). *The effects of academic literacy instruction on engagement and conceptual understanding of biology in ninth grade students.* Aurora, IL: Aurora University.

Peterson, S. E., & Miller, J. A. (2004). Comparing the quality of students' experience during cooperative learning and large group instruction. *Journal of Educational Research, 97*, 123–133.

Rathunde, K., & Csikszentmihalyi, M. (2005a). Middle school students' motivation and quality of experience: A comparison of Montessori and traditional school environments. *American Journal of Education, 111*, 341–371.

Rathunde, K., & Csikszentmihalyi, M. (2005b). The social context of middle school: Teachers, friends, and activities in Montessori and traditional school environments. *Elementary School Journal, 106*, 59–79.

Seligman, M. P., Steen, T. A., Park, N., & Peterson, C. (2005). Positive psychology progress: Empirical validation of interventions. *American Psychologist, 60*(5), 410–421.

Shernoff, D. J. (2012). Engagement and positive youth development: Creating optimal learning environments. In K. R. Harris, S. Graham, & T. Urdan (Eds.), *The APA educational psychology handbook.* Washington, DC: American Psychological Association.

Shernoff, D. J. (2013). *Optimal learning environments to promote student engagement.* New York: Springer.

Shernoff, D. J., & Csikszentmihalyi, M. (2009). Flow in schools: Cultivating engaged learners and optimal learning environments. In R. C. Gilman, E. S. Heubner, & M. J. Furlong (Eds.), *Handbook of positive psychology in schools* (pp. 131–145). New York: Routledge.

Shernoff, D. J., Csikszentmihalyi, M., Schneider, B., & Shernoff, E. S. (2003). Student engagement in high school classrooms from the perspective of flow theory. *School Psychology Quarterly*, *18*, 158–176.
Shernoff, D. J., Tonks, S., Anderson, B., & Dortch, C. (2011). Linking instructional practices with student engagement from moment to moment in high school classrooms. Paper presented at the Annual Meeting of the American Educational Research Association, New Orleans, LA.
Shernoff, D. J., & Vandell, D. L. (2007). Engagement in after-school program activities: Quality of experience from the perspective of participants. *Journal of Youth and Adolescence*, *36*, 891–903. doi:10.1007/s10964-007-9183-5
Strati, A. D., Shernoff, D. J., & Kackar, H. Z. (2012). Flow. In R. Levesque (Ed.), *Encyclopedia of adolescence* (pp. 1050–1059). New York: Springer.
Vandell, D. L., Shernoff, D. J., Pierce, K. M., Bolt, D. M., Dadisman, K., & Brown, B. B. (2005). Activities, engagement, and emotion in after-school programs (and elsewhere). *New Directions for Youth Development*, *105*, 121–129.
Wiggins, G., & McTighe, J. (2005). *Understanding by design*. Upper Saddle River, NJ: Pearson.
Wilhelm, J. D. (2008). *"You gotta be the book": Teaching engaged and reflective reading with adolescents* (2nd ed.). New York: Teachers College Press.

12

Positive Education and Teaching for Wisdom

Michel Ferrari and Christine E. Guthrie

A good education should provide more than technical skills: it should also develop the personal maturity necessary to allow students to live a good and satisfying life that promotes well-being for themselves and for their communities. And, indeed, when asked to say in a word or two what they wanted most for their children, parents most often answered in terms of "happiness," "contentment," "good health," or "kindness" – in essence, their children's well-being (Seligman, 2011; Seligman, Ernst, Gillham, Reivich, & Linkins, 2009). And yet when asked, "What do schools teach?" parents answered things like "thinking skills," "literacy," and "mathematics." But as has been understood since ancient times, we desire skills for the sake of happiness, but only happiness is desired for its own sake (Aristotle, *Nicomachean Ethics*). The field of positive education has emerged in response to this division. Positive education applies the findings of positive psychology to educational contexts, to promote the well-being (or happiness, used here synonymously) of students and school communities. Positive educators argue that academic skills, though important, form only part of the path to a good life; schools should "teach both the skills of well-being and the skills of [academic] achievement" (Seligman et al., 2009, p. 294). What is more, positive education is indirectly associated with improved academic skills by promoting broader attention (Rowe, Hirsh, Anderson, & Smith, 2007), more creative thinking (Isen, Daubman, & Nowicki, 1987), and more holistic thinking (Kuhl, 2000). For this reason, there is increasing interest in incorporating positive education into traditional classrooms.

Since antiquity, wisdom has been considered essential to achieving and sustaining well-being (Alster, 2005), and so we propose that any effort at positive education should incorporate efforts to teach for wisdom. Positive psychologists and contemporary wisdom researchers interested in "the science of wisdom" have used empirical methods to investigate wisdom. Surprisingly, their findings are rarely discussed together. However, both traditions provide new understandings of wisdom

The Wiley Blackwell Handbook of Positive Psychological Interventions, First Edition.
Edited by Acacia C. Parks and Stephen M. Schueller.

and its importance to education. In this chapter we will integrate findings from both traditions.[1]

We begin by reviewing five theories of wisdom in psychology. This review serves three main purposes. First, we wish to distinguish between the treatment of wisdom in positive psychology and in the science of wisdom. Although the two stances are related, they place different emphasis on the role of wisdom in achieving well-being. Second, the various wisdom theories are interrelated conceptually, so we compare and contrast them as we move through the review. Third, some theories of wisdom have been directly applied to wisdom teaching, while others provide useful background to contextualize and assess educational programs. As we move into a discussion of wisdom in positive education, the theoretical overview will allow us to situate wisdom teaching within the various frameworks suggested by positive psychology and by the science of wisdom.

With this groundwork in place, we devote the second half of the chapter to discussing programs that claim to teach for wisdom. We briefly address the general grounding and purpose of positive education as related to wisdom, before moving into specialized wisdom learning. We look at one representative example for each of three current approaches to teaching for wisdom: (i) direct instruction in Project Wisdom/WiseSkills; (ii) thinking-skills training in Sternberg's (1998) balanced curriculum; and (iii) interpretative simulation and self-exploration using the Ontario secondary school English curriculum. We propose that these models are not competing alternatives, but emphasize different aspects of any possible wisdom curriculum. To conclude, we discuss the implications of these teaching programs for best practices in wisdom education and for further research.

Understanding Wisdom: A Variety of Approaches

Above, we alluded to the fact that wisdom has been explored from a diverse set of theoretical perspectives. Here, we will explore these theories in more detail. First, we present the view of positive psychology, where wisdom is one of six major traits that build good character. Cultivating this trait (or "virtue") presents one possible path of many to good character, and to a good life. We will situate this view within positive psychology's broader framework for understanding optimal well-being or happiness (the *Character Strengths and Values* framework, or CSV; Peterson & Seligman, 2004). This framework will provide a reference point as we move through other conceptions of wisdom. We follow by contrasting the positive psychology/CSV stance with the more comprehensive views of wisdom expressed by researchers working in the science of wisdom. For these theorists, achieving and sustaining well-being *requires* wisdom as a "master virtue" (Schwartz & Sharpe, 2006); that is, as a virtue that coordinates the optimal deployment of all the other virtues. First, we discuss wisdom as an ideal personality type with cognitive, reflective, and affective dimensions (Ardelt, 2003). Next, we consider wisdom-as-activity, reflecting either a general expertise (Baltes & Smith, 2008) or a specific kind of thinking and judgment (Sternberg, 1998). Finally, we present a narrative theory of wisdom that considers wisdom to emerge as personally significant events are plotted into narratives, especially autobiographical narratives (Ferrari, Weststrate, & Petro, 2013; Ricoeur, 1992).

Wisdom Theory in Positive Psychology and the CSV

Wisdom as intellectual virtue

Much of positive psychology has revolved around the classification and study of strength and virtue (see Chapter 4). Peterson and Seligman (2004) propose that using strengths is one important way to achieve high levels of subjective well-being (SWB). The authors identify three conceptual levels to this endeavor:

1 *Virtues* are core character traits valued by religious leaders and philosophers at the highest level of abstraction. The CSV framework proposes six such virtues: (i) *courage* (emotional strengths to use one's will to accomplish goals despite internal or external opposition); (ii) *temperance* (emotional strengths that protect one from excess); (iii) *humanity* (interpersonal strengths that tend toward concern for others); (iv) *justice* (civic strengths that support and sustain communal life); (v) *transcendence* (cognitive strengths that meaningfully connect one to the larger universe); and (vi) *wisdom* (cognitive strengths that allow one to acquire and use knowledge).
2 *Character strengths* are the specific processes through which universal virtues are expressed. Peterson and Seligman (2004) identify 24 separate character strengths, although the link to their six-factor virtue structure has been challenged (Shryack, Steger, Krueger, & Kallie, 2010; Singh & Choubisa, 2010). Even so, most of the cognitive strengths associated with wisdom (i.e., curiosity, love of learning, perspective, and creativity) consistently load onto a unique factor, supporting the notion that wisdom is a unique strength with distinct characteristics (Singh & Choubisa, 2010).
3 *Situational themes* are situation-specific habits of mind that lead people to manifest particular character strengths in particular situations. Situational themes differ across contexts (e.g., work situations vs. family situations). A parent might find that when she is in the family context, she manifests kindness towards her child. While in a work context, however, she manifests bravery. Within situations, people manifest strengths through various themes (interior schemata, or external scaffolds) that may be unique to that context or situation. So, for example, an individual who is not habitually creative may be creative in an art class, where the theme of creativity is specifically cultivated and supported; while a highly creative person may find outlets for creativity in other situations such as coaching or cooking.

Across contexts, themes vary most, strengths vary slightly, and virtues are universal and unchanging. Peterson and Seligman (2004) propose that the empirical focus of positive psychology is on assessing and developing character strengths as these are relatively stable across contexts but responsive to intervention. The CSV treats wisdom as a core intellectual virtue that contributes to well-being, but it does not prioritize the role of wisdom among numerous means of achieving well-being.

Wisdom Theories in the Science of Wisdom

Wisdom as personality

Monika Ardelt (2003) considers wisdom to be a latent personality variable with three dimensions:

1 *Cognitive:* understanding of life and a desire to know the truth.
2 *Reflective*: looking at phenomena and events from different perspectives, even if unpleasant.
3 *Affective*: having positive emotions towards others (e.g., sympathy and compassionate love).

Like positive psychologists, Ardelt aims to identify individual differences in character that improve experienced well-being. But, like Schwartz and Sharpe (2006), Ardelt considers wisdom a master virtue that integrates the six character virtues identified by Peterson and Seligman (2004), although it is difficult to imagine a direct mapping to her three dimensions of wisdom (i.e., cognitive, reflective, and affective dimensions of personality).

Ardelt's model of wisdom is one of the most influential in the field. She defines wisdom as an "ideal type" of personality that integrates cognition (knowledge and love of learning), reflection (perspective-taking), and affect (compassion). Wiser individuals more fully integrate these three dimensions. Ardelt has conducted numerous studies to test this model and demonstrate that wisdom is associated with increased well-being and functioning. People clearly distinguish wisdom from knowledge along the lines suggested by her theory; that is, wisdom includes knowledge, but has an emotional dimension that makes that knowledge personally vital (Ardelt, Achenbaum, & Oh, 2013; Ardelt & Ferrari, in press).

Empirical work has established the utility of the Three-Dimensional Wisdom Scale (3D-WS), a self-report measure that assesses each of the three dimensions, as well as confirming the measure's psychometric validity (Ardelt, 2003).[2] Early work demonstrated that the three dimensions of wisdom are important to successful aging (Ardelt, 1997, 1998). Ardelt studied 81 women and 39 men (aged 58–82) and found wisdom to be strongly associated with life satisfaction ($r = .77$, $p < .001$). In fact, wisdom was more predictive of well-being than objective life conditions such as age, socioeconomic status, financial situation, health, physical environment, or social involvement. Ardelt found that high scorers cope with stresses in life more successfully than do low scorers, have greater life satisfaction, and experience greater happiness (see Ardelt et al., 2013 for a review). Ardelt's research on wisdom-as-personality establishes wisdom's importance to living well; in doing so, it provides a possible rationale for attending to wisdom in education.

Wisdom as pragmatic expertise

Paul Baltes and colleagues (Baltes & Smith, 2008; Baltes & Staudinger, 2000) developed the first and most elaborate scientific theory of wisdom, the "Berlin model." Baltes and his colleagues propose that "at the core of this concept [of wisdom] is the notion of the perfect, quasi-utopian integration of knowledge and character, of mind and virtue" (Baltes & Kunzmann, 2003, p. 131), an integration that requires an expertise in the fundamental pragmatics of life. Rather than developing a taxonomy or proposing an ideal type, the Berlin model explains how wisdom operates. In other words, within the wisdom-as-pragmatic-expertise approach, wisdom is expressed through correct action, not just the intellectual virtue of optimally acquiring and using knowledge. Furthermore, it is not enough to only have virtues (whether Ardelt's three dimensions or the CSV's six virtues), as action requires the expert orchestration of virtues.

More specifically, according to the Berlin model wisdom requires expert *factual* and *strategic* knowledge about the fundamental pragmatics of life (i.e., knowledge of human nature, critical life events, and how to conduct oneself in life; Baltes & Kunzmann, 2003; Baltes & Smith, 2008; Baltes & Staudinger, 2000). Life-expertise as wisdom must also meet three additional "meta-criteria": *lifespan contextualism* (i.e., knowing what contexts and events matter to particular people); *relativism of values and life-priorities* (i.e., acknowledging different values and priorities, while still holding certain values to be universal); and *managing uncertainty* (i.e., accepting the limits of human knowledge) (Baltes & Smith, 2008).[3] Baltes' wisdom criteria overlap with the CSV understanding of wisdom and the other virtues. For example, meta-criteria like "relativism of values and life-priorities" and "lifespan contextualism" draw on the strength of "perspective," under the virtue "wisdom" – or perhaps on "social intelligence," under the virtue "humanity." However, while the CSV understanding of wisdom is also knowledge-based, such knowledge is not necessarily about the fundamental pragmatics of life, nor need it be expert knowledge.

Baltes and his colleagues have collected a wide range of empirical data supporting their view of wisdom (see Kunzmann & Baltes, 2005; and Baltes and Smith, 2008 for a review). We note a few of the findings that are pertinent to the current discussion. First, although rare, wisdom is not exclusive to the aged, and in fact, young adults are equally likely to be as wise as older adults. This suggests that interventions that aim to develop wisdom could be appropriate for school-aged youth. However, each phase of life fosters its own specific wisdom-related knowledge, so wisdom learning should be developmentally appropriate. Also, reflective activities such as internal dialogues seem to enhance wisdom-related performance, suggesting a role for this type of activity in teaching for wisdom.

Wisdom as balanced decision-making

In related work, Sternberg (1990, 1998, 2013) considers the essence of wisdom to be the act of making a balanced judgment. Although Sternberg does not make an explicit connection to the Berlin model, this presumably requires an expertise in the fundamental pragmatics of life. For Sternberg, wisdom is more specifically defined as the application of tacit as well as explicit knowledge, as mediated by values toward the achievement of a common good. This is achieved by balancing intrapersonal, interpersonal, and extrapersonal interests over the short term and long term to adapt, shape, and select environments. To be wise, one must balance understanding and action among competing *interests*, immediate and lasting *consequences* of those interests, and the *environment* in which they occur. All of this is in the service of attaining a common good, understood within a system of values, the most important of which perhaps is equity – aligning with the CSV strength of "perspective" (under the virtue of "wisdom") and also with "fairness" (under the virtue of "justice"). It may be helpful here to draw a parallel with casuistry – a case-based approach to applied ethics which operates on the basis that there are no universally-accepted answers to moral dilemmas (Jonson & Toulmin, 1990). For both Baltes and Sternberg, the wisest decisions are contextual, and people must always negotiate unique values and circumstances. This approach acknowledges that there are different conceptions of what constitutes the common good, a finding paralleled in social psychologist Shalom Schwartz's value theory (Schwartz, 1992).

Importantly for positive education, Sternberg is the only psychological researcher to have implemented his theory of wisdom in a public school setting. We will return to this project later in our discussion of teaching for wisdom.

Wisdom as narrative understanding and self-insight

This fourth approach provides a different view of wisdom, considering wisdom to be expressed within detailed fictional or historical cases, or one's own autobiographical narrative (Ferrari, Weststrate, & Petro, 2013). This treatment of wisdom is based in a narrative conception of the self. Theories of "narrative identity" suggest that our stories of self (our autobiographical narratives) are the primary means by which we construct self-identity (McAdams & Pals, 2006; Randall & Kenyon, 2001; Ricoeur, 1992). Reflecting on our own life stories allows us to reassess and learn from our actions – in essence, to become wiser through "narrative understanding" (Brockmeier, 2013; Randall & Kenyon, 2001; Shen, 2001). We can also engage with the richly contextualized narratives of historical or fictional characters in much the same way, becoming wiser through considering the actions of others (Brockmeier, 2013; Ricoeur, 1992). Actors and events (including our own self, and our own life events) are "emplotted" in larger story arcs, as we place events in their wider temporal and thematic contexts. Emplotment is the action through which narrative understanding emerges, and thus it is a primary mechanism for the development of wisdom as deep insight into self and character. The situated, contextual nature of narrative understanding means that exemplars (or "expected cases") provide emotional, subjective standards of wise action (Bruner, 1990, 2002; Oatley, 2011, 2012). We could say that in a narrative theory, the existence of exemplars (like Gandhi, or your grandmother) eliminates the need for an abstracted pattern, rubric, or a rule set to define wisdom. In its use of exemplars, narrative understanding is deeply relational: it allows us to acquire and express wisdom about our links to others and the world; even about the depths of human nature (Shen, 2001).

Although interpretive actions such as emplotment are usually associated with the analysis of fictional narratives, Keith Oatley (2011, 2012; see also Brockmeier, 2013) has argued that these techniques have a greater psychological purpose. He argues that literary fiction could be used to generate truths in psychology in much the same way that thought experiments generate truths in science (Mar & Oatley, 2008). Both thought experiments and fictional narratives involve imaginative simulations, and the plausibility or psychological realism of these simulations allows them to provide new information about the world. Two further examples reinforce the idea that narrative understanding of character is not necessarily tied to fiction or simulation. A movement in journalism known as "new journalism" is adopting literary techniques in order to render true stories more vivid and meaningful (Wolfe, 1975). Also, it has been argued that narrative is critical to the understanding of legal decisions that govern our lives (Amsterdam & Bruner, 2000).

While the relationship between narrative insight and wisdom seems plausible, it is only now being empirically tested. For example, a pilot study by Weststrate (2011) has shown that those who engage in more elaborate autobiographical reasoning about wisdom narratives score higher on the Ardelt 3D-WS wisdom scale – a finding we hope to replicate in a large international study of personal wisdom currently underway.

Wisdom as narrative understanding is a theory that supports wisdom learning in educational settings, as we will describe later in our discussion of teaching for wisdom in secondary school English classrooms.

Summary of theories of wisdom

We opened this discussion by describing positive psychology's CSV framework and its treatment of wisdom as an *intellectual virtue*: one possible route to good character, among many. We then examined four theories that grant primacy to wisdom as the path to a good life. Ardelt's theory treats wisdom as a *personality* variable with cognitive, reflective, and affective dimensions. The *expertise* and *decision-making* theories are similar to one another, emphasizing intellectual knowledge, and seeing wisdom as demonstrated through expert knowledge (Baltes) or skilled judgment in dealing with life problems (Sternberg). The theory of wisdom as *narrative understanding* suggests that it is through our emplotment of events into a story that wisdom can emerge.

Positive Education

As mentioned earlier, positive education applies the research findings of positive psychology to promote well-being or happiness in students and school communities. Despite the obvious allure of positive education, skeptics rightly ask, "can well-being or happiness really be taught?" And, if so, can they be taught in a way that is evidence-based, while still endorsing values parents wish to instill in their children (Spence & Shortt, 2007)? Seligman and others say "yes" and argue that educational programs that promote well-being have other associated benefits. They propose that teaching well-being in schools can lead to reduced rates of depression, increased life satisfaction, and improved learning (Seligman, 2011; Seligman et al., 2009). Seligman's program for teaching well-being is based on the idea, detailed in the CSV, that individuals have a set of signature virtues and that engaging those virtues promotes a good life.

Since the CSV attributes five strengths to the core virtue of wisdom (creativity, curiosity, open-mindedness, love of learning, and perspective), teaching for wisdom from a positive psychology perspective would involve cultivating these five strengths. However, positive education programs target strengths broadly, and few efforts specifically target strengths associated with wisdom[4] (Seligman et al., 2009). However, one interesting example of a strengths-based program that targets the virtue of wisdom is a participatory photography project with refugee youth from Thailand and Colombia (Kia-Keating, 2009). The AjA project aims for both individual and community impact, providing social support and a sense of belonging by connecting students with peers and adult mentors. Among its objectives is the promotion of *perspective-building* or what Ardelt (2003) calls reflection (a core attribute of wisdom). Photography serves as a model for framing and highlighting viewpoints, since project tasks are situated in their larger temporal, social, and geographical contexts. Youth also benefit from serving in an advisory capacity, helping to determine project goals and directions.

Teaching for Wisdom

Whereas "positive education" typically aims to promote a wide range of character strengths, in this section we focus on programs intended specifically to cultivate wisdom. We will address several examples drawing from different practical and theoretical traditions.

Project Wisdom and WiseSkills

While character education programs tend to focus on civic responsibility and moral rectitude (Bercowitz, 2002), some of their goals are shared with positive psychology programs. In fact, both Project Wisdom and WiseSkills promote many of the strengths advocated by Peterson and Seligman (2004). We will discuss these two examples of character education that have emphasized the notion of wisdom.

Project Wisdom, founded by Leslie Matula in 1992, is a widely used character education program in the United States that specifically claims to teach for wisdom through proverbs and maxims. Every school day a short message ("words of wisdom") is read over the school's PA system, or in-house TV, to reach every student and staff member in the school (Project Wisdom, 2012). Their collection of proverbs and maxims is drawn from a range of sources worldwide (e.g., "The music that can deepest reach and cure all ills is cordial speech," from Ralph Waldo Emerson).

The program also provides educators with online access to additional program material such as weekly messages and lesson plans designed to integrate wisdom education into every grade level and course in the curriculum. Classroom tools such as mini-posters are also available, as well as parent resources. Students are encouraged to apply the "words of wisdom" to their own lives. They can also be given a weekly journal that explores a different theme each week: for example, *personal choice.* These journals can be tailored to fit different courses or school settings. According to their website, Project Wisdom is in over 17,000 schools across the US, reaching over 4 million students each day. Entire schools are sometimes involved in related projects. For example, a school in Palm Springs created a wall of over 1,500 ceramic tiles, each with a message inspired by the "words of wisdom" (Mahr, 2005).

The intention to integrate wisdom learning within all courses, at all levels, makes this a promising program. However, rather than emerging from a theory of wisdom, the program came from the founder's experiences as an educator. We have little information about what theory of wisdom the programs are based on, or why these particular messages and activities constitute wisdom. Without an explicit theory-based conception of the role of wisdom this program focuses on character education more than wisdom. This does not mean that the program is without benefit, as a program evaluation found that it had a positive effect on school climate. Specifically, it improved teacher morale, encouraged student conversations about character, and "increase[d] students' self awareness, social awareness, and self management," while decreasing student teasing, bullying, and referrals to the office (Project Wisdom & Manke, 2004, p. 1).

Similar, less widespread programs are being used in other schools. For example, the WiseSkills program revolves around monthly "character themes" such as conflict resolution, media awareness, and "world of wisdom," provided to three key constituents: school, family, and community (Wise Skills Resources, 2012). The *school component* includes teacher resources to teach character throughout the year. For example, the middle school program includes quotations, classroom activities, interdisciplinary projects, and a parent newsletter drawn from the sayings, life stories and life choices of 42 "great people." Teachers are given a classroom package that includes a curriculum notebook, wisdom and character posters, character cards, and "WiseStudent certificates." The *family component* encourages parents to reflect on their own personalities and behavior and includes many family activities. The *community component* suggests practical ways to connect the community to the classroom, for example, by inviting career speakers and engaging in community service projects.

These programs share the strength of engaging the entire school, including both students and staff, and can be extended outwards to families and the school community. We note that these programs modernize the ancient method of fostering wisdom through didactic instruction, proverbs, and examples of wise actions (Alster, 2005; Crenshaw, 2010). A criticism of this approach by Seneca (with contemporary examples) still resonates today:

> "This is what [Oprah] said." But what do you say? "This is [Emerson's] view." What is yours? How long will you march under another's orders? Take command and say something memorable of your own ... It is one thing to remember, another to know. To remember is to safeguard something entrusted to memory. But to know is to make each thing one's own, not to depend on the text and always look back to the teacher ... Let there be a space between you and the text. (Seneca, 1917; from letter 33, composed in the year 64 CE)

We can provide examples of wise actions, and encourage students to learn them, but will this help students to act wisely when faced with their own unique dilemmas? Seneca argues that to be wise goes far beyond parroting back the words of past exemplars – one must take that knowledge and put it to work in one's own life, for example, by making good decisions.

Sternberg's "balanced" curriculum

A more reflective approach to cultivating wisdom requires people to think for themselves and generate their own decisions and actions. Sternberg has developed a curriculum that aims to cultivate balanced judgment, which is the central expression of wisdom in his balance theory (Sternberg, 2001; Sternberg, Jarvin, & Grigorenko, 2009). According to Sternberg's theory, a wise person is intelligent and oriented towards the common good. When making decisions, this individual must be able to balance various relational interests across the short and long term, and maintain sensitivity to the broader context (Sternberg, 2008, 2013). Sternberg's curriculum is the most explicitly theory-based contemporary effort to teach for wisdom in schools, making it unique among the programs we discuss here. Sternberg and colleagues have developed an infused curriculum, incorporating critical and wise thinking into eighth grade History (while still meeting Connecticut curriculum objectives). The 10- to 12-week program has two units (*The Birth of the Nation* and *Slavery in America*) comprising nine topics. Students behave like expert historians, considering original historical sources in an age-appropriate way to develop their own interpretive strategies to make sense of history.

Not only do students study historical events, they are asked to think about them wisely. According to the *Teacher's Manual* for Unit 1, "Wisdom primarily involves the capacity to judge, along with the constraint that this judgment be right, sound, or just. Wisdom is measured both by the means involved in reaching the judgment and also by its end. Wisdom represents an avenue to creating a better, more harmonious world" (Sternberg, 2003, p. 6). So how does Sternberg propose to teach students to think wisely? The balanced curriculum involves activities that foster:

1 *Critical, creative, and practical thinking* (as mediated by attitudes and assumptions) that considers the common good (this maps onto the CSV strength of "social intelligence" under the virtue of humanity).
2 *Dialogical thinking*, that is, an ability to consider a situation from the point of view of different people within a dialogue (e.g., those on both sides of a conflict) (a new strength under the virtue of "self-transcendence", or it might map onto "open-mindedness" under "wisdom").
3 *Dialectical thinking*, that is, thinking that resolves competing points of view from a more integrative perspective (the proverbial Hegelian synthesis of opposites) (a new strength under the virtue of "self-transcendence").
4 *Critical discussion* of actions, as to whether they are wise or foolish (both historically, and from students' own lives) (perhaps associated with the strength "prudence" under the virtue "temperance").
5 *Role modeling* of wise judgment and action on the part of students and teachers (a method that relies on social modeling as a prerequisite to "love of learning" and "perspective" under the virtue "wisdom").
6 *Reflection on values* using maxims (such as those of Project Wisdom or WiseSkills – the content of a body of expert declarative knowledge, as proposed by Baltes).

Teachers are given curriculum materials that include presentation materials, student materials (such as worksheets), and objectives for historical content and wise thinking. Students work with primary sources (for those with reading difficulties, vocabulary lists and simplified versions of the source material are provided). Group work is encouraged because it allows opportunities for wise thinking in dialogue with others.

Sternberg's conception is that wisdom is simply a comprehensive ability (or constellation of abilities) at which students can be more or less expert (this echoes

Baltes' treatment of wisdom as expertise). In later work, Sternberg (2003, 2011) has proposed a "WICS" model of education, in which education should involve *Wisdom*; analytic, creative, and practical *Intelligence*; and *Creativity*, "*Synthesized*." Recently, he has turned towards the development of WICS-based assessment tools to extend and refine current approaches to standardized testing (Sternberg, 2010; Sternberg, Bonney, Gabora, Karelitz, & Coffin, 2010). For example, the Kaleidoscope Project at Tufts University gave prospective students the option to complete a WICS-based admission test in addition to the SAT/ACT (Sternberg, 2012). One wisdom measure asked applicants to write about how to transform one of their high school passions into a project that would benefit society. The Kaleidoscope test was found to predict students' academic performance in their first year of university above SAT/ACT alone, and also predicted engagement in student life. Oklahoma State University is now adopting a similar admissions initiative. There is potential for wider application of these WICS initiatives. For example, WICS-based assessments could provide a new way to chart student progress in positive education programs.

English Teacher Wisdom Project

Critics of Sternberg's balanced curriculum note that his skills-based approach is limited in the case of "blind spots" (when our own motivations are invisible to us), and "action slips" (when we do not do what we know is right; Perkins, 2001; Stanovich, 2001). In our own lives, we may not be able to act as we would in a simulated exercise. Another critique is provided by Ricoeur (1992), who claims that self-insight (and so, wisdom) must draw from both history and literary fiction, suggesting that incorporating wisdom teaching into the History curriculum alone cannot be sufficient to develop wisdom. We emphasize the importance of literature in our own efforts to investigate teaching for wisdom in secondary school English classrooms (Ferrari et al., 2011). Most importantly, we also consider the wisdom of teachers, since it is teachers who must implement any curriculum, whether proverb-based or reflective.

In our pilot study, we interviewed 15 expert and 15 novice teachers about what wisdom means for them and whether the standard Ontario English curriculum can help students learn about life or, more specifically, learn to be wise. Expert teachers had at least 10 years' experience and were nominated by their principals as being exemplary teachers. Novice teachers had not yet formally begun to teach but were nominated by their Curriculum and Instruction teachers as having been exemplary in their practicum. Participants were given the opportunity to discuss three commonly used senior high school English texts (a scene from Shakespeare's *Macbeth*, Bertrand Russell's "What I have lived for" (the prologue to his autobiography), and the Earle Birney poem, "Bushed"). We also asked participants to answer a self-report measure of wisdom, the 3D-WS.

In our preliminary analysis, we compared four narratives: those of the highest and lowest wisdom scorers in both expert and novice teacher groups. Attitudes, strategies, and pedagogical content differed across these four exemplars. In general, we found that although both expert teachers had more knowledge of how to teach English as compared to the novices, only the wiser expert considered it part of his job to provide space for exploring the life themes that could cultivate wisdom. The wisest expert was also the only teacher who specified the desired outcome of his students' life/wisdom learning. Both novices expressed some interest in teaching for wisdom, but struggled with the details.

The least wise expert had a lot of pedagogical content knowledge about how to teach English, but did not consider teaching for wisdom part of her job description, except perhaps indirectly through teaching critical reasoning skills. For example, this teacher discussed exercises and objectives in detail: when discussing "Bushed", she described moving from class discussion of vocabulary to a series of structured lessons on literary analysis, culminating with a "jigsaw" group activity in which students form analyses in teams and then break into teaching groups to share their findings with one another. For this teacher, the ultimate goal is to develop an understanding of "form," "style," and "analy[sis]." But when asked about teaching for wisdom, she responded, "I don't think that's what we do …." For this individual, teaching wisdom is the job of a "poet" or a "religious leader," while teachers need to focus on literacy and other skills.

The least wise novice teacher was more supportive, on the surface, about being able to teach for wisdom. He stated: "I think … in every case, hmm, people at the heart of these three texts have learned or are learning things … and they're making, they've made mistakes and if wisdom is the product of experience which I think it is … these are people who have experienced a lot and have learned something from it …." But when we consider how he proposed to do so, using Bertrand Russell's essay as his example, he seemed overwhelmed by some of the details of the passage. At first, he was enthusiastic about Russell's message of "passion" for life. But Russell's essay also comments on suffering in the world, and here this novice teacher became fixated:

> [Russell] is looking at the world and saying "I feel so bad for the world and for the people of the world for what they've had to suffer and live through but I'm part of that world too, right like I can't help it I can't fix it as much as I'd like to, I've lived my whole life trying and […] it's kind of a lie […] there's a natural order to things and there is the future that I have no control over …."

In the end, this teacher drew a pessimistic message of fatalism that draws attention away from Russell's message about the good life.

By contrast, the wisest novice teacher saw an inspiring message in the texts that can be conveyed to students: "I think that wisdom would be a really great way to connect all these texts and if I had that as my objective to be teaching all these [texts] you know I would begin with that and then design my lesson from there …." Although this novice teacher noted that she would ask students to consider the question "what is wisdom?" she did not detail the nuances of how she would structure these discussions. In Shulman's (2004) terms, she lacked the pedagogical content knowledge about how to teach both English in general and wisdom in particular, which are essential aspects of a "wisdom of practice."

Only the wisest expert teacher had both the rich pedagogical content knowledge about how to teach English, and the factual and strategic (pragmatic) knowledge to engage students deeply with texts that provides opportunities to teach for wisdom. Although this teacher did not think you can teach wisdom directly, he described the importance of taking on difficult life situations as a part of classroom teaching: "You can't teach it [wisdom] but I think it's important, I do, to put kids in a situation where they have to deal with problems, issues that will develop insights, that eventually will culminate in maybe what we call wisdom." When describing teaching Russell's essay, this teacher took a very different stance on Russell's comments on suffering, one much more constructive than that of the novice teacher above:

> What do we do with this "pity for suffering mankind" thing? Students are – there's two times in life when you commit suicide at the greatest rate demographically: teenage years and old age. We understand the old age, you're not well, your friends are gone, all that kind of thing doesn't seem like much to look forward to. Teenagers are so idealistic and haven't had the opportunity to realize that there is life after this terrible thing that's just happened: my girlfriend dumped me, or my parents are upset with what I wanna do with my life or – so there's that, but also how do you deal with the terrible things that happen in the world? [...] So, how do we balance the awful things that happen out there?

This teacher could explain, in the context of his students' lives, why Russell's essay is important and why he hoped students might gain wisdom from studying it. We suggest that this illustrates an expertise about the fundamental pragmatics of life that Baltes considers the essence of wisdom, while also highlighting the theme of balance so central to Sternberg's conception of wisdom.

These preliminary results indicate that it is not enough to have a curriculum designed to promote psychological well-being. Teachers differ in their own wisdom (as captured by the 3D-WS) and in their attitudes toward teaching for wisdom. With that in mind, we need to consider whether teacher training, school settings, and ongoing professional development can support the development of wisdom and a sense of well-being in teachers. Only under such conditions will more teachers be able to model the search for wisdom and well-being, or even its successful outcome in a "good life." Teachers must also be given the opportunity to develop necessary pedagogical content knowledge, and must have the mandate and the appropriate institutional support to incorporate these themes into their classroom practices. Moving forward, it would be important to examine student learning as well as teacher skills and attitudes in order to draw a more complete picture of teaching for wisdom in English classrooms.

Conclusion and Discussion

This chapter began with a review of major psychological conceptions of wisdom. We presented the view of positive psychology; namely that wisdom is one path to expressing good character and achieving a good life, but merely one path of many (Peterson & Seligman, 2004). We contrasted this with theories emerging from the more comprehensive perspective of "the science of wisdom," where wisdom is seen as the foundational path to a good life. Here, we first considered the theory of wisdom as an expression of personality (Ardelt, 2003). Next, we considered theories in which wisdom is a form of activity, expressing either a general expertise (Baltes & Smith, 2008) or a balanced approach to thinking and judgment (Sternberg, 1998). Finally, we considered narrative theories in which wisdom emerges from considering character and action as emplotted in stories, especially autobiographical stories (Ferrari et al., 2013; Ricoeur, 1992). The theories of wisdom as balanced decision-making and as narrative understanding support specific efforts to teach for wisdom, while the other theories provide a rationale for wisdom teaching by empirically establishing the importance of wisdom across the lifespan. From the Berlin project's expertise approach, we can hypothesize that developmental appropriateness and opportunities for reflection are important to wisdom learning. From these various research traditions, we find a growing interest exists in exploring the potential for public schooling to increase students' well-being.

We described the place of wisdom in positive education, and then presented three examples of teaching for wisdom: Project Wisdom/WiseSkills' didactic, proverb-centric approach, Sternberg's balanced History curriculum for wise thinking, and narrative understanding through the Ontario English curriculum. We propose that these models are not competing alternatives, but are variations that emphasize different aspects of a wisdom curriculum. As with ancient wisdom traditions, we can roughly divide these programs into didactic and reflective efforts to teach for wisdom. Project Wisdom and WiseSkills follow a proverbial approach, emphasizing a specific content to be mastered in order to promote psychosocial well-being. Students are asked to articulate the connection between wisdom content and their own lives. However, these programs lack an articulated theory and could integrate content more carefully into the existing curriculum in History or English to maximize the opportunities for reflection and application. Sternberg addresses these concerns in his balanced curriculum, which embeds theoretically grounded wisdom learning within History classes. Students benefit from the challenge of evaluating decisions embedded in historical contexts. Also, Sternberg places the focus not on learning content but on developing the skill of balanced judgment. Although embedding wisdom teaching in the curriculum (rather than adding it on) seems beneficial, we propose that some existing curricular material could be used as-is, if used wisely by teachers. We provided the example of an English class, which takes the idea of teaching for wisdom beyond where the "balanced curriculum" left off. The aim is not specific maxims to be learned, or a single skill (i.e., balanced judgment) to be nurtured. Here, the focus is on the contextualized analysis of character and action through literature. Through narrative understanding, this kind of learning makes meaningful connections to students' lives, and increases self-understanding. This approach highlights the importance of teachers' own skills and attitudes in the successful implementation of a wisdom curriculum. A comprehensive future study seeking to explore teaching for wisdom should include all three of the described approaches. This would allow for assessment of the relative merits of didactic instruction, reflective activities, and teacher education in promoting students' ability to discern what matters in life and how to live a worthwhile life. Wisdom's place in classroom education is still being established, and the research and programs covered provide important foundations for this ongoing work.

Notes

1 Related efforts to improve well-being are not covered here, such as the mindfulness approach of "contemplative education" (see Roeser & Zelazo, 2012, for an overview).

2 Besides the 3D-WS there is also the work of Jason and colleagues (Jason et al., 2001), Brown and Greene (2006), Webster (2007), and Levenson and colleagues (Levenson, Jennings, Aldwin, & Shiraishi, 2005), who have developed their own self-report measures to assess wisdom, which involve a different subset of character strengths that include, for example, awe, humor, and spirituality (virtues specifically identified in the CSV under the virtue "transcendence").

3 Staudinger (1999, 2013) has recently adapted this model to distinguish "general wisdom" (exemplified by advice to others) from "personal wisdom" (exemplified by self-insight).

4 Evidence-based positive education typically aims to develop students' *own* greatest strengths, and to remediate their weaknesses (see Chapter 4).

References

Alster, B. (2005) *Wisdom of ancient Sumer*. Bethesda, MD: CDL Press.

Amsterdam, A. G., & Bruner, J. (2000). *Minding the law*. Cambridge, MA: Harvard University Press.

Ardelt, M. (1997). Wisdom and life satisfaction in old age. *Journal of Gerontology: Psychological Sciences, 52B*, 15–27.

Ardelt, M. (1998). Social crisis and individual growth: The long-term effects of the great depression. *Journal of Aging Studies, 12*, 291–314.

Ardelt, M. (2003). Empirical assessment of a three-dimensional wisdom scale. *Research on Aging, 25*, 275–324.

Ardelt, M., Achenbaum, A., & Oh, H. (2013). The paradoxical nature of personal wisdom and its relation to human development in the reflective, cognitive, and affective domains. In M. Ferrari & N. M. Weststrate (Eds.), *The scientific study of personal wisdom: From contemplative traditions to neuroscience*. New York: Springer.

Ardelt, M., & Ferrari, M. (in press). Wisdom and emotions. In P. Verhaeghen & C. Hertzog (Eds.), *The Oxford handbook of emotion, social cognition, and everyday problem solving during adulthood*. New York: Oxford University Press.

Baltes, P. B., & Kunzmann, U. (2003). Wisdom: The peak of human excellence in the orchestration of mind and virtue. *The Psychologist*, *16*, 131–133.

Baltes, P. B., & Smith, J. (2008). The fascination of wisdom: Its nature, ontogeny, and function. *Perspectives on Psychological Science*, *3*, 56–64.

Baltes, P. B., & Staudinger, U. M. (2000). Wisdom: A metaheuristic (pragmatic) to orchestrate mind and virtue toward excellence. *American Psychologist*, *55*, 122–136.

Berkowitz, M. W. (2002). The science of character education. In W. Damon (Ed.), *Bringing in a new era in character education* (pp. 43–63). Stanford, CA: Hoover Institution Press.

Brockmeier, J. (2013). Fact and fiction: Exploring the narrative mind. In M. Hatavara, L.-C. Hyden, & M. Hyvarinen (Eds.), *The travelling metaphor of narrative*. Amsterdam: John Benjamins.

Brown, S. C., & Greene, J. A. (2006). The wisdom development scale: Translating the conceptual to the concrete. *Journal of College Student Development*, *47*, 1–19.

Bruner, J. (1990). *Acts of meaning*. Cambridge, MA: Harvard University Press.

Bruner, J. (2002). *Making stories: Law, literature, life*. Cambridge, MA: Harvard University Press.

Crenshaw, J. L. (2010). *Old Testament wisdom: An introduction* (3rd ed.). Louisville, KT: Westminster John Knox Press.

Ferrari, M., Peskin, J., Allen, G., Petro, A., Waugh, C., & Martin-Smith, A. (2011). Teaching for wisdom in high school English class. Poster presented at the 2011 Annual Meeting of the Canadian Psychology Association, Toronto, Ont.

Ferrari, M., Weststrate, N. M., & Petro, A. (2013). Stories of wisdom to live by: Developing wisdom in a narrative mode. In M. Ferrari & N. Weststrate (Eds.), *The scientific study of personal wisdom: From contemplative traditions to neuroscience*. Amsterdam: Springer.

Isen, A. M., Daubman, K. A., & Nowicki, G. P. (1987). Positive affect facilitates creative problem solving. *Journal of Personality and Social Psychology*, *52*, 1122–1131.

Jason, L. A., Reichler, A., King, C., Madsen, D., Camacho, J., & Marchese, W. (2001). The measurement of wisdom: A preliminary effort. *Journal of Community Psychology*, *29*, 585–598.

Jonson, A. R., & Toulmin, S. E. (1990). *The abuse of casuistry: A history of moral reasoning*. Los Angeles: University of California Press.

Kia-Keating, M. (2009). Positive psychology and school/community-based youth participatory photography programs. In R. Gilman, E. S. Huebner, & M. J. Furlong (Eds.), *Handbook of positive psychology in schools* (pp. 383–397). New York: Routledge.

Kuhl, J. (2000) A functional-design approach to motivation and self-regulation: The dynamics of personality systems interactions. In M. Boekaerts, P. R. Pintrich, & M. Zeidner (Eds.), *Handbook of self-regulation* (pp. 111–169). San Diego, CA: Academic Press.

Kunzmann, U., & Baltes, P. B. (2005). The psychology of wisdom: Theoretical and empirical challenges. In R. J. Sternberg & J. Jordan (Eds.), *A handbook of wisdom: Psychological perspectives* (pp. 110–135). New York: Cambridge University Press.

Levenson, M. R., Jennings, P. A., Aldwin, C. M., & Shiraishi, R. W. (2005). Self-transcendence: Conceptualization and measurement. *Aging*, *60*, 127–143.

Mahr, C. (2005, June 13). Students craft mosaic of tiles depicting values. *The Desert Sun*. Retrieved from http://www.projectwisdom.com/news/DesertSun.asp

Mar, R. A., & Oatley, K. (2008). The function of fiction is the abstraction and simulation of social experience. *Perspectives on Psychological Science, 3*, 173–192.

McAdams, D. P., & Pals, J. L. (2006). A new big five: Fundamental principles for an integrative science of personality. *American Psychologist, 61*, 204–217.

Oatley, K. (2011). Fiction and its study as gateways to the mind. *Scientific Study of Literature, 1*, 153–164.

Oatley, K. (2012). *The passionate muse: Exploring emotion in stories.* New York: Oxford University Press.

Perkins, D. (2001). Wisdom in the wild. *Educational Psychologist, 36*, 265–268.

Peterson, C., & Seligman, M. E. P. (2004). *Character strengths and virtues: A handbook and classification.* New York: Oxford University Press.

Project Wisdom (2012). *Project Wisdom.* Retrieved from http://www.projectwisdom.com

Project Wisdom & Manke, B. (2004). *Project Wisdom program evaluation 2004.* Retrieved from http://www.projectwisdom.com/ers/ProgramEvaluation_2004.pdf

Randall, W. L., & Kenyon, G. M. (2001). *Ordinary wisdom: Biographical aging and the journey of life.* Westport, CT: Praeger.

Ricoeur, P. (1992). *Oneself as another* (K. Blamey, Trans.). Chicago: University of Chicago Press. (Original work published 1990.)

Roeser, R. W., & Zelazo, P. D. (2012). Contemplative science, education and child development: Introduction to the special section. *Child Development Perspectives, 6*, 143–145.

Rowe, G., Hirsh, J. B., Anderson, A. K., & Smith, E. E. (2007). Positive affect increases the breadth of attentional selection. *PNAS Proceedings of the National Academy of Sciences of the United States of America, 104*, 383–388.

Schwartz, B., & Sharpe, K. (2006). Practical wisdom: Aristotle meets positive psychology. *Journal of Happiness Studies, 7*, 377–395.

Schwartz, S. H. (1992). Universals in the content and structure of values: Theoretical advances and empirical tests in 20 countries. In M. Zanna (Ed.), *Advances in experimental social psychology* (pp. 1–65). New York: Academic Press.

Seligman, M. E. P. (2011). *Flourish: A visionary new understanding of happiness and well-being.* New York: Simon & Schuster.

Seligman, M. E. P., Ernst, R. M., Gillham, J., Reivich, K., & Linkins, M. (2009). Positive education: Positive psychology and classroom interventions. *Oxford Review of Education, 35*, 293–311.

Seneca (1917). *Moral letters to Lucilius* (R. M. Gummere, Trans.). Cambridge, MA: Harvard University Press. (Original work published c. 4 BCE–65 CE.)

Shen, V. (2001). Metaphor and concept in religious narratives. *Inter-Religio, 39*, 3–27.

Shryack, J., Steger, M. F., Krueger, R. F., & Kallie, C. S. (2010). The structure of virtue: An empirical investigation of the dimensionality of the virtues in action inventory of strengths. *Personality and Individual Differences, 48*, 714–719.

Shulman, L. (2004). *The wisdom of practice: Essays on teaching, learning, and learning to teach.* San Francisco, CA: Jossey-Bass.

Singh, K., & Choubisa, R. (2010). Empirical validation of Values in Action-Inventory of Strengths (VIA-IS) in Indian context. *Psychological Studies, 55*, 151–158.

Spence, S. H., & Shortt, A. L. (2007). Research review: Can we justify the widespread dissemination of universal, school-based interventions for the prevention of depression among children and adolescents? *Journal of Child Psychology and Psychiatry, 48*, 526–542.

Stanovich, K. E. (2001). The rationality of educating for wisdom. *Educational Psychologist, 36*, 247–251.

Staudinger, U. M. (1999). Older and wiser? Integrating results on the relationship between age and wisdom-related performance. *International Journal of Behavioral Development, 23*, 641–664.

Staudinger, U. M. (2013). The need to distinguish personal from general wisdom: A short history and empirical evidence. In M. Ferrari & N. M. Weststrate (Eds.), *The scientific study of personal wisdom* (pp. 3–20). Dordrecht: Springer.

Sternberg, R. J. (Ed.) (1990). *Wisdom: Its nature, origins, and development*. New York: Cambridge University Press.

Sternberg, R. J. (1998). A balance theory of wisdom. *Review of General Psychology, 2*, 347–365.

Sternberg, R. J. (2001). Why schools should teach for wisdom: The balance theory of wisdom in educational settings. *Educational Psychologist, 36*, 227–245.

Sternberg, R. J. (2003). *Wisdom, intelligence, and creativity synthesized*. New York: Cambridge University Press.

Sternberg, R. J. (2008). Schools should nurture wisdom. In B. Z. Presseisen (Ed.), *Teaching for intelligence* (2nd ed., pp. 61–88). Thousand Oaks, CA: Corwin.

Sternberg, R. J. (2010). *College admissions for the 21st century*. Cambridge, MA: Harvard University Press.

Sternberg, R. J. (2011). The theory of successful intelligence. In R. J. Sternberg & S. B. Kaufman (Eds.), *Cambridge handbook of intelligence* (pp. 504–527). New York: Cambridge University Press.

Sternberg, R. J. (2012). Why I became an administrator…And why you might become one too: Applying the science of psychology to the life of a university. *Observer, 25*(2). Retrieved from http://www.psychologicalscience.org/index.php/publications/observer/2012/february-12/why-i-became-an-administrator-and-why-you-might-become-one-too.html

Sternberg, R. J. (2013). Wisdom in the balance. In M. Ferrari & N. M. Weststrate (Eds.), *The scientific study of personal wisdom*. Amsterdam: Springer.

Sternberg, R. J., Bonney, C. R., Gabora, L., Karelitz, T., & Coffin, L. (2010). Broadening the spectrum of undergraduate admissions. *College and University, 86*(1), 2–17.

Sternberg, R. J., Jarvin, L., & Grigorenko, E. L. (2009). *Teaching for wisdom, intelligence, creativity, and success*. Thousand Oaks, CA: Sage.

Webster, J. D. (2007). Measuring the character strength of wisdom. *Aging, 65*, 163–183.

Weststrate, N. M. (2011). *Stories of wisdom: A qualitative analysis of autobiographical narratives of relatively wise and unwise individuals*. Unpublished MA thesis. Retrieved from ProQuest Dissertations & Theses (MR76259).

Wise Skills Resources (2012). *WiseSkills*. Retrieved from http://www.wiseskills.com

Wolfe, T. (1975). The new journalism. In T. Wolfe & E. W. Johnson (Eds.), *The new journalism* (pp. 13–68). London: Picador.

Part III
Areas of Application

13

Positive Family Therapy Interventions

Collie W. Conoley, Jane Close Conoley, and Marla E. Pontrelli

Positive psychology research, as well as research contributing to positive psychology, can enrich the practice of family therapy. This chapter discusses that literature and presents constructs, findings, and applications relevant to family therapy. While many positive psychology interventions can enrich individual therapy, family therapy is distinct, thus requiring separate considerations. Family therapy models differ from individual therapy models by incorporating systems theory (von Bertalanffy, 1976), communication theory (Bateson, Jackson, Haley, & Weakland, 1956), and social constructivism (Gergen, 1985), thus requiring specialized therapy models and training. Further, while the constructs can enrich nearly all family therapy models, we center our discussion on the applications to the Positive Family Therapy model (Conoley & Conoley, 2009).

Although a complete explanation distinguishing individual and family therapies is beyond the purpose of this chapter, we present a few critical distinctions between individual and family therapy theories by reviewing some central principles from the theories underlying family therapy.

Systems Theory

Ludwig von Bertalanffy (1976) devised general systems theory as a universal theory that would allow understanding of all living systems. The definition of a human system is people who interact in somewhat predictable patterns. Systems are recursive such that when one person acts, every other person in the system is influenced, which in turn influences the person who initially acted, and so on. Because of mutual influence, each member is a change agent for the family, yet some members have more influence than others. Those with the most influence receive priority but not all of the therapist's attention.

The Wiley Blackwell Handbook of Positive Psychological Interventions, First Edition.
Edited by Acacia C. Parks and Stephen M. Schueller.

The principle of equifinality in systems theory emphasizes that there are many ways that a system could have become where it is at present and many ways that the system could proceed over time. Thus, naming a cause or placing blame is meaningless, just as is the belief that there is only one path to follow to accomplish a goal (von Bertalanffy, 1976).

Like all systems, family systems have purpose and develop over time. Families have the purpose of nurturing the members.

Communication Theory

Communication theory originated with the Palo Alto group (Bateson et al., 1956; Watzlawick, Beavin, & Jackson, 2008), who emphasized interpersonal communication as the central process for understanding mental health. They postulated several communication axioms including: (i) communication continuously occurs in relationships, (ii) everything done in a relationship, even silence, communicates something, (iii) a communication cannot be withdrawn once communicated, (iv) to negate or ignore a perspective (a person's reality) is to communicate a person's unimportance or impotence in the system/family which can lead to counterproductive behavior.

Understanding communication axioms is paramount when working with families, manifested by choice of content, interrupting damaging content, and pursuing neutrality (described below). In individual therapy, a client can explore issues openly and then decide if the uncovered material feels valid. For example, a therapist could ask an individual client what it would be like to abandon her child who creates havoc at home. The client may initially express relief and benefits and then explore the feeling of loss. While this could be beneficial in an individual context, the exploration of abandonment in the presence of children cannot be un-communicated, even if this questioning ends with the parent deciding to work harder to help the child. The family therapist must guide the therapeutic conversation in a manner that does not harm any member of the family.

Another important difference between individual and family therapy based upon communication theory is the need for therapist neutrality in family therapy. Neutrality is viewed as taking every family member's side. The therapist should be seen as curious about each person's perspective or strengths without favoritism toward a person or a perspective (Boscolo, Cecchin, Hoffman, & Penn, 1987; Cecchin, 1987). Following the principle of neutrality in family therapy, a therapist must take an active stance to include each person's perspective in the conversations. Excluding a person's perspective can pathologize or exclude that person as a member of the family. A member who is pathologized or excluded often acts in ways that are counterproductive to the family or him- or herself.

Social Constructivism

Theories of constructivism and social constructivism describe how we create meaning, and thus our reality. Most individual psychotherapies incorporate constructivist theory because they assume the creation of meaning comes from an individual's perception or beliefs about occurrences (Rudes & Guterman, 2007). For constructivists, reality is created by our cognitive processes, therefore many individual therapies focus on changing an individual's cognitions about important issues.

On the other hand, many family therapy theories integrate social constructivism theory because of the focus on relationships. Social constructivism describes reality created through our interactions with each other (Bruner, 2004; Gergen, 1997). The way family members talk about or talk to another member influences each member's reality. Self-concept provides an important illustration of the difference between constructivism and social constructivism. That is, how one comes to know who one is. A constructivist (individual) therapist believes an individual's beliefs create her/his self-concept. Thus, the treatment focuses on changing the individual's beliefs.

A social constructivist (family) therapist believes recursive communication creates self-concept. Following from this view, the way significant others act toward and talk in the presence of an individual forms identity (Gergen, 1997; White & Epston, 1990). A family therapist focuses on changing how each person is spoken to and treated in the family, as well as how each person reacts to other family members.

Some family theorists have advocated for labeling the focus of therapy as a "problem system" rather than a "family system" because whoever converses about the problem creates and maintains the problem (Anderson & Goolishian, 1988). Furthermore, the goal of family therapy is changing the conversations from the problem to a more member-helpful conversation. Initially, the family consistently engages in conversation about "the problem." A major difficulty, therefore, in family therapy is shifting the conversation from the problem to their goals.

Because most often parents maintain intense emotional ties and high frequency of interaction with often more than one child over a long period of time, the goal of family therapy could be viewed as making the parents family therapists. Most family theories support the leadership role of the parents. Most parents care about their children and spend a great deal of time with them, making parents ideal collaborators in developing healthy children. Indeed, changing the child outside the context of the family and then, upon returning to the family, expecting the child to change the family, in order to maintain the child's growth, is not reasonable.

Positive Family Therapy

Positive Family Therapy (PFT; Conoley & Conoley, 2009) uses these theories as a basis and draws from positive psychology research to derive a model of family therapy that builds upon the strengths of a family to enhance the growth of each individual member. PFT specifies a theory of change (the Broaden and Build Theory of positive emotions; Fredrickson, 2001), identifies appropriate therapeutic goals (approach goals), and contains central interventions (strengths-based). We discuss each of these aspects in turn below. Unlike most other therapy models, the presenting problems or problem formulations have very little importance because PFT is a goal-oriented, well-being-focused model that describes problems as warning indicators at best and distractions from progress at worst. PFT deals with the psychological problems encountered by a family by focusing on goals consistent with enhancing family functioning and individual well-being. Goal attainment of small goals and subgoals of the larger goals leads to dissipation of the problematic behaviors or feelings that initiated family therapy. The family leaves with more facilitative communication patterns and knowledge of their strengths, thus promoting continued growth toward larger goals.

Broaden and Build Theory

PFT interventions draw on the Broaden and Build Theory for the theoretical rationale of change. Fredrickson's (1998) Broaden and Build Theory of positive emotions specifies that even brief positive emotions can create long-term beneficial changes. Positive emotions do so by creating openness to new thoughts and behaviors, which subsequently builds long-term resources. Positive emotions and resources exist in a positive feedback loop such that the newly built resources can create more positive emotions, thereby escalating benefits. For example, when experiencing the positive emotion of love, a person is more open to playing with, knowing more deeply, and savoring experiences with another, thus building more intimacy in a relationship. With the longer lasting experience of intimacy, feelings of love are more likely to reappear.

Many forms of psychotherapy aim to increase positive emotions. The unique contribution of the Broaden and Build Theory is the therapeutic process to achieve this aim. Broaden and Build Theory asserts that interventions that foster clients' positive emotions (e.g., curiosity, joy, gratitude, optimism) support creativity, openness to change, and development of resources (Fredrickson, 2008). Therefore, because therapy is a complex interaction that demands creativity and the development of resources, therapeutic interventions help when they support experiences of positive emotions. Therefore, positive emotions are both an important part of the process and end-state of PFT.

Approach Goals

Approach goals target a desirable end-state to reach as opposed to avoidance goals that seek to avert a specified undesirable outcome. A positive psychology framework views approach goals as the preferred path toward growth. In PFT, approach goals direct a family toward positive outcomes, such as cooperation, commitment, or deeper bonds. Conversely, avoidance goals emphasize escaping negative outcomes, such as conflict, rejection, or resentment (Gable, 2006). Most families enter therapy with the goal of ceasing a problem, which is an avoidance goal. For example, in a family with a mother and daughter with a highly conflictual relationship, the daughter may identify her goal as having her mother stop yelling at her. In contrast, an approach goal could be developing an enjoyable relationship with her mother.

The research supports that approach goals are associated with several beneficial outcomes, including more novel and creative solutions (Crowe & Higgins, 1997; Friedman & Forster, 2001), as well as increased motivation, persistence, and openness to attempting challenging activities (Sideridis & Kaplan, 2011), when compared to avoidance goals. Central to family functioning, approach goals increase relationship satisfaction and closeness, as well as the positive emotions of gratitude, love, and compassion (Impett et al., 2010).

Interventions in PFT

Strengths

Interventions in PFT take a strengths-based perspective. Focusing upon strengths for promoting human growth is fundamental to positive psychology. Multiple definitions of strengths and the identification of strengths exist in the literature. The best known research on strengths provides a finite list of strengths, and measures which facilitate research. These include the VIA (Values in Action classification of character strengths; Peterson & Seligman, 2004), Personality Strengths Project (Linley, 2007), and Gallup's Signature Themes of Talent (Hodges & Clifton, 2004). Another perspective advocates for viewing strengths from the perspective of development rather than as fixed traits (Biswas-Dienera, Kashdan, & Minhas, 2011).

While our approach to understanding and using strengths will no doubt evolve, the broad definition of strengths best fits our applied needs. A broad stance means inclusive of many perspectives of strength. Psychotherapy research indicates that attending to a broad definition of client strengths can lead to individual psychotherapy gains beyond the same therapy without the attention to client strengths (Fluckiger & Holtforth, 2008): the therapeutic relationship was enhanced; clients felt more efficacious; and symptoms were reduced.

In PFT, the definition of a strength is a helpful personal asset or quality. Strengths include: (i) abilities such as athletic, cooking, school work, creativity, humor, social skills, coping; (ii) accomplishments such as learning, friendship, job, income, knowledge, physical health; (iii) attitudes/emotions such as prosocial beliefs, love of others, curiosity, hope, enjoyment of activities; (iv) virtues such as kindness, honesty, courage.

Our definition of strengths allows identification during a session. The list is simple and inclusive enough for the therapist to recognize the strengths when revealed during a session. Many of the interventions described in this chapter require the immediate identification of strengths. Focusing on strengths can lead to therapeutic relationship enhancement, creating positive emotions in session, identifying approach goals, modeling attending behaviors, and tools for accomplishing goals.

Paraphrasing

Paraphrasing in therapy entails the therapist selecting the most important stated content to repeat back to the client in fewer words (Hill, 2009). While similar to empathy in that client-revealed information is fed back to the client, paraphrasing differs from empathy by restating the client's verbal communication without going deeper into the hidden meaning or feeling. In PFT, the therapist paraphrases the client's words that state an approach goal, a solution, or a strength. For example:

MOTHER: I am so tired of getting notes from the teacher that Elisa is acting badly. Elisa knows how upset I get and yet she continues to misbehave. I know that she can act better. Last year she made good grades and not one bad note from the teacher.

THERAPIST: So you are certain that she knows how to behave well and she can make good grades. Right?

This paraphrase selects the information describing what the mother wants (a goal), and what the mother has seen Elisa accomplish (a strength). The mother's statement could be further refined to create an approach goal, i.e., increase Elisa's good behavior at school or receive notes praising her behavior. The therapist's interest enhances the importance of the selected content and strengthens the relationship between the therapist and the mother. Additionally, Elisa is reminded that she has the skills to do well and her mother knows she can do well. Paraphrasing increases the likelihood that issues will be presented in terms of strengths and approach goals.

Family therapy benefits from increased neutrality created by paraphrasing and empathizing with an approach goal, a solution, or a strength. In the above example, family members listen to the conversation between the therapist and the mother wondering whose side the therapist will take. The therapist power can tip the scales of social construction by siding with mom's or daughter's reality. If the therapist paraphrases the negative views of Elisa, then Elisa would view the therapist as biased or siding with her mom, breaking the concept of neutrality. Elisa could be ready to defend herself or sink back into non-participation if she feels maligned by the therapist taking her mother's side (negative emotions). However, the therapist can compliment and support Elisa by paraphrasing or empathizing with the positive content. Both Elisa and her mother can feel sided with, leading to more cooperation and positive emotion.

Positive empathy

Therapeutic empathy is the therapist's ability to sense the client's world and share the experience with the client (Elliott, Bohart, Watson, & Greenberg, 2011; Rogers, 1957). Empathy can help a client feel deeply understood and facilitate deeper processing of the content presented by the therapist. Therapeutic empathy remains one of the foremost conditions for establishing the therapeutic alliance, and is a critical precursor to positive change in therapy (Elliott et al., 2011). Empathy differs from paraphrasing as it relates to content that the client does not fully verbalize. Empathy uncovers unstated experiences that may not be fully understood by the client until stated by the therapist. Paraphrasing, on the other hand, draws attention to specific information stated by the client. The empathic content chosen by the therapist should be selected based upon the therapist's theory of psychotherapeutic change.

Positive empathy focuses upon the client's unstated, and perhaps unrecognized, approach goals (Conoley & Conoley, 2009). Focusing on the client's hidden desire, positive empathy can provide the client understanding of a deeply held personal approach goal. For example, if a teenaged client states, "My parents yell at me whenever they see me. I stay in my bedroom when I'm home or I stay away from home when I can. They yell at me for coming home late but they yell at me when I come home early too," a typical empathic response might be, "It seems like you're in a lot of pain because your parents continuously feel angry with you. Sounds like you're feeling hopeless about escaping their disapproval." In contrast, a positive empathic response that focuses upon the hidden, unstated desire might be, "It seems like you want a home that feels enjoyable to you. Maybe even you would like to hear your parents recognize your strengths or what you do right?" Positive empathy not only captures the deeper meaning and positive feelings implied in the client's statement, but also builds a smooth transition to identifying strengths, solutions, and goals. Positive empathy facilitates moving from negative emotions and a problem focus to more positive emotions resulting from remembering better times or maintaining hope for the future, as well as beginning to look for approach goals and solutions.

Preliminary research has demonstrated that positive empathy facilitates the identification of strengths and approach goals. Using an analogue design, positive empathy achieved the same level of depth in the client feeling understood as regular empathy, which focused upon the negative feelings. Positive empathy, however, caused the analogue clients to list more strengths and approach goals as well as fewer avoidance goals (Conoley, Pontrelli, & Nagata, under review). Positive empathy has the potential to communicate a deep level of understanding with the added benefit of uncovering an unstated approach goal (the hidden desire), greater cognitive access to personal strengths, and positive emotions.

Circular questioning

Circular questions use information the therapist gains from an individual as the basis for the next question for another individual or the whole family. The name, circular question, refers to the circular or systemic reintroduction of the information gained by the therapist back into the family system. Circular questioning both informs the family about a member's revelation and gains more information through the questioning process (Boscolo et al., 1987; Scheel & Conoley, 1998; Tomm, 1988). Similar to paraphrasing and positive empathy, circular questioning requires the therapist to select and expand on theory-relevant information. While any information could be selected for circular questioning, PFT therapists select strengths, compliments, and approach goals.

The following extends the example from the section on paraphrasing to include circular questioning:

MOTHER: I am so tired of getting notes from the teacher that Elisa is acting badly. Elisa knows how upset I get and yet she continues to misbehave. I know that she can act better. Last year she made good grades and not one bad note from the teacher.

THERAPIST: So you are certain that she knows how to behave well and she can make good grades. Right? (Paraphrase)

THERAPIST (turning to Elisa): Elisa, did you know your mom had so much confidence in your ability to do well in school? (Circular question)

Asking Elisa about the information gained from her mother reintroduces the information back into the system either to create change or gather more information. Elisa's response could be reintroduced back to her mother or father, thus continuing the circular questioning:

ELISA: Well you wouldn't know it the way she yells at me and calls me stupid all the time.

THERAPIST: How would you like for her to help you get your homework done? (Positive empathy – intuiting that getting homework done is the approach goal)

ELISA: Last year we sat down at the dinner table together. She would read her book and we could talk when I needed help or got bored.

MOTHER: I had forgotten about that. I've been very busy this year. I could do that again ...

Circular questioning kept both family members communicating productively through the therapist. The therapist continually selects productive information for the family member to discuss further. Editing out the negative emotions, blaming, and criticism, the theory of PFT dictates that information is most helpful when it is restated in approach goals and possible solutions. Both Elisa and mother feel supported when circular questions retain neutrality.

Capitalization

Capitalization involves the act of communicating a positive personal event with others and reaping additional benefits beyond the original event that was shared (Langston, 1994). Revealing good news or a strength can increase both individual and relationship well-being when the listener responds in an affirming, enthusiastic manner. Gable, Reis, Impett, and Asher (2004) demonstrated that when a person sharing a positive event receives a celebratory response in reaction to the sharing, many benefits follow. The positive event sharer experiences higher positive affect and greater life satisfaction beyond the initial influence of the original positive event. Among couples, capitalization correlates with higher ratings of intimacy and trust, greater satisfaction with relationships, fewer conflicts, as well as engagement in more fun and relaxing activities (Gable et al., 2004). Subsequent research found that the positive influences of capitalization are not limited to romantic relationships but occur between strangers and friends (Reis et al., 2010) and extend to work experiences as well (Ilies, Keeney, & Scott, 2011).

Also, the listener can benefit from capitalization. The listener experiences increased positive emotions and friendliness toward the sharer of positive information when the listener feels genuine in the active, affirming response, and when the listener believes the sharer accepts the celebration as genuine (Vasquez, Lee, & Conoley, 2012). The relational closeness between the listener and sharer did not matter.

Capitalization can occur between family members as well as between the therapist and a family member. This technique is therapeutic because the shared positive information increases in value, the dyadic relationship is enhanced, and positive feelings increase for both people in the dyad. In modeling capitalization, the therapist demonstrates the techniques and benefits of using capitalization to the family members.

Capitalization can be used almost immediately in the beginning session. During the initial meeting, we often start with a child because they are less likely to start off negatively with a problem and we would like to emphasize their involvement. "What is your name? How old are you? What grade are you in school? What is your favorite subject? What do you do for fun?" When the child answers with a favorite subject or fun activity, the answer reveals a strength. Typically the individual and family members do not think of interest in a subject or enjoying an activity as a strength. In order to increase the individual and family's appreciation of the strength, and to enhance the relationship between the therapist and the individual, the therapist actively celebrates the strength. For example, when a child replies that science is a favorite topic, we respond with excitement and interest. Capitalization research predicts the child will value science more, be more impressed by him/herself, and like us more (Gable et al., 2004). Setting the norm of using capitalization in family therapy signals the importance of this communication style to the family members, increasing the use of this skill among the family members.

Formula First Session Task

Steve de Shazer (1988) describes a first session homework assignment that focuses the family members' attention upon the daily interaction that they enjoy and wish to continue. In the next session each family member is asked to observe something about the family's interactions that should continue, something that is working. The Formula First Session Task (FFST) directs the family members' attention to the strengths of their family at a time when they are consumed with thoughts about what is going wrong. We find the FFST intervention especially useful when the family cannot converge on goals in the first session.

FFST redirects the family members' attention away from the typical focus upon the problem toward identifying family strengths that might contribute to reaching the family members' approach goals. The following is an FFST example:

> Between now and the next time we meet, we would like you to observe, so that you can describe to us next time, what happens in your family that you want to continue to have happen. (de Shazer, 1988, p. 137)

Using the FFST intervention among family, couple, and individual therapy clients produced higher compliance, clarity of treatment goals, and improvement in the presenting problem when compared to a standard problem-focused structural-strategic intervention for family therapy (Adams, Piercy, & Jurich, 1991). At session two, FFST was found to increase perceived problem improvement and outcome expectancy when compared to a problem identification homework assignment (Jordan & Quinn, 1994). FFST fits with the research from positive psychology underscoring the power of focusing on good things that occur daily (Emmons & McCullough, 2003). People who spend time thinking about good things (e.g., what they are grateful for) have more positive emotions, which power broadening of attention and building of resources (Fredrickson, 1998).

Additionally, focusing upon the daily occurrences of positive behaviors influences the family members to become more oriented to the present than the past. Because blame and failure are associated with the past, moving to the present is considered a therapeutic shift. The present and future hold the movement toward approach goals fueled by positive emotions. Additionally becoming mindful of the present time has therapeutic benefits (Eberth & Sedlmeier, 2012; Seligman, Railton, Baumeister, & Sripada, 2013).

The helpful interactions that members identify become the building blocks of further interventions because these experiences are targeted for expansion and maintenance. We observe that family members enjoy hearing from each other about strengths and so we believe that discussing the FFST homework assignment contributes to confidence, hope, and pace of change. The FFST is easy to do and provides the family (and therapist) with an early success. Success breeds hope, which predicts change.

Success finding

After establishing an approach goal, the strengths that contribute to the goal's accomplishment can be uncovered by asking about past success or partial successes in achieving the goal. We call this intervention "success finding." Success finding is modeled after exception finding from Solution Focused Therapy (De Jong & Berg, 1998; de Shazer et al., 2007). Exception-finding interventions ask the client to describe the last time the problem did not occur. In keeping with the approach goal orientation, we prefer the term success finding and instruct clients to "tell us about the last time [the approach goal] occurred or some part of it occurred." The description of the context and interactions surrounding the success or partial success reveals the existing strengths that can contribute to achieving the approach goal.

Melidonis and Bry (1995) found that exception finding in family therapy reduced blaming statements (i.e., put-downs, complaints, or specification of the problem) while increasing positive statements (i.e., positive appraisals or problem solutions) between family members. Thus, the family conversations change toward describing what the family members like about each other and what could be done to make family life better. Asking carefully about the circumstances and details of the past partial successes identifies strengths and building blocks for growth. Additionally, remembering abilities and past successes may increase positive emotions such as hope.

> THERAPIST: When was the last time the marriage felt right? What happened to make it feel like the marriage you want?
>
> WIFE: When Jose and I were first married and before the children came, we used to find the time to talk about each other's day. That felt good. I felt important.
>
> HUSBAND: Yeah, we'd take a walk or lie around in bed and sometimes talk or read the paper and talk about the stories. I guess we got too busy, but we …
>
> THERAPIST (interrupting): What you are saying is very important! So when you take a little time together it feels good. A walk or a talk seems to bring you closer. Is this feeling of closeness something that you want more of in your future? (Watching for non-verbal agreement as the therapist restates the clearer approach goal and links the behavioral strengths to the goal.) Can you think of how to find these moments right now? Can you imagine the setting in which you could be close?

The brief interchange illustrates how a therapist can focus a couple's conversation on an approach goal (closeness) through success finding. Note that the conversation began with a vague goal, feeling closer. Through the success-finding intervention the approach goal of feeling closer became linked with enjoyable time together as well as the past behaviors or strengths (i.e., walking, lying in bed, talking) that facilitate accomplishing the goal.

Visualizing success

Visualization, the imagined representation of an event (Atance & O'Neill, 2001; Beach, 1990), contributes to family therapy by enhancing intentions, motivation, and enactment of facilitative behaviors. Decades of investigation have uncovered the complexities and promise of using visualization in many applications. Visualizing an occurrence increases the belief that the event will happen (Pham & Taylor,

1999) and increases the likelihood that the behavior will occur (Taylor, Pham, Rivkin, & Armor, 1998). In a classic investigation of visualization, Gregory and colleagues (Gregory, Cialdini, & Carpenter, 1982) demonstrated that visualizing the process of buying and enjoying television increased the likelihood of purchasing cable television service in the next month. Visualization benefits diverse outcomes including: increased study time (Pham & Taylor, 1999), commitment to exercise programs (Ten Eyck, Gresky, & Lord, 2008), sports performance (Weinberg, 2008), and therapy attendance (Buckner et al., 2009). Visualization is useful for more cognitively complex issues as well. Taylor et al. (1998) found that students who visualized coping successfully with difficulties experienced better problem-solving, increased positive affect, reduced negative affect, and accessed more social support. Feelings of optimism were increased for clients who wrote down and then visualized their best possible self for five minutes a day over two weeks (Meevissen, Peters, & Alberts, 2011).

The content and context of the material visualized is critical. The most effective content for behavioral enactment appears to include the antecedent steps and action steps, while focusing on the outcome of the action increases motivation (Pham & Taylor, 1999; Ratcliff et al. 1999). The fluency or ease with which a scenario is imaginable influences the believability of eventual accomplishment. Typically concrete descriptions of actions increase the ease of visualizations (Hansen & Wänke, 2010). Matching affective states also enhances visualization (Risen & Critcher, 2011) and believability (Johnson & Tversky, 1983). For example, family members experience difficulty visualizing being pleased with the success of their son when they feel resentment and anger. The timing of visualizing an enjoyable family life is critical to believability.

While most research in visualization explores use by an individual, the strategy is applicable to family therapy. In summarizing the visualization research, the following issues are important: matching the present emotional state with the visualization, and detailed guidance for the experience that includes the antecedent, effective action as well as the successful results. A common way to apply visualization in family therapy is to create an interactive visualization of supportive interactions that encompass goal attainment and maintenance, as in the following intervention, the "miracle question."

The miracle question

The miracle question (de Shazer et al., 2007) is an intervention from Solution Focused Therapy that asks the family members to visualize the disappearance of their problem because of a miracle. The family members visualize and discuss, via circular questions, what occurs in their family system with the absence of the problem. In the discussion the family members concretely describe their conversations, positive feelings, and non-verbal interactions. The intervention combines visualization, approach goals, Broaden and Build, as well as circular questions. The process reveals the systemic nature of reaching the approach goal. Getting people to buy into being part of a miracle is far easier than getting them to own their contribution to a problem that was previously understood to belong to another. That is, a parent can more easily accept that he or she can contribute to a child's growth in emotional regulation than accept that he or she contributed to emotional dis-regulation. Understanding the systemic nature of change empowers each individual in a family and underscores the significance of family therapy. In discussing the aftermath of the miracle, each person hears about and personally describes his or her own contribution to the new miracle life that does not include the problem and moves them toward their approach goal.

Asking the family to create a common visualization uses the power of imagery to carefully construct the antecedent conditions. Introducing the miracle question in a playful, fun manner provides the visceral fit for the positive affect associated with the therapeutic process of goal achievement. Asking the participants to act out the interactions within the session creates more believability in the family's ability to accomplish the goal and, perhaps, even the memory that the goal was accomplished once. The family members take each small step through the interactional nature of the resolution, leading to a systemic understanding and behavioral enactment.

Although Solution Focused Therapy has research support (e.g., Knekt et al., 2008), we found no specific research on the miracle question as a stand-alone intervention. Clinical experience supports its use, but research is sorely needed. However, given the similarity between visualization and the miracle question, it is likely that the miracle question will be beneficial if it follows the same guidelines drawn from the research on visualization.

We implement the miracle question upon formulating an approach goal or at least a problem agreed upon by the family members present in the session. The therapist asks the clients to imagine that the problem that brought them into therapy disappeared magically. The therapist pursues the visualization by asking family members to report on how their lives would be different after the miracle, in minute detail. The therapist emphasizes the description of interactions among the family members in this visualization. For example, the therapist can ask questions such as, "What does your father say to you?" "What expression does he have on his face?" "How do you respond?" "What do you say?" "Are you smiling?" "How does he respond to your smile?"

Responding to the miracle question allows family members to visualize the steps involved in goal achievement. The follow-up questions require each family member to identify with great precision how his or her interactions would be changed by the magical event and how their behaviors would maintain the change. When done in detail, the miracle question leads to a visualization of the goal and its constituent parts. This process outlines with clarity what each person can do to contribute to success. The systemic nature of change is clarified during the process by asking each person to visualize the effects of his/her behavior upon the others and vice versa. No one person begins change; instead, each person can lead change.

The following is an example of the miracle question. The family consists of a mother and son.

THERAPIST (changing voice volume and tone to mysterious and mischievous fun): I'm about to do something very odd. OK? Yes, this is very odd. Who believes in miracles?
(Family members respond with mixed beliefs.)

THERAPIST: Get ready because a miracle is about to happen! OK, this miracle is going to happen tonight!! (Snapping fingers loudly) Just like that! Your problem is gone. Tonight while you sleep it disappeared! Wow! A wonderful miracle huh? (Making eye contact with everyone.) So you wake up in the morning. What is the first sign that the miracle happened? How do you know that your problem is gone?

MOTHER: I would know the miracle happened because when I walked into Juan's room to tell him breakfast is ready, he would be awake and getting dressed.

THERAPIST: OK, great. So mom you would see Juan up and dressing, what would you do? Would you be smiling at him? What would you say?

MOTHER: Yes, I'd smile really big! (She begins smiling)

THERAPIST: Juan look! What do you think of that smile?

JUAN (giggling): I like it.

THERAPIST: Now what are you doing Juan?

JUAN: I'm smiling back at mom.

THERAPIST: Great! Now what were you doing before mom came in your room?

JUAN: I'm getting dressed!

THERAPIST: Wow! How did you manage to do that?

JUAN: I got up when the alarm clock went off and got dressed!

THERAPIST: Wonderful! So let me see if I understand. Juan you heard the alarm clock. And then what did you do?

JUAN: I got up when the alarm clock went off and got dressed!

MOM: That is a miracle!

THERAPIST: Did you hear that Juan! You made your mom smile really big! OK, so mom walks into your room and sees you up and getting dressed. And mom you smile really big right? What are you saying when you see Juan has gotten up by himself and started getting dressed?

MOM: I say "That's not so bad is it?"

THERAPIST: Great! Can you say something that really celebrates him getting up and dressed. Something that lets him know that you are really proud of him and happy?

MOM: Yes, I can say, "Wow look at you! I'm so proud of you!!"

THERAPIST: Perfect! Juan look at your mom. She is so proud of you! And look at that big smile. Is that the miracle you want Juan?

JUAN: Yes, but I don't want her …

THERAPIST (interrupting): So that is what you want! Great! Mom, did you know that is the miracle that Juan wants? Then what happens next?

MOM: I'll go make Juan his favorite breakfast and we can relax, talk, and eat together instead of …

THERAPIST (interrupting): Great! So Juan did you hear that? Mom is making you your favorite breakfast! What will you do when you come to breakfast and see what your mom did for you!

The visualization continues. Notice that the therapist creates repetition, asks about non-verbal and verbal responses, coaches the responses, and implies that each person is influencing the other. Both perspectives of the miracle are repeated. The miracle for mom is that Juan is up and getting dressed on his own. The miracle for Juan is that mom is smiling and happy with him in the morning. After the completion of the miracle question follow-up visualization, the therapist asks a success question, "When was the last time this miracle or part of the miracle happened?" Then the therapist asks, "Will this miracle happen again tomorrow? Juan, how many times will it happen this week?" Then, as a homework assignment, tell the family to make the miracle happen half the number of times Juan guessed.

Catching-your-child-being-virtuous

Parents can be taught to promote children's virtuous behavior via the intervention of catching-your-child-being-virtuous. The intervention is based upon catching-your-child-being-good, which is supported by embedded instruction research (Johnson, McDonnell, Holzwarth, & Hunter, 2004). Catching-your-child-being-virtuous begins with asking the parents to select a maximum of two virtues to nurture in their child. The parents catch the child in the process of performing acts associated with the virtue two to three times daily. Upon catching the child being virtuous, the parent actively, positively compliments the child by stating the behavior and the associated virtue, which is ascribed to the child. The goal is for the child to increase the behaviors associated with the virtue and create a virtuous identity in the process.

The historical intervention, catching-your-child-being-good, is associated with the research on embedded instruction. The strength of embedded instruction is that teaching occurs within the ongoing routines of children without the need of instructing the child (Johnson et al., 2004). The procedure has been effective and highly acceptable to clients (Harrower, 1999; McDonnell, 1998). Our research (Spaventa-Vancil & Conoley, 2012) supports the effectiveness of embedded instruction for increasing the virtues of kindness and persistence when used by a parent with a first to third grade child.

For example, the parents could identify kindness as the virtue to increase in their child. The therapist helps the parents create a list of example behaviors the child might do that would indicate kindness. Following the list of example behaviors, parents are assisted in developing a variety of complimentary statements to use when they observe the target behavior. After a warm telephone call with his grandfather, the parent may say to the child, "I really love the way you talked so nicely to your grandfather. You told him about your day and you asked him about his. And I especially like the way you said, 'I love you' at the end. You are a kind boy!"

Persistence is a particularly important virtue to cultivate in children, who need support to shift attention from immediate states, such as frustration, to the long-term benefits that come from accomplishing a task. Highlighting the benefits that come from being a hard worker is applicable in many situations, such as persisting with a puzzle. For example, the parent could hug the child while saying, "I love the way you work and work until you figure it out! You are trying each piece of the puzzle over and over again until you figure it out. You are a hard worker!" The parent attends to the child's virtuous behavior by actively expressing affection, labeling the prized behaviors, and telling the child he/she is virtuous using the same words over and over.

Family rituals

Family rituals are predictable acts that communicate the family's identity and values. Rituals promote stability and virtues in families (Fiese et al., 2002). Common family rituals include celebrations of birthdays, anniversaries, religious holidays, secular holidays, reunions, weddings, and funerals. In reviewing 50 years of research on rituals, Fiese and her colleagues (2002) found that routines and rituals enhance families in many ways, from better behavior to increased resiliency.

Rituals are more than family routines, but they can be built from routines. Typical family routines are associated with dinnertime, bedtime, chores, and regular telephone visits with relatives. Routines are habitual behaviors for getting something accomplished. Routines make family life easier by providing a predictable, almost automatic, process that feels secure to children and removes some of the effortful decision-making process from the parents. A routine, however, does not involve the symbolic meaning that is at the heart of rituals.

Often families neglect communicating or even remembering the virtues hidden in rituals. Facilitating the family's overt communication of the virtues within a ritual creates heightened awareness for all family members. The initial step of the intervention requires the family to identify their current and past rituals. Families often need prompting through examples to list their rituals. After identifying rituals, the family members are asked to identify the meaning of the rituals. Then the therapist can help associate the virtue that the ritual highlights. Often the family loses the foundational virtues associated with a ritual. For example, the meaning of a birthday celebration is easily forgotten. A family that routinely celebrates birthdays could add a time for recounting why each is grateful for the individual's birth.

Conclusion

We hope the interventions presented in our chapter will be adopted by family therapists and further developed by researchers. Because little research exists specifically examining positive psychology applied in the context of family therapy, we have woven together various findings from within positive psychology to support interventions for family therapy. Experimental studies in social psychology strongly contribute to this endeavor, but must be replicated in clinical samples across a variety of family cultures and contexts to demonstrate their efficacy when applied to family therapy.

Beyond the mechanics of the intervention, we hope that the interventions clearly demonstrate the tenets of PFT (Conoley & Conoley, 2009). A family therapist is responsible for the communication in a session. Understanding that damaging communication must be interrupted is only the first step. The second step is knowing where and how to guide the therapeutic conversation. The positive psychology interventions incorporated into PFT enfranchise each family member in developing their approach goals, using their strengths as solutions, and revealing the systemic nature of change through processes that cultivate positive emotions. Through these interventions, PFT shifts the family members to ask for what they want, notice strengths, and employ relational support in ways that lead the family to effective patterns of communication and the thriving and flourishing of the family system.

References

Adams, J. F., Piercy, F. P., & Jurich, J. A. (1991). Effects of solution focused therapy's "formula first session task" on compliance and outcome in family therapy. *Journal of Marital and Family Therapy, 17*, 277–290.

Anderson, H. D., & Goolishian, H. (1988). Human systems as linguistic systems: Preliminary and evolving ideas about the implications for clinical theory. *Family Process, 27*, 371–393.

Atance, C. M., & O'Neill, D. K. (2001). Episodic future thinking. *Trends in Cognitive Science, 5*, 533–539.

Bateson, G., Jackson, D. D., Haley, J., & Weakland, J. (1956). Toward a theory of schizophrenia. *Behavioral Science, 1*, 251–264.

Beach, L. R. (1990). *Image theory: Decision making in personal and organizational contexts.* New York: John Wiley.

Biswas-Diener, R., Kashdan, T. B., & Minhas, G. (2011). A dynamic approach to psychological strength development and intervention. *Journal of Positive Psychology, 6*, 106–118.

Boscolo, L., Cecchin, G., Hoffman, L., & Penn, P. (1987). *Milan systemic family therapy: Conversations in theory and practice.* New York: Basic Books.

Bruner, J. (2004). The narrative creation of self. In L. E. Angus & J. McLeod (Eds.), *The handbook of narrative and psychotherapy: Practice, theory, and research* (pp. 3–14). Thousand Oaks, CA: Sage Publications.

Buckner, J. D., Cromer, K. R., Merrill, K. A., Mallott, M. A., Schmidt, N. B., Lopez, C. (2009). Pretreatment intervention increases treatment outcomes for patients with anxiety disorders. *Cognitive Therapy and Research, 33*, 126–137.

Cecchin, G. (1987). Hypothesizing, circularity, and neutrality revisited: An invitation to curiosity. *Family Process, 26*, 405–413.

Conoley, C. W., & Conoley, J. C. (2009). *Positive psychology and family therapy: Creative techniques and practical tools for guiding change and enhancing growth.* Hoboken, NJ: John Wiley & Sons.

Conoley, C. W., Pontrelli, M., Nagata, C. (under review). Positive empathy: A new therapeutic skill. Manuscript submitted for publication.

Crowe, E., & Higgins, E. T. (1997). Regulatory focus and strategic inclinations: Promotion and prevention in decision-making. *Organizational Behavior and Human Decision Processes, 69*, 117–132.

De Jong, P., & Berg, I. K. (1998). *Interviewing for solutions.* Belmont, CA: Thomson Brooks/Cole Publishing Co.

de Shazer, S. (1988). *Clues: Investigating solutions in brief therapy.* New York: Norton.

de Shazer, S., Dolan, Y., Korman, H., McCollum, E., Trepper, T., & Berg, I. K. (2007). *More than miracles: The state of the art of solution-focused brief therapy.* New York: Haworth Press.

Eberth, J., & Sedlmeier, P. (2012). The effects of mindfulness meditation: A meta-analysis. *Mindfulness, 3*, 174–189.

Elliott, R., Bohart, A. C., Watson, J. C., & Greenberg, L. S. (2011). Empathy. *Psychotherapy, 48*, 43–49.

Emmons, R. A., & McCullough, M. E. (2003). Counting blessings versus burdens: An experimental investigation of gratitude and subjective well-being in daily life. *Journal of Personality and Social Psychology, 84*(2), 377–389.

Fiese, B. H., Tomcho, T. J., Douglas, M., Josephs, K., Poltrock, S., & Baker, T. (2002). A review of 50 years of research on naturally occurring family routines and rituals: Cause for celebration? *Journal of Family Psychology, 16*, 381–390.

Fluckiger, C., & Holtforth, M. G. (2008). Focusing the therapist's attention on the patient's strengths: A preliminary study to foster a mechanism of change in outpatient psychotherapy. *Journal of Clinical Psychology, 64*(7), 876–890.

Fredrickson, B. L. (1998). What good are positive emotions? *Review of General Psychology, 2*, 300–319.

Fredrickson, B. L. (2001). The role of positive emotions in positive psychology – the broaden-and-build theory of positive emotions. *American Psychologist, 56*, 218–226.

Fredrickson, B. L. (2008). Promoting positive affect. In M. Eid & R. J. Larsen (Eds.), *The science of subjective well-being* (pp. 449–468). New York: Guilford Press.

Friedman, R. S., & Forster, J. (2001). The effects of promotion and prevention cues on creativity. *Journal of Personality and Social Psychology, 81*, 1001–1013.

Gable, S. L. (2006). Approach and avoidance social motives and goals. *Journal of Personality, 74*, 175–222.

Gable, S., Reis, H., Impett, E., & Asher, E. (2004). What do you do when things go right? The intrapersonal and interpersonal benefits of sharing positive events. *Journal of Personality and Social Psychology, 87*, 228–245.

Gergen, K. J. (1985). The social constructionist movement in modern psychology. *American Psychologist, 40*(3), 266–275.

Gergen, K. J. (1997). The place of the psyche in a constructed world. *Theory and Psychology, 7*, 723–746.

Gregory, W. L., Cialdini, R. B., & Carpenter, K. M. (1982). Self relevant scenarios as mediators of likelihood estimates and compliance: Does imagining make it so? *Journal of Personality and Social Psychology, 43*, 89–99.

Hansen, J., & Wänke, M. (2010). Truth from language and truth from fit: The impact of linguistic concreteness and level of construal on subjective truth. *Personality and Social Psychology Bulletin, 36*, 1576–1588.

Harrower, J. (1999). Educational inclusion of children with severe disabilities. *Journal of Positive Behavior Interventions, 1*, 215–230.

Hill, C. (2009). *Helping skills: Facilitating exploration, insight, and action* (3rd ed.). Washington, DC: American Psychological Association.

Hodges, T. D., & Clifton, D. O. (2004). Strengths-based development in practice. In P. A. Linley & S. Joseph (Eds.), *Positive psychology in practice* (pp. 256–268). Hoboken, NJ: John Wiley & Sons.

Ilies, R., Keeney, J., & Scott, B. A. (2011). Work–family interpersonal capitalization: Sharing positive work events at home. *Organizational Behavior and Human Decision Processes, 114*(2), 115–126.

Impett, E. A., Gordon, A. M., Kogan, A., Oveis, C., Gable, S. L., & Keltner, D. (2010). Moving toward more perfect unions: Daily and long-term consequences of approach and avoidance goals in romantic relationships. *Journal of Personality and Social Psychology, 99*, 948–963.

Johnson, E. J., & Tversky, A. (1983). Affect, generalization, and the perception of risk. *Journal of Personality and Social Psychology, 45*, 20–31.

Johnson, J. W., McDonnell, J., Holzwarth, V. N., & Hunter, K. (2004). The efficacy of embedded instruction for students with developmental disabilities enrolled in general education classes. *Journal of Positive Behavior Interventions, 6*, 214–227.

Jordan, K., & Quinn, W. H. (1994). Session two outcome of the formula first session task in problem- and solution-focused approaches. *American Journal of Family Therapy, 22*, 3–16.

Knekt, P., Lindfors, O., Harkanen, T., Valikoski, M., Virtala, E., Laaksonen, M. A., Marttunen, M., Kaipainen, M., Renlund, C., & Helsinki Psychotherapy Study Group (2008) Randomized trial on the effectiveness of long and short-term psychodynamic psychotherapy and solution-focused therapy on psychiatric symptoms during a 3-year follow-up. *Psychological Medicine, 38*, 689–703.

Langston, C. A. (1994). Capitalizing on and coping with daily-life events: Expressive responses to positive events. *Journal of Personality and Social Psychology, 67*, 1112–1125.

Linley, P. A. (2007). Character strengths in the United Kingdom: The VIA inventory of strengths. *Personality and Individual Differences, 43*(2), 341–351.

McDonnell, J. (1998). Instruction for students with severe disabilities in general education settings. *Education and Training in Mental Retardation and Developmental Disabilities, 33*, 199–215.

Meevissen, Y. M. C., Peters, M. L., & Alberts, H. J. E. M. (2011). Become more optimistic by imagining a best possible self: Effects of a two week intervention. *Journal of Behavior Therapy and Experimental Psychiatry, 42*, 371–378.

Melidonis, G. G., & Bry, B. H. (1995). Effects of therapist exceptions questions on blaming and positive statements in families with adolescent behavior problems. *Journal of Family Psychology, 9*, 451–457.

Pham, L. B., & Taylor, S. E. (1999). From thought to action: Effects of process- versus outcome-based mental simulations on performance. *Personality and Social Psychology Bulletin, 25*, 250–260.

Ratcliff, C. D., Czuchry, M., Scarberry, N. C., Thomas, J. C., Dansereau, D. F., & Lord, C. G. (1999). Effects of directed thinking on intentions to engage in beneficial activities: Actions versus reasons. *Journal of Applied Social Psychology, 29*, 994–1009.

Reis, H., Smith, S., Carmichael, C., Caprariello, P., Tsai, F., & Rodrigues, A. (2010). Are you happy for me? How sharing positive events with others provides personal and interpersonal benefits. *Journal of Personality and Social Psychology, 99*, 311–329.

Risen, J. L., & Critcher, C. R. (2011). Visceral fit: While in a visceral state, associated states of the world seem more likely. *Journal of Personality and Social Psychology, 100*, 777–793.

Rogers, C. (1957). The necessary and sufficient conditions of therapeutic personality change. *Journal of Consulting Psychology, 21*, 95–103.

Rudes, J., & Guterman, J. T. (2007). The value of social constructionism for the counseling profession: A reply to Hansen. *Journal of Counseling and Development, 85*, 387–392.

Scheel, M. J., & Conoley, C. W. (1998). Circular questioning and neutrality: An investigation of the process relationship. *Contemporary Family Therapy: An International Journal, 20*, 221–235.

Seligman, M. E., Railton, P., Baumeister, R. F., & Sripada, C. (2013). Navigating into the future or driven by the past. *Perspectives on Psychological Science, 8*, 119–141.

Sideridis, G. D., & Kaplan, A. (2011). Achievement goals and persistence across tasks: The roles of failure and success. *Journal of Experimental Education, 79*, 429–451.

Spaventa-Vancil, K. Z., & Conoley, C. W. (2012, August). Increasing virtues in children. Poster presented at the 120th Annual American Psychological Association, Tampa, FL.

Taylor, S. E., Pham, L. B., Rivkin, I. D., & Armor, D. A. (1998). Harnessing the imagination: Mental simulation, self-regulation, and coping. *American Psychologist, 53*, 429–439.

Ten Eyck, L. L., Gresky, D. P., & Lord, C. G. (2008). Effects of directed thinking on exercise and cardiovascular fitness. *Journal of Applied Biobehavioral Research, 12*, 237–285.

Tomm, K. (1988). Interventive interviewing: III. Intending to ask lineal, circular, strategic, or reflexive questions? *Family Process, 27*, 1–15.

Vasquez, E., Lee, A., & Conoley, C. W. (2012, August) Capitalization's effect on the celebrator. Poster presented at the 120th Annual American Psychological Association, Tampa, FL.

von Bertalanffy, L. (1976). *General system theory: Foundations, development, applications* (rev. ed.). New York: George Braziller.

Watzlawick, P., Beavin, J., & Jackson, D. (2008). *Some tentative axioms of communication.* Piscataway, NJ: Transaction Publishers.

Weinberg, R. (2008). Does imagery work? Effects on performance and mental skills. *Journal of Imagery Research in Sport and Physical Activity, 3*, article 1.

White, M., & Epston, D. (1990). *Narrative means to therapeutic ends.* New York: Guilford Press.

14

Applications of Positive Psychology to Individual Therapy

Jeana L. Magyar-Moe

For hundreds of years, clients have sought out counselors and psychotherapists for the purpose of talking about their struggles, symptoms, and weaknesses, relying on the largely untested assumption that discussing deficits is curative. Research has shown that deficit-based treatment approaches help to ease symptoms of pathology significantly more so than placebos; however, such approaches have not necessarily enhanced symptoms of well-being (Rashid, 2009). Positive psychology grew from dissatisfaction with the principles and practices of deficit-based psychology when professionals within applied fields began to realize the opportunities and benefits afforded through augmenting the traditional scope of clinical practice with strengths-based practices. As Seligman and Csikszentmihalyi (2000) stated: "Treatment is not just fixing what is broken; it is nurturing what is best" (p. 1). Indeed, many researchers have successfully applied positive psychological interventions to a host of clinical issues including depression (Seligman, Rashid, & Parks, 2006; Sin & Lyubomirsky, 2009), schizophrenia (Johnson et al., 2011; Meyer, Johnson, Parks, Iwanski, & Penn, 2012), anxiety (Ruini & Fava, 2009), smoking cessation (Kahler et al., 2014), and substance use (Krentzman, 2013). Furthermore, integration of positive psychology into counseling and psychotherapy enhances conceptualization of well-being and positive functioning and provides useful intervention goals and practices across a wide range of client issues (Magyar-Moe, 2009; Rashid, 2009; Wood & Tarrier, 2010). This chapter presents various ways to use positive psychology in the therapy room with individual clients, and includes a review of several therapeutic approaches based on principles aligned with positive psychology, including Strengths-Based Counseling (Smith, 2006), Strengths-Centered Therapy (Wong, 2006), Quality of Life Therapy (Frisch, 2006), Well-Being Therapy (Ruini & Fava, 2004), Hope Therapy (Lopez, Floyd, Ulven, & Snyder, 2000), and Positive Psychotherapy (Rashid, 2008). Finally, client exercises and activities and therapeutic techniques informed

The Wiley Blackwell Handbook of Positive Psychological Interventions, First Edition.
Edited by Acacia C. Parks and Stephen M. Schueller.

by positive psychology that can be infused into traditional treatment approaches are presented.

Positive Psychological Therapy Models

Engaging in clinical practice from a positive psychology perspective requires an additional focus on well-being and positive functioning to supplement symptom remediation. A complete review of positive psychological assessment is beyond the scope of this chapter, but a more thorough analysis and recommendations are available elsewhere (see Magyar-Moe, 2009). Succinctly, two foundational models that should be utilized in positive psychological assessment and conceptualization include the four-front approach (Wright & Lopez, 2002) and the complete state model of mental health (Keyes & Lopez, 2002). The four-front approach includes assessment of both client weaknesses and strengths as well as destructive and constructive forces in their environments (Wright & Lopez, 2002). The complete state model separates symptoms of mental illness and mental health onto two separate continuums such that clients are classified in one of four possible categories as follows: (i) completely mentally healthy or flourishing (low symptoms of mental illness and high symptoms of well-being); (ii) completely mentally ill or floundering (high symptoms of mental illness and low symptoms of well-being; (iii) incompletely mentally healthy or languishing (low symptoms of mental illness and low symptoms of well-being); or (iv) incompletely mentally ill or struggling (high symptoms of mental illness and high symptoms of well-being; Keyes & Lopez, 2002).

Upon completion of a positive psychological assessment, clinicians working with individual therapy clients can use one or more forms of therapy informed by positive psychology as the primary form of treatment or to augment treatment-as-usual. Multiple examples of such models are reviewed in the following sections.

Strengths-Based Counseling

Strengths-Based Counseling is a model for conducting therapy based on the premises of positive psychology, counseling psychology, prevention, positive youth development, social work, solution-focused therapy, and narrative therapy (Smith, 2006). Strength-Based Counseling progresses through 10 stages. The first three stages build a strong therapeutic alliance, identify the client's strengths, and assess presenting problems. Smith (2006) suggests assessing client problems through questions such as: "What's your theory about why you have this problem?" and "If there were one question that you were hoping I would ask you, what would that question be?" (p. 41). While assessing the client's perceptions of his or her problems, the therapist helps the client identify his or her strengths by teaching the client to reframe his or her life story from a strengths perspective (e.g., helping a client to view oneself as a survivor rather than a victim of child abuse).

Stages four and five refocus the client from the problem and ultimate outcome to solutions and progress. In stage four, therapists instill a sense of hope in clients by providing feedback that increases the focus on efforts or small improvements, rather than the final outcomes of their efforts. In stage five, therapists and clients engage in solution-building conversations that focus on how clients are addressing their problems rather than on the problems themselves. Smith (2006) provides the following questions for eliciting solutions in therapy: "How have you been trying to solve this problem? What works for you, even for a little while? Is there ever a time you remember when the problem did not exist? What was going on in your life when the problem did not exist?" (p. 43). The principles of solution-focused interviewing are key at this stage of the Strengths-Based Counseling process (for a more detailed review of solution-focused therapy, see De Jong & Berg, 2002).

Stage six, building strength and competence, fosters the development of internal and external assets by helping clients to realize that they have the power to effect important changes in their lives. This is accomplished through the use of personal strengths and environmental resources (which should be assessed when using the four-front approach). Stages seven through nine, empowering, changing, and building resilience, are designed to promote agency and facilitate goal pursuits. Major components of these stages include: (a) developing an awareness of how one's problems do not necessarily reside within oneself; (b) seeing change as a process, rather than an isolated event; (c) using strengths to facilitate change; and (d) viewing mistakes that occur *en route* to change as opportunities for learning, rather than as failures. Finally, stage ten consists of evaluating and terminating. During this stage the therapist and client identify the strengths that were most valuable to the change process and honor the progress that has been made (Smith, 2006).

Strength-Centered Therapy

Strength-Centered Therapy (Wong, 2006) is a model of counseling grounded in social constructionism (the idea that knowledge is a product of social consensus) and designed to leverage character strengths and virtues (as defined by Peterson & Seligman, 2004) in the change process. A key aspect of Strength-Centered Therapy, drawn from social constructionism, is the notion that the client's subjective view of his or her own pathology and well-being is more important than the opinion of mental health providers. Hence, in this approach, therapists are not experts who provide information to clients, rather, clients and therapists work together to make meaning of client experiences (Wong, 2006).

Over the course of Strength-Centered Therapy, as practitioners and clients work together to develop new meanings for client experiences, they expand clients' "strength vocabularies" in order to help clients learn to attach their life experiences to that which is positive and adaptive. Strength-Centered Therapy cycles through four phases (explicitizing, envisioning, empowering, and evolving) and typically lasts for a few weeks or months.

In the first phase, explicitizing, therapists help clients name their existing character strengths. In explicitizing strengths, however, therapists must not ignore or overlook the presenting problems and concerns that brought the client to therapy (Wong, 2006). Therapists can validate the client's concerns in a way that also highlights strengths. For example, a client who comes to therapy feeling very sad and exhibiting symptoms of depression can have those feelings validated while at the same time pointing out the courage and bravery necessary to come to therapy and the hope demonstrated through believing therapy might be helpful (Magyar-Moe, 2009). Therapists can also reframe apparent character flaws as strengths (Gelso & Woodhouse, 2003). For example, a child whose mother reports that "she just does not let things go and will not give up until she gets her way" could be assisted to see how such perseverance can actually be a strength when used at appropriate times.

In the envisioning phase (phase two), clients identify the strengths they want to develop and envision how these strengths could be useful for accomplishing their goals for therapy. Therapists can facilitate this through questioning (e.g., "What strengths would you like to develop?" or "What strengths would be useful for helping you to reach your therapy goals?"; Wong, 2006), or a sentence completion exercise (e.g., "I am more likely to achieve my goal of __________ if I am a (an) __________ person"). Once identified, therapists should encourage elaboration of the meanings of the strengths, to ensure that the therapist's understanding of strengths matches the client's.

In phase three, empowering, clients begin to believe that using their strengths can positively affect their lives, thus boosting motivation and promoting a sense of empowerment. Motivation may stem from the development of habits that lead to the effective use of strengths (e.g., reading books from different genres each month in order to develop strengths of wisdom and curiosity). Hence, therapists should work to creatively incorporate exercises and activities that capitalize on and develop existing client strengths. Wong (2006) also recommends that therapists ask their clients to consider connecting with people in their lives who can support them in the strengths-development process. Finally, in this phase, therapists help clients to explore when their strengths are useful and when they could be problematic. For example, a client who is humorous and playful may find these strengths to be helpful when applied to his or her social life and leisure activities, but problematic at work or school, especially if the client becomes a distraction or uses his or her humor in ways that put others down.

Finally, the evolving phase occurs during termination and involves making strengths-development a never-ending process that extends beyond the formal psychotherapeutic process (Wong, 2006). Here, therapists help clients review and celebrate progress. Working together, therapists and clients identify areas for further growth and discuss ways in which clients can use their strengths to address future problems or challenges that might arise.

Quality of Life Therapy

Quality of Life Therapy is a comprehensive approach that blends the tenets of positive psychology with cognitive therapy to promote discovery and progress towards needs, goals, and wishes and increase life quality and satisfaction (Frisch, 2006). Indeed, Quality of Life Therapy is so comprehensive that describing all of the components is beyond the scope of this chapter; however, an overview is provided and therapists interested in learning more can refer directly to Frisch (2006) for more details.

Quality of Life Therapy emphasizes a Whole Life or Life Goal perspective (Frisch, 2006). More specifically, at each stage of treatment interventions are directly connected to the client's life goals, needs, and wishes. In addition, clients are conceptualized in a complete way that incorporates their strengths, weaknesses, life functioning, and psychopathology. Table 14.1 describes the 16 areas of life functioning surveyed in Quality of Life Therapy that can be measured using the Quality of Life Inventory (QOLI; Frisch, 1994).

Quality of Life Therapy is built on a five-fold model of life satisfaction referred to as the CASIO model (Frisch, 2006). Central to this model is the idea that satisfaction in any given area of life is made up of four components, namely a client's (i) objective Circumstances or Characteristics; (ii) subjective Attitudes, perceptions, and interpretations; (iii) Standards of what constitutes fulfillment; and (iv) Importance of each life area for his or her overall well-being. "O" refers to Overall life satisfaction, which is a summation of the individual domains. Thus, a client's overall satisfaction levels can be increased by raising satisfaction in any of the 16 areas of life functioning (Frisch, 2006).

The CASIO model guides clients on how to increase satisfaction, reach goals, and fulfill needs. For example, if a client is dissatisfied in one or more important life areas, a Quality of Life therapist would assist the client to consider ways in which he or she could change his or her Circumstances. This might involve changing careers, ending or beginning relationships, or moving. Next, therapists help clients adjust their Attitudes about the situation by fixing any errors or distorted patterns in thinking. Clients reevaluate and restructure their goals and Standards for fulfillment in a particular life domain to ensure that such standards are realistic. Changing priorities is the fourth change strategy of Quality of Life Therapy. Clients are encouraged to change the Importance that is placed on each life area to conform to what is most under their control. Finally, Overall life satisfaction is promoted by highlighting the life areas that clients are already satisfied with that they may be overlooking due to other immediate concerns (Frisch, 2006).

Quality of Life Therapy also emphasizes self-care including make time for themselves each day in order to relax, to process stressors and worries, and to focus on their key life goals that provide a sense of meaning and purpose in their lives. Frisch (2006) provides several exercises and homework assignments (e.g., "mindful breathing and the guide for worrywarts," "play it again technique," the "five minutes to joy technique," and "mental health day or hour technique") aimed to

Table 14.1 The 16 areas of everyday life functioning that are the foci of Quality of Life Therapy (Frisch, 2006)

Area of life functioning	*Definition*
Health	Being physically fit, not sick, and without pain or disability.
Self-esteem	Liking and respecting yourself in light of your strengths and weaknesses, successes and failures, and ability to handle problems.
Goals-and-values/ spiritual life	(A person's goals-and-values or philosophy of life may or may not include spiritual life.) Goals-and-values are your beliefs about what matters most in life and how you should live, both now and in the future. This includes your goals in life, what you think is right or wrong, and the purpose or meaning of life as you see it. Spiritual life may or may not be an important part of a person's goals-and-values. Spiritual life refers to spiritual or religious beliefs or practices that you pursue on your own or as part of a like-minded spiritual community.
Money (or standard of living)	The money you earn, the things you own (like a car or furniture), and believing that you will have the money and things that you need in the future.
Work	Your career or how you spend most of your time. You may work at a job, at home taking care of your family, or at school as a student. Work includes your duties on the job, the money you earn (if any), and the people you work with.
Play (or recreation)	What you do in your free time to relax, have fun, or improve yourself. This could include watching movies, visiting friends, or pursuing a hobby like sports or gardening.
Learning	Gaining new skills or information about things that interest you. Learning can come from reading books or taking classes on subjects like history, car repair, or using a computer.
Creativity	Using your imagination to come up with new and clever ways to solve everyday problems or to pursue a hobby like painting, photography, or needlework. This can include decorating your home, playing the guitar, or finding a new way to solve a problem at work.
Helping (social service and civic action)	Helping others (not just friends or relatives) in need or helping to make your community a better place to live. Helping can be done on your own or in a group such as a church, a neighborhood association, or a political party. Helping can include doing volunteer work at a school or giving money to a good cause.
Love (or love relationship)	A very close romantic relationship with another person. Love usually includes sexual feelings and feeling loved, cared for, and understood.
Friends (or friendships)	People (not relatives) you know well and care about who have interests and opinions like yours. Friends have fun together, talk about personal problems, and help each other out.

Table 14.1 (*Continued*)

Area of life functioning	*Definition*
Children	How you get along with your child (or children). How you get along as you care for, visit, or play with your child (or children).
Relatives	How you get along with your parents, grandparents, brothers, sisters, aunts, uncles, and in-laws. How you get along when you are doing things together like visiting, talking on the telephone, or helping each other.
Home	Where you live. Your house or apartment and the yard around it. How nice it looks, how big it is, and your rent or house payment.
Neighborhood	The area around your home. How nice it looks, the amount of crime in the area, and how well you like your neighbors.
Community	The whole city, town, or rural area where you live (not just your neighborhood). Community includes how nice the area looks, the amount of crime, and how well you like the people. It also includes places to go for fun such as parks, concerts, sporting events, and restaurants. You may also consider the cost of things you need to buy, the availability of jobs, the government, schools, taxes, and pollution.

increase general happiness, contentment, and life satisfaction, as well as a number of intervention strategies matched to the 16 areas of functioning (e.g., the "emotional honesty" and "find a friend, find a mate" principles for relationship enhancement).

Well-Being Therapy

Well-Being Therapy is a brief, structured, directive, and problem-oriented treatment program that uses client self-observations, structured journaling, and client and therapist interactions in order to increase client well-being (Ruini & Fava, 2004). The goal of Well-Being Therapy is to help clients improve functioning in each of six domains of psychological well-being defined by Ryff (1989): environmental mastery, personal growth, purpose in life, autonomy, self-acceptance, and positive relations with others. In general, the key therapeutic techniques include cognitive restructuring of automatic thoughts, scheduling of activities that will produce a sense of mastery or pleasure, assertiveness training, and problem-solving (Ruini & Fava, 2004).

In order to help clients move from impaired to optimal levels of psychological well-being, therapists guide clients to identify current and previous well-being experiences in their lives, no matter how brief those well-being experiences may have been (Ruini & Fava, 2004). Clients complete homework assignments that entail writing about their well-being experiences and the circumstances of such experiences in a structured diary along with rating each experience on a 1–100-point well-being scale (Ruini & Fava, 2004). After clients gain awareness of the instances of well-being in their lives, the next phase of treatment entails helping clients to identify their thoughts and beliefs that either promote or impede experiencing well-being and engaging in well-being experiences (Ruini & Fava, 2004). This phase of treatment is similar to the identification of automatic thoughts (Beck, Rush, Shaw, & Emery, 1979) or irrational beliefs (Ellis & Becker, 1982) in popular cognitive therapy treatment programs; however, in Well-Being Therapy, the thoughts of interest are those tied to instances of well-being rather than distress (Ruini & Fava, 2004). Examination of automatic thoughts connected to well-being experiences facilitates discovery of those areas of psychological well-being that are free of irrational automatic thoughts as well as those areas that are highly affected by such faulty thinking. Once therapists and clients understand how psychological well-being links to automatic negative thinking patterns, therapists can help clients to challenge or refute their faulty thinking that impedes well-being (using similar techniques to cognitive therapy such as evaluating evidence for thoughts), while also encouraging behaviors and thoughts that are likely to elicit well-being. Finally, therapists educate clients about the six dimensions of psychological well-being and how to assess and improve their functioning in each of these domains.

Hope Therapy

Hope theory asserts that emotions follow from one's thoughts regarding goal pursuits. More specifically, "emotions are a by-product of goal-directed thought – positive emotions reflecting perceived success in the pursuit of goals, and negative emotions reflecting perceived failures" (Snyder, 2000, p. 11). Hope is targeted in therapy because it is malleable and thus can help facilitate therapeutic change (Lopez et al., 2004). Therapists can help clients to create clearer goals, to learn how to produce multiple pathways to reach goals, and to generate the mental energy needed to sustain goal pursuits, thus changing client self-perceptions regarding their abilities to engage in goal-directed and agentic thinking (Lopez et al., 2000). The focus of Hope Therapy is on goals, possibilities, and past successes rather than on problems or failures. Hope Therapy includes four components: Finding, Bonding, Enhancing, and Reminding.

Hope Finding entails uncovering hope via use of narratives or self-report measures of hope. Therapists can introduce narrative strategies through sharing stories of hopeful characters. Through these stories, therapists educate clients about goals, agency, and pathways thinking. Eventually, clients are asked to tell stories from their own lives in which the components of hope can be identified and made explicit. Many times, clients tell stories of hope without even realizing it, hence astute therapists will be able to point out the components of hope in a client's life even if the client was not specifically asked to share a hopeful life experience story (Lopez et al., 2004).

The goal of Hope Bonding is to foster a strong, hopeful working alliance with clients. Indeed, the components of hope overlap considerably with the components of the working alliance (i.e., goals, tasks, and bond) defined by Bordin (1979). More specifically, the goals components of each framework match, tasks relate to pathways thinking, and bond corresponds to agency thinking (Lopez et al., 2000; Magyar-Moe, Edwards, & Lopez, 2001). Hopeful alliances are more likely to form when therapists engage clients in treatment planning and goal setting, especially when these processes engage the elements of hope theory (Lopez et al., 2004).

Hope Enhancing involves increasing hopeful thinking either in general or in a specific hope domain. The Adult Trait Hope Scale can determine a client's current level of dispositional hope (Snyder et al., 1991; see Worksheet 11). With this feedback, therapists can point out components of hope that are strengths for clients as well as components that need further work. Hope Therapy provides several techniques to enhance hope where it is lacking, including goal development, planning, and motivation.

Many clients struggle developing goals because they are uncertain about where to begin. Therapists can guide goal development by asking clients to create a list of their various life domains, prioritizing which are most important, and rating current levels of satisfaction within each domain. Next, positive, specific, and workable goals are collaboratively developed for each life domain (Lopez et al., 2004). For example, a client who says he wants to be happier could be asked questions such as "How would your life be different if you were happier?" or "If you were feeling happier, what would you be doing that you are not currently doing?" Goals should be stated positively, as this facilitates pathways planning and shifts the focus from reducing negative behaviors to increasing positive behaviors (Lopez et al., 2000). For example, rather than losing weight, the goal could be to work out more often and eat healthier. These positively framed goals could then be made even more explicit by defining exactly how often the client will work out and what healthier eating entails.

For clients who struggle with the pathways component of hope, they are taught to break goals into a series of smaller steps and to be creative and flexible in their thinking about how goals can be attained (Lopez et al., 2000). Therapists also challenge clients to come up with as many possible routes to a goal as possible (Lopez et al., 2000).

For clients who struggle with the agency component of hope, therapists aim to increase their motivation to work towards goals by exploring what, in general, serves to motivate the client (Lopez et al., 2000). Therapists can ask clients what has motivated them in the past and how they have overcome previous barriers. In addition, therapists teach the use of positive rather than negative self-talk regarding one's abilities to succeed, and underscore the enjoyment of the process of working toward a goal rather than focusing only on the outcome (Snyder, 1994).

Hope Reminding teaches clients how to self-monitor their hopeful thinking and use hope-enhancing techniques to sustain high hope levels independent of their therapists (Lopez et al., 2004). Relevant assignments include: (i) reviewing hope stories generated during Hope Finding; (ii) identifying a "hope buddy" in their personal lives who can assist in goal planning or support when goal pursuit becomes difficult; (iii) reflecting on successful goal pursuits and what they did that led to the success; or (iv) completing automatic thought records to understand and confront barrier thoughts (Lopez et al., 2004).

Positive Psychotherapy

Positive Psychotherapy is designed to build client strengths and increase positive emotions and meaning in order to alleviate psychopathology and foster happiness (Rashid, 2008; Seligman et al., 2006). Positive psychotherapists elicit and attend to positive emotions and memories while addressing client problems, with the goal of integrating the positive and negative (Rashid, 2008). For example, to help a client cope with a recent tragedy, a therapist engaging in Positive Psychotherapy would focus on the strengths that developed as a result. Positive Psychotherapy is based on two major assumptions (Rashid, 2008). The first is that all people are susceptible to mental illness yet they maintain an inherent capacity for happiness. Hence, positive psychotherapists view clients as autonomous and growth-oriented. The second assumption of Positive Psychotherapy is that client strengths and positive emotions are as genuine and relevant to the therapy process as weaknesses and negative emotions. As such, attending to the positives is crucial in establishing a strong therapeutic alliance and fully understanding a client's psychological repertoire that can be used as a foundation for treatment planning (Rashid, 2008).

The theoretical underpinnings of Positive Psychotherapy stem from Seligman's (2002) theoretical proposition that happiness consists of the pleasant life, the engaged life, and the meaningful life. The pleasant life is achieved when people are able to experience positive emotions about their past, present, and future lives. The engaged life is felt when one is deeply involved and absorbed in what one is doing in multiple life roles, including, love, work, and play. The meaningful life is defined as using one's strengths in the service of something larger than oneself (Seligman, 2002). A full life includes the experience of activities that promote pleasure, engagement, and meaning. The empty life, which occurs when one or more of these elements of the full life are lacking, is hypothesized to be a partial cause of psychological problems (Rashid, 2008).

Rashid (2008) presents an "idealized" model of individual Positive Psychotherapy consisting of 14 sessions. Each of the 14 sessions addresses a different theme or construct from positive psychology and provides clients with a corresponding homework assignment. For example, sessions 1 and 2 focus on identifying the client's character strengths. Clients construct a positive introduction story and complete a measure of character strengths. Other sessions cover concepts such as gratitude, forgiveness, optimism, love and attachment, savoring, and meaning. (See Magyar-Moe, 2009, for detailed descriptions of the 14 sessions of Positive

Psychotherapy and corresponding handouts and homework assignments.) Rashid (2008) emphasizes that a course of Positive Psychotherapy should match the needs of each individual client and therapists should adjust the length of therapy, homework and exercises, and focus of each session accordingly.

Positive Psychotherapy has demonstrated efficacy for the treatment of depression in both individual and group formats (Seligman et al., 2006). Individual Positive Psychotherapy resulted in a reduction of depressive symptoms and more cases of complete remission of depression symptomology compared to those in the treatment-as-usual and treatment-as-usual plus antidepressant medication conditions. In addition to reducing symptoms of depression, Positive Psychotherapy enhanced happiness and had better rates of adherence. In another study, group Positive Psychotherapy was provided to college students with mild or moderate levels of depression. In this study, the students reported greater reduction of depressive symptoms and greater increases in life satisfaction than a no-treatment control group, with superiority lasting throughout a one-year follow-up (Seligman et al., 2006). Many of the homework exercises used in Positive Psychotherapy have been validated through various studies, including web-based studies (Schueller & Parks, 2012; Seligman, Steen, Park, & Peterson, 2005). Based on these results, Rashid (2008) concludes that "Positive Psychotherapy has demonstrated efficacy, with large to medium effect sizes" (p. 205).

Individual Client Exercises Informed by Positive Psychology

A number of exercises are designed to foster various positive psychological constructs and strengths and can be used alone or in conjunction with the positive psychological treatment models previously reviewed. Such exercises are described in the following section.

Forgiveness exercises

Forgiveness exercises are well developed (see Chapter 2). Positive Psychotherapy includes the writing of forgiveness letters but various other options exist as well. These include emotional storytelling, finding benefits in adversity, and letting go of grudges activities.

Forgiveness letters Forgiveness can be utilized to undo anger, bitterness, and other negative emotions. For some, forgiveness even holds the power to transform negative emotions into positive ones. Forgiveness letters are written to individuals against whom clients are holding grudges. Letters address the transgression that occurred and associated client feelings. Clients then pledge to forgive; however, letters should not actually be delivered to the transgressor since forgiveness is a personal event that is not synonymous with reconciliation (Rashid, 2008). An alternative option for writing forgiveness letters is to have clients write forgiveness letters to themselves if they are working to overcome guilt or shame. Finally, clients should be reminded that writing forgiveness letters to people who have passed away but against whom they still hold a grudge can also be therapeutic (Magyar-Moe, 2009).

Emotional storytelling Emotional storytelling consists of having clients systematically write down the emotional upheaval they feel after experiencing a traumatic event, over the course of several timed writing sessions, in order to process intense negative emotions. This technique was popularized by Pennebaker (1997) and has since been referred to as the Pennebaker paradigm.

According to Niederhoffer and Pennebaker (2002), putting emotion-laden experiences into words helps clients to stop avoiding their thoughts and feelings, to start framing these thoughts and feelings into a meaningful framework that allows them to make better sense of the traumatic event, and to reintegrate themselves back into their daily lives and social networks without constantly being distracted by their negative emotions.

Some therapists and clients may wonder why emotional storytelling is a positive psychological exercise because the process of writing about emotional upheaval often has the short-term effect of making clients feel worse, as they are focusing on the negatives in their lives. Indeed, many research participants report feeling anxious, sad, depressed, and frustrated upon writing their stories (Pennebaker, 1989). However, in the long term, many positive health benefits have been found in association with emotional storytelling (Pennebaker, Kiecolt-Glaser, & Glaser, 1988; Petrie, Booth, & Pennebaker, 1998), for a diversity of people, including "all social classes and major racial and ethnic groups in the United States, as well as samples in Mexico City, French-speaking Belgium, the Netherlands, Spain, and Japan" (Niederhoffer & Pennebaker, 2002, p. 575). In addition, participants in emotional storytelling research studies report that despite the initial sadness, anxiety, and frustration experienced after engaging in writing their negative life stories, the writing experience was also very valuable and meaningful. Indeed, 98% of participants indicate that they would participate in emotional storytelling research again if given the opportunity to do so (Pennebaker, 1997).

Emotional storytelling can be a first step in the process of finding forgiveness, given that recalling the hurt is a first step in most models of forgiveness, followed by making meaning out of the transgression experience. Emotional storytelling is one way to help clients progress to the point where they are truly ready to let go of grudges and find forgiveness so that they can experience more positive emotions and satisfaction with life.

Finding benefits in adversity King and Miner (2000) suggest that an alternative to Pennebaker's emotional storytelling entails having clients write about the benefits that have resulted from their traumatic experiences. Indeed, a variety of researchers have found positive relationships between finding meaning in traumatic experiences and effective coping, psychological adjustment, higher self-esteem, and fewer symptoms of depression (Freedman & Enright, 1996; Janoff-Bulman, 1992; Taylor, 1983; Tennen, Affleck, & Mendola, 1991). King and Miner (2000) found that individuals who were instructed to write about only the positive aspects of negative or traumatic events (i.e., writing about the positive aspects and how one has grown or benefited as a result of a negative event), for 20 minutes a day for three days, showed the same health benefits as those who were instructed to write about their most traumatic life experiences. Hence, having clients write about the perceived benefits of their negative experiences may be a great alternative to having them experience or re-experience the pain of their past traumas through emotional storytelling.

Letting go of grudges Reivich (2004) created a forgiveness exercise that works off the principles of both gratitude and forgiveness. More specifically, clients are asked to think about a person against whom they are holding a grudge and then to recall and write down as many things as they can about that person for which they are grateful. The idea is that seeing the person in his or her entirety and recalling gratitude will loosen the grudge and allow the process of forgiveness to proceed.

Gratitude exercises

Putting gratitude into action within counseling and therapy is often achieved through assigning clients to write and deliver detailed gratitude letters to important people in their lives and to maintain daily journals of events they experience for which they are grateful. Indeed, such activities are included within Positive Psychotherapy. Several other exercises that may serve to increase gratitude and thereby life satisfaction are reviewed below (see also Chapter 1).

Couples or family gratitude journals In addition to keeping an individual daily gratitude journal, some clients may find it useful to engage in gratitude activities that involve their significant others or family members. For example, clients who are working on strengthening their marriages or partnerships may find that keeping a gratitude journal with their significant other is useful not only for increasing gratitude, but also for appreciation of one another. Couples are instructed to write down and share three things each day that they are thankful for regarding their partner (e.g., Campbell & Donovan, 2007; Magyar-Moe, Morrow, Jankiewicz, Simmerman, & Titel, 2010). The same activity can be extended to include children or other family members as well.

Altruism exercises

In order to help clients find more meaning in their lives and to experience firsthand how tending to the welfare of others is more satisfying than focusing on pleasure for oneself, clients can be assigned an exercise designed by Seligman called Fun versus Philanthropy (Peterson, 2006). This exercise entails having clients engage in one activity purely for fun or pleasure and then another activity designed to benefit another person. They are then asked to reflect on the similarities and differences between these two experiences. Typically, clients will report that both events led to positive emotions, but the benefits of the philanthropic activity were longer-lasting (Peterson, 2006).

Altruism can also be fostered by encouraging clients to seek out and participate in volunteer activities in their local communities. Indeed, research shows that volunteering is related to higher levels of life satisfaction, good health (Dulin & Hill, 2003; Hunter & Linn, 1981; Krause, Ingersoll-Dayton, Liang, & Sugisawa, 1999; Morrow-Howell, Hinterloth, Rozario, & Tang, 2003), and reductions in symptoms of depression and anxiety (Della Fave & Massimini, 1992). In addition, Myers (2004) reports that when people feel happy they are more willing to help others, and vice versa – when people help others, they are more likely to feel happy. Salovey, Mayer, and Rosenhan (1991) describe this relationship between helping and happiness as the "feel-good, do-good phenomenon."

Optimism exercises

According to learned optimism theory, pessimistic and optimistic people tend to think differently about the bad and good things that happen to them (Seligman, 1991; Seligman, Reivich, Jaycox, & Gillham, 1995). People who are optimistic make external, variable, and specific attributions for failure-like events, rather than the internal, stable, and global attributions made by pessimists. When it comes to explaining successful events or outcomes, the optimist will attribute the success to internal, stable, and global factors, while the pessimist will explain his or her success as the result of external, variable, and specific attributions. Methods to help clients learn to think more optimistically include door opening and closing exercises and ABCDE Disputation.

One door closes, another door opens In this exercise, clients recall three times in their lives when they lost out on something important, when an important plan fell through, or when they experienced rejection, and then work to find the doors that later opened as a result of these seemingly negative events (Rashid, 2008).

ABCDE Disputation Seligman (2002) contends that clients can learn to be more optimistic through intentional disputation of automatic pessimistic thoughts. Clients examine an *A*dverse experience that led them to think like a pessimist. Next, they write down their *B*eliefs about the adverse event and the *C*onsequences of their pessimistic beliefs. Then they *D*ispute their current beliefs in order to feel more *E*nergized and optimistic about the adversity. Optimism is enhanced as clients learn to consider alternative explanations for adverse events and to choose the one that is most temporary and specific (rather than permanent and global; Seligman, 2002).

A note on using positive psychological interventions and exercises

The number of potential positive psychological exercises and homework assignments could be overwhelming for clients if they were assigned all of them. The chances are that most clients will not have a need to complete each activity; therefore, carefully picking and choosing among them those that are most relevant for each individual client is recommended. Vital to this process is tailoring the activities and assignments, as well as the overall treatment plan, to fit client cultural identities and perspectives. Finally, within-session assistance on homework assignments is recommended if clients seem to be struggling with completion on their own outside of the therapy room (Magyar-Moe, 2009).

Conclusion

Throughout this chapter, scholarly information and practical resources have been provided for therapists who are interested in applying positive psychology in therapy with individual clients. As research in positive psychology continues to proliferate, so too will the information relevant to the applications of positive psychology to counseling and therapy. Perhaps in the future, positive psychology will become such an ingrained part of the training and work of all practitioners that there will be no such thing as therapy that is not based in the principles of positive psychology.

References

Beck, A. T., Rush, A. J., Shaw, B. L., & Emery, G. (1979). *Cognitive therapy of depression.* New York: Guilford Press.

Bordin, E. S. (1979). The generalizability of the psychoanalytic concept of the working alliance. *Psychotherapy: Theory, Research and Practice, 16,* 252–260.

Campbell, S., & Donovan, A. (2007). *An examination of the three good things exercise as an interpersonal positive intervention.* Unpublished master's thesis, University of Pennsylvania.

De Jong, P., & Berg, I. K. (2002). *Interviewing for solutions* (2nd ed.). Belmont, CA: Thomson Brooks/Cole Publishing Co.

Della Fave, A., & Massimini, F. (1992). The experience sampling method and the measurement of clinical change: A case of anxiety disorder. In M. deVries (Ed.), *The experience of psychopathology* (pp. 280–289). Cambridge: Cambridge University Press.

Dulin, P. L., & Hill, R. D. (2003). Relationships between altruistic activity and positive and negative affect among low-income older adult service providers. *Aging and Mental Health, 7,* 294–299.

Ellis, A., & Becker, I. (1982). *A guide to personal happiness.* Hollywood, CA: Melvin Powers Wilshire Book Company.

Freedman, S. R., & Enright, R. D. (1996). Forgiveness as an intervention goal with incest survivors. *Journal of Consulting and Clinical Psychology, 64,* 983–992.

Frisch, M. B. (1994). *Manual and treatment guide for the Quality of Life Inventory or QOLI.* Minneapolis, MN: Pearson Assessments.

Frisch, M. B. (2006). *Quality of life therapy: Applying a life satisfaction approach to positive psychology and cognitive therapy.* Hoboken, NJ: John Wiley & Sons.

Gelso, C. J., & Woodhouse, S. (2003). Toward a positive psychotherpay: Focus on human strength. In W. B. Walsh (Ed.), *Counseling psychology and human strengths* (pp. 344–369). New York: Lawrence Erlbaum.

Hunter, K. I., & Linn, M. W. (1981). Psychosocial differences between elderly volunteers and non-volunteers. *International Journal of Aging and Human Development, 12,* 205–213.

Janoff-Bulman, R. (1992). *Shattering assumptions: Towards a new psychology of trauma.* New York: Free Press.

Johnson, D. P., Penn, D. L., Fredrickson, B. L., Kring, A. M., Meyer, P. S., Catalino, L. I., & Brantley, M. (2011). A pilot study of loving-kindness meditation for the negative symptoms of schizophrenia. *Schizophrenia Research, 129,* 137–140.

Kahler, C., Spillane, N., Day, A., Clerkin, E., Parks, A. C., Leventhal, A., & Brown, R. (2014). Positive psychotherapy for smoking cessation: Treatment development, feasibility, and preliminary results. *Journal of Positive Psychology, 9*(1), 19–29.

Keyes, C. L. M., & Lopez, S. J. (2002). Toward a science of mental health: Positive directions in diagnosis and intervention. In C. R. Snyder & S. J. Lopez (Eds.), *Handbook of positive psychology* (pp. 45–62). New York: Oxford University Press.

King, L. A., & Miner, K. N. (2000). Writing about the perceived benefits of traumatic events: Implications for physical health. *Personality and Social Psychology Bulletin, 26,* 220–230.

Krause, N. M., Ingersoll-Dayton, B., Liang, J., & Sugisawa, H. (1999). Religion, social support, and health among Japanese elderly. *Journal of Health and Social Behavior, 40,* 405–421.

Krentzman, A. R. (2013). Review of the application of positive psychology to substance use, addiction, and recovery research. *Psychology of Addictive Behavior, 27,* 151–165.

Lopez, S. J., Floyd, R. K., Ulven, J. C., & Snyder, C. R. (2000). Hope therapy: Helping clients build a house of hope. In C. R. Snyder (Ed.), *Handbook of hope* (pp. 123–150). New York: Academic Press.

Lopez, S. J., Snyder, C. R., Magyar-Moe, J. L., Edwards, L. M., Pedrotti, J. T., Janowski, K., Turner, J. L., & Pressgrove, C. (2004). Strategies for accentuating hope. In P. A. Linley & S. Joseph (Eds.), *Positive psychology in practice* (pp. 388–404). Hoboken, NJ: John Wiley & Sons.

Magyar-Moe, J. L. (2009). *Therapist's guide to positive psychological interventions.* San Diego, CA: Elsevier Academic Press.

Magyar-Moe, J. L., Edwards, L. M., & Lopez, S. J. (2001). A new look at the working alliance: Is there a connection with hope? Unpublished manuscript, Department of Psychological Research and Education, University of Kansas, Lawrence.

Magyar-Moe, J. L., Morrow, C., Jankiewicz, A., Simmerman, D., & Titel, B. (2010). Effects of couples gratitude journaling on relationship satisfaction and well-being. Poster presented at the 118th Annual Convention of the American Psychological Association, San Diego, CA.

Meyer, P. S., Johnson, D. P., Parks, A., Iwanski, C., & Penn, D. L. (2012). Positive living: A pilot study of group positive psychotherapy for people with schizophrenia. *Journal of Positive Psychology, 7,* 239–248.

Morrow-Howell, N., Hinterloth, J., Rozario, P. A., & Tang, F. (2003). Effects of volunteering on the well-being of older adults. *Journals of Gerontology Series B: Psychological Sciences and Social Sciences, 58,* S137–S145.

Myers, D. G. (2004). Digested from D. G. Myers, *The Pursuit of Happiness.* New York: Avon Books. Excerpted from *Psychology* (7th ed.). New York: Worth Publishers.

Niederhoffer, K. G., & Pennebaker, J. W. (2002). Linguistic style matching in social interaction. *Journal of Language and Social Psychology, 21*, 337–360.

Pennebaker, J. W. (1989). Confession, inhibition, and disease. In L. Berkowitz (Ed.), *Advances in experimental social psychology* (Vol. 22, pp. 211–244). New York: Academic Press.

Pennebaker, J. W. (1997). *Opening up: The healing power of expressive writing.* New York: Guilford Press.

Pennebaker, J. W., Kiecolt-Glaser, J., & Glaser, R. (1988). Disclosure of traumas and immune function: Health implications for psychotherapy. *Journal of Consulting and Clinical Psychology, 56*, 239–245.

Peterson, C. (2006). *A primer in positive psychology.* New York: Oxford University Press.

Peterson, C., & Seligman, M. E. P. (2004). *Character strengths and virtues: A handbook and classification.* New York: Oxford University Press.

Petrie, K. P., Booth, R. J., & Pennebaker, J. W. (1998). The immunological effects of thought suppression. *Journal of Personality and Social Psychology, 75*, 1264–1272.

Rashid, T. (2008). Positive psychotherapy. In S. J. Lopez (Ed.), *Positive psychology: Exploring the best in people* (Vol. 4, pp. 187–217). Westport, CT: Praeger Publishers.

Rashid, T. (2009). Positive interventions in clinical practice. *Journal of Clinical Psychology, 65*, 461–466.

Reivich, K. (2004). Letting go of grudges. Assignment instructions for M. E. P. Seligman's Authentic Happiness Coaching Program.

Ruini, C., & Fava, G. A. (2004). Clinical applications of well-being therapy. In P. A. Linley & S. Joseph (Eds.), *Positive psychology in practice* (pp. 371–387). Hoboken, NJ: John Wiley & Sons.

Ruini, C., & Fava, G. A. (2009). Well-being therapy for generalized anxiety disorder. *Journal of Clinical Psychology, 65*, 510–519.

Ryff, C. D. (1989). Happiness is everything, or is it? Explorations on the meaning of psychological well-being. *Journal of Personality and Social Psychology, 57*, 1069–1081.

Salovey, P., Mayer, J. D., & Rosenhan, D. L. (1991). Mood and helping: Mood as a motivator of helping and helping as a regulator of mood. *Review of Personality and Social Psychology, 12*, 215–237.

Schueller, S. M., & Parks, A. C. (2012). Disseminating self-help: Positive psychology exercises in an online trial. *Journal of Medical Internet Research, 14*, e63.

Seligman, M. E. P. (1991). *Learned optimism.* New York: Knopf.

Seligman, M. E. P. (2002). *Authentic happiness: Using the new positive psychology to realize your potential for lasting fulfillment.* New York: Free Press.

Seligman, M. E. P., & Csikszentmihalyi, M. (2000). Positive psychology: An introduction. *American Psychologist, 55*, 5–14.

Seligman, M. E. P., Rashid, T., & Parks, A. C. (2006). Positive psychotherapy. *American Psychologist, 61*, 774–788.

Seligman, M. E. P., Reivich, K. J., Jaycox, L. H., & Gillham, J. (1995). *The optimistic child.* Boston, MA: Houghton, Mifflin and Co.

Seligman, M. E. P., Steen, T. A., Park, N., & Peterson, C. (2005). Positive psychology progress: Empirical validation of interventions. *American Psychologist, 60*, 410–421.

Sin, N. L., & Lyubomirsky, S. (2009). Enhancing well-being and alleviating depressive symptoms with positive psychology interventions: A practice-friendly meta-analysis, *Journal of Clinical Psychology, 65*, 467–487.

Smith, E. (2006). The strengths-based counseling model. *The Counseling Psychologist, 34*, 13–79.

Snyder, C. R. (1994). *The psychology of hope: You can get there from here*. New York: Free Press.

Snyder, C. R. (2000). Hypothesis: There is hope. In C. R. Snyder (Ed.), *Handbook of hope* (pp. 3–20). San Diego, CA: Academic Press.

Snyder, C. R., Harris, C., Anderson, J. R., Holleran, S. A., Irving, L. M., Sigmon, S. T., Yoshinobu, L. R., Gibb, J., Langelle, C., & Harney, P. (1991). The will and the ways: Development of an individual-differences measure of hope. *Journal of Personality and Social Psychology*, *60*, 570–585.

Taylor, S. E. (1983). Adjustment to threatening events: A theory of cognitive adaptation. *American Psychologist*, *38*, 1161–1173.

Tennen, H., Affleck, G., & Mendola, R. (1991). Causal explanations for infertility: Their relation to control appraisals and psychological adjustment. In A. Stanton & C. Dunkel-Schetter (Eds.), *Infertility: Perspectives from stress and coping research* (pp. 109–132). New York: Plenum.

Wong, J. (2006). Strengths-Centered Therapy: A social constructionist, virtue-based psychotherapy. *Psychotherapy: Theory, Research, Practice, and Training*, *43*, 133–146.

Wood, A. M., & Tarrier, N. (2010). Positive clinical psychology: A new vision and strategy for integrated research and practice. *Clinical Psychology Review*, *30*, 819–829.

Wright, B. A., & Lopez, S. J. (2002). Widening the diagnostic focus: A case for including human strengths and environmental resources. In C. R. Snyder & S. J. Lopez (Eds.), *The handbook of positive psychology* (pp. 26–44). New York: Oxford University Press.

15

Evidence-Based Coaching as a Positive Psychological Intervention

Suzy Green and Gordon B. Spence

As has been stated many times by its chief proponents, positive psychology is focused on the application of psychological science to the optimization of human experience (Seligman, 2011). It is therefore no surprise that advances in positive psychological science tend to be closely followed by efforts to develop and validate new positive psychological interventions (PPIs). PPIs are intentional activities that aim to increase well-being through the cultivation of positive feelings, cognitions, and behaviors. Examples of popular PPIs include methods used for identifying and developing strengths (see Chapter 4), exercises for cultivating gratitude (see Chapter 1), and visualizations of one's best possible self (Seligman, Steen, Park, & Peterson, 2005; Sheldon & Lyubomirsky, 2006). Encouragingly, a recent meta-analytic study of 51 PPI-related studies has reported that many of these practical applications are capable of both significantly enhancing well-being and reducing psychopathology (Sin & Lyubomirsky, 2009).

Whilst these developments are welcomed, we note with interest that the PPI literature has developed with little explicit connection to another closely related literature: coaching psychology. This seems odd as these disciplines share similar aims and purposes. In this chapter we will introduce the field of coaching psychology and review a growing empirical literature that is increasingly supportive of evidence-based coaching as an efficacious intervention methodology in a variety of contexts. In addition, we will explore some of the commonalities that exist between PPIs and coaching psychology and argue that efforts to enhance human experience at the individual, group, and organizational levels would be bolstered by greater integration of the two disciplines.

What Is Coaching?

Coaching involves a collaborative relationship formed between a coach and a coachee for the purpose of attaining valued outcomes. Central to the coaching

The Wiley Blackwell Handbook of Positive Psychological Interventions, First Edition.
Edited by Acacia C. Parks and Stephen M. Schueller.

process is the clarification and articulation of personal and professional goals, goals that are generally set to stretch an individual's current capacities (Spence & Grant, 2007). Whilst the coaching process occurs within a supportive, collaborative relationship, it is action-oriented and focused on creating purposeful, positive change. Simply put, it involves both "talking and doing." Importantly, the coach does not assume control of the coachee's change process (by telling them what to do), rather he/she uses Socratic questioning to build self-responsibility for change and discover (or rediscover) the latent strengths and tacit knowledge needed to create the solutions needed for goal attainment to occur (Berg & Szabo, 2005).

In essence, coaching assists individuals to enhance goal striving by: (i) developing a positive or preferred future vision, (ii) identifying desired outcomes, (iii) establishing specific personal goals, (iv) enhancing motivation by identifying strengths and building self-efficacy, (v) identifying resources and formulating action plans, (vi) regularly monitoring and evaluating progress, and (vii) the modification of action plans (based on an ongoing evaluation of progress) (Grant, 2003a). The use of simple process models such as the Goal, Reality, Options, Wrap-up model (GROW; Whitmore, 1996) encourages coachees to take ownership of their goal striving and behavior change by inviting them to set the agenda for each coaching conversation. The GROW model also forms part of an ongoing iterative process that includes the Review and Evaluation (RE-GROW) of goal-directed action over multiple coaching sessions, which permits modifications to goals or action plans as needed. This review–evaluate–modification component of the coaching process creates a "cycle" of self-regulation (see Figure 15.1) that is important for successful behavior change (Grant, 2003b).

Whilst a number of theoretical models and practice perspectives are used to inform coaching (Peltier, 2001), the amalgam of cognitive-behavioral, solution-focused (CB-SF) approaches has been frequently used in coaching interventions (Grant, Passmore, Cavanagh, & Parker, 2010; Spence & Oades, 2011). The coupling together of these approaches has been justified on the basis that both support adaptive self-regulation in subtly different ways: the CB approach via methods (such as thought monitoring and cognitive restructuring) that support more rational, realistic thought–action sequences (Grant, 2003a), and the SF approach via techniques that orient coachees towards desired future states, existing functional behavior, and solution construction (such as goal clarification and exceptions questions; for a detailed description of SF coaching and SF techniques, see Berg & Szabo, 2005; Green, 2011).

Coaching psychology or evidence-based coaching?

At this point it is worth clarifying what is meant by two terms that are widely used within the coaching literature: coaching psychology and evidence-based coaching. According to Grant (2007) *coaching psychology* is the "systematic application of behavioural science [within a coaching context] to the enhancement of life

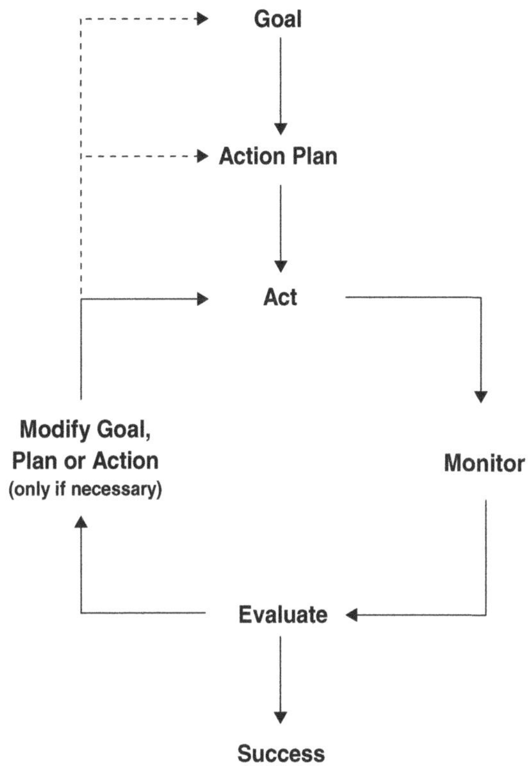

Figure 15.1 Generic model of self-regulation (Grant, 2003b). © Society for Personality Research

experience, work performance and well-being of individuals, groups and organizations" (Grant, 2007, p. 23). As such, coaching psychology is an applied science and somewhat narrowly focused on the use of knowledge from a specific domain (i.e. behavioral science).

In contrast, Stober and Grant (2006) define *evidence-based coaching* as "the intelligent and conscientious use of *best current knowledge* integrated with practitioner expertise in making decisions about how to deliver coaching" (p. 6, italics in original), with "best current knowledge" defined as "up-to-date information from relevant, valid research, theory and practice" (p. 6). Whilst evidence-based coaching is also an applied discipline (as it is focused on how knowledge is used), it represents a broader perspective on coaching as its practice can potentially be informed by knowledge drawn from multiple disciplines (e.g., psychology, sociology, adult learning, education, organizational behavior, business management).

Although this distinction is not critically important within the context of this discussion (as PPIs are encompassed by both definitions), the clarification is useful if confusion is to be avoided for those relatively unfamiliar with the scholarly coaching literature.

What Is the Evidence for Evidence-Based Coaching?

Over the past decade, the coaching literature has repeatedly called for the development of an evidence base that is scientifically rigorous, theoretically informed, unique to the field, and relevant to the needs of its practitioners (Cavanagh & Grant, 2006; Grant, 2006; Spence, 2007). In response, there have been over 400 publications on coaching listed in the behavioral science and business databases since 2005, compared to only 131 such publications in the preceding five years (Grant, 2010). Although these recent publications continue to be dominated by reviews, surveys, and opinion pieces, an encouraging increase in the number of peer-reviewed empirical studies is noted. According to Spence and Oades (2011), a close examination of this literature reveals that 69 publications make some reference to coaching using some theoretical orientation (e.g., CB-SF), practice model (e.g., motivational interviewing), or organizing construct (e.g., emotional intelligence). However, only a few of these have been used as the basis of empirical investigation, with CB-SF coaching being utilized in 6 of the 18 between-subjects studies reported to date.

Whilst the research base is still embryonic, early findings suggest that evidence-based coaching (EBC) impacts an array of psychological characteristics and processes related to goal-directed self-regulation (Grant & Cavanagh, 2011; Spence & Grant, 2013). For example, EBC has been found to increase goal attainment, resilience, hope, and other indicators of well-being in samples of secondary school students, teachers, public sector managers, and adults drawn from the general population. A short summary of findings follows.

Evidence-based coaching in organizations

Although coaching has been widely used in workplaces for several decades and research can be traced back to the early 1990s (e.g., Deviney, 1994), there is still relatively little research that has been reported on its impact and effectiveness. In one of the few randomized controlled trials (RCT) conducted to date, Duijts, Kant, van den Brandt, and Swaen (2008) examined the effectiveness of coaching as a means of reducing work absence due to psychosocial health complaints. In this study, 37 "at risk" employees completed six months of workplace coaching (comprising seven to nine 60-minute sessions) during which coaches helped participants to set a variety of health goals and then supported behavior change by encouraging them to reflect on factors that might have been helping or hindering such change (e.g., high self-efficacy, low social support). Whilst no decrease in absenteeism was observed, there was some evidence that workplace coaching enhanced employee well-being as participants reported significantly lower burnout, along with improvements in general health, life satisfaction, and psychological well-being.

The most comprehensive study of coaching in organizations has recently been concluded by Cavanagh, Atkins, Spence, and Grant (2010). This study sought to understand whether developmental coaching could enhance four key psychological characteristics believed to be important for effective leadership (i.e., perspective-taking capacity (PTC), mindfulness, purpose, and positivity). The participants were 245 managers and leaders drawn from two high-stress work environments (a large law firm and public health service), who were randomly assigned to leadership training only, leadership training plus coaching, or wait-list control conditions. In the coaching condition, participants were encouraged to set relevant work-related goals, and throughout the coaching process were constantly challenged to vary the perspective they held in regard to their challenges (e.g., the tension that exists for nurse managers between delivering quality care to patients and making hospital beds available as quickly as possible).

The major hypothesis of this study was that developmental coaching would help leaders to construct bigger, more complex perspectives that could help them respond to complex, stressful work scenarios with less reactivity, more creativity, and greater behavioral flexibility. The results supported this hypothesis and indicated that coaching significantly enhanced all four leadership qualities (compared to the other conditions), with the gains maintained at a nine-month follow-up. This study is important as it has: (i) identified key leadership variables (e.g., PTC) and examined how coaching can influence the development of those variables, and (ii) confirmed earlier findings (Olivero, Bane, & Kopelman, 1997) that coaching seems to play an important role in the consolidation and transfer of workshop learning.

In addition to these RCTs, there have also been some quasi-experimental studies in the workplace using pre-test and post-test comparisons and non-randomized allocation to an intervention or control group. For example, Gyllensten and Palmer (2005) found that coaching was associated with lower levels of anxiety and workplace stress (compared with a control group), whilst Evers, Brouwers, and Tomic (2006) reported that executive coaching enhanced participants' self-efficacy and perceived ability to set personal goals. In addition, Barrett (2007) found that group coaching was effective for reducing burnout but not for improving productivity.

Evidence-based coaching in education

There is an emerging literature on coaching for teachers or educators that is particularly focused on leadership development (see Denton & Hasbrouck, 2009). For example, Contreras (2009) conducted a within-subject study of 60 school principals using professional leadership coaches, with positive results reported in respect of the principals' capacity to lead effectively. In another study, Grant, Green, and Rynsaardt (2010) studied the impact of "developmental coaching" on teachers. A randomized controlled (pre-post) design was used to explore the impact of coaching on goal attainment, workplace well-being, resilience, and leadership styles. Participants were 44 high school teachers who were randomly assigned to either a 20-week CB-SF coaching intervention or a wait-list control group. Participants in the coaching group received multi-rater (i.e., 360-degree) feedback on their leadership behaviors and, with the help of a tertiary-qualified coach, attempted to use that feedback to develop a more positive, constructive leadership style (by, for example, disputing self-limiting beliefs or displaying greater empathy). The findings indicated that the coaching participants reported significant increases in goal attainment, well-being, and resilience, and also significant reduction in stress. Coaching also appeared to enhance dimensions of constructive leadership (e.g., achievement, humanistic-encouraging), whilst reducing self-reported aggressive/defensive and passive/defensive styles. These findings suggest that coaching, as a professional development methodology, has great potential to contribute to the professional development and well-being of teachers in an educational setting.

Research has also been conducted with student samples. For example, Green, Grant, and Rynsaardt (2007) conducted a randomized controlled trial of EBC with an adolescent population. Fifty-six female senior high school students (mean age = 16 years) were randomly allocated to an individual life coaching group (n = 28) or to a wait-list control group (n = 28). Participants were randomly assigned to a teacher-coach (who had been trained in the use of the EBC model and techniques) and they met one-on-one for 10 sessions over two school terms. Each coaching session involved the setting of session goals, followed by a discussion of what was going on in the student's life. A primary aim of coaching was to raise awareness of personal circumstances and use that awareness to identify resources that could be utilized to move towards personal goals. Students were also assisted to systematically work through the self-regulatory cycle of setting goals, developing (self-generated) action plans, and then monitoring and evaluating progress. The findings indicated that student coachees (compared to controls) experienced significant increases in cognitive hardiness and hope, and a significant decrease in levels of depression, which suggests that evidence-based life coaching may be an effective intervention for high school students.

Whilst these findings from the organizational and educational coaching literatures are encouraging, they should be interpreted cautiously for two reasons. First, recent reviews (e.g., Grant, 2010; Spence & Oades, 2011) indicate that the empirical coaching literature is still relatively small, with few replications and considerable methodological variability. Second, much of the research reported to date appears to lack firm theoretical foundations and seems to have occurred in the absence of clearly articulated, coherent research agendas. Consequently, the evidence base for coaching can best be described as disparate, largely atheoretical, and primarily composed of "one-off" findings. Whilst coaching clearly has some way to go before it could be described as a mature field of study, practitioners are fortunate to have several bodies of relevant knowledge to draw on to inform their work.

The Relationship Between Positive Psychology and Coaching Psychology

Whilst coaching for the enhancement of optimal functioning has existed since the late 1980s when "executive coaching" first emerged, the initial focus was primarily on peak performance and achievement of organizational goals, rather than the enhancement of well-being *per se*. More recently, the emergence of work–life balance as a common goal in executive and organizational settings has resulted in coaching becoming more holistic, and focused on the health and well-being of executives and employees.

By the mid-1990s, interest in using coaching as a way of enhancing personal functioning had spread beyond the organizational context and into the public domain, when life coaching went through its "boom" period (Naughton, 2002). During this time people began engaging the services of "life coaches" to assist with managing a wide range of issues including life transitions (e.g., retirement), career transitions, entrepreneurial ventures, relationship issues, and lifestyle modifications (e.g., improving physical and/or mental health).

Highly complementary disciplines

Gable and Haidt (2005) define positive psychology as "the study of the conditions and processes that contribute to the flourishing (well-being) or optimal functioning of people, groups, and institutions" (p. 103). When this definition is compared to the coaching definitions outlined earlier in this chapter, the link between positive psychology and coaching becomes easy to detect, as both disciplines are focused on the cultivation of optimal functioning and well-being, albeit at different ends of the research–practice continuum. That is, positive psychology dedicates itself primarily to the scientific development and validation of intentional activities designed to cultivate pleasure, engagement, relationships, meaning, and accomplishment (PERMA; Seligman, 2011), whereas coaching psychology focuses exclusively on the application of methods that encourage individuals to set and strive for personally meaningful goals within the framework of a collaborative relationship.

As noted earlier, a critical feature of coaching psychology is the use of knowledge derived from behavioral science to help enhance the personal and professional experience of individuals (Grant, 2007). As such, evidence-based coaches – by definition – seek an evidentiary basis for the methods they use and may draw from a number of relevant literatures to achieve this (e.g., sport, organizational, or counseling psychology), of which positive psychology is one possible option. Nonetheless, as positive psychology is concerned with the conditions that support flourishing within individuals, groups, and communities (Gable & Haidt, 2005), and EBC provides a context for seeking such outcomes, it is possible to view coaching as a form of applied positive psychology. Indeed, Grant and Spence

(2010) have argued that the context provided in coaching is valuable because it permits the presentation of "user-friendly applications of positive psychological knowledge" (p. 177) to individuals who might find them beneficial across multiple domains of life and/or who might not otherwise have exposure to them.

The emergence of positive psychology coaching

Whilst there were some early scholarly publications on the integration and implementation of positive psychology within coaching (e.g., Kauffman & Scoular, 2004), the term positive psychology coaching (PPC) has only become popularized in the last few years as a result of some influential publications (Biswas-Diener, 2010; Biswas-Diener & Dean, 2007). Whilst there are no known scientific studies conducted on PPC, some evidence-based coaching studies have been published using positive psychological constructs as dependent variables. These include the first published randomized controlled trial of CB-SF life coaching for the enhancement of goal striving, well-being, and hope (Green, Oades, & Grant, 2006), and a subsequent study that compared professional and peer life coaching for the enhancement of goal striving and well-being (Spence & Grant, 2007). Whilst the evidence-based coaching methodologies used in these studies did not specifically include positive psychology techniques (i.e., gratitude visits or random acts of kindness), their aim was to increase both goal striving and well-being.

Strategic Integration of Positive Psychology and Coaching Psychology

Whilst both positive psychology and coaching psychology can be utilized to enhance well-being and optimal functioning across a variety of settings, these approaches appear to operate largely in isolation from each other. For example, an organization or school might undertake "leadership coaching" but not necessarily utilize PPIs (such as strengths assessment and development) as part of that intervention. So, the question becomes, "What would be the benefit in providing additional training in positive psychology to staff?" Alternatively, one might ask, "Why might an organization interested in utilizing PPIs (such as gratitude or kindness interventions) provide additional education and training in coaching?"

One reason relates to the potential impact that can occur at different levels of human systems. Whilst both PPIs and EBC are known to enhance well-being at the individual level, the use of social network analysis in recent coaching trials has revealed that workplace coaching (without the use of PPIs) can enhance positivity within organizational teams, creating a "ripple effect" that extends beyond those who are directly involved in coaching interventions (O'Connor & Cavanagh, 2012).

As such, if an organization wanted to create a more engaging, supportive culture, research suggests that PPIs provide useful methods for creating such conditions (e.g., by managers using strengths-spotting with teams), and if these methods are complemented by EBC, change can be further embedded within the system as individuals explore how such methods might be most usefully employed at individual, team, and organizational levels.

Another reason relates to the transfer of learning. Many organizations today invest heavily in learning and development activities for their staff and understandably are keen to maximize those investments by ensuring that what is learnt in the classroom translates into action on the job. In a widely cited study, Olivero, Bane, and Kopelman (1997) reported that coaching substantially enhanced the transfer of workshop training. The researchers argued that there is a qualitative difference in the type of learning that takes place in training and coaching, with training supporting the abstract learning of principles, whilst coaching facilitates the specific *application* of learning by individuals in specific situations. That is, coaching provides the opportunity to practice and obtain constructive feedback regarding the subject matter learnt during training. In this case, any explicit training in positive psychology principles could be enhanced through the use of coaching to support the transfer of training and sustain application in daily life.

As such, we would argue that any organization or educational institution providing training in positive psychology should also consider the use of EBC as a means to increase retention of knowledge, enhance transfer of training, and as an integral part of a sustainability strategy. For example, if after receiving a lesson on "signature strengths" a student is given coaching support and helped toward goals that leverage that student's strengths, the learning is likely to become personalized and the goals more fully owned by the student (Spence & Oades, 2011). If the coaching continued (either on an individual or group basis) additional opportunities would be gained to monitor the progress of the original goal(s) or new goals set in regard to other positive psychology concepts including gratitude, kindness, forgiveness, etc. Coaching then allows individuals to make meaning of the positive psychology concepts in practically applying them to their lives, drawing on the goal-setting and goal-striving methodologies of coaching.

This approach has recently been tested with a sample of primary-aged school boys. In a pilot study, Madden, Green, and Grant (2011) assessed the impact of a strengths-based group coaching program on students' levels of engagement and hope. Using a within-subject design, 38 boys (mean age 10.7 years) participated as part of a personal development/health program at an independent, private primary school. Students were randomly allocated to groups of four or five, with each group receiving eight coaching sessions over two school terms. The Youth Values in Action survey was used to highlight participants' character strengths, and the participants were coached in identifying personally meaningful goals, being persistent in their goal striving, and finding novel ways to use their signature strengths. The results indicated that the strengths-based coaching program was associated with significant increases in the students' self-reported levels of engagement and hope, suggesting that strengths-based coaching programs may form an important part of Positive Education programs.

Similarly, we would also suggest that an organization considering training its staff in EBC techniques consider supporting that initiative through the addition of positive psychology training sessions. For example, recent research has shown that the explicit use of strengths assessment and use in the pursuit of goals enhances goal attainment and well-being (Linley, Nielsen, Gillett, & Biswas-Diener, 2010).

Future Research and Implications

First, future research needs to explore further applications of PPIs and EBC in various domains such as educational institutions and organizations. However, before proceeding with such research, it is important to investigate how these subdisciplines of psychology are best integrated into different contexts, in order to enhance outcomes for individuals, teams, educational institutions, and organizations. This issue was explored by Oades, Robinson, Green, and Spence (2011) who examined how positive psychology principles might be applied within the context of tertiary education. They concluded that there was much that could potentially be gained across all levels of university life (i.e., classroom, social, faculty, local community, and residential) and suggested a range of interventions at each level (see Oades et al., 2011, table 1, p. 434). An interesting possibility is the running of residential environments using strengths-focused techniques (e.g., strengths-spotting), coaching for academic and personal goal attainment, and cross-cultural events to enhance learning.

Second, some attention could be given to understanding the degree to which EBC can be used as a form of empirically-supported self-help (Parks, Schueller, & Tasimi, 2013). Whilst some studies using manualized coaching programs have been reported in the empirical coaching literature (e.g., Grant, 2003a), these have tended to be facilitated programs rather than self-directed. As such, an opportunity exists to develop self-coaching interventions that assist people to engage in purposeful, positive change through the iterative, reflective process that sits at the heart of coaching and involves setting authentic goals and the monitoring and evaluation of one's attempts to attain such goals.

Finally, it is important to determine who the appropriate "audience" is for PPIs and EBC. Whilst some attention has been given to the use of PPIs with clinical populations (e.g., Rashid, 2013), coaching has typically focused on non-clinical rather than clinical populations. Regardless of context, we would suggest that future research consider the issue of mental health status as a part of the engagement process for PPIs or EBC interventions. This is because without a thorough psychological assessment prior to engaging in these interventions, there may be a real danger of an unintended negative outcome. For example, if an adolescent were to undertake a "strengths-based coaching intervention" at school and find it difficult to apply his/her strengths sufficiently to achieve his/her goals (due to, say, an unrecognized depressive disorder), it is possible that the positively intended PPI might only make matters worse. This issue has received some attention in the coaching literature in the past decade, with evidence suggesting that people presenting for life coaching sometimes have significantly high levels of psychological distress (Green, Oades, & Grant, 2006; Spence & Grant, 2007).

Conclusion

Evidence-based coaching, when viewed as a PPI, appears to be a promising approach to the enhancement of personal functioning, although further research is required. With increasing research showing the benefits to well-being from both PPIs and EBC, we would argue that these approaches have real potential to be powerful interventions that increase well-being at the individual, group/team, and organizational level. We have also argued that there is considerable value in further integrating PPIs and EBC. Practical approaches such as Biswas-Diener's (2010) "Practicing Positive Psychology Coaching" seem useful starting points for evidence-based coaching practitioners to begin from.

PPIs and EBC are but two of the approaches currently available to the scientist-practitioner, and they are unlikely to be the intervention of choice for all. We would argue that they do, however, provide a rigorous framework for the application of positive psychology research. They also appear to offer many benefits for those undertaking such an intervention, including the enhancement of both goal striving and well-being.

References

Barrett, P. T. (2007). The effects of group coaching on executive health and team effectiveness: A quasi-experimental field study. *Dissertation Abstracts International Section A*, *67*, 26–40.

Berg, I. K., & Szabo, P. (2005). *Brief coaching for lasting solutions.* New York: Norton.

Biswas-Diener, R. (2010). *Practicing positive psychology coaching: Assessment, activities and strategies for success.* Hoboken, NJ: John Wiley & Sons.

Biswas-Diener, R., & Dean, B. (2007). *Positive psychology coaching: Putting the science of happiness to work for your clients.* Hoboken, NJ: John Wiley & Sons.

Cavanagh, M., Atkins, P., Spence, G. B., & Grant, A. M. (2010). Developing leaders for a complex world: New models of leadership and the use of coaching in creating developmental change among leaders. Symposia presented at the 27th International Congress of Applied Psychology, Melbourne, Australia (July 11–16, 2010).

Cavanagh, M., & Grant, A. M. (2006). Coaching psychology and the scientist-practitioner model. In D. A. Lane & S. Corrie (Eds.), *The modern scientist-practitioner: A guide to practice in psychology* (pp. 146–157). Hove, UK: Routledge.

Contreras, Y. M. (2009). A descriptive study: Coaching school leaders for 21st century schools: A new context for leadership development. *Dissertations available from ProQuest.* Paper 3322839. http://gradworks.umi.com/33/22/3322839.html

Denton, C. A., & Hasbrouck, J. (2009). A description of instructional coaching and its relationship to consultation. *Journal of Educational and Psychological Consultation*, *19*(2), 150–190.

Deviney, D. E. (1994). The effect of coaching using multiple rater feedback to change supervisor behavior. *Dissertation Abstracts International: Section A*, *55*, 144.

Duijts, S. F. A., Kant, I., van den Brandt, P. A., & Swaen, G. M. H. (2008). Effectiveness of a preventive coaching intervention for employees at risk for sickness absence due to psychosocial health complaints: Results of a randomized controlled trial. *Journal of Environmental Medicine*, *50*(7), 765–776.

Evers, W. J. G., Brouwers, A., & Tomic, W. (2006). A quasi-experimental study on management coaching effectiveness, *Consulting Psychology Journal: Practice and Research*, *58*(3), 174–182.

Gable, S., & Haidt, J. (2005). Positive psychology. *Review of General Psychology*, *9*(2), 103–110.

Grant, A. M. (2003a). Towards a psychology of coaching: The impact of coaching on metacognition, mental health and goal attainment. *Dissertation Abstracts International: Section B: The Sciences & Engineering*, *63*(12-B), 6094.

Grant, A. M. (2003b). The impact of life coaching on goal attainment, metacognition and mental health. *Social Behavior and Personality: An International Journal*, *31*(3), 253–263.

Grant, A. M. (2006). An integrative goal-focused approach to executive coaching. In D. R. Stober & A. M. Grant (Eds.), *Evidence based coaching handbook: Putting best practices to work for your clients* (pp. 153–192). Hoboken, NJ: John Wiley & Sons.

Grant, A. M. (2007). Past, present and future: The evolution of professional coaching and coaching psychology. In S. Palmer & A. Whybrow (Eds.), *Handbook of coaching psychology* (pp. 23–39). New York: Routledge.

Grant, A. M. (2010). Workplace, executive and life coaching: An annotated bibliography from the behavioural science and business literature. Unpublished paper, Coaching Psychology Unit, University of Sydney, Australia.

Grant, A. M., & Cavanagh, M. J. (2011). Coaching and positive psychology. In K. M. Sheldon, T. B. Kashdan, & M. F. Steger (Eds.), *Designing positive psychology: Taking stock and moving forward* (pp. 293–309). New York: Oxford University Press.

Grant, A. M., Green, L. S., & Rynsaardt, J. (2010). Developmental coaching for high school teachers: Executive coaching goes to school. *Consulting Psychology Journal: Practice & Research*, *62*(3), 151–168.

Grant, A. M., Passmore, J., Cavanagh, M. J., & Parker, H. (2010). The state of play in coaching. *International Review of Industrial and Organizational Psychology*, *25*, 125–168.

Grant, A. M., & Spence, G. B. (2010). Using coaching and positive psychology to promote a flourishing workforce: A model of goal-striving and mental health. In P. A. Linley, S. Harrington, & N. Garcea (Eds.), *Oxford handbook of positive psychology and work* (pp. 175–188). Oxford: Oxford University Press.

Green, L. S., Oades, L. G., & Grant, A. M. (2006). Cognitive-behavioural, solution-focused life coaching: Enhancing goal striving, well-being, and hope. *Journal of Positive Psychology*, *1*(3), 142–149.

Green, S. (2011). Solution-focused life coaching. In C. Franklin, T. S. Trepper, W. J. Gingerich, & E. E. McCollum (Eds.), *Solution-focused brief therapy: A handbook of evidence-based practice*. New York: Oxford University Press.

Green, S., Grant, A., & Rynsaardt, J. (2007). Evidence-based life coaching for senior high school students: Building hardiness and hope. *International Coaching Psychology Review*, *2*, 24–32.

Gyllensten, K., & Palmer, S. (2005). Can coaching reduce workplace stress? A quasi-experimental study. *International Journal of Evidence Based Coaching and Mentoring*, *3*(2), 75–85.

Kauffman, C., & Scoular, A. (2004). Toward a positive psychology of executive coaching. In P. A. Linley & S. Joseph (Eds.), *Positive psychology in practice* (pp. 287–302). Hoboken, NJ: John Wiley & Sons.

Linley, P. A., Nielsen, K. M., Gillett, R., & Biswas-Diener, R. (2010). Using signature strengths in pursuit of goals: Effects on goal progress, need satisfaction, and well-being, and implications for coaching psychologists. *International Coaching Psychology Review*, *5*(1), 6–15.

Madden, W., Green, L. S., & Grant, A. M. (2011). A pilot study evaluating strengths-based coaching for primary school students: Enhancing engagement and hope. *International Coaching Psychology Review*, *7*(1), 71–83.

Naughton, J. (2002). The coaching boom: Is it the long-awaited alternative to the medical model? *The Psychotherapy Networker*, *26*, 24–33.

Oades, L. G., Robinson, P., Green, L. S., & Spence, G. B. (2011). Towards a positive university. *Journal of Positive Psychology*, *6*(6), 432–439.

O'Connor, S., & Cavanagh, M. (2013). The coaching ripple effect: The effects of developmental coaching on wellbeing across organizational networks. *Psychology of Well-Being: Theory, Research and Practice*, *3*. http://www.psywb.com/content/3/1/2

Olivero, G., Bane, K. D., & Kopelman, R. E. (1997). Executive coaching as a transfer of training tool: Effects on productivity in a public agency. *Public Personnel Management*, *26*(4), 461–469.

Parks, A. C., Schueller, S. M., & Tasimi, A. (2013). Increasing happiness in the general population: Empirically supported self-help? In S. David, I. Boniwell, & A. C. Ayers (Eds.), *The Oxford handbook of happiness* (pp. 962–977). Oxford: Oxford University Press.

Peltier, B. (2001). *The psychology of executive coaching*. New York: Brunner-Routledge.

Rashid, T. (2013). Positive psychology in practice: Positive psychotherapy. In S. David, I. Boniwell, & A. C. Ayers (Eds.), *The Oxford handbook of happiness* (pp. 978–993). Oxford: Oxford University Press.

Seligman, M. E. P. (2011). *Flourish: A visionary new understanding of happiness and well-being*. New York: Free Press.

Seligman, M. E. P., Steen, T. A., Park, N., & Peterson, C. (2005). Positive psychology progress: Empirical validation of interventions. *American Psychologist*, *60*(5), 410–421.

Sheldon, K. M., & Lyubomirsky, S. (2006). How to increase and sustain positive emotion: The effects of expressing gratitude and visualizing best possible selves *Journal of Positive Psychology*, *1*, 73–82.

Sin, N. L., & Lyubomirsky, S. (2009). Enhancing well-being and alleviating depressive symptoms with positive psychology interventions: A practice-friendly meta-analysis. *Journal of Clinical Psychology: In Session*, *65*, 467–487.

Spence, G. B. (2007). Historical support for the further development of evidence-based coaching: The rise and fall of the human potential movement. *Australian Psychologist*, *42*(4), 255–265.

Spence, G. B., & Grant, A. M. (2007). Professional and peer life coaching and the enhancement of goal striving and well-being: An exploratory study. *Journal of Positive Psychology*, *2*(3), 185–194.

Spence, G. B., & Grant, A. M. (2013). Coaching and well-being: A brief review of existing evidence, relevant theory and implications for practitioners. In S. David & I. Boniwell (Eds.), *Oxford handbook of happiness* (pp. 1009–1025). Oxford: Oxford University Press.

Spence, G. B., & Oades, L. G. (2011). Coaching with self-determination in mind: Using theory to advance evidence-based coaching practice. *International Journal of Evidence Based Coaching and Mentoring*, *9*(2), 37–55.

Stober, D. R., & Grant, A. M. (Eds.) (2006). *Evidence based coaching handbook*. Hoboken, NJ: John Wiley & Sons.

Whitmore, J. (1996). *Coaching for performance*. London: Nicholas Brealey.

16

Online Positive Psychological Interventions

State of the Art and Future Directions

Linda Bolier and Katherina Martin Abello

Since the founding of positive psychology in 1998, positive psychological interventions (PPIs) have advanced considerably. Many interventions have demonstrated efficacy to increase well-being and decrease depressive symptoms (Bolier, Haverman, et al., 2013; Sin & Lyubomirsky, 2009). PPIs can benefit already happy individuals looking to become happier, and also have a role in the whole spectrum of mental health interventions, from mental health promotion, to prevention and treatment (Barry, 2001).

In 2011, Martin Seligman, one of the founders of positive psychology, launched the "Flourish 51" initiative that set an ambitious goal: by the year 2051, 51% of the people of the world will be flourishing (Seligman, 2011). This challenge is addressed to health professionals, government leaders, and every person who wishes to improve well-being.

Reaching the Flourish 51 goal requires considerable work. Even if effective methods to increase well-being exist, simply reaching 51% of the world population is a major obstacle. Relatedly, the so-called "mental health gap" refers to the many individuals in need of mental health services lacking access to quality interventions (Kohn, Saxena, Levav, & Saraceno, 2004). Explanations for this gap include limited resources (e.g., money, therapists) and a lack of awareness and recognition of the seriousness of mental disorders. This health gap extends to people with subclinical symptoms, who rarely receive help for such distress; for example, subclinical depressive symptoms are highly prevalent and still lead to serious individual impairment, loss in productivity, and increased health care uptake (Cuijpers & Smit, 2008). Delivering positive psychological interventions could contribute to the Flourish 51 goal and help narrow the mental health gap.

The Wiley Blackwell Handbook of Positive Psychological Interventions, First Edition.
Edited by Acacia C. Parks and Stephen M. Schueller.

People with stress, anxiety, depression, and those simply looking to increase their well-being may be more easily reached with a well-being approach as opposed to a problem-focused approach (Parks, Schueller, & Tasimi, 2013). People may be more attracted to these kinds of interventions, as they identify more with the well-being message.

In addition, in order to close the health gap and allow people to flourish, we need to design interventions that are "non-consumable" (Muñoz, 2010). "Non-consumable" interventions are those that can be used repeatedly to benefit more people without being used up (e.g., unlike therapists' time, medication). Given the capability of repeated use, "non-consumable" interventions, such as self-help, are particularly applicable outside the boundaries of the traditional local health care systems. Many PPIs are already delivered in self-help formats (Bolier, Haverman, et al., 2013; Sin & Lyubomirsky, 2009).

New information and communication technologies (ICT) and the World Wide Web offer an excellent platform to disseminate "non-consumable" self-help well-being interventions. Worldwide internet penetration currently stands at 34%, but is much higher in North America (79%) and Europe (63%; Internet World Stats, 2012). In total, more than two billion people use the internet, with access continuing to rise in both the developed and developing countries.

The use of technology and the internet can also help to increase engagement in positive self-help interventions. Even if people read self-help books, sustained benefit requires translating the acquired knowledge into practice. Devoting the time and effort necessary for sustainable behavioral change often requires some external support. New technologies can potentially increase engagement and translation into real life by leveraging features that create intrinsic rewards and social connectivity (McGonigal, 2011). By expanding access and increasing engagement, new technologies and delivery of interventions via the internet suit the goals of positive psychology and the Flourish 51 initiative.

This chapter will address the following questions: What are online positive psychological interventions (OPPIs)? Who uses OPPIs? What are the benefits of disseminating PPIs via the internet? What OPPIs are currently available and what do we know about their effectiveness? What are the future challenges for OPPIs?

What Are Online Positive Psychological Interventions?

Definition of online interventions

In this chapter we focus on online interventions offered directly to users. Ritterband and colleagues (2003) define online interventions as: "Interventions typically focused on behavioral issues, with the goal of instituting behavior change and subsequent symptom improvement. They are usually self-paced, interactive and tailored to the user, and they make use of the multimedia format offered by the Internet" (p. 527). Given the growing dissemination of interventions in mediums beyond just the internet (e.g., mobile applications, virtual reality, sensors), other terms have been offered (e.g., behavioral intervention technologies, "BITs"; Mohr, Burns, Schueller, Clarke, & Klinkman, 2013). In this chapter, however, we use "online interventions," because this term is (still) adopted more widely.

Online interventions differ on several features (see Proudfoot et al., 2011; Ritterband et al., 2003), including:

1 **Hardware.** Online interventions are offered and accessed via personal computers, tablets (e.g. an iPad), and/or cell-phones.
2 **Professional support.** Interventions vary from self-help with no support, e-mail or telephone support, to adjunct interventions integrated for use within face-to-face interventions.
3 **Program interactivity.** High levels of interactivity help engage people. Online interventions can achieve this through self-tests and feedback, interactive exercises, SMS or e-mail reminders, chat sessions, or games and gaming elements.
4 **Multimedia channels.** The number and type vary widely across interventions (e.g., animations, videos, audio podcasts, images, and 3D virtual reality).
5 **Length and flexibility.** Online interventions span simple, one-time exercises, highly structured extended programs, and highly personalized interventions.
6 **Sharing opportunities.** Consistent with trends in Web 2.0, online interventions increasingly allow for sharing of ideas, emotions, and social support. Social media channels, such as Twitter and Facebook, are gaining in importance in online interventions and empower their participants through interaction with others.

Online positive psychological interventions

In the context of positive psychology, OPPIs expand on definitions of online interventions by including "improvement of well-being and resilience" in addition to "symptom improvement" (Mitchell, Vella-Brodrick, & Klein, 2010). The use of online interventions began during early evaluation of positive psychological interventions aimed to increase well-being in the general population (Seligman, Steen, Park, & Peterson, 2005).

Since then, a vibrant movement in positive psychology is aimed at using opportunities provided by technology and the internet to support people's flourishing. These include "positive computing," or "The study and development of information and communication technology that is consciously designed to support people's psychological flourishing in a way that honors individuals' and communities' different ideas about the good life" (Sander, 2011, p. 311), and "positive technology," or "The use of technology to improve the quality of our personal experience with the goal of increasing wellness, and generating strengths and resilience in individuals, organizations, and society" (Botella et al., 2012, p. 78).

OPPIs align with both these movements. Positive computing and positive technology look further than just adding another theme (well-being) to the range of online intervention themes (such as depression, alcohol, etc.). They aim to improve human experience and engage people to reach their targets in real life, which is clearly aligned with the goals of positive psychology.

For whom?

Many people use the internet for health-related purposes. Besides the long-standing interest in symptoms and medical diagnosis, there is a growing interest in information related to well-being and healthy lifestyle behaviors (Evers, 2006). Relatedly, a large target group for OPPIs exists, including anyone with internet access who is interested in the enhancement of well-being, health, and resilience. Although, one might expect that many of these people would be free of psychiatric symptoms, it has been found that many of the people seeking self-help to improve their well-being have subclinical to even rather severe depressive symptoms (Parks, Della Porta, Pierce, Zilca, & Lyubomirsky, 2012).

If OPPIs are effective at reducing subclinical or clinical levels of distress, they may be a helpful complement to existing mental health resources. Muñoz (2010) offers several examples of how online interventions can be used in addition to other forms of health care for individuals in need, including while on waiting lists for other interventions, as an adjunct intervention during routine care, and after treatment, in order to prevent relapse or recurrence. Furthermore, OPPIs might be used as preventive interventions, to avoid the need for later treatment (Wiederhold & Riva, 2012). Thus, OPPIs provide options across a whole spectrum of mental health interventions, from health promotion and prevention to cure and care (Barry, 2001).

Benefits of Online Positive Psychological Interventions

Self-management/empowerment

OPPIs can engage and empower participants to take charge of their own health and well-being. OPPIs stimulate self-management skills by providing participants with tools to guide their behavior, thoughts, and interactions (see also section on "Persuasion" below). Participants can even get support and/or information from other participants, who provide expertise based on their own experiences. The Health 2.0 movement emphasizes "patient empowerment" by promoting a collaborative approach between patients, caregivers, and professionals. In this approach, the participant is an active and responsible partner in his/her own health and care pathway (Swan, 2009; Van de Belt, Engelen, Berben, & Schoonhoven,

2010). Social media, such as Facebook and Twitter, can be a valuable tool in promoting collaboration and support.

Population strategy by high scalability

Automated self-help interventions are, at least in terms of their potential, highly scalable as the World Wide Web has significant population penetration. A "population strategy" views health and well-being as an issue for populations as well as for individuals (Rose, 1992). It proposes that greater benefits to overall public health can be expected with small boosts in mean levels of health within the population. For positive psychology, a small increase in population well-being may have a larger promoting and preventive effect than treating the small group of people already suffering from mental illness (Huppert, 2009). In this way, interventions with small effect sizes but that reach large groups can still have a major impact on a population's well-being, especially when costs are low. OPPIs meet these criteria as they are low-cost, empowering, and easily accessible.

Effectiveness of Online Positive Psychological Interventions

Examples of online positive psychological interventions

In the boxes below, we present a non-exhaustive selection of OPPIs. These interventions provide examples of existing programs that are appealing and engaging, although some lack empirical support (i.e., randomized controlled trials).

Online positive psychological interventions, a review of randomized controlled studies

Several meta-analyses demonstrate the efficacy of online interventions for a wide range of problems, including depression and anxiety (Spek et al., 2007) and problematic alcohol use (Riper et al., 2009). In positive psychology, however, results have been less conclusive. A review of online positive psychological interventions identified five studies, with three demonstrating improved well-being and three yielding significant decreases in depressive symptoms (Mitchell et al., 2010).

As research on online interventions is accumulating rapidly, we present an updated review to provide a more current overview of the evidence. We used Mitchell et al.'s (2010) study as a starting point and included additional studies retrieved using the following search terms in PsycINFO and PubMed: well-being, happiness, positive psychology, e-health, internet, intervention, effectiveness, and efficacy. We consulted international colleagues for additional studies that may have been missed. The main inclusion criterion was an examination of the effects of an OPPI using a randomized research design. We used the term "online" broadly and included interventions that used recruitment procedures and plain instructions via the internet or e-mail (even if they contained no interactive features, which is a hallmark of online interventions).

Case 1 ResilienceOnline training (USA, PowerThinking Corp)

In 2012, PowerThinking Corp developed ResilienceOnline training, based on Martin Seligman's (1990) work on learned optimism and other research conducted at the University of Pennsylvania. The goal of the program is to help the participant to overcome obstacles and adversity and to support them to achieve their potential. The program includes interactive features including streaming videos with synchronized slides and dynamic content, a self-monitoring test, and an action plan. These materials cover seven resilience skills based on cognitive-behavioral principles, such as the ABC model, thinking traps, and challenging beliefs. It also provides skills to manage stress and to cultivate personal strengths.

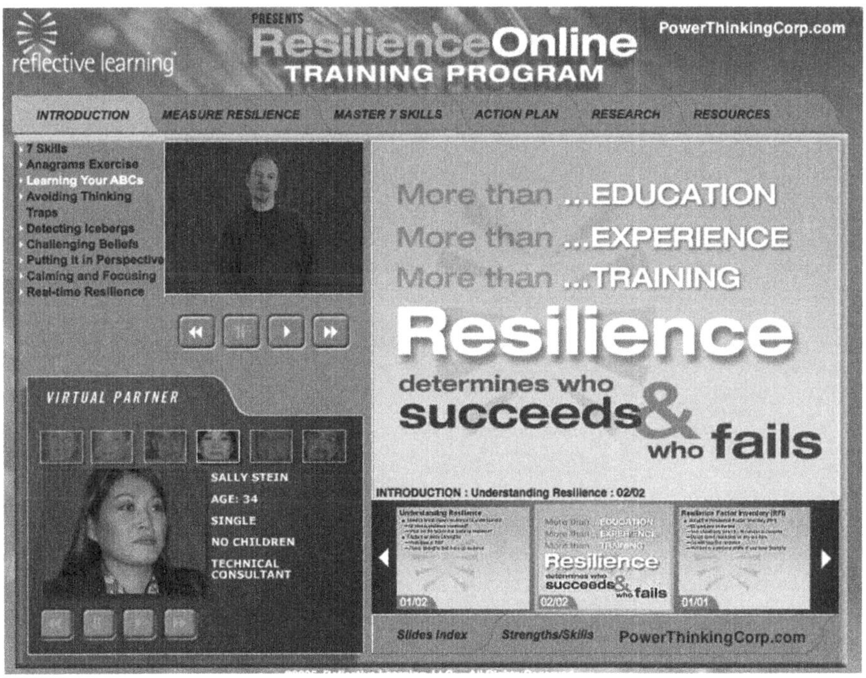

Figure 16.1 ResilienceOnline training

Case 2 Psyfit.nl (The Netherlands, Trimbos Institute)

Psyfit (www.psyfit.nl) is an online unguided self-help intervention that aims to enhance well-being and reduce depressive symptoms. Designed for the general population, it can also be used within a stepped care approach

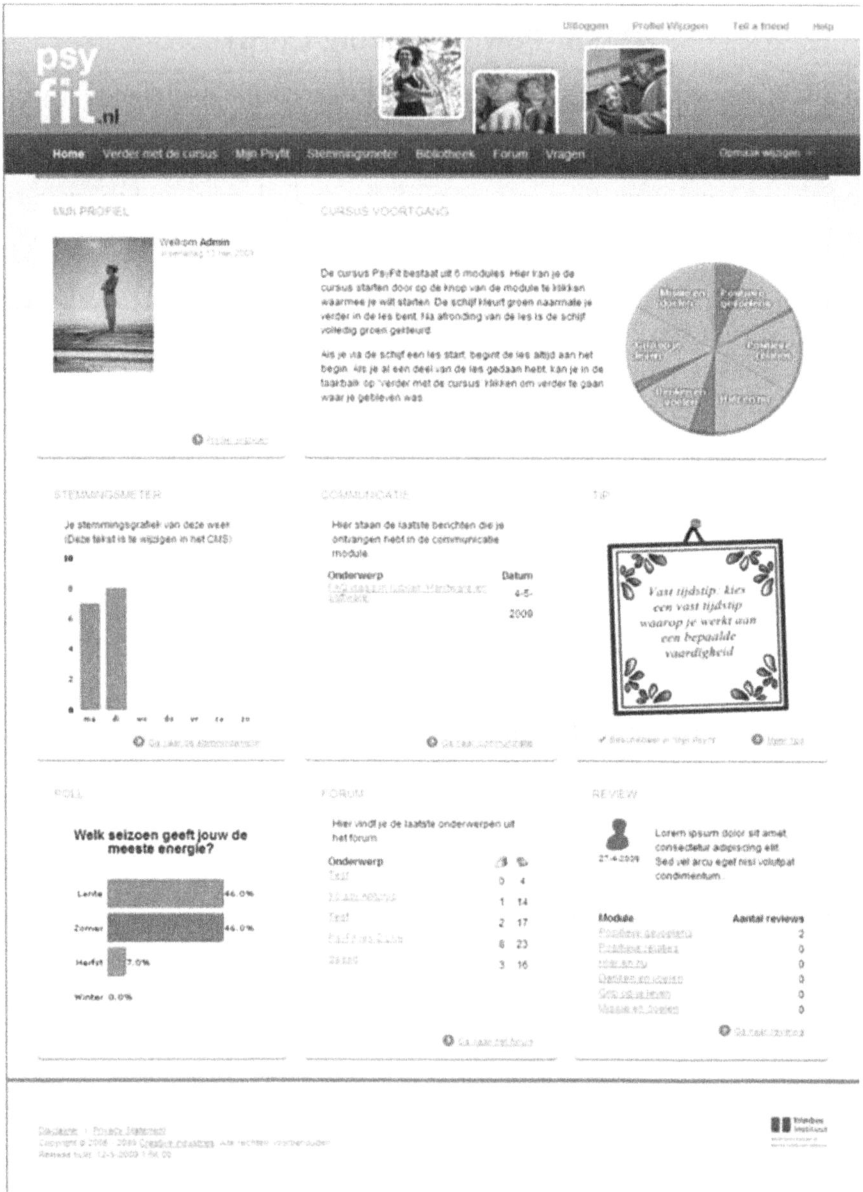

Figure 16.2 Psyfit.nl – mental fitness online

(i.e., offering minimal care first and more intensive care if warranted) for the prevention and treatment of depression. Participants tailor the intervention program to meet their personal needs and monitor their progress through self-administered tests. The program consists of six modules with four lessons each. The modules are (i) mission and goals, (ii) positive feelings, (iii) positive relationships, (iv) living in the moment, (v) optimistic thinking, and (vi) mastering your life (Bolier, Kramer, et al., 2013). This program is also discussed in the literature review of randomized controlled trials.

Case 3 The Happiness Coach (Belgium, ISW Limits & Christelijke Mutualiteit)

Based on Psyfit, the Happiness Coach was developed in Belgium (gelukscoach.plukjegeluk.be) as a comprehensive intervention and part of a broader "Seize your happiness" campaign. The program uses the metaphor of people traveling along a subway and provides a railway map to guide people to their preferred happiness strategies. It includes information, advice, and interactive exercises aimed to change behavior. In one year more than 10,000 people registered for this program (Vansteenwegen, 2011).

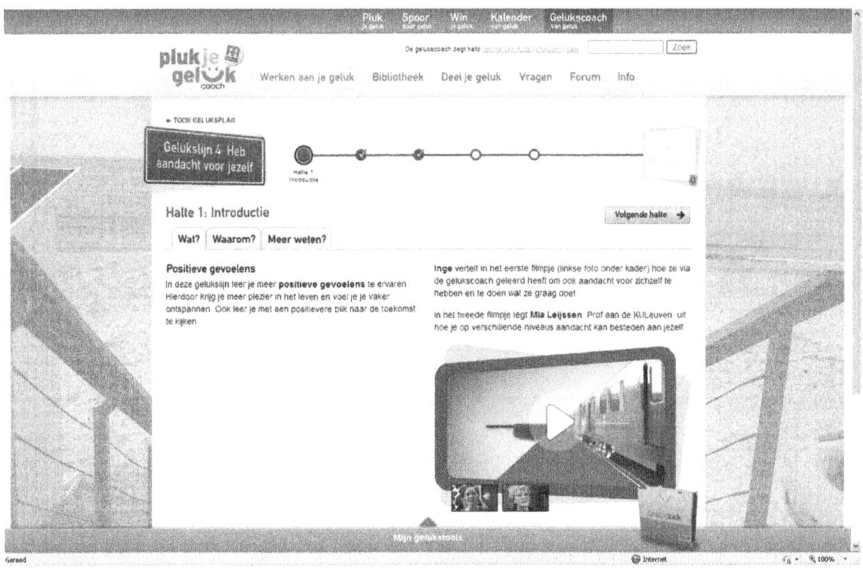

Figure 16.3 The Happiness Coach

Case 4 Live Happy iPhone app (USA, Signal Patterns)

In 2008, Signal Patterns launched the Live Happy iPhone app as the first mobile application in positive psychology based on empirically based principles. The content drew on the comprehensive work of Sonja Lyubomirsky and contained key elements from her book, *The how of happiness* (Lyubomirsky, 2008), and well-known positive psychological exercises, such as savoring the day, doing kind things, and a gratitude journal. In an Experience Sampling Methodology study, mood and happiness improved significantly following use of one or more of the exercises (Parks et al., 2012), demonstrating the effectiveness of these interventions in naturalistic settings.

Figure 16.4 Live Happy iPhone app

In total, 11 studies were found, 10 of which measured well-being, and one of which measured only depressive symptoms (see Table 16.1). Seven of the 10 studies measuring well-being found significant increases (Bolier, Kramer, et al., 2013; Gander, Proyer, Ruch, & Wyss, 2012; Layous, Nelson, & Lyubomirsky, 2013; Luthans, Avey, & Patera, 2008; Mitchell, Stanimirovic, Klein, & Vella-Brodrick,

Table 16.1 Characteristics of studies on the effectiveness of online positive psychological interventions (translated and adapted from Bolier, 2013)

Study	*Intervention*	*Session (number), duration*	*Population*	*Outcome measures*	*Control group*	*N analyzed*	*Attrition rate*	*ITT (Y)/CO*	*Time points*	*Results*	*Cohen's d (pooled)*
Abbott et al., 2009	ResilienceOnline, program to enhance resilience	7, 10w	Working adults	PWB: AHI DEP: DASS-21, WHOQOL-BREF	Waiting list	Ne = 26 Nc = 27	41.5%	Y	Pre, Post	No significant differences between groups on well-being, depression, anxiety, stress, or quality of life	−0.06 (PWB) 0.11 (DEP)
Bolier, 2013 (submitted)	Psyfit, online well-being self-help program to improve mental fitness	4, 4w	Adult population (moderately depressed)	PWB: MHC-SF DEP: CES-D	Waiting list	Ne = 143 Nc = 141	24.6% at post 37.3% at 6 months	Y	Pre, Post, 6m	Significant improvement in PWB and reduction in depressive symptoms at post-test, for depression still significant at follow-up	0.27 (PWB) 0.36 (DEP) (Post) 0.01 (PWB) 0.35 (DEP) (6m)
Gander et al., 2012	9 exercises: Gratitude Visit, 3 Good Things (1 and 2 weeks), strengths, 3 funny things, social exercises	7, 1w 14, 2w	Adult sample	PWB: AHI DEP: CES-D	Placebo (early memo-ries)	Ne = 559 Nc = 63	74%	N	Pre, Post, 1m, 3m, 6m	Significant improvement in PWB for all exercises (except 3 Good Things over 2 weeks) at at least one time period. Significant reduction of depression in 5 out of 9 exercises (not in the 3 Good Things). Largest effects for signature strengths and 3 funny things	0.10 (PWB) −0.05 (DEP) (Post) 0.27 (PWB) −0.07 (DEP) (6m)

(*continued*)

Table 16.1 (*Continued*)

Study	*Intervention*	*Session (number), duration*	*Population*	*Outcome measures*	*Control group*	*N analyzed*	*Attrition rate*	*ITT (Y)/CO*	*Time points*	*Results*	*Cohen's d (pooled)*
Goldstein, 2007	E-mail program Cultivating sacred moments	15, 3w	Adult sample	SWB: SWLS PWB: RPWB	Treatment as usual (therapeutic writing)	Ne = 35 Nc = 38	12%	N	Post, 6w	No differences between groups Both conditions showed significant positive effects for SWB and three out of six areas in PWB. Effects were partly sustained at follow-up	0.06 (SWB) −0.02 (PWB) (Post)
Layous et al., 2013	Best Possible Selves exercise	4, 4w	Students	SWB: PA PWB: NS	Placebo (neutral writing)	Ne = 31 Nc = 38	Unknown	N	Pre, Post	Significant improvement in SWB, non-significant improvement in PWB Online format just as effective as in-person format	0.56 (SWB) 0.24 (PWB)
Luthans et al., 2008	Online well-being program (PsyCap)	2, 2w	Working adults	PWB: PCQ	Placebo (decision-making exercise)	Ne = 187 Nc = 177	5.5%	N	Pre, Post	PWB (PsyCap) significantly increased	0.23 (PWB)

Mitchell et al., 2009	Use your strengths in a new way Online	3, 3w	Adult community sample	SWB: PWI-A, SWLS, PA PWB: OTH DEP: DASS-21	Placebo (information only) Treatment as usual (problem-solving)	Ne = 48 Nc = 54	69.9% at post 83.1% at 3 months	Y	Pre, Post, 3m	Significant increase in cognitive component of SWB (as measured with the PWI-A, not with the SWLS), and not for the affective component No significant decrease in mental symptoms	0.07 (SWB, PWI-A: 0.20) 0.01 (PWB – pleasure scale: 0.13) 0.06 (DEP) (Post)
Parks-Sheiner, 2009 (unpublished)	Online Positive Psychotherapy	42, 6w	Mild to moderately depressed adults	SWB: SWLS, PANAS DEP: CES-D	Waiting list	Ne = 125 Nc = 142 (3m)	47.6% at post	Y	Pre, Post, 1m, 3m	Significant decrease at 3-month follow-up in depressive symptoms in PPT group, but no significant improvement in the PPT group for well-being (significant deterioration of well-being in the control group)	0.21 (DEP) 0.07 (SWB: SWLS) −0.50 (SWB: PA) (3m)

(*continued*)

Table 16.1 (*Continued*)

Study	*Intervention*	*Session (number), duration*	*Population*	*Outcome measures*	*Control group*	*N analyzed*	*Attrition rate*	*ITT (Y)/CO*	*Time points*	*Results*	*Cohen's d (pooled)*
Schueller & Parks, 2012	Group PPT: package of 2, 4, or 6 positive psychology exercises (Active/ Constructive Responding, Gratitude Visit, Life Summary, 3 Good Things, savoring, strengths)	14, 2w 28, 4w 42, 6w	Mild to moderately depressed adults	DEP: CES-D	No inter-vention	Ne = 457 Nc = 204	55.4%	N	Pre, every week during 6 weeks	Significantly fewer depressive symptoms in both the 2-exercise condition and the 4-exercise condition in comparison to the 6-exercise condition. No significant difference (only numerically) with the control group	0.14 (DEP, 2 exercises) 0.16 (DEP, 4 exercises) 0.02 (DEP, 6 exercises)
Seligman et al., 2005	Strengths exercises (2), gratitude (1), positive thinking (2), send by e-mail	7, 1w	Adult sample (moderately depressed)	PWB: SHI DEP: CES-D	Placebo (earliest memo-ries)	Ne = 341 Nc = 70	28.8%	N	Pre, Post, 1m, 3m, 6m	PWB and DEP: at 6-month follow-up significant effects for 3 Good Things and using signature strengths. At 1-month post-test significant effect for Gratitude Visit	0.01 (PWB) 0.17 (DEP) (Post) 0.06 (PWB) 0.14 (DEP) (6m)

Shapira & Mongrain, 2010; Mongrain, Chin, & Shapira, 2011; Sergeant & Mongrain, 2011; Mongrain & Anselmo-Matthews, 2012	3 Good Things, signature strengths, self-compassion, optimism, compassionate action, gratitude intervention	7, 1w	Adult community sample (moderately depressed)	PWB: SHI DEP: CES-D	Placebo (earliest memo-ries)	Ne = 118 Nc = 70	25% at post 75% at 6m	N	Pre, Post, 1m, 3m, 6m	Significant increases in well-being and decreases in depression up to 3–6 months. On the whole, the effects on well-being are smaller than for depression	0.11 (PWB) 0.25 (DEP) (Post) 0.14 (PWB) 0.36 (DEP) (3m)

Abbreviations: AHI = Authentic Happiness Inventory, a revised version of the SHI; CES-D = Centre for Epidemiological Studies – Depression scale; CO = Completers Only analysis; DASS-21 = Depression Anxiety Stress Scale; DEP = Depression; ITT = Intention-To-Treat analysis; m = month; MHC-SF = Mental Health Continuum – Short Form; NS = Need Satisfaction; OTH = Orientations to Happiness; PA = Positive Affect; PANAS = Positive And Negative Affect Scale; PCQ = PsyCap Questionnaire; PWB = Psychological Well-Being; PWI-A = Personal Well-being Index; RPWB = Ryff Psychological Well Being scales; SHI = Steen Happiness Index; SWB = Subjective Well-Being; SWLS = Satisfaction with Life Scale; WHOQOL-BREF = World Health Organization Quality of Life – Brief Version; w = week.

2009; Seligman et al., 2005; Shapira & Mongrain, 2010). Furthermore, of the eight studies measuring depression, five found significant decreases in symptoms (Bolier, Kramer, et al., 2013; Gander et al., 2012; Parks-Sheiner, 2009; Seligman et al., 2005; Shapira & Mongrain, 2010). For significant findings, effect sizes were mostly small. However, given that these interventions were often self-help in nature, this is in line with the results of a previous meta-analytic review of PPIs which found that self-help interventions were typically associated with small effect sizes as opposed to the medium to large effects produced by more intensive face-to-face interventions (Bolier, Haverman, et al., 2013; Sin & Lyubomirsky, 2009).

Three studies found no significant effects on well-being (Abbott, Klein, Hamilton, & Rosenthal, 2009; Goldstein, 2007; Parks-Sheiner, 2009). It is difficult to explain the findings by Abbott et al. (2009) and Parks-Sheiner (2009). Adherence and motivational factors may have played a role in the results achieved by the online programs, which were both fairly demanding. The non-significant result in the study of Goldstein (2007) is more easily explained, as the comparison condition was care-as-usual and both conditions resulted in improvements. Based on this result, OPPIs could be considered as an acceptable alternative intervention, especially when available resources might only be able to provide online interventions rather than other care. Three studies indicated no significant improvement on depression levels compared to the control group (Abbott et al., 2009; Mitchell et al., 2009; Schueller & Parks, 2012). In the studies of Mitchell et al. (2009) and Abbott et al. (2009), lack of significant findings might be due to low levels of depressive symptoms at baseline, providing little room for improvement.

More than half of the interventions in the studies were single-component interventions (Gander et al., 2012; Goldstein, 2007; Layous et al., 2013; Mitchell et al., 2009; Seligman et al., 2005; Shapira & Mongrain, 2010). The others were comprehensive multi-component interventions (Abbott et al., 2009; Bolier, Kramer, et al., 2013; Luthans et al., 2008; Parks-Sheiner, 2009; Schueller & Parks, 2012). Based on the available data, no clear conclusion can be drawn as to which type of intervention is more effective, as both produced some studies with significant results and others with non-significant differences. Results from Schueller and Parks (2012) suggest that more exercises and content might not lead to increased benefits, as the two-exercise and four-exercise conditions were more effective compared to the six-exercise condition. More experimental studies that vary intensity, variety, and duration could provide more evidence to guide the question of single exercises versus extended programs.

Seligman et al. (2005) found the strongest effects for the "Three Good Things" and "Using Your Strengths in a New Way" exercises (sustained effects on well-being and depression after six months). Notably, however, these effects were only partly replicated in the later study of Gander et al. (2012) in which effects were marginal, and a study by Mongrain and Anselmo-Matthews (2012) which found only effects on well-being but not depression for these interventions.

It is important to underscore the limitations of these evaluations. Many trials had high drop-out rates, a common problem in online trials (Eysenbach, 2005). Although 4 of the 11 studies conducted an intention-to-treat analysis (Abbott et al., 2009; Bolier, Kramer, et al., 2013; Mitchell et al., 2009; Parks-Sheiner, 2009), which attempts to address drop-out and reduce bias by including every participant in the analysis, the other studies conducted only a completers-only analysis, which includes those who complete all questionnaires. A completers-only analysis biases the results and limits the generalizability when factors (e.g., motivation, personality, disorder) correspond to differential drop-out.

In conclusion, some empirical data support the hypothesis that online positive psychological interventions can effectively enhance well-being and reduce depressive symptoms, in the short and long term. However, effects for online programs appear to be smaller than for offline programs, indicating an "effectiveness gap" (Mitchell et al., 2010). Only one study directly compared an online and offline intervention, showing no differences between them (Layous et al., 2013). Despite this preliminary evidence, more research is needed to extend the current body of evidence. Future studies should also address more nuanced questions including examining mediation and moderation to determine what works and for whom.

The Future of Online Positive Psychological Interventions

Research to date shows that internet dissemination of positive psychological interventions holds promise for mental health and well-being. However, actual large-scale delivery and uptake of OPPIs lags this potential. Addressing several questions, however, could help realize this potential, such as: What is necessary to make OPPIs work in the real world? Can alternative research designs (e.g., besides randomized clinical trials) inform development and implementation? What innovations have to be made to keep up with new technologies? In this part of the chapter we explore some of the ways in which OPPIs could address these issues in the future.

Persuasion

Improving well-being is a dynamic and active process. People have to take action and change their behavior, cognitions, and attitudes to reach this goal. Lyubomirsky, Dickerhoof, Boehm, & Sheldon (2011) conclude that increasing well-being requires effective positive psychology exercises, motivation, and continuous effort devoted to the interventions, and an individual "fit" with the personality, motives, strengths, and needs of the person completing the intervention (see also Chapter 22). Persuasive elements in OPPIs can promote adherence and improve effectiveness by helping people stay involved. Technical design elements within an online intervention can arouse and prolong motivation for sustained behavioral change even in the absence of professional support (Fogg, 2003). A systematic review suggested that persuasive elements in interventions explain a substantial amount of the variance in adherence and intervention effectiveness (Kelders, Kok, Ossebaard, & Van Gemert-Pijnen, 2012). Therefore, it is recommended that OPPI designs learn from the literature on persuasive design, especially because the examination of persuasive elements in OPPIs is still scarce. Following the Persuasive Systems Design model (Oinas-Kukkonen & Harjumaa, 2009), designers are advised to consider, for example:

- **Tailoring content** and instructions to the participants' needs, interests, strengths profiles, or personality. Some empirical evidence shows that tailoring positive psychology exercises can indeed effectively enhance intervention engagement and adherence (Schueller, 2010, 2011).
- **Prompts and reminders:** messages or brief feedback via e-mail, SMS, or social media. Prompts can be automated but can also be tailored to the specific needs of a participant. This can lead to a greater exposure and therefore a more effective intervention (Crutzen et al., 2011; Fry & Neff, 2009).
- **Goal setting and action planning.** The opportunity to set goals and to make an action plan through a website has a significant effect on desired behavior and may lead to prolonged exposure to the intervention (Webb, Joseph, Yardley, & Michie, 2010).
- **Serious gaming and storytelling.** Video games can attract and maintain attention and offer an opportunity for positive psychology to make exercises challenging and fun (Baranowski, Buday, Thompson, & Baranowski, 2008). They link very closely to the aims of positive psychology because (many) people inherently enjoy the activity of playing, and the gaming experience can be applied to change real-life behavior (McGonigal, 2011).
- **Self-monitoring.** Self-screening and monitoring of personal well-being status can actively support the achievement of goals. Online questionnaires can support this, but a more convenient option is to monitor using mobile apps that might even be able to collect data passively.
- **Social support and sharing.** Social influence is a powerful persuasive strategy to motivate people. Online interventions can facilitate learning by demonstrating the behavior of others (social learning), and can shape behavior by providing comparisons with one's past performance or the performance of others (social comparison). Online-based social platforms (e.g., peer groups) can facilitate sharing of experiences and supporting change (Swan, 2009). Social networks, such as Facebook and Twitter, can also be used in online interventions to bring people together and disseminate ideas and interventions (McGonigal, 2011; Swan, 2009). Positive psychology exercises (e.g., "Three Good Things") have already been set up as a Facebook application (Munson, Lauterbach, Newman, & Resnick, 2010).

Quality standards for interventions

Although qualified positive psychology professionals, researchers, organizations, and institutions develop online interventions, commercial developers also create these sites. Multiple contributors advance the development of OPPIs and may promote interdisciplinary collaboration between positive psychology professionals, technologists, and commercial developers to create novel applications of positive psychological theory. However, to protect consumers, the merits of these interventions need to be addressed. A quality seal for OPPIs could help consumers choose from the many interventions that populate the web. Although international quality standards for online interventions have not yet been developed, a certifying instrument and quality seal have been developed in the Netherlands for this purpose (Fischer, Nabitz, & Riper, 2010). A collaborative project between the Trimbos Institute and the health care agencies for the Ministry of Health provides potential participants with a comprehensive review of the quality of online interventions. Each intervention undergoes a systematic quality evaluation. Furthermore, participants can review the interventions themselves by completing an online rating questionnaire. Interventions that promote well-being or resilience will be part of this evaluation process. The Beacon website is a similar initiative that provides a database of internet and mobile interventions, along with a summary of the research evidence, intended for a lay audience (Christensen et al., 2010).

A quality system for OPPIs should at least cover four main criteria:

- **User friendliness:** This criterion includes items such as usability, contact possibilities and quality of service, and the professionalism of the design (look and feel).
- **Effectiveness (evidence-based):** This aspect emphasizes the importance of the research basis for the program and evidence of its benefits.
- **Transparency:** The developer of an online intervention should provide full access to information about the organization behind the intervention, the developers, the costs involved, possible contraindications, objectives of the program, amount of time a participant is expected to use the intervention in order to get positive results, and privacy issues.
- **Technical aspects and security:** The organization responsible for the intervention should guarantee the availability of the program (uptime), scalability and security in terms of data protection, software updates, installation of security patches, and back-up.

Quality standards for research designs

The real-world impact of online interventions is sometimes questioned because of the disparity between the positive effects found in RCTs, and the outcomes produced when disseminated in naturalistic settings or to widespread audiences. Although RCTs are needed to establish efficacy of online positive psychological interventions, other forms of research are necessary to ensure a good fit between the technology, the participants, and the dissemination context. Traditional RCTs alone are insufficient to keep up with the rapid pace at which technology develops and thus OPPIs evolve. Van Gemert-Pijnen et al. (2011) propose a holistic framework for the design, evaluation, and implementation of online interventions that is useful for researchers, developers, and marketers of OPPIs. The framework recommends a mixed-method approach, combining both qualitative and quantitative methods. In the early stages of development, formative evaluation aims to improve the product through a cyclic, iterative design process. This process should involve the relevant stakeholders (end-users, professionals who are going to work with the product, health care providers, etc.). Important elements during this development stage include testing prototypes, assessing usability, and conducting a requirements analysis to facilitate subsequent upscaling. Process evaluations, including small-scale pilot testing of initial prototypes, can identify considerations or problems for future implementation and dissemination. Summative evaluation is necessary after developing the intervention. This includes addressing the benefits to well-being, and actual use of the intervention, and may involve conducting an RCT.

Evaluating online intervention trials involves specific challenges and issues (Proudfoot et al., 2011). For example, as previously mentioned, poor adherence and high drop-outs are typical of online trials (Eysenbach, 2005), and also in positive psychology (e.g. Bolier, Kramer, et al., 2013; Mongrain & Anselmo-Matthews, 2012). In RCTs it is justly recommended to conduct an analysis of everyone included in the trial, regardless of drop-out status (intention-to-treat analysis). As a sensitivity analysis, we recommend conducting completers-only analyses as well, to better understand the characteristics of the subpopulation that did not drop out and the effects of the intervention for this group. Another critical issue is to evaluate not just well-being outcomes, but adherence, or the actual use of the intervention as well. This can be assessed via analyzing web statistics: log files, login times, and unique webpage viewing, if technological features are created to capture this data. Use data may link to outcomes or provide additional information useful for subsequent development and refinement of OPPIs. Perceived usefulness of the program assessed using participant satisfaction rates should also contribute to the evaluation process (Danaher & Seeley, 2009).

Creating a business model

In order to facilitate the upscaling of OPPIs to the mass market it is crucial that they are developed on the basis of a sustainable business model. This model should define how the intervention will generate revenue for the continued maintenance, hosting, and updating, along with an implementation strategy. Implementation must ensure that the OPPI will achieve its full potential under real-world conditions and circumstances (Van Limburg et al., 2011). For most OPPIs, it is unlikely that they will be covered through insurance as they are wellness-based and not illness-based. To make them accessible to the general public, the developer should carefully consider the balance between the needed revenue stream and affordability for the user.

Another possibility for OPPIs to generate revenue would be to provide "the software of the program as a service" (SAAS) to stakeholders such as health care institutions, hospitals, schools, and companies. They could integrate the information, tools, and modules into their websites to add value to their products and services by providing OPPIs to clients and/or workers. Costs could be paid for with the funds generated from the licenses.

Co-creation also has the potential to contribute to the development of a sustainable model for OPPIs, by leveraging resources from different stakeholders to keep the cost low for each individual. For example, cooperation may be possible with a hosting provider, an ICT company, or with a university in exchange for research data.

Conclusion

The available literature shows that the field of online interventions provides positive psychology researchers and practitioners with many opportunities to develop enjoyable, engaging, and scalable interventions. Preliminary evidence suggests that some OPPIs can effectively enhance well-being and reduce depressive symptoms. However, the mixed findings within the small number of studies suggest that much remains to be learned about which OPPIs are effective and what are their effective ingredients. Researchers and practitioners interested in OPPIs should learn from related fields and integrate principles of persuasive technology design to enhance the use and efficacy of these interventions. OPPIs need to take full advantage of the technological medium to be highly interactive, personalized, and supportive of the intrinsic motivation of participants. In addition, researchers and developers should consider how the development and evaluation differ for online interventions in comparison to their offline counterparts.

Not only do new technologies offer a convenient way of delivering established interventions, they can also have a profound impact on how we shape our lives and how we relate to one another. Sander (2011) describes the process of "democratization" of positive psychology through the use of new technologies: knowledge becomes available to a greater number of people, and they can use it in accordance with their own values to make their lives happier and more meaningful. The general public can use OPPIs without professional guidance to enhance their well-being and lead more fulfilling lives. Policy-makers, companies, psychologists, and practitioners can provide these resources as stand-alone interventions, as first-line treatments in stepped care programs, or as supplements to face-to-face, traditional interventions. The challenge we are faced with is to develop interventions that are based on research of the highest possible quality, the most up-to-date knowledge, and novel uses of emerging technology, to make a true contribution to human flourishing.

References

Abbott, J. A., Klein, B., Hamilton, C., & Rosenthal, A. (2009). The impact of online resilience training for sales managers on wellbeing and performance. *E-Journal of Applied Psychology, 5*, 89–95.

Baranowski, T., Buday, R., Thompson, D. I., & Baranowski, J. (2008). Playing for real: Video games and stories for health-related behavior change. *American Journal of Preventive Medicine, 34*, 74–82.

Barry, M. M. (2001). Promoting mental health: Theoretical frameworks for practice. *International Journal of Mental Health Promotion, 3*, 25–34.

Bolier, L. (2013). Positieve psychologie online. In E. Bohlmeijer, L. Bolier, G. Westerhof, & J. A. Walburg (Eds.), *Handboek positieve psychologie* (pp. 360–361). Amsterdam: Boom Publishing

Bolier, L., Haverman, M., Westerhof, G. J., Riper, H., Smit, F., & Bohlmeijer, E. (2013). Positive psychology interventions: A meta-analysis of randomized controlled studies. *BMC Public Health, 13*, 119.

Bolier, L., Kramer, J., Westerhof, G. J., Haverman, M., Riper, H., Walburg, J. A., et al. (2013). Psyfit, internet-based intervention to promote mental fitness for mildly depressed adults: Results of a randomized controlled trial. Manuscript submitted for publication.

Botella, C., Riva, G., Gaggioli, A., Wiederhold, B. K., Alcaniz, M., & Baños, R. M (2012). The present and future of positive technologies. *Cyberpsychology, Behavior, and Social Networking, 15*, 78–84.

Christensen, H., Murray, K., Calear, A. L., Bennett, K., Bennett, A., & Griffiths, K. M. (2010). Beacon: A web portal to high-quality mental health websites for use by health professionals and the public. *Medical Journal of Australia, 7*, S40–S44.

Crutzen, R., de Nooijer, J., Brouwer, W., Oenema, A., Brug, J., & de Vries, N. K. (2011). Strategies to facilitate exposure to internet-delivered health behavior change interventions aimed at adolescents or young adults: A systematic review. *Health Education & Behavior, 38*, 49–62.

Cuijpers, P., & Smit, F. (2008). Subklinische depressie: Een klinisch relevante conditie? (Subclinical depression: A clinically relevant condition?). *Tijdschrift voor Psychiatrie, 50*, 519–528.

Danaher, B. G., & Seeley, J. R. (2009). Methodological issues in research on web-based behavioral interventions. *Annals of Behavioral Medicine, 38*, 28–39.

Evers, K. E. (2006). eHealth promotion: the use of the internet for health promotion. *American Journal of Health Promotion, 20*, 1–7.

Eysenbach, G. (2005). The law of attrition. *Journal of Medical Internet Research, 7*, e11.

Fischer, E., Nabitz, U., & Riper, H. (2010). *Kwaliteitsbeoordeling e-mental health* (Quality assurance e-mental health). Utrecht: Trimbos-instituut.

Fogg, B. J. (2003). *Persuasive technology: Using computers for what we think and do.* San Francisco: Morgan Kaufman Publishers.

Fry, J. P., & Neff, R. A. (2009). Periodic prompts and reminders in health promotion and health behavior interventions: Systematic review. *Journal of Medical Internet Research, 11*, 1–15.

Gander, F., Proyer, R. T., Ruch, W., & Wyss, T. (2012). Strength-based positive interventions: Further evidence for their potential in enhancing well-being and alleviating depression. *Journal of Happiness Studies, 14*, 1241–1259.

Goldstein, E. D. (2007). Sacred moments: Implications on well-being and stress. *Journal of Clinical Psychology*, *63*, 1001–1019.

Huppert, F. A. (2009). A new approach to reducing disorder and improving well-being. *Perspectives on Psychological Science*, *4*, 108–111.

Internet World Stats (2012). http://www.internetworldstats.com/stats.htm. Bogota: Miniwatts Marketing Group.

Kelders, S. M., Kok, R. N., Ossebaard, H. C., & Van Gemert-Pijnen, J. E. W. C. (2012). Persuasive system design does matter: A systematic review of adherence to web-based interventions. *Journal of Medical Internet Research*, *14*, e152.

Kohn, R., Saxena, S., Levav, I., & Saraceno, B. (2004). The treatment gap in mental health care. *Bulletin of the World Health Organization*, *82*, 858–866.

Layous, K., Nelson, K. S., & Lyubomirsky, S. (2013). What is the optimal way to deliver a positive activity intervention? The case of writing about one's best possible selves. *Journal of Happiness Studies*, *14*, 635–654.

Luthans, F., Avey, J. B., & Patera, J. L. (2008). Experimental analysis of a web-based training intervention to develop positive psychological capital. *Academy of Management Learning and Education*, *7*, 209–221.

Lyubomirsky, S. (2008). *The how of happiness: A practical approach to getting the life you want.* London: Sphere.

Lyubomirsky, S., Dickerhoof, R., Boehm, J. K., & Sheldon, K. M. (2011). Becoming happier takes both a will and a proper way: An experimental longitudinal intervention to boost well-being. *Emotion*, *11*, 391–402.

McGonigal (2011). *Reality is broken: Why games make us better and how they can change the world.* New York: Penguin Books.

Mitchell, J., Stanimirovic, R., Klein, B., & Vella-Brodrick, D. (2009). A randomised controlled trial of a self-guided internet intervention promoting well-being. *Computers in Human Behavior*, *25*, 749–760.

Mitchell, J., Vella-Brodrick, D., & Klein, B. (2010). Positive psychology and the internet: A mental health opportunity. *Electronic Journal of Applied Psychology*, *6*, 30–41.

Mohr, D. C., Burns, M. N., Schueller, S. M., Clarke, G., & Klinkman, M. (2013). Behavioral intervention technologies: Evidence review and recommendations for future research. *General Hospital Psychiatry*, *35*, 332–338.

Mongrain, M., & Anselmo-Matthews, T. (2012). Do positive psychology exercises work? A replication of Seligman et al. (2005). *Journal of Clinical Psychology*, *68*, 382–389.

Mongrain, M., Chin, J., & Shapira, L. (2011). Practicing compassion increases happiness and self-esteem. *Journal of Happiness Studies*, *12*, 963–981.

Muñoz, R. F. (2010). Using evidence-based internet interventions to reduce health disparities worldwide. *Journal of Medical Internet Research*, *12*, e60.

Munson, S., Lauterbach, D., Newman, M., & Resnick, P. (2010). Happier together: Integrating a wellness application into a social network site. In T. Ploug, P. F. V. Hasle, & H. Oinas-Kukkonen (Eds.), *Lecture notes in computer science* (Vol. 6137, pp. 27–39). Berlin Heidelberg: Springer-Verlag.

Oinas-Kukkonen, H., & Harjumaa, M. (2009). Persuasive systems design: Key issues, process model, and system features. *Communications of the Association for Information Systems*, *24*(28), 485–500.

Parks, A. C., Della Porta, M. D., Pierce, R. S., Zilca, R., & Lyubomirsky, S. (2012). Pursuing happiness in everyday life: The characteristics and behaviors of online happiness seekers. *Emotion*, *12*, 1222–1234.

Parks, A. C., Schueller, S. M., & Tasimi, A. (2013). Increasing happiness in the general population: Empirically supported self-help? In S. David, I. Boniwell, & A. C. Ayers (Eds.), *Oxford handbook of happiness* (pp. 962–977). Oxford: Oxford University Press.

Parks-Sheiner, A. C. (2009). *Positive psychotherapy: Building a model of empirically supported self-help.* Doctoral dissertation. ProQuest Information & Learning. Paper AAI3363580. http://repository.upenn.edu/dissertations/AAI3363580

Proudfoot, J., Klein, B., Barak, A., Carlbring, P., Cuijpers, P., Lange, A., Ritterband, L., & Andersson, G. (2011). Establishing guidelines for executing and reporting internet intervention research. *Cognitive Behaviour Therapy, 40*, 82–97.

Riper, H., van Straten, A., Keuken, M., Smit, F., Schippers, G., & Cuijpers, P. (2009). Curbing problem drinking with personalized-feedback interventions: A meta-analysis. *American Journal of Preventive Medicine, 36*, 247–255.

Ritterband, L. M., Gonder-Frederick, L. A., Cox, D. J., Clifton, A. D., West, R. W., & Borowitz, S. M. (2003). Internet interventions: In review, in use, and into the future. *Professional Psychology: Research and Practice, 34*, 527–534.

Rose, G. (1992). *The strategy of preventive medicine.* Oxford: Oxford University Press.

Sander, T. (2011). Positive computing. In R. Biswas-Diener (Ed.), *Positive psychology as social change* (pp. 309–326). New York: Springer.

Schueller, S. M. (2010). Preferences for positive psychology exercises. *Journal of Positive Psychology, 5*, 192–203.

Schueller, S. M. (2011). To each his own well-being boosting intervention: Using preference to guide selection. *Journal of Positive Psychology, 6*, 300–313.

Schueller, S. M., & Parks, A. C. (2012). Disseminating self-help: Positive psychology exercises in an online trial. *Journal of Medical Internet Research, 14*, e63.

Seligman, M. E. P. (1990). *Learned optimism.* New York: Knopf.

Seligman, M. (2011). Flourish 51. Retrieved from http://www.actionforhappiness.org/news/flourish-51

Seligman, M. E. P., Steen, T. A., Park, N., & Peterson, C. (2005). Positive psychology progress: Empirical validation of interventions. *American Psychologist, 60*, 410–421.

Sergeant, S., & Mongrain, M. (2012). Are positive psychology exercises helpful for people with depressive personality styles? *Journal of Positive Psychology, 6*, 260–272.

Shapira, L. B., & Mongrain, M. (2010). The benefits of self-compassion and optimism exercises for individuals vulnerable to depression. *Journal of Positive Psychology, 5*, 377–389.

Sin, N. L., & Lyubomirsky, S. (2009). Enhancing well-being and alleviating depressive symptoms with positive psychology interventions: A practice-friendly meta-analysis. *Journal of Clinical Psychology, 65*, 467–487.

Spek, V., Cuijpers, P., Nyklicek, I., Riper, H., Keyzer, J., & Pop, V. (2007). Internet-based cognitive behaviour therapy for symptoms of depression and anxiety: A meta-analysis. *Psychological Medicine, 37*, 319–328.

Swan, M. (2009). Emerging patient-driven health care models: An examination of health social networks, consumer personalized medicine and quantified self-tracking. *International Journal of Environmental Research and Public Health, 6*, 492–525.

Van de Belt, T., Engelen, L., Berben, S., & Schoonhoven, L. (2010). Definition of Health 2.0 and Medicine 2.0: A systematic review. *Journal of Medical Internet Research, 12*(2), e18.

Van Gemert-Pijnen, J., Nijland, N., Van Limburg, M., Ossebaard, H. C., Kelders, S. M., Eysenbach, G., & Seydel, E. R. (2011). A holistic framework to improve the uptake and impact of eHealth technologies. *Journal of Medical Internet Research, 13*(4), e111.

Van Limburg, M., van Gemert-Pijnen, J. E., Nijland, N., Ossebaard, H. C., Hendrix, R. M., & Seydel, E. R. (2011). Why business modeling is crucial in the development of eHealth technologies. *Journal of Medical Internet Research, 13*(4), e124.

Vansteenwegen, D. (2011). Onderzoeksrapport De gelukscoach – een online programma om meer uit je leven te halen en te werken aan geluk (Research report happiness coach). Leuven: ISW Limits.

Webb, T. L., Joseph, J., Yardley, L., & Michie, S. (2010). Using the internet to promote health behavior change: A systematic review and meta-analysis of the impact of theoretical basis, use of behavior change techniques, and mode of delivery and efficacy. *Journal of Medical Internet Research, 12*(1), e4.

Wiederhold, B. K., & Riva, G. (2012). Positive technology supports shift to preventive, integrative health. *Cyberpsychology, Behavior and Social Networking, 15*, 67–68.

17

Resilience Interventions for Youth

Craig Springer, Justin Misurell, Amy Kranzler, Lindsay Liotta, and Jane Gillham

Most children are exposed to some form of adversity, stress, or trauma over the course of their development. Some face daily stressors such as bullying, family conflict, or poverty. Others experience acute traumas such as child abuse, neglect, and exposure to domestic violence. Yet despite frequent exposure to adversity, most adults and children display a capacity for continued growth indicating enormous resilience to stress, trauma, and loss (Bonanno, 2004; Masten, 2001). Consequently, an increasing interest exists in understanding the personal and environmental factors that contribute to resilience, in order to inform the development of programs that further promote resilience, well-being, and positive development in youth. In this chapter, we briefly describe two universal prevention programs, the Penn Resiliency Project and the Positive Psychology Program. Both programs employ concepts from the fields of positive psychology and cognitive-behavioral therapy to reduce risk factors and bolster pre-existing individual strengths among adolescents, in order to prepare them to face life's daily stressors and prevent the development of pathology. However, while prevention programs such as these are effective, few treatment interventions employ knowledge from these fields to promote resilience and positive growth among youth already exposed to trauma and loss. Therefore the majority of this chapter focuses on a novel treatment, Game-Based Cognitive-Behavioral Therapy, which further builds upon theory and knowledge from the fields of positive psychology and cognitive-behavioral therapy to promote resilience, well-being, and post-traumatic growth among youth who have been sexually abused.

Positive Prevention Programs

The Penn Resiliency Program

The Penn Resiliency Program (PRP) is a cognitive-behavioral and social problem-solving prevention program designed to promote resilience and prevent symptoms of depression and anxiety in youth (Gillham, Jaycox, Reivich, Seligman, & Silver,

The Wiley Blackwell Handbook of Positive Psychological Interventions, First Edition.
Edited by Acacia C. Parks and Stephen M. Schueller.

1990). We provide here a short overview of the intervention; for a more detailed description of the PRP curriculum, see Gillham, Brunwasser, and Freres (2008).

The primary goal of PRP is to prepare children and adolescents to handle the daily stressors and challenges that are a common part of life for most youth. As part of this goal, the program works to foster youth's individual strengths in areas related to resilience such as emotional competence, self-control, problem-solving, social competence, self-efficacy, and realistic optimism (Reivich & Shatté, 2002). To accomplish this, two components comprise PRP. The first component focuses on increasing resilience by targeting cognitive skills. Youth learn about Ellis's Adversity–Beliefs–Consequences (ABC) model (Ellis, 1962), that our beliefs and interpretations of events mediate their impact on emotions and behaviors. They learn to recognize their internal "self-talk," and how to detect negative cognitions and maladaptive thinking styles, such as pessimistic and catastrophic thinking. Youth evaluate the accuracy of their thoughts and challenge their negative thoughts by considering alternative explanations. Through this process, they learn to replace self-defeating patterns with more flexible and realistically optimistic interpretations. In this way, PRP often increases both self-efficacy and optimism in youth, by reducing inaccurate and overly pessimistic cognitive patterns.

In the second component of PRP, youth are taught problem-solving and coping skills to help them manage difficult emotions and situations. They learn techniques to increase assertiveness, negotiation, decision-making, social problem-solving, and relaxation. Further, youth are taught how to apply these skills across many domains of their lives, including relationships with friends and family and academic achievement. In this way, the PRP builds resilience in youth by promoting positive relationships and strong connections to school and family, factors that have consistently been associated with reduced depression, substance use, violence, and other risky behaviors (e.g., Resnick et al., 1997).

Teachers, counselors, or clinicians teach PRP in twelve weekly group sessions of 90–120 minutes each. An interactive curriculum increases engagement and student enjoyment. Lessons include skits, role-plays, short stories, cartoons, and games. Instead of didactic lecturing, lessons use group discussions that draw on examples provided by group members. This increases the relevance and interest of material presented, and the enjoyment of participants.

PRP has now been evaluated in over 19 studies and found to be effective in reducing symptoms of depression for at least 12 months (Brunwasser, Gillham, & Kim, 2009). Several studies have found that the program has positive effects on improving healthy cognitions and reducing cognitive styles related to depression, including hopelessness, and negative automatic thoughts (e.g., Cardemil, Reivich, & Seligman, 2002; Gillham, Reivich, Jaycox, & Seligman, 1995). In addition, research suggests that PRP may have positive effects on behavioral problems and anxiety (Roberts, Kane, Bishop, Matthews, & Thompson, 2004; Roberts, Kane, Thomson, Bishop, & Hart, 2003). This research suggests that PRP is an effective prevention program for youth.

PRP incorporates knowledge from the fields of cognitive-behavioral therapy and positive psychology to promote youth resilience. The program utilizes an engaging and interactive curriculum to foster youth's ability to respond to both severe and daily stressors and setbacks, and prevent the development of pathology. To accomplish this, lessons encourage the development of individual strengths, social and emotional competence, healthy cognitive styles, and effective problem-solving skills, all of which are associated with increased resilience to stressors. The PRP program has been implemented as both a targeted intervention for at-risk youth, as well as a universal prevention program. In both formats, the PRP program aims to prepare youth for the many forms of adversity and stressors that life may present to them.

The Positive Psychology Program

While the Penn Resiliency Program focuses on preparing youth to respond effectively to stressors and setbacks, the Positive Psychology Program (PPP; Reivich et al., 2007) is focused on increasing well-being more generally, regardless of the presence of stressors. As such, the PPP incorporates knowledge from the field of positive psychology to increase well-being by helping youth develop an increased capacity for positive emotions, build close relationships, and engage in meaningful activities. In addition, the program helps high school students identify their signature character strengths and increase their use of these strengths in their daily lives.

The curriculum is based on Seligman's (2002) three pathways to happiness; and therefore it includes lessons that comprise three different units, which teach the pleasant life, the engaged life, and the meaningful life. As part of the pleasant life unit, youth learn about savoring, gratitude, and optimism. For example, participants each write a letter expressing gratitude to someone who has helped them whom they have not yet thanked. As part of the engaged life unit, youth engage in several activities that help them identify their individual strengths, and ways to apply these in their daily lives. As part of the meaningful life unit, youth reflect on different interpretations of meaning from excerpts by philosophers, writers, and leaders, and develop their own perspectives on life meaning.

Each of these lessons is embedded within the Language Arts curriculum, and taught through writing assignments, class discussions, and journal reflections. This program is still in the early stages of evaluation, but has been demonstrated to increase social skills (e.g., cooperation, assertiveness, empathy), and students' reports of enjoyment and engagement in school, while improving Language Arts achievement through the 11th grade (Seligman, Ernst, Gillham, Reivich, & Linkins, 2009). Based on initial evaluations, this program provides an effective method of teaching well-being and resilience to high school-age adolescents within the context of their existing Language Arts curriculum. For a more detailed description of the PPP curriculum, see Seligman and colleagues (2009).

While the Penn Resiliency Project builds resilience by preparing youth to effectively cope with challenges and stressors, the Positive Psychology Program builds resilience by fostering general well-being and positive intrapersonal and interpersonal resources among youth. Rather than simply preventing maladaptive responses to stressors, this approach also promotes positive growth by helping students identify and build upon their strengths. By promoting self-efficacy, positive emotions, and individual strengths, the PPP curriculum thereby increases youth capacity to cope with adversity. Despite these differences, both strategies effectively employ knowledge from the field of positive psychology to build resilience preventatively, before youth encounter significant stressors.

A Positive Treatment Program: Game-Based Cognitive-Behavioral Therapy for Child Sexual Abuse

While prevention programs such as PRP and PPP have been developed for both healthy and at-risk youth, few treatment interventions incorporate concepts from positive psychology to promote resilience and positive development among youth already exposed to trauma. However, the positive psychology literature has highlighted the particular importance of facilitating resilience and post-traumatic growth among children exposed to severe stressors and trauma (Helgeson, Reynolds, & Tomich, 2006; Ickovics et al., 2006; McElheran et al., 2012). This section will therefore describe one novel therapeutic model, Game-Based Cognitive-Behavioral Therapy (GB-CBT), which incorporates positive psychology concepts in order to treat youth exposed to trauma (Springer & Misurell, 2010). The underlying theory and rationale of the model will be presented first, followed by detailed descriptions of game examples. As GB-CBT was initially designed to address trauma among survivors of child sexual abuse (CSA) aged 5–10 years old, we focus our discussion on GB-CBT for this population. We conclude, however, with several examples of adaptations of this model for other populations.

Game-Based Cognitive-Behavioral Therapy (GB-CBT) is an integrative group treatment model, incorporating structured play activities with evidence-based cognitive-behavioral practices for survivors and families impacted by trauma. The GB-CBT model enhances positive growth and development by focusing on youth strengths, creating a healing, enriching, and positive therapeutic environment, and increasing knowledge through experiential learning.

Treatment is administered to children and caregivers through 12 sessions of 90 minutes each. A group for caregivers parallels the children's group by utilizing therapeutic games to create an appealing and supportive forum for parents to process their children's trauma, learn about their children's treatment, and receive parenting education. GB-CBT for CSA was originally developed and studied within an urban outpatient center providing services for predominantly economically disadvantaged African American and Latino families. Careful considerations have therefore been made to enhance the model's cultural responsiveness (Misurell & Springer, 2013).

Theoretical framework

There is increasing recognition that positive emotions are essential for bolstering coping and resilience in the face of adversity (Lyubomirsky & Della Porta, 2010). According to the broaden-and-build theory (Fredrickson, 2001), positive emotions broaden one's repertoire of thoughts and actions, which leads individuals to engage in constructive activities (e.g., playing with peers) that can enhance and build important personal resources such as social support. In the face of stressors, positive emotions have been associated with a style of coping characterized by a broad perspective on problems, seeing beyond immediate stressors, and generating multiple courses of action. In this way, in the aftermath of traumatic experiences, positive emotions can help promote the development of effective coping mechanisms. Consistent with this theory, post-crisis experiences of positive emotions have been found to buffer people against depression, following the September 11 terrorist attacks (Fredrickson, Tugade, Waugh, & Larkin, 2003), and increase post-traumatic growth among bereaved caregivers (Moskowitz, 2001).

While the role of positive emotions in promoting adaptive coping and post-traumatic growth has been identified, the majority of literature studying the consequences of CSA has focused on the negative impact of the experience on future behavioral and emotional functioning (Berliner, 2011). Survivors of CSA have been found to experience a host of post-traumatic stress difficulties (e.g., re-experiencing, hyperarousal, and avoidance), internalizing symptoms (e.g., anxiety, depression, and anger), externalizing problems (e.g., oppositionality, conduct problems, and risk-taking behaviors), sexual behaviors (e.g., promiscuity, sexual aggression, and sexual preoccupation), and social difficulties (e.g., poor self-esteem, peer-related problems, and distortions about oneself; Kendall-Tackett, Williams, & Finkelhor, 1993; Pereda, Guilera, Forns, & Gomez-Benito, 2009). However, more recently, there has been a shift toward recognizing that there are not only negative consequences but also potential opportunities for growth following a traumatic experience (O'Dougherty Wright, Crawford, & Sebastian, 2007). According to Frazier and Berman (2008), some survivors of sexual trauma have indicated that they have experienced improvements in their sense of self, relationships with others, empathy for others, and sense of purpose.

GB-CBT is an integrative model combining aspects of cognitive-behavioral therapy (CBT), play therapy, and positive psychology. It provides an innovative platform for increasing positive functioning of children and families in addition to addressing the adverse impact of sexual trauma. The GB-CBT model uniquely builds on the power of positive emotion to increase learning and effective coping by embedding skills in the context of games and rewards that create a positive learning environment for children. GB-CBT was formulated on the principle that happiness and enjoyment increase interest in learning and skill acquisition (Springer & Misurell, 2010). Enhancing engagement is particularly relevant for treatment of sexual trauma, when subject matter can be difficult and uncomfortable. This is consistent with literature suggesting that strategies that facilitate flow and engagement are invaluable for learning to take place (Shernoff & Csikszentmihalyi, 2009; see Chapter 11). Indeed research suggests that the inclusion of play improves the ability of children to relate to the content of CSA interventions (Drewes, 2009), and increases the efficacy of cognitive-behavioral interventions for CSA (Cavett & Drewes, 2012; Drewes & Cavett, 2012; Sánchez-Meca, Rosa-Alcázar, & López-Soler, 2011). Accordingly, opportunities for enjoyment and engagement are incorporated into the overarching GB-CBT session structure as well as the individual activities that are utilized for skill building and abuse processing.

In addition, as in PRP and PPP, the GB-CBT curriculum fosters youth individual strengths by focusing on both helping youth develop new skills, as well as identifying and bolstering pre-existing internal resources. These individual strengths are highlighted throughout the program and recognized as important tools for youth to employ as they cope with their abuse experience. For example, as part of the preparation for their graduation ceremony, youth are encouraged to use their signature strengths (e.g., artistic talent, poetry, and writing) to develop a final project that reflects what they have learned in the group, which they present to parents at graduation. In this way, the graduation ceremony celebrates the individual strengths that have helped each child cope with his or her experience. Additionally, rather than relating to youth as victims, the GB-CBT program is structured to empower youth, by focusing on their ability to achieve mastery of skills that are not only directly related to their trauma but can also be applied to other areas of their lives. For instance, GB-CBT facilitates the development of many characteristics discussed elsewhere in this volume, including empathy (Chapter 6), courage (Chapter 9), purpose (Chapter 5), assertiveness, and a sense of belonging through participation in collaborative group games.

Group structure

The structure of GB-CBT group sessions draws upon traditional behavioral therapy approaches that have been well researched for addressing motivation and disruptive behaviors (e.g., token economies, behavioral expectations, and differential attention; Christopherson & Mortweet, 2005; Martin & Pear, 2007). Every session has the same organizational format, containing an introductory ritual, psychoeducation, role-plays, structured therapeutic games, processing, and a closing ritual. By providing clear expectations and a consistent, reliable, and familiar routine, children and families are able to experience the feeling of safety and develop trust in each other, allowing them to fully express themselves and practice new skills without judgment. Group clinicians also focus on identifying positive behaviors among group members, to increase their utilization of pre-existing strengths and to incorporate the use of new patterns of behavior. Furthermore, the therapeutic topics covered through GB-CBT are based on the research and development of Trauma-Focused Cognitive-Behavioral Therapy (TF-CBT; Cohen, Mannarino, & Deblinger, 2006; Saywitz, Mannarino, Berliner, & Cohen, 2000).

Topics covered in GB-CBT include emotional regulation, psychoeducation about child sexual abuse and healthy sexuality, gradual exposure for trauma, and personal safety skills training (Springer & Misurell, 2010).

As mentioned earlier, play therapy, a common intervention for CSA (Gallo-Lopez, 2006; Kelly & Odenwalt, 2006), also greatly contributed to the formation of the primary therapeutic technique utilized in GB-CBT: developmentally appropriate games (DAGs; Springer & Misurell, 2010). DAGs are goal-oriented, rule-governed, structured activities that children can participate in at their own ability level (Reddy et al., 2005). DAGs have been utilized to improve treatment outcomes for a variety of childhood behavior disorders and problems, including social skills deficits and attention-deficit/hyperactivity disorder (ADHD; Reddy et al., 2005; Springer & Reddy, 2010). These techniques enhance motivation and provide an enjoyable atmosphere for learning, thereby increasing positive emotion, engagement, and interest in the therapeutic process. DAGs contribute to skill acquisition through experiential learning and by providing multiple opportunities for rehearsal. It is expected that using DAGs creates a more naturalistic environment within therapy and, thus, can increase the generalization of skills outside of therapy. Furthermore, DAGs are particularly useful in facilitating gradual exposure to trauma cues in a safe manner, and assist in reducing experiential avoidance (Misurell, Springer, & Tryon, 2011; Springer & Misurell, 2010; Springer, Misurell, & Hiller, 2012). To support the process of learning, psychoeducation and role-plays are also utilized.

The group format of GB-CBT is built upon Yalom's (1995) work, which identified a number of beneficial effects of group treatment, including instilling hope, communicating a sense of universality, and providing opportunities for imitative learning and cohesion. GB-CBT harnesses the power of group therapy to promote positive growth for survivors of CSA and their families in a number of ways. Through the use of group games, children and caregivers learn that they can have fun, nourishing, and rejuvenating experiences despite the trauma they have endured. In this way, they realize that there is hope for a brighter future when the pain and suffering of the past no longer have a hold on their functioning. By creating a group of peers from similar backgrounds who have experienced sexual abuse, GB-CBT enables children and their caregivers to understand that they are not alone and to appreciate the commonality of their experiences. Clinicians facilitating activities serve as positive role models for the children and caregivers participating in GB-CBT groups, and provide opportunities for imitative learning which encourages the development of effective social skills. Additionally, over the course of treatment, as group cohesion builds, participants often emerge as positive role models for their peers.

Therapeutic topics

Therapeutic topics contained within the GB-CBT curriculum encourage recovery and growth through nine skill areas: (i) rapport and communication skills building, (ii) personal space identification, (iii) emotional expression, (iv) anger management, (v) psychoeducation about CSA, physical abuse, and personal safety, (vi) gradual exposure and abuse processing, (vii) personal safety skills training, (viii) coping with difficult emotions and relaxation skills, and (ix) reflecting on the past and planning for the future. Each topical area builds upon previous skills and is sequenced to effectively facilitate group cohesion and the processing of abuse and trauma.

Conducting a GB-CBT group

At the beginning of a new GB-CBT group, clinicians introduce the structure of sessions and utilize games to build rapport, bolster communications skills, and create group cohesion. Group rules establish a sense of trust, safety, and behavioral expectations, thereby encouraging group members to accept new challenges, share with peers, and learn new skills. Incentives are provided for participation in games and activities, good sportsmanship, and following of group rules. This structure promotes bravery both implicitly and explicitly. Furthermore, the structure of the group embodies standards of fairness as all group members have opportunities to earn equal rewards.

From the beginning of treatment, children learn that the group is fun and engaging, and that interactive games emphasize teamwork. Furthermore, humor is encouraged throughout therapy in order to enhance interest in topical material and to facilitate healing. Group leaders convey that while the subject matter is serious, the process of learning can be both fun and enjoyable. Initial games and role-plays provide opportunities for group members to introduce themselves and learn the value of authentic and genuine communication.

Survivors of CSA often have difficulty understanding personal boundaries and body awareness. This may be a result of personal violations committed by trusted individuals who had betrayed them through grooming and abuse. As such, conceptions of personal space are covered and simplified for the purposes of the group. Through role-plays and therapeutic games, children learn to identify appropriate personal space and build social intelligence by recognizing how one's body and communication style may impact others. Children also practice demonstrating courage and assertiveness by letting others know when someone commits a personal space violation.

As the group progresses, clinicians work with children to bolster their emotional expression skills in an effort to help them develop a richer understanding of themselves and their experiences. Children first work on increasing their emotional vocabularies, then practice demonstrating body language and facial expressions, and finally work on linking feelings to experiences. Social intelligence is developed through games and activities designed to help children learn to identify and respond empathically to emotions in others. In many cases, survivors of CSA struggle with anger and emotional distress in the wake of their abuse experiences. Furthermore, other traumas and life challenges may have contributed to emotional regulation difficulties. As such, anger management strategies are also presented and practiced through role-plays and therapeutic games. By practicing anger management strategies children learn the value of self-regulation and hone skills needed to better regulate and cope with difficult emotions.

Prior to providing opportunities for group members to process their sexual abuse experiences, therapeutic games are used to provide psychoeducation about CSA, physical abuse, and personal safety. Typically, children have a number of misconceptions and experience anxiety and resistance in relation to these topics. Games help to debunk myths about abuse, introduce preliminary strategies for staying safe, and encourage children to develop a love of learning, curiosity, and open-mindedness for acquiring this new material. Additionally, children discover that abuse has impacted many other children and that they have the capacity to heal.

Once a safe and supportive therapeutic environment has been established, group cohesion has solidified, and psychoeducation about abuse has been covered, GB-CBT moves to gradual exposure and abuse processing. Through therapeutic games and activities, children are given opportunities to disclose and process their individual abuse experiences in a supportive and nurturing peer environment. Children receive encouragement and positive feedback from peers and adults emphasizing their bravery and courage in discussing their abuse. Furthermore, children are encouraged to take a leadership role in sharing and supporting those who are struggling. Through increased positive emotion and empowerment after sharing and listening, children develop a sense of empathy, support, and gratitude for others. Furthermore, children develop self-confidence in their ability to overcome life struggles and a sense of optimism for their future. Children learn to forgive those in their life who have disappointed them (e.g., parents for failing to keep them safe), failed to support them (e.g., relatives who did not believe the allegations), and in some cases, betrayed their trust (e.g., perpetrator).

While it is recognized that adults have primary responsibility for keeping children safe, personal safety skills are reintroduced after gradual exposure and abuse processing, to empower children to work through challenging situations. Children learn several strategies for staying safe, and are assisted in developing personal safety plans in the event that they are faced with abuse or other threatening situations. Therapeutic games develop children's assertiveness and bravery skills. Children practice identifying risky situations, rehearse effective response strategies, and are encouraged to be persistent even when initial attempts are unsuccessful.

As the GB-CBT group concludes, additional coping and relaxation skills are introduced and practiced to enhance children's ongoing emotional balance. Therapeutic games are played to rehearse diaphragmatic breathing, progressive muscle relaxation, and visualization. These activities help children strengthen their self-regulation skills and increase prudence. Emphasis on a non-abuse-related topic during the final session of group helps children shift from the past to a present and future focus.

The program culminates in a graduation ceremony in which therapeutic accomplishments are celebrated and positive growth is highlighted. Clinicians, caregivers, and children express positive remarks, reflect on their experiences, and discuss hopes and plans for the future. The graduation ceremony provides a forum for group members and their families to express their gratitude and appreciation of life.

Group game examples

The following section provides a sampling of structured, therapeutic games that are utilized during the children's group, illustrating how some of the aforementioned skills are taught through the use of games.

Emotional regulation skill development game example: "Hand-Off Madness" "Hand-Off Madness" is a game that provides children with opportunities to learn and practice emotional regulation techniques. It involves simulating a frustrating situation in which children are encouraged to use appropriate coping strategies to enhance their self-regulation skills. During "Hand-Off Madness" children pass a ping-pong ball to one another, using plastic spoons, in an attempt to circulate it amongst all group members without dropping the ball. In an effort to induce an emotional investment in the game, group facilitators inform children that past groups were able to successfully complete the task. Because of the difficulty of the task, it is inevitable that the ball will drop, causing anger and frustration among group members. When this occurs, children are encouraged to utilize appropriate coping strategies (e.g., deep breathing), and are provided with reinforcement for effectively utilizing them. This game provides a forum for children to practice applying emotional regulation skills in a highly relatable and relevant manner, by simulating a frustrating situation that resembles common occurrences.

Psychoeducation game example: "Life Size Wheel of Knowledge" Psychoeducation is delivered in a fun, interactive format through the "Life Size Wheel of Knowledge." When playing "Life Size Wheel of Knowledge," the therapeutic room is transformed into a board game. Group clinicians position themselves throughout the room to create separate stations, containing a category of topics that include sexual abuse, physical abuse, and personal safety. Each child is given a "knowledge wheel," which is a handout containing a circle subdivided into numbered sections corresponding to the categories. Children are instructed to roll a die and go to the station corresponding to that number. At each station, children are asked a question from the corresponding category. If the child answers correctly, a designation is placed on their "knowledge wheel," and they are instructed to roll the die again to determine the next station that they must complete. If they answer incorrectly, children are given the correct answer and provided with additional questions until they are able to provide a correct answer. Children are provided with incentives based on the order in which they fully complete their "knowledge wheel." By embedding psychoeducation about abuse in the context of this game, children are motivated and engaged, often laughing with enjoyment, as they absorb material that is often uncomfortable and difficult to learn.

Passive disclosure game example: "Who, What, Where in a Hat" This game facilitates children's disclosure of abuse-related material in a non-verbal manner. During this game, children learn about the commonalities of their abuse experiences and realize that they are not alone. Children receive three pieces of colored paper and write down who sexually abused them, where they were when they were sexually abused, and what occurred when they were sexually abused (e.g., what part of their body was touched by what part of the alleged perpetrator). Children then fold each paper and place it in a container (e.g., a hat). Once all papers are collected, group leaders select the responses from the container that correspond with the question, "Who sexually abused you?" Children are asked to raise their hands if the response read is applicable to them. In order to highlight the commonalities of experiences group clinicians expand on each response. For example, if a response indicated "father," as the abuser, children who were touched by their father would be asked to raise their hand. With their hands raised, children would be told that a father is a family member and, as such, anyone abused by a family member should raise their hand. A third level of expansion may include anyone who knew the perpetrator before the abuse took place. The same procedure is followed for answering the questions, "Where were you abused?" and "What happened to you?" At the conclusion of the game, group clinicians facilitate processing of the activity, explicitly emphasizing the commonality of experiences shared between members of the group.

Caregiver group

Non-offending caregivers are involved in a parallel group that covers all the major topics addressed in the children's group. This enables caregivers to understand and support their children through the therapeutic process and helps caregivers to broaden their own coping repertoires, thus experiencing positive growth themselves. Caregivers learn parenting skills to enhance their ability to create a positive and supportive environment for their children. Another focus of the caregiver group is to encourage caregivers to limit their focus on the negative experiences of the past, increase their sense of appreciation and gratitude, and recognize their children's, as well as their own, potential for positive growth. DAGs allow caregivers to actively participate in therapy and experience the process as a pleasant, engaging, and non-threatening experience. The strength of humor is highly encouraged during all sessions, is promoted through many of the games, and serves as a valuable tool for helping group members participate and express themselves openly. Additionally, the use of games assists in facilitating the development of group cohesion as group members get to know one another through an interactive medium. While initially reluctant to play games, within a short period of time caregivers are laughing, engaging, and having fun.

Caregiver group games

Rapport-building game example: "Getting to Know You Stack" "Getting to Know You Stack" acquaints group members with one another, while allowing them to share their individual preferences, life experiences, and values. This game involves the use of cards with one-point and three-point questions containing surface level (e.g., "What is your favorite movie?") and more personal questions (e.g., "What happened to your child?"), respectively. Group members are seated around a table and take turns rolling a die. Following their roll, the stack of cards is passed from person to person the number of times corresponding to the die (e.g., if a group member rolls a four, then they will pass the stack four persons to the right). When a group member receives the stack of cards, they pick a card from the top of the pile and decide whether they will answer the one-point question, the three-point question, or both for four points. The objective for group members is to earn the most points. From our experience, the positive interactions promoted by this game establish a foundation for open, positive, and honest interactions throughout treatment.

Parent management training game example: "What if my child did …?" "What if my child did …?" is another game utilized to enhance the cohesion of the group, while allowing caregivers to exchange parenting strategies and expand their repertoire of responses to parenting scenarios. As part of this game, group clinicians ask caregivers to write down how they would respond to common scenarios involving their children. After each scenario is presented, caregivers' responses are collected and group members vote on which represents the most effective strategy. Group members receive points for the number of votes their answer received.

Empirical research

Preliminary research on GB-CBT has found it to be effective for reducing internalizing symptoms, including depression and anxiety, trauma-related symptoms, externalizing behavior problems, including oppositional and conduct behaviors, and sexually inappropriate behaviors (Misurell et al., 2011; Springer et al., 2012). Additionally, GB-CBT was found to improve children's knowledge of abuse and personal safety skills (Misurell et al., 2011; Springer et al., 2012). Furthermore, findings indicate that clinical gains have been maintained for up to three months following treatment (Springer et al., 2012).

Following the initial success of the GB-CBT group model, a federal appropriations grant was obtained in order to deliver the model in an individual and conjoint family therapy format (Springer & Misurell, 2012). Preliminary data analyses suggest that the GB-CBT individual model is effective in addressing internalizing symptoms, externalizing behaviors, trauma-related symptoms, and sexually inappropriate behaviors, and appears to improve children's knowledge of abuse and personal safety skills (Misurell, Springer, Acosta, Liotta, & Kranzler, 2013).

Future directions

While GB-CBT was initially developed to treat CSA, the curriculum can be adapted for use with a range of disorders. GB-CBT is unique in its approach, employing games to foster positive emotions that enable individuals to engage more easily and meaningfully with information and activities that are otherwise often difficult and uncomfortable. GB-CBT builds positive social support networks, instills hope, and empowers individuals to gain new skills and apply them in the real world. For these reasons, the game-based model may offer similar advantages to treatments designed for other clinical populations including: children with disruptive behavior disorders (e.g., ADHD), anxiety disorders (e.g., social anxiety, specific phobias, and obsessive-compulsive disorder), depression, medical illnesses (e.g., oncology, serious physical illness, pain management), and/or other traumas (e.g., physical abuse, exposure to violence). As the model continues to evolve, efforts should be made to implement GB-CBT among non-clinical populations of children, such as in schools and other organizations for youth, in order to enhance character strengths and facilitate learning.

Currently, efforts are being made to disseminate the use of the GB-CBT model through presentations and trainings. Given the delicacy with which many topics must be treated in therapy, opportunities for comprehensive training for clinicians unfamiliar with GB-CBT should accompany efforts to disseminate the model. This is particularly important when working with vulnerable populations, in order to maximize the therapeutic value of games, while ensuring that treatment honors the importance and significance of client experiences.

Future research should investigate the impact of GB-CBT on children's life satisfaction, enjoyment of treatment, self-efficacy, and overall well-being. Additionally, research should assess the interaction between resilience and clinical outcomes for children in the GB-CBT program. Considerations for including measures that assess positive growth and resilience in children and families following participation in GB-CBT are currently underway.

Conclusion

We have outlined several interventions that employ current knowledge from the field of positive psychology to build resilience among youth, both prophylactically and in response to stress and trauma. Programs such as PRP and PPP have been implemented as both targeted and universal prevention strategies, building youth resilience by cultivating the intrapersonal and interpersonal resources that increase adaptive well-being and help youth cope effectively with stressors. These programs incorporate both knowledge from the field of cognitive-behavioral therapy about effective cognitive styles, as well as knowledge from the field of positive psychology such as the importance of identifying and using individual character strengths, building positive emotions and relationships, and promoting self-efficacy and realistic optimism.

As the field of psychology grows to recognize the importance of these factors in promoting resilience, there is great promise for their incorporation into treatment programs for youth with trauma experiences. We have outlined here one such treatment model, Game-Based Cognitive-Behavioral Therapy, which capitalizes on the power of positive emotions to help youth cope with experiences of sexual abuse. By incorporating knowledge from the field of positive psychology, GB-CBT seeks not only to reduce the adverse effects of child sexual abuse, but also to promote resilience and post-traumatic growth. By embedding lessons in developmentally appropriate games, GB-CBT cultivates a positive environment in which youth can more easily engage with difficult material about sexual abuse. Youth learn that while the subject matter is serious, the process of learning can be both enjoyable and meaningful. The group format allows youth to cultivate interpersonal resources, as they engage in collaborative games and are reinforced for supporting one another through the disclosure process. Furthermore, GB-CBT empowers youth to identify and use their individual strengths as they cope with their abuse experience.

In the context of both universal and targeted prevention, as well as treatment interventions for youth who have been exposed to traumatic experiences, positive psychology research can guide our understanding of the factors that enable youth to flourish in the face of adversity. Unfortunately, we cannot protect youth from the many forms of adversity they may encounter. However, as we describe in this chapter, we *can* prepare them with the resources and skills they need to bolster their own strengths and face life's challenges with resilience.

References

Berliner, L. (2011). Sexual abuse of children. In J. E. B Myers (Ed.), *The APSAC handbook on child maltreatment* (3rd ed., pp. 51–71). London: Sage Publications.

Bonanno, G. A. (2004). Loss, trauma and human resilience: Have we underestimated the human capacity to thrive after extremely aversive events? *American Psychologist*, *59*, 20–28.

Brunwasser, S. M., Gillham, J. E., & Kim, E. S. (2009). A meta-analytic review of the Penn Resiliency Program's effect on depressive symptoms. *Journal of Consulting and Clinical Psychology*, *77*, 1042–1054. doi:10.1037/a0017671

Cardemil, E. V., Reivich, K. J., & Seligman, M. E. P. (2002). The prevention of depressive symptoms in low-income minority middle school students. *Prevention and Treatment*, *5*(8). doi:10.1037/1522-3736.5.1.58a

Cavett, A. M., & Drewes, A. A. (2012). Play applications and trauma-specific components. In J. A Cohen, A. P. Mannarino, & E. Deblinger (Eds.), *Trauma-focused CBT for children and adolescents: Treatment applications* (pp. 124–148). New York: Guilford Press.

Christopherson, E. R., & Mortweet, S. L. (2005). *Treatments that work with children: Empirically supported strategies for managing childhood problems.* Washington, DC: APA Press.

Cohen, J. A., Mannarino, A. P., & Deblinger, E. (2006). *Treating trauma and traumatic grief in children and adolescents.* New York: Guilford Press.

Drewes, A. A. (2009). *Blending play therapy with cognitive behavioral therapy: Evidence-based and other effective treatments and techniques.* New York: John Wiley & Sons.

Drewes, A. A., & Cavett, A. M. (2012). Play applications and skill components. In J. A Cohen, A. P. Mannarino, & E. Deblinger (Eds.), *Trauma-focused CBT for children and adolescents: Treatment applications* (pp. 105–123). New York: Guilford Press.

Ellis, A. (1962). *Reason and emotion in psychotherapy.* New York: Lyle Stuart.

Frazier, P., & Berman, M. I. (2008). Posttraumatic growth following sexual assault. In S. Joseph & P. A. Linley (Eds.), *Trauma, recovery, growth: Positive psychology studies on posttraumatic stress* (pp. 161–184). Hoboken, NJ: John Wiley & Sons.

Fredrickson, B. L. (2001). The role of positive emotions in positive psychology: The broaden-and-build theory of positive emotions. *American Psychologist, 56*, 218–226. doi:10.1037/0003-066X.56.3.218

Fredrickson, B. L., Tugade, M. M., Waugh, C. E., & Larkin, G. R. (2003). What good are positive emotions in crisis? A prospective study of resilience and emotions following the terrorist attacks on the United States on September 11th, 2001. *Journal of Personality and Social Psychology, 84*, 365–376. doi:10.1037/0022-3514.84.2.365

Gallo-Lopez, L. (2006). A creative play therapy approach to the group treatment of young sexually abused children. In C. E. Scheafer & H. G. Kaduson (Eds.), *Short-term play therapy for children* (2nd ed., pp. 245–272). New York: Guilford Press.

Gillham, J. E., Brunwasser, S. M., & Freres, D. R. (2008). Preventing depression in early adolescence: The Penn Resiliency Program. In J. R. Z. Abela & B. L. Hankin (Eds.), *Handbook of depression in children and adolescents* (pp. 309–332). New York: Guilford Press.

Gillham, J. E., Jaycox, L. H., Reivich, K. J., Seligman, M. E. P., & Silver, T. (1990). The Penn Resiliency Program. Unpublished manual, University of Pennsylvania, Philadelphia.

Gillham, J. E., Reivich, K. J., Jaycox, L. H., & Seligman, M. E. P. (1995). Preventing depressive symptoms in schoolchildren: Two year follow-up. *Psychological Science, 6*, 343–351. doi:10.1111/j.1467-9280.1995.tb00524.x

Helgeson, V. S., Reynolds, K. A., & Tomich, P. L. (2006). A meta-analytic review of benefit finding and growth. *Journal of Consulting and Clinical Psychology, 74*, 797–816. doi:10.1037/0022-006X.74.5.797

Ickovics, J. R., Meade, C. S., Kershaw, T. S., Milan, S., Lewis, J. B., & Ethier, K. A. (2006). Urban teens: Trauma, posttraumatic growth, and emotional distress among female adolescents. *Journal of Consulting and Clinical Psychology, 75*, 841–850. doi:10.1037/0022-006X.74.5.841

Kelly, M. M., & Odenwalt, H. C. (2006). Treatment of sexually abused children. In C. E. Schaefer & H. G. Kaduson (Eds.), *Contemporary play therapy: Theory, research, and practice* (pp. 186–211). New York: Guilford Press.

Kendall-Tackett, K. A., Williams, L. M., & Finkelhor, D. (1993). The impact of sexual abuse on children: A review of and synthesis of recent empirical studies. *Psychological Bulletin, 113*, 164–190.

Lyubomirsky, S., & Della Porta, M. D. (2010). Boosting happiness, buttressing resilience: Results from cognitive and behavioral interventions. In J. W. Reich, A. J. Zautra, & J. S. Hall (Eds.), *Handbook of adult resilience* (pp. 450–464). New York: Guilford Press.

Martin, G., & Pear, J. (2007). *Behavior modification: What it is and how to do it* (8th ed.). Upper Saddle River, NJ: Pearson-Prentice Hall.

Masten, A. S. (2001). Ordinary magic: Resilience processes in development. *American Psychologist, 56*, 227–238. doi:10.1037/0003-066X.56.3.227

McElheran, M., Briscoe-Smith, A., Khaylis, A., Westrup, D., Hayward, C., & Gore-Felton, C. (2012). A conceptual model of post-traumatic growth among children and adolescents in the aftermath of sexual abuse. *Counseling Psychology Quarterly, 25*, 73–82. doi: 10.1080/09515070.2012.665225

Misurell, J. R., & Springer, C. (2013). Developing culturally responsive evidence-based practice: A Game-Based Cognitive-Behavioral Group Therapy (GB-CBT) program for African-American and Latino families impacted by child sexual abuse (CSA). *Journal of Child and Family Studies, 22*, 137–149. doi 10.1007/s10826-011-9560-2

Misurell, J. R., Springer, C., Acosta, L., Liotta, L., & Kranzler, A. (2013). Game-Based Cognitive-Behavioral Therapy Individual Model (GB-CBT-IM) for child sexual abuse (CSA): A preliminary outcome study. Unpublished manuscript.

Misurell, J. R., Springer, C., & Tryon, W. (2011). Game-Based Cognitive-Behavioral Therapy (GB-CBT) group program for children who have experienced sexual abuse: A preliminary investigation. *Journal of Child Sexual Abuse, 20*, 14–36.

Moskowitz, J. T. (2001). Emotion and coping. In T. J. Mayne & G. A. Bonnano (Eds.), *Emotion: Current issues and future directions* (pp. 311–336). New York: Guilford Press.

O'Dougherty Wright, M., Crawford, E., & Sebastian, K. (2007). Positive resolution of childhood sexual abuse experiences: The role of coping, benefit-finding, and meaning-making. *Journal of Family Violence, 22*, 597–608. doi:10.1007/s10896-007-9111-1

Pereda, N., Guilera, G., Forns, M., & Gomez-Benito, J. (2009). The prevalence of child sexual abuse in community and student samples: A meta-analysis. *Clinical Psychology Review, 29*, 328–338. doi:10.1016/j.cpr.2009.02.007

Reddy, L. A., Springer, C., Files-Hall, T. M., Schmelzer-Benisz, E., Hauch, Y., Braunstein, D., & Atamanoff, T. (2005). Child ADHD multimodal program: An empirically supported intervention for young children with ADHD. In L. A. Reddy, T. M. Files-Hall, & C. E. Schaefer (Eds.), *Empirically based play interventions for children* (pp. 145–167). Washington, DC: American Psychological Association.

Reivich, K. J., Seligman, M. E. P., Gillham, J., Linkins, M., Peterson, C., Schwartz, B., et al. (2007). Positive psychology program for high school students: Lessons for the pleasant life, the good life, and the meaningful life. Unpublished manuscript, Wallingford-Swarthmore School District, University of Pennsylvania, and Swarthmore College.

Reivich, K., & Shatté, A. (2002). *The resilience factor: 7 essential skills for overcoming life's inevitable obstacles.* New York: Broadway Books.

Resnick, M. D., Bearman, P., Blum, R. W., Bauman, K. E., Harris, K. M., Jones, J., et al. (1997). Protecting adolescents from harm: Findings from the National Longitudinal Study on Adolescent Health. *Journal of the American Medical Association, 278*, 823–832.

Roberts, C., Kane, R., Bishop, B., Matthews, H., & Thompson, H. (2004). The prevention of depressive symptoms in rural children: A follow-up study. *International Journal of Mental Health Promotion, 6*, 4–16.

Roberts, C., Kane, R., Thomson, H., Bishop, B., & Hart, B. (2003). The prevention of depressive symptoms in rural school children: A randomized controlled trial. *Journal of Consulting and Clinical Psychology*, *71*, 622–628. doi:10.1037/0022-006X.71.3.622

Sánchez-Meca, J., Rosa-Alcázar, A. I., & López-Soler, C. (2011). The psychological treatment of sexual abuse in children and adolescents: A meta-analysis. *International Journal of Clinical and Health Psychology*, *11*, 67–93.

Saywitz, K. J., Mannarino, A. P., Berliner, L., & Cohen, J. A. (2000). Treatment for sexually abused children and adolescents. *American Psychologist*, *22*, 1040–1049.

Seligman, M. E. P. (2002). *Authentic happiness: Using the new positive psychology to realize your potential for lasting fulfillment.* New York: Free Press.

Seligman, M. E. P., Ernst, R. M., Gillham, J., Reivich, K., & Linkins, M. (2009). Positive education: Positive psychology and classroom interventions. *Oxford Review of Education*, *35*, 293–311. doi:10.1080/03054980902934563

Shernoff, D. J. & Csikszentmihalyi, M. (2009). Flow in schools: Cultivating engaged learners and optimal learning environments. In R. Gilman, E. S. Huebner, & M. J. Furlong (Eds.), *Handbook of positive psychology in schools* (pp. 131–145). New York: Routledge.

Springer, C., & Misurell, J. R. (2010). Game-Based Cognitive-Behavioral Therapy (GB-CBT): An innovative group treatment program for children who have been sexually abused. *Journal of Child and Adolescent Trauma*, *3*, 163–180.

Springer, C., & Misurell, J. R. (2012). Game-based cognitive-behavioral therapy individual model for child sexual abuse. *International Journal of Play Therapy*, *21*, 188–201.

Springer, C., Misurell, J. R., & Hiller, A. (2012). Game-Based Cognitive-Behavioral Therapy (GB-CBT) group program for children who have experienced sexual abuse: A three-month follow-up investigation. *Journal of Child Sexual Abuse*, *21*, 646–664. doi: 10.1080/10538712.2012.722592

Springer, C., & Reddy, L. A. (2010). Measuring parental treatment adherence in a multimodal treatment program for children with ADHD: A preliminary investigation. *Child and Family Behavior Therapy*, *32*, 272–290. doi: 10.1080/07317107.2010.51552

Yalom, I. D. (1995). *The theory and practice of group psychotherapy* (4th ed.). New York: Basic Books.

18

Positive Social Identity Interventions

Finding a Conduit for Well-Being in Stigmatized Group Memberships

Thomas C. Ball and Michelle R. Nario-Redmond

A preponderance of evidence suggests that social groups are a critical determinant of self-concept, capable of dictating beliefs and regulating behaviors (Tajfel & Turner, 1986; Turner, Hogg, Oakes, Reicher, & Wetherell, 1987). Particularly relevant for a discussion of positive psychological interventions, belonging to a group can promote health and well-being, especially in the face of social disadvantage, associated stigma, and other stressful conditions (Branscombe & Ellemers, 1998; Matheson & Cole, 2004). Despite this wealth of research, applied methods for improving well-being (e.g., positive psychological interventions) through social identification are lacking (see Haslam, Jetten, Postmes, & Haslam, 2009). This chapter aims to establish a basis for interventions that emphasize the significance of social identities. To do so, we review evidence on the influence of identification with social groups on health and well-being for members of stigmatized categories (i.e., social groups characterized by traits that are devalued and marginalized by society). Although this research has not traditionally influenced positive psychology, its application might help create novel and useful positive psychological interventions. We begin with an overview of Social Identity Theory (SIT; Tajfel & Turner, 1986), followed by an overview of the evidence on social identification and its ties to well-being. After establishing this empirical foundation, we shift to an applied focus, using positive psychological interventions as a model for implementing practices designed to promote well-being in members of stigmatized groups via social identity. Lastly, we propose ideas and directions for future research on positive social identity interventions that facilitate well-being.

The Wiley Blackwell Handbook of Positive Psychological Interventions, First Edition.
Edited by Acacia C. Parks and Stephen M. Schueller.

The Construction of Social Identity

According to SIT, people are motivated to achieve a positive sense of self, which is composed of both personal and social identities (Tajfel & Turner, 1979). Personal identities are attributes that define individuals as unique from others (personality traits, talents, strengths, and physical characteristics), while social identities derive from memberships in social groups (e.g., gender, nationality, occupation). For social identities, the social context helps determine which aspects of the self are relevant to regulating one's own behavior in line with group expectations (Turner, Oakes, Haslam, & McGarty, 1994). Therefore, depending on the social context, individuals will often use their group memberships strategically to maintain or enhance self-worth by distinguishing how their own *ingroups* compare positively to *outgroups*, or groups to which they do not belong (Tajfel & Turner, 1986). This might involve highlighting one's deafness as a protective advantage over hearing individuals when working in a construction zone.

Regardless if memberships are ascribed from birth (e.g., gender) or achieved over time (e.g., occupation), social identification depends on the extent to which the individual *self*-categorizes and accepts these group memberships as self-defining (Deaux, 1992; Turner et al., 1987). For example, one may inherit a family-based cultural or religious identity but may not accept this identity as part of one's self-concept. Leach and colleagues (2008) proposed that social identification is composed of two dimensions: one's feelings toward and membership in a group (i.e., group-level self-investment), and one's beliefs about the group and its members, including the self (i.e., group-level self-definition).

For members of stigmatized groups (e.g., ethnic or sexual minority, physically or mentally disabled, etc.), feelings and beliefs about one's group memberships are complicated by pervasive societal devaluation, which one may or may not have internalized as applicable to one's self (Camp, Finlay, & Lyons, 2002). Importantly, an individual's response to stigma depends on how one's disadvantaged status is appraised, and the attributions made to explain one's particular circumstances (Branscombe, Schmitt, & Harvey, 1999). Stigmatized persons are also motivated to maintain positive self-regard, but may do so by embracing their stigmatized memberships rather than eschewing or disavowing these socially devalued groups (Crocker & Major, 1989). For example, an individual may feel ashamed of their association with a group and believe the group inferior to others, or may feel pride and believe the group to be worthy of equal rights.

In addition to evaluative appraisals about group status, social identification also depends on factors related to stigma temporality, visibility, and the perceived permeability of intergroup boundaries. Individuals who do not expect to be discriminated against in the near future (e.g., young people; Garstka, Schmitt, Branscombe, & Hummert, 2004), or who appraise their stigmatized circumstances to be temporary (e.g., broken leg), impermanent (e.g., gender status prior to transitional surgery), or relatively easy to escape (e.g., removal of body piercings), tend not to identify with the social group (Branscombe & Ellemers, 1998; Jetten, Branscombe, Schmitt, & Spears, 2001). When stigmas are less visible, individuals can also deny or minimize their association to certain groups, especially if they view the stigmatized status of the group as legitimate and deserved, or have internalized hegemonic cultural standards (e.g., homosexuality is immoral) (McVittie, Goodall, & McKinlay, 2008).

Finally, social identification is context-specific and depends on which aspects of the self-concept are made salient within different interaction contexts (Turner et al., 1987). For example, being the only female or minority in the room may occasion a readiness to identify with a particular social group, but only if that social group has been accepted as part of one's self-definition. However, to the extent that individuals define themselves in group-membership terms, they typically regulate their attitudes and behavior in line with group-defining characteristics and are more likely to internalize group beliefs (Tarrant & Butler, 2011; White, Hogg, & Terry, 2002). For example, a group norm for gay men prescribes a slim, muscular body (Yelland & Tiggemann, 2003). Thus, gay men who strongly identify with that group might be more likely to possess a gym membership than gay men who minimize the significance of their sexual identity. Some have argued that those who strongly identify with their groups may even self-stereotype (e.g., African American men might view themselves as athletic and thus play more sports) as a way to signal their commitment to and representation of the group (Latrofoa, Vaes, Pastore, & Cadinu, 2009), and this may also help perpetuate group stereotypes (Pickett, Bonner, & Coleman, 2002).

Evidence for Group Identification as a Predictor of Health and Well-Being

Given the often self-protective nature of identity-affirming behaviors such as self-stereotyping, much research has focused on social identity implications for individuals' well-being and the contingencies surrounding this process. Several studies demonstrate that social identification predicts mental (e.g., life satisfaction, personal and collective self-esteem) and physical (e.g., immune system function and physical recovery) well-being (Branscombe et al., 1999; Cohen, 2004; Sani, Magrin, Scrignaro, & McCollum, 2010). For example, higher identification with family as a group is associated with more self-reported happiness, psychological well-being, and general health, and less anxiety, depression, loneliness, and stress (Sani, Herrera, & Bowe, 2009). However, for stigmatized groups, membership can also threaten self-esteem, especially when the group confronts pervasive discrimination, negative stereotypes, and prejudice (e.g., Branscombe et al., 1999). Research consistently shows that the stress and marginalization associated with real and perceived discrimination can undermine psychological well-being (Armenta & Hunt, 2009; Herek, Gillis, & Cogan, 2009; Schmitt, Branscombe, Kobrynowicz, & Owen, 2002).

Although the negative consequences of experiencing stigma have been well documented, many members of stigmatized groups still report increased well-being from identifying with those groups. For example, Fernández and colleagues recently found that quality of life was higher among those with dwarfism who positively identified as "little people" (Fernández, Branscombe, Gómez, & Morales, 2012). Similarly, studies focusing on specific stigmas, including race (Mossakowski, 2003), sexual orientation (Luhtanen, 2003), disability (Nario-Redmond, Noel, & Fern, 2012), acquired brain injury (Jones et al., 2011), old age (Garstka et al., 2004), and mental illness (Corrigan & Watson, 2002), have all shown social identification as a predictor of psychological well-being. In some cases, this relationship is mediated in part by the social support that groups provide to their members (Haslam, O'Brien, Jetten, Vormedal, & Penna, 2005). In fact the use of social networks and other effective coping strategies may be the main reason research has failed to find consistent differences in well-being between members of stigmatized and non-stigmatized groups (Crabtree, Haslam, Postmes, & Haslam, 2010; Crocker, Major, & Steele, 1998). Indeed, individuals' attempts to cope with devaluation, and the effectiveness and applicability of coping strategies, depend in part on the extent to which individuals identify themselves as *belonging* to a socially disadvantaged group (Crabtree et al., 2010; Nario-Redmond et al., 2012; Outten, Schmitt, Garcia, & Branscombe, 2009). That is, strongly identified group members tend to use different strategies to combat stigma compared to those less identified with the group. For instance, strongly identified group members might employ socially creative strategies that reappraise stigmatized traits as desirable (e.g., black is beautiful, fat acceptance), or reclaim terms of disparagement as signifiers of group pride (e.g., queer power).

Social identification can also confer a protective effect through collective action efforts that advocate for equal rights to improve the status of the group (Jackson, Sullivan, Harnish, & Hodge, 1996; Nario-Redmond et al., 2012). In fact, those who identify strongly as members of a disadvantaged class are more likely to view their lower status as illegitimate, socially produced, and amenable to change through group advocacy and collective action (Tajfel & Turner, 1986).

Thus, self-identifying as a member of a traditionally devalued group is not necessarily a chronic detriment to individuals' sense of value, and may instead serve a self-protective function in the face of stigma and other identity threats.

Similarly, identification with one's group can also serve as a buffer to protect self-worth when confronted with negative feedback, social rejection, and discrimination. For example, if rejected for a new job, someone who self-identifies as a member of the gay community can attribute this negative outcome to the homophobia of others, and thereby avoid self-blame. Such attributional strategies allow group members to avoid negative psychological outcomes by shifting the blame to marginalization and prejudice. Attributional strategies have been shown to enhance perceptions of self-worth in several groups (for a review, see Major, Quinton, & McCoy, 2002).

Moderators of the Well-Being Benefits of Group Identification

Research has identified certain factors that modify the generally positive relationship between social identification and well-being. One important variable is the extent to which individuals disclose or conceal stigmatized identities. For example, a study involving HIV-positive men demonstrated that disclosure of sexual orientation and HIV status both correlate with improved immune responses (Strachan, Murray, Russo, & Roy-Byrne, 2007), and, in keeping with prior research, higher group identification among those with HIV also predicts greater physical and psychological well-being (Molero, Fuster, Jetten, & Moriano, 2011). Furthermore, concealment of HIV status predicts more rapid disease progression and vulnerability to infection (Cole, Kemeny, Taylor, Visscher, & Fahey, 1996). Indeed, members of stigmatized groups who conceal their group identity experience increased depression and/or lower quality of life. This is the case among gay men and lesbian women (Beals, Peplau, & Gable, 2009), mental health clients (Corrigan et al., 2010), people with disabilities (Fitzgerald & Patterson, 1995), and ethnic minorities (Mossakowski, 2003). In short, group membership predicts well-being for individuals willing to disclose or acknowledge these memberships. Even if disclosure is irrelevant to interpersonal goals, the deliberate concealment and denial associated with self-stigma can undermine individual perceptions of self-authenticity and community support (Gill, 1997; Sani et al., 2010).

In sum, much evidence from the social psychological literature confirms that even when confronted with significant threats to identity due to pervasive discrimination and social stigma, social identification has positive implications for well-being across sexual and ethnic minorities, physical and cognitive disability, and many other stigmatized groups. That is, people who are positively identified as group members demonstrate strong feelings of self-worth and overall psychological well-being (for a review, see Major & O'Brien, 2005). Moreover, the disclosure of group identities predicts the strength of identification, which in turn may instigate collective coping strategies, including stigma reappraisal, attributions to discrimination, and direct political actions promoting social justice for the group overall (Nario-Redmond et al., 2012). These strategies, which are more likely among highly identified group members, also contribute uniquely to identity enhancement and improved well-being. Using the above body of literature as a foundation, the following sections outline several interventions designed to use group identity as a means of promoting enhanced well-being and feelings of self-worth.

Positive Social Identity Interventions

Similar to positive psychology's use of research on happiness and its various predictors to inform positive psychological interventions, social identity research could be used to construct interventions designed to promote well-being based on reliable findings from the social identity literature (e.g., lesbian women might consider how the lesbian, gay, and bisexual [LGB] community or group-related qualities have improved their lives by contemplating how they have thrived not *in spite of* but *because of* their sexuality). Although the social identity approach to bolstering well-being has not been widely tested in many applied contexts (see Haslam et al., 2009), several measures of social identity, degree of identification, identity disclosure, and continuity of identity have been published elsewhere (Leach et al., 2008; Nario-Redmond, Biernat, Eidelman, & Palenske, 2004) and could be used in pre–post intervention research to assess the impact of social identification on well-being and the impact of interventions on the development and well-being consequences of new social identities. For example, Leach and colleagues' (2008) model of social identification measures centrality of group identification with items such as, "I often think about the fact that I am [group]," and "The fact that I am [group] is an important part of my identity." Some of these measures, along with short-form versions of validated health, mood, and well-being scales (e.g., social support, burnout, traumatic experiences, life satisfaction, happiness), appear in Jetten, Haslam, and Haslam's (2012) edited volume, the *The social cure: Identity, health and well-being*, including recommendations and a methodology for assessing key aspects of identity and well-being, and thus the positive potential for social identity interventions. As a first step, Haslam and colleagues (2009) suggest surveying clients' existing group memberships and prospects for maintaining and cultivating future self-categorizations by focusing on the meanings ascribed to each along with their personal significance.

Of the factors involved in assessment, the potential for acceptance of a group membership as self-defining may be among the most critical. This may or may not require public or direct disclosure of one's group membership status to others, although, as discussed above, disclosure has been associated with personal affirmation and quality of life (Corrigan et al., 2010). Initially, identification as a member of a particular group may reflect a more personal recognition of some categorization as part of one's *emerging* or *possible* self-definitions. Nonetheless, social identity interventions may necessitate consideration of a client's readiness to accept certain groups as self-defining and the salience of alternative identities (i.e., social context), which can be manipulated in both subtle and deliberate ways.[1]

After establishing this background via self- or clinician-guided assessment of one's existing and potential group identifications and their applicability for interventional purposes, one may begin to consider specific strategies to capitalize upon the benefits of particular social identifications. We divide the discussion of proposed intervention methods into three broad categories: social self-definition/redefinition interventions, social identity affirmation interventions, and collective action interventions. The first seeks to establish a foundation for interventions by identifying or encouraging new social identifications that may confer positive outcomes and promote well-being. The latter two focus on interventions capitalizing on existing group memberships to promote well-being through a range of methods, including cognitive reframing of the interpretations ascribed to various groups, and behavioral plans that emphasize the strengths associated with memberships and activities that involve connecting with the larger community.

Social self-definition/redefinition interventions

By identifying or encouraging clients to consider various social categorizations that are at least potentially self-inclusive, practitioners can develop an inventory of group memberships to springboard a discussion of the significance and meanings each client associates with different social groups. Depending on therapeutic goals, one intervention technique might involve facilitating the consideration of new identities by having clients imagine themselves as members of groups to which they might belong (e.g., consumer, patient-advocate, survivor) but have yet to internalize or accept as self-defining. This approach draws on perspective-taking interventions shown to induce empathy and change attitudes toward stigmatized groups and their members (Batson, Chang, Orr, & Rowland, 2002). Such interventions may encourage shifts in self-perception that simultaneously reduce "readiness" to align oneself with groups associated with detrimental behaviors (e.g., partiers), while facilitating identification with groups defined by more empowering norms or health-promoting behaviors (e.g., activists, athletes) (Clucas & St. Claire, 2010; Terry & Hogg, 1996). For example, some individuals with acquired brain injury (ABI) reported improved quality of life and post-traumatic growth following severe head injuries (McGrath & Linley, 2006; Wood, 2008), which was critically related to a process of empowerment through self-redefinition (e.g., transformed survivor as opposed to helpless victim) and identity change. Specifically, Jones et al. (2011) found that the strength of one's identification as an ABI survivor was the single best predictor of life satisfaction, followed by the number of positive relationships with others formed post-injury; and both of these variables fully mediated the relationship between injury severity and life satisfaction. Furthermore, the strength of one's survivor identity was positively correlated with the number of positive relationships formed post-injury. Thus the more positive connections one has with fellow ingroup members, the more strongly one should identify with the group.

Interventions involving the active pursuit of new identities may also counter the negative effects associated with the loss of past identities by providing new avenues of social support, belonging, and purpose (Haslam et al., 2009). For instance, following retirement, one might avoid the detrimental effects of losing one's sense of self as provider by constructing new social identities – such as mentor or community volunteer – that can promote self-efficacy. Interventions that initiate or support client interest in reconnecting with former identity categories (or increasing involvement in current but less active identity groups) can also provide continuity between past and present social identity classifications. To illustrate the latter, Haslam and colleagues (2008) found that those who maintained important group memberships following a stroke reported higher life satisfaction. Interventions that help clients to create new identities can also be beneficial by providing individuals with multiple identity resources to draw from in times of need. Indeed, multiple social identities may help buffer individuals from the challenges of major life transitions and health disruptions (Haslam et al., 2010; Iyer, Jetten, Tsivrikos, Haslam, & Postmes, 2009; Putnam, 2000).

Practitioners may be instrumental in helping clients reconsider the potential benefits of connecting with traditionally stigmatized groups (e.g., survivor groups, disability advocacy organizations, or LGB alliances). These benefits include increased contact with fellow group members who are intimately familiar with the experiences and specific challenges they confront as targets of stigma, and who can provide important feedback disrupting overgeneralized assumptions about the group (Camp et al., 2002). However, to instantiate or germinate a new identity category requires a relevant basis for self-identification. That is, one cannot spontaneously establish and draw well-being from new group memberships, as social identification is contingent upon a meaningful acceptance of the group as part of the self. Practitioners, therefore, must consider aspects of the client's self that can be cultivated and encouraged through identification (Haslam et al., 2009). After establishing a meaningful basis for social identification, individuals can begin to explore methods that draw upon and affirm their group memberships as sources of well-being, through behavior demonstrations and active involvement with these groups, for example. The following two sections illustrate some intervention ideas through which specific health-enhancing benefits can be derived by affirming affiliations with specific group memberships and by enacting group-relevant behaviors.

Social identity affirmation interventions

One identity-oriented method of bolstering well-being involves leveraging the positive aspects of one's existing group memberships through cognitive affirmation strategies and behavioral techniques that exemplify and reinforce those positive aspects. For instance, in keeping with traditional practices within positive psychology (see Seligman, Parks, & Steen, 2004), emphasizing ingroup strengths and engaging in activities that use group-relevant strengths can enhance well-being. Thus, it may be beneficial to identify and cultivate those positive traits that derive from (or are accredited to) a particular social identity. For example, those who self-identify as LGB can draw on an elaborate ingroup schema inclusive of both positive stereotypic exemplars (e.g., proud, fashionable) and various subtypes (e.g., activist, artist) from which to select depending on one's goals and the situational context. Similarly, within the transgender community, cross-dressing can serve as a behavioral expression of group identity that predicts fewer depressive symptoms and a sense of well-being (Blanchard & Steiner, 1985). The ability to view the meaning of one's sexual identity as dynamic opens new avenues for deriving self-efficacy, empowering beliefs about one's ability to effectively combat stigma. Cognitively, this might involve reframing one's experiences with anti-gay stigma as an opportunity for growth. For example, growing up LGB might foster a sense of compassion for others, or resilience in the face of adversity, or having prevailed in spite of societal devaluation (Shih, 2004), thus emerging as an even stronger individual.

Toward this end, LGB members could cultivate a sense of gratitude for the ways in which their sexual identity has been a boon to their overall development (Riggle & Rostosky, 2012). Once an individual has identified some of the specific strengths they have developed from group memberships, he/she can engage in activities designed to tap into these strengths. For instance, LGB members who experienced teasing about their sexuality during childhood might volunteer for an anti-bullying hotline, allowing them to share their strategic perspectives with others who might not have considered externalizing interpretations (e.g., "We are fine; it is the bullies who are prejudiced against us"). In this context, drawing upon one's group-relevant experience facilitates the role of "mentor" and could be considered an identity-related strength.

Engaging in meaningful activities that might not be possible or effective without one's LGB identity accomplishes two primary goals. First, it makes the positive aspects of having gone through life as LGB more salient, which could generate a greater appreciation for one's LGB status or further affirm its positive aspects (e.g., being sensitive and empathetic to the plight of other stigmatized youth). Second, it makes these strengths concrete and manifested as goal-directed behaviors. For example, embracing the gay stereotype associated with physical fitness and a lean physique could promote new practices around healthy eating and exercise.

Collective action interventions

Social identification can also instigate the seeking and provision of actual social support from ingroups as repositories of material and instrumental resources ranging from information and companionship to general acceptance and validation of experiences (Wills, 1991). Indeed, merely being part of a larger community of individuals whose shared experiences legitimize one's worldview is an invaluable source of social support and belongingness. The collective action approach goes further however, to leverage social identity into action on behalf of the group as a means of affirming and enhancing identity (Tajfel & Turner, 1986). For example, a sense of social identification may impel individuals with an obligation to enact their identities, thereby demonstrating their commitment to the group, through fundraising or other collective actions aimed at confronting social injustice through awareness campaigns, public protests, or even pride parades. Even symbolic manifestations of group identity (e.g., bumper stickers, badges) can substitute for behavioral expressions as a means of performing identity, particularly if newly accepted, uncertain, or aspirational (Simon, Trötschel, & Dähne, 2008).

Therefore, while social identification often functions as an antecedent to collective action for those participating in a variety of social movements, ranging from fat acceptance to the rights of women, LGB, and disabled people (Baron-Cohen & Klin, 2006; Little, 2010; Simon, 2004), social identification can also be strengthened as a consequence of social movement participation. That is, there is a reciprocal relationship between participation in collective action efforts and the reinvention of self that may further contribute to social identity affirmation and the use of social supports. Collective action strategies directly engage fellow group members as sources of support for one another and as vehicles for collective agency and social change on behalf of the group. This might also include seeking comfort from members of the LGB community after being the target of an anti-gay crime, or banding together to advocate for gay rights and the freedom to marry. The mere presence of other ingroup members may provide a sense of collective agency, which both fosters and enhances beliefs about effectively coping with stigma through shared goals and experiences.

In describing the deployment of social identity as an avenue for the improvement of well-being, Jetten and colleagues' (2012) model of social identity risk emphasizes the importance of an available community with goals that are accessible to individuals (e.g., an LGB center). Assuming a local or online community exists or could be created, group-sponsored activities serve to reinforce one's sense of belonging to a cohesive entity while encouraging the development of new relationships. Thus practitioners can encourage clients to find meaningful engagement by joining a local LGB center, or fat acceptance or disability rights event. Each of these examples allows members of stigmatized communities to surround themselves with similar others while working toward common goals that reinforce core values of the group.

Discussion and Future Directions

This chapter provides an introductory glimpse of possible positive social identity interventions geared toward members of stigmatized groups, and how these practices could improve well-being. We have argued that self-identified members of stigmatized groups might uniquely benefit from their group memberships by emphasizing collective self-definition and identity affirmation strategies. These strategies include cognitive approaches (i.e., imagining of alternative identities and their associated strengths), and behavioral approaches (i.e., enacting collective identities as communal supports and change agents to improve individual well-being and the overall status of the group). The social identity approach postulates that the acceptance of group identities and the use of associated coping strategies are effective means of enhancing self-worth among people who identify with stigmatized groups. As we have proposed in this chapter, this line of research and its findings regarding well-being among members of stigmatized groups require further empirical testing in applied settings using intervention methodology similar to how the study of positive psychology has been applied to positive psychological interventions. Although these suggested techniques can inform practice, more data are necessary to support their long-term efficacy at improving self-worth, and to identify the techniques that contribute most to well-being.

Researchers must transcend speculation and begin developing interventions grounded in the SIT literature such as those proposed in this chapter. The applied research with vulnerable populations that is beginning to emerge should facilitate studies that extend social identity research to practical positive psychological interventions. Future research needs to move beyond simply measuring whether people belong to and interact with a certain number of groups, to investigate the meanings people ascribe to the groups to which they belong, how important these groups are to self-definition, how group norms and values intersect with individual goals, and the impact of member status or typicality for specific health outcomes. For example, newer members of an addiction recovery group or those who identify less strongly as "sober" may be perceived as having less credibility in terms of maintaining sobriety but may also be more open to program alternatives compared to those who have adopted the group's core values or made more public commitments to conform to group-endorsed abstinence norms.

Practitioners might also consider uncovering new, adaptive social identity aspirations in line with therapeutic goals or self-determination objectives. In addition, more research is needed to discover the key mediating variables involved in producing social identity change, and the relative contributions of positive mood, perceived or actual social support, and the internalization or resistance of group norms to well-being outcomes (Crabtree et al., 2010; Terry & Hogg, 1996). Intervention strategies designed to promote identification with specific group-level treatments or organizations (e.g., addiction recovery or cancer survivors) could also compare the independent and interactive effects of social identification and other positive psychological interventions (e.g., signature strengths, gratitude, savoring, optimism) designed with particular populations in mind.

In addition to its potential applications within a client–practitioner framework, positive social identity interventions might be feasible in more accessible or less formalized modalities, such as self-help approaches. For some stigmatized populations, this might even be a benefit, because individuals with invisible stigmas (e.g., LGB) may initially be less willing to disclose their sexual identity, even to a professional. Self-administered mode of delivery would be more financially accessible than regular sessions with a clinician. For those with more visible or detectable stigmas (ABI, stroke, sensory or physical disability, weight or gender identity), the identity work of considering one's belonging to and acceptance of certain identity categories, previously avoided, may be facilitated by perspective taking and contact with those who have already embraced the group as a positive aspect of self (Jones et al., 2011).

While the psychological benefits of identification with stigmatized social groups have been well documented, it is also worth considering potential negative consequences of group identification and thus social identity interventions. As others have noted, more research is needed on the potential disadvantages or unintended consequences associated with group separatism from the mainstream: backlash, onerous obligations, and mindless compliance (see Crabtree et al., 2010; Crisp, Stone, & Hall, 2006). Furthermore, some group memberships may not only be unhelpful, but actually harmful (e.g., fraternity or dieting clubs promoting unhealthy risk-taking). Indeed, some group memberships have been shown to impact the perception of illness and symptoms (St. Claire & He, 2009), reactions to stress, adjustment to trauma, and health-related decision-making (Berkman & Syme, 1979). In addition, adopting group norms and expectations may not always promote healthy behaviors, as some norms may emphasize unrealistic standards (e.g., weight; Lindly, Nario-Redmond, & Noel, 2013; body image; Tiggemann, Martins, & Kirkbride, 2007; Yelland & Tiggemann, 2003). For example, gay men have been found to be at higher risk for body dissatisfaction and dysmorphia (Beren, Hayden, Wilfley, & Grilo, 1996), which may be related to the extent they have internalized the gay-male stereotype as part of their self-definition (Ball & Nario-Redmond, 2013).

Conclusion

Drawing on the vast literature documenting the positive effects of social identification, this chapter provides some preliminary suggestions from which positive social identity interventions can be initiated. The relative absence of interventions grounded in SIT necessitates their development with attention to the existing literature for theoretical rationale and a focus on validating these interventions. Much work needs to be done before this goal can be realized, however. Next steps include not only empirically evaluating the effects of various intervention strategies, but also investigating their interactions with specific groups. Strategies that work for LGB community members may not necessarily work for individuals within the disability community due to each group's distinct experiences. Therefore we must proceed with caution and an appreciation for the unique elements and history surrounding different social groups. Failure to do so may lead to interventions causing more harm than good.

It should also be noted that while we have chosen to focus on stigmatized group memberships, social identities are beneficial even in cases without stigma. Indeed, a shared group identity among members of a bowling league may have similar benefits to its constituents to a shared group identity in a sobriety group. The common thread that promotes well-being across various groups stems from the collective experience and beneficial coping strategies resulting from group membership. That is, social identification promotes well-being to the extent the group provides a meaningful basis for shared self-representation among constituents. In addition to promoting well-being, this approach may have the advantage of being accessible to a wider population than traditional therapeutic interventions, by virtue of it being less cost-prohibitive and possessing viability within a self-help framework. Many positive psychological interventions share the benefits associated with improved well-being, but a social identity approach capitalizes on the taken-for-granted group-based aspects of self-definition that are critical to the adoption of group-relevant behaviors and beliefs. Echoing the importance of looking beyond the self for sources of empowerment, Seligman and colleagues remind, "Although the pursuit of gratifications involves deploying our strengths ... happiness comes from using these strengths to belong to and in the service of something larger than ourselves" (Seligman, Parks, & Steen, 2004, p. 1380). The untapped potential of social identities to promote wellness through interventions represents a new frontier for research, one that has only begun to be explored.

Note

1 Experimental manipulations have tested bogus pipeline techniques (Ellemers, Spears, & Doosje, 1997) and open-ended formats to induce temporary or hypothetical group memberships where participants are asked to describe how they differ from typical ingroup (low identification) or outgroup members (high identification), confirming the effectiveness of these approaches (Simon, Trötschel, & Dähne, 2008).

References

Armenta, B. E., & Hunt, J. S. (2009). Responding to societal devaluation: Effects of perceived personal and group discrimination on the group identification and self-esteem of Latinos/as. *Group Processes and Intergroup Relations*, *12*, 23–39.

Ball, T. C., & Nario-Redmond, M. R. (2013). Gay identity and body satisfaction: The mediating effects of self-stereotyping. Manuscript in preparation, Hiram College, Hiram, OH.

Baron-Cohen, S., & Klin, A. (2006). What's so special about Asperger syndrome? *Brain and Cognition*, *61*, 1–4.

Batson, C. D., Chang, J., Orr, R., & Rowland, J. (2002). Empathy, attitudes, and action: Can feeling for a member of a stigmatized group motivate one to help the group? *Personality and Social Psychology Bulletin*, *28*, 1656–1666.

Beals, K. P., Peplau, L. A., & Gable, S. L. (2009). Stigma management and well-being: The role of perceived social support, emotional processing, and suppression. *Personality and Social Psychology Bulletin*, *35*, 867–879.

Beren, S. E., Hayden, H. A., Wilfley, D. E., & Grilo, C. M. (1996). The influence of sexual orientation on body dissatisfaction in adult men and women. *International Journal of Eating Disorders*, *20*, 135–141.

Berkman, L. F., & Syme, L. (1979). Social networks, host resistance, and mortality: A nine-year follow-up study of Alameda County residents. *American Journal of Epidemiology*, *109*, 186–204.

Blanchard, R., & Steiner, B. (1985) Gender reorientation, psychological adjustment, and involvement with female partners in female-to-male transsexuals. *Archives of Sexual Behavior*, *112*, 149–157.

Branscombe, N. R., & Ellemers, N. (1998). Coping with group-based discrimination: Individualistic versus group-level strategies. In J. K. Swim & C. Stangor (Eds.), *Prejudice: The target's perspective* (pp. 243–266). New York: Academic Press.

Branscombe, N. R., Schmitt, M. T., & Harvey, R. D. (1999). Perceiving pervasive discrimination among African Americans: Implications for group identification and well-being. *Journal of Personality and Social Psychology*, *77*, 135–149.

Camp, D. L., Finlay, W. M. L., & Lyons, E. (2002). Is low self-esteem an inevitable consequence of stigma? An example from women with chronic mental health problems. *Social Science and Medicine*, *55*, 823–834.

Clucas, C., & St. Claire, L. (2010). The effect of the patient role and feeling respected on patient health-related outcomes. *Applied Psychology: Health and Well-Being*, *2*, 298–322.

Cohen, S. (2004). Social relationships and health. *American Psychologist*, *59*, 676–684.

Cole, S. W., Kemeny, M. E., Taylor, S. E., Visscher, B. R., & Fahey, J. L. (1996). Accelerated course of human immunodeficiency virus infection in gay men who conceal their homosexual identity. *Psychosomatic Medicine*, *58*, 219–231.

Corrigan, P. W., Morris, S., Larson, J. E., Rafacz, J., Wassel, A., Michaels, P., Wilkniss, S., Batia, K., & Rüsch, N. (2010). Self-stigma and coming out about one's mental illness. *Journal of Community Psychology*, *38*, 1–17.

Corrigan, P. W., & Watson, A. C. (2002). The paradox of self-stigma and mental illness. *Clinical Psychology: Science and Practice*, *9*, 35–53.

Crabtree, J. W., Haslam, S. A., Postmes, T., & Haslam, C. (2010). Mental health support groups, stigma, and self-esteem: Positive and negative implications of group identification. *Journal of Social Issues*, *66*, 553–569.

Crisp, R. J., Stone, C. H., & Hall, N. R. (2006). Recategorization and subgroup identification: Predicting and preventing threats from common ingroups. *Personality and Social Psychology Bulletin*, *32*, 230–243.

Crocker, J., & Major, B. (1989). Social stigma and self-esteem: The self-protective properties of stigma. *Psychological Review*, *96*, 608–630.

Crocker, J., Major, B., & Steele, C. (1998). Social stigma. In D. Gilbert, S. T. Fiske, & G. Lindzey (Eds.), *The handbook of social psychology* (pp. 504–553). Boston, MA: McGraw-Hill.

Deaux, K. (1992). Personalizing identity and socializing self. In G. Breakwell (Ed.), *Social psychology of identity and the self-concept* (pp. 9–33). London: Academic Press.

Ellemers, N., Spears, R., & Doosje, B. (1997). Sticking together or falling apart: Ingroup identification as a psychological determinant of group commitment versus individual mobility. *Journal of Personality and Social Psychology*, *72*, 617–626.

Fernández, S., Branscombe, N. R., Gómez, Á., & Morales, J. F. (2012). Influence of the social context on use of surgical-lengthening and group-empowering coping strategies among people with dwarfism. *Rehabilitation Psychology*, *57*, 224–235.

Fitzgerald, M. H., & Patterson, K. A. (1995). The hidden disability dilemma for the preservation of self. *Journal of Occupational Science*, *2*, 13–21.

Garstka, T. A., Schmitt, M. T., Branscombe, N. R., & Hummert, M. L. (2004). How young and older adults differ in their responses to perceived age discrimination. *Psychology and Aging*, *19*, 326–335.

Gill, C. J. (1997). Four types of integration in disability identity development. *Journal of Vocational Rehabilitation*, *9*, 39–46.

Haslam, C., Haslam, S. A., Jetten, J., Bevins, A., Ravenscroft, S., & Tonks, J. (2010). The social treatment: The benefits of group interventions in residential care settings. *Psychology and Aging*, *25*, 157–167.

Haslam, C., Holme, A., Haslam, S. A., Iyer, A., Jetten, J., & Williams, W. H. (2008). Maintaining group memberships: Social identity predicts well-being after stroke. *Neuropsychological Rehabilitation*, *18*, 671–691.

Haslam, S. A., Jetten, J., Postmes, T., & Haslam, C. (2009). Social identity, health and well-being: An emerging agenda for applied psychology. *Applied Psychology: An International Review*, *58*, 1–23.

Haslam, S. A., O'Brien, A., Jetten, J., Vormedal, K., & Penna, S. (2005). Taking the strain: Social identity, social support and the experience of stress. *British Journal of Social Psychology*, *44*, 355–370.

Herek, G. M., Gillis, J. R., & Cogan, J. C. (2009). Internalized stigma among sexual minority adults: Insights from a social psychological perspective. *Journal of Counseling Psychology*, *56*, 32–43.

Iyer, A., Jetten, J., Tsivrikos, D., Haslam, S. A., & Postmes, T. (2009). The more (and the more compatible) the merrier: Multiple group memberships and identity compatibility as predictors of adjustment after life transitions. *British Journal of Social Psychology*, *48*, 707–733.

Jackson, L. A., Sullivan, L. A., Harnish, R., & Hodge, C. (1996). Achieving positive social identity: Social mobility, social creativity, and permeability of group boundaries. *Journal of Personality and Social Psychology*, *70*, 241–254.

Jetten, J., Branscombe, N. R., Schmitt, M. T., & Spears, R. (2001). Rebels with a cause: Group identification as a response to perceived discrimination from the mainstream. *Personality and Social Psychology Bulletin*, *27*, 1204–1213.

Jetten, J., Haslam, C., & Haslam, S. A. (2012). *The social cure: Identity, health and well-being*. New York: Psychology Press.

Jones, J. M., Haslam, S. A., Jetten, J., Williams, W. H., Morris, R., & Saroyan, S. (2011). That which does not kill you can make you stronger (and more satisfied with life): The contribution of personal and social changes to well-being after brain injury. *Psychology and Health*, *26*, 353–369.

Latrofoa, M., Vaes, J., Pastore, M., & Cadinu, M. (2009). "United we stand, divided we fall"! The protective function of self-stereotyping for stigmatized members' psychological well-being. *Applied Psychology: An International Review*, *58*, 84–104.

Leach, C. W., Zomeren, M. V., Zebel, S., Vliek, M. L. W., Ouerkerk, J. W., & Spears, R. (2008). Group-level self-definition and self-investment: A hierarchical (multicomponent) model of in-group identification. *Journal of Personality and Social Psychology*, *95*, 144–165.

Lindly, O., Nario-Redmond, M. R., & Noel, J. G. (2013). Creatively re-defining fat: Identification predicts strategic responses to stigma, ingroup attitudes and well-being. Manuscript in preparation, Hiram College, Hiram, OH.

Little, D. (2010). Identity, efficacy, and disability rights movement recruitment. *Disability Studies Quarterly*, *30*. Retrieved from http://www.dsq-sds.org/article/view/1013/1226

Luhtanen, R. K. (2003). Identity, stigma management and well-being: A comparison of lesbians/bisexual women and gay/bisexual men. *Journal of Lesbian Studies*, *7*, 85–100.

Major, B. N., & O'Brien, L. T. (2005). The social psychology of stigma. *Annual Review of Psychology*, *56*, 393–421.

Major, B., Quinton, W. J., & McCoy, S. K. (2002). Antecedents and consequences of attributions to discrimination: Theoretical and empirical advances. *Advances in Experimental Social Psychology*, *34*, 251–330.

Matheson, K., & Cole, B. (2004). Coping with a threatened group identity: Psychological and neuroendocrine responses. *Journal of Experimental Social Psychology*, *40*, 777–786.

McGrath, J. C., & Linley, P. A. (2006). Post-traumatic growth in acquired brain injury. A preliminary small scale study. *Brain Injury*, *20*, 767–773.

McVittie, C., Goodall, K. E., & McKinlay, A. (2008). Resisting having learning disabilities by managing relative abilities. *British Journal of Learning Disabilities*, *36*, 256–262.

Molero, F., Fuster, M. J., Jetten, J., & Moriano, J. A. (2011). Living with HIV/AIDS: A psychosocial perspective on coping with prejudice and discrimination. *Journal of Applied Social Psychology*, *41*, 609–626.

Mossakowski, K. N. (2003). Coping with perceived discrimination: Does ethnic identity protect mental health? *Journal of Health and Social Behavior*, *44*, 318–331.

Nario-Redmond, M. R., Biernat, M., Eidelman, S., & Palenske, D. J. (2004). The social and personal identities scale: A measure of the differential importance ascribed to social and personal self-categorizations. *Self and Identity*, *3*, 143–175.

Nario-Redmond, M. R., Noel, J. G., & Fern, E. (2012). Redefining disability, re-imagining the self: Disability identification predicts self-esteem and strategic responses to stigma. *Self and Identity*, *12*, 468–488.

Outten, R. H., Schmitt, M. T., Garcia, D. M., & Branscombe, N. R. (2009). Coping options: Missing links between minority group identification and psychological well-being. *International Association of Applied Psychology*, *58*, 146–170.

Pickett, C. L., Bonner, B. L., & Coleman, J. M. (2002). Motivated self-stereotyping: Heightened assimilation and differentiation needs result in increased levels of positive and negative self-stereotyping. *Journal of Personality and Social Psychology*, *82*, 543–562.

Putnam, R. D. (2000). *Bowling alone: The collapse and revival of American community.* New York: Simon & Schuster.

Riggle, E. D. B., & Rostosky, S. S. (2012). *A positive view of LGBTQ: Embracing identity and cultivating well-being.* Lanham, MD: Rowman & Littlefield.

Sani, F., Herrera, M., & Bowe, M. (2009). Perceived collective continuity and ingroup identification as defense against death awareness. *Journal of Experimental Social Psychology*, *45*, 242–245.

Sani, F., Magrin, M. E., Scrignaro, M., & McCollum, R. (2010). Ingroup identification mediates the effects of subjective ingroup status on mental health. *British Journal of Social Psychology*, *49*, 883–893.

Schmitt, M. T., Branscombe, N. R., Kobrynowicz, D., & Owen, S. (2002). Perceiving discrimination against one's gender group has different implications for wellbeing in women and men. *Personality and Social Psychology Bulletin*, *28*, 197–210.

Seligman, M. E. P., Parks, A. C., & Steen, T. (2004). A balanced psychology and a full life. *Philosophical Transactions of the Royal Society B*, *359*, 1379–1381.

Shih, M. (2004). Positive stigma: Examining resilience and empowerment in overcoming stigma. *Annals of the American Academy of Political and Social Science*, *591*, 175–185.

Simon, B. (2004). *Identity in modern society: A social psychological perspective.* Oxford: Blackwell.

Simon, B., Trötschel, R., & Dähne, D. (2008). Identity affirmation and social movement support. *European Journal of Social Psychology*, *38*, 935–946.

St. Claire, L., & He, Y. Q. (2009). How do I know if I need a hearing aid? Further support for the self-categorization approach to symptom perception. *Applied Psychology: An International Review*, *58*, 24–41.

Strachan, E. D., Murray, W. R., Russo, J., & Roy-Byrne, P. P. (2007). Disclosure of HIV status and sexual orientation independently predicts increased absolute CD4 cell counts over time for psychiatric patients. *Psychosomatic Medicine*, *69*, 74–80.

Tajfel, H., & Turner, J. (1979). An integrative theory of intergroup conflict. In W. G. Austin & S. Worchel (Eds.), *The social psychology of intergroup relations* (pp. 33–47). Monterey, CA: Brooks/Cole.

Tajfel, H., & Turner, J. C. (1986). The social identity theory of inter-group behavior. In S. Worchel and L. W. Austin (Eds.), *Psychology of intergroup relations* (pp. 7–24). Chicago, IL: Nelson-Hall.

Tarrant, M., & Butler, K. (2011). Effects of self-categorization on intentions to perform health behaviors. *British Journal of Social Psychology, 50*, 121–139.

Terry, D. J., & Hogg, M. A. (1996). Group norms and the attitude–behavior relationship: A role for group identification. *Personality and Social Psychology Bulletin, 22*, 776–793.

Tiggemann, M., Martins, Y., & Kirkbride, A. (2007). Oh to be lean and muscular: Body image ideals in gay and heterosexual men. *Psychology of Men and Masculinity, 8*, 15–24.

Turner, J. C., Hogg, M. A., Oakes, P. J., Reicher, S. D., & Wetherell, M. S. (1987). *Rediscovering the social group: A self-categorization theory*. Oxford: Blackwell.

Turner, J. C., Oakes, P. J., Haslam, S. A., & McGarty, C. (1994). Self and collective: Cognition and social context. *Personality and Social Psychology Bulletin, 20*, 454–463.

White, K. M., Hogg, M. A., & Terry, D. J. (2002). Improving attitude–behavior correspondence through exposure to normative support from a salient ingroup. *Basic and Applied Social Psychology, 24*, 91–103.

Wills, T. A. (1991). Social support and interpersonal relationships. In M. S. Clark (Ed.), *Prosocial behavior* (pp. 265–289). Newbury Park, CA: Sage.

Wood, R. Ll. (2008). Long-term outcome of serious traumatic brain injury. *European Journal of Anaesthesiology, 25*, 115–122.

Yelland, C., & Tiggemann, M. (2003). Muscularity and the gay ideal: Body dissatisfaction and disordered eating in homosexual men. *Eating Behaviors, 4*, 107–116.

19

Adapting a Positive Psychological Intervention for People with Schizophrenia

Piper S. Meyer

Researchers in the field of positive psychology have studied the conditions and processes associated with achieving greater happiness and enhanced well-being. Recently, research has focused on strategies that practitioners can use to promote positive psychological resources and well-being through intentional activities to cultivate positive feelings, behaviors, or thoughts. These approaches or treatments are referred to as positive psychological interventions (PPIs). As reported elsewhere in this volume, PPIs have shown increases in both happiness and well-being in non-clinical samples (Lyubomirsky, Dickerhoof, Boehm, & Sheldon, 2011; Ruini, Belaise, Brombin, Caffo, & Fava, 2006), but for the most part, researchers have only speculated on the role of PPIs in a clinical population (Fava & Tomba, 2009; Lyubomirsky & Della Porta, 2012; Seligman, 2011). A recent meta-analysis found that PPIs can decrease depressive symptoms (Sin, Della Porta, & Lyubomirsky, 2011), and one initial study has examined the efficacy of PPIs in the treatment of major depression (Seligman, Rashid, & Parks, 2006). Although, researchers have suggested a role for PPIs in other clinical populations such as those with anxiety disorders (Fava et al., 2005), there has been very little discussion about how these strategies could be used in the treatment of people with more severe and disabling disorders.

The following chapter examines an adaptation of a PPI for persons with schizophrenia. The chapter begins with a brief overview of the common symptoms, deficits, and obstacles that persons with schizophrenia face, followed by a description of the current state of psychosocial treatment for schizophrenia. Next, the role of psychological recovery (i.e., a process that includes multiple elements such as reductions in symptoms, life satisfaction, and the ability to function in the community, socially, and vocationally; Bellack, 2006) in treatment for schizophrenia is reviewed and discussed as a treatment target. The chapter continues with a

The Wiley Blackwell Handbook of Positive Psychological Interventions, First Edition.
Edited by Acacia C. Parks and Stephen M. Schueller.

description of the adaptation of a PPI for persons with schizophrenia. Next, results are presented from a pilot study that used the adapted materials. Lastly, the chapter ends with lessons learned and suggestions for adapting a PPI for other special populations.

Understanding Schizophrenia Symptoms, Treatment, and Recovery

Schizophrenia affects 1 to 2% of persons in the general population (Jablensky, 1997). Persons diagnosed with schizophrenia struggle with a wide array of symptoms and challenges. These symptoms can include hallucinations and delusions as well as blunted affect, anhedonia, and avolition. In addition, the disorder can have a profound impact on cognition, mood, language, behavior, and role functioning (e.g., work and social relationships).

Schizophrenia was originally labeled *dementia praecox* (or premature dementia) most notably by Emil Kraepelin in the 1890s (1971) and portrayed along with other serious mental disorders as a devastating disorder with a chronic and debilitating course of illness. Over the last several decades treatment for schizophrenia has become more advanced, focusing on decreasing the severity of symptoms and improving social and vocational functioning. There have been significant advances in the use of individual interventions including cognitive-behavioral therapy along with the rise of evidence-based practices such as Illness Management and Recovery, Supported Employment, and Assertive Community Treatment, which have led to a change in the long-term perspective on treatment for schizophrenia (Dixon et al., 2010). In fact long-term outcome studies have shown that between 40 and 70% of individuals with schizophrenia show full or partial remission of symptoms or functional impairments over their lifetime (Harding, Zubin, & Strauss, 1987; Harrison et al., 2001).

Recently, there has been a change in the concept of recovery from mental illness, brought on by the rise of the mental health consumer movement (Chamberlin, 1978; Davidson, 2009). Interventions used to treat schizophrenia, both pharmacological and psychosocial, have often defined recovery as the removal of symptoms. However, the removal of symptoms is not always associated with progress in recovery. Studies have shown that the removal of symptoms may benefit some, while many others do not experience significant improvements in well-being or functioning (Bellack, 2006; Lambert et al., 2006). Similar findings can be found in research on affective disorders (Rafanelli et al., 2000; Seligman, Rashid, & Parks, 2006). The concept of recovery has broadened the traditional definition of remission beyond the minimization of symptoms, relapses, and impairments. Instead recovery is based on a personally meaningful definition provided by the individual receiving treatment, often with a focus away from pathology and towards improved psychological and psychosocial functioning (Deegan, 1992; Madera,

1988). One often cited definition of recovery is, "Recovery involves the development of a new meaning and purpose in one's life as one grows beyond the catastrophic effects of mental illness" (Anthony, 1993, p. 21). Important themes of recovery have emerged across the different definitions and they include: hope and optimism, self-determination and self-respect, coping, and openness to discovery and new experiences (Ralph, 2000). As a consequence, individuals with schizophrenia and other mental illnesses have placed a greater emphasis on the process of recovering and changes in functional outcomes in order to experience a full and rewarding life (Meyer & Mueser, 2011).

The Role of Positive Psychological Interventions in Recovery

Despite the advances in interventions for people with schizophrenia and the increased focus on improving symptoms, studies have shown that a large percentage of individuals taking antipsychotic medications will discontinue their medications (up to 74%) (Lieberman et al., 2005). Both pharmacological and psychosocial treatments also have moderate to high non-compliance rates that range from 13 to 52% (Nose, Barbui, & Tansella, 2003; Villeneuve, Potvin, Lesage, & Nicole, 2010). In addition, even when pharmacological treatment is helpful, an equally large number of individuals (up to 60%) will experience treatment-resistant symptoms despite compliance with medications (Lindenmayer, 2000). The problems associated with current interventions for schizophrenia, along with the increased interest in developing recovery-based interventions, suggest that the field is ready to explore some alternative treatment options.

The broadened definition of recovery is aimed primarily at living a more meaningful and gratifying life. Interventions that are specifically designed to restore deficits are less likely to teach skills that directly impact finding meaning or purpose in one's life, and therefore these interventions may be less likely to improve well-being. In addition, interventions targeting well-being may also result in a longer lasting and more well-rounded recovery (Davidson, 2010). According to the broaden-and-build theory, positive emotions broaden a person's thoughts and behavioral options, and the accrual of these moments over time leads to the building of personal resources including purpose in life and social support (Fredrickson, 2001). Studies have also shown that enhancing positive emotions leads to an upward spiral of well-being (Fredrickson, Cohn, Coffey, Pek, & Finkel, 2008; Fredrickson & Joiner, 2002; Garland et al., 2010). Positive psychological interventions designed to generate more positive emotions and enhance the experience of positive emotions offer a new perspective on strategies to help persons with schizophrenia make greater progress towards recovery, and possibly lead to increases in well-being.

PPIs have traditionally focused on persons in the general population or persons with mild to moderate symptoms, but support for their effectiveness in clinical populations is growing (Sin & Lyubomirsky, 2009). Researchers are beginning to investigate the impact of positive psychological interventions on more severe affective and anxiety disorders such as major depressive disorder and post-traumatic stress disorder (Fava & Tomba, 2009). Some researchers have proposed that PPIs may be more effective in treating the residual symptoms or preventing relapse through the development of meaningful coping skills (Fava, Ruini, & Belaise, 2007; Sin et al., 2011). However, these studies suggest there are important factors that contribute to increased success in PPIs, including: positive psychology exercises that are guided by a provider, interventions that are longer in duration, interventions where persons can volunteer, participants who have a supportive social network, and interventions with a variety of exercises to choose from to increase the person–activity fit (Sin & Lyubomirsky, 2009; Sin et al., 2011).

The focus of PPIs has been on building strengths and promoting positive emotions, thoughts, and behaviors. PPIs offer a unique opportunity to promote recovery and increase well-being through the experience of selected effortful activities. As described above, the traditional interventions for schizophrenia are not designed to directly enhance well-being in this population. PPIs may facilitate the process of recovery and boost coping skills through strength building and increasing opportunities to find meaning and purpose in life. As a result, individuals may also experience better symptom management, reductions in residual symptoms, and fewer relapses.

Adapting Positive Psychotherapy for Persons with Schizophrenia

The first step in selecting which PPI could have the greatest impact on recovery and be successfully adapted for people with schizophrenia was to consider similar characteristics between evidence-based practices in this population and current PPIs. Evidence-based interventions for schizophrenia have focused on teaching skills to remediate social and cognitive deficits, and enhance coping and relapse prevention strategies, and educating persons about the symptoms and medications associated with mental illness. Important therapeutic elements in evidence-based psychotherapy for people with schizophrenia include working toward personal goals, providing structure within the session, and developing a rapport and therapeutic alliance (Dickerson & Lehman, 2006). The focus of PPIs has been to develop activities that increase positive emotions and attributes. Two of the current PPIs include Positive Psychotherapy (PPT) (Seligman et al., 2006), in which people learn multiple positive psychology exercises to increase positive emotions, and Well-Being Therapy (WBT; Fava & Ruini, 2003), which uses cognitive restructuring techniques to reinforce beliefs that promote well-being.

Positive Psychotherapy (PPT), developed by Parks and Seligman (2007), has several elements in common with interventions designed for people with schizophrenia. First, the exercises are behaviorally based and can be easily broken down into smaller steps. Second, the exercises in PPT can be demonstrated in session. Both of these strategies are used in social skills-training interventions with people with schizophrenia, where specific social skills are broken down into small steps with instructions and then the skill is demonstrated and practiced in session (Bellack, 2004). Third, the intervention offers a variety of exercises that the participants can try out during the intervention and then discuss options to individualize and incorporate them into their daily lives. One important element of the recovery movement has been the ability to provide individualized treatment and create and respect choice in treatment (Davidson et al., 2007; Dickerson & Lehman, 2006). Fourth, the treatment uses a sequence and structure in the therapy sessions. These four elements suggest that PPT could be a good fit for people with schizophrenia.

WBT is based on cognitive-behavioral therapy and Ryff's model of psychological well-being (Ryff, 1989). WBT uses structured sessions in a sequence that teach the cognitive model and focus on improving coping skills. In addition, WBT uses cognitive restructuring techniques that are similar to those used in cognitive-behavioral treatments for psychosis (Tai & Turkington, 2009). However, WBT emphasizes both understanding areas of distress and symptoms as well as monitoring periods of well-being (Fava, 1999). Since the aim of piloting a PPI in this population was to help persons make progress towards recovery with less of an emphasis on symptoms and areas of distress, PPT was a better fit to meet this goal.

The original PPT intervention as described by Seligman et al. (2006) included six behavioral exercises (Using Your Strengths, Three Good Things, Biography, Gratitude Visit, Active-Constructive Responding, and Savoring). Each session lasted for 1.5 hours weekly for eight weeks. In the revised manual, Parks and Seligman (2007) added an additional exercise (Positive Service) for participants to use one of their strengths in service of something larger than themselves. The original implementation of PPT included a group intervention and an individual intervention. We decided to implement PPT in the group format, which is similar to successful implementations of social skills training and Illness Management and Recovery, another evidence-based intervention focused on skills and recovery (Bellack, 2004; Meyer, Gingerich, & Mueser, 2010). When we adapted the PPT intervention for a pilot study, we conducted two groups that were recruited from local outpatient clinics in central North Carolina. The methods and outcome measures are described in greater detail in Meyer, Johnson, Parks, Iwanski, and Penn (2012). I will briefly describe our findings from this pilot study below.

Before implementing PPT with this population we made a few additional modifications to the manual – which we called "Positive Living" – to address common cognitive impairments associated with schizophrenia and to enhance the connection with recovery. These changes included extending the length of the intervention and the addition of three elements to aid in teaching and reinforcing the skills (positive goal, mindfulness minute, and worksheets for each exercise). We extended the number of sessions from 8 to 10. The first additional session was added to the strength exercise. Participants filled out a brief version of the VIA (Values in Action) strengths inventory during the session, rather than taking the computerized version at home. Many of our participants do not have regular access to a computer or the internet, so we decided to make completing the strengths inventory part of a session. Also, by reviewing the strengths inventory in session, the group leaders were able to answer any questions that participants had about the items, and read over items with the participants when they did not understand. The second additional session was added to the Positive Service exercise. This exercise involves trying out some activity or skill in the community, which can be challenging for some participants, so we provided an extra week to problem-solve obstacles and allow a second opportunity to try out this strategy.

Each exercise was adapted to fit this population by building in-session skills practice and helping participants make a specific and detailed plan to use the exercises outside of the session. For example, one exercise teaches participants about the benefits of active-constructive responding, related to work by Gable, Reis, Impett, and Asher (2004). We borrowed techniques from social skills training to teach this exercise which included: breaking down the skill into smaller steps, providing a demonstration to show participants what the skill looks like, doing a role-play to practice the skill, and helping the participants set up an assignment to practice the exercise (Bellack, Mueser, Gingerich, & Agresta, 2004). In session, an active-constructive response was broken down into steps, demonstrated by one of the group leaders, and then the group leaders engaged at least one participant in a role-play to practice the skill. For example, one exercise teaches participants about the benefits of responding actively and constructively to good news, related to work by Gable et al. (2004). At the end of the group, each participant brainstorms ideas for possible persons who might have some good news and generates ideas for how to respond for the home practice.

The two new additions to the manual were the positive goal and the mindfulness minute. After completing the strengths inventory during session three, participants were asked to select one positive goal to break down into smaller steps that could be followed up at the beginning of the next seven sessions. An example of the positive goal tracking sheet that was used in the Positive Living group can be found in Figure 19.1. Participants in the group were instructed to choose a positive goal: something that they had wanted to try and had never had the opportunity, or a goal that would use one of their top five strengths. The establishment of personally meaningful goals is another common feature among psychosocial treatments for schizophrenia that allows an individual to focus on increasing hope and recovery (Clarke, Oades, Crowe, & Deane, 2006; Meyer et al., 2010). The purpose of adding the positive goal was to increase active participation in treatment and to promote self-determination, by allowing the participant to choose a goal that was important and pursue something positive. The second new component that was added to the Positive Living manual was the mindfulness minute. Mindfulness has been linked to positive emotions, increased well-being, and savoring, which is a closely related concept (Brown & Ryan, 2003; Bryant & Veroff,

Positive Living Goal Tracking Sheet (Review weekly)
Adapted from the IMR Goal Tracking Sheet

Name:____________________ **Date that Positive Goal was Set:**____________________

Positive (strengths-based) Goal:

Short-term Goals (place a √ after steps achieved):

Short-term Goal 1	**Steps** →	**Modified Steps**
	1.	1.
	2.	2.
	3.	3.
Achieved: ☐	4.	4.
Modified: ☐		
Short-term Goal 2	**Steps** →	**Modified Steps**
	1.	1.
	2.	2.
Achieved: ☐	3.	3.
Modified: ☐	4.	4.

Figure 19.1 Example of Positive Living goal tracking sheet

2007). Mindfulness has also been shown to be helpful and useful in the management of psychosis (Tai & Turkington, 2009). In the Positive Living group, each session began and ended with a brief mindfulness exercise that instructed participants to focus on a specific sensation. Later, when teaching the savoring exercise, the mindfulness practice was linked to savoring. To help participants follow along in session and practice the skills, we created a worksheet for each of the nine exercises. The worksheets were also helpful in setting up the home practice of the exercise before leaving the session. An example of a worksheet that was created for the savoring exercise is found in Figure 19.2.

Results from the Positive Living Pilot Study

As reported in Meyer et al. (2012), we conducted an uncontrolled pilot study of Positive Living with 16 participants in two groups with a diagnosis of schizophrenia or schizoaffective disorder. Participants were assessed at baseline, post-intervention, and a three-month follow-up. The results indicated that the intervention was feasible in this population, with a <20% drop-out rate and an attendance rate of 77%. Participants also responded favorably to the intervention using a satisfaction questionnaire. Some comments that participants made about

Savoring

What are some experiences you find pleasurable in your normal daily routine?______

____

____

____

Every day this week savor at least 2 experiences (for example, your morning coffee, the sun on your face, dinner with family/friends). Spend at least 2-3 minutes savoring each experience.

Remember the pointers for savoring:
(1) Sharing your experience with others, (2) Take mental photographs or even a physical souvenir of the event and reminisce about it later with others, (3) Don't be afraid to congratulate yourself, (4) Focus your perceptions on certain elements and block out others, (5) Let yourself get totally immersed and try not to think, just sense.

What are some possible savoring experiences that could incorporate your strengths?__

____

____

____

____

List your Savoring Experiences each day over the next week and rate the intensity of emotion that you experience from 1 (not at all intense) to 10 (the most intense feeling you've ever had)

	Savoring Experience #1 Intensity Rating	Savoring Experience#2 Intensity Rating
Monday		
Tuesday		
Wednesday		
Thursday		
Friday		
Saturday		
Sunday		

Figure 19.2 Savoring exercise worksheet

what was positive or helpful about the intervention were: "The experience has let me know that I am not alone battling my illness ... It has made me a happier person overall"; "I am less fearful, less anxious about everything"; and "It has made me more aware of my strengths, and has allowed me to open up more to others."

Participants reported significant improvements on the primary outcomes (overall well-being, hope, savoring, and self-reported psychological symptoms) at both post-intervention and the three-month follow-up. Self-esteem improved significantly from baseline to post-intervention but was not maintained at follow-up. Additional exploratory analyses suggested that participants experienced significant improvements in recovery related to hope/confidence and goal orientation at the end of the intervention and at the three-month follow-up. Unexpectedly, participants reported a significant decrease in psychotic and paranoid symptoms that was maintained through the three-month follow-up, but depression was only significantly decreased at the end of the intervention.

In the Positive Living group, participants rarely discussed their symptoms or diagnosis but reported gains in both the broad area of well-being and clinical functioning, where they were reporting greater control in their lives and higher levels of recovery along with increases in hope. These findings were somewhat similar to other PPIs that have been associated with decreases in depressive symptoms, but suggest that PPIs may have the potential to reduce the effects of symptoms through improved coping strategies, gains in happiness and well-being, and promoting the process of recovery from mental illness (Fava, Rafanelli, Cazzaro, Conti, & Grandi, 1998; Lyubomirsky & Della Porta, 2012; Seligman et al., 2006). Indeed, a recent study has found similar results that link a positive psychology concept with progress in the stages of recovery. In this study, persons with a severe mental illness who were in the later stages of psychological recovery (e.g., rebuilding and growth stages associated with working toward a positive identity and living a meaningful life) were more likely to set approach-oriented goals rather than avoidance goals (Clarke, Oades, & Crowe, 2012). Approach goals have also been associated with gains in well-being (Church, Elliot, & Sheldon, 1997). The improvements in well-being, symptoms, and recovery that we found in the Positive Living groups suggest that PPIs may offer persons with schizophrenia an opportunity to progress further in their recovery.

Recommendations for the Adaptation of Positive Psychological Interventions

The process of adapting positive psychotherapy for people with schizophrenia was a rewarding experience that was well received by the participants. In adapting the original intervention, there were some important considerations to keep in mind that would be useful to practitioners interested in adapting PPIs for other special populations. First, it is important to understand the current obstacles or challenges that persons in the special population face, whether that is cognitive deficits or difficulties in motivation. For people with schizophrenia, we had to consider deficits in memory or attention, and therefore we decided to make adjustments to how we presented the information (e.g., broken down into smaller chunks and eliciting personal examples) and how we asked participants to practice the exercises outside of the group (e.g., using the worksheets as a written reminder).

Second, it can be helpful to review common teaching strategies or treatment approaches currently used in the special population that could be modified and used to teach a positive psychology skill. For example, a commonly used technique in schizophrenia treatment that is used to teach a new skill is skills training (Bellack et al., 2004). This technique, described above in relation to active-constructive responding, could easily be utilized in several of the exercises to break down the skill into small steps, demonstrated during the session, allowing the participants to practice in session with feedback, and setting up a home practice to use the skills outside of the session.

Third, there are often concerns about how feasible an intervention such as a PPI can be in a novel population. Modifying the original protocol to meet the special needs of a population can increase the success of the implementation. This might include things such as using two practitioners to lead the group instead of one, or focusing on two to three exercises over the course of the group instead of all seven of them, or using technology (e.g., text messaging or reminders on cell-phones) to help reinforce the importance and success in completing the homework outside of the session.

Lastly, before starting a group, it can be helpful to pilot a couple of exercises with a few clients to see what other adaptations may be helpful. For example, the first time we conducted the group we realized that many participants found it too overwhelming to try to think of at least three good things at the end of every day, but they could work towards writing down at least one good thing at the end of the day. Additional modifications to consider when piloting the exercises may be the wording that is used to describe the exercises, which may need to be simplified, and planning the order of the exercises that best fits the special population.

Conclusion

PPIs have a role in the treatment of clinical populations, but there is much to be learned. People with schizophrenia had a good response to the Positive Living group and reported that the exercises were helpful in their recovery. In this and other clinical populations, it is unclear when this type of intervention could be most effective. Some researchers have suggested using it when persons are clinically stable but experiencing residual symptoms, but there may also be a role for PPIs when teaching coping strategies for distressing symptoms or supporting a person in a more functional recovery that could alter the illness process (Dickerson & Lehman, 2006; Fava & Tomba, 2009). The method of delivery of a PPI could also vary. The Positive Living group format was well received, but recently we included the adapted exercises from the Positive Living group in a multi-site trial of an individual therapy aimed at persons with first-episode psychosis. Researchers have found good outcomes using both individual and group interventions (Fava & Ruini, 2003; Lyubomirsky & Della Porta, 2012; Seligman et al., 2006). Lastly, future studies should consider expanding the treatment targets for PPIs. In our pilot study, we had preliminary findings that suggested positive outcomes in the traditional targets of well-being and satisfaction with life. However, the exploratory outcome data also suggested that the intervention may have an impact on other clinical and recovery outcomes, such as symptoms and social functioning (Meyer et al., 2012).

As treatment for mental disorders moves away from the emphasis on psychopathology to a more integrated concept of wellness and recovery, it will be important to consider how PPIs can be effective tools in clinical practice. Positive psychology strategies and interventions represent a treatment approach that can facilitate changes through positive emotions, positive thoughts, and positive events (Lyubomirsky & Della Porta, 2012). The experience of positive emotions has been described as having an "undoing effect" on the harmful effects from negative emotions (Fredrickson & Levenson, 1998). Treatment interventions that incorporate positive psychology strategies offer a distraction or a "time-out" from the experience of symptoms or negative emotions, create meaningful coping skills that are aimed at counteracting negative or dysfunctional thoughts, and provide persons in treatment with moments to experience positive activities or events that bring persons closer to a full recovery (Lyubomirsky & Della Porta, 2012).

References

Anthony, W. A. (1993). Recovery from mental illness: The guiding vision of the mental health service system in the 1990s. *Psychosocial Rehabilitation Journal, 37*, 586–594.

Bellack, A. S. (2004). Skills training for people with severe mental illness. *Psychiatric Rehabilitation Journal, 27*(4), 375–391.

Bellack, A. S. (2006). Scientific and consumer models of recovery in schizophrenia: Concordance, contrasts, and implications. *Schizophrenia Bulletin, 32*(3), 432–442.

Bellack, A. S., Mueser, K. T., Gingerich, S., & Agresta, J. (2004). *Social skills training for schizophrenia*. New York: Guilford Press.

Brown, K. W., & Ryan, R. M. (2003). The benefits of being present: Mindfulness and its role in psychological well-being. *Journal of Personality and Social Psychology, 84*(4), 822–848.

Bryant, F. B., & Veroff, J. (2007). *Savoring: A new model of positive experience*. Mahwah, NJ: Lawrence Erlbaum Associates.

Chamberlin, J. (1978). *On our own: Patient-controlled alternatives to the mental health system*. New York: Hawthorn Books.

Church, M. A., Elliot, A. J., & Sheldon, K. M. (1997). Avoidance personal goals and subjective well-being. *Personality and Social Psychology Bulletin, 23*(9), 915–927.

Clarke, S., Oades, L. G., & Crowe, T. P. (2012). Recovery in mental health: A movement towards well-being and meaning in contrast to an avoidance of symptoms. *Psychiatric Rehabilitation Journal, 35*(4), 297–304. doi:10.2975/35.4.2012.297.304

Clarke, S., Oades, L. G., Crowe, T. P., & Deane, F. P. (2006). Collaborative goal technology: Theory and practice. *Psychiatric Rehabilitation Journal, 30*(2), 129–136.

Davidson, L. (2009). *A practical guide to recovery-oriented practice: Tools for transforming mental health care*. Oxford: Oxford University Press.

Davidson, L. (2010). PORT through a recovery lens. *Schizophrenia Bulletin*, *36*(1), 107–108.

Davidson, L., Tondora, J., O'Connell, M. J., Kirk, T., Jr., Rockholz, P., & Evans, A. C. (2007). Creating a recovery-oriented system of behavioral health care: Moving from concept to reality. *Psychiatric Rehabilitation Journal*, *31*(1), 23–31.

Deegan, P. E. (1992). The Independent Living Movement and people with psychiatric disabilities: Taking back control over our own lives. *Psychosocial Rehabilitation Journal*, *15*(3), 3–19.

Dickerson, F. B., & Lehman, A. F. (2006). Evidence-based psychotherapy for schizophrenia. *Journal of Nervous and Mental Disease*, *194*(1), 3–9. doi:10.1097/01.nmd.0000195316.86036.8a

Dixon, L. B., Dickerson, F., Bellack, A. S., Bennett, M., Dickinson, D., Goldberg, R. W., ... Kreyenbuhl, J. (2010). The 2009 schizophrenia PORT psychosocial treatment recommendations and summary statements. *Schizophrenia Bulletin*, *36*(1), 48–70.

Fava, G. A. (1999). Well-being therapy: Conceptual and technical issues. *Psychotherapy and Psychosomatics*, *68*(4), 171–179.

Fava, G. A., Rafanelli, C., Cazzaro, M., Conti, S., & Grandi, S. (1998). Well-being therapy. A novel psychotherapeutic approach for residual symptoms of affective disorders. *Psychological Medicine*, *28*(2), 475–480.

Fava, G. A., & Ruini, C. (2003). Development and characteristics of a well-being enhancing psychotherapeutic strategy: Well-being therapy. *Journal of Behavior Therapy and Experimental Psychiatry*, *34*(1), 45–63.

Fava, G. A., Ruini, C., & Belaise, C. (2007). The concept of recovery in major depression. *Psychological Medicine*, *37*(3), 307–317.

Fava, G. A., Ruini, C., Rafanelli, C., Finos, L., Salmaso, L., Mangelli, L., & Sirigatti, S. (2005). Well-being therapy of generalized anxiety disorder. *Psychotherapy and Psychosomatics*, *74*(1), 26–30. doi:PPS2005074001026 [pii] 10.1159/000082023

Fava, G. A., & Tomba, E. (2009). Increasing psychological well-being and resilience by psychotherapeutic methods. *Journal of Personality*, *77*(6), 1903–1934. doi:10.1111/j.1467-6494.2009.00604.x

Fredrickson, B. L. (2001). The role of positive emotions in positive psychology: The broaden-and-build theory of positive emotions. *American Psychologist*, *56*(3), 218–226.

Fredrickson, B. L., Cohn, M. A., Coffey, K. A., Pek, J., & Finkel, S. M. (2008). Open hearts build lives: Positive emotions, induced through loving-kindness meditation, build consequential personal resources. *Journal of Personality and Social Psychology*, *95*(5), 1045–1062.

Fredrickson, B. L., & Joiner, T. (2002). Positive emotions trigger upward spirals toward emotional well-being. *Psychological Science*, *13*(2), 172–175.

Fredrickson, B. L., & Levenson, R. W. (1998). Positive emotions speed recovery from the cardiovascular sequelae of negative emotions. *Cognition and Emotion*, *12*(2), 191–220.

Gable, S. L., Reis, H. T., Impett, E. A., & Asher, E. R. (2004). What do you do when things go right? The intrapersonal and interpersonal benefits of sharing positive events. *Journal of Personality and Social Psychology*, *87*(2), 228–245. doi:10.1037/0022-3514.87.2.228

Garland, E. L., Fredrickson, B., Kring, A. M., Johnson, D. P., Meyer, P. S., & Penn, D. L. (2010). Upward spirals of positive emotions counter downward spirals of negativity: Insights from the broaden-and-build theory and affective neuroscience on the treatment of emotion dysfunctions and deficits in psychopathology. *Clinical Psychology Review*, *30*(7), 849–864.

Harding, C. M., Zubin, J., & Strauss, J. S. (1987). Chronicity in schizophrenia: Fact, partial fact, or artifact? *Hospital and Community Psychiatry*, *38*(5), 477–486.

Harrison, G., Hopper, K., Craig, T., Laska, E., Siegel, C., Wanderling, J., ... Wiersma, D. (2001). Recovery from psychotic illness: A 15- and 25-year international follow-up study. *British Journal of Psychiatry: The Journal of Mental Science*, *178*, 506–517.

Jablensky, A. (1997). The 100-year epidemiology of schizophrenia. *Schizophrenia Research*, *28*(2–3), 111–125.

Kraepelin, E. (1971). *Dementia praecox and paraphrenia* (R. M. Barclay, Trans.). New York: Krieger.

Lambert, M., Schimmelmann, B. G., Naber, D., Schacht, A., Karow, A., Wagner, T., & Czekalla, J. (2006). Prediction of remission as a combination of symptomatic and functional remission and adequate subjective well-being in 2960 patients with schizophrenia. *Journal of Clinical Psychiatry*, *67*(11), 1690–1697.

Lieberman, J. A., Stroup, T. S., McEvoy, J. P., Swartz, M. S., Rosenheck, R. A., Perkins, D. O., ... Hsiao, J. K. (2005). Effectiveness of antipsychotic drugs in patients with chronic schizophrenia. *New England Journal of Medicine*, *353*(12), 1209–1223. doi:10.1056/NEJMoa051688

Lindenmayer, J. P. (2000). Treatment refractory schizophrenia. *The Psychiatric Quarterly*, *71*(4), 373–384.

Lyubomirsky, S., & Della Porta, M. D. (2012). Boosting happiness, buttressing resilience: Results from cognitive and behavioral interventions. In J. W. Reich, A. J. Zautra, & J. Hall (Eds.), *Handbook of adult resilience* (pp. 450–464). New York: Guilford Press.

Lyubomirsky, S., Dickerhoof, R., Boehm, J. K., & Sheldon, K. M. (2011). Becoming happier takes both a will and a proper way: An experimental longitudinal intervention to boost well-being. *Emotion*, *11*(2), 391–402. doi:10.1037/a0022575

Madera, E. J. (1988). Seven principles in self help: Understanding how self-help groups help. *New Program Initiatives in Mental Health* (May, pp. 3–4). Newsletter published by the New Jersey State Division of Mental Health and Hospitals.

Meyer, P. S., Gingerich, S., & Mueser, K. T. (2010). A guide to implementation and clinical practice of illness management and recovery for people with schizophrenia. In A. Rubin, D. W. Springer, & K. Trawver (Eds.), *Clinician's guide to evidence-based practice: Psychosocial treatment of schizophrenia* (pp. 23–87). Hoboken, NJ: John Wiley & Sons.

Meyer, P. S., Johnson, D. P., Parks, A., Iwanski, C., & Penn, D. L. (2012). Positive Living: A pilot study of group positive psychotherapy for people with schizophrenia. *Journal of Positive Psychology*, *7*(3), 239–248.

Meyer, P. S., & Mueser, K. T. (2011). Resiliency in individuals with serious mental illness. In S. M. Southwick, B. T. Litz, D. Charney, & M. J. Friedman (Eds.), *Resilience and mental health: Challenges across the lifespan* (pp. 276–288). Cambridge: Cambridge University Press.

Nose, M., Barbui, C., & Tansella, M. (2003). How often do patients with psychosis fail to adhere to treatment programmes? A systematic review. *Psychological Medicine*, *33*(7), 1149–1160.

Parks, A., & Seligman, M. E. (2007). 8-week group positive psychotherapy (PPT) manual. Unpublished manuscript.

Rafanelli, C., Park, S. K., Ruini, C., Ottolini, F., Cazzaro, M., & Fava, G. A. (2000). Rating well-being and distress. *Stress Medicine, 16*, 55–61.

Ralph, R. O. (2000). Recovery. *Psychiatric Rehabilitation Skills, 4*, 480–517.

Ruini, C., Belaise, C., Brombin, C., Caffo, E., & Fava, G. A. (2006). Well-being therapy in school settings: a pilot study. *Psychotherapy and Psychosomatics, 75*(6), 331–336. doi:10.1159/000095438

Ryff, C. D. (1989). Happiness is everything, or is it? Explorations on the meaning of psychological well-being. *Journal of Personality and Social Psychology, 57*(6), 1069–1081.

Seligman, M. E. (2011). *Flourish: A visionary new understanding of happiness and well-being.* New York: Free Press.

Seligman, M. E., Rashid, T., & Parks, A. C. (2006). Positive Psychotherapy. *American Psychologist, 61*(8), 774–788.

Sin, N. L., Della Porta, M. D., & Lyubomirsky, S. (2011). Tailoring positive psychology interventions to treat depressed individuals. In S. I. Donaldson, M. Csikszentmihalyi, & J. Nakamura (Eds.), *Applied positive psychology: Improving everyday life, health, schools, work, and society* (pp. 79–96). New York: Routledge/Taylor & Francis.

Sin, N. L., & Lyubomirsky, S. (2009). Enhancing well-being and alleviating depressive symptoms with positive psychology interventions: A practice-friendly meta-analysis. *Journal of Clinical Psychology, 65*(5), 467–487.

Tai, S., & Turkington, D. (2009). The evolution of cognitive behavior therapy for schizophrenia: Current practice and recent developments. *Schizophrenia Bulletin, 35*(5), 865–873. doi:10.1093/schbul/sbp080

Villeneuve, K., Potvin, S., Lesage, A., & Nicole, L. (2010). Meta-analysis of rates of dropout from psychosocial treatment among persons with schizophrenia spectrum disorder. *Schizophrenia Research, 121*(1–3), 266–270. doi:10.1016/j.schres.2010.04.003

20

Adapting Positive Psychology for Smoking Cessation

Anne M. Day, Elise M. Clerkin, Nichea S. Spillane, and Christopher W. Kahler

Growing interest in positive psychology has led to an increase in research on positive psychological interventions (PPIs). Rather than focusing on correcting deficits and decreasing negative emotion, PPIs focus on sources of individual strength and on enhancing happiness and positive emotions (Seligman, Rashid, & Parks, 2006; Sin & Lyubomirsky, 2009).

The role of emotion in smoking cessation has been extensively studied, and research indicates that treatments that include a component designed to reduce negative affect have been effective in assisting some individuals with quitting, particularly those with high depressive symptoms (Brown et al., 2001; Brown et al., 2007; Haas, Munoz, Humfleet, Reus, & Hall, 2004; Hall, Muñoz, & Reus, 1994; Hall et al., 1996; Hall et al., 1998). However, for individuals with no history of depression, mood management shows little or no benefit, and has even been associated with increased depressive symptoms after the completion of treatment (Kahler et al., 2002). Therefore, existing treatments that focus on negative affect reduction may be appropriate only for those individuals with psychiatric comorbidity.

Recent research indicates that positive emotions and related traits, such as anhedonia (i.e., an inability to experience pleasure), are important predictors of smoking cessation success above and beyond the effects of negative affect and other depressive symptoms, suggesting that the two exert independent effects on smoking cessation. For example, one study found that low positive affect had a stronger influence on cessation treatment success than negative affect or somatic features (Leventhal, Ramsey, Brown, LaChance, & Kahler, 2008). Of particular importance, decreases in positive affect in the weeks *prior* to quitting and lower levels of positive affect *on quit day* are associated with greater risk of smoking lapse (Strong et al., 2009). Thus, positive affect may be an important, but less-studied, target for smoking cessation treatments. PPIs, then, may be ideal for smoking cessation,

The Wiley Blackwell Handbook of Positive Psychological Interventions, First Edition.
Edited by Acacia C. Parks and Stephen M. Schueller.

where helping individuals to increase their experience of positive emotions, build psychological and social resources for coping with stress, and develop less cynical and more optimistic cognitions, may lead to better smoking outcomes.

In this chapter, we describe the development of a manual that integrates standard smoking cessation treatment with Positive Psychotherapy (PPT; Seligman, Steen, Park, & Peterson, 2005; Seligman et al., 2006), in an effort to increase positive affect in smokers seeking cessation treatment. Standard smoking cessation programs include discussion of a quit date, previous quit attempts, factors associated with quitting (e.g., the need for social support), how to plan for and cope with high-risk situations, and proper use of the nicotine patch (Fiore et al., 2008; Kahler et al., 2008). Traditional smoking cessation programs do not discuss or emphasize the role of emotions, unless the individual considers certain emotions to confer risk for relapse. In its initial implementations (Seligman et al., 2005; Seligman et al., 2006), PPT was delivered in a group format and combined different exercises (PPIs) that led to greater positive affect, a decrease in depressive symptoms, and enhanced well-being for participants, even after the treatment concluded. By combining and integrating PPT with traditional smoking cessation strategies, we postulate that PPT will enhance positive affect both prior to the quit attempt and in the early stages of abstinence, and therefore increase cessation.

The PPT for Smoking Cessation manual was developed in an iterative fashion, with treatment providers meeting on a weekly basis for discussion of the elements of the therapy and how participants were receiving the treatment. The primary considerations in evaluating the positive-emotion-focused interventions were: (i) how well the content matched with the stage of the quit smoking process participants were in (e.g., preparation, initial quitting, or maintenance); (ii) the ease with which participants reported carrying out the exercise; and (iii) the extent to which participants described the exercises as useful for their quit smoking efforts.

Below, we describe the specific interventions that are incorporated in the final Positive Psychotherapy for Smoking Cessation (PPT-S) manual, along with clinical considerations of each technique and their inclusion in the treatment. We do not provide specific details on sample selection and treatment outcomes, as those will be published elsewhere in detail. The chapter concludes with recommendations for researchers and clinicians.

General Information on PPT-S

PPT-S was adapted from the original PPT manual (Parks & Seligman, 2007) which used an eight-session group treatment to enhance positive emotions. There are three ways in which the PPT-S manual deviates from the original manual. First, in the original protocol, individuals engaged in a Positive Introduction during the first session, which included using signature strengths to tell a narrative about one's life. However, we modified the Positive Introduction exercise slightly to be consistent with our smoking cessation focus. During the first session, we did have participants provide an example of how they had employed one of their strengths, and throughout treatment, we utilized participants' signature strengths to enhance and complement each of the PPIs that were used (described below). The second deviation was with the removal of Positive Service, an intervention designed to assist individuals with using their signature strengths to engage in community service (Parks & Seligman, 2007). Lastly, while PPT was originally delivered in a group format, we chose an individually delivered treatment. We have had success in the past administering smoking cessation treatment individually (Kahler et al., 2008), and the individual approach was shown in a recent meta-analysis to yield the largest effects for PPT (Sin & Lyubomirsky, 2009).

The treatment consists of six sessions spread across six weeks, with a two-week break between the fifth and sixth sessions (i.e., sessions 1–5 are each a week apart). The quit date is the third session, in order to provide each participant with two weeks of PPT homework assignments prior to the quit date. The first session averages 60 minutes, while the remaining sessions are completed in approximately 30 minutes. Participants are provided with eight weeks of transdermal nicotine patch, consistent with the federal guidelines for smoking cessation treatment (Fiore et al., 2008). Participants begin using the patch on the morning of their quit day (i.e., session 3). In addition, they are provided with information about quitting smoking, and, at each session, are encouraged to identify and plan for "high-risk" situations – those that the participant feels are the most likely to lead to a relapse after their quit date.

Homework

In the first session, we discuss the importance of homework in order to establish the expectation that individuals will complete the assignments so as to maximize their benefit from the treatment. This is an important component to the treatment, as we have found that many of our participants have not been to a therapist before and the idea of homework is new to them. The importance of practicing the PPT strategies is emphasized. For example, clients receive a participant manual with worksheets and spend time in each session troubleshooting obstacles that might arise regarding the completion of homework. Individuals are encouraged to keep homework sheets in a place where they are most likely to remember them (e.g., next to their bed or in their car).

Participants' Introduction to PPT

Prior to the first session of PPT-S, participants complete the VIA (Values in Action) Character Strengths Survey (Peterson & Seligman, 2004) to assess signature strengths/virtues, such as love of learning, bravery, social intelligence, and appreciation of beauty and excellence (see Chapter 4). In the first session, participants are provided with information about their top five character strengths according to the survey. After providing an explanation of each strength, therapists guide participants through an exercise that asks them to consider ways that these strengths fit with how they view themselves. Participants are also asked to provide examples of ways in which they use their strengths. There were participants for whom focusing on the top strengths was difficult, and who instead chose to focus on the strengths near the end of the list (i.e., the signature strengths the participant scored least highly on: "This is true, I don't have much Self Regulation ..."). As a result, therapists stress that none of the qualities from the VIA survey are "weaknesses," despite their order – rather, the strengths listed at the top are *relative* to the other qualities and will thus be the ones that receive the most focus in treatment.

The first point at which we utilize signature strengths to assist with smoking cessation is in the first session, when we include a discussion of how these qualities may be helpful in one's quit attempt. Participants are specifically encouraged to use their signature strengths to handle high-risk situations and to remain smoke-free. As an example, a woman whose top strength is love of learning might seek out additional information about the health benefits of quitting smoking. A man whose top strength is bravery might be encouraged to think of craving to smoke as an opportunity to face the challenge rather than shrinking away from it. Table 20.1 contains additional examples of other strength-based strategies for quitting smoking.

After participants are oriented to the PPT intervention, the process of assigning activities begins. Below, we outline each activity and provide some observations based on our attempts to teach that activity to participants.

Three Good Things (Week 1 and Beyond)

The first take-home exercise that participants are asked to complete is Three Good Things, which has been shown to boost happiness in a way that accumulates over time (Seligman et al., 2005). Participants are asked to spend a few minutes at the end of each day writing down three positive things, large or small, that happened during their day. The purpose of this exercise is to assist participants with maintaining a focus on the positive aspects of their life in order to boost their mood. Participants are given this assignment during the first week and are asked to continue it during each week of treatment. During week 3, or quit week, participants are asked to specifically focus on good things related to quitting smoking. At this time, therapists encourage participants to think of and include aspects of quitting in the three good things that they write down each day.

The Three Good Things exercise has a number of advantages as an initial PPT exercise. It is easy for participants to understand and can be completed easily. In addition, it is easy to explain both how the exercise is designed to boost mood, as well as how the exercise can be integrated into the participant's quit attempt

Table 20.1 Signature strengths and strategies for quitting smoking

Strength	*Strategy for quitting*
Appreciation of beauty and excellence	Utilize savoring of beautiful experiences to boost mood; consider how quitting smoking will make the world a more beautiful place.
Bravery	Write down the rating of your strongest craving on a scale of 0 (not at all) to 100 (extreme craving). See how high a rating you are able to get through without smoking.
Creativity	Think of a unique way to get through a craving.
Curiosity	Learn as much as you can about the benefits of quitting smoking.
Fairness	Treat quitting smoking with an open mind.
Forgiveness	Forgive yourself when you have a craving; don't let your mood get too low.
Gratitude	Thank yourself for making the choice to quit.
Honesty	Remind yourself that you have chosen to be a non-smoker, and that this is consistent with your values.
Hope	Write down your goals of how to use the money you save from smoking, or the activities you can engage in now that you have quit; make plans of how to reach these goals.
Humility	Let the accomplishment of quitting smoking speak for itself.
Humor	Make fun of yourself, if only by saying, "there I go again."
Judgment	Use your ability to change your mind to allow yourself to think of yourself as a non-smoker.
Kindness	Be kind to yourself – don't get too down on yourself for having a craving; do your body a favor by not having a cigarette.
Leadership	Organize a social get-together for your friends that is incompatible with smoking.
Love	Congratulate yourself and your ability to quit smoking each day.
Love of learning	Learn as much as you can about the benefits of quitting smoking.
Perseverance	Consider quitting smoking to be the ultimate perseverance through difficult times.
Perspective	Think about how your quitting will help others as well as yourself.
Prudence	Think about the benefits of quitting smoking.
Self-regulation	Think about the long-term gain of quitting smoking.
Social intelligence	Ask friends and family for support when you have a craving.
Spirituality	Ask your "higher power" for assistance with managing a craving.
Teamwork	Ask yourself how quitting contributes to making a better world.
Zest	Put up stickers or notes in your house "cheerleading" your quit attempt.

(i.e., noticing positive aspects of quitting smoking). Once quit date occurs (session 3), incorporating good things about quitting smoking seems particularly valuable. For instance, some participants reported an increased sense of taste or smell (e.g., able to enjoy dinner), positive social interactions with non-smokers supportive of their attempt to quit, and increased productivity at work after eliminating repeated breaks to smoke.

One of the challenges that arose with many participants was not writing down their good things, which seemingly led to poor memory for events by the time the following session arrived. Without specific notes, participants tended to describe vague recollections (e.g., "I realized I have great friends"), as opposed to specific positive experiences. Unfortunately, this likely diminished the effectiveness of the exercise to train participants' attention to the positive things happening around them. Another related challenge was that participants would list the same good things over and over each week, which presumably limited the benefit of monitoring one's attention and attuning it to positive, novel events.

When participants provide vague stories or list the same ideas repeatedly, clinicians remind participants of the purpose of the exercise (i.e., to become more in touch with the positive things happening in one's life, which should then boost one's mood). Clinicians and participants also engage in problem-solving around completion of the assignment (e.g., keep the Three Good Things list by the bed; make it part of an evening routine).

Gratitude Visit (Week 2)

The homework assignment for the second session is for participants to write a gratitude letter and deliver it in person to someone who helped them in their life and whom they want to thank more fully, with the idea that expressing gratitude helps enhance appreciation and strengthen relationships (Seligman et al., 2006). In an effort to further adapt standard PPT to smoking, participants are also instructed to let the person know about their commitment to quit smoking, as a means to gain greater support for their non-smoking lifestyle. The steps that are included in the assignment are: to write down one's thoughts, to read the letter to the person, and to recruit support for quitting smoking.

An essential element of utilizing this intervention is to gauge the participant's level of comfort with writing. If the participant seems very averse to writing in general, we stress the use of a "letter prompt" form, which includes open-ended items related to the assignment (e.g., the form prompts participants to consider the three things he or she appreciates about the other person; specific things he or she admires, etc.). In addition, clinicians can provide an introduction that participants can use if they feel the process of reading a letter about gratitude to a friend or family member is awkward. The introduction is different from the prompt in that it provides a framework for beginning the letter (e.g., "As you might know, I have been going to appointments each week …").

This activity has the potential to be particularly beneficial because it not only boosts well-being, but it can also enhance the quality of relationships and/or broaden social networks, which is important, as social support is a predictor of quitting success and maintenance of smoking cessation (Mermelstein, Cohen, Lichtenstein, Baer, & Kamarck, 1986; Murray, Johnston, Dolce, & Lee, 1995; Wagner, Burg, & Sirois, 2004). In some cases, participants chose to write a gratitude letter to individuals from whom they had become estranged, or to individuals they were not particularly close with (e.g., a friend's parent, a former co-worker). One of the participants wrote a gratitude letter to his mother who was in a nursing home, to thank her for her support over the years. He delivered this letter on Mother's Day and later told his treatment provider that the letter engendered a lot of positive emotion for both him and his mother. Critically, the exercise not only enhanced the quality of existing relationships, but also effectively broadened and strengthened the individual's social network at a time when it was needed – at the end of week 2, just before the quit date was to occur at session 3.

One of the major challenges that arose in the implementation of this assignment was that participants often left out one or more of the steps. For instance, participants would not write down their thoughts about gratitude and instead tried to provide the recipient with broad statements ("I appreciate what you've done for me") in person. Or, participants might write down thoughts, but not deliver the letter in person. For instance, one individual relayed her gratitude message in a public social networking forum. Another challenge that arose with the gratitude letter was participants using this as an opportunity to express complaints ("I really love you, but …"). Given this concern, we stress that the point of the exercise is not to give a balanced view or a constructive critique, but instead to focus exclusively on the aspects of the other person that the participant feels most grateful for.

Savoring (Week 3)

In the third session, participants are introduced to techniques for savoring and complete an in-session exercise aimed at helping them to slow down and fully engage in day-to-day activities. The homework assignment for this session is to savor at least two experiences per day (e.g., their morning coffee; the sun on their face), for at least 2–3 minutes per experience. Participants are provided with instructions to "pay attention to and let yourself get the full enjoyment from something you do." They are additionally given suggestions for how to maximize their savoring experience, and are asked to write down the two things they savored each day. We used the same suggestions for maximizing savoring that are included in the original manual (Parks & Seligman, 2007), which are:

1 Sharing with others: You can seek out others to share the experience and tell others how much you value the moment. This is probably the single best way to savor pleasure.

2 Memory-building: Take mental photographs or even a physical souvenir of the event and reminisce about it later with others.
3 Self-congratulation: Do not be afraid of pride. Tell yourself how impressed others are and remember how long you have waited for this to happen.
4 Sharpening perceptions: Focus on certain elements and block out others.
5 Absorption: Let yourself get totally immersed and try not to think, just sense.

Overall, this activity is especially well received by participants. One participant discussed how he savored the time that he spent with his wife. He expressed how this had a positive impact on his relationship and how supported he felt by his wife. One benefit of this activity is the opportunity to incorporate the use of signature strengths to facilitate savoring. For example, someone with high appreciation of beauty and excellence might choose to pursue opportunities to savor things that are aesthetically pleasing, whereas someone with high gratitude might savor the things for which they are grateful as they are experiencing them. This technique also provides the opportunity to discuss how savoring certain things is easier as a non-smoker (e.g., tastes, smells).

One potential challenge in implementing this technique is managing the ways in which certain signature strengths might get in the way of savoring. For example, a participant high in vitality/zest might find it difficult to slow down and savor, while being high in curiosity or love of learning might make it difficult to stop thinking and just experience the moment. Being familiar with each participant's signature strengths allows for a comprehensive discussion of how certain characteristics might make completion of this activity more or less difficult for the participant.

Active-Constructive Responding (Week 4)

The next assignment is to engage in active-constructive responding, a communication style developed from relationship research that indicates that responding to another person's good news in an active, engaged, genuinely interested way can enhance relationship satisfaction (Gable, Gonzaga, & Strachman, 2006; Gable, Reis, Impett, & Asher, 2004). For one week, participants are asked to go out of their way to respond actively and constructively to good news that others shared. They are also asked to write about these experiences by noting the good news, their response to the good news, and how the other person responded. The key elements to effectively engaging in active-constructive responding are: (i) genuine excitement; (ii) outwardly displaying excitement; and (iii) capitalizing on the event, which includes prolonging discussion of the good news, asking for more details, telling other people about it, encouraging your friend to tell other people, and/or suggesting celebratory activities (Parks & Seligman, 2007). For example, if a friend shares news of a promotion at work, the participant could respond in an active-constructive way (e.g., "Awesome! When did you hear? Have you called your mom? Let's grab a drink after work to celebrate!"). One participant had a great opportunity to practice this technique when interacting with his adult child. His daughter had recently received a college scholarship and he took her out to lunch to celebrate and discuss how wonderful this opportunity was for her to be able to go to school. This participant later expressed to his treatment provider how the experience improved his overall relationship with his daughter and made him feel supported in his quit attempt.

One challenge that arose from this exercise occurred when participants responded in an active and constructive way, but others did not respond in the same way to the participants' good news. For these participants, the exercise had the potential to highlight relationship dissatisfaction. In these circumstances, treatment providers highlighted that they were modeling a skill that others may emulate. There were also participants whose personality did not lend itself to this activity without engendering a feeling of phony interest. These individuals were encouraged to engage in the activity only to the extent that it felt natural, with the idea that to come across as unauthentic would be counter to the activity's purpose. One individual, for instance, found that he could simply modify the method to ask only one additional question of an individual after receiving his or her good news. This allowed the participant to feel genuine while still responding actively and constructively.

Savoring Acts of Kindness (Week 5)

The last happiness-boosting exercise that participants are assigned involves being more aware of times when they are acting in a friendly, generous, charitable, or considerate manner. Participants are asked to become more aware of this behavior toward another person or the environment, and to write it down. Of note, the task was previously called Counting Kindnesses (Otake, Shimai, Tanaka-Matsumi, Otsui, & Fredrickson, 2006), and participants were asked to record and count specific instances of kind behavior. However, some participants were concerned about "gloating" about how many charitable acts they had performed. This seemed particularly true among participants who identified as religious, with one participant expressing, "The Bible would look down on counting the kind things one does." Thus, the exercise was eventually modified from Counting Kindnesses to Savoring Kindnesses, and participants are simply asked to notice and write down (as opposed to notice, write down, and count) kind acts that either they notice others doing or that they engage in themselves. Treatment providers also emphasize that there is no specific number of good things participants "should" do each day.

Changing the terminology from counting to savoring seemed to alleviate some concerns, but individuals still reported difficulty with the activity. For some, paying attention to one's own kind acts highlighted the extent to which it was evident that others did not treat them in the same way. When this occurs, providers remind participants of the purpose of the activity, which is to turn their attention to the positive things happening in their lives, particularly those things that are the result of the participant's own kind actions. To focus on the deficits that others evidence is counter to the purpose of the activity, and participants are supported in their efforts to maintain a positive attentional focus in their lives.

Closing Thoughts and Memory Building (Week 6)

The final session concludes with a summary and time to consider what was most useful in the treatment. Participants are asked to reflect on their journey of becoming a non-smoker, and they are encouraged to give feedback on the happiness-boosting exercises and consider ways to utilize them in their lives on a regular basis after treatment ends.

Additional Exercises

Positive Service (from Parks & Seligman, 2007) was initially included in the PPT-S manual, and participants were asked to choose two domains in which they wanted to serve (e.g., politics, religion, family, science, community) by exercising their strengths. Our sense was that participants found this task difficult to implement and did not fully engage in the activity. One important distinction between the original implementation of this PPI and the current manual is that participants in this study are coming in for smoking cessation treatment, not traditional Positive Psychotherapy. Thus, their goal was not to have increased happiness, but to quit smoking. By the later sessions, some participants had returned to smoking, and thus asking for commitment to substantial changes outside of the treatment did not seem feasible.

General Reflections

Overall, the strategies of PPT were easy to implement and utilize for smoking cessation. The techniques are easy to explain, inexpensive, require nothing other than pen/paper, and can be individualized using signature strengths. In addition, participants seemed to enjoy the focus on their strengths, and clinicians enjoyed guiding participants through this protocol.

In behavioral change interventions (e.g., addictions, weight loss), focusing on a person's strengths at the beginning of treatment is unique. Like standard smoking cessation treatments, most behavioral interventions are based on identifying learned habits, planning for high-risk situations, and eliciting support from family and friends during treatment. Discussion of emotion is often limited to negative affect, or circumstances under which negative affect might influence craving, commitment to change, or ability to utilize learned strategies. The use of PPT for smoking cessation has not been fully established, but our impression was that focusing on strengths and positive affect helped to build rapport and mobilize a person's personal resources to assist with behavior change.

Recommendations

The timing of the PPT exercises appeared to be an important factor in how participants perceived their utility. For example, starting with Three Good Things was a good first exercise because of its relative simplicity, compared to an activity such as active-constructive responding. In addition, activities assigned in the last two sessions may have had less of an impact on smoking cessation outcomes because participants had initiated their quit attempt several weeks earlier and were finishing with the study. Future research might examine timing of the interventions as a variable that influences outcome, or modify later interventions to be maintenance-related (e.g., encouraging loved ones to be active-constructive about quit-related successes). An alternative method might be to reinforce only a few activities early on in smoking cessation in order to establish positive affect during early abstinence, and not ask individuals to engage in so many different PPIs.

Many of our participants were successful in utilizing social support during this study, and, anecdotally, PPT had a positive impact on their relationships with friends and family. In the future, if PPT proves to be effective in helping people quit smoking, researchers might want to examine the role that PPT plays in enhancing social relationships, which could ultimately serve as a mediator of the relation between treatment and smoking cessation success.

There were many opportunities for participants to incorporate hand-held technology into their completion of study assignments. For instance, some participants used the notes function on smartphones, or reminder/alarm functions to remind themselves about the Three Good Things exercise. Employing technology was particularly helpful in ensuring homework completion, and providers were supportive of participants who chose to complete their assignments in this way. PPIs have already received support for implementation over the web (Seligman et al., 2005) and using smartphone apps (Parks, Della Porta, Pierce, Zilca, & Lyubomirsky, 2012), and there is growing interest in the use of smartphone apps to assist with smoking cessation (Abroms, Padmanabhan, Thaweethai, & Phillips, 2011). Future research might work to combine the two efforts of PPT and smoking cessation apps to aid individuals with quitting. For example, research might determine whether activities such as the gratitude letter need to be delivered in person, or whether they are equally effective at boosting mood when delivered onto a public social networking site. Alternatively, individuals might post Three Good Things or share savoring experiences on a social networking site, or engage in active-constructive responding in response to news they read online (vs. news they hear about in person).

Conclusion

Smoking cessation strategies have been bolstered for some individuals by the inclusion of a mood management component, but low positive affect continues to be predictive of relapse and is not specifically addressed in most smoking cessation interventions. We developed a manual utilizing empirically-validated PPIs to enhance positive mood prior to and during a smoking quit attempt. We found that participants liked the interventions, were able to complete the assignments, and clinicians enjoyed providing the treatment.

References

Abroms, L. C., Padmanabhan, N., Thaweethai, L., & Phillips, T. (2011). iPhone apps for smoking cessation: A content analysis. *American Journal of Preventive Medicine, 40*(3), 279–285. doi:10.1016/j.amepre.2008.09.040] [Medline: 19135907].2009-00505-01110.1016/j.amepre.2008.09.040

Brown, R. A., Kahler, C. W., Niaura, R., Abrams, D. B., Sales, S. D., Ramsey, S. E., et al. (2001). Cognitive-behavioral treatment for depression in smoking cessation. *Journal of Consulting and Clinical Psychology, 69*, 471–480.

Brown, R. A., Niaura, R., Lloyd-Richardson, E. E., Strong, D. R., Kahler, C. W., Abrantes, A. M., et al. (2007). Bupropion and cognitive-behavioral treatment for depression in smoking cessation. *Nicotine and Tobacco Research, 9*(7), 721–730.

Covey, L. S., Glassman, A. H., & Stetner, F. (1990). Depression and depressive symptoms in smoking cessation. *Comprehensive Psychiatry, 31*(4), 350–354.

Fiore, M. C., Jaén, C., Baker, T., et al. (2008). *Treating tobacco use and dependence: 2008 update*. Rockville, MD: US Department of Health and Human Services, Public Health Service.

Gable, S. L., Gonzaga, G. C., & Strachman, A. (2006). Will you be there for me when things go right? Supportive responses to positive event disclosures. *Journal of Personality and Social Psychology, 91*(5), 904–917. doi:10.1037/0022-3514.79.6.953

Gable, S. L., Reis, H. T., Impett, E. A., & Asher, E. R. (2004). What do you do when things go right? The intrapersonal and interpersonal benefits of sharing positive events. *Journal of Personality and Social Psychology, 87*(2), 228–245. doi:10.1037/0022-3514.60.2.241

Haas, A. L., Munoz, R. F., Humfleet, G. L., Reus, V. I., & Hall, S. M. (2004). Influences of mood, depression history, and treatment modality on outcomes in smoking cessation. *Journal of Consulting and Clinical Psychology, 72*(4), 563–570.

Hall, S. M., Muñoz, R. F., & Reus, V. I. (1994). Cognitive-behavioral intervention increases abstinence rates for depressive-history smokers. *Journal of Consulting and Clinical Psychology, 62*(1), 141–146.

Hall, S. M., Muñoz, R. F., Reus, V. I., Sees, K. L., Duncan, C., Humfleet, G. L., et al. (1996). Mood management and nicotine gum in smoking treatment: A therapeutic contact and placebo-controlled study. *Journal of Consulting and Clinical Psychology, 64*(5), 1003–1009.

Hall, S. M., Reus, V. I., Muñoz, R. F., Sees, K. L., Humfleet, G. L., Hartz, D. T., et al. (1998). Nortriptyline and cognitive-behavioral therapy in the treatment of cigarette smoking. *Archive of General Psychiatry, 55*, 683–690.

Kahler, C. W., Brown, R. A., Ramsey, S. E., Niaura, R., Abrams, D. B., Goldstein, M. G., et al. (2002). Negative mood, depressive symptoms, and major depression after smoking cessation treatment in smokers with a history of major depressive disorder. *Journal of Abnormal Psychology, 111*(4), 670–675.

Kahler, C. W., Metrik, J., LaChance, H. R., Ramsey, S. E., Abrams, D. B., Monti, P. M., & Brown, R. A. (2008). Addressing heavy drinking in smoking cessation treatment: A randomized clinical trial. *Journal of Consulting and Clinical Psychology, 76*(5), 852–862. doi:10.1037/a0012717

Leventhal, A. M., Ramsey, S. E., Brown, R. A., LaChance, H. A., & Kahler, C. W. (2008). Dimensions of depressive symptoms and smoking cessation. *Nicotine and Tobacco Research, 10*(3), 507–517.

Mermelstein, R., Cohen, S., Lichtenstein, E., Baer, J. S., & Kamarck, T. (1986). Social support and smoking cessation and maintenance. *Journal of Consulting and Clinical Psychology, 54*(4), 447–453. doi:10.1037/0022-006x.54.4.447

Murray, R. P., Johnston, J. J., Dolce, J. J., & Lee, W. W. (1995). Social support for smoking cessation and abstinence: The Lung Health Study. *Addictive Behaviors, 20*(2), 159–170. doi:10.1016/s0306-4603(99)80001-x

Otake, K., Shimai, S., Tanaka-Matsumi, J., Otsui, K., & Fredrickson, B. L. (2006). Happy people become happier through kindness: A counting kindnesses intervention. *Journal of Happiness Studies, 7*(3), 361–375.

Parks, A. C., Della Porta, M. D., Pierce, R. S., Zilca, R., & Lyubomirsky, S. (2012). Pursuing happiness in everyday life: A naturalistic investigation of online happiness seekers. *Emotion, 12*(6), 1222–1234.

Parks, A. C., & Seligman, M. E. P. (2007). *8-week group Positive Psychotherapy (PPT) manual.* Unpublished manual, available by request.

Peterson, C., & Seligman, M. E. P. (2004). *Character strengths and virtues: A classification and handbook.* New York: Oxford University Press/Washington, DC: American Psychological Association.

Seligman, M. E. P., Rashid, T., & Parks, A. C. (2006). Positive psychotherapy. *American Psychologist, 61*(8), 774–788. doi:10.1037/1089-2680.5.4.323

Seligman, M. E. P., Steen, T. A., Park, N., & Peterson, C. (2005). Positive psychology progress: Empirical validation of interventions. *American Psychologist, 60*(5), 410–421. doi:10.1037/0003-066X.60.5.410

Sin, N. L., & Lyubomirsky, S. (2009). Enhancing well-being and alleviating depressive symptoms with positive psychology interventions: A practice-friendly meta-analysis. *Journal of Clinical Psychology, 65*(5), 467–487. doi:10.1037/0003-066x.54.3.165

Strong, D. R., Kahler, C. W., Leventhal, A. M., Abrantes, A. M., Richardson, E. E., Niaura, R., & Brown, R. A. (2009). Impact of bupropion and CBT for depression on positive affect, negative affect, and urges to smoke during cessation treatment. *Nicotine and Tobacco Research, 11*(10), 1142–1153.

Wagner, J., Burg, M., & Sirois, B. (2004). Social support and the transtheoretical model: Relationship of social support to smoking cessation stage, decisional balance, process use, and temptation. *Addictive Behaviors, 29*(5), 1039–1043. doi:10.1037/0022-006x.56.4.520

Part IV
Special Considerations

21

Making Happiness Last

Using the Hedonic Adaptation Prevention Model to Extend the Success of Positive Interventions

Katherine Jacobs Bao and Sonja Lyubomirsky

So basic is the idea of the pursuit of happiness that the US Declaration of Independence positions it on an equal footing with life and liberty. Yet, as the never-ending supply of self-help books suggests, people undertake this journey with some difficulty. Many studies have demonstrated the efficacy of various positive activities in raising levels of well-being (see elsewhere in this volume; see also Sin & Lyubomirsky, 2009, for a meta-analysis). However, the answer is clearly not as simple as implementing a positive activity and becoming happier forever. Any boosts in happiness that do occur are likely to abate with time, due to a process called hedonic adaptation (Frederick & Loewenstein, 1999; Lyubomirsky, 2011; Wilson & Gilbert, 2008). Thus, hedonic adaptation serves as a barrier to becoming lastingly happier – unwelcome news to happiness seekers – but, fortunately, it also carries the keys to its own undoing. Just as mapping a virus's mechanisms enables a microbiologist to design a potent new drug, by learning about hedonic adaptation, psychologists can craft positive activities that resist adaptation and produce sustainable well-being.

Becoming Happier

Before researchers can begin developing ways to increase people's happiness, they must ask the question of whether such increases are even possible. The sustainable happiness model (Lyubomirsky, Sheldon, & Schkade, 2005) addresses this question by examining the contributions of genetic factors, life circumstances, and intentional activities to people's happiness. Although uncontrollable factors such as genetics and life circumstances explain half of the variance in individuals'

The Wiley Blackwell Handbook of Positive Psychological Interventions, First Edition.
Edited by Acacia C. Parks and Stephen M. Schueller.

levels of happiness, more than a third is left unexplained and may be bolstered by intentional activities. Because intentional activities are performed deliberately and volitionally, they are under the individual's control. They include positive activities that are carried out in order to become happier, such as writing gratitude letters (see Chapter 1; Boehm, Lyubomirsky, & Sheldon, 2011; Lyubomirsky, Dickerhoof, Boehm, & Sheldon, 2011), counting one's blessings (Lyubomirsky, Sheldon, & Schkade, 2005), performing acts of kindness (Lyubomirsky et al., 2005; Sheldon, Boehm, & Lyubomirsky, 2012), reliving positive events (Lyubomirsky, Sousa, & Dickerhoof, 2006), savoring positive experiences (see Chapter 3), building strengths (see Chapter 4), promoting meaning and purpose (see Chapter 5), and nurturing relationships (Lyubomirsky, 2008).

Psychologists from multiple laboratories have empirically studied a variety of positive activity-based interventions. A meta-analysis of these results suggests that positive interventions are, on average, effective at increasing well-being and decreasing depression (Sin & Lyubomirsky, 2009), providing persuasive evidence that it is possible to become happier.

Barriers to Becoming Happier

Although performing positive activities has been found to bring about increases in happiness, research on hedonic adaptation suggests that those increases may subside with time. To our knowledge, the longest published intervention included follow-ups of only 15 months (Cohn & Fredrickson, 2010), so the standard rate of adaptation to positive interventions is difficult to determine. One positive intervention study showed decreases in depression and increases in life satisfaction at a six-month follow-up, but by the one-year follow-up, participants had already started to return to baseline levels (Seligman, Rashid, & Parks, 2006). Researchers have shown that people adapt to negative events such as unemployment (Lucas, Clark, Georgellis, & Diener, 2004), divorce (Lucas, 2005), and widowhood (Lucas, Clark, Georgellis, & Diener, 2003), as well as to positive events such as starting a new job (Boswell, Boudreau, & Tichy, 2005) and getting married (Lucas et al., 2003). Given the variety of circumstances subject to hedonic adaptation, it seems likely that people would adapt to positive interventions as well. In this way, hedonic adaptation may serve as an under-studied obstacle to sustainably increasing happiness via positive activities.

According to the hedonic adaptation prevention model (Lyubomirsky, 2011; Sheldon & Lyubomirsky, 2012; see Figure 21.1), adaptation unfolds via two paths – through decreases in positive emotions (bottom path) and through increases in aspirations (top path). In this first path, when a person experiences a positive change that involves initiating a new positive activity, such as performing acts of kindness for people around her on a regular basis, that change will generate a stream of positive events, such as helping a friend prepare for a test, or more generally meeting new people and thinking of new kind acts to perform.

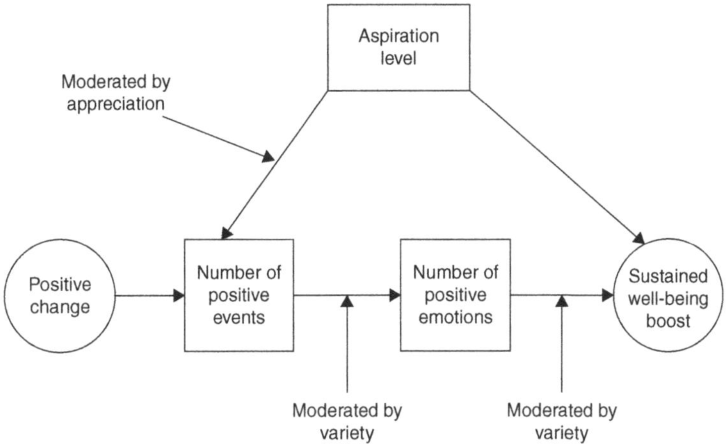

Figure 21.1 Hedonic adaptation prevention model (adapted from Sheldon & Lyubomirsky, 2012)

These positive events will trigger increases in positive emotions, such as gratitude, inspiration, and appreciation, which then boost well-being. However, over time, practicing kindness produces fewer and fewer novel positive events, and thus fewer positive emotions, so well-being will begin to decline or fail to rise. For example, a person performing kind acts for his neighbors will likely run out of ideas for novel kind acts, causing him to repeat previous deeds. As a result, he will obtain less enjoyment than the first time he performed a kindness, when the act – and its reward – was exciting, fresh, and new. Thus, the person begins to adapt. In this case, positive events and positive emotions, which are both associated with higher well-being, mediate the adaptation process.

As illustrated in Figure 21.1, another path that underlies the process of adaptation involves a rise in people's aspiration levels, which typically occurs after they experience or initiate a positive change (e.g., starting a positive activity) and the subsequent increase in positive events. Aspirations, in this context, refer to people's hopes and desires regarding the positive change. Over time, the positive events resulting from the positive change begin to become expected and predictable. Predictable events are less interesting or stimulating than unexpected or novel events, and thus do not lift a person's well-being to the same degree. Higher aspirations, then, are associated with lower well-being. For example, after the person who practices kindness improves her relationships and feels more compassion and competence, she begins to expect to experience those events and to feel those emotions. As a result, every kind act she performs leads to less of a gain in well-being, because her standard for what is required to maintain the same level of well-being has been raised. Those positive events and emotions she has begun to experience have become her new "normal," and thus she requires even greater numbers of events and emotions to increase in well-being (Gruber, Mauss, & Tamir, 2011; Kesebir & Diener, 2008). She may even begin expecting and feeling deserving of gratitude from those she helps, so when those higher aspirations are not met, the result may be disappointment or letdown.

The hedonic adaptation prevention model posits that both paths underlying the course of adaptation are moderated by several key variables, including variety and appreciation (see Figure 21.1; see also Lyubomirsky, 2011). First, the more varied the positive events, the longer it takes to adapt to them. A joke told twice garners few laughs, but a comedian with a wealth of material keeps us chuckling. So a person who helps others in different ways adapts less rapidly than someone who always sends flowers. Second, the less people appreciate (i.e., are aware of and grateful for) a positive change, whether a new hobby, a new relationship, or a new car, the more quickly they adapt. Appreciation may slow adaptation by guarding against social comparisons and increasing expectations (Layard, 2005). For example, if the individual stops being aware and appreciative of the rewards she obtains from performing acts of kindness – that is, she begins to take those rewards for granted – then completing this activity will produce less of a boost in her well-being. Thus, striving to increase appreciation of positive changes, as well as injecting variety, may be critical to forestalling adaptation.

How to Sustain Happiness through Positive Activities

Fortunately, hedonic adaptation is not an insurmountable barrier to sustainable happiness. Researchers can apply their knowledge of the mediators and moderators of adaptation to maximize the effectiveness of positive interventions. Indeed, some interventions have already tested the role of these variables. We discuss these previous relevant studies regarding activities that may be relatively more resistant to adaptation, as well as make suggestions for modifications that can be made to existing interventions to decelerate the adaptation process.

Positive emotions and events

As mentioned above, two important mediators of hedonic adaptation are positive events and positive emotions. Experiencing more positive events (e.g., compliments), and consequently more positive emotions (e.g., gladness), has been theorized to maintain increases in well-being (Lyubomirsky, 2011; Sheldon & Lyubomirsky, 2012). Thus, any one positive activity needs to produce a great deal of positive events and positive emotions in order for the individual to sustain any boost obtained from that activity. Research from our laboratory has supported this idea, showing that both more positive emotions (chosen from a checklist; e.g., "enthusiasm" or "curiosity") and more positive events (listed by participants; e.g., "I told a joke and everyone laughed") predict slower adaptation rates when people receive a stream of personalized positive feedback about their top strengths (e.g., "Your top strength is humor"; Boehm, 2010). Furthermore, another study showed that when participants continued to think about a positive change they had made (e.g., beginning an exercise program), they experienced more positive emotions associated with that change, and thus remained happier (Sheldon & Lyubomirsky, 2012).

Choosing the right activities Notably, certain types of activities may be better at producing streams of positive events and emotions than others. For example, performing acts of kindness may be especially powerful at generating lots of positive events and emotions. Philanthropic acts have been shown to activate brain areas that are associated with pleasure and euphoria (Moll et al., 2006). Also, by performing acts of kindness, people may establish new social connections, strengthen existing relationships, or participate in activities in which they do not normally participate. Each of these possibilities may be associated with new positive experiences or events. Research from our laboratory suggests that performing acts of kindness is indeed associated with increases in well-being (Lyubomirsky et al., 2005).

A related positive activity that is likely to elicit many positive emotions and events is nurturing relationships. Relationships are complicated, dynamic, and ever-changing, and thus involve abundant events and changes, both positive and negative. By focusing on their relationships and trying to improve them, individuals may experience more frequent positive events and emotions, thereby slowing adaptation. For example, if a husband decides he wants to improve his relationship with his wife, he may start to show her more affection, take her out on regular dates, or surprise her with flowers. In return, his wife may reciprocate his affection and show more appreciation for him and the effort he is putting into their marriage. Thus, due to the social nature of this exercise, the husband will enjoy more time together (i.e., positive events) and feel more affection and love (i.e., positive emotions) from his acts directly, but also from his wife's reactions (e.g., feeling appreciated). Furthermore, his wife is likely to experience comparable events and emotions, so the benefits extend not only to the person who chooses to engage in this activity, but to their partner as well. Thus, the dynamic nature of social relationships may provide individuals unique opportunities to multiply positive events and positive emotions in their lives.

A third strategy or activity that is likely to produce copious positive events and emotions is the pursuit of goals that are intrinsic and self-determined. Intrinsic, self-determined goals are those that people work toward because they enjoy doing so, rather than chasing the goal for external, controlled reasons (Deci & Ryan, 2000; Sheldon & Elliot, 1999; Sheldon & Kasser, 1995). The pursuit of intrinsic, self-determined goals is associated with increased happiness because such pursuits accrue positive experiences (see Sheldon, 2002, for a review). Consider a young woman who wishes to become a doctor because she enjoys learning about medicine, is a good student, and likes helping others. In this case, her goal is intrinsically motivated, but the same goal would be extrinsically motivated if she aspired to be a doctor for the high salary or prestige. By enjoying the process, the future doctor experiences many more positive events and emotions than if she worked for the goal purely for external reasons. Thus, if she chooses to increase her happiness by pursuing intrinsic goals – a type of positive activity – she is much less likely to adapt to that activity, and is likely to remain happier for longer, than someone who chooses to pursue extrinsic goals.

Modifying activities One enhancement that could be made to most positive interventions to slow adaptation is to make the intervention social. For example, people could participate in the intervention with a friend rather than by themselves. By adding a social element, the experimenter increases opportunities for a greater variety and number of positive experiences and emotions. For example, a person who decides to begin performing regular acts of kindness with a friend may discuss the acts he performed each week and obtain positive feedback from his friend. His friend may also give him new ideas. By experiencing more positive events and positive emotions, the pair may also be less likely to quit their happiness-enhancing program, because they are not adapting to its rewards and are continuing to benefit from doing acts of kindness week after week. Thus, the social element of the activity may allow them to sustain their increases in happiness for a longer period of time.

Aspirations

Another key mediator of hedonic adaptation is aspiration level. As described above, higher aspirations speed up adaptation because as they increase, people need more positive events and emotions just to maintain their original level of happiness. For example, if a woman is striving to become happier by imagining her best possible self once a week, she may experience a number of positive events the first time she completes the exercise. However, as she continues to do so week after week, she may begin to expect to experience those same events, which will likely become less intense and less frequent as the exercise becomes less novel. As a result, her boosts in happiness will become less frequent, and she will gradually return to the level of well-being she experienced before she started. She may also raise her aspiration levels, so that she starts to anticipate feeling an even larger boost each time and to aspire to ever-higher levels of happiness. As it is unlikely that her activity will continue to meet those raised expectations, her well-being will suffer as a result, bringing her closer to her baseline happiness levels.

When designing happiness interventions, it is important for researchers to keep the optimal level of happiness in mind. If participants' aspirations about the happiness level they wish to achieve are too high, then no positive intervention is going to have long-term benefits, because they are never going to be satisfied with the results and will always want more. Thus, participants should approach interventions with reasonable aspirations or expectations about the potential outcomes of the positive activities they will be prompted to perform.

An effective way to avoid the emergence of ever-higher aspirations may be to pursue intrinsic or self-determined goals. If individuals enjoy the pursuit of the goal, rather than just its attainment, they will be less focused on the end product of "increased happiness" and thus less likely to develop high outcome aspirations. Supporting this idea, in one study, participants who completed positive activities for intrinsic reasons reported greater increases in well-being than those with extrinsic reasons (Dickerhoof, 2007). Thus, as discussed earlier, intrinsic goal pursuit may be associated with larger boosts in happiness and slowed adaptation as compared to pursuing extrinsic goals.

Finally, to avoid increasing aspirations as individuals complete a particular happiness-enhancing activity, they could make an effort to remain conscious of their reference point. That is, as a person progresses in performing positive activities, he may begin to compare his happiness this week to his happiness last week, rather than to his initial happiness level. Because he is likely to experience the biggest boost in happiness near the beginning of the intervention, he may be disappointed when later weeks provide a lesser boost. If he simply takes time to remember where he started, he may remain happier than if he keeps shifting his reference point to the previous week's level.

Variety

As discussed earlier, an abundance of positive events and emotions generated by a particular positive activity – whether that activity involves committing acts of kindness, writing gratitude letters, or pursuing intrinsic goals – leads to increases in well-being. This relationship, however, is moderated by variety, such that the more variable the positive events and emotions, the longer the boost in well-being is maintained. If a person decides to express gratitude more frequently, but ends up writing gratitude letters to the same person every week, he will obtain less and less of a boost in happiness with each letter. If he had written to different people each week – and focused on different reasons that he is thankful – then the boost from each letter would have remained more constant, allowing him to maintain the increase in happiness from the positive activity.

A number of studies have provided empirical support for the importance of variety. For example, one investigation examined how people seek to become happier in the real world by engaging in positive activities (Parks, Della Porta, Pierce, Zilca, & Lyubomirsky, 2012, Study 2). The researchers found that participants, on average, were simultaneously undertaking seven different activities to increase their happiness. Additionally, completing a greater number of different happiness activities on an iPhone application predicted increases in positive mood (Study 3). Thus, variety in what people do in their real lives as they strive to become happier is both common and efficacious. Finally, in an experimental study, participants who completed different acts of kindness each week experienced increases in happiness, whereas those who performed the same act each week did not (Sheldon, Boehm, & Lyubomirsky, 2012).

In one happiness intervention, participants were asked to make changes in either their circumstances or activities. Those who reported more variety in their lives after making the change experienced larger increases in happiness (Sheldon & Lyubomirsky, 2009). Furthermore, those assigned to make a change to their activities (e.g., joining a club) were rewarded with a larger boost in well-being than those assigned to make a change to their circumstances (e.g., making a purchase). The experiences associated with changes in activities are likely more variable than those resulting from changes in circumstances, thus the larger boost. Joining a club may entail meeting new people, making friends, learning a new skill, or spending time doing something one enjoys. Making a new purchase is likely to be associated with fewer unique experiences, which are often limited to interacting with the purchased item. Consequently, the individual is less likely to adapt to changes in activities due to the greater variety in experiences.

These studies provide examples for how people can modify the ways that they engage in positive activities, such that their well-being gains are sustained. First, completing multiple activities at once (unlike most experimental settings where a single activity is completed, one at a time) may lead to larger and longer-lasting happiness boosts. This is apparently already common in people's real-world behavior (Parks et al., 2012, Study 2). A person who engages in multiple activities will likely obtain larger boosts in well-being than if she engages in just one activity, and therefore it will take longer for her well-being to return to baseline levels. Also, because it takes longer to become bored when performing a variety of activities, she may continue participating in those activities for longer, thus maintaining the well-being boost.

Second, if people do perform the same activity each week, it is important that they do not carry it out in the same way each time. For example, if a husband chooses to improve his romantic relationship, he can vary the activity by focusing on being a better listener the first week, writing his wife a love letter the next week, and then giving his wife a thoughtful present. Choosing different types of actions to improve his relationship will increase the variability of the activity and thus slow adaptation.

A third way to strengthen the effectiveness of a happiness-increasing program is to alternate which activities are performed. A person could begin an intervention by performing acts of kindness for a couple of weeks, then switch to writing letters of gratitude, and so on. By alternating or cycling through activities, the individual has less opportunity to adapt to each individual activity, and the resumption of an old activity may reset the adaptation process. Researchers have found that interrupting a positive activity increases people's enjoyment of the activity, presumably because the distraction restarts the adaptation process (Nelson & Meyvis, 2008). Furthermore, the newness of each activity may generate a larger boost, which might prolong the return to baseline. In this way, varying the activities may decelerate adaptation.

Appreciation

Appreciation is another important moderator of the hedonic adaptation process. Appreciating a life change, such as beginning a new positive activity or set of activities, slows down adaptation, allowing people to sustain the boost in happiness from that change. In an intervention where participants made a change to either their circumstances or activities, those who reported maintaining awareness of the change (regardless of which type) experienced more positive moods than those who did not remain aware of the change (Sheldon & Lyubomirsky, 2009). Thus, if a person stops to think about and appreciate her positive change, she will maintain her increased happiness for longer. As Allen Ginsberg once said, "You own twice as much rug if you're twice as *aware* of the rug" (2000, pp. 145–146). That is, if you are not aware of what you have, then it is as if you do not actually have it. Because awareness and attention are so integral to people's experiences (James, 1890), being mindful and aware of the positivity in their lives is a considerable contributor to their happiness.

Choosing the right activities Increasing appreciation is the implicit or explicit goal of several types of positive activities. For example, researchers have tested the effects of increasing attention to positive life events via listing "three good things." In one such intervention, participants were asked to think of three good things that happened on a particular day, to write them down, and to describe why they occurred (Seligman, Steen, Park, & Peterson, 2005). Participants who completed this exercise reported increases in well-being and decreases in depressive symptoms. The Three Good Things exercise forces people to appreciate the good things that happened each day by attending to them, and, therefore, by appreciating them.

Gratitude-based positive activities also essentially work to increase appreciation. Counting one's blessings, for example, is associated with increases in well-being (Emmons & McCullough, 2003; Lyubomirsky et al., 2005; see Chapter 1). In this exercise, people strive each day or each week to think about things for which they are grateful. The exercise compels them to appreciate recent events or experiences, thus fostering well-being gains. Gratitude-based activities force people to re-appreciate the individuals, circumstances, and experiences of their lives and therefore obtain the maximum enjoyment from life. This process slows adaptation by extending the boost in well-being that each of those individuals, circumstances, and experiences provides.

Modifying activities Existing positive activities can be altered to directly increase appreciation in ways that maintain boosts in well-being long after the activity or set of activities is completed. For example, after penning a series of gratitude letters, the writer could maintain the positive benefits by saving the gratitude letters she has written, and an individual who spent several weeks writing down three good things that happened to her every day could display a master list of all those daily "three good things" lists in a prominent place where she might frequently see it. Finally, reminders during the course of an activity (especially after some time has passed) to savor or appreciate the activity as it is occurring may act as a way to infuse appreciation after it has begun to subside.

Conclusion

Human beings are liable to adapt to everything, and especially to positive changes in their lives. Although the pervasiveness of adaptation to positive changes may seem disheartening, the process is both functional and evolutionarily adaptive (Frederick & Loewenstein, 1999). When individuals experience high levels of positive or negative affect, they cannot help but focus on those intense feelings. This attention on their affect can make it difficult to function, because people need to focus on their basic needs in order to survive. Thus, humans hedonically adapt as a means of reducing high arousal, allowing them to direct their attention to more important needs, as well as to novel opportunities and threats. Furthermore, if people did not adapt to positive events or achievements, they might become complacent with the status quo and never strive to accomplish more.

Hedonic adaptation to the rewards of positive activities, however, holds few, if any, benefits, because these rewards are not likely to increase arousal to the point of impaired functioning. Fortunately, such adaptation can be actively and intentionally forestalled, even thwarted, if people heed the recommendations offered in this chapter. Individuals can increase the number of positive events and emotions experienced by engaging in certain types of positive activities (e.g., acts of kindness, nurturing relationships, intrinsic goal pursuit) or by making their positive activities more social in nature. Aspirations can be lowered or kept in check by pursuing intrinsic goals and keeping one's optimal happiness level and reference point in mind. Variety can be added to happiness-increasing programs by completing multiple activities at once, alternating which activities are performed, and performing the activities in a different way each time. Finally, people can augment their appreciation by completing activities that call their attention to the positives in their lives (e.g., savoring and listing "three good things") and gratitude-based activities (e.g., counting one's blessings and writing gratitude letters).

An activity that combines all of these elements is likely to provide the best opportunity for impeding adaptation. Accordingly, people who attempt happiness-enhancing programs should consider the risks of adaptation that present themselves at various points in their program, and researchers should do the same when designing happiness-enhancing interventions. Although the process of adaptation may seem inevitable, by attending to these problems, both practitioners and experimenters may be able to thwart the process of adaptation, and successfully increase happiness – if not forever, then for a very long time.

References

Boehm, J. K. (2010). Getting used to the good things in life: Hedonic adaptation to positive life events (Doctoral dissertation, University of California, Riverside). *Dissertation Abstracts International*, *70*, 5229B.

Boehm, J. K., Lyubomirsky, S., & Sheldon, K. M. (2011). A longitudinal experimental study comparing the effectiveness of happiness-enhancing strategies in Anglo Americans and Asian Americans. *Cognition and Emotion*, *25*, 1152–1167.

Boswell, W. R., Boudreau, J. W., & Tichy, J. (2005). The relationship between employee job change and job satisfaction: The honeymoon-hangover effect. *Journal of Applied Psychology*, *90*, 882–892.

Cohn, M. A., & Fredrickson, B. L, (2010). In search of durable positive psychology interventions: Predictors and consequences of long-term positive behavior change. *Journal of Positive Psychology*, *5*, 355–366.

Deci, E. L., & Ryan, R. M. (2000). The "what" and "why" of goal pursuits: Human needs and the self-determination of behavior. *Psychological Inquiry*, *4*, 227–268.

Dickerhoof, R. (2007). Expressing optimism and gratitude: A longitudinal investigation of cognitive strategies to increase well-being (Doctoral dissertation, University of California, Riverside). *Dissertation Abstracts International*, *68*, 4174.

Emmons, R. A., & McCullough, M. E. (2003). Counting blessings versus burdens: An experimental investigation of gratitude and subjective well-being in daily life. *Journal of Personality and Social Psychology*, *84*, 377–389.

Frederick, S., & Loewenstein, G. (1999). Hedonic adaptation. In D. Kahneman, E. Diener, & N. Schwarz (Eds.), *Well-being: The foundations of hedonic psychology* (pp. 302–329). New York: Russell Sage Foundation.

Ginsberg, A. (2000). Letter to the Wall Street Journal. In B. Morgan (Ed.), *Deliberate prose: Selected essays 1952–1995* (pp. 145–146). New York: Harper Perennial.

Gruber, J., Mauss, I. B., & Tamir, M. (2011). A dark side of happiness? How, when, and why happiness is not always good. *Perspectives on Psychological Science*, *6*, 222–233.

James, W. (1890). *Principles of psychology*. New York: Henry Holt and Company.

Kesebir, P., & Diener, E. (2008). In pursuit of happiness: Empirical answers to philosophical questions. *Perspectives on Psychological Science*, *3*, 117–125.

Layard, R. (2005). *Happiness: Lessons from a new science*. New York: Penguin.

Lucas, R. E. (2005). Time does not heal all wounds: A longitudinal study of reaction and adaptation to divorce. *Psychological Science*, *16*, 945–950.

Lucas, R. E., Clark, A. E., Georgellis, Y., & Diener, E. (2003). Re-examining adaptation and the set point model of happiness: Reactions to changes in marital status. *Journal of Personality and Social Psychology*, *84*, 527–539.

Lucas, R. E., Clark, A. E., Georgellis, Y., & Diener, E. (2004). Unemployment alters the set point for life satisfaction. *Psychological Science*, *15*, 8–13.

Lyubomirsky, S. (2008). *The how of happiness: A scientific approach to getting the life you want*. New York: Penguin.

Lyubomirsky, S. (2011). Hedonic adaptation to positive and negative experiences. In S. Folkman (Ed.), *Oxford handbook of stress, health, and coping* (pp. 200–224). New York: Oxford University Press.

Lyubomirsky, S., Dickerhoof, R., Boehm, J. K., & Sheldon, K. M. (2011). Becoming happier takes both a will and a proper way: An experimental longitudinal intervention to boost well-being. *Emotion*, *11*, 391–402.

Lyubomirsky, S., Sheldon, K. M., & Schkade, D. (2005). Pursuing happiness: The architecture of sustainable change. *Review of General Psychology*, *9*, 111–131.

Lyubomirsky, S., Sousa, L., & Dickerhoof, R. (2006). The costs and benefits of writing, talking, and thinking about life's triumphs and defeats. *Journal of Personality and Social Psychology*, *90*, 692–708.

Moll, J., Krueger, F., Zahn, R., Pardini, M., de Oliveira-Souza, R., & Grafman, J. (2006). Human fronto-mesolimbic networks guide decisions about charitable donation. *Proceedings of the National Academy of Sciences*, *103*, 15623–15628.

Nelson, L. D., & Meyvis, T. (2008). Interrupted consumption: Disrupting adaptation to hedonic experiences. *Journal of Marketing Research*, *45*, 654–664.

Parks, A. C., Della Porta, M. D., Pierce, R. S., Zilca, R., & Lyubomirsky, S. (2012). Pursuing happiness in everyday life: A naturalistic investigation of online happiness seekers. *Emotion*, *12*(6), 1222–1234.

Seligman, M. E. P., Rashid, T., & Parks, A. C. (2006). Positive psychotherapy. *American Psychologist*, *61*, 774–788.

Seligman, M. E., Steen, T. A., Park, N., & Peterson, C. (2005). Positive psychology progress: Empirical validation of interventions. *American Psychologist*, *60*, 410–421.

Sheldon, K. M. (2002). The self-concordance model of healthy goal-striving: When personal goals correctly represent the person. In E. L. Deci & R. M. Ryan (Eds.), *Handbook of self-determination research* (pp. 65–86). Rochester, NY: University of Rochester Press.

Sheldon, K. M., Boehm, J. K., & Lyubomirsky, S. (2012). Variety is the spice of happiness: The hedonic adaptation prevention (HAP) model. In I. Boniwell & S. David (Eds.), *Oxford handbook of happiness* (pp. 901–914). Oxford: Oxford University Press.

Sheldon, K. M., & Elliot, A. J. (1999). Goal striving, need-satisfaction, and longitudinal well-being: The self-concordance model. *Journal of Personality and Social Psychology*, *76*, 482–497.

Sheldon, K. M., & Kasser, T. (1995). Coherence and congruence: Two aspects of personality integration. *Journal of Personality and Social Psychology*, *68*, 531–543.

Sheldon, K. M., & Lyubomirsky, S. (2009). Change your actions, not your circumstances: An experimental test of the sustainable happiness model. In B. Radcliff & A. K. Dutt (Eds.), *Happiness, economics, and politics* (pp. 324–342). New York: Edward Elgar.

Sheldon, K. M., & Lyubomirsky, S. (2012). The challenge of staying happier: Testing the hedonic adaptation prevention (HAP) model. *Personality and Social Psychology Bulletin*, *38*, 670–680.

Sin, N. L., & Lyubomirsky, S. (2009). Enhancing well-being and alleviating depressive symptoms with positive activity interventions: A practice-friendly meta-analysis. *Journal of Clinical Psychology*, *65*, 467–487.

Wilson, T. D., & Gilbert, D. T. (2008). Explaining away: A model of affective adaptation. *Perspectives on Psychological Science*, *3*, 370–386.

22

Person–Activity Fit in Positive Psychological Interventions

Stephen M. Schueller

Introduction

The road to happiness might better be thought of as a set of interweaving highways rather than a single interstate. With regards to positive psychology, researchers, practitioners, and laypeople have proposed diverse strategies for increasing happiness. Duckworth, Steen, and Seligman (2005) surmised that well over 100 positive interventions exist. In a meta-analytic review, Sin and Lyubomirsky (2009) identified 51 research studies of positive psychological interventions (although some of these studies investigated similar techniques). In creating an empirical science of these strategies, researchers begin with the question, "Which ones actually work?" The empirical literature, exemplified by this volume, has demonstrated that a variety of strategies can make people lastingly happier. On average, positive psychological interventions lead to moderate boosts in well-being and help alleviate depressive symptoms, suggesting that not only do these exercises work, but that they work well (Sin & Lyubomirsky, 2009).

Initial validation, however, investigates how much people on average benefit from a given intervention compared to some other intervention, placebo, or no-intervention control. This determines if a technique works and whether researchers and practitioners should disseminate it. Unfortunately, it does not speak to whether or not a specific technique is likely to work for a given person. This question requires a more nuanced view of efficacy that considers how and why performing a given intervention impacts well-being and explores the influence of individual characteristics, contextual variables, and cultural values on outcomes (see the positive activity model; Lyubomirsky & Layous, 2013). Matching hypotheses make intuitive sense and are backed by anecdotal evidence. Those with experience of applying positive psychological interventions have likely encountered people who claim that a selected skill "just doesn't work" for them. Chris Peterson, one of the founders and intellectual leaders of positive psychology,

The Wiley Blackwell Handbook of Positive Psychological Interventions, First Edition.
Edited by Acacia C. Parks and Stephen M. Schueller.

apparently could never bring himself to write a gratitude letter despite assigning the task to students time and time again (Lyubomirsky, 2008). On a first attempt to write a gratitude letter, he felt forced and insincere, using his strength of humor to avoid being embarrassingly sentimental. Eventually he realized that this hindered the efficacy of completing a gratitude letter and to benefit he needed to act in a way that was consistent with the intent of the intervention rather than his natural personality tendencies. In this example, Peterson was able to overcome his personality and benefit; however, most people have more difficulty doing this and thus fail to benefit from some exercises, as was initially the case with Peterson.

This illustrates the person-to-person variability in benefits gained from different positive psychology strategies. Just as people gain fulfillment in their lives from different careers, leisure activities, and family life (and different weighting on each of these aspects), various personality characteristics might affect the benefits accrued from positive psychological interventions. This chapter reviews the historical, theoretical, and empirical underpinnings of the notion of person–activity fit. In this chapter, I will discuss why matching people to interventions might be beneficial, and present evidence supporting this notion. I will also review research that identifies the most important factors in determining fit so that readers might be better able to select interventions for the people they work with. Lastly, I will discuss considerations for making sequences of positive psychological interventions more personalized, and open research questions that could advance person–activity fit and personalization if explored.

Why Person–Activity Fit?

A relevant starting point is to question whether a science of person–activity fit is warranted; one might argue that people would be better served by receiving some standard set of interventions. Providing standard interventions (or standard sets of interventions) requires fewer resources and promotes comparison of research results. Theories that emphasize the universality of human needs would seem to suggest that interventions should be targeting these needs and that investigating (and prioritizing) an individual's unique wants and propensities might be taking away from activities that meet their underlying psychological needs. For example, Self-Determination Theory (SDT) proposes that people have basic psychological needs of autonomy, competence, and relatedness, and that activities that meet these needs are best posed to contribute to psychological well-being (Deci & Ryan, 1985; Sheldon & Cooper, 2008). Along these lines, in a study of goal setting and attainment, Sheldon and Schüler (2011) found that predispositions towards certain motives (i.e., need for affiliation, need for achievement) did not predict the amount of well-being participants received from goals that were consistent with these motives; instead, need fulfillment based on SDT's proposed universal psychological needs led to larger boosts in well-being.

Even within the framework of SDT, however, findings support the notion that fit plays some role in determining the benefits one would accrue from engaging in an activity. First, SDT points to the importance of internal, self-concordant motivation. Self-concordance refers to the degree to which an individual pursues an activity based on his or her own personal values and interests (Sheldon & Houser-Marko, 2001). Indeed, self-concordant activities are engaged in more often and lead to better outcomes in several domains of behavior change. For example, internally motivated individuals are more likely to follow an exercise regime (Ryan, Frederick, Lepes, Rubio, & Sheldon, 1997) and show better adherence to medication and behavioral recommendations for diabetes management (Greening, Stoppelbein, Moll, Palardy, & Hocking, 2004). Therefore, even a theory like SDT, which revolves around the idea of universal needs, also acknowledges that individual differences matter.

Even when given a standard set of positive psychological interventions, individuals tend to select and use a subset of the techniques (Parks, Della Porta, Pierce, Zilca, & Lyubomirsky, 2012). Research should follow up on this observation in order to make specific recommendations rather than promoting the same set of options for all people.

Historical Precedents for Person–Activity Fit in Interventions

Addressing person–activity fit is critical for the field as practitioners turn more and more to individualized and personalized health care. In psychology, the notion of matching people to interventions has a long history of interest from clinicians and researchers. Drawing on his clinical experiences, Freud (1940/1964) suggested that psychological minded patients benefit more from interpretation whereas less sophisticated patients respond better to direct suggestion. Along these lines, the key research question is not whether or not a strategy leads to benefits, but "What treatment by whom is most effective for this individual with that specific problem, and under which set of circumstances?" (Paul, 1967, p. 111). Positive psychologists have been attuned to this as they develop interventions, acknowledging that "any one activity will not help everyone become happier" (Lyubomirsky, Sheldon, & Schkade, 2005, p. 121), and researchers have been encouraged to consider such questions as "is there a personality type for whom some exercises 'take' and others do not?" (Seligman, Steen, Park, & Peterson, 2005, p. 420).

Unfortunately, these pearls of clinical wisdom and calls for research have not been met by impressive or consistent findings. One of the largest studies of person–treatment matching undertaken, Project MATCH, found little support for the existence of any person-by-treatment interactions within substance abuse intervention research, leaving many to conclude that matching individuals to treatment is unimportant and that providing efficacious interventions to the masses is the best approach (Project Match Research Group, 1997). Project MATCH and other similar research paradigms contain many methodological features that reduce the likelihood that researchers might be able to identify person–treatment interactions even if they exist. One critical factor is that although participant characteristics are often measured using psychometrically validated measures with high levels of specificity, differences between treatment conditions are conceptualized on a gross level (Shoham & Insel, 2011). That is, to determine whether interpersonal therapy is more or less effective than cognitive therapy for people with a given characteristic (i.e., level of extraversion, depressive symptoms, age, etc.), researchers also need to measure variation in the delivery of the intervention (e.g., what components do participants receive, do, etc.). As many interventions are complex, multi-faceted, and extended interactions, it is difficult to conduct studies of person–activity fit using these interventions.

Positive psychological interventions might be in a better position to consider questions of person–activity fit than therapies (e.g., cognitive therapy, interpersonal therapy). Positive psychological interventions are often brief strategies that focus on a single repeated behavior (e.g., write down three good things each day; Emmons & McCullough, 2003) or strength (e.g., optimism; Lyubomirksy, Dickerhoof, Boehm, & Sheldon, 2011) that they aim to promote. In fact, in the previously mentioned meta-analytic review of positive psychological interventions, 39% of interventions were only four weeks or shorter. Thus, positive psychological interventions can be thought of more as kernels or elements of content rather than a single unified treatment model such as those used in Project MATCH. Although there are obvious exceptions to this rule, such as Positive Psychotherapy (Seligman, Rashid, & Parks, 2006) or Well-Being Therapy (Fava & Ruini, 2003), the bulk of research on positive psychological interventions covers single-shot intervention techniques. This chapter will focus its review on these briefer, "single-shot" interventions, because this is where most of the research on person–activity fit has accumulated.

Theories of Person–Activity Fit

Assuming that an activity or set of activities exists that will provide greater benefits for a given individual, it is then worth discussing how one might determine which activity would be the best "fit" and why that activity might be the most beneficial. In general, theories of person–activity fit can be divided into those that capitalize on one's strengths and those that compensate for one's weaknesses (Cronbach & Snow, 1977). Lyubomirsky (2008) describes this distinction more colloquially as being between those interventions that fit with our source of unhappiness and those that suit our strengths or our lifestyle.

Capitalization or strengths-based perspectives believe that people benefit the most from practicing activities that are consistent with their strengths, talents, values, cultures, or other variables. Using an educational example, whereas a verbal learner might perform best on a spelling test after carefully repeating the words aloud, a socially motivated achiever might do best after participating in a mock spelling bee with classmates. Capitalization or strengths-based approaches might produce greater benefits as people are more engaged in these activities and thus more motivated to complete them. This additional motivation might correspond to increased time and effort devoted to an intervention that builds off one's strengths.

Compensation refers to identifying strategies that help overcome deficits or weaknesses. These approaches emphasize balance by working on skills or characteristics one lacks, but needs in order to become a well-rounded person. An intervention that focuses on compensation would help teach skills a person does not possess or require a person to engage in activities that he does not usually engage in. For example, a verbal learner might be best helped by developing his spatial learning skills, or an independent achiever would do best in an exercise that encourages him to work in a group. I refer to the compensation approach of matching as the "head through the clouds" idea that a person gains the most benefit by experiencing something that they would not otherwise do and therefore adding a new behavior or cognitive strategy to their repertoire. This might build insight, resources, or understanding that would not happen by just further developing one's strengths, and might create a more "well-rounded" person. I will consider each of these approaches in turn.

Strengths

A strengths perspective is most consistent with the tenets of positive psychology and will likely be familiar to readers of this volume. Strengths-based perspectives in clinical practice focus on determining the characteristics and resources that help people function and cope even in the face of stressors. Applying notions of strengths to the question of person–activity fit, the most effective strategies should be those that are consistent with an individual's characteristics. Clinical research on the efficacy of treatments for depression provides initial support that interventions drawing on strengths might produce the most benefit. In the National Institute of Mental Health (NIMH) Depression Collaborative Research Program, a large-scale study of the effectiveness of psychotherapy for major depressive disorder, the patients who benefited most from cognitive-behavioral therapy were those with the lowest initial level of cognitive dysfunction, whereas the individuals who benefited most from interpersonal therapy were those who started out highest in social skills (Elkin, 1994). In both of these cases, these variables are constructs that were suggested to be the active ingredients of each treatment. These results provide support from the clinical literature that building on a strength may be an important factor in determining the best fit for an individual. Theoretically, then, what is it that drives strengths-based approaches to lead to enhanced benefits?

Cronbach and Snow (1977) express a preference for strengths-based approaches because they believe an intervention addressing a weakness runs the risk of becoming boring, helplessness-inducing, or might damage motivation. Thus, drawing on strengths will be more intrinsically rewarding. Using strengths promotes flow experiences and helps bring out the best in a person (Seligman, 2002). Working on strengths might also increase the likelihood that the activity will be self-sustaining. Spontaneous usage of a positive intervention after the skill has been taught is one way that the activity might lead to larger and more sustainable boosts in well-being. Even brief interventions have been shown to have long-term effects on well-being; however, it appears that the individuals who experience sustainable boosts in happiness are those who continue to practice the intervention techniques even after they are no longer required to do so (Seligman et al., 2005).

Indeed, it is this intrinsic motivation to continue practicing strengths-based activities that makes them superior to those that focus on weaknesses in the long term. In a series of studies that compared the strengths and weakness approach head-to-head, the typical signature strengths exercise was modified by requiring participants to do an activity that drew either on one of their top five "signature strengths," or on one of their bottom five strengths, which were considered "weaknesses" (Haidt, 2002, 2004). Every day for two weeks participants either engaged in an activity that used one of their five "signature strengths," or worked on a weakness. After the two weeks there were no differences in terms of happiness, self-esteem, or self-reported health. This is not surprising, as the VIA (Values in Action) classification of strengths only includes characteristics that are thought to be beneficial and valued for their own sake (Peterson & Seligman, 2004). Even if one does not have the strength of self-discipline, if one continues to engage in it, it might boost one's well-being. Looking at the long-term effectiveness of the different strategies, however, demonstrated that boosts in well-being were only maintained amongst the group who used their strengths and not amongst the group who worked on weaknesses. Participants who worked on strengths reported enjoying the intervention more than those who worked on weaknesses, and continued to do activities that used their strengths after the end of the intervention. These participants who continued to engage in the exercise had more long-lasting benefits from the intervention. Participants who were asked to work on their bottom five strengths from the VIA questionnaire were more than happy to stop working on those aspects once the intervention ended. This is consistent with the idea that working on a strength is self-perpetuating whereas working on a weakness can be boring, futile, disheartening, and reduces the motivation to continue.

Models within personality theory posit the same outcome. The Affect Congruence Model of interactionism, for example, posits that situations that are a better fit for a person's personality will result in more benefits, specifically higher levels of positive affect (Emmons, Diener, & Larsen, 1986). Studies of person/situation interactionism, however, have found mixed results. For example, with regards to introversion/extraversion, some studies find that extraverts enjoy social interactions more than introverts, whereas other studies find that extraverts respond more positively to any situation (Emmons & Diener, 1986; Emmons et al., 1986; Lucas & Diener, 2001). Advancing evidence in personality theory suggests that personality is much more dynamic than the stable, consistent, individual differences that classical personality theory proposed (see Chapter 27). More dynamic models of personality highlight the need to better understand contextual and cultural variables that might play a role in person–activity fit (Biswas-Diener, Kashdan, & Minhas, 2011).

In positive psychology, one of the most commonly referenced strengths activities is the "Using Your Signature Strength" exercise. A careful reading of the instructions indicates that participants are encouraged to use the strength in a new and different way each day (as summarized in Seligman et al., 2005). This highlights an important theoretical point about person–activity fit. Regardless of whether the activity is consistent with a person's strengths, values, interests, or inclinations, in order for an activity to effectively increase happiness, it must get him or her to engage in a *new* behavior or cognitive activity. The issue of recommending interventions to people will be considered in more detail later.

Weaknesses

An exercise could also help a person by working on their weaknesses or engaging them in activities that they do not typically do. These might be dissimilar to their personality dispositions, for example having an introvert perform an exercise that requires social interaction such as delivering a gratitude letter. Strategies that are disparate from one's predispositions might provide insight, understanding, compensate for deficits, build skills that were otherwise lacking, or perhaps just be a break from the quotidian routine that one has settled into. Working on one's deficits might promote balance and make a person a more well-rounded individual, developing a variety of skills to promote well-being and cope with life's stressors. Additionally, people increase in skills more quickly after initial attempts. Thus, in addressing one's deficits one might experience faster growth than when working with strong and well-developed skills (Biswas-Diener et al., 2011). This is a strategy I referred to earlier as the "head through the clouds" perspective. This metaphor is meant to help create an image of a person bursting through the clouds as they develop new insight or new skills from trying something different. Life at times traps people in a pattern of doing the same thing or relying on the same skill over and over again. This perspective highlights the need for flexibility, which might actually be a crucial component to promoting psychological health (Kashdan & Rottenberg, 2010).

As an example of the benefits of addressing one's weaknesses and the notion that this might represent a good "fit" activity, consider a sports metaphor. Dwight Howard, a professional basketball player with the Houston Rockets, is one of the premier players in the NBA. In several years of his career he has led the league in various statistics including rebounding, blocks, and field goal percentage. One might think that the activity that would provide the best "fit" for Dwight would be to continue to refine his rebounding and his stellar defense (he has also won the Defensive Player of the Year Award in three consecutive years). However, Dwight also has one of the lowest free throw percentages in the league. In the 2012/2013 season he missed 366 free throws (as a reference point only 16 other players even attempted more than 366 free throws) shooting a meager 49%. In fact, he missed more free throws in that season than his then teammate Steve Nash did in his entire 17-year career. If Dwight had improved his free throw shooting percentage to the league average, he would have averaged over two more points per game. Thus, the best way for Dwight to be considered a better, more well-rounded (and happier) basketball player might be to spend less time in practice standing near the post and more time on the free throw line.

The best "fit" for any intervention, including positive psychological interventions, therefore, might be the one that develops a person into the most well-rounded individual, using compensation to capitalize on novelty rather than pre-existing strengths or interests. As Schwartz and Sharpe (2006) state, "more of any one of the strengths is not necessarily better; in fact nurturing a single signature strength can produce deformations of character" (p. 380). Adopting this perspective, however, might appear less beneficial than a strengths perspective using certain methods of evaluation. For example, working on one's deficits might be less fun in the moment and lead to a decrease in short-term subjective well-being but ultimately lead to large and lasting long-term benefits that might increase an individual's well-being. Returning to Dwight Howard, he might not enjoy the practice required to improve his free throw shooting percentage (this might correspond to why he is such a poor free throw shooter to begin with) but an improved percentage might improve his personal statistics, his team's chances of winning, and the likelihood of winning future individual awards. Even if in the short term working on free throws decreases his well-being it is hard to argue that winning a Most Valuable Player award would not produce increased joy and satisfaction in the long term. Moving beyond this example and returning to positive psychology, it could be that an isolated introvert who rarely expresses gratitude would have the most to gain by completing a Gratitude Visit exercise, with the letter written to a fellow student who helped him out during a group project. Although, while writing the letter, he might feel apprehensive and nervous about how the other student might react, delivering the letter could then lead to increased social connections, satisfying a basic need to build social relationships, and increase his connectedness to others in his community (see Deci & Ryan, 1985; Seligman, 2011).

Thus, although, at first glance, weakness approaches might seem inconsistent with basic tenets of positive psychology, their application to person–activity fit requires consideration. I will now turn to a review of existing evidence of person–activity fit to discuss some areas in which person–activity interactions have been demonstrated within the field of positive psychology.

Specific Examples of Person–Activity Fit

Personality

One area that might predict person–activity fit is personality characteristics. Personality refers to the patterns of affect, behaviors, and cognitions, which are stable across time. In this way, individual differences in a person are thought to predispose them to benefit from particular activities. In studies of this nature, a variety of personality characteristics have been assessed *a priori* and then multiple intervention strategies are compared to see if people who score high on a given personality characteristic gain more or less benefit from a specified intervention. In a series of studies, I investigated if personality could serve as a prognostic variable for several positive psychology exercises (Schueller, 2012). In the first study, 150 undergraduate students were randomly assigned to receive one of five positive psychology exercises and completed the assigned exercise over a six-week period. In addition to measures of personality, participants also completed measures of well-being. The interaction term between extraversion and condition was not significant ($F(4, 139) = 2.36$, $p = .056$), but suggestive that some differences might exist in individual interventions. Planned contrast analyses, however, supported that extraversion was an important variable that related differential benefits from the various exercises assigned. Extraverts benefited more from the Gratitude Visit and Savoring exercises, whereas introverts benefited more from the active-constructive responding, signature strengths, and blessings exercises. Given the non-significant interaction, however, this study was replicated in a second sample that examined if performing a gratitude visit either in person or over the phone would change the direction of these findings. This study would remove the in-person interaction component that was believed to be driving the reduced efficacy of the intervention for introverts, who shy away from social interaction and prefer solitude (such as that provided by the gratitude journaling "blessings" exercise). Indeed, introverts received larger boosts in well-being when instructed to perform the gratitude visit over the phone. Pooling the participants who completed the gratitude visit in person across these two studies using meta-analytic techniques supported that the gratitude visit produced larger increases in well-being for extraverts than for introverts. These findings provide some support for the notion that broad personality traits might predict which exercises would provide the best "fit" for a given person.

Within an intervention, the specific instructions can be modified to be more consistent with personality predispositions. Giannopoulos and Vella-Brodrick (2011) adopted this approach and modified the blessings exercise to evaluate experiences that related to different orientations to happiness (Peterson, Park, & Seligman, 2005). Participants were randomly assigned to one of four groups, with each group reflecting on three events from the day that they found either (a) pleasurable, (b) engaging, or (c) meaningful, or (d) one event from each of the three categories. People's responses to the Orientation to Happiness Questionnaire were used to determine if people with an orientation to a particular pathway to happiness would receive greater benefits in well-being if they reflected on events consistent with that pathway. Participants' scores on the Mental Health Continuum – Short Form increased in all of the intervention groups, with the largest increases coming in the condition which reflected on an event in each category (pleasure, engagement, and meaning). Person–activity fit was partially supported, as an interaction emerged immediately post-intervention but not at a two-week follow-up. The researchers found, however, that this matching followed a deficits perspective. That is, at post-test, those individuals who were assigned to an intervention that was different from their dominant orientation to happiness received the largest increases in well-being.

A series of studies have looked at personality dispositions that relate to increased levels of psychopathology in order to investigate questions of person–activity fit. These are useful characteristics to consider because findings following from these personality traits could help shape recommendations for people with specific diagnoses or suggest strategies that might be most beneficial if provided in a preventive manner. These studies evaluated interventions that promoted self-compassion and optimism (Shapira & Mongrain, 2010), involved performing acts of compassion towards others (Mongrain, Chin, & Shapira, 2010), and required participants to review events they were grateful for or listen to uplifting music (Sergeant & Mongrain, 2011).

An internet sample was recruited from ads placed on Facebook and the exercises were then disseminated through an online web portal entitled "Project HOPE." Project HOPE involved the delivery of various positive psychological interventions that contributed to several research studies. In one study, participants who entered via the "Project HOPE" web portal were randomly assigned to a self-compassion, optimism, or control condition (Shapira & Mongrain, 2010). In the compassion condition, participants were directed to reflect on a stressful experience and to write a letter to oneself in order to soothe and comfort oneself. In the optimism condition, participants wrote on their future, imagining they are in a better place and reflecting on the steps it took them to get there. These interventions were effective strategies at boosting well-being. To investigate person–activity fit, the researchers also examined interactions based on different aspects related to depressogenic characteristics including self-criticism and connectedness. The results regarding practicing self-compassion were mixed, however, as findings supported that individuals high in connectedness benefited more from the self-compassion exercise, but other predictions, such as that those who were self-critical would benefit, were not supported. Their conclusion was that connected individuals have developed skills to nurture others and this exercise invited them to use those skills on themselves. Indeed, the directions for the self-compassion exercise instructed participants to "think about what you would say to a friend in your position, or what a friend would say to you in this situation" (Shapira & Mongrain, 2010, p. 380), a task that might be more easily accomplished by someone who is connected and thus has more frequent and compassionate interactions with others.

Furthermore, within this same study, different data analytic methods produced different conclusions regarding whether those high in self-criticism benefited more from the self-compassion and optimism condition. Although results of a completers analysis supported these predictions, results from multi-level modeling failed to replicate the findings. This illustrates one of the difficulties of research on person–activity fit. Investigating moderation hypotheses requires statistical tests that might be unpowered with some methods without large samples.

Using the same recruitment procedures, participants from the same web portal were invited to participate in a study in which they received a gratitude exercise (listing five things that they were grateful for), a music exercise (listening to three or four uplifting songs of their choosing), or a control condition, for a week-long intervention period (Sergeant & Mongrain, 2011). The researchers predicted that the gratitude exercise would appeal to self-critics and that the music exercise would appeal to needy individuals, two personality styles selected due to their relation to increased vulnerability to depressive disorders. Although they found some support for the fit of the gratitude exercise for individuals high in self-criticism, as they experienced greater increases in happiness, self-esteem, and decreases in physical symptom severity, they did not find that the music condition was a good fit for individuals high in neediness. In fact, those high in neediness did not respond well to either the gratitude or music condition. It is difficult to decipher from these results whether this shows that individuals high in neediness were a poor fit for the two exercises selected in this study, or if neediness is a prognostic variable that indicates poor response to any treatment.

In a third study using the same recruitment procedures and web portal to administer interventions, participants were either instructed to perform a compassionate action for someone else or assigned to a control condition in which they wrote about an early memory (Mongrain et al., 2010). Again interested in person–activity fit, the researchers examined whether an anxious attachment style, as measured by a self-report questionnaire, predicted response to the exercise. Indeed, people with an anxious attachment style reported a greater decrease in depressive symptoms after completing the intervention than those who scored low on the measure of anxious attachment. Although this study only demonstrated these findings in the short term, and these results were not replicated in the analyses which assessed change over time throughout the six-month follow-up period, it provides some support that completing compassionate acts for others might be a useful strategy for those with an anxious attachment style. Compassionate actions might promote other-focus and promote social interactions that can draw anxiously attached individuals away from focusing on themselves and their anxious symptoms. Certainly, the effects of a brief intervention would likely diminish over time, especially if participants did not continue to use the intervention strategies. In the case of this intervention, it could be that performing compassionate actions might be novel to an anxiously attached sample and thus they did not continue to practice these actions once the intervention period ended. This would be consistent with the notion that working to overcome one's deficits might be beneficial in the short term but is not self-maintaining after the intervention period ends.

Overall, these studies of personality characteristics offer promising support for the notion that person–activity fit is important, but demonstrate the challenges of conducting this research. First, researchers often use a small sample of interventions, and unless the selected interventions have opposite effects (as in individuals high on the variable benefit from one intervention and not the other and vice versa for individuals low on that trait), it is difficult to determine if the selected characteristic is a prescriptive variable (which speaks to "fit" for a given intervention) or a prognostic variable (which relates to either positive or negative outcomes overall). Second, conducting analyses of moderation is often underpowered in some statistical tests and requires large samples, replication and summation across samples, or strong *a priori* theoretically driven hypotheses and tests to reach significance. Lastly, the selection of which variables to include is not straightforward, yet measuring too many variables leads to difficulties in conducting multiple tests and thus reducing power again.

Motivation

Another way to conceptualize person–activity fit is through looking at an individual's self-reported "fit" for a given intervention technique. This is the strategy advocated by Lyubomirsky (2008) in her research-based self-help book, *The how of happiness.* Before presenting the activities, Lyubomirsky provides a questionnaire to help determine which strategies might be the most effective to boost one's own happiness. This questionnaire is based on the notion that activities that best represent one's interests and values will produce more self-concordant motivation and thus individuals will put more time and effort into completing these activities and gain more benefits.

In a study investigating this theory, participants were randomly assigned to a writing condition either based on expressing gratitude, thinking about one's best possible self, or reviewing one's day (Sheldon & Lyubomirsky, 2006). Before completing the exercise participants answered questions that described why they would engage in the exercise, either for their own interest and benefit or based on external and introjected motivation. Results supported that self-concordant motivation did in fact relate to continued practice of the techniques over time and that higher levels of initial self-concordant motivation corresponded to greater decreases in negative mood as participants practiced the exercise over time.

In a subsequent study, self-selection was manipulated by including two separate recruitment procedures (Lyubomirsky et al., 2011). The same study was advertised to undergraduate students as both an opportunity to take part in a study on "happiness interventions" or one on "cognitive exercises." It was predicted that students who sought to participate in a study on happiness interventions would be more interested and thus motivated to improve their own happiness and thus experience larger boosts in well-being. Within each of these groups, participants were randomly assigned into the same set of conditions: a gratitude exercise, an optimism exercise, or a control condition. The proposed active interventions led to increases in happiness only for the motivated group. Furthermore, within this group, effort invested was related to larger boosts in happiness. It was not reported whether effort was greater overall in the self-selected versus the non-self-selected group but this would not be surprising given the pattern of results. From these findings, it might be that motivation is not just an important consideration for fit but actually essential. To quote the authors, "becoming happier takes both a will and a proper way" (Lyubomirsky et al., 2011, p. 391).

Ethnicity

Other aspects of person–activity fit may represent broader concepts than individual characteristics. Instead, there might be aspects of the group or culture one belongs to that might affect whether or not one benefits from a given intervention (see Chapter 23). In clinical practice, modifications to manuals developed might be necessary for new ethnic, cultural, or income groups (see Muñoz & Mendelson, 2005). In recent applications of positive psychology techniques, practices were adapted to be relevant for dissemination in the United States military (Reivich, Seligman, & McBride, 2011). However, it could be that modifications and adaptations are not enough and that different content on the basis of one's cultural group might be more beneficial. Findings along these lines would help advance the understanding of person–activity matching questions.

In order to address the differential efficacy of positive psychology techniques amongst different cultural groups, Boehm, Lyubomirsky, and Sheldon (2011) recruited an Anglo American and an Asian American community-dwelling sample using community-based websites, fliers, and newspaper advertisements. They specifically targeted sources that would be able to recruit low acculturated, predominantly foreign-born Asian Americans. For example, some of their ads were placed in a Chinese language newspaper. A total of 220 participants were randomly assigned to a gratitude, optimism, or control condition. These participants practiced the strategy for a six-week period and completed measures of subjective well-being. Although, overall, the gratitude and optimism conditions produced greater increases in subjective well-being than the control condition, these benefits were greater for the Anglo American group than for the Asian American group. It could be that strategies that enhance positive emotions are less relevant for participants from an Eastern background. Instead, Asian participants might benefit more from techniques that emphasize a balance between positive and negative emotions (see Leu, Wang, & Koo, 2011).

Different cultures have also shown differential benefits from the widely used Penn Resiliency Program (PRP). This program worked better for Latinos than for African American middle school children at both six-month (Cardemil, Reivich, & Seligman, 2002) and two-year (Cardemil, Reivich, Beevers, Seligman, & James, 2007) follow-ups. Interestingly, in both this and the previous example, cultural matching identified groups who did not benefit from the intervention but did not find interventions from which those groups did benefit. Again, this presents difficulty in interpretation of the findings. It could be that the content of the intervention was not beneficial for these cultural groups, or it could be that not enough care was taken to translate and modify the techniques to make them culturally appropriate. Further research is needed to evaluate whether PRP could be adapted to be relevant for African American students (as PRP is the basis of the program that was adapted for the US military), or if the skills and strategies are not relevant for that cultural group.

Implications and Future Directions

This review of the literature on person–activity fit illustrates some promising support, methodological limitations, and open questions. Overall, enough studies have provided evidence supporting the idea that specific strategies might produce more benefits for a given individual that it is worthwhile to consider person–activity fit both in researching and applying positive psychological interventions. Unfortunately, the studies presented here often conceptualize the individual characteristics and the meaning of person–activity fit in different ways. This chapter has reviewed evidence that has supported person–activity fit within areas of personality characteristics, motivation, and culture. Furthermore, most of these studies investigated only a small subset of the possible positive interventions. This volume has demonstrated that positive psychological interventions include a vast and disparate selection of strategies. When only a small set of interventions are used within a single study it is difficult to determine if null findings for one characteristic means that the variable of interest merely indicates poor fit, poor prognosis, or both. Comparing across studies is complicated when studies do not use similar measures to investigate the person part of the person–activity fit equation. Lastly, failure to consider fit might lead to an underestimation of effect sizes if all participants receive the same intervention within a study. This is especially concerning if variables that might predict fit are non-normally distributed within samples of those seeking positive interventions, as Parks and colleagues (2012) demonstrated was the case with depressive symptoms. Thus fit should continue to be explored in future studies of positive interventions.

Personalized Positive Psychology

Even with these findings on person–activity fit, it remains difficult for researchers and practitioners to answer the question that most interests consumers of positive psychological interventions: Which strategy should I use? In a series of studies, I attempted to address this question by laying the foundation for personalized positive psychology programs. In an initial study, six positive psychology exercises were disseminated through an online web portal (Schueller, 2010). Participants rated their preference for each intervention after completing it. Submitting these ratings to a factor analysis produced three groups of two exercises each. Participants who preferred the Active-Constructive Responding exercise tended to also prefer the savoring exercise, those who preferred the Gratitude Visit exercise also preferred the strengths exercise, and those who preferred the blessings exercise also preferred the Life Summary exercise (see Schueller, 2010, for a description of these exercises). In a further study, these groupings were used to form the basis of a recommendation system, providing some participants with a second exercise based on their rated preference for a first exercise and other participants with simply two randomly assigned exercises (Schueller, 2011). Participants were unaware that a matching framework was used for any participants. Thus they could not be influenced by the belief that an exercise was specifically selected for them. Using this matching framework increased participants' preference for the second exercise and was related to increased (although not significantly so) well-being compared to participants in the unmatched group.

These studies demonstrate a promising future direction for integrating the work of various studies on person–activity fit, creating individualized packages of positive psychology content for each person. As research advances, it may be possible to incorporate more than just preference to make recommendations, but instead rely on variables such as personality characteristics, motivation, and culture.

To accomplish this, researchers need to be more mindful of the variables they measure and report. It would be extremely useful if researchers who study positive psychological interventions and practitioners who apply them could create a consensus of common characteristics that should be evaluated and collect data in such a way that it could be generalized across studies. Furthermore, the science of person–activity fit can be advanced by improved frequency and granularity of data collection.

Another important future direction of person–activity fit is an expansion of the variables used to measure people and interventions. It would be interesting to see more studies take on contextual and cultural variables to add to the literature that considers personality characteristics. As previously discussed, recent research has challenged the idea of personality as a stable, fixed aspect and highlighted the variability of personality traits across situations (see Chapter 27). Contextual variables might be able to indicate the optimal timing or sequence of interventions. It could be that the intervention that is best for a given person in the morning is not the best intervention at night. For example, gratitude affects sleep quality in that it improves pre-sleep cognitions, suggesting that it might be best to do it at night before bed (Wood, Joseph, Lloyd, & Atkins, 2009). The strategies that help alleviate a negative mood might not be the same as those that capitalize on a positive mood, and thus certain activities may be more or less appropriate in a given moment.

Overall, the literature suggests that individual considerations should be taken into account when selecting intervention strategies. Returning to where we started, the road to happiness is not the same for all people and positive psychologists need to ensure that the roadmap their interventions offer is helpful for highlighting the various available routes.

References

Biswas-Diener, R., Kashdan, T. B., & Minhas, G. (2011). A dynamic approach to psychological strength development and intervention. *Journal of Positive Psychology*, *6*, 106–118.

Boehm, J. K., Lyubomirsky, S., & Sheldon, K. M. (2011). A longitudinal experimental study comparing the effectiveness of happiness-enhancing strategies in Anglo Americans and Asian Americans. *Cognition and Emotion*, *25*, 1152–1167.

Cardemil, E. V., Reivich, K. J., Beevers, C. G., Seligman, M. E. P., & James, J. (2007). The prevention of depressive symptoms in low-income, minority children: Two-year follow-up. *Behaviour Research and Therapy, 45*, 313–327.

Cardemil, E. V., Reivich, K. J., & Seligman, M. E. P. (2002). The prevention of depressive symptoms in low-income minority middle-school students. *Prevention and Treatment, 5*.

Cronbach, L. J., & Snow, R. E. (1977). *Aptitudes and instructional methods: A handbook for research interactions.* New York: Irvington Publishers, Inc.

Deci, E. L., & Ryan, R. M. (1985). *Intrinsic motivation and self-determination in human behavior.* New York: Plenum Press.

Duckworth, A. L., Steen, T. A., & Seligman, M. E. P. (2005). Positive psychology in clinical practice. *Annual Review of Clinical Psychology, 1*, 629–651.

Elkin, I. (1994). The NIMH Treatment of Depression Collaborative Research Program: Where we began and where we are. In A. E. Bergin & S. L. Garfield (Eds.), *Handbook of psychotherapy and behavior change* (4th ed., pp. 114–139). Oxford: John Wiley & Sons.

Emmons, R. A., & Diener, E. (1986). An interactional approach to the study of personality and emotion. *Journal of Personality, 54*, 371–384.

Emmons, R. A., Diener, E., & Larsen, R. J. (1986). Choice and avoidance of everyday situations and affect congruence: Two models of reciprocal interactionism. *Journal of Personality and Social Psychology, 51*, 815–826.

Emmons, R. A., & McCullough, M. E. (2003). Counting blessings versus burdens: An experimental investigation of gratitude and subjective well-being in daily life. *Journal of Personality and Social Psychology, 84*, 377–389.

Fava, G. A., & Ruini, C. (2003). Development and characteristics of a well-being enhancing psychotherapeutic strategy: Well-being therapy. *Journal of Behavior Therapy and Experimental Psychiatry, 34*, 45–63.

Freud, S. (1964). An outline of psychoanalysis. In J. Strachey (Ed. and Trans.), *The standard edition of the complete psychological works of Sigmund Freud* (Vol. *23*, pp. 137–207). London: Hogarth. (Original work published 1940.)

Giannopoulos, V. L., & Vella-Brodrick, D. A. (2011). Effects of positive interventions and orientations to happiness on subjective well-being. *Journal of Positive Psychology, 6*, 95–105.

Greening, L., Stoppelbein, L., Moll, G., Palardy, N., & Hocking, M. (2004). Intrinsic motivation and glycemic control in adolescents with Type 1 diabetes. *Diabetes Care, 27*, 1517.

Haidt, J. (2002). It's more fun to work on strengths than weaknesses (but it may be better for you). Unpublished manuscript, University of Virginia.

Haidt, J. (2004). Noble pleasures last longer than self-indulgent pleasures, especially when they match strengths and are socially shared. Unpublished manuscript, University of Virginia.

Kashdan, T. B., & Rottenberg, J. (2010). Psychological flexibility as a fundamental aspect of health. *Clinical Psychology Review, 30*, 865–878.

Leu, J., Wang, J., & Koo, K. (2011). Are positive emotions just as "positive" across cultures? *Emotion, 11*, 994–999.

Lucas, R. E., & Diener, E. (2001). Understanding extraverts' enjoyment of social situations: The importance of pleasantness. *Journal of Personality and Social Psychology, 81*, 343–356.

Lyubomirsky, S. (2008). *The how of happiness: A scientific approach to getting the life you want.* New York: Penguin.

Lyubomirsky, S., Dickerhoof, R., Boehm, J. K., & Sheldon, K. M. (2011). Becoming happier takes both a will and a proper way: An experimental longitudinal intervention to boost well-being. *Emotion, 11*, 391–402.

Lyubomirsky, S., & Layous, K. (2013). How do simple positive activities increase well-being? *Current Directions in Psychological Science*, *22*, 57–62.

Lyubomirsky, S., Sheldon, K. M., & Schkade, D. (2005). Pursuing happiness: The architecture of sustainable change. *Review of General Psychology*, *9*, 111–131.

Mongrain, M., Chin, J. M., & Shapira, L. B. (2010). Practicing compassion increases happiness and self-esteem. *Journal of Happiness Studies*, *12*, 963–981.

Muñoz, R. F., & Mendelson, T. (2005). Toward evidence-based interventions for diverse populations: The San Francisco General Hospital prevention and treatment manuals. *Journal of Consulting and Clinical Psychology*, *73*, 790–799.

Parks, A. C., Della Porta, M. D., Pierce, R. S., Zilca, R., & Lyubomirsky, S. (2012). Pursuing happiness in everyday life: A naturalistic investigation of online happiness seekers. *Emotion*, *12*, 1222–1234.

Paul, G. L. (1967). Strategy of outcome research in psychotherapy. *Journal of Consulting Psychology*, *31*, 109–118.

Peterson, C., Park, N., & Seligman, M. E. P. (2005). Orientations to happiness and life satisfaction: The full versus the empty life. *Journal of Happiness Studies*, *6*, 25–41.

Peterson, C., & Seligman, M. E. P. (2004). *Character strengths and virtues: A handbook and classification*. New York: Oxford University Press.

Project Match Research Group (1997). Matching alcoholism treatments to client heterogeneity: Project MATCH posttreatment drinking outcomes. *Journal of Studies on Alcohol*, *58*, 7–29.

Reivich, K. J., Seligman, M. E. P., & McBride, S. (2011). Master resilience training in the U.S. army. *American Psychologist*, *66*, 25–34.

Ryan, R. M., Frederick, C. M., Lepes, D., Rubio, N., & Sheldon, K. M. (1997). Intrinsic motivation and exercise adherence. *International Journal of Sports Psychology*, *28*, 335–354.

Schueller, S. M. (2010). Preferences for positive psychology exercises. *Journal of Positive Psychology*, *5*, 192–203.

Schueller, S. M. (2011). To each his own well-being boosting intervention: Using preference to guide selection. *Journal of Positive Psychology*, *6*, 300–313.

Schueller, S. M. (2012). Personality fit and positive interventions: Extraverted and introverted individuals benefit from different happiness increasing strategies. *Psychology*, *12A*, 1166–1173.

Schwartz, B., & Sharpe, K. E. (2006). Practical wisdom: Aristotle meets positive psychology. *Journal of Happiness Studies*, *7*, 377–395.

Seligman, M. E. P. (2002). *Authentic happiness*. New York: Free Press.

Seligman, M. E. P. (2011). *Flourish: A visionary new understanding of happiness and well-being*. New York: Free Press.

Seligman, M. E. P., Rashid, T., & Parks, A. C. (2006). Positive psychotherapy. *American Psychologist*, *61*, 774–788.

Seligman, M. E. P., Steen, T. A., Park, N., & Peterson, C. (2005) Positive psychology progress: Empirical validation of interventions. *American Psychologist*, *60*, 410–421.

Sergeant, S., & Mongrain, M. (2011). Are positive psychology exercises helpful for people with depressive personality styles? *Journal of Positive Psychology*, *6*, 260–272.

Shapira, L. B., & Mongrain, M. (2010). The benefits of self-compassion and optimism exercises for individuals vulnerable to depression. *Journal of Positive Psychology*, *5*, 377–389.

Sheldon, K. M., & Cooper, M. L. (2008). Goal striving within agentic and communal roles: Separate but functionally similar pathways to enhanced well-being. *Journal of Personality*, *76*, 415–448.

Sheldon, K. M., & Houser-Marko, L. (2001). Self-concordance, goal attainment, and the pursuit of happiness: Can there be an upward spiral? *Journal of Personality and Social Psychology*, *80*, 152–165.

Sheldon, K. M., & Lyubomirsky, S. (2006). How to increase and sustain positive emotion: The effects of expressing gratitude and visualizing best possible selves. *Journal of Positive Psychology*, *1*, 73–82.

Sheldon, K. M., & Schüler, J. (2011). Wanting, having, and needing: Integrating motive disposition theory and self-determination theory. *Journal of Personality and Social Psychology*, *101*, 1106–1123.

Shoham, V., & Insel, T. R. (2011). Rebooting for whom? Portfolios, technology, and personalized intervention. *Perspectives on Psychological Science*, *6*, 478–482.

Sin, N. L., & Lyubomirsky, S. (2009). Enhancing well-being and alleviating depressive symptoms with positive psychology interventions: A practice-friendly meta-analysis. *Journal of Clinical Psychology*, *65*, 467–487.

Wood, A. M., Joseph, S., Lloyd, J., & Atkins, S. (2009). Gratitude influences sleep through the mechanisms of pre-sleep cognitions. *Journal of Psychosomatic Research*, *66*, 43–48.

23

Taking Culture into Account with Positive Psychological Interventions

Jennifer Teramoto Pedrotti

Within the field of positive psychology, many scholars have noted that attention must be paid to culture in order to understand how various behaviors may play out as positive characteristics within different groups (Christopher & Hickinbottom, 2008; Pedrotti, Edwards, & Lopez, 2009; Snyder, Lopez, & Pedrotti, 2011; Sue & Constantine, 2003). Though some have posited that certain characteristics or virtues may "transcend" culture (Seligman & Csikszentmihalyi, 2000, p. 5), other research has offered data that suggest that culture does "count" in terms of definition, manifestation, interaction with other constructs, and in level of import of particular characteristics (Pedrotti et al., 2009). These potential differences must be considered in developing positive interventions that are multiculturally competent across a variety of cultural facets, and in researching these treatments. In being mindful that cultural facets play a role in deciding how to develop the most effective intervention to increase happiness, work toward forgiveness, or enhance hope, practitioners who use positive psychological techniques are better able to reach a broad spectrum of individuals. In addition, culture must be considered when measuring the effectiveness of these positive interventions so as to interpret the results accurately.

In general, culture must be treated as a broad concept, particularly in today's diverse society; as such, it includes identity facets along a variety of different spectra. In addition to important facets such as race and ethnicity, many psychologists (both in practice and in research) include facets such as gender, nation of origin, sexual orientation, generation, religion, socioeconomic status, and disability as viable cultural markers (see Chapter 18; Hays, 2008). Each of these facets may offer a contribution to the development of a person's worldview, and as such each must be considered in developing and executing a multiculturally competent positive psychological intervention. Failure to consider these myriad cultural facets as

The Wiley Blackwell Handbook of Positive Psychological Interventions, First Edition.
Edited by Acacia C. Parks and Stephen M. Schueller.

overarching influences early on in the development process may lead to difficulty in communication, misinterpretation of responses, or lack of development of a close working alliance (Sue & Sue, 2008).

To this end, counselors aiming toward developing and implementing multiculturally competent interventions in the field of positive psychology must first check in with their clients so as to gain a good understanding of the salience of various cultural facets within each. It is important to note that the pieces that a particular individual finds to be salient to him- or herself regarding cultural identity may be visible or invisible to others around them (Hays, 2008). Facets like sexual orientation or nation of origin may not have physical markers that point to these particular identity facets, and even if status along these facets is visible, one is still unable to interpret the amount of identification with these without checking in with the individual. Facets such as race or ethnicity are sometimes visible and thus may be "guessed" at, but again are not always clear to others. Finally, some facets may change with time or development, and yet vestiges of the "old" may remain with the "new." A good example of this last circumstance is with regard to socioeconomic status; research shows that even when socioeconomic status changes to more wealthy with age or time, individuals may carry with them the cultural identity of their socioeconomic status of origin as opposed to their current situation (Mossakowski, 2008). Accurately gleaning this information from potential participants can allow a careful treatment of culture in any positive psychological intervention, thus assisting in facilitating an inclusive and effective style of intervention. The role culture may play in a discussion of positive characteristics is varied. Some of the ways in which culture must be considered in developing appropriate and effective positive interventions will now be detailed.

The Role of Culture in Positive Interventions

In current literature within the field of positive psychology, researchers are more commonly noting that culture plays a significant role in many aspects of understanding and measurement of various positive characteristics (Christopher & Hickinbottom, 2008; Pedrotti et al., 2009; Snyder et al., 2011; Sue & Constantine, 2003). Identification with various cultural groups or facets may lead to different definitions, manifestations, and valuing of these characteristics and traits. In this section, evidence is presented regarding these cultural nuances in order to assist practitioners in developing culturally competent interventions within the field of positive psychology. First, evidence showing differences in definitions of various positive constructs across cultural groups will be reviewed. Next, discussion is provided about differential relationships and correlations found between some of these constructs. Third, findings regarding different manifestations of positive characteristics and their levels of import across cultures are presented. In addition, suggestions are given to researchers who study positive psychological interventions in the hope that accurate and culturally competent interpretations of evidence can be obtained.

Definitional differences across cultures

When developing any intervention, the variables of study must of course first be operationalized. For example, in developing a positive intervention to increase hope in children, one must first identify what behaviors and/or attitudes will show that a change has occurred in the hope level of the participants. Research shows that cultural background may play a role in the definitions various constructs are given. For example, Uchida, Norasakkunkit, and Kitayama (2004) identified "substantial cultural variations" (p. 223) in accepted definitions of happiness across different cultures. In comparing East Asian participants with North American individuals, Uchida and colleagues note distinct differences between these groups in self-construal; i.e., Eastern ideology has more of a focus on the group, whereas Western norms dictate more of a focus on the self or individual. These differences appear to play a strong role in conceptualizations of happiness when looking at the responses given by the participants in this study. Uchida and colleagues found that within Western participants ideas of happiness were grounded as contingent upon "both personal achievement and positivity of the personal self" (2004, p. 227), while East Asian understandings of happiness focused more strongly on harmony within the social sphere and balance in relationships. Though both groups speak about "happiness" in their lives, the meaning of this term differs cross-culturally (Uchida et al., 2004).

This definitional difference has great implications for considering development of a happiness-increasing intervention. Designed within a European American framework (i.e., individualistic), components of this intervention might include tasks such as self-reflection regarding how well one is doing in one's life overall, and efforts to promote personal meaning with the aim of increasing happiness. While this may have the desired effect on a participant who operates from a Western framework culturally, this same positive result may not be found in working with clients from Eastern cultural backgrounds. As an example, consider an exercise designed to promote personal meaning offered to both an Asian client and a Caucasian client that asks each to take some self-reflection time to ponder what each personally thinks of various activities in their present life. In this scenario the therapist aims to help clients to decrease demands on their time spent on activities that the client does not find personally meaningful, perhaps in order to decrease guilt over saying no to requests in favor of using one's time to pursue personally meaningful activities. The Caucasian client may find this exercise very useful to figure out what is most important to them and then prioritize this; and this exercise would likely lead to more well-being in their life. In contrast, the Asian client might socially injure him- or herself if he or she chose to neglect social demands that may have little personal importance, but carry great weight in terms of their social purpose and meaning. As mentioned above, social harmony has been found to be closely related to well-being in Eastern-oriented individuals (Uchida et al., 2004). Thus, the culturally unaware therapist may inadvertently decrease the well-being of the Asian client (as a function of creating social conflict), while simultaneously increasing the well-being of the Caucasian client. Even treatment modality of such an exercise (e.g., individual versus group presentation) may be more or less successful depending on which cultural group a practitioner wants to benefit from the intervention.

As a second example, wisdom is another construct that may be defined differently in individuals from different cultural backgrounds. Researchers comparing American and Slovak college students found that on measures of wisdom, students from the United States placed much more of an emphasis on the *cognitive* aspects of wisdom in defining this construct as opposed to the Slovak students who placed significantly more focus on the *affective* aspects (Benedikovičová & Ardelt, 2008). In addition, Yang (2008) noted in other research that the description of wise people offered by individuals from Taiwan contained a more balanced treatment of cognitive factors (e.g., problem-solving, intelligence, and planning) and affective factors (e.g., humbleness, compassion, open-mindedness) as compared to individuals from the United States, who emphasized solely cognitive aspects. Thus, different tasks and activities would need to be employed to design an intervention to increase wisdom in these different groups, such that this increase would be authentic in whichever population it was being attempted. A positive intervention designed to increase wisdom in Taiwanese or Slovak groups would have to include a strong affective component in order for the participants to feel that wisdom had increased. This affective component might not play much of a role in increasing wisdom from the view of a participant in the United States. Thus, definitional differences that exist between cultures can have overarching effects on design, and success, of particular positive interventions.

Differential relationships between positive constructs

Differences may also exist in relationships between various constructs in different cultural groups. This points to the idea that assorted positive characteristics and traits may interact differently with one another as a function of the cultural facets of the individual or group. Constructs may have a different direction of correlation depending on cultural group (e.g., Leu, Wang, & Koo, 2011; Uchida & Kitayama, 2009), and because of this different connotations (e.g., positive in one culture and negative in another; Chang, 2001), or different predictors in different cultures (e.g., Chang & Banks, 2007). In developing any positive psychological intervention, a practitioner needs to know the way in which these constructs function with and relate to one another in order to effect change in the desired direction, and ultimately in deciding which direction is the desired outcome.

Practitioners may often work to decrease a less desired characteristic or state by increasing other negatively correlated characteristics. For example, in working to decrease pessimism or depression, one might consider a treatment program designed to increase optimism. Chang (2001) investigated these associations (i.e., optimism, pessimism, and depression) in Chinese American and Caucasian American participants, and found that though levels of pessimism differed when comparing these two groups (Chinese American participants had significantly more pessimism), they did not differ in levels of optimism or depression. This finding was surprising as much previous research that did not look at racial or ethnic differences found that these constructs (optimism × pessimism and optimism × depression) were negatively correlated (Gillham, Shatté, Reivich, & Seligman, 2001). In looking more closely at these associations, Chang found that optimism and depression were not negatively correlated in the Chinese American sample, and in addition, problem-solving (a positive trait often found to be negatively correlated with depression) was *positively* correlated with pessimism within this portion of the sample. Though the inverse relationships between depression or pessimism, and optimism may be taken for granted by someone from a Western cultural framework, these associations were made salient in primarily majority culture, United States samples. In addition, the values given to optimism (positive) and pessimism (negative) are derived from this majority culture worldview. Here, it appears that pessimism may play a functional role within the Chinese American sample and thus could be touted as a positive characteristic associated with better problem-solving. If this cultural difference in association between these variables is not attended to, one might design a positive intervention to decrease pessimism in order to also decrease depression. While this may have the desired effect in a Caucasian American sample, the practitioner runs the risk of having no effect on the Chinese American participants at best, and at worst risks decreasing problem-solving ability in these participants.

Different relationships between positive and negative affect have also been found in studies with other constructs. Several researchers have found that in many Asian cultures, positive correlations often exist between positive and negative emotions as compared to the inverse correlations found between these variables in United States samples (primarily Caucasian American participants; Kitayama, Markus, & Kurokawa, 2000; Spencer-Rodgers, Peng, & Wang, 2010). Kitayama and colleagues (2000) interpret these findings as being rooted in a desire for balance in Eastern cultures as compared to a more linear wish for happiness in and of itself in Western-oriented cultures such as the United States, which others have also posited (Pedrotti et al., 2009; Uchida et al., 2004). Along these same lines, Leu and colleagues (2011) found that increasing positive emotions had no significant effect in decreasing depression in immigrant Asians in their study, while the opposite was true in the European American participants in this same study. Leu and colleagues (2011) and Uchida and Kitayama (2009) note that in Japanese populations, happiness is often discussed more in terms of potential negative social backlash that may occur as a result of jealousy of others around them who are not as happy. This is in stark contrast to European American samples who more often discuss happiness in terms of benefits to the self (Markus & Kitayama, 1991; Uchida & Kitayama, 2009; Uchida et al., 2004). Thus in designing an intervention to increase happiness, a practitioner must be mindful of the desire for balance, and of the potential negative connotation with extreme happiness, in working with participants from Asian backgrounds as opposed to those with a more Western mindset.

Chang and Banks (2007) offer a final example in a study looking at predictors of agentic thinking (i.e., motivation to work toward various goals as a component of Snyder and colleagues' [1991] model of hope) across various racial groups, this time within one context: the United States. While life satisfaction was found to be the best predictor of agentic thinking in the Caucasian American sample, this variable was not able to significantly predict agentic thinking at all in the Latino sample, and was not the best predictor of agentic thinking within Asian American and African American samples. The best predictor of agentic thinking in Latino Americans was found to be rational problem-solving, while in Asian American and African American samples, the best predictor was found to be positive affect (Chang & Banks, 2007). With these differential relationships existing in different cultural groups, it would be prudent to consider culture in developing an intervention for promoting any positive trait, as different routes may be successful in different cultural groups.

In each of the above examples, a practitioner would be well-advised to consider the cultural makeup of their client before embarking on designing a positive psychological intervention. Without taking this care, practitioners run the risk of misinterpreting actual change in behavior or attitude at best, or in worst case scenarios decreasing a functional trait (e.g., pessimism in Asian participants) within some clients. Having a clear understanding of how culture may relate to, and thus play a role in enhancement or development of, positive traits can help practitioners to be more culturally competent in their offerings of such interventions.

Different manifestation of positive characteristics

Research has found that even when definitions are the same or similar, culture may play a role in the manifestations of various positive characteristics. This information is important in giving practitioners the ability to establish whether or not a change has occurred in a particular trait, or whether change in a particular trait is needed at all. For example, Kadiangandu, Gauché, Vinsonneau, and Mullet (2007) found that the positive characteristic of forgiveness may look very different in different cultural populations. While Western-focused definitions of this construct focus strongly on the *intra*personal process that one goes through in order to forgive a transgressor (e.g., McCullough, 2000), Kadiangandu and colleagues (2007) found that, in a sample of Congolese individuals, forgiveness in this cultural group focused more on the *inter*personal process between victim and transgressor. In the Congolese culture, the valuing of social harmony and a collectivist mindset require forgiveness to include a social piece in order to facilitate these cultural goals. This has implications both for creating an intervention (i.e., an interpersonal component would be essential with Congolese participants) and in noting the effectiveness of the intervention for those in Congolese culture (i.e., unless the interpersonal component was included in the outcome assessment, it would be difficult to comment on the effectiveness of the intervention).

Other examples of different manifestation as a function of culture are also present in the literature. Lu and Gilmour (2004), for example, note that happiness is touted as a less intense experience in a sample from China, as compared to a sample taken from the United States. Chinese participants in this study noted that happiness was a pleasant emotion and brought satisfaction and contentment but, as above, took care to mention balance in experience of happiness and unhappiness as an important factor. Lu and Gilmour note that in the American (and primarily Caucasian) accounts of happiness, more extremes were described and levels of happiness were referred to more often. Thus, what is viewed as a manifestation of happiness may not be the same across cultural groups. Practitioners working with Chinese populations (and possibly other Asian groups; Uchida & Kitayama, 2009) may not recognize these less intense manifestations of happiness (as compared to majority individuals in the United States), or may rate the intervention as less successful for Chinese populations, if they are not aware of these cultural differences. In addition, research appears to show that this less intense expression of happiness is culturally functional for Chinese individuals (Leu et al., 2011; Uchida & Kitayama, 2009). Thus a practitioner without this cultural knowledge who pushes a Chinese client toward a more intense manifestation of happiness may actually be damaging this individual's success at interacting harmoniously with his or her cultural group. This example shows the complexity of the influence one's own culture has in implementing various interventions. When the desired outcome of the intervention is defined solely by the cultural framework of the practitioner, there is a clear risk of unintended damage to the clients involved who are of different cultural backgrounds from the practitioner.

Flow is a positive state of "profound task absorption, cognitive efficiency, and intrinsic enjoyment that makes a person feel one with the activity in which s/he is involved" (Moneta, 2004, p. 115), and has been illustrated with examples such as artists who become lost in their work, oblivious to time and/or physical needs such as food or sleep. In Csikszentmihalyi's (1990) research on this positive state, he found that the optimal conditions for inducing the flow state were situations in which both challenge and skills were perceived to be *high* by the individual; indeed Csikszentmihalyi states that these are "required" for a flow state to be achieved. Moneta's (2004) work, however, found that his Chinese participants did not report a state of flow in this high challenge/high skill situation and instead required a *moderate* challenge/high skill situation in order to achieve the flow state. This difference was attributed to desire for attention to detail in Chinese culture, with the idea that this attention could not be given in situations that were too high in challenge (Moneta, 2004). Thus, interventions desiring to elicit a particular positive characteristic such as flow may need to take cultural values into account in order to design effective conditions for a diverse set of clients.

Finally, it is important to note that different cultural groups may value different traits as the "most positive" or the "most important" within their lives. Lu and

Gilmour (2004) found that although happiness was touted as the "supreme goal in life" (pp. 285–286) among their American (mostly Caucasian) participants, this high ranking of happiness was "totally absent from the Chinese students' [responses]" (p. 286). Within the United States the pursuit of happiness is viewed as so important to the framework of the country that it is included in the US Constitution. Thus, its increase is often a primary goal of researchers who operate from this cultural background. Lu and Gilmour's research brings forth the point that an intervention to increase happiness may or may not be valued at the same level by individuals who do not operate from this framework. In past work, some have posited that "everyone wants to be happy" (Myers, 1993); this current research points to the fact that this may not be the case and as such practitioners must take this information into account when creating new positive psychological interventions.

Attention to Cultural Facets Other than Race, Ethnicity, and Nation of Origin

The previous examples have mostly compared viewpoints, definitions, manifestations and the like between ethnic or racial groups or between different nations. It is also likely that other cultural facets such as generation, socioeconomic status, or gender, might play a role in defining certain positive traits, how they are manifested, and thus how one might best develop interventions to increase them. For example, Ardelt (2009) found that women more often discuss the *affective* component of the positive characteristic of wisdom, whereas men more often discuss the *cognitive* components. Here gender creates a cultural difference that leads to different definitions and understandings of wisdom. In addition, gender may interact with the generation of the individual studied to create a different manifestation of the construct of wisdom. In 1993 Orwoll and Achenbaum reported that men exhibit wisdom in more public settings, while women more commonly complete wise acts in private settings. Current research, however, shows that these gender differences in manifestation of wisdom are not present in younger cohorts (though they are still found in older generations), who may have more egalitarian gender roles due to today's different norms (Ardelt, 2009). Thus, considering multiple cultural facets (e.g., gender, race, ethnicity, generation, socioeconomic status, etc.), and their potential interactions with one another, may also be prudent for practitioners embarking on the creation of positive interventions.

Suggestions for Researchers

Researchers who study the effects of positive interventions must take the previously made points into account, but there are additional points to consider from a research perspective. In particular, the following issues are highlighted below: attention to equivalence (construct, linguistic, and metric), avoidance of setting up deficit models, broadening research to include larger samples of underrepresented groups, and addressing cultural differences other than the East/West differences. Following are several suggestions to this end.

Attention to equivalence issues

In comparing results across cultural groups, researchers must make sure, as noted above for practitioners, that the construct being studied is equivalent in the different cultures; however, even when this is the case, the instruments used to measure these constructs must also be able to measure these traits equivalently across these cultural groups. Linguistic equivalence, for example, must be established when measures for these positive traits are translated into languages other than the one in which they were originally developed (Mio, Barker, & Tumambing, 2009). Idioms, common phrases, and vocabulary may not translate well, depending on the phraseology used in the scale, and as such appropriate procedures of translation and back-translation must be taken into consideration. In addition, some cultural groups may be more or less averse to taking risks, or toward exhibiting extreme declarations, and as such even the commonly used Likert scale can have different meanings to different cultural groups (Mio et al., 2009). If a 10-point scale is used, for example, with 1 denoting a low level of a particular trait and 10 denoting a high level of that same trait, these two numbers (1 and 10) are to be the outside markers of the measurement of this particular trait. Mio and colleagues state that some cultures may be more cautious about making extreme statements regarding their views and, as such, the ends of the continuum (i.e., 1 and 10) may never be used by members of this type of culture. In this case, the markers of 2 and 9 may be as low or as high as members of these cultures are willing to go. This creates issues in metric equivalence for use of these scales with risk-averse cultures. As such, researchers must take care to note these cultural factors before making comparisons between groups.

Avoiding deficit models

Researchers must also take care not to set up what others have termed *deficit models* between cultures (Sue & Sue, 2008). When a particular theoretical framework is devised within one culture and then used within another culture, researchers run the risk of unintentionally pathologizing a particular group (Clauss-Ehlers, 2008; Pedrotti et al., 2009). For example, in the previously mentioned example of optimism and pessimism with the Chinese American and Caucasian American participants (Chang, 2001), the construct of pessimism is shown to be a potential source of strength for the Chinese American sample; notably pessimism was positively linked to problem-solving. If this functional effect had not been identified by Chang in his research because of his more thorough investigation of the nature of this construct, it would be easy to deduce that Chinese participants were lacking in some way due to their high levels of pessimism (a trait found to be problematic in Caucasian American samples because of its links to depression). In this way a deficit model would be set up, with Chinese Americans having a more pathological presentation in terms of the optimism–pessimism continuum. Thus researchers must fully investigate the traits they are measuring, and the effects of the interventions upon them, as a function of cultural differences. At the same time researchers must refrain from making ethnocentric judgments about which traits are "better" or "worse."

Over-sampling underrepresented groups

With the aim of taking care to avoid the pathologization of particular cultural groups, researchers attempting to evaluate any interventions might find that over-sampling of underrepresented cultural groups may be appropriate to more fully investigate various constructs within different cultural groups (Heppner, Wampold, & Kivlighan, 2008). This method would also be beneficial in measuring outcome of positive interventions. In looking at Chang's (2001; Chang & Banks, 2007) work, and the work of others, it can be seen that in sampling groups other than majority culture, differences often emerge. It is only through these types of data collection that we can become aware of the definitions, manifestations, and level of import of various constructs within different groups. It is also possible, of course, that similarities across cultures also exist and this type of data could help practitioners to distinguish when the *same* treatment across cultures may also be *equal* treatment. In obtaining this information researchers can then better advise practitioners on developing culturally appropriate and multiculturally competent interventions in the realm of positive psychology.

Moving beyond East/West distinctions and including multicultural studies

In addition, at present much of the research available has compared populations within Western versus Eastern (particularly Japanese and Chinese) cultures. While this vein of research is undoubtedly important, descriptions of Latino and African American samples are currently found to be lacking in the literature (Kim-Prieto & Eid, 2004; Suh & Oishi, 2004). Finally, *cross*-cultural (i.e., comparisons between inhabitants of different countries) may not reflect *multi*cultural distinctions (i.e., comparisons between different cultural groups living within one context such as the United States; Matsumoto & Yoo, 2006). Moneta's (2004) findings regarding Chinese individuals from Hong Kong, for example, may not be replicated in looking at Chinese *American* individuals. More studies such as Chang and Banks' (2007) investigation of hope in different cultural populations within the United States must be conducted before it can be determined if cross-cultural findings are replicated in these multicultural contexts.

Conclusion

In the field of positive psychology, some have posited that certain characteristics may be present across cultures to the extent that they approach universality (Myers, 1993; Peterson & Seligman, 2004). In the above examples, it is clear that while a term such as "happiness" may be used across cultural groups, it may not have the same definition, correlation to other constructs, manifestation, or ranking of importance. As such, it must be understood that the mere presence of discussion of a particular trait or state within a culture may not mean that a trait is truly "universal." In addition, measurement may not have been adequate or accurate in some studies due to potential lack of construct, linguistic, and/or metric equivalence. Construct equivalence has particular relevance in gaining clear cross-cultural and multicultural information about a particular construct. Because of potential problems with this type of equivalence, a construct such as "happiness" may be defined in a particular way in one culture and then *that conceptualization* of "happiness" is measured in another culture. This conceptualization, however, may or may not be accurate as "happiness" for the second cultural group. Thus, studies that look carefully at these qualitative differences between positive psychological traits and states are invaluable.

Currently, it is still the case that much of the literature and study on members of racial, ethnic, and other minority groups in the field of psychology in general is limited (Sue & Sue, 2008). Positive psychology in its design of culturally competent interventions must also be furthered by more research devoted to multicultural and cross-cultural differences and similarities. As more research is conducted in this area, as noted in the examples in this chapter, it seems clear that culture does "count" in the creation, implementation, and interpretation of outcomes of positive psychological interventions. If practitioners and researchers in this area of the field work to increase the cultural competence of these interventions, a more broad and inclusive positive psychology will emerge, allowing this area of the field to be accessible to all.

References

Ardelt, M. (2009). How similar are wise men and women? A comparison across two age cohorts. *Research in Human Development*, *6*, 9–26. doi:10.1080/15427600902779354

Benedikovičová, J., & Ardelt, M. (2008). The three dimensional wisdom scale in cross-cultural context: A comparison between American and Slovak college students. *Studia Psychologica*, *50*, 179–190.

Chang, E. C. (2001). Cultural influences on optimism and pessimism: Differences in Western and Eastern construals of the self. In E. C. Chang (Ed.), *Optimism and pessimism: Implications for theory, research, and practice* (pp. 257–280). Washington, DC: American Psychological Association.

Chang, E. C., & Banks, K. H. (2007). The color and texture of hope: Some preliminary findings and implications for hope theory and counseling among diverse racial/ethnic groups. *Cultural Diversity and Ethnic Minority Psychology, 13*, 94–103. doi:10.1037/1099-9809.13.2.94

Christopher, J. C., & Hickinbottom, S. (2008). Positive psychology, ethnocentrism, and the disguised ideology of individualism. *Theory and Psychology, 18*, 563–589. doi:10.1177/0959354308093396.

Clauss-Ehlers, C. S. (2008). Sociocultural factors, resilience, and coping: Support for a culturally sensitive measure of resilience. *Journal of Applied Developmental Psychology, 29*, 197–212. doi:10.1016/j.appdev.2008.02.004

Csikszentmihalyi, M. (1990). *Flow: The psychology of optimal experience.* New York: Harper & Row.

Gillham, J. E., Shatté, A. J., Reivich, K. J., & Seligman, M. E. P. (2001). Optimism, pessimism, and explanatory style. In E. C. Chang (Ed.), *Optimism and pessimism: Implications for theory, research, and practice* (pp. 53–75). Washington, DC: American Psychological Association.

Hays, P. A. (2008). *Addressing cultural competencies in practice* (2nd ed.) *Assessment, diagnosis, and therapy.* Washington, DC: American Psychological Association.

Heppner, P. P., Wampold, B. E., & Kivlighan, D. (2008). *Research design in counseling.* Belmont, CA: Thomson.

Kadiangandu, J. K., Gauché, M., Vinsonneau, G., & Mullet, E. (2007). Conceptualizations of forgiveness: Collectivist-Congolese versus individualist-French viewpoints. *Journal of Cross-Cultural Psychology, 38*, 432–437. doi:10.1177/0022022107302312

Kim-Prieto, C., & Eid, M. (2004). Norms for experiencing emotions in sub-Saharan Africa. *Journal of Happiness Studies, 5*, 242–268.

Kitayama, S., Markus, H. R., & Kurokawa, M. (2000). Culture, emotion, and well-being: Good feelings in Japan and the United States. *Cognition and Emotion, 14*, 93–124.

Leu, J., Wang, J., & Koo, K. (2011). Are positive emotions just as "positive" across cultures? *Cognition and Emotion, 11*, 994–999. doi:10.1037/a0021332

Lu, L., & Gilmour, R. (2004). Culture and conceptions of happiness: Individual oriented and social oriented SWB. *Journal of Happiness Studies, 5*, 269–291.

Markus, H. R., & Kitayama, S. (1991). Culture and self: Implications for cognition, emotion and motivation. *Psychological Review, 98*, 224–253.

Matsumoto, D., & Yoo, S. H. (2006). Toward a new generation of cross-cultural research. *Perspectives on Psychological Science, 1*, 234–250. doi:10.1111/j.1745-6916.2006.00014x

McCullough, M. E. (2000). Forgiveness as a human strength: Theory, measurement, and links to well-being. *Journal of Social and Clinical Psychology, 19*, 43–55.

Mio, J. S., Barker, L. A., & Tumambing, J. (2009). *Multicultural psychology: Understanding our diverse communities.* New York: McGraw-Hill.

Moneta, G. B. (2004). The flow experience across cultures. *Journal of Happiness Studies, 5*, 115–121.

Mossakowski, K. N. (2008). Dissecting the influence of race, ethnicity, and socioeconomic status on mental health in young adulthood. *Research on Aging, 30*, 649–671. doi:10.1177/0164027508322693

Myers, D. G. (1993). *The pursuit of happiness.* New York: HarperCollins.

Orwoll, L., & Achenbaum, W. A. (1993). Gender and the development of wisdom. *Human Development, 36*, 274–296.

Pedrotti, J. T., Edwards, L. M., & Lopez, S. J. (2009). Positive psychology within a cultural context. In S. J. Lopez & C. R. Snyder (Eds.), *Oxford handbook of positive psychology* (pp. 49–57). New York: Oxford University Press.

Peterson, C., & Seligman, M. E. P. (2004). *Character strengths and virtues: A handbook and classification*. Washington, DC: American Psychological Association.

Seligman, M. E. P., & Csikszentmihalyi, M. (2000). Positive psychology: An introduction. *American Psychologist, 55*, 5–14.

Snyder, C. R., Harris, C., Anderson, J. R., Holleran, S. A., Irving, L. M., Sigmon, S. T., ... Wu, W. Y. (1991). The will and the ways: Development and validation of an individual-differences measure of hope. *Journal of Personality and Social Psychology, 60*, 570–585.

Snyder, C. R., Lopez, S. J., & Pedrotti, J. T. (2011). *Positive psychology: The scientific and practical explorations of human strengths*. Thousand Oaks, CA: Sage.

Spencer-Rodgers, J., Peng, K., & Wang, L. (2010). Dialecticism and the co-occurrence of positive and negative emotions across cultures. *Journal of Cross-Cultural Psychology, 41*, 109–115. doi:10.1177/0022022109349508

Sue, D. W., & Constantine, M. G. (2003). Optimal human functioning in people of color in the United States. In W. B. Walsh (Ed.), *Counseling psychology and optimal human functioning* (pp. 151–169). Mahwah, NJ: Lawrence Erlbaum.

Sue, D. W., & Sue, D. (2008). *Counseling the culturally diverse: Theory and practice*. Hoboken, NJ: John Wiley & Sons.

Suh, E. M., & Oishi, S. (2004). Cultural and subjective well-being: An introduction to the special issue. *Journal of Happiness Studies, 5*, 219–222.

Uchida, Y., & Kitayama, S. (2009). Happiness and unhappiness in east and west: Themes and variations. *Emotion, 9*, 441–456. doi:10.1037/a0015634

Uchida, Y, Norasakkunkit, V., & Kitayama, S. (2004). Cultural constructions of happiness: Theory and empirical evidence. *Journal of Happiness Studies, 5*, 223–239.

Yang, S. (2008). Real-life contextual manifestations of wisdom. *International Journal of Aging and Human Development, 67*, 273–303. doi:10.2190/AG.67.4a

24

Dovetailing Ethical Practice and Positive Psychology to Promote Integrity, Industriousness, Innovation, and Impact

Dianne A. Vella-Brodrick

It is well understood that being free from mental illness is important for mental health. Relatedly, a growing recognition in psychology and related fields is the importance of the presence of well-being as a significant contributor to mental health (Keyes, 2007). Consistent with this perspective, Seligman (2011) envisions that by the year 2051 more than half of the world's population can be flourishing. To achieve this vision requires the development of initiatives for enhancing positive emotions, psychological well-being, and optimal functioning, and application of these on a global scale.

Although Seligman (2011) has set an ambitious target, it is well intentioned given the benefits of flourishing. Flourishing individuals experience a multitude of desirable outcomes that benefit both themselves and society, including better psychosocial functioning, reduced health care costs, and higher work productivity, compared to non-flourishing individuals (Keyes, 2007). Hence, it comes as no surprise that many people and organizations support this goal, including governments, educators, and workplace managers. For example, the UK government is actively promoting well-being as a central goal and is encouraging people to engage in five evidence-based strategies for enhancing well-being, namely, to "connect, be active, take notice, keep learning, and give" (Aked, Marks, Cordon, & Thompson, 2008). The government of Bhutan has recognized the importance of happiness as a primary indicator of national success with the creation of an index of "gross national happiness" to contrast economic indicators typically adopted by many nations (Centre for Bhutan Studies, 2009). The integration of positive education in schools throughout the world is also burgeoning, as is evident from the extensive work undertaken at Geelong Grammar School

The Wiley Blackwell Handbook of Positive Psychological Interventions, First Edition.
Edited by Acacia C. Parks and Stephen M. Schueller.

(Seligman, Ernst, Gillham, Reivich, & Linkins, 2009). Organizations such as Camp Quality are also infusing positive psychology practices such as gratitude, savoring, and laughter activities into their daily practices, with great success (Langley, 2013).

Scholars and practitioners of positive psychology are actively promoting well-being through the development, evaluation, and dissemination of well-being interventions and programs. This has led to a reinvigoration of pre-existing methods and the development of new approaches often referred to as positive psychological interventions (PPIs; Sin & Lyubomirsky, 2009) or positive activity interventions (PAIs; Layous, Chancellor, Lyubomirsky, Wang, & Doraiswamy, 2011). While those working within well-being frameworks have been instrumental in promoting and creating positive change in how mental health is approached, their eagerness to make a difference needs to be balanced with careful deliberation about the best strategies to employ for progressing their mission. To influence health policy and attract funding – both necessary factors for creating significant change in mental health – the case for investing in well-being strategies needs to be strong and clear and potential ramifications need to be considered. This means that those working within the boundaries of positive psychology must rise to the challenge and adopt a scientific and ethical framework in the conduct of their work.

Although consumers are not restricted by what they can attempt in their pursuit of well-being and happiness, it is the responsibility of the "expert" (e.g., psychologist, scholar, coach, or therapist), as the professional, to adhere to scientific and ethical standards. The challenge for positive psychology is to create standards that promote the greater good (i.e., the welfare of recipients and the reputation of the profession) without over-regulating and stifling its professionals in their service delivery. This chapter raises and discusses some contentious issues with the intent of encouraging all those associated with the enhancement of well-being, particularly under the auspices of positive psychology, to adopt a sound and ethical approach to their work. I hope to prompt those in the well-being field to honestly appraise their practices with an understanding and acceptance that although all disciplines and professionals have their shortcomings, this does not preclude the necessity of developing standards. Acknowledging these shortcomings enables the field to move forward to remedy the situation. Although most who identify with positive psychology have good intentions and sound ethical practices, more explicit discourse, education, and training around best practice will increase awareness of expectations and subsequently the consistency of excellent conduct.

In line with ethical practice, I note my background, potential biases, and goals, as these will likely influence the views expressed in this chapter. First, I am an advocate of positive psychology and I am currently the Secretary for the International Positive Psychology Association (IPPA). Second, I am also an ambassador for ethical practice, having trained postgraduate psychology students in ethical and professional practice for over a decade. My aim is to stimulate discussion and action around the intersection between positive psychology and ethics in hopes of strengthening the utility and longevity of positive psychology.

The primary focus of this chapter is to promote the importance of ethical standards for the attainment of scientific goals and best practice within positive psychology. In this chapter I often refer to ethics, professional practice, and science as an inseparable trio. Although these are distinct concepts, their conceptual overlap is important for the purpose of this chapter. They all refer to standards of excellence to which all professions should aspire. To introduce this trio I will first present and critique scientific and professional standards. Following this, I will examine some key ethical issues associated with positive interventions and explore the prospect of a positive ethical framework for positive psychology. In conclusion, I recommend four primary ethical principles to guide the practice of positive psychology: integrity, industriousness, innovation, and impact. I argue that positive psychology would benefit from having more explicit and widely disseminated practice frameworks and that the principles of integrity, industriousness, innovation, and impact are particularly pertinent for positive psychology at this point in time.

Ethical, Professional, and Scientific Standards

Seligman and Csikszentmihalyi (2000) have emphasized that positive psychology has strong scientific underpinnings. However, despite the reference to psychology in its title, positive psychology is not firmly embedded within psychology or any other existing scientific discipline. Despite many calls to integrate positive psychology with mainstream psychology (e.g., Linley, Joseph, Harrington, & Wood, 2006) or subfields such as clinical psychology (i.e., positive clinical psychology; Wood & Tarrier, 2010), to do so would overlook the contributions to positive psychology from other fields and professionals, including, but not limited to, economics, business, law, coaching, philosophy, education, and public policy. Given this diversity, it appears that positive psychology is best served acting as an independent entity where it can partner with and benefit so many disciplines, not just psychology. This position does not preclude positive psychology from being embedded in science, but it may make the process more difficult.

The formation of its own professional association, namely the International Positive Psychology Association (IPPA), reinforces the autonomous nature of positive psychology and is an important first step in acknowledging the formal presence of positive psychology. It also validates positive psychology as a specialized and worthy field of study and practice. In only a few years, the IPPA has developed a large membership base of around 1,500 members and has held three international meetings and several leader series conference calls with the aim of promoting and exchanging knowledge related to the science, teaching, and practice of positive psychology. The IPPA is to be applauded on what it has achieved thus far, but it has more work to do over the coming years. Typically professional associations develop practice guidelines to minimize any potential harm to service recipients and to the reputation of the field. Many professional associations also require formal engagement in and documentation of professional development activities.

This aims to promote competent practice for optimal outcomes and should be added to the IPPA's agenda, at least as a point of discussion.

One possible reason why ethical guidelines do not yet exist specifically for the field of positive psychology is that the diverse membership base of the profession prohibits a unified starting point. The IPPA membership base further demonstrates the diversity of professionals who identify with positive psychology. This level of inclusivity is founded on the premise that an interdisciplinary approach to understanding what makes life worthwhile is likely to yield more varied and fruitful outcomes. Although this is a reasonable stance to adopt and one that should be commended based on collaborative merits, it can result in inconsistent practice standards and diffused ethical responsibilities. Not all professions adhere to the same standards of conduct, as these standards depend on the nature of the service and the specific goals of the profession. Similarly, the value attributed to different ethical principles (e.g., duty of care, confidentiality, or competence) may vary across professions. Furthermore, the level of professional training in ethics and professional practice vary across disciplines. Thus, the differing backgrounds of members can advance novel and interdisciplinary thinking but can limit the widespread endorsement of ethical standards.

Although attending to ethical and professional responsibilities may seem a daunting and unappealing task for some, it is nevertheless a necessary one. According to O'Gorman (2007), one of the main criteria for establishing whether a working group qualifies as a profession depends on whether they ascribe to a code of ethics. These codes need to be endorsed and regulated by the members of the profession at large such that they represent the values of that professional group. Fortunately many other professions, including psychology, have already successfully devised their own practice standards. This provides a pre-existing knowledge base on ethical codes for consultation. For example, the American Psychological Association (2002) has identified (a) beneficence and non-maleficence, (b) fidelity and responsibility, (c) integrity, (d) justice, and (e) respect for people's rights and dignity, as its primary guiding ethical principles. Other professions have variations of these core principles. For example, core principles of the medical profession include respect for autonomy, beneficence, non-maleficence, and justice (Gillon, 1994). Now may be the right time for positive psychology to invest more fully in the development of ethical, professional, and scientific standards and to draw on existing resources which may be helpful in this endeavor.

Why Are Ethical, Professional, and Scientific Standards Necessary for Positive Psychology?

Positive psychology is at an exciting juncture where many new interventions are being developed and implemented in a variety of contexts, including education (Seligman et al., 2009), workplaces (Turner, Barling, & Zacharatos, 2002), and health settings (Harris & Thoresen, 2006). It is important when developing, evaluating, and disseminating interventions, to strike a balance between establishing the necessary scientific basis and maximizing the real-world utility. The temptation to be hasty in the application of positive interventions is high, particularly in light of their intuitive appeal and the public demand for such resources. Hence, professional and scientific standards are necessary to guide when a new intervention should be disseminated for general use.

An overarching principle in positive psychology is to ground practice in science. For instance, Seligman (2003) has stated:

> For Positive Psychology to flourish we need interventions that work and we need a systematic program of interventions that is scientifically proven to raise the level of human well-being. Unless we test the efficacy of our interventions we will be appropriately labelled "just another boosterism" or even "charlatans."

Establishing a scientific evidence base for positive psychology involves progressing through a sequence of steps including observation and hypothesis creation, development and evaluation, and dissemination of knowledge and interventions to real-world settings. Throughout these steps, a scientific approach requires that impact be quantified and qualified using rigorous and objective standards. In the practice of positive psychology and especially the dissemination of positive psychological interventions, it is imperative that client welfare and respect are included as a critical outcome. This will help build trusting relationships with clients, consumers, stakeholders, and the broader community, and maintain the credibility of positive psychology. The following section will examine some ethical, professional, and scientific issues associated with positive interventions and will make recommendations for addressing these.

What Do Positive Psychological Interventions Include?

Positive interventions are defined by their intended outcomes and the methods employed to achieve these outcomes. According to Sin and Lyubomirsky (2009), positive psychological interventions incite "positive feelings, behaviors or cognitions" (p. 468). Their examples of PPIs include mindfulness, positive writing, and gratitude interventions. They also stipulate that processes focused on alleviating illness or deficiencies, as opposed to strengths, do not qualify as PPIs. More specifically, positive interventions aim to enhance well-being using positive processes such as strength identification and use, instilling hope, savoring positive experiences, and the expression of gratitude. So while they may simultaneously improve other factors such as depression and anxiety, their primary aim is to enhance, heighten, and/or prolong at least one component of well-being such as pleasure, engagement, or meaning. However, positive interventions are used in several settings demonstrating their usefulness for alleviating distress. Indeed, many health professionals include positive interventions within an eclectic framework, integrating them along with traditional clinical methods such as cognitive-behavioral therapy (CBT). For example, well-being therapy has been sequentially added to CBT for the treatment of generalized anxiety disorders and can produce greater symptom reduction and enhanced well-being than when CBT alone is used (Fava et al., 2005; Fava & Tomba, 2009). Positive interventions are also beneficial for individuals experiencing depressive symptoms. A case in point is the work on positive psychotherapy by Seligman and colleagues that demonstrated significant reductions in depressive symptoms compared to treatment as usual, including therapy provided at a university counseling center and medication (Seligman, Rashid, & Parks, 2006). Furthermore, Layous et al. (2011) concluded that positive interventions may be beneficial as a sole therapeutic intervention for individuals with mild depression or as an adjunctive therapy for those who are only partially responding to medication. It would seem, then, that positive psychology can be quite versatile in its administration, process, and potential outcomes and does not lie exclusively within the boundaries of the positive "side." This is not always consistent with definitions or perceptions of PPIs such as those outlined earlier. Such definitions and examples of PPIs open up some stimulating discussion about the boundaries of positive psychology, particularly in relation to a positive and negative divide in mental health (see also Gable & Haidt, 2005).

The positive and negative divide

The divide between positive and negative is not helpful or representative of best practice and more work is needed to remove this dichotomy and create a more blended and inclusive concept of mental health. The salient point is that an exclusive focus on positive or negative aspects may not be productive, effective, or ethical. This is not to say that emphasizing the need for positive processes and outcomes is not warranted amidst the barrage of material on dysfunction in mainstream psychology (Rand & Snyder, 2003), but this positive emphasis needs to be integrated with existing work so that a more comprehensive understanding of treating the affective spectrum is developed.

The way in which positive psychology is marketed and defined may need to be expanded to avoid the negative and positive divide and so that it aligns more closely with practice. As the practice of positive psychology is diverse, it can at times involve exposure to issues associated with mental illness. This brings with it a number of added responsibilities, and proponents of positive psychology need to be cognizant of these. The following section will discuss some of the core issues and responsibilities associated with positive psychology as a practice which can span the full spectrum of mental health.

Avoiding harm (non-malificence) of positive interventions

In addition to the expectation that clients will benefit in some predicted and desirable way from our professional service or prescribed interventions, mental health professionals are employed to "do no harm." Thus it is necessary to monitor and report multiple outcomes, including adverse ones, so that this feedback can improve future interventions. Some may hold the position that positive interventions designed for the average person are harmless, and therefore that the field of positive psychology need not concern itself with too many regulations. It is problematic, however, to assume that because positive interventions focus on positive outcomes and methods, they are risk-free. For example, through strengths identification processes, clients may come to realize that they are lacking particular strengths they value (e.g., a new mother may show concern because she does not report any "humanity" signature strengths such as love in her VIA [Values in Action] survey). This may cause distress, which if not managed adequately can lead to more long-lasting adversity for the individual. Even the process of exploring what makes life engaging and meaningful can involve confronting some deep and sensitive issues and may uncover psychopathology. Those working within a positive psychology framework should not underestimate potential risks and need to take responsible action to ameliorate any adversities.

Working with people is complex and it is not possible to simply prevent, subtract, or ignore client experiences which are negative or indicative of a mental illness, even when adopting a positive psychology framework. While referral is an ethical and feasible option, some understanding of clinical issues is warranted in order to first recognize the clinical issue, second, acknowledge and address it appropriately, and third, determine if continuing with the positive approach is conducive to client welfare. As some evidence suggests that positive psychology practitioners may play a useful role in reducing symptoms of depression (Sin & Lyubomirsky, 2009), when working directly with depressed individuals it is likely that at least some positive psychology practitioners will be working with clinical populations. In these cases, the importance of competent practice, nonmaleficence, and duty of care is amplified.

Efficacy (beneficence) of positive interventions

A critical question concerning positive interventions is what extent of evidence is required before an intervention can be promoted and disseminated for general use. Although it is plausible that an overemphasis on the verification of the efficacy of interventions can delay their application and potential benefit, positive psychology must adhere to some standards if it is to uphold its scientific status and safeguard users. Standards relating to the level and quality of evidence required to denote a positive intervention as efficacious and effective need to be proposed and agreed upon. Standards exist in other disciplines, thus beginning this process of inquiry from scratch is not necessary. Positive psychology should draw on these resources to develop and provide standards that will suit its needs. It is not my intent in this chapter to review all options or propose a set of standards but rather to identify some of the key aspects relevant to positive interventions.

In some fields, such as the medical profession, this is sometimes referred to as "substantial evidence" and is typically considered to be at least "two adequate and well-controlled clinical trials." In psychology, the issue of empirically supported treatments (ESTs) has been addressed by the American Psychological Association Division 12 (Clinical Psychology) Taskforce (Chambless et al., 1998), which has emphasized the importance of evidence-based practice by formulating two categories: (a) well-established ESTs, and (b) probably efficacious ESTs. Designation as a well-established EST requires, among other criteria, at least two between-group studies demonstrating statistically significant effects favoring the new intervention in comparison to a psychological placebo or another treatment (or equivalent effects for the latter provided studies have adequate sample sizes). Probably efficacious ESTs would require at least two experiments showing that the treatment is superior to a wait-list control group. This raises the issue of what is the ideal comparison group (Devilly & McFarlane, 2009), along with the debate as to whether a control group is appropriate and ethical. Some regulating bodies such as the revised Declaration of Helsinki (World Medical Association, 2000) have stipulated that when an effective method is already available, this should serve as the comparison method against which to evaluate the new method (Devilly & McFarlane, 2009). Although these deliberations are still in progress, it is clear that positive psychology research needs to move closer in this direction. To date many positive interventions have been compared with a non-active control or with comparison groups which do not meet the aforementioned standards and fail to provide strong evidence for the efficacy of these interventions (see Wood & Tarrier, 2010). In addition it is not sufficient to simply state whether an intervention is efficacious or not. Rather, one must specify whether the body of evidence is sufficient to support its use in a particular context, with a particular person or group, and for a particular purpose.

The strong emphasis placed on establishing the efficacy of interventions using the randomized controlled trial "gold standard," however, can come at the expense of the ecological (external) validity of this data. Effectiveness studies focus on whether interventions work in the real world as opposed to the tightly controlled conditions required for a randomized controlled trial (Glasgow, Lichtenstein, & Marcus, 2003). If results are to be generalized, it is important to examine if interventions found to be efficacious in these tightly controlled laboratory settings are equally effective in the real-world context. Effectiveness studies should also address factors that moderate the benefits accrued from interventions, particularly participant characteristics and context. A related issue is whether a statistically significant change as a result of an intervention has any real-world value. Jacobson and colleagues (Jacobson, Roberts, Berns, & McGlinchey, 1999) developed the concept of clinical significance to quantify a level of change as a result of a clinical intervention that corresponds to a real-world benefit. Many clinical interventions also focus on moving individuals from being "cases" (i.e., people who meet diagnostic criteria for a mental disorder) to being free from disorder. In the case of positive interventions, it is unclear at what point a change in levels of happiness, positive emotions, or life satisfaction produces some level of real-world meaning. These recommendations would serve as a useful guide for the evaluation and dissemination of positive psychology work, and some discussion around these standards would benefit the field.

Other noteworthy factors associated with positive interventions include standardization and program integrity. Interventions are evaluated under certain circumstances that may be important for their efficacy thus meriting that conditions are replicated in future administrations (Glasgow et al., 2003). To maximize the likelihood of a standardized intervention with high program integrity, the tested intervention needs to be sufficiently detailed and manualized, particularly for more complex interventions. Specific training in the content or delivery of particular programs or interventions may also be necessary. Clearly describing the method (i.e., participant characteristics, measures administered, delivery mode, and exact instructions) is critical to replicate and extend work. To assess if the program was delivered as planned and completed by participants as prescribed, manipulation checks are also recommended (Dusenbury, Brannigan, Falco, & Hansen, 2003). Similarly, information about program adherence should be collected using surveys or through programmed electronic data-gathering systems if the interventions are completed in electronic form. Any deviations from the intended plan need to be noted and considered in the interpretation of the results.

Competency and training issues associated with positive interventions

Inherent in producing effective positive interventions is the principle of competence, whereby scholars, teachers, and practitioners are required to have sufficient training to either carry out high-quality research, or promote learning and practice informed by findings with acceptable levels of evidence. In particular, some training in understanding research findings and their practical implications is needed for those within positive psychology. Additionally, scholars need to make their work more concise, palatable, and accessible. Presenting findings in various mediums, allocating more funding towards research involving practitioner and industry partners, and the utilization of open access publications will also help to disseminate research findings and promote the scientist-practitioner model (Chwalisz, 2003). Publishing review papers and meta-analyses, especially in outlets aimed at a more widespread audience (e.g., Lyubomirsky & Layous, 2013), which outline the findings from rigorous empirical studies, can also assist with this goal. For example, in positive psychology some influential meta-analyses summarize outcomes and moderators of positive interventions (Sin & Lyubomirsky, 2009) and the benefits associated with increased happiness and positive affect (Lyubomirsky, King, & Diener, 2005). Essentially, the inclusion of both randomized controlled trials and ecological studies will contribute to securing the long-term position of positive psychology in improving mental health.

Competency is a prevailing issue for those working within the field of positive psychology, given that the standard of training is so varied. No accreditation body monitors the practice of positive psychology. Having psychology in the title raises some additional complexities as it can imply that those working in the field of positive psychology are "positive psychologists" when in reality many members are not licensed psychologists and some do not have any psychology training. This may be misleading to the public who can be naïve to these subtle distinctions. Practicing members of the IPPA, especially those without a background in psychology, may need to undergo some psychology training related to, for example, ethics, research, and professional practice. In addition, university courses in positive psychology should consider including modules specifically on research, ethics, and professional practice in their teaching programs, just like other disciplines, which have core subjects that are required in order to be accredited. This may already be the case with some existing programs but no formal body is currently overseeing this, or at the very least making recommendations about the core content material of academic positive psychology programs.

Another related issue concerns professional development (PD) requirements. Most other professions, including teachers, nurses, accountants, and psychologists, are required to keep abreast of the latest developments in their field of specialization. PD is considered an essential aspect of being a responsible and competent professional (Jasper, 2006). Hence, most professions mandate that their members undertake regular PD activities and accrue a certain level of training points per cycle (e.g., every two years) to maintain their membership. As yet, positive psychology does not have a formal PD system in place. Creating a PD system is important to encourage members to stay aware of the latest developments given the rapid development within positive psychology. Establishing a PD system compatible with the needs of the broad positive psychology network is worth pursuing and would provide more "street" credibility which should ultimately translate to better practice.

Acknowledgment of prior work

Critics of positive psychology, such as Held (2004), have asserted that although positive psychology is relatively new, the topic of focus is not. It is well known that philosophers have pondered for centuries over what makes life worth living (see Deci & Ryan, 2008). Positive psychology has also been compared with previous work in psychology, particularly humanistic psychology (Held, 2004; Robbins, 2008). For example, well before the inception of positive psychology, William James, Abraham Maslow, and Carl Rogers demonstrated scholarly interest in understanding the positive side of humans, as some positive psychologists such as Linley et al. (2006) and Seligman and Csikszentmihalyi (2000) have rightfully acknowledged. However, just because positive psychology is not entirely original and it draws on previous works, this does not mean that it has nothing new or valuable to contribute. Often, with the inception of new ideas, frameworks, theories, and findings, an old topic of inquiry can be examined with new insights, methods, and questions. Furthermore, new fields create opportunities to formally evaluate previously untested but well used methods drawn from related areas, especially applied fields such as humanistic psychology (Resnick, Warmoth, & Serlin (2001) and coaching (Biswas-Diener & Dean, 2007).

Overall, the scholarly standards within medical and mental health professions, while not perfect, are very high. A constant and vibrant deliberation is necessary to identify what else can be done to improve standards. Positive psychology, as a scientific community, needs to actively engage in these deliberations. At present much of the research on positive interventions does not meet these high standards, but with some forethought and planning, more work can move in this direction. The progress of positive psychology over such a short period is impressive, but more work is needed if the field is to secure its position as a reputable profession. The assimilation of ethics, professionalism, and science into positive psychology practices is necessary for the success and longevity of positive psychology. The next section will present an initial ethical framework specifically for the field of positive psychology, to consider and discuss further.

Positive psychology and ethics – the ideal partnership

It would be ironic if positive psychology and formal positive psychology organizations did not emphasize the importance of ethical practice. Positive psychology and ethics form an ideal partnership, as I have argued elsewhere (Vella-Brodrick, 2011). Both fields endorse excellence and seek to understand and promote best practice. This is especially the case for principle-based ethics, which provide aspirational standards, as opposed to rule-based ethics, which emphasize what not to do rather than what to do. Advocates of positive psychology are most likely to respond best to an ethical system that illuminates exemplary behavior rather than one that serves mainly to sanction inappropriate behavior. The key will be to develop ethical standards that represent the deepest values and aspirations of the profession, so that "ethics" can be viewed with fervor rather than with contempt, and as something intrinsic and inherent in what we do rather than as an external constraint.

Positive psychology is at a critical juncture as it is still in its formative stages. It must find a way to ensure that its members from diverse backgrounds can meet standards and are aware of what not to do as well as what to do. The latter is often represented as a series of principles that reflect best practice standards and provide broad and overarching guidance without being overly prescriptive about the processes to achieve these higher-order qualities. It may, therefore, be helpful for those who identify with positive psychology to first develop these higher-order ethical principles with sufficient flexibility to provide guidance without compromising its diversity. The following section commences this process.

Recommendations for the Field of Positive Psychology to Flourish: Integrity, Industriousness, Innovation, and Impact

I propose four guiding principles for the field of positive psychology to consider, namely integrity, industriousness, innovation, and impact. While other principles may also apply, I offer these specific principles because they provide a broad and encompassing standpoint and demonstrate to advocates of positive psychology what is needed for the field to continue to flourish.

Integrity

From a professional perspective, integrity involves having an unreserved respect for and adherence to ethical principles. It also involves staying true to the science, teaching, and practice of one's field of expertise. Integrity is a point of reference, similar to a moral compass, which steers individuals towards honest, sound, and morally upright behavior. With a large contingency of junior members who need guidance and mentorship, it would be advantageous for the field to clearly articulate practice standards to which these members can be held, and which can serve as guidelines for professional development. The development of practice standards would also help educate the diverse membership group in the professional requirements endorsed by the field. Integrity is the cornerstone of ethical practice and should permeate all work conducted under the auspices of positive psychology.

Industriousness

Industriousness refers to diligence, conscientiousness, and a work ethic that values hard work and quality output. To date advocates of positive psychology have worked hard to establish the field. They have created journals, conferences, university courses, online courses, discussion forums, and a professional association. However, considerable work still remains to be done. It is imperative that scholars and practitioners within positive psychology establish shared goals and work collectively towards achieving these (e.g., Seligman's "Flourish 51" goal). The unique value of positive psychology needs to be clearly identified in this process. Also more work is needed to integrate important developments from other disciplines such as neuroscience, philosophy, business, and economics. Although this requires those in positive psychology to keep abreast of cutting-edge works from a broad array of disciplines, this level of industriousness can produce higher-quality and more transformational work.

Innovation

Innovation is about contributing something new and valuable. The process of being innovative involves translating ideas, often of a scientific or technical nature, into a valuable and unique commodity that can satisfy a particular need, expectation, or gap. It often involves imagination and initiative to achieve such an outcome. As positive psychology is perceived by many to be closely aligned with psychology, it must demonstrate the unique contributions it can make to methods and outcomes. Positive psychology needs to review its accomplishments to date to build a strong, collective case for why positive psychology is needed and to identify gaps and needs that could be addressed by further work.

Innovation can also occur through multidisciplinary and complementary partnerships where multiple parties view the project through different lenses. Positive psychology has advantages in this respect because of the diverse backgrounds many in the field bring with them. This diversity can be mobilized to incite creativity and innovation, whether it be in conference format, research projects, or professional training forums.

Impact

By concisely illustrating how positive psychology has made a difference to its stakeholders, its impact will be more readily felt and acknowledged and its implementation more widely sought and funded. Ultimately it should be the goal of positive psychology to leave a strong positive impression on society in a way that can be quantified. It is necessary for positive psychology to determine a set of metrics which reasonably represent impact. Some metrics can include scholarly and social contributions. For example, the quality of journals in which one publishes one's work, the number of times work is cited by others, whether one's work has contributed to policy, whether external funding has been received, whether the community is interested in hearing about the work (e.g., media), and how many opportunities have arisen to deliver an intervention to an intended group, are all indicators of impact. The more coverage there is of quality work, the more likelihood of positive impact. Impact should also address whether these findings benefit people in the real world. Scholarly publications, even widely read and cited ones, need to lead to work that creates positive change in the real world. Positive psychologists need to ensure that their work does not only transform the research literature but the world as well.

Moving Forward to Dovetail, and Not Just Join, Positive Psychology and Ethical/Professional Practice

Positive psychology has many options regarding professional standards. These range from doing nothing at all to creating a highly regulated profession with clearly articulated ethical standards. As with most situations, both extremes are not ideal. However, some initial discussions around a proposed set of principles, such as those I have put forward in this chapter, as well as some frank discussions about addressing gray areas of practice, may prove helpful. Many within positive psychology have a wealth of experience, and guidance from these experienced members or those with specific expertise relevant to the issues raised in this chapter, could prove invaluable to others and the profession at large. No profession or professional is perfect. A first step in ethical practice is to acknowledge this statement and to draw on the necessary resources (internal and external) to help guide decision-making and practice. This is what personal and professional growth is all about. Asking some key questions and responding honestly to these may provide valuable insight. Below I offer a preliminary set of questions based on the four principles I presented earlier, for contemplation and discussion among those working in positive psychology.

Key questions to ask yourself as indicators of best ethical practice

- Have I checked what the extent of the evidence is before I recommend a positive intervention? (integrity)
- Do I know how to differentiate a scientifically sound research study from a less rigorous one? If not, how do I learn this? (integrity and industriousness)
- Have I used an appropriate comparison group in my research study? (integrity)
- Am I up to date with the latest findings on positive interventions? (integrity and industriousness)
- Have I consulted with relevant others about how well my proposed intervention might work in the real world? (integrity, industriousness, and impact)
- Do I need more training in a particular intervention, method, or theory? If so, what course can I take on this? (integrity and industriousness)
- Who can I connect with to exchange ideas and knowledge? (industriousness and impact)
- Is the work I am doing valuable to clients or the broader community or is it adding new scientific insights? (innovation)
- What steps am I taking to assess the outcomes (both positive and negative) that I have achieved through my work? (integrity, impact)
- What have I done recently that demonstrates high integrity and work ethic and how can others learn from this approach? (integrity)
- What work in positive psychology or in other relevant disciplines is at the forefront? What can I learn from this work? (industriousness and innovation)

Conclusion

Formulating the standards of a profession is a collective effort that involves a systematic and consultative process. The (aspirational) recommendations made throughout this chapter require considerable leadership, resources, and hard work, but I have presented justification for why this work needs to occur. Consequently, my intention in writing this chapter was not to create "the" ethical framework for positive psychology but rather to stimulate discourse about the standards of practice for the field and to underscore the importance of commencing this deliberate journey. Given the exuberance, competence, and productivity demonstrated in such a short time by the leaders and members of the broader positive psychology community and the IPPA, formally addressing such issues would be a timely challenge. These ethical factors will play a significant role in establishing the scientific credibility and longevity of positive psychology and will enable the positive psychology community to enact the aspirational qualities it so highly and vocally espouses. The question is not so much about whether or not positive psychology needs to be more explicit about developing and espousing ethical standards, but rather about how to do this to ensure that positive psychology and ethics dovetail harmoniously together to achieve its ambitious goals.

References

Aked, J., Marks, N., Cordon, C., & Thompson, S. (2008). *Five ways to well-being: The evidence.* London: New Economics Foundation.

American Psychological Association (2002). Ethical principles of psychologists and code of conduct. *American Psychologist, 57,* 1060–1073.

Biswas-Diener, R., & Dean, B. (2007). *Positive psychology coaching: Putting the science of happiness to work for your clients.* New York: John Wiley & Sons.

Centre for Bhutan Studies (2009). Gross national happiness. Retrieved May 29, 2009, from http://www.grossnationalhappiness.com/

Chambless, D. L., Baker, M. J., Baucom, D. H., Beutler, L., Calhoun, K. S., Crits-Christoph, P., … Woody, S. A. (1998). Update on empirically validated therapies II. *Clinical Psychologist, 51,* 3–16.

Chwalisz, K. (2003). Evidence-based practice: A framework for twenty-first-century scientist-practitioner training. *The Counseling Psychologist, 31,* 497–528. doi:10.1177/0011000003256347

Deci, E. L., & Ryan, R. M. (2008). Self-determination theory: A macrotheory of human motivation, development, and health. *Canadian Psychology–Psychologie Canadienne, 49,* 182–185. doi:10.1037/a0012801

Devilly, G. J., & McFarlane, A. C. (2009). When wait lists are not feasible, nothing is a thing that does not need to be done. *Journal of Consulting and Clinical Psychology, 77,* 1159–1168. doi:10.1037/a0016878.supp

Dusenbury, L., Brannigan, R., Falco, M., & Hansen, W. B. (2003). A review of research on fidelity of implementation: Implications for drug abuse prevention in school settings. *Health Education Research, 18,* 237–256.

Fava, G. A., Ruini, C., Rafanelli, C., Finos, L., Salmaso, L., Mangelli, L., & Sirigatti, S. (2005). Well-being therapy of generalized anxiety disorder. *Psychotherapy and Psychosomatics, 74,* 26–30. doi:10.1159/000082023

Fava, G. A., & Tomba, E. (2009). Increasing psychological well-being and resilience by psychotherapeutic methods. *Journal of Personality, 77,* 1903–1934. doi:10.1111/j.1467-6494.2009.00604.x

Gable, S. L., & Haidt, J. (2005). What (and why) is positive psychology? *Review of General Psychology, 9,* 103–110. doi:10.1037/1089-2680.9.2.103

Gillon, R. (1994). Medical ethics: Four principles plus attention to scope. *British Medical Journal, 309*, 184–188.

Glasgow, R. E., Lichtenstein, E., & Marcus, A. C. (2003). Why don't we see more translation of health promotion research to practice? Rethinking the efficacy-to-effectiveness transition. *American Journal of Public Health, 93*, 1261–1267.

Harris, A. H. S., & Thoresen, C. E. (2006). Extending the influence of positive psychology interventions into health care settings: Lessons from self-efficacy and forgiveness. *Journal of Positive Psychology, 1*, 27–36.

Held, B. S. (2004). The negative side of positive psychology. *Journal of Humanistic Psychology, 44*, 9–46. doi:10.1177/0022167803259645

Jacobson, N. S., Roberts, L. J., Berns, S. B., & McGlinchey, J. B. (1999). Methods for defining and determining the clinical significance of treatment effects: Description, application, and alternatives. *Journal of Consulting and Clinical Psychology, 67*, 300–307.

Jasper, M. (2006). *Professional development, reflection, and decision-making*. Oxford: Blackwell Publishing.

Keyes, C. L. M. (2007). Promoting and protecting mental health as flourishing: A complementary strategy for improving national mental health. *American Psychologist, 62*, 95–108. doi:10.1037/0003-066x.62.2.95

Langley, S. (2013). Positive relationships at work. In S. Roffey (Ed.), *Positive relationships: Evidence based practice across the world* (pp. 163–180). London: Springer.

Layous, K., Chancellor, J., Lyubomirsky, S., Wang, L., & Doraiswamy, P. M. (2011). Delivering happiness: Translating positive psychology intervention research for treating major and minor depressive disorders. *Journal of Alternative and Complementary Medicine, 17*, 675–683. doi:10.1089/acm.2011.0139

Linley, P. A., Joseph, S., Harrington, S., & Wood, A. M. (2006). Positive psychology: Past, present, and (possible) future. *Journal of Positive Psychology, 1*, 3–16. doi:10.1080/17439760500372796

Lyubomirsky, S., King, L., & Diener, E. (2005). The benefits of frequent positive affect: Does happiness lead to success? *Psychological Bulletin, 131*, 803–855.

Lyubomirsky, S., & Layous, K. (2013). How do simple positive activities increase well-being? *Current Directions in Psychological Science, 22*, 57–62. doi:10.1177/0963721412469809

O'Gorman, J. (2007). *Psychology as a profession in Australia*. Bowen Hills, Qld: Australian Academic Press.

Rand, K. L., & Snyder, C. R. (2003). A reply to Dr. Lazarus, the evocator emeritus. *Psychological Inquiry, 14*, 148–153.

Resnick, S., Warmoth, A., & Serlin, I. A. (2001). The humanistic psychology and positive psychology connection: Implications for psychotherapy. *Journal of Humanistic Psychology, 41*, 73–101. doi:10.1177/0022167801411006

Robbins, B. D. (2008). What is the good life? Positive psychology and the renaissance of humanistic psychology. *The Humanistic Psychologist, 36*, 96–112. doi:10.1080/08873260802110988

Seligman, M. E. P. (2003, June). Testing positive interventions. Retrieved October 25, 2011 from http://www.authentichappiness.sas.upenn.edu/newsletter.aspx?id=50

Seligman, M. E. P. (2011). *Flourish: A visionary new understanding of happiness and well-being*. New York: Free Press.

Seligman, M. E., & Csikszentmihalyi, M. (2000). Positive psychology: An introduction. *American Psychologist, 55*, 5–14.

Seligman, M. E. P., Ernst, R. M., Gillham, J., Reivich, K., & Linkins, M. (2009). Positive education: Positive psychology and classroom interventions. *Oxford Review of Education*, *35*, 293–311. doi:10.1080/03054980902934563

Seligman, M. E. P., Rashid, T., & Parks, A. C. (2006). Positive psychotherapy. *American Psychologist*, *61*, 774–788. doi:10.1037/0003-066x.61.8.774

Sin, N. L., & Lyubomirsky, S. (2009). Enhancing well-being and alleviating depressive symptoms with positive psychology interventions: A practice-friendly meta-analysis. *Journal of Clinical Psychology*, *65*, 467–487. doi:http://dx.doi.org/10.1002/jclp.20593

Turner, N., Barling, J., & Zacharatos, A. (2002). Positive psychology at work. In C. R. Snyder & S. J. Lopez (Eds.), *Handbook of positive psychology* (pp. 715–728). New York: Oxford University Press.

Vella-Brodrick, D. A. (2011). The moral of the story: The importance of applying an ethics lens to the teaching of positive psychology. *Journal of Positive Psychology*, *6*, 320–325. doi:10.1080/17439760.2011.580773

Wood, A. M., & Tarrier, N. (2010). Positive clinical psychology: A new vision and strategy for integrated research and practice. *Clinical Psychology Review*, *30*, 819–829.

World Medical Association (2000). Ethical principles for medical research involving human subjects. Paper presented at the 52nd Assembly, Declaration of Helsinki, Edinburgh. http://www.wma.net/e/policy/b3.htm

25

Beyond Life Satisfaction

A Scientific Approach to Well-Being Gives Us Much More to Measure

José L. Duarte

Subjective well-being (SWB) has long been the cardinal outcome assessed by positive psychology practitioners and researchers (Diener, Suh, Lucas, & Smith, 1999). Theorized as a combination of self-reported life satisfaction and the ratio of positive to negative emotions (Diener & Suh, 1997), SWB is a global (rather than domain-specific) outcome measure, and because it relies on self-reports, is fairly easy to capture. However, it is an incomplete measure of well-being – the well-being of a richly complex organism cannot be reduced solely to satisfaction and affective propensities. The exclusive use of SWB also leaves practitioners and researchers at a disadvantage – because it draws on a narrow range of variables, it will be more difficult to detect intervention impacts. For example, if participants initially score a mean of 5 on a seven-point scale of life satisfaction (which is consistent with population values; see Pavot & Diener, 1993), the efficacy of the intervention rests entirely on movement within the limited range of that single variable. But marked improvements might occur in a number of other well-being domains, and researchers and practitioners would be wise to look for them.

This chapter offers several approaches for measuring well-being outcomes beyond SWB. First, I explain why life satisfaction is an incomplete measure of well-being, and I argue that well-being requires an approach that incorporates additional factors. I then introduce five ideas for additional outcome measures that positive psychology practitioners and researchers[1] might consider when evaluating their interventions: (i) exploring nuanced outcome *patterns*, spanning multiple life domains and specific emotions; (ii) adopting *behavioral* measures of well-being; (iii) leveraging new technologies that enable continuous and pervasive physiological data collection during day-to-day life (experience-sampling); (iv) measuring

The Wiley Blackwell Handbook of Positive Psychological Interventions, First Edition.
Edited by Acacia C. Parks and Stephen M. Schueller.

meaning in life; and (v) assessing the well-being of *close others* to *vicariously* gauge a person's well-being and explore potential network effects.

Subjective Well-Being and Human Nature

As noted above, SWB is measured via self-report scales of life satisfaction and affective/emotional states. The Satisfaction with Life Scale (SWLS; Diener, Emmons, Larsen, & Griffin, 1985) is a well-established and widely used measure of life satisfaction (Pavot & Diener, 2008). It includes items such as: "I am satisfied with my life" and the more abstract "If I could live my life over, I would change almost nothing." The affective component of SWB is typically gauged by measures that tap into both positive and negative affect, such as the Positive and Negative Affect Schedule (PANAS; Watson, Clark, & Tellegen, 1988). The PANAS asks respondents to what extent they experience a given affective state (either presently or looking back over some specified time period), such as alert, afraid, irritated, or enthusiastic.

One problem with these standard measures of SWB is that they do not measure well-being completely. Well-being (how well one is doing) and life satisfaction (the extent to which one is satisfied with one's life) are conceptually and empirically distinct. Although they are certainly not opposites, they have several key differences. Satisfaction is by definition an introspective concept. In contrast, well-being need not carry an introspective implication – we can speak of the well-being of all sorts of organisms and ecologies, not needing any creature to introspect on abstract questions. More importantly, life satisfaction is not an accurate proxy for well-being. Researchers would do well to extend beyond life satisfaction and affect, and assess well-being as the multi-faceted construct that it is. To support this point, I will first offer a rigorous scientific method by which we can define human well-being, and then I will illustrate a number of ways in which life satisfaction does not correspond to facets of well-being.

Historically, when positive psychology has expanded beyond SWB it has drawn on eudaimonic approaches to well-being. Eudaimonia is an alternative to hedonia in defining well-being. The hedonic approach rests on self-reported life satisfaction and affect. In this model, a person's satisfaction ratings are authoritative. Self-report is not merely a method of convenience here – it is the only thing that matters, because a hedonic approach is subjective *by definition*. The eudaimonic approach adds several facets of well-being that extend beyond satisfaction – e.g., positive relationships (Seligman, 2011), autonomy (Ryff, 1989), and meaning in life (Seligman, 2011), to name a few. The concept of eudaimonia was introduced by Aristotle (1986), and describes the life of excellence and virtue – it is not centrally about happiness, but rather about living in accordance with a set of cardinal virtues. The modern "eudaimonic" conceptions of well-being offered by positive psychology theorists are somewhat softer visions than Aristotle's, focusing more on presumed human *needs* than on prescriptive virtues (see Waterman, 2013, for a review), but they do sometimes carry value-judgments, which I will discuss later.

A long-standing debate among positive psychology researchers centers on which of these approaches – hedonic or eudaimonic – is most appropriate for the study of well-being or happiness. As Kashdan, Biswas-Diener, and King (2008) summarize, advocates of the hedonic approach argue that psychology is "centrally about mental states." Some eudaimonists distrust this approach because they worry that people can *feel happy* even if they are doing terrible things (Annas, 2004) – in this view, happiness is an incomplete construct, missing key elements of the good life. In response, hedonic theorists argue that any model of happiness or well-being that includes more than a person's self-reported satisfaction/happiness – particularly one that contains notions of *virtue* – will remain subjective and ultimately biased by the notion of virtue adopted.

Being forced to choose either a hedonic or eudaimonic approach is unnecessary, as a *third approach* can solve the above issues. Kashdan et al. (2008) aptly note that a philosophical definition of the good life is problematic for behavioral scientists. Models like Seligman's (2011) seem particularly tailored to the *intellectual* life, with a high-minded interpretation of the meaningful life and "accomplishment" treated as basic components of human well-being. However, it is a mistake to retreat to the position that human well-being is reducible to a saccharine mix of self-reported satisfaction and positivity scores. This position is vulnerable to biases related to self-presentation and self-deception and may provide a version of well-being akin to reality TV's version of reality. That is, a version of well-being that distorts the truth to present a version that appeals more to other people.

Moreover, human beings do not run on happiness. Just as a self-report questionnaire would be insufficient to define physical health, a self-report measure cannot suffice for psychological well-being. A more scientific approach would focus on human nature – on what human beings need in order to flourish – just as animal welfare researchers have laid out the core elements of what flourishing means for a particular species (Botreau, Veissier, Butterworth, Bracke, & Keeling, 2007). Core components should be *basic* needs and capacities – basic in that if left unsatisfied or undeveloped, a person could not be considered to be doing well, regardless of his level of life satisfaction. This approach and a eudaimonic approach share some features – for example, social support/positive relationships are surely a fundamental human need (Baumeister & Leary, 1995; Ryan & Deci, 2000; Sheldon, Elliot, Kim, & Kasser, 2001). However, other components of eudaimonic models will likely fail to satisfy this scientific standard, which is to be expected, since such models are not typically framed around scientifically verified fundamentals of human nature.

Conceptions of human well-being should be consistent with definitions of well-being for living organisms in general. Well-being is a *naturalistic* concept – the definition of well-being for any given organism necessarily springs from basic facts about that organism's *nature*. These include facts about its physical needs and proper physiological functioning, its innate behaviors and optimal environment, and for mammals at least, its capacity for mental distress. Human beings are organisms, and all organisms have a nature (however flexible ours may be). Human *physical* needs and health indicators are relatively easy to identify and have been the focus of centuries of medical research. It is more challenging to identify the components of human *psychological* well-being, but it is ultimately a scientifically driven task – it is not subjective.

Definitions of well-being need to include these other scientifically derived factors. Beyond social relationships, other well-supported constructs include efficacy and autonomy (see self-determination theory; Deci & Ryan, 2000, 2008; Ryan & Deci, 2000), and purpose and meaning in life (see Chapter 5). Self-efficacy or confidence is a good candidate because life requires sustained and effective interaction with the environment/world. The particular skills and behaviors necessary to successfully navigate the social world may vary across time and culture, but an individual's self-reported sense of efficacy controls for this variation, and provides information about how well an individual is doing. Even better, practitioners can assess a person's *actual competence* in some domains (e.g., social skills), independent of a person's self-confidence, which I will explore later in the chapter.

Other plausible components of well-being include autonomy (importantly, at a level of fundamentality and breadth that would accommodate collectivist cultures), purpose, and meaning (as long as it is a non-partisan, neutral conception of meaning, bearing witness to coal miners and kindergarten teachers, not just deep-thinking psychology professors). In light of the preceding arguments, I offer the following definition of well-being: that state of affairs where an organism amply meets its basic needs and robustly employs its core capacities. A flower is doing well if it draws from rich, nutritious soil, basks in good light, blooms broadly, spawns good pollen, and attracts competent bees to collect it. An eagle pegs the needle of well-being if she has an ample hunting range, lays viable eggs in a secure nest, can spot rabbits a mile away, and flies true. A human being is doing well if she is physically healthy, has quality friendships and social bonds, can think through routine problems and regulate short-term impulses for the sake of larger goals, and is happy (for the philosophical foundations of this approach, see Harris, 2011, and Aristotle, 1986).

Life Satisfaction Will Not Reliably Capture Well-Being

Even if positive psychology practitioners accept that life satisfaction and well-being are not identical, they still might be willing to lean on life satisfaction if it is a clean proxy for – or index of – well-being. This might be the case if life satisfaction tracked well-being as a feedback mechanism. That is, a person who is doing well across domains should report high life satisfaction, and a person who is languishing in at least one domain should report lower life satisfaction. This seems like a reasonable position and it would be very surprising if life satisfaction and well-being were *completely* unrelated. However, I suggest reasons why life satisfaction will not tell the whole story (cf. Diener, Inglehart, & Tay, 2013):

- Much like the human thirst and hunger mechanisms (Greenleaf, 1992), we should expect the life satisfaction mechanism to be an imperfect feedback mechanism.
- Life satisfaction seems to exhibit a *contentment bias.* That is people generally report being *slightly* happy (above the midpoint of any scale), across time and culture (see more below).
- Because of their limited range and resolution (e.g., a handful of items, seven-point scales), typical life satisfaction measures will sometimes fail to track changes in well-being (for a discussion, see Deyo & Inui, 1984; Fitzpatrick et al., 1992).
- Therefore, practitioners are less likely to observe effects of their interventions if they measure only life satisfaction and affect. Measuring a broad, multi-faceted well-being construct gives more potential effects to report (Diener, Oishi, & Lucas, 2009), and those effects may be *substantively important.*

Evidence for a contentment bias centers on two facts: (i) most people are happy (Diener & Diener, 1996); (ii) mean societal happiness levels do not change much over the generations (Diener & Diener, 1996). This holds even across cultures – even though people in different cultures have different conceptions of happiness (Rojas & Vitterso, 2007), they still tend to report being slightly happy.

That most people are happy – across generations and cultures – implies a type of *positivity bias* (Cacioppo, Gardner, & Berntson, 1999). I refer to this specific case of the positivity bias, the tendency of individuals to rate themselves as slightly above the mean on measures of life satisfaction, as a *contentment bias.* In light of this, people tend to settle on a particular point (e.g., 5 out of 7 on the Satisfaction with Life Scale; Diener & Diener, 1996), and this response is likely to be consistent – that is, it may not change easily in response to changes in one's life, even those resulting in greater well-being. Although a complete discussion of the causes for this bias is beyond the scope of this chapter, researchers have noted raising aspirations (Sheldon & Lyubomirsky, 2012) and stable temperamental underpinnings (Diener & Lucas, 1999) as possibilities. This bias has implications for measurement and people's self-report on scales of life satisfaction. A slightly positive life satisfaction rating, because it is so common, might correspond to a wide range of objective well-being levels. For example, a 5 on the Satisfaction with Life Scale (range = 1–7) would not necessarily correspond to a 5 on a hypothetical composite 1–7 well-being index (an index that combines social support, self-efficacy, meaning, etc.). Rather, people who report Satisfaction with Life Scale scores of 5 would likely have varying scores on this composite measure (e.g., with a range of 4–6). Therefore, this contentment bias is likely to obscure significant variation in actual well-being, and will also obscure moderate *changes* in well-being levels, like those triggered by interventions.

Available Models of Well-Being

In order to measure well-being outcomes, it is important to have a definition or model of well-being and its components. I have offered one definition of well-being, but even if practitioners and researchers do not adopt this definition, they should still define and justify their specific model and measure variables consistent with that model. If a practitioner thinks that well-being consists of five facets, including life satisfaction, he or she should measure as many of those facets as possible. In recent years, numerous models of well-being have been proposed by theorists and empirical researchers (listed in Table 25.1 below). Some of them are grounded in the classic hedonic and eudaimonic distinction. These models take a *sociocultural* approach, by observing how people seem to be pursuing happiness in today's culture and building their model from such observations. For example, Seligman (2011) stipulates that to be included in his model, a component must meet three criteria: it contributes to well-being; people pursue it for its own sake; and it is defined and measured independently of the others. He posits that positive emotions, positive relationships, meaning, engagement, and accomplishment meet these criteria.

In contrast to the sociocultural approaches are *functional* approaches. These approaches focus on mental health or basic psychological needs (Table 25.2). Ryff and Singer (1998) offer six facets of well-being: autonomy, environmental mastery, positive relations, self-acceptance, purpose, and personal growth. Deci and Ryan (2000) posit only the first three of those factors in their model, while Keyes (2005) includes all six of Ryff and Singer's facets and adds three more: positive affect, avowed life satisfaction, and various grouped dimensions of social well-being.

A well-developed model of well-being helps solve the first problem noted in this chapter – the problem of measuring well-being obliquely or indirectly by simply asking participants to rate their life satisfaction – by capturing all the theorized components of well-being *directly*. For instance, if meaning, engagement, and

Table 25.1 Sociocultural classically grounded models of well-being

	Model			
Component type	*Classic*	*Seligman (2002)*	*Seligman (2011)*	*Wong (2011)*
Hedonic	Hedonia	Positive emotion	Positive emotion	Hedonia
Meaning	Eudaimonia	Meaningful life	Life meaning	Eudaimonia
Substantive additions		Engagement	Engagement Positive relationships Accomplishment	Prudential engagement Chaironic

Table 25.2 Functional models of well-being

Ryff and Singer (1998)	*Deci and Ryan (2000)*	*Keyes (2005)*
Autonomy	Autonomy	Autonomy
Environmental mastery	Competence	Environmental mastery
Positive relations	Relatedness/belonging	Positive relations
Self-acceptance		Self-acceptance
Purpose in life		Purpose in life
Personal growth		Personal growth
		Social well-being (social acceptance, actualization, contribution, coherence, and integration)
		Positive affect
		Avowed life satisfaction/ happiness

social support are part of the theorized model, then measuring well-being requires practitioners to assess meaning, engagement, and social support.

Comprehensive models also help solve a second problem – the fact that participants are generally not experts in psychological well-being (e.g., psychologists), just as they are generally not experts in physical well-being (e.g., doctors). This means that practitioners should not expect that participants can integrate and summarize all the components of well-being when they rate their life satisfaction – participants might not necessarily *know* what the relevant components are, and they may not automatically register in satisfaction ratings. For example, we would not expect people to be able to give themselves a comprehensive medical examination and report the diagnoses to their doctor for recordkeeping purposes. A methodical approach to well-being directly assesses the various components of well-being instead of relying on a client or participant's snapshot rating of life satisfaction. This might include a dozen nuanced questions about social support, or a half-dozen questions about self-acceptance. Furthermore, temporal resolution can be increased by including questions that probe daily experience more closely, rather than calling for quick snapshot judgments of well-being as a whole. Measuring to a specified model allows practitioners to develop a richer set of hypotheses, and brings underlying mechanisms into focus.

Domain-Specific Patterns

Given the presumed multi-faceted nature of well-being and consistent with the functional models cited above, it makes sense to evaluate interventions in terms of the *specific* outcome patterns they are predicted to produce. It is doubtful that a domain-specific intervention (e.g., forgiveness, wisdom, etc.) will have the same impact on *all* components of well-being. Rather, one might predict certain components that the intervention would influence more than others. Working from their theoretical model, practitioners should be able to predict a *pattern* of outcomes shaped by their interventions, and test those predictions. This is similar to the practice of demonstrating convergent and divergent validity for a psychological measure, as a positive psychological intervention should produce change on the relevant outcomes but not on other outcomes. One benefit of this approach is that it forces practitioners to think through the specific *pathways* and *mechanisms* through which their interventions work.

Instead of measuring broad positive/negative affect, practitioners would do better to measure a host of specific emotions. For example, whereas the original PANAS-PA (Watson et al., 1988) measures general positive affect or *activation* – particularly high-energy positive engagement with the environment – the revised PANAS-X (Watson & Clark, 1999) adds specific (and low-activation) positive emotions including joviality, self-assurance, and serenity. In several of the models of well-being cited above, emotions like compassion, contentment, gratitude, love, authentic pride (Tracy & Robins, 2007), and moral elevation (Silvers & Haidt, 2008) are extremely relevant. At least two available measures gauge these and other positive emotions. The Modified Discrete Emotions Scale (mDES) (Fredrickson, 2013) includes eight negative and ten positive emotions, such as gratitude, pride, contentment, and inspiration. The Dispositional Positive Emotions Scale (DPES) (Shiota, Keltner, & John, 2006) captures seven positive emotions across 38 items, including awe, pride, humor, and contentment.

Consider the following example. Assume that: (i) you are launching an intervention aimed at spurring acts of forgiveness; (ii) you think the Ryff and Singer (1998) model of psychological well-being is most useful; and (iii) you want to account for discrete emotions in addition to positive affect as such – that is, you want to measure the extent to which participants experience various discrete emotions in their daily lives. (Table 25.3 lists the components of the model.)

Table 25.3 Possible outcomes of interest

Domains of psychological well-being (Ryff & Singer, 1998)	*Discrete positive emotions*	
Environmental mastery	Gratitude	Pride
Autonomy	Love	Contentment
Purpose in life	Compassion	Amusement
Positive relations	Awe	Moral elevation
Personal growth	Admiration	Curiosity/interest
Self-acceptance	Enthusiasm	Joy

The next step is to predict the specific effects of your intervention, constructing an outcome *profile* from a constellation of well-being indicators. Given that your intervention focuses on *forgiveness*, what pattern of outcomes might you predict? If participants engage in acts of forgiveness, you might expect their *positive relations* with others to strengthen or increase in number. You might also predict a greater sense of *environmental mastery* because forgiveness can be a difficult and onerous task. Having done something they had previously thought impossible, participants might feel less intimidated by other challenges. As for discrete emotions, you might expect someone who has systematically engaged in acts of forgiveness to experience more *compassion* (toward the forgiven and others in general), *pride* (at having forgiven), and *contentment* (freed from the distraction of festering wounds).

So far, I have focused on self-report measures. Fundamentally, these measures still address *subjective* elements of well-being. I noted previously that people are not necessarily experts in well-being. This problem is partially mitigated by an approach that cues participants to specific domains (e.g., social support, environmental mastery, etc.), rather than global assessments (i.e., life satisfaction). A complete assessment of well-being will supplement self-report with a host of objective measures of behavior and wellness.

Behavioral Measures

In addition to assessing mental states, emotions, and global self-ratings, researchers would be wise to measure behavior. One step in that direction is to use self-report measures that tap more explicitly into behaviors (Henricksen & Stephens, 2013; Warner & Vroman, 2011). It might be useful to consider the *skills* and *capacities* relevant to well-being and that positive psychological interventions aim to promote. For example, self-regulation, the need to forgo or delay immediate gratifications in favor of more important long-term goals, is an important capacity linked to well-being and achievement (Mischel, Ebbesen, & Raskoff Zeiss, 1972). People with weak self-regulatory capacities often fall short of optimal functioning (e.g., Baumeister & Heatherton, 1996). Self-regulatory capacity could be included as an outcome measure and tested directly in a variety of established ways.

Resilience is another good candidate. Adapting to change and recovering from stressors is another ability fundamental to optimal human functioning. Researchers can assess resilience directly in the laboratory. For example, Waugh, Fredrickson, and Taylor (2008) tracked participants' affective responses while anticipating aversive stimuli (unsettling photos), as well as their affective responses during and after the stimuli. This method captures how quickly an individual recovers from an aversive event or stimulus, mirroring research that measures cardiovascular recovery times after exercise as an index of fitness and mortality (Cole, Blackstone, Pashkow, Snader, & Lauer, 1999).

Because social connectedness is a basic human need, certain social skills might be included as a component of well-being. As such, researchers could directly observe and measure various social skills as targets of an intervention. Vacharkulksemsuk and Fredrickson (2012) found, for example, that behavioral synchrony mediated the effect of self-disclosure on rapport with an interaction partner. A researcher could theorize behavioral synchrony as a core component of social skill or social responding, and hypothesize that a mindfulness intervention would increase behavioral synchrony in a pre and post design. Synchrony could be gauged in a laboratory setting. Vacharkulksemsuk and Fredrickson (2012) accomplished this by having coders rate simultaneous movement, tempo similarity, and coordination from videos of participant interactions.

In the previous section I suggested measuring discrete emotions. A behavioral measure could assess an individual's *capacity* to experience a given emotion. This could be done by inducing the emotion in the laboratory – e.g., using video clips or other stimuli (Silvers & Haidt, 2008). An alternative approach would be a recall exercise, in which a participant is asked to recall a time when she experienced a given emotion and to write about it (e.g., Griskevicius, Shiota, & Neufeld, 2010).

Experience Sampling – You Can Make an App for That

The recent proliferation of smartphones has dramatically expanded the potential for rich experience-sampling methods. Most smartphones now include accelerometers, gyroscopes, and GPS tracking, and of course easily facilitate two-way text communication between researchers and participants. Data obtained from these sensors can be used to infer mental states relevant to well-being. Accelerometer data, for example, have been used to identify specific patterns of activity that correlate with depressed mood (Burns et al., 2011; Yoshiuchi et al., 2006). Smartphone data presents an opportunity for positive psychology researchers as it draws from a portable and increasingly ubiquitous device. Current generation smartphones offer the capability to access data from accelerometers, visible Bluetooth signals, call and message logs, video cameras, and microphones. Burns et al. (2011) pilot-tested a mobile application called Mobilyze that used user and contextual data to infer mood states. Although the system demonstrated reasonable accuracy at predicting contextual states, its prediction of mood performed more poorly.

Given sufficient resources, researchers and practitioners can use smartphones to deliver interventions and collect data by building their own customized applications. Such applications could include self-report fields (e.g., affect) timed in whichever way the researcher specified, and could also present reminders to participants (e.g., if the intervention is designed to get people to interrupt long periods of inactivity). Custom applications are not expensive – they can be contracted to software developers for as little as $3,000 (Maxwell, 2011). However, it should be noted that contracting design out to a software developer rather than working in tandem with a developer throughout the design process might result in an application that meets the original design specifications but may overlook important features. Given their more flexible open-source design, Android applications may prove more feasible than iPhone apps, but researchers will have to navigate these issues based on their particular needs. Lastly, practitioners may find that it makes more sense to procure an app that is already available in the relevant app stores (some are free). This is a constantly changing area, so rather than list specific apps here, I encourage practitioners to search for the latest positive psychology apps.

In addition to smartphones, researchers can use other activity-tracking devices such as the Nike Fuel Band, Jawbone UP, or the Fitbit. These devices are light wristbands that include accelerometers and other sensors, and track movement, steps, calories, and in the case of Fitbit, sleep duration and quality. Currently, though, as these devices are targeted at consumers, researchers may have a difficult time accessing data due to restrictions on the application programming interfaces. Devices developed for researchers are available, but often more expensive.

Meaning

Meaning features prominently in many eudaimonic models of well-being (e.g., Ryff & Singer, 1998; Seligman, 2011; Wong, 2011) and is a target of several positive psychological interventions (see Chapter 5). *Meaning* can be defined in vastly different ways. Baumeister and Vohs (2002) focus on predicted properties of things in the environment (e.g., water being wet), while terror management theorists refer to a human need to manage existential concerns by ascribing a death-transcendent significance to their lives (Landau, Greenberg, Solomon, Pyszczynski, & Martens, 2006). Some positive psychology theorists (e.g., Seligman, 2011) define meaning as serving something (i.e., a cause or purpose) that one views as greater than oneself.

Embedding particular philosophical perspectives into the scientific study of well-being, however, is invalid, and the measurement of meaning is particularly prone to difficulties here. An example of a valid neutral approach is the Meaning in Life Questionnaire (Steger, Frazier, Oishi, & Kaler, 2006), which includes items such as "I understand my life's meaning" and "My life has a clear sense of purpose." These items are appropriately neutral and do not presuppose a certain framework or values. Conversely, the Meaning in Life Scale (Jim, Purnell, Richardson, Golden-Kreutz, & Andersen, 2006) includes items such as "I feel a sense of harmony within myself" and "I find comfort in my faith or spiritual beliefs." These items narrowly define meaning around concepts of harmony and faith, potentially leaving some participants out of the conversation (e.g., atheists, secular humanists, scientists). Researchers should take care to measure meaning in a value-neutral fashion, unless there are strong theoretical reasons for focusing on a narrower conception.

Extended Well-Being – Including Close Others' Welfare as an Extension of One's Own

An innovative alternative to self-report ratings of well-being and personality has been the use of *peer ratings*. Researchers ask close others – family and friends – to rate the participant's apparent well-being, life satisfaction, extraversion, etc. The premise is that close others are in a position to observe such traits, and that tapping their judgments overcomes some of the limitations of self-report. For example, peer ratings of life satisfaction converge somewhat with self-report (Pavot, Diener, Colvin, & Sandvik, 1991), and can validate purported relationships between life satisfaction and other self-focused constructs (Schimmack & Diener, 2003). This approach can be taken further by having clients' or participants' close others rate *their own* well-being, rather than the participant's.

Individual well-being may manifest itself beyond the individual. A flourishing – or languishing – individual does not operate in a vacuum. In fact, for some researchers, how well one's close others are doing might be part of the *definition* of well-being. This will likely be intuitive for researchers in collectivistic cultures, but it may be a useful consideration in non-collectivistic cultures as well.

The nature of the intervention will be relevant here. For example, if the intervention is designed to strengthen social bonds or relationship skills, an outcome measure that aggregates the participant's and close others' well-being might make perfect sense. And even less explicitly relational interventions – e.g., a mindfulness intervention – might yield significant effects on participants' loved ones, co-workers, etc. Evidence from the Framingham Heart Study suggests that happiness is contagious across households (Fowler & Christakis, 2008), and researchers might consider how their interventions will impact the well-being of specific close others, informed by their theoretical models and the nature of the intervention. Moreover, the manner in which well-being spreads can be mathematically modeled in ways that may provide useful information – for example, well-being might be more likely to spread to same-sex friends compared to opposite-sex friends. Researchers have several methods at their disposal, from the network analysis algorithm used by Fowler and Christakis to the epidemiological methods used to model a zombie outbreak (Munz, Hudea, Imad, & Smith, 2009).

An Index of Well-Being

A multi-faceted conception of well-being – a conception that rests on a variety of separately measured components – logically implies that an integrated well-being index may be useful. That is, if researchers and practitioners collect scores on a host of well-being outcome variables, they may want to integrate them and speak of *well-being* as a unified outcome variable. It will often be necessary to report each outcome factor separately (social support, meaning in life, efficacy, etc.), but a comprehensive index may be useful. Such an index invites us to think about the respective weights assigned to each factor. After all, it is implausible that a well-developed theory of well-being would weigh each factor equally – it is statistically unlikely that every factor contributes equally to human well-being (e.g., social support may be more important than autonomy, and would therefore be weighed more heavily).

Surprisingly, many prevailing models of well-being (Seligman, 2011; Wong, 2011) do not address the issue of how much each of their factors should contribute to well-being. One reason for this is that the weighting of these factors could vary across individuals, groups, or cultures. For example, it would be reasonable to weigh autonomy less heavily in collectivistic or familial cultures. However, if the weighting could be determined, the next generation of positive psychological interventions might be able to be tailored to an individual's specific well-being index. For example, an introvert may need less social support or social time than an extravert, thus warranting positive psychological interventions that do not emphasize social components (see Schueller, 2012). As positive psychology advances and matures, individual differences should evolve from mere *predictors* of outcomes into personalized *profiles* relevant to the interventions best suited for that individual.

Conclusion

A multi-faceted model of well-being provides greater insight into the effects of interventions than subjective well-being approaches. The more different facets of well-being are explored, the more this work can contribute to the understanding of the factors that shape it and the best ways to measure it. Fortunately, the measurement of well-being has advanced considerably in recent years, and new methods can provide richer, higher resolution insights into the effects of our interventions. A full scientific conception of well-being will look beyond life satisfaction and affect and measure behavior, psychophysiology, observer reports, and the well-being of close others.

Practitioners stand to benefit from a comprehensive approach in a number of ways. For example, a practitioner interested in adaptive functioning might behaviorally assess self-regulatory capacity or resilience, just as a physical trainer would assess aerobic capacity. This can provide a more accurate view of what the practitioner is aiming to improve. Just as a physical trainer would not be satisfied by only asking clients how fit they are, a practitioner should not be satisfied with only asking clients if they are satisfied with their lives.

The measures and methods covered in this chapter provide only a start. As the science of human well-being and its assessment continues to advance, practitioners will have ever more options for the evaluation of interventions. Beyond the components and measures of well-being outlined in this chapter, several future directions come to mind. It is likely that smartphone apps will become more accurate in determining mood from conversation quality, social support, and voice characteristics. Early efforts have already been piloted (Lu et al., 2012).

Another promising outcome variable is goal fulfillment. Pursuing life goals is central to most human lives. The extent to which people are able to achieve their goals may be worth measuring directly, as an aspect of well-being, augmenting self-report measures of efficacy (Ryff, 1989). Lastly, the capacity to experience certain emotions might be a promising avenue of research. For example, people likely vary in their capacity to be *deeply moved*, or to experience emotions such as inspiration or awe. This capacity might relate to other facets of well-being, or it could explain a range of behaviors. In any case, the way forward is to treat psychological well-being similarly to physical health – as a multi-faceted construct grounded in facts of human nature that is unlikely to be measurable via a brief quiz.

Note

1 This chapter is intended for researchers and positive psychology practitioners. I sometimes refer to one or the other throughout the chapter, but readers may take each point as relevant for both audiences.

References

Annas, J. (2004). Happiness as achievement. *Daedalus*, *133*, 44–51.

Aristotle (1986). *Nicomachean ethics*. New York: Macmillan. (Original work published in the fourth century BCE.)

Baumeister, R. F., & Heatherton, T. F. (1996). Self-regulation failure: An overview. *Psychological Inquiry*, *7*, 1–15.

Baumeister, R. F., & Leary, M. R. (1995). The need to belong: Desire for interpersonal attachments as a fundamental human motivation. *Psychological Bulletin*, *117*, 497–529.

Baumeister, R. F., & Vohs, K. D. (2002). The pursuit of meaningfulness in life. In C. R. Snyder & S. J. Lopez (Eds.), *Handbook of positive psychology* (pp. 608–618). New York: Oxford University Press.

Botreau, R., Veissier, I., Butterworth, A., Bracke, M. B. M., & Keeling, L. J. (2007). Definition of criteria for overall assessment of animal welfare. *Animal Welfare*, *16*, 225–228.

Burns, M. N., Begale, M., Duffecy, J., Gergle, D., Karr, C. J., Giangrande, E., & Mohr, D. C. (2011). Harnessing context sensing to develop a mobile intervention for depression. *Journal of Medical Internet Research*, *13*, e55.

Cacioppo, J. T., Gardner, W. L., & Berntson, G. G. (1999). The affect system has parallel and integrative processing components: Form follows function. *Journal of Personality and Social Psychology*, *76*(5), 839–855.

Cole, C. R., Blackstone, E. H., Pashkow, F. J., Snader, C. E., & Lauer, M. S. (1999). Heart-rate recovery immediately after exercise as a predictor of mortality. *New England Journal of Medicine*, *341*, 1351–1357.

Deci, E. L., & Ryan, R. M. (2000). The "what" and "why" of goal pursuits: Human needs and the self-determination of behavior. *Psychological Inquiry*, *11*, 227–268.

Deci, E. L., & Ryan, R. M. (2008). Self-determination theory: A macrotheory of human motivation, development, and health. *Canadian Psychology/Psychologie canadienne*, *49*, 182–185.

Deyo, R. A., & Inui, T. S. (1984). Toward clinical applications of health status measures: Sensitivity of scales to clinically important changes. *Health Services Research*, *19*, 275–289.

Diener, E., & Diener, C. (1996). Most people are happy. *Psychological Science*, *7*(3), 181–185.

Diener, E. D., Emmons, R. A., Larsen, R. J., & Griffin, S. (1985). The Satisfaction with Life Scale. *Journal of Personality Assessment*, *49*, 71–75.

Diener, E., Ingelhart, R., & Tay, L. (2013). Theory and validity of life satisfaction scales. *Social Indicators Research*, *112*, 497–527.

Diener, E., & Lucas, R. E. (1999). Personality and subjective well-being. In D. Kahneman, E. Diener, & N. Schwarz (Eds.), *Well-being: The foundations of a hedonic psychology* (pp. 213–229). New York: Russell Sage Foundation.

Diener, E., Oishi, S., & Lucas, R. E. (2009). Subjective well-being: The science of happiness and life satisfaction. In S. J. Lopez & C. R. Snyder (Eds.), *Oxford handbook of positive psychology* (2nd ed., pp. 187–194). New York: Oxford University Press.

Diener, E., & Suh, E. (1997). Measuring quality of life: Economic, social, and subjective indicators. *Social Indicators Research*, *40*, 189–216.

Diener, E., Suh, E. M., Lucas, R. E., & Smith, H. L. (1999). Subjective well-being: Three decades of progress. *Psychological Bulletin*, *125*, 276–302.

Fitzpatrick, R., Fletcher, A., Gore, S., Jones, D., Spiegelhalter, D., & Cox, D. (1992). Quality of life measures in health care. I: Applications and issues in assessment. *British Medical Journal*, *305*, 1074–1077.

Fowler, J. H., & Christakis, N. A. (2008). The dynamic spread of happiness in a large social network. *British Medical Journal*, *337*, a2338.

Fredrickson, B. L. (2013). Positive emotions broaden and build. In P. G. Devine & E. A. Plant (Eds.), *Advances in Experimental Social Psychology* (pp. 1–54). New York: Elsevier.

Greenleaf, J. E. (1992). Problem: Thirst, drinking behavior, and involuntary dehydration. *Medicine and Science in Sports and Exercise*, *24*, 645–656.

Griskevicius, V., Shiota, M. N., & Neufeld, S. L. (2010). Influence of different positive emotions on persuasion processing: A functional evolutionary approach. *Emotion*, *10*, 190–206.

Harris, S. (2011). *The moral landscape: How science can determine human values.* New York: Free Press.

Henricksen, A., & Stephens, C. (2013). The happiness-enhancing activities and positive practices inventory (HAPPI): Development and validation. *Journal of Happiness Studies*, *14*, 81–98.

Jim, H. S., Purnell, J. Q., Richardson, S. A., Golden-Kreutz, D., & Andersen, B. L. (2006). Measuring meaning in life following cancer. *Quality of Life Research*, *15*, 1355–1371.

Kashdan, T. B., Biswas-Diener, R., & King, L. A. (2008). Reconsidering happiness: The costs of distinguishing between hedonics and eudaimonia. *Journal of Positive Psychology*, *3*(4), 219–233.

Keyes, C. L. M. (2005). Mental illness and/or mental health? Investigating axioms of the complete state model of health. *Journal of Consulting and Clinical Psychology*, *73*, 539–548.

Landau, M. J., Greenberg, J., Solomon, S., Pyszczynski, T., & Martens, A. (2006). Windows into nothingness: Terror management, meaninglessness, and negative reactions to modern art. *Journal of Personality and Social Psychology*, *90*, 879–892.

Lu, H., Rabbi, M., Chittaranjan, G. T., Frauendorfer, D., Mast, M. S., Campbell, A. T., ... Choudhury, T. (2012). StressSense: Detecting stress in unconstrained acoustic environments using smartphones. In *Proceedings of the 14th International Conference on Ubiquitous Computing*. Retrieved from http://www.idiap.ch/~gatica/publications/LuRabbiChittaranjanFrauendorferSchmidCampbellGaticaChoudhury-ubicomp12.pdf

Maxwell, A. (2011, February 24). Is developing a mobile app worth the cost? Retrieved from http://mashable.com/2011/02/24/mobile-app-dev-cost

Mischel, W., Ebbesen, E. B., & Raskoff Zeiss, A. (1972). Cognitive and attentional mechanisms in delay of gratification. *Journal of Personality and Social Psychology*, *21*, 204–218.

Munz, P., Hudea, I., Imad, J., & Smith, R. J. (2009). When zombies attack! Mathematical modelling of an outbreak of zombie infection. *Infectious Disease Modelling Research Progress*, 133–150.

Pavot, W., & Diener, E. (1993). Review of the Satisfaction with Life Scale. *Psychological Assessment*, *5*, 165–177.

Pavot, W., & Diener, E. (2008). The Satisfaction with Life Scale and the emerging construct of life satisfaction. *Journal of Positive Psychology*, *3*, 137–152.

Pavot, W., Diener, E., Colvin, C. R., & Sandvik, E. (1991). Further validation of the Satisfaction with Life Scale: Evidence for the cross-method convergence of well-being measures. *Journal of Personality Assessment*, *57*, 149–161.

Rojas, M., & Vitterso, J. (2007). Conceptual referent for happiness: Cross-country comparisons. *Journal of Social Research and Policy*, *1*, 103–116.

Ryan, R. M., & Deci, E. L. (2000). Self-determination theory and the facilitation of intrinsic motivation, social development, and well-being. *American Psychologist*, *55*, 68–78.

Ryff, C. D. (1989). Happiness is everything, or is it? Explorations on the meaning of psychological well-being. *Journal of Personality and Social Psychology*, *57*, 1069–1081.

Ryff, C. D., & Singer, B. (1998). The contours of positive human health. *Psychological Inquiry*, *9*, 1–28.

Schimmack, U., & Diener, E. (2003). Predictive validity of explicit and implicit self-esteem for subjective well-being. *Journal of Research in Personality*, *37*, 100–106.

Schueller, S. M. (2012). Personality fit and positive interventions: Extraverted and introverted individuals benefit from different happiness increasing strategies. *Psychology*, *3*, 1166–1173.

Seligman, M. E. P. (2002). *Authentic happiness*. New York: Free Press.

Seligman, M. E. P. (2011). *Flourish: A visionary new understanding of happiness and well-being*. New York: Free Press.

Sheldon, K. M., Elliot, A. J., Kim, Y., & Kasser, T. (2001). What is satisfying about satisfying events? Testing 10 candidate psychological needs. *Journal of Personality and Social Psychology*, *80*, 325–339.

Sheldon, K. M., & Lyubomirsky, S. (2012). The challenge of staying happier: Testing the Hedonic Adaptation Prevention model. *Personality and Social Psychology Bulletin*, *38*, 670–680.

Shiota, M. N., Keltner, D., & John, O. P. (2006). Positive emotion dispositions differentially associated with Big Five personality and attachment style. *Journal of Positive Psychology*, *1*, 61–71.

Silvers, J. A., & Haidt, J. (2008). Moral elevation can induce nursing. *Emotion*, *8*, 291–295.

Steger, M. F., Frazier, P., Oishi, S., & Kaler, M. (2006). The meaning in life questionnaire: Assessing the presence of and search for meaning in life. *Journal of Counseling Psychology*, *53*, 80–93.

Tracy, J. L., & Robins, R. W. (2007). The psychological structure of pride: A tale of two facets. *Journal of Personality and Social Psychology*, *92*, 506–525.

Vacharkulksemsuk, T., & Fredrickson, B. L. (2012). Strangers in sync: Achieving embodied rapport through shared movements. *Journal of Experimental Social Psychology*, *48*, 399–402.

Warner, R. M., & Vroman, K. G. (2011). Happiness inducing behaviors in everyday life: An empirical assessment of "The how of happiness." *Journal of Happiness Studies*, *12*, 1063–1082.

Waterman, A. S. (2013). *The best within us: Positive psychology perspectives on eudaimonia*. Washington, DC: American Psychological Association.

Watson, D., & Clark, L. A. (1999). The PANAS-X: Manual for the positive and negative affect schedule–expanded form. Retrieved from http://ir.uiowa.edu/cgi/viewcontent.cgi?article=1011&context=psychology_pubs

Watson, D., Clark, L. A., & Tellegen, A. (1988). Development and validation of brief measures of positive and negative affect: The PANAS scales. *Journal of Personality and Social Psychology*, *54*, 1063–1070.

Waugh, C. E., Fredrickson, B. L., & Taylor, S. F. (2008). Adapting to life's slings and arrows: Individual differences in resilience when recovering from an anticipated threat. *Journal of Research in Personality*, *42*, 1031–1046.

Wong, P. T. P. (2011). Positive psychology 2.0: Towards a balanced interactive model of the good life. *Canadian Psychology /Psychologie canadienne*, *52*, 69–81.

Yoshiuchi, K., Nakahara, R., Kumano, H., Kuboki, T., Togo, F., Watanabe, E., … Aoyagi, Y. (2006). Yearlong physical activity and depressive symptoms in older Japanese adults: Cross-sectional data from the Nakanojo study. *American Journal of Geriatric Psychiatry*, *14*, 621–624.

26

Positive Psychological Interventions and Self-Perceptions

A Cautionary Tale

Kasley M. Killam and Young-Hoon Kim

According to Allport (1937), "an impartial and objective attitude toward oneself is held to be a primary virtue, basic to the development of all others … if any trait of personality is intrinsically desirable, it is the disposition and ability to see oneself in perspective" (p. 422). Similarly, Jahoda (1953) claimed that a hallmark of healthy individuals is considering "matters one wishes were different, without distorting them to fit these wishes" (p. 349). In line with the viewpoints of these and other forerunners in psychology, this chapter presents a case for positive psychological interventions that promote positive yet realistic self-perceptions. Our recommendation arises from research showing that unrealistically positive self-perceptions – deemed self-enhancement – can actually hinder a person from succeeding and functioning optimally, whereas accurate self-perceptions yield a host of beneficial outcomes. In particular, we have conducted experiments directly comparing self-enhancement to accurate self-perceptions and consistently found that the former is detrimental, whereas the latter promotes academic excellence, motivation to improve and achieve, and psychological well-being. Likewise, robust research from within positive psychology supports this claim, which we will review in this chapter. Taking into account this body of evidence, interventions may be most effective in helping people to flourish if they encourage positive but realistic self-perceptions and if they provide effective methods to advance from a current, realistic self to a future, idealistic self. Indeed, in order to improve, be more successful, and lead fulfilling, meaningful lives, individuals need to have an accurate sense of themselves, their current abilities, and their current shortcomings, and to take action accordingly.

Furthermore, emphasizing realistic self-perceptions within positive psychological interventions separates positive psychology from other trends that promote artificial positive thinking. These trends, such as the self-esteem movement, the

The Wiley Blackwell Handbook of Positive Psychological Interventions, First Edition.
Edited by Acacia C. Parks and Stephen M. Schueller.

power-of-positive-thinking movement, or *The Secret*, to name a few, are often combined with science-based positive psychology by laypeople and media sources. This chapter attests their distinction and importantly asserts that self-enhancement, which is a self-focused form of artificial positive thinking, is not beneficial and can be harmful. The same may be said of the aforementioned trends insomuch as they induce unrealistic, inflated self-perceptions. Indeed, the evidence presented in this chapter exemplifies the theme that positive psychology is not about merely thinking positively and experiencing positive emotions, which distinguishes positive psychological interventions from other unscientific practices by acknowledging the potential risks of promoting self-enhancement, instead endorsing accurate self-perceptions, and providing active, effective ways to improve, build skills, strengths, and relationships, form healthy habits, and, in short, to prosper enduringly. To be sure, positive psychology is focused on uncovering what enables us to be our best and how to cultivate lasting fulfillment – it is the scientific investigation of optimal functioning – and we hope that the following discussions will offer insight into how interventions can better achieve that goal by taking into account research on self-enhancement.

Cautions from Self-Enhancement Research

As Mark Twain observed, "We do not deal much in facts when we are contemplating ourselves." Along these lines, individuals who self-enhance uphold favorable self-perceptions that are not supported by objective criteria. This bias is extremely common, even though people are capable of perceiving themselves accurately (Alicke, Klotz, Breitenbecher, Yurak, & Vredenburg, 1995; John & Robins, 1994; Kim, Chiu, & Zou, 2010; Kruger & Dunning, 1999; Taylor & Brown, 1988).

Despite the pervasiveness of self-enhancement, investigators have documented many corresponding undesirable effects. Outcomes include poorer social skills; lower academic performance, self-esteem, resilience, and motivation to improve; higher levels of depression, dejection, and maladjustment; and maladaptive attitudes such as defensiveness, narcissism, hostility, and arrogance (e.g. Colvin, Block, & Funder, 1995; Gresham, Lane, MacMillan, Bocian, & Ward, 2000; Kim & Chiu, 2011; Kim et al., 2010; Kurt & Paulhus, 2008; Kwan, John, Robins, & Kuang, 2008). These consequences are incompatible with achieving a flourishing, optimal life. Indeed, someone who self-enhances may not be able to make personal progress due to such factors as low motivation and improper time allocation (Försterling & Morgenstern, 2002; Kim et al., 2010). This line of evidence is supported theoretically, as well. For example, people who perceive themselves as better than they actually are do not acknowledge a need to improve, and subsequently will not engage in additional effort because they are not motivated by a need to improve, and therefore cannot advance themselves. On the other hand, people who perceive themselves realistically take into account both their strengths and shortcomings, can identify the need for improvement, will not be impaired by a lack of achievement motivation, and can apply effort appropriately in a given domain.

Congruent with this reasoning, we have repeatedly shown the detrimental effects of self-enhancement and identified positive outcomes that arise from accurate self-perceptions. To begin, in a study by Kim and colleagues (2010), 283 university students completed a math test and were given either positive bogus feedback, negative bogus feedback, or no feedback about their performance, to induce self-enhancement, self-effacement (which we will discuss in a later section), or their own self-perceptions, respectively. Given that tests are familiar to students, they are able to perceive their performance fairly accurately. Indeed, in a pilot study to confirm this point, 83% of students accurately assessed their math test performance, or were off by only one mark, when given monetary incentive for accuracy. Thus, in the experiment, when participants perceived their performance on the math test as only "alright" but were informed that they performed very well compared to 800 other university students, these individuals experienced induced self-enhancement. Subsequently, participants were informed that they would complete another math test with different questions, supposedly to evaluate the impact of noise on performance, and were given the choice of seven noise levels (ranging from no noise at all to very loud noise). The experimenters stated that louder noise can severely degrade performance on math tests, regardless of test takers' actual math ability, and then asked the participants to choose a noise level. Those with induced self-enhancement (i.e., low actual performance but high performance feedback) chose higher levels of noise than those with accurate self-perceptions, indicating self-handicapping. This finding was theoretically consistent with the authors' hypothesis: people who receive feedback that is more positive than their initial self-perceptions are pleased, adopt self-enhancement, and are motivated to protect the enhanced identity. However, based on their knowledge of previous math test ability, these individuals know that the enhanced self-perception is not realistic. Thus, they will self-handicap to provide an excuse for any subsequent discrepancy in performance, so that they can justify maintaining a desirable, enhanced self-perception. In this case, by choosing to work in a noisier environment despite knowing that doing so could negatively impact their performance, participants with induced self-enhancement created an anticipatory excuse to account for lower performance on the second math test, thereby enabling maintenance of their enhanced self-perception from the first math test. For the purposes of this chapter, we want to underline that while self-handicapping may enable preservation of an enhanced self-perception, it also by definition inhibits a person from performing optimally. Therefore, the finding that self-enhancement induces greater self-handicapping behavior is one compelling example of how self-enhancement is detrimental and impedes individuals from achieving their best.

In another study, 136 university students also completed a math test and were provided bogus performance feedback in the same way (Kim et al., 2010). Then, these students were given the option to wait for eight minutes or to use the time to work on an ungraded tutorial exercise consisting of anagrams, which they were informed would augment their performance on a subsequent, graded task. The authors used the number of anagrams attempted to indicate preparatory effort, finding that participants with induced self-enhancement attempted fewer anagrams and therefore invested less preparatory effort into the task. In this way, self-enhancement was again associated with more self-handicapping and furthermore with lower achievement motivation, which can only hinder a person from succeeding or flourishing. Indeed, additional studies showed that self-enhancers achieved lower task performance and actually had lower grade point averages (GPAs) than accurate self-perceivers (Kim et al., 2010). Moreover, in a final study, students who perceived themselves as ranking higher in a course than they actually ranked, signifying self-enhancement, reported lower levels of subjective well-being. This emotional outcome was in line with theoretical predictions, because individuals who self-enhance are constantly wary of having their enhanced self-perceptions disproven and therefore experience intensified concerns and emotional distress related to evaluative situations. In short, self-enhancement has inhibiting effects that oppose the exact aims of positive psychological interventions.

Similarly, we examined the effects of self-enhancement in direct comparison to accurate self-perceptions over four years (Kim, Killam, Shigeto, & Grison, 2013). In order to provide an objective comparison, we identified self-enhancers as students who self-assessed their exam grades as higher than they actually scored, whereas we pinpointed participants as having accurate self-perceptions if their self-assessments matched their actual exam grades. Given that exam-taking is a familiar task for students, they have fairly accurate knowledge of their exam performance and so can accurately self-perceive in that domain. Our analysis showed that students who self-enhanced in the first semester of their undergraduate degree consistently attained lower GPAs each semester thereafter until graduation, compared to those who accurately self-perceived. Furthermore, the individuals with accurate self-perceptions improved academically over the four years to a greater extent than did the self-enhancers.

In another study, people who self-enhanced in the same way demonstrated lower motivation to improve their performance on an assigned task, as indicated by their responses to a survey about achievement motivation and by their self-handicapping behaviors, than those with accurate self-perceptions (Kim et al., 2013). As well, they reported stronger emotional distress, as shown by higher self-rated levels of agitation emotions (e.g., uneasy, on edge, tense) and dejection emotions (e.g., discouraged, low, upset). Notably, these results were apparent among European American, Asian American, Chinese, Japanese, and Korean participants, which underscores cross-cultural relevance of this phenomenon. Therefore, regardless of whether they arise from knowledge or belief, accurate self-perceptions are beneficial and help to structure growth and well-being, in line with the goals of positive psychological interventions.

Finally, of particular interest to clinical practitioners, Kim and Chiu (2011) posited that self-enhancement would predict the highest levels of depression and the lowest levels of self-esteem, whereas the opposite would be true for accurate self-perceptions. Participants completed a verbal test, ranked their performance in comparison to peers at their school, and self-assessed how many questions they answered correctly. They also filled out the Beck Depression Inventory-II (BDI-II; Beck, Steer, & Brown, 1996) and the Rosenberg Self-Esteem Scale (Rosenberg, 1965). To construct an objective measure of self-enhancement, individuals who ranked themselves as higher than their actual rank and who claimed to have answered more questions correctly than they actually did were considered self-enhancers. In comparison to individuals with accurate self-perceptions (i.e., those who ranked themselves accurately and who reported the true amount of correct answers), self-enhancers were more depressed and had lower self-esteem. Overall, these examples from our research offer ample reason to acknowledge the problems associated with self-enhancement and the benefits of realistic self-perceptions, especially for elements like performance, motivation, and well-being that contribute to flourishing.

In light of these findings, we wish to caution that positive psychological interventions could be ineffective in fostering optimal living if they either directly or inadvertently encourage unrealistically positive self-perceptions. Endorsing an honest self-perception better prepares people to thrive, both in the short and long term. Hence, given the problems associated with self-enhancement and the benefits accompanying accurate self-perceptions, we advise for interventions that influence a person's self-perception to strive to be realistic, albeit still being positive.

Emphasizing Positive yet Realistic Self-Perceptions

We will now discuss two examples from other areas of positive psychology research that support our assertion. First, a certain amount of negative emotion is advantageous. According to Fredrickson and Losada (2005), "problems can occur with too much positivity" and "appropriate negativity may play an important role" for human flourishing (p. 684). Appropriate negativity is defined as time-limited and connected to specific circumstances, rather than global and dominant. Accordingly, the authors determined that flourishing mental health corresponds with a ratio of positive to negative affect between 3:1 and 13:1, indicating that there is an upper limit above which positive emotions are no longer beneficial and that a person at his or her best still experiences some negative emotions. Therefore, Fredrickson and Losada (2005) emphasized that "positivity must be both appropriate and genuine" (p. 685), which opposes the feigned positivity that characterizes self-enhancement. This notion points to a realistic balance between positive and negative and is mirrored in our caution against self-enhancement. In short, the value of negative emotions is attuned with encouraging realistic self-perceptions that take into account both the positive and negative aspects of an individual.

Second, accurate self-perceptions may contribute to experiencing flow. An essential quality of the flow state is a matching of skill level with challenge; indeed, flow requires "perceived challenges, or opportunities for action, that stretch (neither overmatching nor underutilizing) existing skills" and "a sense that one is engaging challenges at a level appropriate to one's capacities" (Nakamura & Csikszentmihalyi, 2002, p. 90). Thus, individuals aiming to trigger flow must engage in activities that are at an appropriate level, which we suggest is determined by realistic self-perception of their skills. Indeed, the importance of accurately perceiving one's abilities is apparent from the impact of mismatched skills and challenge level: "If challenges begin to exceed skills, one first becomes vigilant and then anxious; if skills begin to exceed challenges, one first relaxes and then becomes bored" (Nakamura & Csikszentmihalyi, 2002, p. 90). Even though this matching is subjective, it stands to reason that a realistic self-perception (based on belief or knowledge) would better enable people to gauge their skills and therefore succeed at identifying appropriately challenging activities to promote flow. Insomuch as flow is a desirable, optimal state and the ability to evaluate skill and challenge levels is useful for its occurrence, accurate self-perceptions can be valuable.

Progressing from Current to Ideal Self

In addition to advocating for accurate albeit positive self-perceptions, we aim to draw attention to the necessity of interventions that are habit-forming and skill-building. As Lyubomirsky, Sheldon, and Schkade (2005) pointed out, scientific research has focused on increasing happiness, but not sufficiently on *sustaining* those increases. To fill this void, interventions have the opportunity to guide people in building *and* upholding fulfilling lives. In this way, individuals can methodologically advance from their initial state to one of lasting prosperity and wellness. We will refer to several existing interventions to illustrate this theme in greater detail.

To begin, in various positive psychological interventions, individuals think about their ideal selves, thereby focusing on a positive self-perception. For instance, during the "Best Possible Self" exercise, participants visualize and write about the best version of themselves (King, 2001). They are instructed to "imagine yourself in the future, after everything has gone as well as it possibly could. You have worked hard and succeeded at accomplishing all of your life goals. Think of this as the realization of your life dreams, and of your own best potentials" (Sheldon & Lyubomirsky, 2006, p. 77). This intervention has been associated with various benefits, such as increased subjective well-being (King, 2001) and positive affect (Sheldon & Lyubomirsky, 2006). Similarly, in a study by Seligman, Rashid, and Parks (2006), participants considered their ideal selves in this way: "Imagine that you have passed away after living a fruitful and satisfying life. What would you want your obituary to say? Write a 1–2 page essay summarizing what you would like to be remembered for the most" (p. 776). Another example is an optimism intervention in which participants wrote a letter to their current selves from the perspective of their future selves, imagining that their issues were resolved and giving advice to their current selves; this activity was linked with reduced depressive symptoms for up to three months and increased happiness for up to six months (Shapira & Mongrain, 2010). We commend these interventions for providing activities that raise well-being.

However, to ensure that envisioning oneself as better than one is currently does not induce a kind of self-enhancement, and therefore to avoid the consequences associated with unrealistically positive self-perceptions, we propose that interventions not only induce thinking about an ideal self, but also offer active ways for people to achieve that envisioned better self. One possible limitation of such activities is that, although they have been shown to invoke beneficial outcomes, they may not guide comprehensive self-progress on their own. We believe that positive psychological interventions can strive to achieve the latter, such as by including components of goal setting and planning goal attainment, which in itself has been shown to increase levels of life satisfaction and positive affect (MacLeod, Coates, & Hetherton, 2008). Accordingly, after a person completes this kind of activity, positive interventions could be used to systematically bring to fruition the person's ideal self. Indeed, there is support for this suggestion: in the aforementioned example of an optimism intervention, the imagined future self's advice for resolving issues actually "may have helped participants engage in active coping by delineating the next steps they needed to take to achieve their ideal goal state" (Shapira & Mongrain, 2010, p. 387). We would like to emphasize the importance of these "steps." As we have learned from our experiments on self-enhancement, for individuals to progress toward their ideal, future selves, they need to accurately perceive their realistic, current selves, gauge the discrepancies with their ideal, imagined selves, and then develop active ways to build skills and bridge the gap. After all, optimal functioning is not passive. For instance, individuals in a flow state are "tackling a series of goals, continuously processing feedback about progress, and adjusting action based on this feedback" (Nakamura & Csikszentmihalyi, 2002, p. 90). Similarly, developing well-being requires applied effort to both carry out and maintain happiness-boosting activities (Lyubomirsky et al., 2005).

As well, research on grit – that is, "perseverance and passion for long-term goals" (Duckworth, Peterson, Matthews, & Kelly, 2007, p. 1087) – reinforces our case further. Specifically, people who excel in a given domain are those who engage in deliberate practice to improve (Duckworth, Kirby, Tsukayama, Berstein, & Ericsson, 2011). In order to do so, we suggest that individuals must first hold realistic understandings of their abilities and shortcomings so that they can strategically apply themselves and improve. The grit model's emphasis on effort underscores a helpful approach for interventions. In the context of positive psychology, knowing what steps to take next, with the goal of improving and flourishing, may require an accurate self-perception at the outset. Subsequently, interventions can provide tangible methods for progressing to an ideal self. Therefore, we propose that realistic self-perception is a prerequisite and interventions are the courses one takes to flourish. In other words, accurate self-perceptions are an essential starting point, and thereafter positive psychological interventions have the opportunity to help people build sustainably better lives.

Along these lines, hope interventions may offer an example of both envisioning an ideal self and providing a structure to achieve that ideal self. For instance, Feldman and Dreher (2012) aimed to increase hopeful, goal-directed thinking among college students. During their intervention, participants chose a personally relevant goal; were taught about hope, goal pathways, and agency; wrote about steps to take to achieve the goal, possible obstacles, and accompanying resolutions; and visualized engaging in the steps, overcoming obstacles, and ultimately achieving the goal. Afterward, these individuals showed greater hope and sense of purpose and, most relevant to our discussion, had made more progress on their goals one month later than people in the control conditions. Thus, focusing on active ways to improve is important during interventions, so that tangible progress can be made from the current self to an ideal, flourishing self.

Likewise, Lyubomirsky and colleagues (2011) concluded that positive interventions require both "a will" to engage in the activity – that is, personal motivation or desire, as shown by self-selection for and continued effort with the intervention – and "a proper way" – that is, a suitable, efficacious activity. This claim is especially true if the effects are to endure; as the authors reported, "sustainable increases in happiness are possible, but only if pursued under optimal conditions, such as when people are motivated to perform a positive activity, when they bring to bear effort and persistence, and when the activity is a legitimately efficacious one" (Lyubomirsky, Dickerhoof, Boehm, & Sheldon, 2011, p. 397). In other words, positive psychological interventions have the potential to systematically aid motivated individuals in not only reaching, but also maintaining a more flourishing life through more focus on deliberate steps. After all, temporarily boosting happiness is valuable progress, but fostering enduring fulfillment is the ultimate goal of interventions.

One final example is Louis' (2011) distinction between positive interventions that only include talent identification and those that extend their scope to cultivate strength development. The former is a "process of identifying, understanding, and affirming talent themes" but does not provide instruction for developing skills further (Louis, 2011, p. 205). In contrast, the latter method identifies talents and then includes specific activities and strategies to build and refine strengths. Students who only trained in a talent identification intervention shifted toward a fixed mindset regarding capabilities and character, which could inhibit them from applying their talents in useful ways. Talent identification focuses on positive qualities without motivating the person to acknowledge negative qualities; it is akin to self-enhancement that entails an unrealistically positive self-perception but does not give rise to recognition of negative aspects of oneself or to improvement motivation. In sum, strengths interventions "must extend beyond helping participants understand and appreciate their unique signature talent themes to include an emphasis on the effort required to develop talents" (Louis, 2011, p. 212).

In summary, we caution that mere thinking about an ideal self may be risky or insufficient for comprehensive flourishing, which highlights the need for interventions to provide structured ways to advance, foster habits, and build strengths toward actualization of that ideal self. Doing so can help to differentiate positive psychology, with its roots in scientific evidence and efficacious results, from folk theories and popular trends that advocate unqualified positive thinking.

The Self-Perception Equilibrium

We would like to note two stipulations. Specifically, by taking into account the harm caused by self-effacement and the value of self-compassion, we wish to highlight that accurate self-perceptions do not necessitate being overly self-critical and indeed should still embrace an optimistic, kind approach to oneself.

First, akin to self-enhancement yielding a host of negative effects, swinging the pendulum too far in the opposite direction is also problematic. Notably, self-effacement – unrealistically *negative* self-perceptions, or unfavorable self-perceptions that are not supported by objective criteria – has been found to be ubiquitously detrimental. One consequence is that individuals who self-efface tend to be depressed and have low self-esteem (Taylor & Brown, 1988). Nonetheless, congruent with our overarching assertion, some self-critique is adaptive. According to Sedikides and Luke (2008), self-enhancement can be beneficial if offset by self-criticism, as indicated by higher optimism, self-esteem, and life satisfaction. On the whole, a balanced, realistic self-perception is ideal. Simply put, "mentally healthy people have a relatively accurate sense of self, are willing to present this imperfect self to the social world, and distort reality primarily to maintain manageable levels of anxiety" (Colvin & Griffo, 2008, p. 124).

Second, accurate self-perceptions should still be *positive*, and upholding an optimistic, accepting view of oneself can be compatible with being realistic. For instance, individuals who demonstrate high self-compassion maintain higher intrinsic motivation after disappointment, cope with negative feelings using adaptive emotion-focused strategies, adopt mastery goals, demonstrate more positive relationship behaviors, are shielded from anxiety, and gain psychological well-being (Neff & Beretvas, 2013; Neff, Hsieh, & Dejitterat, 2005; Neff, Kirkpatrick, & Rude, 2007). More precisely, self-compassion consists of being caring and understanding with oneself about shortcomings, recognizing that everyone is imperfect, and mindfully acknowledging negative emotions (Neff & Beretvas, 2013). Thus, working with negative aspects of oneself is not at the expense of a positive, compassionate self-perception, and this balance lays the foundation for flourishing. Additionally, positive interventions may find value in adopting this line of research: a mindful self-compassion program was shown to increase well-being immediately and at 6- and 12-month follow-ups (Neff & Germer, 2013).

One final consideration was raised in a meta-analysis by Schueller and Seligman (2012). They found that positive psychological interventions that employed cognitive rather than behavioral exercises led to greater increases in *subjective well-being*. Thus, in line with envisioning an ideal self, interventions that change what we think about ourselves can certainly have positive effects on subjective measures. However, they may not be the most effective way to develop ourselves on more objective measures related to flourishing, which is shown by the detrimental consequences associated with self-enhancement and the benefits that come from realistic self-perceptions. A highly favorable self-perception does not necessarily equate with positive, tangible outcomes. Thus, while thinking positively about oneself may yield some benefits, we contend that individuals truly improve and prosper through cultivating accurate self-perceptions and taking strategic action to move forward.

Conclusion

The underlying message of this chapter is that cultivating honest self-perceptions better prepares individuals to flourish. Evidence from our research on self-enhancement and from other areas of positive psychology highlights that positive is beneficial insomuch as it is grounded in reality; accurate self-perceptions help people to become the best they can be. We hope to have demonstrated that "the goal of individuals becoming competent, constructive critics of themselves is of the utmost importance to their ability to lead full, satisfying, participatory lives" (Bergner, 2008, p. 243). Therefore, we emphasize that positive psychological interventions must avoid encouraging self-enhancing tendencies, thereby helping people to develop their ideal selves, and do so in a way that emphasizes effort to actively build talents and skills. Lastly, we hope to have made a case for distinguishing positive psychology from artificial positive thinking through the use of empirically supported, active interventions.

Acknowledgment

This work was supported by the National Research Foundation of Korea Grant, funded by the Korean Government (NRF-2012S1A5A8023903).

References

Alicke, M. D., Klotz, M. L., Breitenbecher, D. L., Yurak, T. J., & Vredenburg, D. S. (1995). Personal contact, individuation, and the better-than-average effect. *Journal of Personality and Social Psychology*, *68*, 804–825.

Allport, G. W. (1937). *Personality: A psychological interpretation*. New York: Henry Holt and Company.

Beck, A. T., Steer, R. A., & Brown, G. K. (1996). *Manual for the Beck Depression Inventory-II*. San Antonio, TX: The Psychological Corporation.

Bergner, R. M. (2008). On promoting adaptive self-criticism in psychotherapy. In E. Chang (Ed.), *Self-criticism and self-enhancement: Theory, research, and clinical implications* (pp. 225–245). Washington, DC: American Psychological Association.

Colvin, C. R., Block, J., & Funder, D. C. (1995). Overly positive self-evaluations and personality: Negative implications for mental health. *Journal of Personality and Social Psychology, 68*, 1152–1162.

Colvin, C. R., & Griffo, R. (2008). On the psychological costs of self-enhancement. In E. Chang (Ed.), *Self-criticism and self-enhancement: Theory, research, and clinical implications* (pp. 123–140). Washington, DC: American Psychological Association.

Duckworth, A. L., Kirby, T. A., Tsukayama, E., Berstein, H., & Ericsson, K. A. (2011). Deliberate practice spells success: Why grittier competitors triumph at the national spelling bee. *Social Psychological and Personality Science, 2*, 174–181.

Duckworth, A. L., Peterson, C., Matthews, M. D., & Kelly, D. R. (2007). Grit: Perseverance and passion for long-term goals. *Journal of Personality and Social Psychology, 92*, 1087–1101.

Feldman, D. B., & Dreher, D. E. (2012). Can hope be changed in 90 minutes? Testing the efficacy of a single-session goal-pursuit intervention for college students. *Journal of Happiness Studies, 13*, 745–759.

Försterling, F., & Morgenstern, M. (2002). Accuracy of self-assessment and task performance: Does it pay to know the truth? *Journal of Educational Psychology, 94*, 576–585.

Fredrickson, B. L., & Losada, M. F. (2005). Positive affect and the complex dynamics of human flourishing. *American Psychologist, 60*, 678–686.

Gresham, F. M., Lane, K, L., MacMillan, D. L., Bocian, K. M., & Ward, S. L. (2000). Effects of positive and negative illusory biases: Comparison across social and academic self-concept domains. *Journal of School Psychology, 38*, 151–175.

Jahoda, M. (1953). The meaning of psychological health. *Social Casework, 34*, 349–354.

John, O. P., & Robins, R. (1994). Accuracy and bias in self-perception: Individual differences in self-enhancement and the role of narcissism. *Journal of Personality and Social Psychology, 66*, 206–219.

Kim, Y.-H., & Chiu, C.-Y. (2011). Emotional costs of inaccurate self-assessments: Both self-effacement and self-enhancement can lead to dejection. *Emotion, 11*, 1096–1104.

Kim, Y.-H., Chiu, C.-Y., & Zou, Z. (2010). Know thyself: Motivated misperceptions of actual performance undermine subjective wellbeing, future performance, and achievement motivation. *Journal of Personality and Social Psychology, 99*, 395–409.

Kim, Y.-H., Killam, K. M., Shigeto, A., & Grison, S. (2013). Illusory self-perceptions: Long-term, cross-cultural consequences for academic performance, and short-term impairments to improvement motivation and emotional functioning. Unpublished manuscript, Yonsei University.

King, L. A. (2001). The health benefits of writing about life goals. *Personality and Social Psychology Bulletin, 27*, 798–807.

Kruger, J., & Dunning, D. (1999). Unskilled and unaware of it: How difficulties in recognizing one's own competence lead to inflated self-assessments. *Journal of Personality and Social Psychology, 77*, 1121–1134.

Kurt, A., & Paulhus, D. L. (2008). Moderators of the adaptiveness of self-enhancement: Operationalization, motivational domain, adjustment facet, and evaluator. *Journal of Research in Personality, 42*, 839–853.

Kwan, V. S., John, O. P., Robins, R. W., & Kuang, L. L. (2008). Conceptualizing and assessing self-enhancement bias: A componential approach. *Journal of Personality and Social Psychology, 94*, 1062–1077.

Louis, M. C. (2011). Strengths interventions in higher education: The effect of identification versus development approaches on implicit self-theory. *Journal of Positive Psychology*, *6*, 204–215.

Lyubomirsky, S., Dickerhoof, R., Boehm, J. K., & Sheldon, K. M. (2011). Becoming happier takes both a will and a proper way: An experimental longitudinal intervention to boost well-being. *Emotion*, *11*, 391–402.

Lyubomirsky, S., Sheldon, K. M., & Schkade, D. (2005). Pursuing happiness: The architecture of sustainable change. *Review of General Psychology*, *9*, 111–131.

MacLeod, A. K., Coates, E., & Hetherton, J. (2008). Increasing well-being through teaching goal-setting and planning skills: Results of a brief intervention. *Journal of Happiness Studies*, *9*, 185–196.

Nakamura, J., & Csikszentmihalyi, M. (2002). The concept of flow. In C. R. Snyder & S. J. Lopez (Eds.), *Handbook of positive psychology* (pp. 89–105). New York: Oxford University Press.

Neff, K. D., & Beretvas, S. N. (2013). The role of self-compassion in romantic relationships. *Self and Identity*, *12*, 78–98.

Neff, K. D., & Germer, K. D. (2013). A pilot study and randomized controlled trial of the mindful self-compassion program. *Journal of Clinical Psychology*, *69*, 28–44.

Neff, K. D., Hsieh, Y.-P., & Dejitterat, K. (2005). Self-compassion, achievement goals, and coping with academic failure. *Self and Identity*, *4*, 263–287.

Neff, K. D., Kirkpatrick, K. L., & Rude, S. S. (2007). Self-compassion and adaptive psychological functioning. *Journal of Research in Personality*, *41*, 139–154.

Rosenberg, M. (1965). *Society and the adolescent self-image*. Princeton, NJ: Princeton University Press.

Ryff, C. D. (1989). Happiness is everything, or is it? Explorations on the meaning of psychological well-being. *Journal of Personality and Social Psychology*, *57*, 1069–1081.

Ryff, C. D., & Keyes, C. L. M. (1995). The structures of psychological well-being revisited. *Journal of Personality and Social Psychology*, *69*, 719–727.

Schueller, S. M., & Seligman, M. E. P. (2012). Positive psychology interventions enhance subjective well-being: A meta-analysis. Unpublished manuscript, University of Pennsylvania.

Sedikides, C., & Luke, M. (2008). On when self-enhancement and self-criticism function adaptively and maladaptively. In E. C. Chang (Ed.), *Self-criticism and self-enhancement: Theory, research, and clinical implications* (pp. 181–198). Washington, DC: American Psychological Association.

Seligman, M. E. P., Rashid, T., & Parks, A. C. (2006). Positive psychotherapy. *American Psychologist*, *61*, 774–788.

Shapira, L. B., & Mongrain, M. (2010). The benefits of self-compassion and optimism exercises for individuals vulnerable to depression. *Journal of Positive Psychology*, *5*, 377–389.

Sheldon, K. M., & Lyubomirsky, S. (2006). How to increase and sustain positive emotion: The effects of expressing gratitude and visualizing best possible selves. *Journal of Positive Psychology*, *2*, 73–82.

Taylor, S. E., & Brown, J. D. (1988). Illusion and well-being: A social psychological perspective on mental health. *Psychological Bulletin*, *103*, 193–210.

27

Act Well to Be Well

The Promise of Changing Personality States to Promote Well-Being

Laura E. R. Blackie, Ann Marie Roepke, Marie J. C. Forgeard, Eranda Jayawickreme, and William Fleeson

Throughout the history of psychology and psychotherapy, much attention has been devoted to developing interventions that reduce negative affect and impairment (i.e., depression, distress, and anxiety), while relatively little attention has been devoted to interventions that enhance positive well-being and psychological thriving (Seligman & Csikszentmihalyi, 2000). The aim of positive psychology is to identify the psychological and social-contextual factors that facilitate optimal well-being, focusing specifically on three related topics: positive subjective experiences (e.g., happiness), positive traits (e.g., optimism), and the role that social institutions have in fostering both positive experiences and traits (Peterson & Seligman, 2004). Thus, the underlying assumption is that specific dispositional traits can serve as catalysts for psychological well-being. In this chapter, we show that this assumption receives strong empirical support from the personality psychology literature, and, consequentially, that interventions that target these specific traits may be quite effective in promoting optimal well-being. Specifically, we review empirical evidence that has demonstrated that enacting certain trait-relevant behaviors enhances well-being (Fleeson, Malanos, & Achille, 2002; McNiel, Lowman, & Fleeson, in press; Zelenski, Santoro, & Whelan, 2012), and propose a behavioral intervention approach that could serve to increase positive affect, work performance, creative thinking, and even facilitate psychological growth in the aftermath of adversity.

The Wiley Blackwell Handbook of Positive Psychological Interventions, First Edition.
Edited by Acacia C. Parks and Stephen M. Schueller.

The Study of Personality

Personality psychology is the study of individual differences in characteristic patterns of cognition, affect, and behavior, and the psychological mechanisms that underlie these differences (Funder, 2001). The goals of personality psychology have been diverse, but have included at least the following four goals: characterizing individuals; identifying internal processes that link the various parts of the person together; explaining why individuals differ from one another; and providing a foundation for improving people's lives (Fleeson, 2012). This fourth function – providing the basis for interventions that enhance well-being – is certainly not a light or uncontroversial undertaking. However, if we acknowledge that personality helps to shape people's lives, then we find that changing an individual's personality might provide an exciting opportunity to change that person's well-being. Despite the widespread belief that personality is stable, a large literature on normative personality trait change has revealed moderate, mostly positive, amounts of trait change across the lifespan (Roberts, Walton, & Viechtbauer, 2006). Given that non-negligible personality change occurs, it leaves open the possibility that individuals may be able to have an influence on how they change (Edmonds, Jackson, Fayard, & Roberts, 2008).

There has been considerable research in personality science on the study of traits. Personality traits are often defined as consistent patterns of thoughts, feelings, and behaviors that distinguish one individual from another (Johnson, 1997). The trait approach to personality is largely descriptive, commonly focusing on describing an individual's disposition in terms of broad, general tendencies to think and behave in certain ways (Funder, 2001). Five broad traits have consistently emerged in studies that use factor analytic methodology; extraversion, agreeableness, openness to experience, conscientiousness, and neuroticism are the "Big Five" personality traits that help to organize a wide range of other, more nuanced traits and behaviors (John & Srivastava, 1999). The predictive power of these broad personality traits has been shown to be considerably influential on many important outcomes in life including academic achievement, job performance, marital quality, mental health, and even length of life (Noftle & Robins, 2007; Ozer & Benet-Martinez, 2006). For example, the effect of conscientiousness on job performance is equivalent to the effect of IQ on job performance, and this relationship has been shown to be robust and consistent with self-reports of job performance, supervisor ratings, and objective indicators of performance (Ozer & Benet-Martinez, 2006). Furthermore, there has been no important domain of life that has *not* been shown to be impacted substantially by the Big Five personality traits. Even the length of one's life is at least in part a function of one's personality traits. Extensive longitudinal studies spanning the course of almost 70 years have shown that people who are relatively high in the personality trait of conscientiousness live years longer than those with lower levels (Friedman et al., 1993, 1995; Kern & Friedman, 2008; Kern, Friedman, Martin, Reynolds,

& Luong, 2009). Perhaps surprisingly, the magnitude of this effect is about the same as the effect of coronary heart disease or cholesterol on length of life, roughly five years (Friedman et al., 1993).

However, the trait perspective has been called into question: evidence demonstrating that the consistency between a typical individual's trait-relevant behaviors across different situations was relatively low (e.g., the typical individual enacted fewer extraverted behaviors during a seminar than during a party) led some researchers to dismiss the notion of traits and conclude that "personality" was actually due to variation in situational cues (Mischel, 1968; see Fleeson, 2004, 2008, for a review). The person–situation debate dominated personality psychology until fairly recently and as a consequence the two major approaches to the study of personality (i.e., trait and social-cognitive) developed largely in isolation from one another (Fleeson, 2012). The density distributions model (Fleeson, 2001, 2012) offered a promising resolution to this debate. Simply stated, Fleeson (2001, 2004) argues that possessing a specific trait – such as extraversion – is simply akin to behaving in an extraverted manner (e.g., talkative, bold, and assertive) slightly more often. In other words, while an individual's behavior varies quite rapidly and frequently across different occasions, his/her behavior is both stable and distinct from other individuals when averaged across a larger period of time such as a few days or a week. Thus, personality traits are stable in the sense that there is reliable between-person variation, and flexible in the sense that there is also substantial within-person variation in an individual's behavior depending on situational cues. Thus, the model focuses on "personality states," which are similar to personality traits in affective, cognitive, and behavioral content, but are manifested for a few minutes or hours rather than for months or years (Cattell, Cattell, & Rhymer, 1947; Fleeson, 2001).

Convincing evidence supports this integrative approach, indicating that personality is not constrained to a single set of stable characteristics, but rather that the individual can respond flexibly in different ways to bring about desired outcomes. For example, in sharp contrast to an earlier perspective that claimed that personality traits were fixed and reside within the person, it has been found that individuals experience small, but mostly positive changes in personality traits across their lifespan (Roberts et al., 2006). Additionally, recent evidence has shown that personality change can even occur in response to a major life event (e.g., retirement), suggesting that the causes of personality trait change are much broader than intrinsic maturation (Specht, Egloff, & Schmukle, 2011). Finally, and of particular relevance to this chapter, individuals have demonstrated the ability to change their trait-relevant behavior in the moment when prompted by a relevant situational cue (Fleeson, 2007). For example, Fleeson observed an increase in participants' level of state extraversion when they were in a situation that involved interacting with a friendly individual. Additionally, research has demonstrated that individuals can also change their trait-relevant behavior in the moment when instructed with an experimental manipulation (see the next section; Fleeson et al., 2002; McNiel & Fleeson, 2006; McNiel, Lowman, & Fleeson, 2010; Zelenski et al., 2012). These and other studies consistent with the density distributions model have implications for the development of interventions that facilitate positive well-being: by shifting people's personality *states*, interventions may also change people's personality *traits*, and improve their well-being as a result.

Application of Manipulating Personality States to Increase Positive Affect

The density distributions model has implications for the literature on increasing well-being. Extensive research into the model has focused on the relationship between extraversion states and positive affect, examining whether enacting extraversion can increase one's positive affect, regardless of one's trait level of extraversion or introversion (Fleeson et al., 2002; McNiel & Fleeson, 2006; McNiel et al., 2010). This question has important implications for positive psychology, because positive affect is considered an integral part of well-being (Diener, Suh, Lucas, & Smith, 1999; Forgeard, Jayawickreme, Kern, & Seligman, 2011; Jayawickreme, Forgeard, & Seligman, 2012). The results of several different experience-sampling studies confirm that participants report feeling happier when acting extraverted (Fleeson et al., 2002; Wilt, Noftle, Fleeson, & Spain, 2012). In addition, Fleeson et al. (2002) found that a simple manipulation that instructed participants to act extraverted in a group discussion (e.g., talkative, energetic, and assertive) increased participants' self-reported positive affect compared to participants who were instructed to act introverted in the discussion (e.g., reserved, passive, and quiet). This manipulation was found to be effective regardless of whether participants were normally extraverted or introverted. The results of these studies have important clinical implications, because they suggest that individuals might be able to enhance aspects of their well-being by self-regulating their extraverted behaviors.

Thus, interventions that instruct individuals to enact behavioral states of specific personality traits may offer a simple and effective way to enhance positive well-being. The value of this intervention approach is further strengthened when it is compared to prevailing evidence-based therapies and treatments that are used to alleviate symptoms of distress. For example, a personality-focused intervention approach is in some ways similar to behavioral activation strategies that are used to effectively treat symptoms of depression, such as social withdrawal, inactivity, and anhedonia (Jacobson, Martell, & Dimidjian, 2001). Behavioral activation is a simple procedure in which therapists help individuals identify one or two actions that could impact how they are feeling, and then create a plan for carrying out these activities. By initiating such activities, the individual can begin a process of behavioral change, symptom reduction, and hope (Wright, Basco, & Thase, 2006). Behavioral activation treatment is tailored to each client's goals and life situation (i.e., the unique factors that exacerbate depressive symptoms or that improve a person's sense of pleasure or mastery), such that joining a social organization might alleviate depressive symptoms for an individual whose depression is being exacerbated by feelings of loneliness and isolation. Essentially, behavioral activation requires acting as if one is not depressed in order to cultivate cognitive and affective improvements. Notably, many of the activities that individuals and their therapists select probably require the individual to act in a more extraverted manner: spending more time with friends, trying new hobbies, acting more assertive/bold, or even simply leaving the house more often may represent increases in the individual's enactment of extraverted states. As such, an intervention that more explicitly instructed participants to enact extraverted states of behavior that were relevant to their goals might be equally effective in treating certain symptoms of depression, shifting the balance of positive to negative affect, and reinforcing the other goals the client identified in therapy (McNiel et al., 2010).

Although positive affect is an integral component of well-being, it is not the entirety of well-being. Recent theoretical approaches emphasize that psychological well-being also encompasses constructs like meaning and autonomy; accomplishment, mastery, and competence; positive relationships/relatedness; and engagement (Ryan and Deci, 2000; Ryff & Singer, 1998; Schueller & Seligman, 2010). The relationship between these constructs and the Big Five personality traits is not as well understood as the relationship between positive affect and extraversion. It is certainly conceivable that behavioral manipulations that encourage people to enact traits like openness to experience or agreeableness might impact these individuals' sense of engagement, meaning, accomplishment, or relatedness. In addition, behavioral manipulations that increase one component of well-being could potentially exert detrimental effects on another component of well-being. For these reasons, interventionists must be clear about precisely which aspect(s) of well-being they are targeting, and aware of which aspects of well-being might also change (for the better or worse) even if these aspects are neither targeted nor measured.

Application of Enacting Personality States to Facilitate Well-Being

The behavioral intervention approach outlined in this chapter offers diverse and exciting applications. In this section, we discuss the implications of this model with reference to three specific areas: work performance, creative thinking, and post-traumatic growth. We take the view that "well-being" is not simply encompassed by subjective reports of well-feeling, rather it must also translate to "well-living" (i.e., positive functioning in important life domains; Jayawickreme et al., 2012). Thus, in this section, we discuss how enacting certain personality states might facilitate both well-feeling and well-living in three specific contexts.

Work performance

Personality has been shown to be an important predictor of performance at work. Results of meta-analyses examining relationships between Big Five personality traits and work performance tend to show that conscientiousness and emotional stability consistently have a positive relation with overall work performance across various occupational groups, while extraversion and openness to experience have positive effects that are limited to the context of performance during job training (Barrick & Mount, 1991; Barrick, Mount, & Judge, 2001; see also Chiaburu, Oh, Berry, Li, & Gardner, 2011).

Although the relationship between personality and job performance was initially investigated for personnel selection purposes (Barrick & Mount, 1991), implications of results evidenced by this area of research suggest promising avenues for the cultivation of personality states that are favorable to work performance. Thus, an employee might learn to act in a conscientious manner at work (e.g., by acting more planful, careful, responsible) – that is, to move his or her distribution of conscientious behaviors to the right – while preserving the flexibility to act in a non-conscientious manner at times, especially in settings where the importance of conscientiousness may not be as important (why wear matched socks on the weekend?). Thus, the usefulness of the density distributions model may lie in helping to foster a flexible and strategic attitude with regards to the cultivation of adaptive personality states (Minbashian, Wood, & Beckmann, 2010). Furthering the importance of flexibility in personality, recent research also pointed out the curvilinear nature of the relationships between conscientiousness, emotional stability, and work performance (Le et al., 2011); very high levels of conscientiousness may be detrimental to work performance if it is reflected by rigidity and inflexibility, and increased levels of emotional stability may not be needed beyond a certain point. The level of complexity of the work performed by employees appears to determine the optimal level of conscientiousness and emotional stability needed (the apex of the inverted U curve).

Creative thinking

The density distributions model may also have implications for the cultivation of more specific abilities. We discuss here the example of creative thinking (for other approaches to enhancing creativity, see Chapter 7). Perhaps the most important and reliable predictor of creativity is the personality trait of openness to experience (Feist, 1998; King, McKee, & Broyles, 1996; McCrae, 1987). Yet, to the best of our knowledge, little systematic research has been conducted on the potential to use open states as a tool to foster creative thinking. The density distributions model provides a tangible way to foster creative thinking by asking individuals to behave in an open manner, for example by acting inquisitive, philosophical, curious, or imaginative. Future experimental studies are needed to determine whether this hypothesized intervention would result in reliable increases in creative thinking, a promising yet untested approach. Interventions focusing on other personality states/traits that have been related to creativity, such as independence, nonconformity, playfulness, persistence, or tolerance of ambiguity (for a review, see Runco, 2007), may also constitute fruitful avenues to investigate.

Finally, personality dispositions may also act as a moderator of other determinants of creativity. The effect of short-term positive and negative emotional inductions has for example been shown to influence the creativity of individuals high in dispositional mood, but not the creativity of individuals low in dispositional mood (Forgeard, 2011).

Post-traumatic growth

There is also reason to predict that enacting behaviorally based personality states may effectively facilitate positive psychological growth after experiences of personal adversity. In recent years, a growing literature on post-traumatic growth (PTG) has reported that some individuals continue to grow and develop in the aftermath of personal adversity (Tedeschi, Park, & Calhoun, 1998; Zoellner & Maercker, 2006). Specifically, PTG is defined as "positive psychological change experienced as a result of the struggle with highly challenging life circumstances" (Tedeschi & Calhoun, 2004, p. 1). In contrast to clinical and psycho-cognitive theories, PTG is less concerned with the course of mental illness and maladaptive behaviors that result from life-threatening experiences, and more focused on how negative events can be overcome and personal adversity can serve as a springboard for positive growth and development. PTG has been observed across a diverse range of threatening experiences including diagnosis with cancer, heart attacks, diagnosis with HIV, and sexual assault (Tedeschi & Calhoun, 2004). Although there are several different ways in which PTG can be manifested, the most commonly reported outcomes are changes in the perception of the self (e.g., increased feelings of self-efficacy and resilience), more intimate relationships with family and friends, a deeper understanding of spirituality, and a re-evaluation of life goals and priorities with a greater appreciation for the simple pleasures in life (Tedeschi & Calhoun, 1996).

Currently, there is considerable debate as to the cognitive processes or mechanisms of PTG. While an extensive review is beyond the scope of this chapter, a recent review paper identified that the personality traits of openness to experience, extraversion, and agreeableness were associated with greater self-reported levels of PTG (Linley & Joseph, 2004). Thus, individuals who typically behave in a more open, extraverted, and/or agreeable manner might be more likely to experience positive psychological growth following personal adversity. Notably, these findings are correlational; therefore it remains unclear whether openness, extraversion, and agreeableness facilitate greater PTG; whether PTG increases the manifestations of these three traits; or whether a third variable explains the relationship. Regardless, these correlational findings present several intriguing leads. If careful prospective research indicates that these personality traits are indeed likely to promote growth, then interventionists might help individuals to behaviorally enact these traits in relevant domains before and/or after their exposure to adverse experiences. For instance, researchers might identify relevant behavioral manifestations of openness to experience, and then help trauma survivors to "try on" these open behaviors in order to explore opportunities to grow and extract meaning from their struggle with difficult events.

To create effective interventions based on personality traits like openness to experience, strong behavioral markers of these traits would need to be identified first. The personality psychology literature can be a rich source for these behavioral markers: for instance, Goldberg's (1992) research provides a large variety of adjectives and behavioral markers that reliably assess the Big Five personality traits, and this list has been successfully used in various tests of the density distributions model (Fleeson, 2001; Fleeson et al., 2002; Fleeson & Gallagher, 2009). Thus, using a similar strategy and instructing individuals to behave in an agreeable manner (e.g., cooperative, trustful, and kind) or in an open manner (e.g., creative, inquisitive, and imaginative) could offer an effective means with which to facilitate PTG in those attempting to come to terms with a stressful life event. It would, however, be necessary to determine the effectiveness of these interventions in an experimental setting with a manipulation akin to that employed by Fleeson et al. (2002) before applying them to more vulnerable populations.

In general, researchers and interventionists must be very cautious in determining when/if to implement any post-traumatic growth intervention for a particular individual or group. People who are struggling with post-traumatic stress symptoms should never be encouraged to use post-traumatic growth interventions as a replacement for effective post-traumatic stress disorder (PTSD) treatment. Established evidence-based treatments, including prolonged exposure and other cognitive-behavioral therapies, are more appropriate treatment options for trauma survivors at this point in their recovery (Powers, Halpern, Ferenschak, Gillihan, & Foa, 2010). Post-traumatic growth interventions/strategies will likely be most appropriate after successful PTSD treatment, as an adjunct or component of ongoing PTSD treatment, or for individuals who are somewhat less distressed and not in need of professional PTSD treatment.

Future Directions

In addition to the Big Five personality traits of extraversion, agreeableness, and openness to experience, research has suggested that dispositional optimism – a favorable outlook and positive expectancies with regards to the future (Scheier & Carver, 1985) – also facilitates positive psychological growth and adjustment in the aftermath of personal adversity (e.g., see Hart, Vella, & Mohr, 2008; Milam, 2004). Similarly, dispositional hope – defined as a positive motivational state in which the individual feels capable of successfully planning and attaining their goals (see Snyder et al., 1991) – has been positively associated with self-reported levels of PTG after traumatic events such as war or diagnosis with cancer (e.g., Ai, Tice, Whitsett, Ishisaka, & Chim, 2007; Ho, Rajandram, Chan, Samman, McGrath, & Zwahlen, 2011). Although there are individual differences in dispositional optimism and hope (Scheier & Carver, 1985; Snyder et al., 1991), it remains an open question as to whether strong behavioral markers can be identified for these two traits. The density distributions approach certainly considers cognitive states in addition to behavioral states, as well as the importance of the cognitive mechanisms that underlie these states (e.g., Cantor, 1990). Thus, an intervention that can promote thinking in an optimistic way (e.g., positive appraisal) and encourage the client to behave in such a manner when appropriate (e.g., pursuing opportunities) is also likely to offer an effective means to facilitate well-being and PTG in the aftermath of adversity.

Additionally, factors such as social support and active disclosure to others who have had a similar experience have also been shown to facilitate positive psychological growth after a traumatic life event (Tedeschi & Calhoun, 2004). It is thought that these processes help survivors to create a new narrative, understand the changes they are experiencing, and eventually integrate these changes into a new self-schema. Thus, the success of the behavioral interventions suggested in this chapter (i.e., enacting personality states of extraversion, agreeableness, and openness to experience) might well be amplified when administered in supportive social environments, such as peer-support groups.

Finally, although there is strong theoretical support for the interventions proposed in this chapter (Fleeson et al., 2002; McNiel & Fleeson, 2006; McNiel et al., 2010; Zelenski et al., 2012), there are still many open questions that remain. The existing literature can offer no answers on the duration of the interventions, how many therapy sessions are necessary, or how the intervention is best administered (e.g., by a clinical practitioner, self-help manual, mutual aid group, or internet-based program). However, the literature on similar therapy techniques, such as the behavioral activation strategies discussed earlier (Jacobson et al., 2001), suggests that our behavioral interventions may be most effective when administered weekly by a qualified practitioner over the course of 16 consecutive weeks. These assumptions would, however, need to be tested in randomized, controlled double-blind trials in future research.

Conclusion

In this chapter, we have outlined a theoretical approach to personality that has clear implications for the development of interventions to facilitate positive well-being. Personality appears to make a difference in people's lives, which means that one way to improve one's own life may be to adjust one's personality – not an uncontroversial or light undertaking. Nonetheless, by shifting people's personality *states*, interventions may also change people's personality *traits*, and improve their well-being as a result.

Acknowledgments

This publication was made possible through the support of a grant from the John Templeton Foundation. The opinions expressed in this publication are those of the authors and do not necessarily reflect the views of the John Templeton Foundation. Additional funding for this project was generously provided by Eva Kedar, PhD.

References

Ai, A. L., Tice, N. T., Whitsett, D. D., Ishisaka, T., & Chim, M. (2007). Posttraumatic symptoms and growth of Kosovar war refugees: The influence of hope and cognitive coping. *Journal of Positive Psychology, 2*, 55–65.

Barrick, M. R., & Mount, M. K. (1991). The Big Five personality dimensions and job performance: A meta-analysis. *Personnel Psychology, 44*, 1–26.

Barrick, M. R., Mount, M. K., & Judge, T. A. (2001). Personality and performance at the beginning of the new millennium: What do we know and where do we go next? *International Journal of Selection and Assessment, 9*, 9–30.

Cantor, N. (1990). From thought to behavior: "Having" and "doing" in the study of personality and cognition. *American Psychologist, 45*, 735–750.

Cattell, R. B., Cattell, A. K. S., & Rhymer, R. M. (1947). P-technique demonstrated in determining psycho-physiological source traits in a normal individual. *Psychometrika, 12*, 267–288.

Chiaburu, D. S., Oh, I.-S., Berry, C. M., Li, N., & Gardner, R. G. (2011). The five-factor model of personality traits and organizational citizenship behaviors: A meta-analysis. *Journal of Applied Psychology, 96*, 1140–1166.

Diener, E., Suh, E. M., Lucas, R. E., & Smith, H. L. (1999). Subjective well-being: Three decades of progress. *Psychological Bulletin, 125*, 276–302.

Edmonds, G. W., Jackson, J. J., Fayard, J. V., & Roberts, B. W. (2008). Is character fate, or is there hope to change my personality yet? *Social and Personality Psychology Compass, 2*, 399–413.

Feist, G. J. (1998). A meta-analysis of personality in scientific and artistic creativity. *Personality and Social Psychology Review, 2*, 290–309.

Fleeson, W. (2001). Toward a structure- and process-integrated view of personality: Traits as density distributions of states. *Journal of Personality and Social Psychology, 80*, 1011–1027.

Fleeson, W. (2004). Moving personality beyond the person-situation debate. The challenge and the opportunity of within-person variability. *Current Directions in Psychological Science, 13*, 83–87.

Fleeson, W. (2007). Situation-based contingencies underlying trait-content manifestation in behavior. *Journal of Personality, 75*, 825–862.

Fleeson, W. (2008). The end of the person-situation debate: The emerging synthesis in the answer to the consistency question. *Social and Personality Psychology Compass, 2*, 1667–1684.

Fleeson, W. (2012). Perspectives on the person: Rapid growth and opportunities for integration. In K. Deaux and M. Snyder (Eds.), *The Oxford handbook of personality and social psychology*. New York: Oxford University Press.

Fleeson, W., & Gallagher, M. P. (2009). The implications of Big Five standing for the distribution of trait manifestation in behavior: Fifteen experience-sampling studies and a meta-analysis. *Journal of Personality and Social Psychology, 97*, 1097–1114.

Fleeson, W., Malanos, A. B., & Achille, N. M. (2002). An intraindividual process approach to the relationship between extraversion and positive affect: Is acting extraverted as "good" as being extraverted? *Journal of Personality and Social Psychology*, *83*, 1409–1422.

Forgeard, M. J. C. (2011). Happy people thrive on adversity: Pre-existing mood moderates the effect of emotion inductions on creative thinking. *Personality and Individual Differences*, *51*, 904–909.

Forgeard, M. J. C., Jayawickreme, E., Kern, M. L., & Seligman, M. E. P. (2011). Doing the right thing: Measuring wellbeing for public policy. *International Journal of Wellbeing*, *1*, 79–106.

Friedman, H. S., Tucker, J., Schwartz, J. E., Martin, L. R., Tomlinson-Keasey, C., Wingard, D., & Criqui, M. (1995). Childhood conscientiousness and longevity: Health behaviors and cause of death. *Journal of Personality and Social Psychology*, *68*, 696–703.

Friedman, H. S., Tucker, J., Tomlinson-Keasey, C., Schwartz, J., Wingard, D., & Criqui, M. H. (1993). Does childhood personality predict longevity? *Journal of Personality and Social Psychology*, *65*, 176–185.

Funder, D. C. (2001). Personality. *Annual Review of Psychology*, *52*, 197–221.

Goldberg, L. R. (1992). The development of markers for the Big-Five factor structure. *Psychological Assessment*, *4*, 26–42.

Hart, S. L., Vella, L., & Mohr, D. C. (2008). Relationships among depressive symptoms, benefit finding, optimism, and positive affect in multiple sclerosis patients after psychotherapy for depression. *Health Psychology*, *27*, 230–238.

Ho, S., Rajandram, R. K., Chan, N., Samman, N., McGrath, C., & Zwahlen, R. A. (2011). The roles of hope and optimism on posttraumatic growth in oral cavity cancer patients. *Oral Oncology*, *47*, 121–124.

Jacobson, N. S., Martell, C. R., & Dimidjian, S. (2001). Behavioral activation treatment for depression: Returning to contextual roots. *Clinical Psychology: Science and Practice*, *8*, 255–270.

Jayawickreme, E., Forgeard, M. J. C., & Seligman, M. E. P. (2012). The engine of well-being. *Review of General Psychology*, *16*(4), 327–342.

John, O. P., & Srivastava, S. (1999). The Big Five trait taxonomy: History, measurement, and theoretical perspectives. In L. A. Pervin & O. P. John (Eds.), *Handbook of personality: Theory and research* (2nd ed., pp. 102–138). New York: Guilford Press.

Johnson, J. A. (1997). Units of analysis for the description and explanation of personality. In R. Hogan, J. Johnson, & S. Briggs (Eds.), *Handbook of personality psychology*. San Diego, CA: Academic Press.

Kern, M. L., & Friedman, H. S. (2008). Do conscientious individuals live longer? A quantitative review. *Health Psychology*, *27*, 505–512.

Kern, M. L., Friedman, H. S., Martin, L. R., Reynolds, C. A., & Luong, G. (2009). Conscientiousness, career success, and longevity: A lifespan analysis. *Annals of Behavioral Medicine*, *37*, 154–163.

King, L. A., McKee, L. W., & Broyles, S. J. (1996). Creativity and the five-factor model. *Journal of Research in Personality*, *30*, 189–203.

Le, H., Oh, I.-S., Robbins, S. B., Ilies, R., Holland, E., & Westrick, P. (2011). Too much of a good thing: Curvilinear relationships between personality traits and job performance. *Journal of Applied Psychology*, *96*, 113–133.

Linley, P. A., & Joseph, S. (2004). Positive changes following trauma and adversity: A review. *Journal of Traumatic Stress*, *17*, 11–21.

McCrae, R. R. (1987). Creativity, divergent thinking, and openness to experience. *Journal of Personality and Social Psychology*, *52*, 1258–1265.

McNiel, J. M., & Fleeson, W. (2006). The causal effects of extraversion on positive affect and neuroticism on negative affect: Manipulating state extraversion and state neuroticism in an experimental approach. *Journal of Research in Personality*, *40*, 529–550.

McNiel, J. M., Lowman, J. C., & Fleeson, W. (2010). The effect of state extraversion on four types of affect. *European Journal of Personality*, *24*, 18–35.

McNiel, J. M., Lowman, J. C., & Fleeson, W. (in press). Does becoming extraverted causally increase positive affect? Ruling out tautological explanations by assessing the effect on four types of affect. Manuscript submitted for publication.

Milam, J. E. (2004). Posttraumatic growth among HIV/AIDS patients. *Journal of Applied Social Psychology*, *34*, 2353–2376.

Minbashian, A., Wood, R. E., & Beckmann, N. (2010). Task-contingent conscientiousness as a unit of personality at work. *Journal of Applied Psychology*, *95*, 793–806.

Mischel, W. (1968). *Personality and assessment.* New York: John Wiley & Sons.

Noftle, E. E., & Robins, R. W. (2007). Personality predictors of academic outcomes: Big Five correlates of GPA and SAT scores. *Journal of Personality and Social Psychology*, *93*, 116–130.

Ozer, D. J., & Benet-Martinez, V. (2006). Personality and the prediction of consequential outcomes. *Annual Review of Psychology*, *57*, 401–421.

Peterson, C., & Seligman, M. E. P. (2004). *Character strengths and virtues: A handbook and classification.* Washington, DC: Oxford University Press.

Powers, M. B., Halpern, J. M., Ferenschak, M. P., Gillihan, S. J., & Foa, E. B. (2010). A meta-analytic review of prolonged exposure for posttraumatic stress disorder. *Clinical Psychology Review*, *30*(6), 635–641.

Roberts, B. W., Walton, K. E., & Viechtbauer, W. (2006). Patterns of mean-level change in personality traits across the life course: A meta-analysis of longitudinal studies. *Psychological Bulletin*, *132*, 1–25.

Runco, M. (2007). *Creativity: Theory and themes: Research, development, and practice.* Burlington, MA: Elsevier Academic Press.

Ryan, R. M., & Deci, E. L. (2000). Self-determination theory and the facilitation of intrinsic motivation, social development, and well-being. *American Psychologist*, *55*, 68–78.

Ryff, C. D., & Singer, B. (1998). The contours of positive human health. *Psychological Inquiry*, *9*, 1–28.

Scheier, M. F., & Carver, C. S. (1985). Optimism, coping, and health: Assessment and implications of generalized outcomes expectancies. *Health Psychology*, *4*, 219–247.

Schueller, S. M., & Seligman, M. E. P. (2010). Pursuit of pleasure, engagement, and meaning: Relationships to subjective and objective measures of well-being. *Journal of Positive Psychology*, *5*, 253–263.

Seligman, M. E. P., & Csikszentmihalyi, M. (2000). Positive psychology: An introduction. *American Psychologist*, *55*, 5–14.

Snyder, C. R., Harris, C., Anderson, J. R., Holleran, S. A., Irving, L. M., Sigmon, S. T., ... Harney, P. (1991). The will and the ways: Development and validation of an individual-differences measure of hope. *Journal of Personality and Social Psychology*, *60*, 570–585.

Specht, J., Egloff, B., & Schmukle, S. C. (2011). Stability and change of personality across the life course: The impact of age and major life events on mean-level and rank-order stability of the big five. *Journal of Personality and Social Psychology*, *101*, 862–882.

Tedeschi, R. G., & Calhoun, L. G. (1996). The posttraumatic growth inventory: Measuring the positive legacy of trauma. *Journal of Traumatic Stress*, *9*, 455–471.

Tedeschi, R. G., & Calhoun, L. G. (2004) Posttraumatic growth: Conceptual foundations and empirical evidence. *Psychological Inquiry*, *15*, 1–18.

Tedeschi, R. G., Park, C. L., & Calhoun, L. G. (1998). Posttraumatic growth: Conceptual issues. In R. G. Tedeschi, C. L. Park, & L. G. Calhoun (Eds.), *Posttraumatic growth: Positive changes in the aftermath of crisis* (pp. 1–23). Mahwah, NJ: Lawrence Erlbaum Associates.

Wilt, J., Noftle, E. E., Fleeson, W., & Spain, J. S. (2012). The dynamic role of personality states in mediating the relationship between extraversion and positive affect. *Journal of Personality*, *80*(5), 1205–1236.

Wright, J. H., Basco, M. R., & Thase, M. E. (2006). *Learning cognitive-behavior therapy: An illustrated guide*. Washington, DC: American Psychiatric Publishing, Inc.

Zelenski, J. M., Santoro, M. S., & Whelan, D. C. (2012, August 22). Would introverts be better off if they acted more like extraverts? Exploring emotional and cognitive consequences of counterdispositional behavior. *Emotion*, *12*, 290–303. doi:10.1037/a0025169

Zoellner, T., & Maercker, A. (2006). Posttraumatic growth in clinical psychology: A critical review and introduction of a two component model. *Clinical Psychology Review*, *26*, 626–665.

Index

The Wiley Blackwell Handbook of Positive Psychological Interventions, First Edition.
Edited by Acacia C. Parks and Stephen M. Schueller.

Lightning Source UK Ltd.
Milton Keynes UK
UKOW07n2126210616

276778UK00002B/2/P

9 781119 950561